New Horizons of PUBLIC ADMINISTRATION

MOHIT BHATTACHARYA

Formerly, Centenary Professor of Public Administration

JAWAHAR PUBLISHERS & DISTRIBUTORS

Published by
JAWAHAR PUBLISHERS & DISTRIBUTORS

First Published, 2000
Second Revised Edition, 2002
Third Revised Edition, 2003
Fourth Revised Edition, 2006
Reprint 2007
Fifth Revised Edition, 2008
Sixth Revised Edition, 2011
Seventh Revised Edition, 2013
Reprint 2018, 2019, 2020, 2025

ISBN-978-81-7361-066-0

Price : ₹575

JAWAHAR PUBLISHERS & DISTRIBUTORS
15, DDA Market, Ber Sarai (Opposite JNU Old Campus), New Delhi-11
Mob: 9811347103

Exclusively Distributed By

UDH PUBLISHERS & DISTRIBUTORS PVT LTD
Think of Books, Think of UDH
4762/63, Gali No 23 Ansari Road, Daryaganj New Delhi 110
(O) : 011-4156-2603, 4156-2623 | (W) : 08929972547 (Wha
E-mail : udhbooks@gmail.com | ordersudh@gmail.com

To My Grand Children;

SREEJATO & DIGONTO

'Intellectuals in making'

Preface to the Seventh Edition

Public Administration has been suffering till now from the old and nagging 'identity crisis'. Yet, it is now a much more robust and diversified field. 'Change' is the law of life. So, it is nothing unnatural for public administration to diversify and branch out in new directions. Four particular aspects need special emphasis in today's circumstances. One, the role of the 'public' need no longer be looked at as a passive recipient of public benediction. There is an urgent need today to integrate the 'public' more firmly with the administrative processes - especially in those areas where the active role of the citizenry has to be acknowledged. Two, technolgy, particularly the new information and communication technology (ICT) has to be integrally connected with today's public administration. Three, 'globalization' is a fact of this century, as our lives everywhere are becoming increasingly connected with 'global' level happenings, be it 'economy' or 'environment'. Four, new facets of administration such as 'disaster','corruption'.'social accountability' need to be included as new agenda items in our academic curricula.

All in all, as a dynamic 'field', public administration has been growing and assuming a more and more complex character which is a sign of'hope' and not of'crisis'. As a core book,'New Horizons' has been constantly updated in keeping with the dynamic nature of our field. The author expects constructive responses from scholars and administrators to improve the book further in future.

The author is grateful to the publishers for bringing out a quality publication in record time.

N. Potomac, Maryland (USA)

Preface to the First Edition

Public Administration as a discipline used to be concerned earlier about its identity. Most textbooks have dealt with the subject from this traditional point of view. Under the impact of powerful domestic and international forces and new conceptualisations of administrative reality, the discipline today is more concerned about explaining diversity, complexity and interactivity. Globalisation and opening up of the economy is a reality now. The earlier role of exclusivity is no longer being accorded to the state and government. In a complex state-society relational situation, the focus has been shifting more and more toward society. Networking with other organisations, rather than exclusivity of government, is what is happening in the practising world of governance. There are new phrases being coined to characterise the new public administration. The *"New Public Management"*, *"Reinventing Government"*, *"Entrepreneurial Government"* are some of the new concepts being introduced in the subject to connote the present and evolving scenario of public management. This book covers all these and many other new themes of contemporary importance.

The present publication marks a continuation of the authors interest in the subject as expressed in the earlier publication : *Public Administration.* Some of the old concerns have continued to remain important but the present book is different from the earlier one in (a) orientation and (b) contents. The orientation is such that the newer concepts and realities have been sought to be captured in this volume and in terms of contents, more than half of the book covers new themes. Even in the old themes like "public-private debate" or 'development administration', the latest thoughts on them have been incorporated to update knowledge appropriately.

In a way, this is an altogether new venture, to gather at one place the stock of new ideas and thoughts and to present newer interpretations on older themes.

The author sincerely thanks all the well-wishers, scholars, colleagues in the discipline and above all, the dear students who have always been the main inspiration behind this endeavour.

Thanks are due to the publishers, who have taken pains to ensure that the publication becomes a quality one.

At home, the patience and quite encouragement of the ever-caring wife needs to be openly acknowledged. For any fault or blemishes, of course, the author alone has to be blamed.

Mohit Bhattacharya

Kolkata
September, 1998

Contents

Chapter 1

Public Administration: Nature, Scope & Evolution

Concrete understanding of public administration is easy. We board a train or a bus run by a government agency Patients are admitted to government-run hospitals. The police constables maintain law and order. So, there are innumerable activities that the government undertakes. Welfare state means more government functions. In the third world, government is involved in many sectors of social life: economic, cultural, social, regulatory, productive and many others. This has been necessary because of the management need for socio-economic leadership from the government. Unlike the developed West, the Third World's development has basically been government-led. Public administration as visible public-serving activity is before everyone's gaze.

Public administration is a system of organisation and action oriented with performance of these activities. It can best be looked at as an instrument that is used for the realisation of the goals of government. Just as societies have their political systems and economic systems, they also have their public administrative systems.

As an aspect of government activity, public administration has been coexisting with every political system as the action part of government for the fulfilment of the objectives set by the political decision makers. Functioning of the machineries of government has attracted the attention of scholars and observers since the time of recorded history. Kautilya's *Arthasastra*, the *Mahabharata* and the *Raniayana* contain many insightful observations about the organisation and working of government. In the history of western political thought, Aristotle's *Politics* and Machiavelli's *The Prince* are important contributions to both political and administrative issues and ideas.

As a field of systematic study, public administration cannot, however, claim a long history. In the eighteenth century, the German scholars in Western Europe felt interested in this branch of academic inquiry. Two great systems of public administration had developed in the West: the Anglo-American and the French. The first, as Leonard White has pointed out, has been "based on a deep-seated preference for self-government in local communities, wide citizen participation, dispersion of authority, well-established responsibility of the administrative system to the legislative body and the responsibility of officials to the ordinary civil courts at the instance of the private citizen". In contrast, the French system which was formulated by Napoleon has been "based on the concentration of executive power, on the dominance of national over local authorities, on the professionalization of the public service and its psychological separation from the body of citizens and on the responsibility of officials to a separate set of administrative courts."

Despite such sharp contrasts, the two systems have come much closer over the years with democratic and industrial changes in the West in recent times. With the growing importance of government in the wake of expanding public functions, public administration became highly complex and more and more specialised. The need for better management of public affairs through scientific studies and analysis of government working and for training of public employees was voiced by practitioners and academics alike. It is in the United States of America that the need was more keenly felt, although the Germans started administrative analysis much earlier in practical terms. An essay by Woodrow Wilson published in 1887 is considered to be the symbolic harbinger of a fairly autonomous inquiry. To quote Wilson's memorable comment:

"There should be a science of administration which shall seek to straighten the paths of government, to make its business less business like, to strengthen and purify its organisation and to crown its duties with dutifulness."[1]

Woodrow Wilson's contribution to public administration can be seen from four interlinked indicators:

i) Advocacy of a 'science of administration';
ii) Emphasis on the special nature- of administration distinguishing administration from politics;
iii) Apparent predilection for private or business administration;
iv) Prompt initiative for comparative study of administration.

Wilson's 1887 article on 'The Science of Administration', which is regarded as the foundation essay for the field, was written at a time (in the late nineteenth century) when the topic of public administration was established as a profession and an academic study. The crying need was to eliminate corruption, improve efficiency and streamline service delivery system in pursuit of public interest. In the 1880s reformers reacted sharply against abuses at all levels: the city, state and national governments. One of the voices of reform was Woodrow Wilson. A lawyer trained at the University of Virginia, he went on to study political economy at Johns Hopkins University. His interest was simply designing governments and policies. Wilson accordingly, shifted his focus from Great Britain to Germany, particularly Prussia, to learn from the German ethos—one of the leading centres of public administrative development.

A Science of Administration

Wilson's advocacy that "there should be a science of administration" has to be seen in the historical context. Writing against the background of widespread corruption, 'science' meant to Wilson a systematic and disciplined body of knowledge which he thought would be the latest fruit of the science of politics. Also he was critical of the fact that the American administrative practice was devoid of any scientific method. By contrast, he thought administrative science was well developed in Europe in the hands of the French and German academics. European governments, in his view, were independent of popular assent. There were more "governments" in those countries and a natural desire to discover newer principles of administration. An important reason for the slow growth of the science of administration in America was, in Wilson's view, the reigning concept of popular sovereignty—"the multitudinous voice called public opinion". More important than the arid debate on constitutional principles was the need for the systematic analysis of administration leading to the development of a 'science of administration'. Hence, Wilson wrote: "It is setting harder to run a constitution than to write one." In his view, the real challenge was not simply how authority would be defined but how it was to be actually used on regular basis by those administrators who must operate the ongoing functions of government and implement new policies.

Pollhcs-Administration Dichotomy

When Wilson said that administration was "removed from the hurry and strife of politics," the stress was to curve out an untarnished field essential for proper and efficient management of governments business. His objective was clear but his statement was possibly naive. His basic argument was that administrators could concentrate on operating the government rather than on substituting their judgement for that of elected representatives. It was this idea that came to be called the politics-administration dichotomy. He sought to make a distinction between 'political activity' and 'administrative activity' in public organisations. Administration, in his view, lies outside the sphere of politics and administrative issues are not political questions.

Although Wilson is regarded as the originator of the idea of politics-administration dichotomy, it will be unfair to present only an one-sided view. As other scholars have pointed out, Wilson was well aware of the fact that public administration was essentially political in nature. He wrote later in 1891: "Administration cannot be divorced from its connections with the other branches of Public Law without being distorted and robbed of its true significance. Its foundations are those deep and permanent principles of Politics."[2]

Public Administration and Management or Business Administration

Wilson wanted to make government business "less un-businesslike'. As he wrote, "Administration is business and like business it does not involve itself in questions of politics." Analysts have pointed out that the "basic premise of Wilson's argument was that the affairs of public administration were synonymous with those of private administration. The central concerns of business administration viz., economy, efficiency and effectiveness, should also be the concerns of public administration.

Again, there are others who are quick to observe that what Wilson wanted was that "administrators could study mechanisms or administration not only in use by other governments but also by those employed in private industry".

Wilson knew it very well that government was different. As Wilson himself wrote, "Business like the administrations of government may and should be—but it is not business. It is organic life."[3] While professionalization was advocated in the management of government, Wilson was well aware of the wider agenda of public administration.

Comparative Public Administration

Wilson may be regarded as the founder of comparative public administration. He became a student of German so that he could study the practices of the then leading (Prussian) government in the development of public administration techniques. Despite his advocacy of comparative method, Wilson was clear in his mind that administration stands on different bases in democratic and other states. He recognized that lessons learned from other countries would have to be "filtered through the cultural lens of the person seeking to learn those lessons and borrow techniques. One need not accept Prussian government and life styles to learn from their public management experience".[4]

To conclude, Wilson was a scholar-administrator who was deeply engrossed both in the theory and practice of government. His writings were conditioned by the tone and temper of his times. Peter Self observes, his basic postulate was that "it was possible to achieve a self-sufficient 'science' of administrative means, so constructed as to leave administrators perfectly amenable to political leadership (of any type) while remaining free of political considerations in the conduct of their work. Wilson's theories may have been naive, but they provided an ideological basis for measures which most people approved: namely the curbing of political patronage, the advancement of professional skills and a tighter framework of internal administrative co-ordination."[5]

Defining the Discipline

Public administration as a specialised academic field deals essentially with the machinery and procedures of government as these are used in the effective performance of government activities. Administration has been defined as a co-operative human effort toward achieving some common goals. Thus defined, administration can be found in various institutional settings such as a business firm, a hospital, a university, a government department and so on. As an aspect of this generic concept, public administration is that species of administration which operates within a specific political setting. It is a means by which the policy decisions made by the political decision makers are carried out. "Public administration is decision making, planning the work to be done, formulating objectives and goals, working with the legislature and citizen organisations to gain public support and funds for government programmes, establishing and revising organisation, directing and supervising employees, providing leadership, communicating and receiving communications, determining work methods and procedures, appraising performance, exercising controls and other functions performed by government executives and supervisors. It is the action part of government, the means by which the purposes and goals of government are realised."[6] Dwight Waldo, the veteran public administration analyst, cautioned us against the dangers of 'defining' public administration. As Waldo said, "The immediate effect of all one sentence or one paragraph definitions of public administration is mental paralysis rather than enlightenment and stimulation." All definitions seek to narrow down and limit the meaning of objects and in this effort, clarity and understanding suffer. Being an action and executive field of government, public administration has never had a settled boundary. The activities of government have expanded and contracted on contextual circumstances. An academic subject seeking to develop a body of knowledge on public administration has to reckon with the shifting boundaries of government in society.

The basic concerns of public administration as a field of study would therefore include (a) structures of public organisations dealing mainly with the way executive organisations are formed, readjusted and reformed, (b) administrative processes denoting the dynamic aspects of organisation such as communication, control and decision-making, (c) bureaucratic behaviour with emphasis on the interpersonal and inter-group relationships in organisaii mal settings and (d) organisation-environment interactions covering the influential and meaningful relationships that are found to exist between public administration and its surrounding forces and factors in the environment. The study of structures, processes and behaviour has been greatly facilitated by the emerging sub-discipline of organisation theory. Its impact on public administration as an academic field has been considerable in recent times. Efforts have been made to relate public administration to its environment 'in much the same way that the science of ecology is concerned with the mutual relations between organisms and their environment.'[7]

The 'public' aspect in public administration lends special character to it. The adjective can be looked at formally to mean 'government'. So, public administration is government administration, the focus being specifically on public bureaucracy. This is the meaning commonly used in discussing public administration. A wider meaning of 'public' administration has sought to expand its ambit by including any administration that has considerable impact on the public. From this aspect, a private electricity undertaking like the Calcutta Electric Supply Corporation can be considered a fit subject of discussion under public administration. It is, however, in the first sense that public administration is usually considered. There has been a view point that 'government' as a phenomenon is so diverse and multifaceted that no single discipline can monopolise its study. Topics like political science, sociology, economics, business administration and others have been discussing several aspects of government and its administration from the vis-a-vis of each discipline. The discipline of Public Administration has to acknowledge this diversity of approaches and yet build up its own ways of dealing with the phenomenon of administration. As Resenbloom has opined it, "Public administration does involve *activity*, it is concerned with *politics* and *policy making*, it tends to be concentrated in the *executive* branch of government, it does differ from private administration and it is concerned with implementing law." Necessarily, the discipline of Public Administration has to have a wide scope. Correspondingly, its definition has to reflect its omnibus character. To quote Rosenbloom again, "Public Administration is the use of managerial, legal and political theories and processes to fulfil legislative, executive and judicial governmental mandates for the provision of regulatory and service functions for the society as a whole or for some segments of it."

One may go a step further and add that economic, sociological and behavioural science theories are all relevant to the study of public administration.

The Public Interest

Discussions of public administration have generally been concerned with efficiency and economy. The underlying idea has been to see that administration becomes result-oriented and productive by spending least resources. Alongside this efficient approach, there has been a growing concern about what may broadly be called 'morality' or 'ethics' in public administration. Government has a universalistic character. It has to serve the common good without making any sort of distinction between man and man. Efficiency in government has thus a moral tone. It is against this background that a broad theory of public interest has emerged to provide a general framework for the functioning of public administration.

The concern for public interest can be traced to a variety of reasons. Indeed, the members of the bureaucracy constitute a power elite. They are likely to take decisions in self-interest or under pressure from powerful interest groups. In either case, public interest may be in jeopardy. Another argument has been that the bureaucracy is a mindless machine that turns out decisions mechanically. The rule-bound administration may look very neat and tidy, but it may not be able to serve the wider cause of public interest. Still another argument can be derived from Herbert Simon's discussion on administrative decision making.[8] According to Simon, administrative decisions are often based on grounds other than those of efficiency and economy. Social and psychological factors greatly influence the way decisions are taken by the decision-makers.

The importance of sense of public interest as a wider ethical commitment in public administration assumes significance in this context. As it has been very aptly commented upon:

"The most frequently hidden agenda in the deliberations of public servants is the effect of substantive or procedural decisions upon the personal lives and fortunes of those deliberating, and yet the very call to serve a larger public often evokes a degree of selflessness and nobility on the part of public servants beyond the capacity of cynics to recognise or to believe. Man's feet may wallow in the bog of self-interest, but his eyes and ears are strangely attuned to calls from the mountaintop. As moral philosophy has insistently claimed, there is a fundamental moral distinction between the propositions:'I want this because it serves my interest' and 'I want this because it is right."[9]

Philosophies of public interest fall broadly into four classes. The very *intuitionist philosophy* seeks to justify existing practices by pointing out that in conflicting situations, the administrator chooses an alternative by intuition. In other words, what the administrator actually does is an intuitionist solution which seems to him the right course of action under given circumstances. This philosophy does not provide any guideline for action, nor does it spell out an explicit theory of public interest.

Perfectionism, the second philosophical school, views public interest from the standpoint of promotion of excellence in all spheres of social activities. Public resources, according to this school of thought, should be spent in such a way that the best members of the society benefit most from the expenditure. Thus conceived, perfectionism is an elitist philosophy and obviously anti-egalitarian; as such, it is not compatible with democratic theory.

Utilitarianism, as propounded by Jeremy Bentham and John Stuart Mill, has been the most influential school of thought in the determination of public interest. According to utilitarian philosophy, the public interest is served when a public policy makes everyone slightly better off even though it makes a few individuals slightly worse off. Under the utilitarian calculus public interest is judged by the augmentation of the net balance of social satisfaction.

The fourth major ethical framework for public administration can be derived from the *Theory of Justice* as propounded by the philosopher, John Rawls, in his monumental work on the subject.[10] Rawls's principles are essentially an elaboration of the Anglo-Saxon concept of fairness and these come close to what is called in economics 'Pareto optimality'. Rawls suggests two basic principles of justice to test public interest. One of these is that "each person is to have an equal right to the most extensive basic liberty compatible with a similar liberty for others".The other principle postulates that "social and economic inequalities are to be arranged so that they are both (a) reasonably expected to be to everyone's advantage and (b) attached to positions and offices open to all." In case of conflict between these two principles, the second principle is expected to prevail and give way to the first. Rational decision-making in public administration has to have an ethical framework.The principles ofjohn Rawls provide an operating logic for the determination of public interest by the decision-makers.

The intuitionist philosophy justifies status quo and is of very little help in actual administrative situations. The perfectionist philosophy favours excellence at the expense of social equality. It is patently anti-democratic. Utilitarian calculus has the merit of emphasising total social good but it also accepts the position that few may be worse off. Compared to all these philosophical positions, the formulation of Rawls seems much more balanced and, as rightly observed by Nicholas Henry, it represents a workable way for determining the public interest by public administrators.[11]

Evolution of Public Administration

The study of public administration, as Peter Self points out,'developed as an offshoot of political science or public law and until recently administration as an academic subject was the very plain step-sister of these older disciplines.'[12] It has not always been easy to get access to government departments; hence the world of administration has rarely been an open one. Also, the technicalities of administration have not been particularly interesting to the scholars. With the expansion of government activities and with more and more concern for both efficiency and accountability, discussions slowly started on better performance of the public sector. The movement for governmental reform gathered momentum especially in the United States of America, where intellectual efforts were systematically expanded for the steady development of an exclusive body of knowledge on the structure and functioning of public administration.

The evolution of public administration as a specialised field of study falls into a number of critical stages. *The first stage* can be called the era of politics-administration dichotomy.

Politics-administration dichotomy is often traced to the Wilsonian call for a science of administration, which, as Waldo has pointed out. goes back to much earlier European administrative traditions. It has been questioned: to what extent Wilson desired separation between the two.

Functionally, administration was separated from politics. Administration, it was argued, is concerned with implementation of policy decisions taken politically. Frank Goodnow sought to conceptually distinguish the two functions.[13] According to him,"Politics has to do with policies or expressions of the state wilP'and "Administration has to do with the execution of these policies." Apart from this analytic distinction, the institutional locations of these two functions were differentiated. The location of politics was identified as the legislature and the higher echelons of government where major policy-decisions would be made and the larger questions of allocation of values decided upon. By contrast, the location of administration was identified' as the executive arm of government, the bureaucracy.

The processes of administration, it was argued, have a certain regularity and concreteness about them and these are amenable to scientific investigations which are likely to lead to a science of administration.

The *second stage of evolution* is marked by the tendency to reinforce the idea of politics-administration dichotomy and to evolve a value-free 'science of management'.The 'public' aspect of public administration was virtually dropped at this stage and the focus was almost wholly on efficiency. This stage can be called the stage of orthodoxy, as efforts were underway to delineate firmly the boundaries of a new discipline of 'management'. Public administration merged into the new science. The questions of 'value' were no longer bothering the new science of administration. Politics as practised by the politicians was considered irrelevant. Scientific management to efficiently handle the 'business' of administration became the slogan. Principles of management were worked out as ready-made aids to practitioners. The administrative practitioners and the business schools joined hands to emphasise the mechanistic aspect of management untrammelled by the whims of politicians and the frailties of human beings.

The merger of public administration and general management has not been a totally fruitless friendship. Certain aspects of administration such as the structures and processes of public organisations were put to more rigorous analysis but the excesses of scientific management triggered a series of reactions against the mechanistic concept of administration which the new movement sought to establish. Studies on private firms revealed new data about the actual working of organisations. The findings might have their origins in private management, but these were general enough to embrace all organisations both private and public.

The most notable contribution, in this connection, came from the famous Hawthorne experiments in the late 1920s executed by a group of scholars at the Hawthorne Plant of the Western Electric Company.[14] The experiments, focussed upon work groups, shook the foundation of the scientific management school by demonstrating the powerful influence of social and psychological factors on the work situation. The mechanistic notion of organisation was exploded by showing that manipulation of monetary rewards and the physical aspects of the work situation had very limited impact on the worker and productivity.

The Hawthorne experiments pioneered a movement which came to be known as the Human Relations approach to management, marking the *third stage of evolution* of administrative thought. Its impact was felt much more widely on public administration in the post-war period. This approach to organisational analysis drew attention to the formation and effect of work groups in the organisation, the force of informal organisation in the formal set up, the phenomena of leadership and conflicts and cooperation among groups in the organisational setting. In short, the human relations approach brought out the limitations of the machine concept of organisation in 'scientific management' thought. By drawing attention to the social and psychological factors of work situation, it underscored the vital importance of the "human side of the enterprise".

The *fourth stage* was heralded by two significant publications in the 1940s—Herbert Simon's *Administrative Behaviour* and Robert Dahl's essay entitled 'The Science of Public Administration: Three Problems'[15] Simons book is a critique of the older public administration. More importantly, it sets forth the rigorous requirements of scientific analysis in public administration. About some of the classical "principles", Simon's conclusion was that these were unscientifically derived and were "no more than proverbs".[16] He rejected the politics-administration dichotomy; at the same time he brought in the perspective of logical positivism in the study of policy-making and the relation of means and ends. Drawing on the perspectives and methodology of 'behaviourism' in psychology and social psychology, *Administrative Behaviour* pleaded for the raising of scientific rigour in public administration. The substantive focus was on "decision-making" and as Simon insisted, "If any 'theory' is involved, it is that decision-making is the heart of administration and that the vocabulary of administrative theory must be derived from the logic and psychology of human choice".[17]

Simon's approach provided an alternative definition of public administration and widened the scope of the subject by relating it to psychology, sociology, economics and political science. In the development of the 'discipline', he identified two mutually supportive streams of thought. One was engaged in the development of a pure science of administration which called for a good grounding in social psychology. Another stream was dealing with a broad range of values and working out prescriptions for public policy

The second approach was, in Simon's view, analytically is very far-ranging. It would imply swallowing up of the whole of political science and absorption of economics and sociology as well. Public administration, he feared, would lose its identity in the second approach. But he favoured the coexistence of both the streams of thought for the growth and development of the discipline.

As he noted, "there does not appear any reason why these two developments in the field of public administration should not go side by side, for they in no way conflict or contradict. But the workers in this field must keep clearly in mind in which area, at any given time, they propose to work".[18]

Dahl's essay identified three important problems in the evolution of science on public administration:

i) The first problem arises from the frequent impossibility of excluding normative considerations from the problems of public administration. Scientific means to achieve efficiency must be found on some clarification of ends.
ii) The second problem arises from the 'inescapable fact that a science of public administration must be a study of certain aspects of human behaviour.' Dahl criticised the 'machine' concept of organisation and argued that the study of administration must embrace the whole psychological man.
iii) The third problem relates to the conception of the principles of administration. Referring to the study of public administration in the United States, he commented on the narrow and parochial nature of the intellectual pursuits. There was a tendency, as he pointed out, to enunciate universal principles based on a few examples drawn from limited national and historical settings.

To quote Dahl, "The study of public administration inevitably must become a much more broadly based discipline, resting not on a narrowly defined knowledge of techniques and processes, but rather extending to the varying historical, sociological, economic and other conditioning factors

This last point has been taken up as a challenge and considerable efforts have been expended so far in the study of public administration in the developing countries in a bid to "establishing propositions about administrative behaviour which transcend national boundaries."[19]

The next stage of the evolution of public administration coincides with a general concern in the social sciences for public policy analysis. Earlier Simon had mentioned the public policy perspective in administrative analysis. With the abandonment of politics-administration dichotomy, the public policy approach became intellectually easier. Evidences from the practical world of administration have also been revealing the close nexus between politics and administration.

As government seeks to formulate and implement more and more welfare programmes, concern for policy studies in public administration starts gathering momentum. At this stage, the study of public administration has been gaining in social 'relevance' no doubt; but the boundaries of the academic field are not as clearly distinguishable now as it used to be in the olden days of politics-administration dichotomy. Moshers comment is particularly relevant in this context:

"Public administration cannot demark any subcontinent as its exclusive province unless it consists of such mundane matters as classifying budget expenditures, drawing organisational charts and mapping procedures. In fact, it would appear that any definition of this field would be either so encompassing as to call forth the wrath or ridicule of others, or so limiting as to stultify its own disciples. Perhaps, it is best that it not be defined.

It is more an area of interest than a discipline, more a focus than a separate science It is necessarily cross-disciplinary. The overlapping and vague boundaries should be viewed as a resource, even though they are irritating to some with orderly minds."[20]

New Public Administration

The evolutionary perspective must include an account of the New Public Administration movement which marked a turning point in the growth of the discipline.

The disciplinary orthodoxy of public administration has certainly boosted up the ego of public administration experts. But the discipline's alienation from political science has caused concern to scholars in both political science and public administration. It has been argued that unless the two disciplines mix freely without losing their identities, understanding of government would be lopsided and inadequate. The basic purpose and cohesion of public administration would be heightened by closer association with political science. One forceful view has been that 'the study of administration is just another expression for the study of politics'.

In the late 1960s, some of the best *of* the younger generation of American scholars pioneered a new movement in American public administration which came to be known as the 'new public administration'. The young academics, although nurtured and schooled in the era of positive government, were actually sensitive to the failings of American democracy. The scholars gathered at Minnowbrook under the patronage of Dwight Waldo and challenged the 'givens' of orthodox public administration and pluralist political science. It was a time of turbulence when the young scholars vociferously demanded restoration of values and public purpose in government. Affected by the turbulence of the war in Vietnam and the urban riots, the younger generation expressed their concern about all institutions, especially government. Two volumes[21] were produced to herald a new brand of public administration oriented toward political theory. As Wallace Sayre has summed up the sentiment, "public administration is ultimately a problem in political theory."

The new counter-culture has demanded the primacy of politics in administration. There has been an ideological conviction that in the USA "the bureaucratic instruments of power utilized by the political establishments and studied with academic detachment by the intellectual establishments are among the most oppressive institutions of American society."

The literature on new public administration lays emphasis .on four major themes: *Relevance, Values, Equity* and *Change.*

The theme of relevance is more a reinterpretation than an original quest. Public administration has traditionally been interested in efficiency and economy. The new public administration movement discovered was that the discipline had little to say about contemporary problems and issues.

Management-oriented public administration curriculum was found 'irrelevant' and the demand was to deal explicitly with the political and administrative implications of administrative action.

Another aspect of the 'relevance' issue relates to the character of the knowledge itself. The question that was asked was: public administration knowledge for what? Is.it the purpose of public administration to facilitate use of administrative knowledge for the perpetuation of political power? Some of the important questions raised at Minnowbrook were:

(a) What standards of decision do we use to select which questions ought to be studied and how to study them ?
(b) Who defines our questions and priorities for us ?
(c) To what extent are we aware of the social and moral implications of knowledge in Public Administration ?
(d) What are the uses of Public Administration as a social and political science ?
(e) Does Public Administration presently yield knowledge useful to certain institutions in society (usually the dominant ones) and not to others?

These are obviously very disturbing questions, challenging the status quo in public administration. The new movement demanded radical curriculum change to facilitate meaningful studies oriented toward the realities of public life.

Values

The new public administration explicitly announced its basic normative concern in administrative analysis. It openly rejected the value-neutral position taken by behavioural political science and management-oriented public administration.Value-neutrality in public administration is an impossibility and the discipline should explicitly espouse the cause of the disadvantaged sections in society. The champions of the new movement advocate openness about the values being served through administrative action. This, they thought, would help unmask the "neutrality" position of actual administration and facilitate evaluation of impact of administrative action and outcomes. As one spokesman of the new movement comments:

"The new public administrator "is less 'generic' and more 'public' than his forbear, less 'descriptive' and more 'prescriptive', less 'institution-oriented' and more 'client-impact oriented', less 'neutral' and 'more normative' and it is hoped, no less scientific."[22]

Social Equity

The protagonists of new public administration do not hesitate to demonstrate their open partisanship. In their view, the distributive functions and impact of governmental institutions should be public administration's basic concern. One manifestation of this philosophy seems almost neo-Benthamite:

"The purpose of public organisation is the reduction of economic, social and psychic suffering and the enhancement of life opportunities for those inside and outside the organisation."[23]

Frederickson has gone a step further and adopted a bold social-equity attitude:

"A Public Administration which fails to work for changes which tries to redress the deprivation of minorities will likely be eventually used to repress those minorities."[24]

This is an aggressive action-oriented stance inviting public administration analysis to work for the removal of the wrongs of society and openly taking side with the socially deprived groups. The new Public Administration movement thus challenged public administration to make it more proactive to major social issues.

Change

To serve the cause of social equity is to actively work for social change. This is the motto of new public administration. The attack is on the status quo and against the powerful interests entrenched in permanent institutions. The new public administration is unwilling to allow enslavement to permanent institutions' that steadily grow into self-perpetuating power centres of dominant interests. The Minnowbrook participants explored ways of institutionalizing change and remedying the bureaucratic tendencies of big organisations.

This movement that started at Minnowbrook has been criticised as anti-theoretic, anti-positivist and anti-management (in the manipulative sense). Its positive value lies in bringing public administration closer to political science. In fact, the movement has been successful in integrating public administration with the basic concerns of political theory. The client oriented, normative and socially conscious public administration, as advocated by the new movement, is of direct relevance for the 'third world' countries as well, where public administration is in *dire* need of de-bureaucratization and basic, qualitative transformation.

The essential message of 'new public administration' has not been missed by mainstream scholars of public administration. There is, in this movement, a streak of idealism, a concern for quantity of life and 'a desire to ameliorate the lot of the more deprived members of society'. As it has been righdy observed;

"We need urgently to inject a good deal of the New Public Administration Thinking into the policy-making process and we need to do this not only as a reminder of the new kinds of questions society is increasingly asking of governments but also as a corrective to those other relatively new and currently dominant influences which see in quantitative analysis and mechanistic techniques the solution to most of man's ills".[25]

Dwight Waldo characterised NPA as follows:

"Its adherents were 'centrally involved in change in the American Society for Public Administration designed to give it a more forward stance... it is unlikely to transform radically public administration short run, but long run there is a possibility; and in any case it now is and will continue to be a yeasty addition to the entire complex of theories, techniques and aspirations."[26] (p.xiv)

And Fredericksons comment on newness of NPA is as follows: "To affix the label 'new' to anything is risky business. The risk is doubled when newness is attributed to idea, thoughts, concepts, paradigms, theories... the newness is in the way the fabric is woven, not necessarily in the threads that are used and the newness is in arguments as to the proper use of the fabric—however threadbare"

Minnowbrook-II (1988)

During Minnowbrook-I in September 1968, the mood of the discipline of public administration was such that it sought to identify values and ethics as the critical issue of the 1970s.

By contrast, in 1988 the social environment of Minnowbrook-II was markedly different from that of its predecessor. The context of public administrative reality in post- Reaganite America- changed in favour of less directly performing government and governance, more privatisation and contracting out, more voluntarism and social capacity- building and more third- party government. The values of public purpose came to be steadily replaced by the emerging values of private interest.

Minnowbrook-II was designed to compare and contrast the changing epochs of public administration.[25] The first Minnowbrook conference was attended by scholars most of whom had political science background. However, in contrast, the second conference included many individuals who had been trained in policy analysis and policy studies, economics, planning, urban studies and law. The composition of the members attending the Conference (1988) influenced the tone and temper of the discussions at Minnowbrook -II. If the 1968 conference had been radical and confrontational, the 1988 conference was, by contrast, more practical and respectful to the 'seniors' in the profession. In terms of thematic coverage, many of the topics of the first conference found place in the second conference also. More particularly, themes like ethics, social equity, human relations, reconciling public administration and democracy and general concern for the academic field featured at Minnowbrook-II, ensuring thereby continuity in intellectual interest. At the same time inclusion of some of the themes that were not so prominent in 1968 such as leadership, constitutional and legal perspective, technology policy and economic perspectives gave the second gathering an identity of its own. Looking back, it seems that Minnowbrook-I represented a well-intentioned but overambitious optimism. As against this, Minnowbrook-II exuded pragmatism and confirmed the inevitability of government .as a tool for strengthening society. In the changed perspective, public administration was called upon to renew its capacity to cope with the problems of the emerging future. This would involve two linkages: between theory and practice on one side and between public administrators and other government - related officials, on the other.

A comparison between the two Minnowbrooks brings out both continuity in thinking and an eagerness to break new grounds. As one of the participants has pointed out, the following five major themes of Minnowbrook-II[27] were related to the legacy of Minnowbrook -I:

1. Concerns for social equity that predominated at the first conference and was acknowledged as important in 1988 also.
2. Democratic values and the centrality of public administration strongly reaffirmed in 1988 with special focus on ethics, accountability and administrative leadership.
3. Continuity of the earlier (Minnowbrook -I) debate between normative and behavioural perspectives with special emphasis on epistemological questions regarding how people learn about the field.
4. Acceptance of the heterogeneous nature of work force in response to social diversity including the emerging gender dimension and the need for free interchange between 'generalists' and 'specialists'.
5. Changing outlook on 'government' in Minnowbrook-II as government was no longer seen as the train on which people wanted to ride. Privatisation was taken for granted in many enterprises and public servants appeared more as conservators than change agents.

Minnowbrook-II, thus, sought to establish its identity by focusing on the current and future vision of the field of public administration. The distinctive character of the second conference is evident from its emphasis on the following thrust areas:

1. The second conference set its visions onto the near future, without trying to be radical. There was a tacit acceptance of the fact that the environment of public administration is exceedingly complex and the problems are of huge proportions. Hence, a meaningful long-term vision is neither reasonable nor feasible.

2. The scholars in the discipline,while aware of their indebtedness to other disciplines, exhibited a strong sense of intellectual parochialism.The general mood was not to lose disciplinary identity. Rather there was keenness to rebuild the discipline *de novo.*
3. Even if'privatisation' was accepted tacitly. there was a strong adversarial attitude towards business. The Minnowbrook-II world-view was expressed in terms of a curious tension between capitalism and democracy that resulted in "an unusual form of a truncated capitalist economy operating within a truncated democracy". Against this backdrop, public administration has to rely on the best that business offers as well as the best that the non-profit public sector offers.
4. Public personnel practices came in for closer scrutiny and the discussions underlined the need for innovative personnel practices in order to move away from public managers' current inability to hire employees on a timely basis, promote the best employees and reinforce high productivity.
5. As regards technology policy, the participants had been generally unwilling to deal with the technological issues. "Technology was faulted more than vaunted" and there was general reluctance to idolise technology as a necessary tool for improving public policy.
6. The specifics of iyhat government should do were avoided. "Even in the midst of discussions on the inevitability of administrators exerting control over policy agendas, the politics - administration dichotomy appears to be alive and well".

An Overview

The optimism engendered by the vision of a new public administration capable of solving important societal problems had dissipated. Minnowbrook-II was caught in a mood ofconstrained hopefulness'. The first conference (1968) offered a challenge to public administration to become proactive with regard to burning social issues. By contrast, the second conference in 1988 held in the midst of governmental cutback and 'privatisation' policy, 'retreated from an action perspective to cerebral examinations of democracy, ethics, responsibility, philosophy and even economics'.The outcomes of Minnowbrook-II were therefore more pragmatic and less radical.[28]

Minnowbrook III Conference (2008)

Following the Minnowbrook tradition, the third Conference — Minnowbrook III - was held during September 3-7, 2008 at the Syracuse University's Minnowbrook Conference Center in the Adirondack Mountains[29].The gathering was coordinated by Rosemary O'Leary, Distinguished Professor at Syracuse University. Professor O'Leary circulated in advance a notice alerting prospective scholars and researchers, who would like to attend the Third Conference, about the 'themes' to be discussed at the Conference. The purposes of Minnowbrook'III, as the circular read, are:

- To Exchange Knowledge of current and emerging public service challenges and solutions in a variety of settings and cultures. Sessions will focus on the international public sector, collaborative governance and the training of the next generation of public servants.
- To Develop a Network of scholars to support future collaboration and the exchange

of ideas concerning improvements in public service.
- To Disseminate the BEST PAPERS PRESENTED at the Conference as a specially edited 'reader' for courses in schools of public policy and management around the world.

This notice gives an idea about the new directions of thinking charted out for the Third Conference. It seems the overall idea informing the Conference had been to focus on the comparative aspects of administrative studies centred on the challenges of public sector management in a variety of settings and cultures. Also, with a view to improving 'practice' in a changed and 'globalised' context, the issue of'training of the next generation of public servants' attracted the attention of the organisers. Attaching considerable importance to the central theme of'Improvements in public service', the Conference floated the idea of 'developing a network of scholars' to support future collabbrations and exchange of ideas.

Conference Theme

Against the background of the ascendancy of 'neo-liberal' ideology, advocating 'downsizing' of government and opening up more space for the 'market' and non-government agencies, the Conference theme was very thoughtfully chosen. It was focused on 'The Future of Public Administration, Public Management and Public Service'. The Conference was organised in two phases.

A 'pre-conference workshop' was organised for the benefit of emerging scholars nominated by senior scholars in the field. The 56 invited attendees were more diverse than previous Minnowbrook conferences in terms of race, gender and nationality, involving for the most part assistant professors but including several tenured associate professors.

The Minnowbrook III Phase One (September 3-5):

Phase One was devoted to the summaries of concerns and future directions representing a dozen fc/cal areas presented to senior scholars and attendees at the opening session of Phase Two. The themes for discussion were wide-ranging including academic-practitioner relations; democratic performance management; financial management; globalisation/comparative perspectives; information technology ahd management; law, politics and public administration management; leadership; methods/interdisciplinary; networks; performance measurement; public administration values and theory; social equity and justice and transparency and accountability.

The group, interested as it was in globalised perspectives, encouraged a renaissance of comparative studies as the world has become increasingly interdependent. The essence of the comparative approach has been context-sensitive with emphases on institutional and cultural contexts which, in the opinion of the attendees, should be incorporated into more rigorous research. The group that discussed research methods proposed a statement of commitment document, informally referred to as a pledge or a manifesto, asking new scholars to serve as 'change agents' regarding the use and teaching of research methods and the responsiveness of the peer-review process. One element of this was more attention to the method of action research to increase engagement with the issues and practice of public administration; another was a commitment to methodological pluralism.

Another group interested in 'public administration values and theory' offered a reformulation of public administration, defining public administration as: "a socially-embedded process of collective relationships, dialogue and action to promote human flourishing for all." Questions arising from the reformulation included how public administration might recognize competing values and how to encourage a critical consciousness regarding public administration.

The Minnowbrook III Phase Two (September 5-7)

Phase two was held at Lake Placid, New York. It was a more traditional academic conference to which scholars throughout the world were invited to submit proposals. About 300 proposals were submitted of which 80 were accepted. Two hundred twenty scholars and practitioners from 13 countries participated. Following the opening session presentations from Phase One participants, the emerging scholars and senior scholars met in roundtable format to discuss the specific ideas presented. In most subsequent sessions, participants limited paper presentations to allow for enhanced discussion of the material in reference to the ideas presented and developed in the opening roundtables.

Minnowbrook III dwelt at length on the issue of 'public administration in dark times focusing on some questions for the future of the field. Major highlights of the discussion are as under:

The Conference took serious note of the contemporary international scenario and the overall impression was that 'humanity is living in dark times—war, terrorism, climate change, economic calamity' and the list could go on. So, the question that was being posed was: Does public administration have the governance capacity to address effectively the seemingly insurmountable problems that characterize dark times? The short and imprecise answer is no, but not for reasons typically argued by scholars and pundits. We agree that sustainable resources for public agencies and programs are diminishing on a daily basis, that public coffers are strained and in some cases, completely drained, that public sector labour markets are largely broken and in distress and that fungible supplies of political support for policies and programs are declining at break-neck pace across all levels of government and throughout the world. These are serious problems. At their root, however, lies an even more disturbing problem, namely that in its pursuit of the right answers to narrow administrative questions (an important but exclusive task), public administration has failed to consider what it means to govern in dark times and therefore, to claim its role in shaping societal affairs.

The concern thus was "how can public administration grapple with the complex and intractable realities of'dark times'". An attempt was made to look back at the seminal contributions of scholars such as Arendt, Stivers and Isaac and to see how far it would be feasible to build on their contributions. So, there was a serious intellectual heart searching going on among the attendee scholars, examining and expanding the seminal ideas of great predecessors about "governance in dark times."

It was argued that public administration often failed to address grave social issues because:

(1) The field does not adequately recognize itself as a de facto arbiter of political conflict and consequently as a discipline responsible for shaping societal affairs;

(2) The field suffers from a bureaucratic pathology that reduces its abilities to do the first. Therefore, the suggestion was to try to reinvigorate the democratic ethos which might help public administration improve its governance capacities amidst such troubling circumstances and realities. Finally, returning to the Minnowbrook III conference and looking to the work of its Phase One groups, some big questions were posed in respect of the future of public administration. It was decided that the goal was not to bemoan the field but rather to

spark debate and identify potential opportunities for public administration to better address issues of governance in dark times.

The overall intellectual reaction had been that public administration, both as a field of academic study and as a professional practice, was not addressing adequately and timely the vital questions about governance in 'dark times'.

Looking Back to Look Forward

Looking back, Minnowbrook I was organised in 1968 by Dwight Waldo, who assembled a group of "young" public administration scholars to evaluate the state of the field. The participants found the field inadequate in its" set of concepts and ideas to explain the modern world of administration" and formulated the ideas of "New Public Administration". It was an action-oriented perspective that embraced normative inquiry and advocated for social equity and citizen participation among other issues.

Minnowbrook II, held in 1988 with a cohort of the 1960s scholars and a cohort new scholars, was designed to compare and contrast the changing epochs of public administration. This conservative mission "retreated from an action perspective to cerebral examinations of... the classics" and produced discussions that were more practical and less radical than those at the first Minnowbrook.

The differences between Minnowbrooks I and II may have had a lot to do with the state of society in the 1960s (which were characterized by political upheaval and radical social change), as compared to the 1980s (which were relatively stable). Thus, the differing perspectives and missions of the first two conferences reflect the respective tone and temper of the times.

One might think that Minnowbrook III, held in 2008, would have had more in common with Minnowbrook I than with Minnowbrook IL Between Minnowbrooks II and III, there were extraordinary changes in the world:

- The fall of the Berlin Wall;
- The end of the Cold war;
- The uniting of European Union under a single monetary system;
- The emergence of China as a superpower;
- Iran and North Korea joining the nuclear age;
- Terrorist attacks on US soil;
- US military actions in Iraq and Afghanistan;
- The emergence of climate change as a planetary threat;
- The need to find sustainable clean energy sources;
- The destruction of New Orleans by hurricane Katrina;
- The emergence and supersonic speed of new technologies;
- The corporate credit crisis and global financial crisis, to name but a few.

The optimists might argue that public administration was reasserting its role and leading the way in addressing these and other problems, it nevertheless seemed that the time was right for participant scholars to discuss these issues, debate possible solutions and propose new directions for the field. The organisers of the conference seem to have agreed; the mission for Minnowbrook III was to "critique the current state of public administration, public management and public service today and examine the future of the field."

To achieve this mission, as earlier pointed out, Minnowbrook III was organised in two parts. For the "Phase One" workshop, new scholars wrote brief critiques of the field in advance and then, at the conference site, self-organised into small groups around topics of interest and reported back to everyone during whole-group sessions. "Phase Two" followed a more traditional conference format. During Phase One, the expectation was that there would be rich discussions about public administration in dark times, although in fact there was little acknowledgement of these issues.

In reflecting on that phase, it seems that the galaxy of new scholars largely avoided the opportunity to address big questions of the field, in favour of ongoing, traditional research agendas. Although a number of new scholar-critiques had been quite provocative* few, however, raised issues relating to the 'dark times'.This omission continued into the small discussion groups that assembled around issues such as the academic/ practitioner divide, networks, information technology, public administration theory, methodology, comparative administration, globalisation, performance measurement, transparency and accountability, leadership, law, social equity and financial management. Although, there was nothing inherently wrong with these and other topics discussed; they were surely important and worthy of consideration. Yet, at the end of the day there was a feeling that the scholars could do much more and raise more significant questions about 'public administration in dark times'. However, absent in the reports from the small groups and in the other whole-group deliberations was noteworthy discussion about the urgent issues that the field and humanity face. To be fair, some heavy-handed critiques emerged in peripheral discussions but they never made it onto the floor for consideration by the whole group of participants.

Concluding Observations

Lack or studied avoidance of more lively debate was possibly the result of the new scholars' need (rather selfish though) to expand personal research agendas with like minded individuals in a safe and supportive setting. As one commentator has observed: 'Perhaps it was a function of the fact that tenure clocks are/were ticking for most of us, leaving little time for engagement of the "big questions," and barely enough time to get out a series of articles'. Perhaps it was related to the fact that the participants were, for the most part, new to each other and did not have the time to build the bonds of trust needed for such potentially divisive discussions. Perhaps the void is a signal that the loss of deliberative spaces has seeped into the realm of the Academy. Whatever the reason, one cannot but bemoan the fact that there was a missed opportunity to address the problems of public administration in dark times and to find new approaches and ways to collectively search out future growth trajectories of the discipline.

In a word, therefore, Minnowbrook III seems like a good gathering without being able to reap a rich intellectual harvest at a time when the discipline of public administration badly needed a new direction and a way out of the nagging 'identity crisis'.

Public Choice Approach

Another landmark in the evolution of the discipline is the emergence of the 'public choice' approach to public administration. The public choice school has been developed by a number of eminent scholars in a variety of ways. Essentially, a critique of the bureaucratic model of administration, the public choice approach deals with the possibility of institutional pluralism in the provision of public goods and services. Plurality of governments and public agencies is supported on the ground of consumers' preferences. Vincent Ostrom, one of the protagonists of the public choice school, has set a concept of'democratic administration' alongside the conventional idea of bureaucratic administration. In brief, Ostrom's argument is as follows:

"Perfection in the hierarchical ordering of a professionally trained public service accountable to a single centre of power will reduce the capability of a larger administrative system to respond to diverse preferences among citizens for many different public goods and services and cope with diverse environmental conditions."

"A variety of different organisational arrangements can be used to provide different public goods and services. Such organisations can be coordinated through various multi-organisational arrangements..."

The public choice school, thus, locates pubtic administration within the domain of politics and an appropriate theory of political organisation.[30]

Esssentially it questions the hegemony of bureaucracy that seeks to promote self-aggrandizement and unnecessarily inflate government. Bureaucracy has thus to be pruned by down-sizing government and passing on many of the functions of government to the private sector.'Market' forces, when allowed free play, may function better than government.

The public choice school of economists challenged the conventional beliefs about the public spiritedness of politicians and bureaucrats.

Two underlying assumptions have been: (a) individuals act rationally with adequate information and ordered preferences; and (b) individuals are utility maximisers. They seek more satisfaction for the same on outlay. The essential question raised by public choice advocates is: how far politics and administration can be treated as an exchange relationship as in economic dealings. While the theory has drawn timely attention to the failings *of* autonomous bureaucracy, it is too sweeping a statement that takes values and public spiritedness completely out of administration. Replacement of public administration by market exchange is too simplistic an idea to be taken seriously.

Critical Theory and Public Organisations

The 'scientific' study of public administration has often strayed away from the normative concerns of democratic government. As earlier explained, the 'public choice' approach has been an attempt to construct a theory of public organisations in tune with consumers' interest and individual preferences. Mono centric, hierarchical, bureaucratic administration has been found to be incompatible with some of the basic norms of a humanist and liberal democracy.

The development of 'critical theory' as a philosophical and practical discipline has greatly influenced social sciences in general and public administration in particular reiterating the need for the humanization of public organisations that exert so much influence on social life and the work place.

The critical perspective has been elaborated by an array of eminent scholars.[31] Following closely the work of Jurgen Habermas, the best known exponent of the critical theory, we can identify salient aspects of the critical approach that have special relevance to the study of public organisations.

Like Weber, Habermas refers to the preponderance of technical efficiency in a modern state through the operation of public bureaucracy. As the society gets increasingly bureaucratised, social power and discretion tend to be concentrated in the hands of bureaucratic state apparatus. The trend toward over-bureaucratization causes concern about the social role of the bureaucracy which can be inquired into from the critical perspective.

The expanding role of the public bureaucracy

is not matched by its popular acceptance. Paradoxically enough there is increasing criticism of the bureaucracy as a self-aggrandising force alienated from the public who can rarely repose trust in it. Public interest and bureaucratic interests seem at many places at loggerheads, which was also the contention of the public choice school.

Despite a great variety of management structures and styles, the common assumption has been that management is basically technical in nature whose primary motive is to produce predictable results by manipulating human beings and materials. Positivistic assumptions pervade mainstream public administration. Administrative 'science' is credited with the power to provide instrumental statements which can be profitably used by practising managers to regulate the behaviour of the subordinates and to control environmental uncertainties. The search for efficiency has led to the depersonalisation and rigidity of the administrative processes. Organisational inmates, especially those at the operative level, are looked at as data to be manipulated at will or directed as and when necessary by the superiors. Within the organisation, the human beings are thus separated from one another and are treated as impersonal objects.

The mainstream literature in public administration has thus been obsessed with the ideas of control and regulation, order and efficiency, [illegible] predictability and rationality. Intra-organisationally, such an approach to organisation has led to alienation from work and fellow workers. As regards organisation-client relationship, the alienation takes the forms of organisational distrust and occasional hostility to the working of bureaucracy.

A critical theory of public organisation would be interested in improving the quality of organisational life. It would inquire about the conditions of power and dependence in an organisation and try to reveal the inherent contradictions ih hierarchical relationships as embedded in a bureaucracy.

The critical approach would concentrate on the distorted patterns of communication that characterise present-day organisations both in terms of internal and external relationships. As organisations structure interpersonal relationships in hierarchical terms, the structural arrangement stands in the way of free flow of communication among human beings within the organisation as equal members of a common enterprise. Same holds good for organisation-client relationship, whereby the organisation tends to look at the client as a burden and the client in turn tends to view the organisation as unhelpful. In such a situation, the organisational design and operation run counter to the basic purposes of a democratic public service.

The critical approach would suggest a different style of management altogether, directed not so much towards contftrf as helping individuals to discover and pursue their own developmental needs. The basic thrust of critical theory of public organisation is towards reaffirmation of a commitment to the democratization of all kinds of social relationships. This could be by locating and removing the disabilities that have blocked the surfacing of true needs of individuals in social and political spheres.

THE PUBLIC SERVICE APPROACH

Public administration as a discipline has been experiencing currently an unusual uncertainty about approaches to the study of administration. Historically, there have been shifting stances from Taylorism to systems theory via behaviour and other process theories such as those on decision-making, leadership, coordination and communication and so on and so forth. The uniqueness of current turmoil lies in raising 'fundamental' questions about the role of the state itself under the bewildering pressures coining from within and without the state (e.g., globalisation).

The two discipline—shaking approaches, in this context, are (a) reinventing government approach of Osbourne and Gabbler and (b) new public management approach of the neo-liberal school of thought. The first approach has sought to reorient governmental studies from the point of view of core competence of government which has been termed as 'steering' rather than 'rowing'. By contrast, the second approach has been focused on the 'downsising' of government (from the point of view of scope) and on enhanced management competence using information technology, introducing critical performance appraisal and allowing the 'market' to function in its designated sphere.

The neo-liberal philosophy, as the critics point out, has functioned to the detriment of larger 'public interest', affecting particularly the poor and the marginalized.

The other consequence of'downsizing' has been to be the central position of government as the core regulator of society.

There have been many reactions to the 'neo-liberal' approach to government; more importantly, it has been suggested that the neo-liberal view, by apotheosizing 'market' has failed to appreciate the critical role of public institutions—the government—in the maintenance and development of society. In their path-breaking publication entitled. 'The New Public Service: Serving, Not Steering' (M.E. Sharpe, 2002) Denhardt and Denhardt have succinctly put the central role of government as 'service'.'Government', as they forcefully argue, 'shouldn't be run like a business, it should be run like a democracy'. Public interest and democratic citizenship are the hall marks of government. As the sense of service and community would be expanding, public employees would be having better self-estimation and sense of dignity and self-respect. They would in fact be reconnected with the citizens. As the public servants would be inviting citizens to participate in the governance process, their will emerge a new culture of co-governance with the administrators and citizens working together for the common good of the society. This new attitude and new involvement—co-governance—is what Denhardt and Denhardt call 'the New Public Service'. As it has been observed,'Administrators are realizing that they have much to gain by 'listening' to the public rather than 'telling' and by 'serving' rather than 'steering'. At the invitation of public servants, even their urging, ordinary citizens are once again becoming engaged in the governance process. Citizens and public officials are working together to define and to address common problems in a cooperative and mutually beneficial way".

What Denhardt and Denhardt describe is more an expectation—a normative stand—in order to sensitize us to the democracy-diminishing trend inherent in the neo-liberal philosophy with its accent on 'market' and de-emphasis on 'government'. It is a timely warning and an appropriate cautionary note against the trendy 'down-sizing' movement in public administration.

Summing Up

To sum up, public administration as a discipline is still in the process of establishing its identity. The evolutionary process is indicative of the shifting boundaries of the discipline in response to constantly emerging social needs. As administrative practices are called upon to respond to new problems and challenges surfacing in the wake of social change, the discipline has correspondingly to shed its formalistic and insular "efficiency" orientation of the older genre. It seems the norms of democracy are seeking entry into public organisations and the concern for distributive justice is assuming critical significance as a major administrative agenda item.

At the same time, since the eighties there has been a noticeable change in public administration discourse, upholding a new 'public management' doctrine (being discussed separately) favouring more and more market-orientation, as distinguished from 'state' or government orientation. Another new development is the steady rise of what has been called third-party administration. The conventional view has been that all government programmes are carried out by the government's own employees. This is true to a great extent no doubt. But in reality much of government's work is farmed out to other semi-government, private and non-government organisations. Local government, for instance, does many agency functions on behalf of the central government. Similarly, many development programmes are often handed over to non-government organisations. Many government activities such as road building, housing etc. are contracted out to private agencies. The current trend is towards leaner and thinner government and as many activities as possible, it is being argued, should be handed over to private parties including NG Os. This trend will in course of time involve new modes of control, financing and monitoring of "third party administration" by the government.

REFERENCES

1. Woodrow Wilson, "The Study of Administration", in Dwight Waldo (ed.) *Ideas and Issues in Public Administration,* McGraw-Hill, 1953.
2. Arthur S. Link, *The Papers cf Woodrow Wilson,* vol. 7 (1890-92), Princeton University Press, 1968.
3. Quoted in Phillip J. Cooper at al, *Public Administration for the Twenty-First Century,* Harecourt Brae Co., 1998, p. 11.
4. Phillip J. Cooper et al, op. cit., p.374.
5. Peter Self, *Administrative Theories and Politics,* S. Chand A' Co. Ltd., New Delhi, 1984, p.20.
6. John J. Corson and Joseph P. Harris, *Public Administration in Modern Society,* McGraw-Hill, 1963, p. 12.
7. Ferrel Heady, *Public Administration: A Comparative Perspective,* Prentice-Hall, 1966, p, 24.
8. Herbert Simon, *Administrative Behaviour,* The Free Press, New York, 1947.
9. Stephen K. Bailey, "Ethics and the Public Service", in *Public Administration, Concepts and Cases* by Richard J. Stillman II (ed.), Houghton Mifflin Company, 1976. An important book in this context is *Morality and Administration in Democratic Government* by Paul H. Appleby, Louisiana State University Press, 1952.
10. John Rawls, *A Theory of Justice,* Harvard University Press, 1971.
11. Nicholas Henry, *Public Administration and Public Affairs,* Prentice-Hall, 1975, pp. 43-4.
12. Peter Self, *Administrative Theories and Politics,* George Allen & Unwin Ltd. London, 1972 p. 12
13. Frank J. Goodnow, *Policy and Administration:* Macmillan, New York, 1900.
14. Fritz J. Roethlisberger and William J. Dickson, *Management and the Worker: An Account of a Reserarch Program Conducted by the Western Electric Company Hawthorne works, Chicago,* Harvard University Press, 1939.
15. R. H. Dahl, "The Science of Public Administration: Three Problems", *Public Administration Review;* 7 (1947).
16. Simon, op. cit., p. 44.
17. Simon, ibid, p. xiv.
18. Simon, "A Comment on 'The Science of Public Administration", *Public Administration Review,* 7 (Winter 1947), p. 202.
19. Ferrel Heady, op. cit., p. 3.
20. F C. Mosher, "Research in Public Administration", *Public Administration Review,* 16 (Summer 1956).
21. The two volumes are: Frank Marini (ed.), *Toward a New Public Administration,* Chandler, 1971; Dwight Waldo (ed.) *Public Administration in a time of Turbulence,* Chandler, 1971. (The second volume is strictly not a new public administration document.)

22. Frederickson, "Toward a New Public Administration" in Marini (ed.), op. cit.
23. Marini op. cit., p. 32.
24. Ibid., p. 311.
25. Quoted in Flix A. Nigro, Lloyd d. Nigro, pp.4-5, *Modern Public Administration,* Harper & Row Publications, New York, 1980.
26. Quoted in H. George Frederickson, *New Public Administration,* the University of Alabama Press, 1980.
27. Minnowbrook-II has been covered in some details in *Public Administration Review,* March - April 1989.
28. Mary Ellen Guy, "Minnowbrook -II: Conclusion", *PAR,* March- April 1989.
29. For detailed discussion see Rosemary O'Leary, David M.Van Şlyke and Soonhee Kim (eds.),The FutureofPublicAdministrationAroundtheWorld, Georgetown University Press, 2011.
30. Robert E. Cleary, "Dialogue^ Negotiation and the Advancement of Democracy: Reflections on Minnowbrook -II", *PAR,* March- April 1989.
31. See in this connection, Vincent Ostrom, *The IntellectualCrisisinAmericanPublicAdministration,* University of Alabama Press, 1974, pp. 111-113.
32. Major works on the critical perspective are included in Andrew Arato and Eike Gebhardt (eds.) *The Essential Frankfurt School Reader, Urizen Books, 197%.*

CHAPTER 2

Organisational Effectiveness

Traditionally, there has been the one-dimensional definition of organisational effectiveness: if an organisation has 'successfully' achieved its objective, it is considered effective". Effectiveness is thus a matter of comparing results with intentions.

This goal attainment theory has been challenged by organisational researchers on the ground that (a) organisations have multiple goals: some are official (openly announced) goals and others are operative goals (more realistic short-term goals); in real practice organisations, move in many directions and it is a simplistic notion to talk about one, overriding goal:

(a) The organisational goals are often in conflicting relationship; one department, say health, would like to go for an aggressive immunisation programme, but its move may by blocked by the finance department by withdrawing fund.

(b) There is a weak relationship between organisational goal and individual behaviour. In real life, decisions are taken by members of the organisation without preset goals. In times of crisis or emergency, stresses and strains, the managers are compelled to take short-term decisions to cope with the problems at hand. Rarely there is much opportunity for rational long-term, goal directed behaviour.

Multiple Criteria: Organisations and their subuniqs are no doubt purposeful and they are expected to attain goals. But 'model of organisational effectiveness must encompass more than goal attainment' and organisational theorists have identified 'a wide variety of effectiveness criteria in which the goal achievement approach is one of several dimensions'.

Palumbo and Moody have shortlisted the following effectiveness criteria out of a large number of *indicators of organisational growth and stability:*

i) **Outcomes:** The first is the traditional performance measurement criterion in terms of outcomes or goal attainment. For instance, in the case of a primary health centre, an important criterion would be: how many patients were treated at the centre? There are, of course, conceptual problems here in regard to measurement of 'treatment' (whether 'treating' or 'curing' would be acceptable criterion).

ii) **Adaptation:** In terms of open systems theory, achievement of results is linked to the organisation's coping ability with the environment. It is organisational survival and continuity that would be the ultimate criterion of effectiveness. Flexibility and adaptability, not strict adherence to goals, would be the hallmark of effectiveness. Thus conceived, organisational effectiveness is the "ability of an organisation, in either relative or absolute terms, to exploit its environment in the acquisition of scarce and valued resources'".[2]

iii) **System health:** The open systems theory suggests that organisations have to strike a balance between production goals and maintenance goals. A local police organisation tnay make an all-out effort to prevent crime by deploying a larger number of police men on patrol duty supported by a fleet of vehicles. It would howeyer be a short-term gain, as the good result (crime prevention/detection) need to be sustained on the basis of a longer-term policy. What is important is to make sure that the equipments used (vehicles) are maintained regularly and kept in good shape for longer term use (not merely one-shot achievement). Also, the basic human resource (the policemen) should be trained and retrained and motivated to do the job on regular basis as against one-time campaign basis, which is very common in police organisations. Thus, maintenance of infrastructure and human resources development are of crucial significance for maintaining organisational health. Only then can one be sure of organisational effectiveness on sustained basis.

Summing Up: Organisational effectiveness is thus a complex, multi-dimensioned problem. As it has been very well summarised:

"Trying to view organisational effectiveness as a single dimension is much like trying to visualize a cube without depth preparation—the result is distortion"[3]

In discussing effectiveness, one should take note of the fact that effectiveness criteria do not remain static; nor do they remain the same in the course of an organisation's life.

It has been observed that an entrepreneurial leadership pushes the organisation towards productivity; by contrast, the general trend in bureaucratic organisation has been towards stability. Even within a bureaucratic organisation, in normal times, effectiveness criteria may favour stability and predictability; but in emergencies (e.g. flood or drought relief) the same organisation would prefer more flexibility and adaptability in search of effectiveness.

Efficiency in Government

The original call for efficiency in government operations can be traced to the old Wilsonian dictum that it was necessary "to straighten the paths of government, to make its business less un-businesslike...". In public administration 'efficiency' has always been the prime consideration, as government has been considered proverbially sick and inefficient. Government is big business.The range and scale of government activities have been increasing with more and more involvement of government in the regulation of supply of commodities and services for ;the benefit of the people. This is particularly true of the post-colonial developing countries where governments have a crucial role to play in bringing about radical socio-economic changes. Expansion of government activities must be matched, by efficient management of the public sector. Experience shows, however, that government is not as efficient as it should be. Allegations are often heard that money is not well spent on government projects; or, when funds are spent, the results are not commensurate with investments. There are frequent complaints of administrative red tape, delays and corruptions. Government may be inefficient, but it has got to be efficient in public interest. It is in this context that efficiency in government assumes critical significance. Peter

Drucker, the well-known management scientist, writes that the service (government) institution is in a fundamentally different 'business' from business. "It is different in its purpose. It has different values. It needs different objectives and it makes a different contribution to society. 'Performance and results' are quite different in a service institution from what they are in a business. 'Managing for performance' is the one area in which the service institution differs significantly from business".[4]

Logically, one has to consider efficiency in government in a different perspective. It need not be equated with what goes on in private management. The differences between public and business administration can be looked at from the input and the output side of the account, as suggested by Peter Self. Public administration is very much exposed to 'politics'. Demands very often come from the political system and the administrative system has to respond to them. "Business firms", to quote Peter Self, "are not directly integrated with the political system in the way that all administrative agencies (including even most public corporations) necessarily are. Administrative agencies inhabit a political instead of a market environment and the political system articulates demands and monitors results in quite different ways from the market system."[5]

Public administration has greater similarity with business administration, when considered from the output side of the account. The technical nature of the activities undertaken by an organisation has a decisive impact on the structure of the organisation. Many a time, the outputs of public administration and those of business administration are found to be much the same. In this connection the six-fold classification of administrative outputs by Peter Self is as follows:

(a) *Public utilities* such as electricity, railways etc.
(b) *Social services* such as education, health etc.
(c) *Scientific and technical services* such as research and development in science and technology, agriculture etc.
(d) *Military and paramilitary services* such as defence, police etc.
(e) *Basic powers of regulation and assistance* such as regulation of competition, regulation relating to safety and health of industrial workers etc.
(f) *Overall planning* of the economy, the environment and social welfare.

Services included in the first three items in the list have built-in technical requirements that have to be adhered to by all organisations, irrespective of their location in the public or private sector. Of course, if an electricity undertaking is in the private sector, it is likely to be much more insulated from public pressures and influences than would be the case if it were in the public sector. Its scale of operation and linkages with other organisations also would be much more limited. Services, when provided through the public sector, would have to reckon with social costs which private management may not take into account. The pollution problem of a thermal plant, for instance, will figure more prominently in a public sector electricity undertaking.

The last three items in the list of administrative outputs have very few genuine parallels in business organisation, they are unique to government.

Clearly, more urgent services, monopolistic and semi-monopolistic services and functions which are inherently public in nature such as defence and law and order maintenance are confined to government. The scope of government activities has never been static in history; it expands or shrinks with political regime variations.

Meaning of Efficiency

Coming back to our initial search for a meaning of the term 'efficiency' in government, it can be suggested that efficiency needs to be related to the objective of an organisation. Government activities are very wide ranging. Some of these lead to the production of concrete, measurable outputs such as water supply, roads, irrigation and so on. Others are maintenance and regulatory functions. Law and order maintenance, licensing, public health regulations are a few examples of such functions. There are a few others that entail balancing of diverse policy goals. Desmond Keeling in his book, *Management in Government,* suggested a three-fold classification of the tasks of government. In the first category, the administrative tasks call for quasi-judicial attitudes and methods. The diplomatic tasks, a second category, involve reconciliation among a number of diverse goals. The third category embracing the management tasks requires the most efficient use of resources. Keeling's classification suggests different efficiency tests for different tasks.

In business administration, efficiency is usually measured in terms of resource use. It is a matter of input-output relationship, the implication being the least cost approach to organisational performance. Efficiency is thus considered in terms of 'profit' earning. The profit test may be applicable to some of the production or commercial units in the public sector. But to assess performance in the public sector merely by the profit indicator would be taking a narrow view of the role of this sector. More than efficiency, 'effectiveness' assumes critical significance in the appraisal of government performance. Effectiveness refers to successful achievement of specific policy goals. Cost reduction should, of course, be kept in mind. But, resource use should not be taken as constraint on performance. In times of crisis such as severe drought or devastating flood, government cannot sit down and calculate the, costs of operations to reduce expenditure. Iminediate relief rather than minimum cost weighs heavily in government mind in such circumstances. Peter Self's observation in tl)is context is very relevant. As he says "Business management is guided by specific but socially narrow tests of resource efficiency, which car. be confined to the firm in question.The equivalent tests for government must refer ultimately to the welfare of the whole society, as politically articulated".[6]

Three kinds of efficiency seem important in public administration. Firstly, *administrative or management efficiency* is as relevant to business administration as to government administration. Good organisations, appropriate methods and procedures and the use of management techniques such as work study, network technique etc. are equally useful in public administration, as it seeks to promote efficiency.

Secondly, *policy efficiency* has peculiar significance for government organisation. This kind of efficiency refers to the making of right policy decisions and the choice of appropriate programmes to achieve the defined objectives. For instance, government may spend huge sums of money on a new rail line but the cost will be in fructuous if the new line does not help to achieve the planned objectives such as regional development through free flow of commodities, services and people. Many a time, government projects yield results after a fairly long period. Still, in making public investment decisions the achievement of larger policy objectives has to be kept in mind. This is how policy efficiency can be ensured in government.

A third kind of efficiency can be related to the satisfaction of the public. This can be called *service efficiency.*[7] Government efficiency, specially where programmes are directed toward specific target groups, has to be measured in terms of accessibility to citizens and their overall satisfaction derived from the enjoyment of designated services and facilities. Development programmes meant for the small farmers (SFDA) and for other weaker sections of the community such as the marginal farmers and rural artisans should keep the service efficiency in mind. Clientele development and satisfaction would determine the efficiency of these development programmes.

REFERENCES

1. Dennis Palumbo and Steven Maynard Moody, *Contemporary Public Administration,* Longman, New York and London, 1991. Chapter 3 contains a detailed, analytical discussion on organisational effectiveness.
2. As noted in Palumbo and Moody, op. cit.
3. As noted in Palumbo and Moody, op. cit.
4. Peter F. Drucker, "Managing the Public Service Institution", in Stilman, op. cit.
5. Op. cit., p. 262.
6. Op. cit. p. 269.
7. A. W. Johnson, "Efficiency in Government and Business", in *Public Administration in Canada* edited by A. M. Williams and W. D. K. Kernaghan, Methuen, 1968.

Chapter 3

Public-Private Dichotomy

It needs to be emphasised, in continuation of the discussion in the previous chapter, that government has to function within defined constitutional rules and regulations. There is a certain legalism inherent in government operations. Business administration is not as hamstrung as public administration by innumerable rules and regulations that are supposed to control the working of the public sector in public interest.

The distinction between the public and the private sector is greatly influenced by the political philosophy of each nation. In the USA, for instance, the private sector plays a very important role in the American economy and society. The public sector is in many ways dependent on the private sector for the supply of goods and services. Hence, the tendency in that country is towards blurring of lines rather than a distinct bifurcation of responsibilities. In India, by contrast, the public sector had earlier been the dominant sector in a situation of mixed economy. The steady diminution of the public sector in India, if it continues as a matter of new public policy, is expected to draw in course of time a sharper distinction between the public and private management.

In a nutshell, it may be suggested that considerations of general welfare should be the common concern of public and business administration. Private management can ignore the larger public interest only at its peril. At the other end, public administration can hardly ignore the needs of efficient management. Continued maladministration may ultimately lead to the shrinkage of its areas of concern. The current advocacy of 'privatisation' is indicative of this trend.

The distinction between business and public administration has broadly been summed up as follows:

1. The major purpose of public administration is to serve the public; hence general welfare and, in specific cases, cliental satisfaction are the ends that public administration must serve. Business administration, by contrast, is basically oriented toward earning profit for the business proprietors. Inability to earn profits will soori drive a private enterprise out of business.
2. Public administration has to operate strictly according to laws, rules and regulations. Adherence to law brings in a degree of rigidity in operation in the public sector. There is always the fear of audit or other aberrations from regulations that act as a constraint on performance. Contrastingly, business administration is relatively free from similar constraints of law and regulations. There are of course general laws regulating business, but individual business firms have considerable flexibility to adapt their operations to changing situations. This is possible because of their relative freedom

from specific laws and rules that abound in public administration.

3. The actions of public administration agencies are much more exposed to the public gaze. An achievement rarely gets publicity, but a little fault hits the newspaper headline. Organisations like the police have to be on their toes to make sure that their operations do not incur the public wrath. This wide publicity is not to be found in business administration, nor is it so very closely watched by the public and the publicity media.
4. In public administration, any show of discrimination, or partiality will evoke public censure or legislative commotion. Hence, the administrators are to be very consistent and impartial in their dealings with the public. In business administration, discrimination is freely practised. In the choice of products and in fixing prices, business administration overtly practises discrimination which is almost a part of business culture.
5. Public administration, especially at higher reach of government, is exceedingly complex. There are many pulls and pressures, many minds have to meet and discuss, consultations go on in several rounds of meetings. Activities in one department have ramifications that spread over several other departments. By contrast, business administration is, generally speaking, much more well-knit and single-minded in operation. There is much less complexity in organisation and operations. The pulls and pressures are certainly much less, as compared to public sector operations.
6. It is political direction that gives public administration its special character. Politics is at the core of public administration and at higher echelons the civil servants must have the tact and mature understanding to work and live with politicians. This speciality of public administration marks it out clearly from business administration.

The distinction between public administration and business or private administration need not, however, be blown out of proportions. There are several aspects of public management that are generic; that is, they are similar in both public administration and private management. There are many grey areas where the line of separation between the two is not so marked. For instance, a publre organisation like a milk dairy or a state transport undertaking has to function on business or commercial lines. It has, therefore, to emulate some of the methods and practices of business management. At the other end, private business is increasingly being subjected to government regulation in public interest. The kind of'mixed' economy that prevails in India under strong government direction is practically an endorsement of public-private coexistence and cooperation.

Privatisation Movement

At this stage, a note on the recent "privatisation" movement will be in order. 'Privatisation' as it emerged in the lexicon of management in the eighties, came to be defined narrowly as 'to make private, especially to change from public to private control or ownership'. It has now come to acquire a broader meaning symbolising a new way of looking at society's needs and redefining the role of government in meeting them. It means relying more on society's private institutions and less on government to satisfy the needs of the people.

The Privatisation movement has been spurred by at least four major forces:

i) **Pragmatic:** The goal being better government and a more cost-effective one;
ii) **Ideological:** The goal being to ideologically reduce the role of government in societal needs fulfilment vis-a-vis private institutions;
iii) **Commercial:** The goal being to get more business by having more of government spending redirected towards commercial interests;
iv) **Populist:** The goal being to achieve a better society by giving people greater power to satisfy their common needs.

Privatisation has been conceived as a strategic approach to improve governmental productivity and thereby to give people more for their money. Attempts to improve governmental performance have taken many forms such as budgeting reform, introduction of management techniques and even large-scale reforms through reforms committees and commissions. In terms of consequences, however, such reform efforts have generally been unsuccessful.The latest move to 'privatise* is not to belitde the importance of 'government' but to improve the productivity of public organisations. Cost-conscious public officials and other productivity-oriented groups are now favouring privatisation 'as an important tool for better public management and as the key to more cost-effective government*.

Methods of Privatisation

Following are the categorisation of E.S. Savas[1], different methods of privatisation can be broadly classified as:

(a) Divestment,
(b) Delegation, and
(c) Displacement

Divestment stands for shedding an enterprise or asset. This involves a positive step by government whereby an enterprise or asset is either sold or given away as an ongoing business, or an enterprise may be closed down and the assets sold away.

Delegation requires a continuing, active role for government. In this method government delegates to the private sector part of or all of the activity of producing goods and services, but retains responsibility for overseeing the result. Delegation can be carried out by contract, franchise, grant, voucher, or mandate. Local government, for instance, often contracts for services such as solid waste collection.

The third method—**Displacement—**is somewhat passive process that leads to a government's entity being displaced more or less gradually by the private sector as markets develop to satisfy needs. Displacement may occur by default (government not being able to provide services such as transport), by withdrawal (deliberately government vacates an area and allows private sector to take it up) and by deregulation—a method enabling the private sector to challenge a government monopoly and even displace it altogether. The discussions here point towards a new way of looking at privatisation, which is government-strengthening and not quite anti-public sector.

How Different is Public Sector?

Public-private distinction, as Dwight Waldo has remarked, is no longer a sharp one, at least in the United States and there is a movement 'towards a ring and mixing of the two'.[2] An extreme view taken by Barry Bozeman is that 'all organisations are public because public authority affects some of the behaviour or process of all organisations. All organisations, in his view, share public' and 'private' features.[3]

It is understandable that as government gets more and more involved in business and as business-like approaches are increasingly taken in governmental operations, there is bound to be the blurring of lines between the public and private sectors.

On the other side, there are scholars who point out the special nature of public administration. Note, in this connection, Wallace Sayre's comment: 'Business and public organisations are alike only in all unimportant respects'[4]. The crucial distinction has been identified as public administration's basis in rule of law. Public organisations do publics business in terms of law. They administer law. 'Every element of their being - their structure, staffing, budget and purpose - is the product of legal authority. Every action taken by a public administrator ultimately must be traceable to a legal grant of authority'[5].

Also public organisations have distinctive processes and they work in different environment. Public scrutiny, balancing of political interests and accountability through a variety of agencies and processes such as the legislature, the judiciary, the media and the public mark out public administration as a distinctly different enterprise and very importantly, it is the challenge of public service that distinguishes public from private administration.

A Balanced View

Public administration as practical governmental activities for societal management is carried on at different levels—centre, state and local —within the broad governing philosophy as delineated in the constitution. Thus, the Indian Constitution provides the philosophical framework and major conditions (e.g. fundamental rights of citizens, directive principles etc.) that public administration in India at any level has to reckon with. The Constitution creates both opportunities and constraints for administration. For instance, there are opportunities created by reservation of public appointments. The office of the Comptroller and Auditor General looks after the accounts and audit of governments at all levels. The legislatures both at the centre and in the states pass the budget and hold the executive accountable. Under the Constitution, the judiciary listens to cases against government agencies lodged by aggrieved citizens. Thus, the basic principles of government and some of the major control mechanisms are laid down in the Constitution.This is something unique to public management.

Secondly, the public agencies and private business face the 'market' very differently. The private firms' face the market more direcdy. If the firms are unable to produce products or services at competitive prices, their clients move to alternative sources and this affects the firms income badly.

Public agencies, by contrast, do not face competitive markets for their products and services. The prices of government 'goods' are usually fixed through budget exercises. Through taxation, resources are raised by government. User charges are also imposed on certain occasions, but the general trend is that government agencies operate as legal monopolies, sometimes services are provided to everyone at a fixed cost. For instance, the charge for 'Speed Post' is the same for everybody.

In public interest, government has to produce certain goods and services which would otherwise not be provided by private firms. These goods and services are called 'public goods or collective goods.' Highways, education, water supply, public welfare are some examples of 'public goods'. Society as a whole derives benefit from these; hence, the cost of these goods and services is borne by the society as a whole.

For this kind of fiscal management, the market is less constraining in the public than in the private sector.

Thirdly, public administration enjoys a position superior to private management because of its direct link with the state's sovereign power.'The actions of public administrators have the forces of law and the coercive power of government behind them'. Private firms can approach the courts for any wrong doing, but their actions are not binding in the same sense and cannot be enforced through legitimate coercive power, as in the case of a government agency.

As Rosenbloom has emphasised the distinctiveness:

"Public administration is concerned with administration of the public interest. It is constrained by constitutions and relatively unconstrained by market forces atid it is considered a public trust exercised on behalf of the sovereign".[6]

The social complexities of modern age have been generating newer pressures for government control and regulation. Environmental management, pollution control, natural resources conservation, child labour prohibition, regulation of information network and broadcasting—all these and many more activities are increasing the burden of public management. Private management has no such parallel macro-social management. Hence, there is considerable truth in the statement that public administration is not simply a kind of technology but a special form of moral endeavour. In a moral and basic sense, public administration has to serve 'a higher purpose'.

What is clearly discernible is that the nature of public service management is ^hanging fast. The change is from a system characterised by bureaucratic hierarchies to one with a much more diversified pattern. There is now much more focus on quality of services, there is more emphasis now on the role of'market' and there is emphasis now on multi-agency partnerships. Government is now being called upon to play more and more 'enabling* role than the traditional 'doing' role. At the same time, old management themes and styles persist. Obviously, the 'new' and the 'old' sometimes coexist and sometimes conflict with each other.

REFERENCES

1. E.S. Savas, "A Taxonomy of Privatization Strategics", *Policy Studies Review,* 1990.
2. Dwight Waldo, *The Enterprise of Public Administration: A Summary View,* Chander and Sharp, 1980.
3. Barry Bozeman, *All Organisations are Public: Bridging Public and Private Organisation Theories,* Jossey-Bass, 1987.
4. Wallace Sayre, "The Unhappy Bureaucrats: Views Ironic, Helpful, Indignant", *Public Administration Review,* 18 Summer, 1958.
5. James W. Fesler and Donald F. Kettl, *The Politics of the Administrative Process,* Chatham House Publications, Inc., New Jersey, 1991.
6. Rosenbloom, *Public Administration,* op.cit.

CHAPTER 4

Approaches, Principles and Theories

Approaches are standpoints that fix the vision and outlook. In public administration, three major approaches or standpoints deserve mention:

(a) **Institutional Approach:** It lays emphasis on structures, organisation, constitutional framework and laws and procedures. Classical analysts belong to this category.

(b) **Managerial Approach:** This has for its focus operational issues and problems–the internal goings on in the organisation. Processes and producing results are its major concerns.

(c) **Political Approach:** It concentrates on power and interests in organisational life; influences coming from outside and public interest issues that dominate public organisation. The role of the state and the changing functions of the public sector fall in this way of thinking. All these approaches are relevant for public administration analysis.

Both theory and practice need to coalesce to help understand the functioning of governments and to work out administrative policies and practices in the interest of efficient management and clientele satisfaction. Bureaucratic structure, processes and behaviour have been the central concerns of the subject. It differs from political science, as it demarcates a narrow area of intellectual inquiry focussed basically on the executive organisation and operations of the government. Public interest being at the core of governmental functioning, it also differs from the management sciences. The subject does, of course, borrow heavily from the latter. As regards its nexus with political science, it is now widely acknowledged that public administration as governmental organisation and activities is embedded in politics and is shaped and influenced by it. There is even an extreme view suggesting that public administration is politics and the classical view of politics-administration dichotomy is unrealistic and untenable.

ADMINISTRATIVE THEORIES

What passes for'theory'in public administration norms needs to be accepted cautiously. The word 'theory' is often very loosely used. In social science discussions the question of 'value' as preferred state of things appears again and again. It is possible to talk of value theory in the sense that there can be generalisations about individual and/or collective expressions of preferences grown out of life-experiences. An administrator might be holding a view that the universities should be headed by officers from the All-India Services. Implied in his viewpoint is a preference for the administrator as the appropriate power-wielder. Discussions on administration abound in suggestions and recommendations that take the form of 'should be'. To a careful observer, these are value judgements or statements of preferences which are not always explicitly expressed.

Scientific inquiry must evolve causal theories that would help analyse concrete situations and would have predictive use. As David Easton puts it:

"The accumulation of data through acceptable techniques does not alone give us adequate knowledge. Knowledge becomes critical and reliable as it increases in generality and internally consistent organisation, when, in short, it is cast in the form of systematic generalised statements applicable to large numbers of particular cases".[1]

Causal theory, in this sense of generalisation and statement of probabilistic relationship between facts, needs to be worked out in public administration. But at the present state of the subject, such theories are more talked about than really existing.

As a subject of study, public administration has been everybody's field. The practising administrators and academics of all sorts have something to say on one or the other aspects of administration. In fact a coherent, concentrated and organised body of knowledge on the phenomenon of public administration is still evolving. The state of 'theory', under such circumstances, cannot be expected to be satisfactory. As Martin Landau comments rather sarcastically, administrative theory is "marked by a plethora of competing schools, a polyglot of languages and accordingly, a confusion of logic. There is neither a common research tradition nor the necessary consensus for a common field of inquiry. Each of the competing schools questions the others, adventurism is rampant and commonly accepted standards of control do not exist".[2] Peter Self similarly points out that various kinds of 'theories' have grown up around public administration "that are derived from many or no academic disciplines".[3]

It is this discomforting situation that prompted Herbert Simon to look for a fairly definite locus of public administration, which can then be subjected to rigorous scientific analysis. Admittedly, theory-building in public administration is not an easy task, as there are various kinds of public organisations, administrative structures and processes. Generalised statements have also to be tested in different cultural situations before they could be accepted as universal.

Traditionally, administrative theorising has been- the work of practitioners and reformers, particularly in the United States of America. Practitioners like Frederick Taylor in America did anchor their ideas in administrative reality. But at the same time, they had their own ideas about 'good organisation' which they had imperceptibly tried to promote. Administrative theories have, therefore, to be understood against the socio-economic background of the theorists and the historical time period of their existence. Ideas that often pass for 'theories' are most likely to contain implied biases grown out of the socio-historical situation of a writer.

Despite such limitations, which are common to social sciences in general, attempts at theorising in public administration have been going on for a long time. Case study method has been very popular, especially in the U.S.A., to portray micro situations, which could be developed inductively into general propositions about administration.

There is now a large compilation known as *organisation theory* dealing mainly with formal organisations. Governmental activities are undertaken within a specific organisational matrix. The growth and evolution of public organisations, their structures and operational processes and the behaviour of the members of those organisations are interesting subjects of study. Theory-building can be possible if more and more empirical studies are made of the various kinds of public organisations. The evolving discipline of organisation theory is in many ways helpful in understanding the organisation and working of public organisations. It needs to be pointed out, however, that most writings on organisation theory are based on the study of business administration. The special features of government organisations are often ignored or not properly understood by organisation theorists. Since its empirical base is primarily in business administration, organisation theory has to be carefully adapted to the study of public administration. Nevertheless, it has emerged in recent times as a powerful tool of analysis of public administration as well.

The most important paradigm in public administration has been the Weberian concept of bureaucracy. Generations of scholars on government organisations have relied heavily on the structural and behavioural implications of Webers theoretical formulation. The Weberian formulation, as we will discuss later, has remained a general conceptual framework for the understanding of the nature of bureaucracy. Organisational complexities of contemporary public organisations in terms of structures, processes and behaviour cannot, however, all be fully comprehended by reference to Weberian theory alone.

Theoretical concerns in public administration have thus to be pursued in a somewhat eclectic fashion. Organisation theory can be helpful, provided its application takes care of the special features of public administration and is related to government organisation. Weberian formulation continues to be the dominant paradigm in the study of administration. Since public administration is peculiarly embedded in politics, administrative analyses have necessarily to draw mostly on political science. With intense intermingling of politics and administration, theories in political science become fairly freely interchangeable with those in public administration. 'Principles' are practical recipes growing out of the world of work and practice. They do not have the rigour and durability of 'theories'. Scientific management which we owe mainly to Taylor laid down some of such 'principles' or action prescriptions.

Organisation Theories

The theories of public administration, as the previous discussion points out, are drawn on from a variety of sources. The term 'administration' refers to an activity or function. Organisation, by contrast, stands for the object within which administration resides and takes place. Conceptually, organisation has wider connotation than administration. Hence instead of talking about administrative theories, we prefer the phrase organisation theories. The basic character of the theories of organisation and an understanding of the nature and typologies of organisation should therefore engage our attention first.

Nature and Typologies of Organisation

Organisation theory has been described as the study of structure and functioning of organisations and the behaviour of groups and individuals within them. Drawing primarily on the disciplines of sociology and psychology, as also on economics and, to a lesser extent, on production engineering, a new science of organisation has been emerging.

We need to distinguish here complex *formal* organisations from what is called social organisations. Formal organisations have been defined as those which have been established for the explicit purpose of achieving certain goals. They possess rules designed to anticipate and shape behaviour in the direction of these goals. Further they have formal status structure with clearly marked lines of communication and authority. Where social life is carried on without a framework of explicit goals or rules which define a formal status structure, it is usually thought more appropriate to use the term 'social organisation'.

The study of formal organisation has been prompted by many considerations. As human life is affected more and more by numerous large scale, complex organisations, it has been felt necessary to study them scientifically. To quote an eminent organisation theorist, "No matter what you have to do with an organisation—whether you are going to study it, work in it, consult for it, subvert it, or use it in the interest of another organisation—you must have some view of the nature of the beast with which you are dealing".[4] There is also the practical need to understand organisations to produce better results. How is it that one organisation produces more than another? How does an organisation produce at the lowest cost, relative to other organisations? These and similar other questions of great practical value can be answered only by systematic and scientific study of organisations.

Organisation theory, therefore, has value both as pursuit of knowledge about organisations and as a practical aid to actual organisational problem-solving.

The scope of our field can be delineated with reference to the three characteristics common to all organisations: structure, processes and behaviour.

Organisations have been studied from a variety of perspectives. The situation has been likened by Mason Haire, a leading writer, to the proverbial story of the blind men describing an elephant: each believing he is describing a different animal.

It is possible, despite considerable variability[7], to distil a certain amount of common viewpoints expressed about organisations. The fact remains, however, that study of organisations is not the exclusive province of any single discipline. Each disciplinary orientation tends to focus on a particular aspect or set of features of organisations.

Economists, for instance, tend to deal with how organisations allocate resources and how decisions are made under conditions of uncertainty. *Industrial engineers* focus on the technological underpinning of organisational activities. *Sociologists* have been mainly concerned with the structure of organisations and the ways in which organisations try to cope with their external social environments. *Psychologists* have been interested in the behaviour of individuals and groups within organisations. Again, such issues as power and authority in organisational settings have attracted the attention of *political scientists.*

In essence, therefore, the analysis of organisations is a fertile meeting ground for a number of disciplines and has the distinct character of an interdisciplinary field. Turning to definition, the term *'organisation'* is not easy to define. In fact, March and Simon in their widely referred book. *Organisations* choose not to define this word but instead state "it is easier and probably more useful, to give examples ot formal organisations than to define the term".

From a representative sample of some of the widely cited definitions, a summary of fundamental characteristics of organisations can be abstracted:

Organisations consist of individuals and groups; their existence is geared to achieve certain goals and objectives and they operate by means of differentiated functions and intended rational coordination.

Organisations can thus be understood in the context of their objectives, human context and operational modes.

Since formal organisations are highly complex entities, classificatory schemes should represent this complexity. The essence of the typological effort really lies in the determination of the critical variables for differentiating the phenomena under investigation.

We can now review some of the efforts made to classify organisations and consider some possible future directions for taxonomic efforts.

Typologies by Goal or Functions

Talcott Parsons[5] has a scheme of classification based on the type of function or goal served by the organisation. Here the concern is with the linkages between organisations and the wider society. The four types of organisations distinguished on this basis are:

i) *Production organisation:* This type of organisation makes things which are consumed by the society.

ii) *Political organisation:* It is oriented toward political goals. It generates and allocates power within the society.

iii) *Integrative organisation:* It seeks to settle conflicts, direct motivations toward the fulfilment of institutionalised expectations and ensures that the parts of society work together.

iv) *Pattern maintenance . organisation:* It attempts to provide societal continuity through educational, cultural and expressive activities.

The same approach has been further elaborated by Katz and Kahn.[6] Their typologies are: (a) *production or economic organisation;* (b) managerial or *political organisation* (concerned with adjudication, coordination and control of resources, people and subsystems); (c) *adaptive organisation* (that creates knowledge and develop and test theories) e.g. universities, research organisations etc.; (d) *maintenance organisation* (which is devoted to the socialization of people for their roles in other organisations and the larger society), e.g. church, school, health and welfare institutions.

Katz and Kahn also refer to organisational characteristics as they highlight these major functions. They select four basic characteristics that seem important for organisational operations.

First: the differentiation can be on the basis of the 'through-put'. There are organisations that transform *objects* and others that *transform* people.

Second:There can be differentiation between *expressive* and *instrumental* orientations on the part of organisation members. Expressive orientations are characteristic of organisations in which members participate for some intrinsic satisfaction gained from participation. An instrumental orientation is one in which participation is for the purpose of receiving some material reward.

Third: Another basis of differentiation is the *organisation's* structure itself. Organisations vary according to the degree to which their boundaries are open and permeable; the degree to which the structure is differentiated, both horizontally and vertically, into sub-units and hierarchical levels and the nature of allocation system within the organisation.

Fourtlr.The final basis of differentiation is the manner in which organisations attempt to utilise the energy or resources at their disposal. These ranges from those organisations that seek to maintain equilibrium, in terms of not expanding or contracting the amount of input or output, to those that seek to maximise the utilization of input so that more resources are kept in the organisation than spent.

Typologies on the Basis of Compliance

Etzioni[7] uses compliance as the major source of

differentiation between organisations. Compliance is the manner in which lower participants in an organisation respond to the authority system of the organisation. It is expressed through the nature of the lower participant's involvement in the organisation. When *coercion* is the basis of authority, compliance is *alienated;* when *remuneration* is the basis of authority, compliance takes a *calculative* (utilitarian) turn; when authority base is *normative* (expressed through persuasion), compliance is moral. Most organisations would thus fall into congruent types where three types of authority would combine with three types of compliance.

TYpologies on the Basis of the Consumer

Another formulation by Blau and Scott[8] is based on the principle of *cui bono* or who benefits. The main consideration is who is the direct consumer of the output of the organisation, or who the prime beneficiary is? Four basic types are derived on this basis.

The first is the *mutual-benefit association,* in which the members themselves are the prime beneficiaries of the organisation's actions.

The second type is the *business concern* where the owners are the prime beneficiaries.

The third type is the *service organisation* where the clients served are the prime beneficiaries.

Finally, there is the *commonweal organisation* in which the public at large receives the major benefits.

These taxonomic efforts are useful no doubt, but these do not differentiate clearly between organisations in terms of the variables that are considered important. These are mainly deductive in the sense that some characteristics have been considered important and then a system has been sought to be developed around the major variables. There have been some attempts to constructaempirically derived taxonomy of organisations. Following such efforts, it is now thought that empirical demonstration of relationships between organisational characteristics might serve the major basis for organisational classification especially in government.

Two Approaches

Studies on organisation have been an ongoing process and the body of knowledge now available as organisation theory is the product of constantly evolving discussions on the phenomenon of organisation. The theories in this field are naturally very diverse, as various writers have written for different purposes and differing from disciplinary bases. Keeping in mind our interest in public administration, a convenient way of looking at the large body of literature on organisations would be to concentrate on the broader and more general theories or 'principles' that help us to understand the design or structural problems as these are related to efficient performance of organisational tasks.

Writings on organisation can broadly be classified into two basic categories. *One group* stands out as a distinct cluster because of its substantive interest in finding out and advocating *"one best way" of* structuring organisation. This stream of thought has been called the 'universal design theory'. The second group, by contrast, is much less orthodox and more flexible, as it concedes a degree of structural fluidity and adjustment in response to such factors as technology and environmental changes. This second group has been labelled 'situational design theory' The two contrasting streams of thought are also known as 'closed system' and 'open system' approaches to organisational analysis.

Under universal design theory, influential

thoughts that have relevance to public administration can be identified as:

(a) Scientific management school;
(b) Classical theory of management, or administrative management theory;
(c) Bureaucratic theory

Scientific Management: In the later part of the nineteenth century and early part of the present, the Scientific Management Movement was initiated by Frederick W. Taylor (1856-1915) who began his career as an apprentice in a small machinery-making shop in Philadelphia. Later he rose to the position of a machinist foreman and in that capacity he became interested in improving methods of work and efficiency in organisation. With his pragmatic concern for efficiency, he placed emphasis on planning, standardising and improving human effort at the level of the worker. He was keen to find out scientifically 'the one best way' of doing each task and thus to increase productivity in the organisation. Increased productivity, according to him, would benefit employer and employee alike and in this process bring about a 'mental revolution.' "By maximising the productive efficiency of each worker, scientific management would also maximise the earnings of workers and employers. Hence, all conflict between capital and labour would be resolved by the findings of science".[9]

The focus of scientific management was rather narrow, as it essentially concentrated on the work done at the lowest level in the organisations. The purpose was to analyse the relationships between the physical nature of work and the physiological nature of workers to determine job definitions.

Objective analysis of facts and data collected at the work place would provide the basis of determining the one best way to organise work. Also, it was the management's responsibility alone to find out this one best way. To quote Taylor:

"It is only through enforced standardization of methods, enforced adoption of the best implements and working conditions and enforced cooperation that this faster work can be assumed and the duty of enforcing the adoption of standards and of enforcing this cooperation rests with the management alone."[10]

The essence of scientific management was stated by Taylor thus:-

First: Develop a science for each element of a man's work which replaces the old rule-of-thumb method.

Second: Scientifically select and then train, teach and develop the workman, whereas in the past he chose his own work and trained himself as best he could.

Third: Heartily cooperate with the men so as to insure all of the work being done in accordance with scientific principles.

Fourth: There is almost an equal division of the work and the responsibility between the management and the workmen. The management takes over all work for which they are better fitted than the workmen, while in the past; almost all of the work and the greater part of the responsibility were thrown upon the men.

Taylor and his associates such as Henry Gantt and Frank and Lillian Gilbreth wrote books and articles spreading the principles of scientific management far and wide. These writings had profound impact on industrial structures and practices in the U.S.A, and Europe. Gantt became well known for the invention of the Gantt chart on which process of work could be plotted continuously against time. Gilbreth s system became known as 'speed work' as it involved reduction in the amount of work through the elimination of unnecessary motions. Taylor initiated improved methods of work, but Gilbreth s work to find out the best way of doing each job was much more far-reaching and laid the foundation of modern motion-study techniques. The other contribution of Gilbreth was the 'flow process chart'. An operation is broken down into steps that may be performed by several workers. This helps to discover whether some of the steps in the operation can be eliminated or shortened.

The main features of scientific management are as follows:

1. The separation of Planning and Execution was one of the basic tenets of Taylorism.
2. *Concept of Functional Forcmanship* was evolved to underline the need for so dividing the work, of management that each man at the supervisory level would have as few functions as possible.
3. *Motion and time study:* The best way to do a work and the standard time for completion of the task. Motion study is to determine a preferable work method with consideration to raw materials, tools and equipments, hand and body motion etc.
4. *Time Study* is the fixing of appropriate time to complete a task after the preferred way is determined.
5. The Taylor system introduced a differential piecework plan of payment to encourage workmen to put forth their best efforts.

Criticism

Taylor's scientific management was soon opposed both by managers and workers. Managers did not like the substitution of the scientific methods for their own judgement and discretion. Workers were opposed to time study procedures and standardisation of all aspects of their performance, as they did not like to be treated as machines. Greatest resistance came from the labour leaders who found in Taylorism a threat to their role and to the growth of trade union movement. It was Taylor s conviction that effective cooperation between employer and employees would flow from better management through the application of the scientific principles. Unions would then be unnecessary.

Taylor and his followers had viewed organisation mechanistically. They were essentially practitioners who were interested in improving workers' performance at the level of the shop floor. The neglect of the human side of the organisation has been one of the major criticisms of Taylorism. Nevertheless, the ideas of scientific management greatly influenced administrative thought and management practices in subsequent years. The conceptual framework adopted later by the administrative management theorists was derived basically from Taylors ideas. Clear delineation of authority and responsibility, the use of standards in control, separation of planning from operation, the functional organisation, incentive system for workers, the principle of management by exception and task specialisation—these were Taylor's ideas that greatly influenced management thought in later periods.

Classical Theory of Management

Scientific management also in the classical mould as developed by Taylor and his followers was narrowly conceived as it focussed on efficiency at the operative level. During the first half of this century, a broader approach to organisation was initiated by a group of writers whose interest was chiefly in formal organisation structure and the basic management process. March and Simon have characterised this body of knowledge as 'administrative management theory' and its proponents were called 'departmentalists'. This is also known as the traditional or classical theory of management. The combination of the definition of the field as proposed by Wilson and the Scientific Management and Departmentalists prescriptions for organisational management and structure (relying heavily on hierarchy as a primary mechanism for control and coordination constituted the core of the classical approach to public administration. Weber is also related to the classical approach, but his analysis covered much wider ground.

Henri Fayol, a French engineer who was chief executive of a large coal and steel company from 1888 to 1918, was one of the earliest writers on the general theory of management. He believed that there was a single 'administrative science' whose principles were applicable not only to business but also to government, religious and other organisations. In 1916, he published a paper entitled 'General and Industrial Management' which was later brought out in a book form. Even now, this is considered one of the classics of management thought. Knowledge of administration rather than technical knowledge, according to Fayol, is what is needed at higher levels of an organisation. He defined the primary function of administration as

1. To plan
2. To organise both men and materials
3. To command or to tell the subordinates what to do
4. To coordinate
5. To control.

For the guidance of practising administrators, Fayol laid down a number of principles, as he said:

"The soundness and good working order of the body corporate depend on a certain numbei of conditions termed indiscriminately principle, laws and rules. For preference I shall adopt the term principles while dissociating it from any suggestion of rigidity, for there is nothing rigid or absolute in management affairs, it is all a question of proportion. Seldom do we have to apply the same principle twice in identical conditions; allowance must be made for different changing conditions."[11]

Fayol's Principles of Management. Fayol evolved fourteen principles of management which may be briefly stated as follows:

1. **Division of work.** The object of division of work is to derive the benefits from the principle of specialisation which can be applied not only in technical work but in all other work as well. Unlike Taylor. Fayol pointed out that the division of work has its obvious limits.
2. **Authority and responsibility.** Authority and responsibility are correlated terms. Responsibility is the essential counterpart of authority and they go hand in hand together. An ideal manager is expected to have official authority arising from official position as well as his inherent personal authority. Such personal authority is 'compounded of intelligence, experience, moral worth, ability to lead, past service, etc'.
3. **Discipline.** 'Discipline is in essence obedience, application, energy behaviour and outward marks of respect' shown by employees. 'Discipline is what the leaders make it' through the observance of agreements, because agreements spell out the formalities of discipline. Three requisites of discipline are (a) good supervisors at all levels, (b) clear and fair agreements and (c) judicious application of penalties or sanctions.
4. **Unity of command.** This principle requires that an employee should receive

orders from one superior only. Dual command wrecks havoc in all concerns, 'since authority is undermined, discipline is in jeopardy, order disturbed and stability threatened'.

5. **Unity of direction.** Fayol discussed this principle of unity of direction in a different way from that of unity of command. While unity of direction is concerned with the functioning of the body corporate, unity of command is only concerned with the functioning of personnel at different levels. For the accomplishment of a group of activities having the same objectives, there should be one head and one plan. 'A body with two heads is in the society as in the animal sphere a monster and has difficulty in surviving.'
6. **Subordination of individual interest to general interest.** Common interest must prevail over individual interest but some factors like ambition, laziness, weakness and others tend to reduce the importance of general interest.
7. **Remuneration of personnel.** As the price of services rendered, remuneration should be fair and satisfactory to both the parties.
8. **Centralisation.** Everything which goes to increase the importance of the subordinate's role is decentralisation; everything which goes to reduce it is centralization. The question of centralisation or decentralisation holds the key to the effective utilisation of all faculties of the personnel.
9. **Scalar chain.** It is the chain of superiors or the line of authority from the highest executive to the lowest one for the purpose of communication. The need for swift action should be reconciled with due regard to the line of authority by using 'gang.plank' or direct contact.
10. **Order.** This is a principle of organisation relating to things and persons. Material order requires 'a place for everything and everything in its place' while social order demands the engagements of 'the right man in the right place'.
11. **Equity.** Equity is greater than justice, since it 'results from the combination of kindliness and justice'. The application of equity requires much good sense, experience and good nature with a view to securing devotion and loyalty from employees.
12. **Stability of tenure.** Stability of tenure is essential to get an employee accustomed to doing a new work and to enable him to perform it well.
13. **Initiative.** The freedom to propose a plan and to execute it is what is known as initiative that increases zeal and energy on the part of human beings. Since initiative is one of 'the keenest satisfactions for an intelligent man to experience', Fayol advised managers to secure as much initiative from employees as possible.
14. **Esprit-de-corps.** It rests on the adage 'union is strength'. It is also an extension of the principle of unity of command whereby teamwork is ensured. To maintain proper *esprit-de-corps* in the enterprise, organisational politics and abuse of written communication are to be guarded against.

Universality of Management Principles

In his monograph, **General and Industrial Management,** as well as in his public speeches, Fayol has time and gain pointed out the universality of management principles. To quote from his monograph, "This (Management) code is indispensable. Be it a case of commerce, industry, politics, religion, war or philanthropy, in every concern there is a management function to be performed and for its performance there must be principles"

Parkinson's Law

Parkinson in his book, **Parkinson's Law,** has written satirically on political organisation and public administration and has developed a list of principles.

1. Administrators create work for each other by artificial means and swell their 'rank' by more than five per cent every year, irrespective of the volume of work to be done. That is, the empire - building tendency prevails in such situations. Managers who manipulate the organisation structure to maximise their personal prestige and benefits are referred to as empire builders.
2. Executives increase the number of subordinates so as to move one level upward in the organisational structure and they refrain from increasing their rivals who may bar their further promotion.
3. Organisations grow more stupid as years roll by, since executives select subordinates who are less smart than themselves with a view to preventing their potential rivals.
4. Committees tend to groW in size until they lose their effectiveness. At that state, the inbreeding of small committees takes place and they in turn grow and the process is repeated.
5. In committee meetings, according to the **law of triviality,** the time spent on subjects varies in inverse proportion to the sum involved. Because of the members' ability to comprehend small things easily, the discussion of petty matters is prolonged by way of curtailing the deliberation of important and expensive propositions.
6. The grandeur of buildings and facilities reaches its climax when the organisation starts decaying.
7. Expenditures of an organisation rise to eat up the available money. This is particularly true in respect of budget-based institutions.

Peter Principle. Another so called principle, the Peter principle, involves a cynical notion of errors in selecting managerial candidates. According to Lawrence J.Peter and Raymond Hall, managers tend to be promoted until they reach to the level of their incompetence. Once a manager is promoted to a position, this very success may lead him to earn promotion to a higher position, irrespective of his personal skill and capacity. This is an open censure of mechanical promotion.

Administrative management theory, as it evolved later, was founded on the fourteen principles of Fayol. Unlike Taylor whoso main focus was the shop level worker, Fayol was concerned with 'management' and the tasks of the manager. His principles were meant to raise management to the level of a science. In laying down the ground rules of management, he acknowledged the need for flexibility and timely adjustments.

Fayol's Followers

After Fayol, his line of thought was further elaborated by a number of writers during the 1920s and 1930s. The names of Luther Gulick and Lyndall Urwick deserve special mention in this connection. They had wide experience in industry and government and had been active as practical reformers Inefficiency at the municipal government level in the U.S.A, came in for severe criticism as city administration suffered badly under the spoils system and incompetent political bosses. Municipal reform movement was extended to state and federal levels and the reformers sought to justify administrative changes in terms of the 'principles' of Administration. In 1937. Gulick and Urwick edited *Papers on the Science of Administration,* which was a report to President Roosevelt's Committee on Administrative Management. As they said:

"It is the general thesis of this paper that there are principles which can be arrived at inductively from the study of human organisation which should govern arrangements for human association of any kind. These principles can be studied as a technical question, irrespective of the purpose of the enterprise, the personnel comprising it, or any constitutional, political or social theory underlying its creation".

This is an assertion of positivism and universalism. Administration is a science and the principles are universally applicable. In their enthusiasm for scientism Gulick and Urwick laid down seven principles of administration that came to be expressed as POSDCORB (planning, organising, staffing, directing, coordinating, reporting and budgeting). Their general approach can be summed up as follows:

(a) There must be a close match between people and organisational structure.
(b) Unity of command is essential to the organisation.
(c) Departmental structure should be based on purpose, process, persons and place.
(d) Responsibility should be commensurate with authority. Delegation should be carefully planned.
(e) Spans of control should be rightly constructed in an organisation.
(f) Source of authority should be clearly concentrated in one top executive.

Two General Motors executives in the U.S.A, James D. Mooney and Alan C. Reiley, made important contributions to administrative management theory.They laid emphasis on four major principles:

(a) The principle of coordination in pursuit of unity of action,
(b) The scalar principle emphasising hierarchy in organisational design,
(c) The functional principle to be followed in organising tasks into departments,
(d) The staff principle for giving advice and information alongside line management for the exercise of authority.

Their writings popularised such devices as organisational charts and manuals.

Mary Parker Follett

Special mention should be made'of Mary Parker Follett, a contemporary theorist, who contributed significantly to the development of management thought but at the same time differed from other writers of the period. Organisation was, to her, a social system and management a social process. Psychological and sociological aspects of management were given prominence in her writings. Unlike most of her contemporaries, she attached special significance to lateral coordination, authority acceptance in an organisation, integration of individuals and organisation as well as administrative change. In many ways, Follett can be looked at as the harbinger of behavioural science approach to organisational analysis.[12]

Of many of her innovative ideas, four deserve special mention. *First, social conflict,* in her view, is inevitable; it is neither good nor bad and it all depends on how conflict is put to use. Conflict can be used to produce harmony, not simply victory or accommodation.

Second, cooperation in an organisation, according to Follett, is a process and an outcome, not a precondition. This goes against the dominant paradigm in organisation theory literature that organisation is a cooperative social system.

Third, group process constitutes a critical theme in Follett's thought process. As she said, individuals achieve their true expression in group relationships; individual activities realise increased range and enhanced significance in the group setting.

Fourth, communication in an organisation, in her view, should flow horizontally. This is in refutation of the classical view that communication should follow the formal chain of command. According to Follett, *control* in the organisation is pluralistic and cumulative. Here also, her view runs counter to the conventional idea of control being concentrated in the apex of the organisational pyramid. She has argued that *authority* should flow from the 'law of the situation', rather than be based on personal imposition. In a novel way, she has conceptualised *leadership* as the 'ability to create functional unity in the organisation through proper correlation of controls instead of personal power to command based on position.'

A person well ahead of her time, Follett presented innovative ideas that have influenced behavioural analysis of organisational life very significantly.

CRITICISM

The classical theory has many critics; it has many adherents as well. It goes to the credit of the classical theorists to point out that 'management' in an organisation deserves careful observation and analysis. The 'principles' identified by them have been followed in the structuring of organisations. Many of these are still found useful in organisational analysis. In the evolution of administrative theory, the classical theory occupies a prominent place for its contribution to some of the main organising principles and for its emphasis on the importance of management in organisation.

The critics, however, have not spared the classical theorists. A few major criticisms are as follows:

1. The classical principles are lacking in specificity and hence are not very helpful for the practising administrator. For example, the principle of division of work and specialisation is easy to understand, but it tells very little about how the task in an Cfrganisation should actually be divided. The principle of span of control, which looks apparently acceptable, does not provide a specific guideline. In actual situations, the span of control has been found to be much wider than what the principle suggests and yet the organisations concerned have operated successfully.
2. The classical principles cannot be wholly followed and some of the principles contradict others. Thus, a short span of control and a short chain of command do not go together. Herbert Simon has severely criticised the classical theorists and has righdy dismissed the principles as 'no more than proverbs'. He has pointed out the serious contradictions thus:

One of the most important uses to which authority is put in an organisation is to bring about specialization'in the work of making decisions, so that each decision is made at the point in the organisation where it can be made most expertly.... 'if an accountant in a school department is subordinate to an educator then the finance department cannot issue direct orders to him regarding the technical, accounting aspects of his work. Similarly, the director of motor vehicles in the public works department will be unable to issue direct orders on care of motor equipment to the fire-truck driver...

The principle of unity of command is perhaps more defensible if narrowed down to the following: In case two authoritative commands conflict, there should be a single determinate person whom the subordinate is expected to obey and the sanctions of authority should be applied against the subordinate only to enforce his obedience to that one person... Even this narrower concept of unity of command conflicts with the principle of specialization, for whenever disagreement does occur and the organisation members revert to formal lines of authority, then only those types of specialization which are represented in the hierarchy of authority can impress themselves on decision.[13]

Gulick's recommendation for departmentalisation has been criticised by Simon for its ambiguity. An education department, as he points out, can be looked at as a 'purpose' organisation (meant for education) or a clientele organisation (for children). Similarly, the forest service organisation could be thought of being based on purpose, clientele, or area.

Classical theory has been most severely criticised by the behavioural scientists. It has been characterised as too mechanistic and incompatible with human nature. March and Simon[14] have called it the 'machine model' theory, while Warren Bennis has observed that the focus of classical theory is on 'organisations without -people'.[15]

As earlier pointed out, the classical theory, despite such criticisms, has its importance in the history of administrative thought. Its proper evaluation has to be made against the historical time period of its birth. What the classical theorists wrote was naturally conditioned by the state of society and technology of their time.

The classical viewpoint can be considered as a first approximation to theory in the development of concepts of organisation and management. The ideas of the classical theorists regarding unity of command, delegation of authority, span of control and departmentalisation are still much in use in the structuring of organisation. Many of the present day management theorists accept the basic framework of the classical school and seek to enrich it with the recent developments in the behavioural and management sciences. Essentially, however, the so-called theories of the classical school are principles, as these are practice-derived prescriptions to help management produce planned results. Subsequent developments in the nature of work and technology have, of course, brought about radical changes in formal organisations and organisation theory.

REFERENCES

1. David Easton, *The Political System,* Scientific Book Agency, Calcutta, 1971, p. 55.
2. M. Landau, "Sociology as the Study of Formal Organisation" in *The Study of Organizational Behaviour,* American Society for Public Administration, Washington, DC., 1966.
3. Op. cit., p. 12.
4. Charles Perrow, Organizational Analysis: A Sociological View, Tavistock, London, 1970, p. 1.
5. Talcott Parsons, *Structure and Process m Modern Societies,* Free Press, New York, 1960.
6. Daniel Katz and Robert L. Kahn, *The Social Psychology of Organizations,* John Wiley & Sons, New York, 1966.
7. A. Etzioni, *A Comparative Analysis of Complex Organizations,* Free Press, New York, 1961,
8. P. M. Blau and W. R. Scott, Formal Organizations, Chandler, San Francisco. 1962.

9. Reinhard Bendix, *Work and Authority in Industry,* John Wiley & Sons, New York, 1956, pp. 274-5.
10. F. W. Taylor, "The Principles of Scientific Management", *Scientific Management,* Harper & Row, New York, 1947, 1947. p. 140.
11. Henri Fayol. *General and Industrial Management,* trans, by Constance Stores, Sir Issac Pitman & Sons. Ltd. London. 1949.
12. H.C., Metcalf and Lyndall Urwi (eds.), *Dynamic Administration: The Collected Papers of Mary Parker Follett,* Harper & Row, New York, 1941.
13. Op. cit., pp. 23-6.
14. James G. March and Herbert A. Simon, *Organizations,* John Wiley & Sons, New York, 1958, p. 36.
15. Warren G. Bennis, "Leadership Theory and Administrative".

Chapter 5

Bureaucratic Theory

In coin .1 parlance, bureaucracy is equated with public administration. The organisation and working of bureaucracy have always remained the core concern of public administration.

The pedigree of the term 'bureaucracy' is not quite clear. As Morstein Marx points out,"it was first used in the French form *bureaucratic* by a French Minister of Commerce in the eighteenth century to refer to the government in operation. spread to Germany during the nineteenth century as *burokratie,* and has since found its way into English and many other languages".[1]

Classical writings on bureaucracy can be traced to several sources. The central concern with writers on bureaucracy has been to find out whether bureaucracy is an administrative apparatus for the implementation of social goals; alternatively, has it become the master dictating the general goals to be pursued. The major contributions have come from Marx, Max Weber and Roberto Michels. The most scholarly writing on the subject is by Max Weber (1864-1920). To note the contributions of other writers very briefly, one can say that the concept of bureaucracy does not occupy a central position in Marx's thought. But he had his views on bureaucracy and its relations to the power structure of society. According to Marx, bureaucracy like the state itself is an instrument by which the dominant class exercises its domination over the other social classes. According to this logic, the interests of bureaucracy are closely linked to those of the dominant class and the state. The Marxist ideas were later elaborated and modified by Lenin and Trotsky. A brief sketch of Marx's thought on bureaucracy is presented below which may be contrasted with Weber's views on the subject and be usefully deployed to the search for "alternatives" in the Third World nations.

In public administration, it needs to be emphasised that the general trend of theory-building, especially in the hands of scholars in the U.S.A., has been along the orthodox Weberian line. Enhancement of rationality in ordering and operating organisations has been the chief concern. Largely divorced from wider social concern, most of the American ideas have been basically mechanistic and highly conservative. Public organisations originate and exist in political situations which in turn reflect the contemporaneous social conditions in a country. Under conditions of developed capitalism the state of public organisations in most Western nations can be related to the needs of the specific socio-economic formation. It is now being argued by writers in Asia, Africa and Latin America that the administrative theories formulated in the capitalist milieu may not fit the organisational needs of what is called the Third World countries. Most of these countries are engaged in rapid socio-economic transformation under varying ideological labels. What kinds of organisations can be created for this purpose? How can these be manned and managed? What can be done to ensure public participation and public accountability? These and other related questions are now being raised in course of a serious search for new organisational paradigms in the context of the less developing nations.

Marx on Bureaucracy

As Wright observes, "Marxists have generally continued to focus on the dynamics and contradictions of capitalist society seen as a total system, while paying relatively little attention to the organisational dynamics of the state." In his earlier writings Marx showed interest in the internal organisation of the state. He analysed specific events as a journalist and later made a pretty thoroughgoing job in conceptualising the role of the bureaucracy in the corpus of state organisation. One has to examine carefully if in his monumental macro social theory there are explicitly stated ideas about the role, structure and working of public organisations. While trying to develop a critique of the political economy of capitalism in 19th century Europe, Marx has been a sensitive and keen observer of contemporary European public administrative organisations. His writings on 'administration' are scattered over numerous books, monographs, letters and editorial comments. It was never his purpose to build up a theory of public administration as such. From his many-faceted writings, each discipline has tried to scrape as much as possible. Public administration has been rather late in joining this effort to look for disciplinary cues in Marx. We would, indeed, benefit from such efforts as public administration experts, but to dismember Marx is to destroy him. Marx's ideas on 'administration' must be related to his wider macro-social concern that cannot be tortured into disciplinary cubicles.

More precisely, Marx's ideas on bun uicracy and administration need to be situated within his sociology of politics. Scientific treatment of bureaucracy is generally attributed to Max Weber. But much before him, Marx wrote very incisively on the bureaucratic structure and behaviour and the relationship of bureaucracy with the state and the society.

In the evolution of Marx's own thoughts, the encounter with politico-administrative realities of his time provoked his writings on different administrative situations. Taking over as chief editor of *Die Rhcimschc Zeitung,* he wrote articles in the newspaper on free press and state censorship and on the law on thefts of wood. He pointed out the repressive character of bureaucracy's censorship of the press and the? contrast between the apparent role of the legislature as a framer of 'universal laws' and its real role of promoting particular interests. Censorship, he commented, is a bureaucratic instrument for maintaining politics as a private and reserved domain of a particular class. Commenting on the legislative debate over thefts of wood, Marx observed that the customary rights of poor peasants to take dead wood from the forests were sought to be criminalised to defend the property rights of private owners of the forests. The political system thus appeared clearly as an instrument of the private interest, as against universal interest.

It is in his critique of Hegel's *Philosophy of Right* that Marx (1843) came out openly questioning Hegel's basic political theory and the idolisation of the state. Conceiving bureaucracy as a bridge between the state and the civil society, Hegel regarded bureaucracy as the medium through which particular interests were translated into general interests. Controverting Hegel's assumption that bureaucracy has the insight and the universal will Marx argued that bureaucracy does not know better, since hierarchical and functional differentiation leads to a mere combination and mutual reinforcement of incompetence. The superior docs not know

the specifics of the case, the subordinate does not know the general principles; and none can **appreciate** the totality of a situation. Bureaucracy as a whole has a corporate particular interest to **defend** against other specific corporations and classes in society. So, the external relations of bureaucracy are of a conflicting and 'private' nature. Within bureaucracy, the relations form an interplay of particular strategies. Information and other resources are manipulated to serve the private ambitions of individual careerists and the competition for power among rival bureaucratic cliques. In sum, bureaucracy symbolises the particularisation or privatisation of the civil society. It is a bearer of private interests and a reinforcement of the private spirit.

Bureaucracy; as Marx saw it in the Feudal-Capitalist Prussian situation, is a form of society dominated by the state and its tendency is to separate itself from the content. It assumes a {formalism' and as such presents itself as a superior 'consciousness' — as the will of the **state.** Thus a particular interest lays claim to universality while the general interest is reduced to the status of a special interest. It is a tissue of practical illusions. It embodies and furthers the illusion that the state is indispensable and rational. Examinations to recruit bureaucrats are a formality. These do not reflect an objective bond between the individual and the state; rather they stress the need for a dual knowledge—one required for life in civil society and one required for life in the state. The examination is merely a baptism into bureaucratic knowledge, he noted.

In terms of competence, the bureaucrat cannot be a rational actor. The hierarchy of structure means a hierarchy of knowledge; Comprehensive knowledge is not possible in a situation where knowledge is deliberately split up. Reality is conceived in dual terms, one practical and one bureaucratic. The real beings are treated according to bureaucratic perceptions and the image the world of bureaucracy forms of them. The bureaucracy reserves to itself the rationality condensed in the social world, sets up a monopoly over it and the consequence is that rationality is changed into its opposite.' Thus Marx's view stands in sharp contrast to the Weberian conception of bureaucracy as rationalisation of organisation.

Another attribute that Marx exposes clearly is much more serious. Bureaucracy changes knowledge into secrecy and competence into mystery. Its actual operations are surrounded by secrecy. The higher functionaries do not reveal their secrets to their subordinate, while the closed character of bureaucracy as a corporate body protects its secrets from the view of outsiders.

The truth, as Marx says, is that bureaucracy captures and holds the substance of the state. It stands between the state and public opinion to prevent profanation of the state, the crown on the bureaucratic pyramid. The bureaucratic mentality expresses itself fully in the worship of authority. The only bond between bureaucratic minds is passive obedience to the next higher tank in the hierarchy.

Marx's observations on the changing role of bureaucracy can be found prominently in his most brilliant political pamphlet *The 18th Brumairc of Louis Bonaparte.* During and after the French Revolution (1789) the bureaucracy had facilitated the class rule of the bourgeoisie. It continued to be the instrument of the class under Louis Philippe and the parliamentary republic. There was apparent independence of the state under Second Bonaparte. But, as Marx pointed out, "the state power is not suspended in mid-air. Bonaparte represents a class—the most numerous class of French small-holding peasantry." Referring to the huge executive body in the then France, Marx called it an appalling, parasitic body which enmeshes the body of French society like a net and chokes all its pores. It sprang up in the days of the absolute monarchy, with the decay of the feudal system, which it helped to hasten. Again, when the state power rests on the large mass of small-holding peasants, the situation suits the flourishing of an all-powerful and innumerable bureaucracy, as an apparatus of uniform action from a supreme centre on all points of this uniform mass.

Marx's analysis of the role of the bureaucracy under feudal capitalist Prussian situation and the classical capitalist French situation needs to be supplemented by his fragmentary writings on the British Civil Service in his *Capital*. Referring to the enactment of the Factory Laws at the end of a process of power struggle between the establishment reflecting agrarian and commercial interests and the industrial middle class, Marx ndted the contribution of the corps of Factory Inspectors and the Health Inspectors in terms of recording of crucial facts. This fraction of the Civil Service argued the case in terms of long term interests as well as responsibilities of government for the common good of all. The inspectors, as Marx points out, had to overcome the resistance of their own Home Secretary and the Justices of the Peace. This episode exposes the availability of a number of mechanisms to transform social pressures into public policies: workers' complaints to Factory Inspectors, Press campaign, petitions to Parliament. It also serves to demonstrate the possibility of occasional control over the state and the bureaucracy by the civil society. No doubt, here, as some critics have pointed out, Marx's account points to a double-edged consequence: small concessions by the capitalist state may not have endangered its continued existence; rather the concessions insured the reproduction of the working population. But, at the same time, the bureaucracy and the state appear malleable and somewhat amenable to pressures posing thereby a possibility of gradual reform of the regime.

If we leave out this fragmentary reference in *Capital*, the fact remains that in his later writings Marx did not engage in detailed discussions on bureaucracy or state administration. He was more and more engrossed in the real momentum of developed capitalism as originating in the struggle between the capitalist and the worker, in the face of which bureaucracy had no choices but to act formally and negatively. As he said, 'where bourgeois life and activity begin, the power of the state bureaucracy ends.'

This is obviously a very hurried glance at a phenomenon which admittedly deserves more careful analysis. To this one can add Marx's description of the Paris Commune as the direct antithesis to the Empire and the positive form of the republic. This is portrayed in more idealistic terms, as compared to his earlier observations on the actual form and forking of bureaucracy under capitalism. If the purpose of theory is to comprehend reality succinctly and synoptically, it is his earlier observations that contain the elements of a bureaucratic theory that is in many ways useful in explaining the bureaucratic phenomena in many of the developing countries. Also, one should mention another line of thought that Marx called the 'labour processes' in the capitalist system which illuminates the work organisation in production organisations. This has been further elaborated by writers like Braverman and Stephen Mafglin. Even one can stretch out to include Gramsci's thoughts on the Factory Council in this stream of explanation. Public administration as a discipline has not cared much for Marx's views on bureaucracy. It has generally been held that bureaucracy is subsumed in Marx's macro theorisation of the capitalist state. Recent Marxist scholarship admits the concept of 'relative autonomy' of the state, opening up thereby a fresh line of thought on the analysis of bureaucracy as a fairly autonomous social category.[2]

Roberto Michels

The other important contributor, Michels, concentrated his analysis on the internal politics of large central organisations, as he drew attention to the striking phenomenon of elite domination in organisations. Basing his observations on the internal structure of the German Socialist Party (which was supposed to be organised along democratic principles), he discovered that the system was oligarchic as power was unevenly distributed in the party hierarchy. He concluded that all big organisations tended to develop a bureaucratic structure which ruled out the possibility of internal democracy. The writing of Michels has thrown light on democracy-bureaucracy conflict.

The Weberian Model

Since a comprehensive theory of bureaucracy is attributed to Max Weber, his formulation deserves careful analysis. His thought has influenced generations of scholars on bureaucracy and formal organisation. As one of the founders of modern sociology, his writings covered a wide range of subjects including economics, sociology and administration. Historically, he was contemporary with the scientific management movement and the earlier writers on classical administrative thought. His ideas on 'bureaucracy' need to be placed in the larger framework of his writings on the economic and political structure of society He traced the impact of religious views on the growth of capitalism and dealt on the relationship between industrialisation and organisational structure. His thoughts on bureaucracy evolved out of the larger considerations of socio-historical forces that led to the growth of complex organisations. Thus, Webers ideas on bureaucracy form an integral part of his macro view of history and social theory.

The Origins of Bureaucracy

Weber went back into ancient history in order to find out the chief reasons for the rise of bureaucratic government in the modern state. As he observed, the avocation system of Roman administration could be traced to Greek practices. There was no colonial officer in Rome despite the vast Roman empire. Provincial governors were sent out on an annual tenure supported by a very limited staff. Julius Caesar's effort to create a permanent civil service ended in failure. In this respect, Augustus and Hadrian were, to some extent, successful. A full-blown bureaucracy had come into being by the reign of Diocletian. The fall of Rome was as much due to the burgeoning bureaucracy as to the creeping corruption of the ruling class. The Roman bureaucracy held sway over the weak rulers and rode roughshod over civil liberties. They had compelled imposition of special taxes to oil the wheels of a vast administrative machine. Here Weber found the clue he was searching for. Bureaucratic administration, he observed, could survive only when there would be a developed money economy capable of sustained economic growth. To quote Weber, "The development of the money economy, in so far as a pecuniary compensation of the officials is concerned, is a presupposition of bureaucracy."This was not the case with Rome and her provinces which were not far removed from a subsistence economy. So, the Romans could not afford a large bureaucratic structure.

A developing economy is able to produce a surplus of food and commodities and this surplus forms the basis of payment of salaries to the members of the civil service. Increasing need for public revenue compels the state to develop a rational system ot public finance. To quote Weber, "a stable system of taxation is the precondition for the permanent existence of bureaucratic administration."

The developed post-subsistence economy may not automatically lead to the emergence of bureaucratic administration, as the rulers in the newly emerging states may still continue to use privilege as a matter of policy and distribute public services on the basis of personal whim and traditional status. The bourgeoisie wanted security of their newly acquired wealth and property. Stable economy could be guaranteed by stable administration. To the newly emerging middle class, bureaucratic administration with its emphasis on uniform and stable rules and regulations was therefore almost a godsend. In Weber's view, a second prerequisite of bureaucratic growth was the demand of a larger middle class for the benefits of mass democracy, especially for social and economic equality. Bureaucratic development, as Weber observed, was closely associated with the negation of the practice of according special privileges. To quote Weber, "Bureaucracy inevitably accompanies modern mass democracy....These results from the characteristic principle of bureaucracy: the abstract regularity of the execution of authority, which is a result of the demand for 'equality' before the law and the principled rejection of doing business, 'from case to case'."

The development of money economy and the emergence of mass democracy prepared the ground for the rise and growth of bureaucratic administration. But these, in Weber's view, were not the cause of bureaucratic ascendancy in the modern state. The real causes could be traced to the human motivations springing from what Weber called the Protestant ethic and the spirit of capitalism. According to Weber, the Protestant ethic was instrumental in bringing about a revolution in human existential condition. A radical transformation took place from an insular feudalism to a worldly asceticism. Protestantism engendered a social psychology supportive of rational planning, personal discipline, technology and bureaucratic organisation. Capitalism advanced on the principle of survival of the fittest in the market place. In the face of fierce economic competition, capitalist enterprises needed a highly efficient organisational form. The bureaucratic principles gave the enterprises the capacity to accomplish economic planning to maintain a stable market for goods and services. It was on the demand of the capitalist enterprises that corporate principles of administration were soon transferred to public agencies. Thus bureaucratic government and bureaucratic capitalism went hand in hand together.

It was Weber's contention that capitalism and bureaucratic administration were bolstered up by the psychology of work generated by sixteenth century religious radicalism. Early monasticism of the Catholic faith laid stress upon a **Pope and** priests to act as spiritual policemen and to forgive sins. By contrast, the anxiety of worrying about one's fate here on earth, Weber observed, caused the Puritans to work too hard, to devote themselves to a worldly asceticism and to pursue their worldly vocations religiously. The Reformation thus created a spiritual climate for the blossoming of bureaucracy.

Theory of Domination

Weber was interested in a full-blown discussion on bureaucracy as a sociological phenomenon.[3] His thought needs to be placed in the more general context of his theory of domination. Domination refers to a power relationship between the rulers and the ruled. In any kind of established authority, there exist a number of beliefs that legitimises the exercise of power in the eyes of the leaders and the led. The other important element in this approach is the notion of the administrative apparatus. **Domination** when exercised over a large, number of people necessitates an administrative staff which will execute demands and serve as a budge between the ruler and the ruled. The beliefs about legitimating and the administrative apparatus constitute the two important criteria for the Weberian construction of typology of domination. Weber identified three types of legitimating, each corresponding to i pa ticular type of domination.

1. *Charismatic domination:* Charisma literally means gift of grace. By virtue of possession of charisma or an exceptional quality, a hero or a leader casts a spell over his followers, who accept his domination because of their faith in the person. In such type of domination,/he admin nrrative apparatus is very loose and unstable. It usually consists of the most faithful followers or disciples who play the role of the intermediary between the leader and the followers.
2. *Traditional domination:* The legitimating in this form comes from the belief in the goodness of the past, in the appropriateness of traditional ways of doing things. This kind of patrimonial authority receives ready obedience because of a peculiar faith in traditional status and personal loyalty to the dominant person. The administrative apparatus in this kind of domination would consist of the personal retainers, servants and relatives. Under feudal system, the feudal lords, interposed between the king and the people, constituted the administrative apparatus.
3. *Legal domination:* Legitimating of legal type of domination is based on the belief in the rightness of law. People obey the laws because they believe that these are enacted by a proper, objective procedure. The typical administrative apparatus corresponding to this kind of domination is bureaucracy. The position of the bureaucrat, his relations with the ruler, the ruled and his colleagues are regulated by impersonal rules. These rules delineate in a rational way the hierarchy, the rights and duties of every position and the methods of recruitment, promotion and other conditions of service.

Bureaucratic Structure

In designing the legal-rational authority system, Weber formulated the following structuring propositions:

1. Official tasks are organised on a continuous, regulated basis.
2. These tasks are subdivided into functionally distinct spheres, each furnished with the requisite authority and sanctions.
3. Offices are arranged hierarchically, the rights of control and compliant between them being specified.
4. Official work is conducted according to the rules which are either technical or legal. In either case, trained men are necessary.
5. The resources of the organisation are quite distinct from those of the members as private individuals.
6. The holder of an office cannot appropriate the office.
7. Administration is based on written documents or files. This tends to make the office the hub of the modern organisation.
8. Legal authority systems can take many forms, but are seen at their purest in a bureaucratic administrative staff.

These eight principles of authority informed the organisation of the bureaucratic administrative staff, in Webers view. Following this line pf thought, the defining characteristics of the bureaucracy in its most rational form were identified as follows:

1. The administrative staff members are engaged in the discharge of only the impersonal duties of their offices; they are personally free.
2. There is a clear hierarchy of offices.
3. The functions of the offices are clearly specified.
4. Officials are appointed on-the basis of a contract.
5. They are selected on the basis of professional qualifications, ideally substantiated by a diploma gained through competitive examination.
6. They have a money salary and usually pension rights. The salary is graded according to position in the hierarchy. The official can always leave the post and under certain circumstances it may also be terminated.
7. The officials post is his sole or major occupation.
8. There is a career structure and promotion is possible both by seniority or merit and according to the judgment of superiors.
9. The official may appropriate neither the post nor the resources that go with it.
10. He is subjected to a unified control and disciplinary system.

"These ten features" as Martin Albrow puts it, "constituted Max Webers ideal, pure or most rational type of bureaucracy".[4]

Weberian formulation has been characterised as value neutral; it simply provides a conceptualisation of a form of social organisation with certain characteristics. It can be examined from three different points of view which are not, of course, mutually exclusive. Firstly bureaucracy can be viewed in terms of purely structural characteristics. In fact, the structural dimension has attracted the most attention in the discussions on bureaucracy. The features like division of work and hierarchy have been identified as important aspects of structure. Secondly, bureaucracy has been sought to be defined in terms of behavioural characteristics. Certain patterns of behaviour form an integral part of the conception. To quote Weber, "When fully developed, bureaucracy also stands in a specific sense under the principle of *sine ira ac studio.* Its specific nature, which is welcomed by capitalism, develops more perfectly the more the bureaucracy is 'dehumanised', the more completely it succeeds in eliminating official business love, hatred and all purely personal, irrational and emotional elements which escape calculation. This is the specific nature of bureaucracy and its special virtue."[5]

Thirdly, bureaucracy has been looked at from the point of view of achievement of purpose. This is an instrumental view of bureaucracy. As Peter Blau suggests, it should be considered as an "organisation that maximises efficiency in administration or an institutionalised method of organised social conduct in the interests of administrative efficiency."[6]

All these approaches have their respective values and the critics ofWeber have often taken one or the other view as the starting point of their criticism.

In evaluating Weber, one has to understand that Weber wanted to construct an "ideal type" or a mental map of a "fully developed" bureaucracy. The ideal type is a mental construct that cannot be found in reality. It is an abstraction and as such exaggerates certain features and deemphasises certain others with a view to convey an image or an idea.

In Weberian formulation, bureaucracy is not

to be confused with the civil services. It refers to the sociological concept of rationalisation of collective activities. As a form or design of organisation it assures predictability of behaviour of organisational members. The bureaucratic form, according to Weber, is the most efficient organisational form for large scale, complex administration that has been developed in the modern world so far. It is superior to any other form in decision precision, stability, maintenance of discipline and reliability. For the heads of organisations, it makes possible a high degree of calculability of results. Bureaucracy compares to other forms of organisations as does the machine with non-mechanical modes of production. As Weber wrote: "The development of the modern form of the organisation of corporate groups in all fields is nothing less than identical with the development and continual spread of bureaucratic administration. This is true of church and state, of armies, political parties and economic enterprises, organisations to promote all kinds of causes, private associations, clubs and many others. Its development is, to take the most striking case, the most crucial phenomenon of the modern Western State.... The whole pattern of every day life is cut to fit this framework. For bureaucratic administration is, other things being Qqual, always, from a formal, technical point of view, the most rational type. For the needs of -mass administration today, it is completely indispensable. The choice is only that between bureaucracy and dilettantism in the field of administration."[7]

Characteristics of Bureaucracy

The growth of capitalism, according to Weber, facilitated the birth and development of bureaucracy. As he wrote, "Today, it is primarily the capitalist market economy which demands that the official business of the administration be dischargedprecisely, unambiguously, continuously and with as much speed as possible." In his view, the very large modern capitalist enterprises proved to be the "unequalled models of strict bureaucratic organisation".[8]

A major technical advantage of bureaucratic organisation, according to Weber, is the optimum possibility that bureaucratization offers "for carrying through the principle of specializing administrative functions according to purely objective considerations". There is room for steady improvement of functioning through training and constant practice. The objective discharge of business means, as Weber explained, the discharge of business'according to calculable rules and without regard for persons'.

While discussing the permanent character of the bureaucratic machine and its socio-economic consequences, Weber made some incisive comments on how the bureaucracy tends to operate in practice. A fully developed bureaucracy, he argues, is among those social structures which are the hardest to destroy. As an instrument of 'socialising' relations of power, bureaucracy is practically unshatterable. The individual bureaucrat is reduced to "a single cop in an ever-moving mechanism which prescribes to him an essentially fixed route of march."

On the part of the ruled, the bureaucratic apparatus of authority, once it comes into existence, becomes almost fixed and unalterable. "More and more the material fate of the masses depends upon the steady and correct functioning of the increasingly bureaucratic organisations of private capitalism."

Weber had foreseen the far-reaching socio-economic consequences of bureaucratization. But he thought that the distribution of economic and social power in a specific country and the particular spheres of activities placed under bureaucratic control would go to determine the actual results of bureaucratization.

He was very emphatic on the idea that the consequences of bureaucracy would ultimately depend "upon the direction which the powers using the apparatus given to it."

In Weber's view, despite the fact that "the modern state is undergoing bureaucratization", whether the power of bureaucracy as such has been increasing cannot be decided *a priori*. As he argued, "The drawing in of economic interest groups or other non-official experts, or the drawing in of non-expert lay representatives, the establishment of local, inter-local, or central parliamentary or other representative bodies, or of occupational associations—these *seem* to run directly against the bureaucratic tendency."

There are hints in these remarks of possible de-bureaucratise in a polity that would be able to develop countervailing institutions and associational groups.

Weber had, however, admitted that normally, the power position of a fully developed bureaucracy was everywhere overpowering. The political master is no match for the expert bureaucrat. Another feature of bureaucracy, as he pointed out, is to increase the superiority of the professionally informed by keeping their knowledge and intentions secret. The concept of the 'official secret' is an invention of bureaucracy, as it tries to hide its knowledge and actions from criticisms. It does not want to divulge information even to the representative parliament. As Weber puts it, "Bureaucracy naturally welcomes a poorly informed and hence a powerless parliament, at least in so far as ignorance somehow agrees with the bureaucracy's interests."

Three Aspects of Weber's Theory

David Beetham in his seminal work on *Max Weber and the Theory of Modern Politics* draws attention to three aspects of Weber's theory of bureaucracy. *First* was his familiar conception of bureaucracy as a technically efficient instrument of administration. Here, Webers main emphasis is on the purely technical, instrumental nature of bureaucracy.The *second* aspect of his theory refers to bureaucracy's inherent tendency to exceed its instrumental function and to become a separate force in society. As a separate power group, a separate status stratum within society at large, bureaucracy is capable of usurping the societal goal-setting function which properly belongs to the politician. As Beetham observes, "central to this second conception of bureaucracy, therefore, was an account of its inherent limitations,'what it can not achieve; where the emphasis in *Economy and Society* was on the technical superiority of bureaucracy, Weber's political writings were concentrated explicitly on its negative side, on what it could not achieve." The *third* aspect of Weber's theory involved a conception of bureaucracy as reflecting the class structure of society. It was unable to free itself from the outlook of the social classes from which it was recruited and to which it was allied.

Relying on Weber's writings on German politics and later political writings, Beetham has thus presented a very different and modified version of Weber's conceptualization of bureaucracy[9] Weber's concern about the power position of a fully developed bureaucracy has also been noted by Alfred Diamant. According to Diamant, Weber's treatment of bureaucracy reflects a dualism in his thought. The severe rationality of his ideal-type construct leads him to consider bureaucracy as a neutral tool. But his own political experiences convinced him that the power interests of bureaucracy might threaten the mastery of political 'leadership."[10]

In his most important essay in political polemics, *Parliament and Government in the Newly Organized Germany* (1918), Weber wrote explicitly on the problem of beamtenherrschaft or rule by officials which, in his view, was different from bureaucracy. How to prevent the inherent tendency of bureaucracy to accumulate power bothered him very much. As Albrow points out, Weber was, therefore, considering a number of mechanisms for limiting the scope of systems of authority generally and bureaucracy in particular. Five mechanisms identified by Albrow[11] in Weber's writings are:

i) Collegiality
ii) The Separation of Powers
iii) Amateur Administration
iv) Direct Democracy
v) Representation.

Collegiality or the collegial principle is the opposite of monocracy. As soon as more than one person would be involved in decision-making, as of right, the collegial principle would come into being. Weber referred to several forms of collegiality such as the Roman consulate, the British Cabinet, various kinds of senates and parliaments. While acknowledging the role of collegiality in limiting bureaucracy, he had also pointed out its disadvantages in terms of speed of decision and fixing of responsibility.

Separation of powers meant dividing responsibility for the same function between two or more bodies. In such an arrangement, a compromise has to be reached between the involved bodies. Weber referred to the compromise over the budget which historically had to be reached by the British monarch and Parliament. Such a system, in Weber's view, is inherently unstable.

The phenomenon of *amateur administration* refers to a situation when the government does not pay its administrators and depends upon those who have the resources to permit their spending time in unremunerated activity. This system is no match for administration by professionals and experts under conditions of modern society.

The principle of *direct democracy* may take many forms such as short term of office, selection by lot and possibility of recall.

The underlying idea has been to place the officials under the guidance of an assembly to ensure their accountability to the people.

Historically, charismatic and traditional leaders claimed to have represented their followers. The peculiarity of the modern age is the existence of collegial *representative bodies.* Their members are selected by vote and are free to make decisions and share in authority over those who elect them. It is the existence and operation of political parties that make this system work. It was through this medium that Weber saw the greatest possibility of a check on bureaucracy.

Leadership recruited and developed in Parliament in Weber's view, provided the only means of controlling the administration. To quote Weber, "It is only this school of intensive work in the realities of administration...that equips an assembly to be a selecting ground, not for mere demagogues, but for effective politicians with a grasp of reality, of which the English Parliament is the supreme example. Only this kind of relationship between officials and professional politicians guarantees the continuous control of the administration and through this the political education of both leaders and led".[12]

Weber was conscious of the fact that in empirical situations bureaucracy tended to exceed its instrumental function. For a check on the usurpation role of bureaucracy, he relied on the proper selection process of politicians with the capacity for leadership and the control of the administrative apparatus.

Critique of Weber

The Weberian model has been criticised from a variety of standpoints. It has been generally characterised as "machine theory" and a closed system model taking little account of organisational interactions with the environment. The Weberian model, the critics point out, is subject to the dysfunctional consequences of failing to consider the individual or behavioural aspects of the people in the organisation. The bureaucratic design can at best function in a stable environment; it will be unsuitable for an unstable environmental situation.

Secondly, the structural features of bureaucracy, according to the critics, might be suitable for routine and repetitive tasks, but these would produce dysfunctional consequences in terms of human behaviour if the jobs would involve innovation and creativity.

Robert K. Merton, the eminent social scientist, points out that although close control by the rule favours reliability and predictability of employee behaviour, at the same time it accounts for lack of flexibility and a tendency sets in to turn means into ends.[13] The instrumental and formalistic aspects of the bureaucratic job become more important than the substantive ones (e.g. service to the people) and the effectiveness of the whole system suffers accordingly. Selznick[14] conceives the central dilemma in bureaucracy as arising out of the need for delegation of power to organisational sub-systems. The increasing complexity of organisational tasks compels decentralisation and delegation of responsibility to intermediaries. Such a measure brings forth the organisational paradox of goal displacement, the bifurcation of interest between the central system and its decentralised sub-units.[15]

To quote Mertom "An effective bureaucracy demands reliability of response and strict devotion to regulation. Such devotion to the rules leads to their transformation into absolutes they are no longer conceived as relative to a given set of purposes. This interferes with ready adaptation under special conditions not clearly envisaged by those who draw up the general rules. Thus the very elements which conduce toward efficiency in general produce inefficiency in specific instances. Those very devices which increase the probability of conformances also lead to an over concern with strict adherence to regulations which induces timidity, consumerism and techniques".

Alvin Gouldner[16] advances the thesis that bureaucratic techniques produce their own reactions. Organisational rules tend to define the minimum levels of acceptable behaviour. As managers become aware of their subordinates' behaviour, they respond by enacting additional rules and procedures. This leads to tension between managers and subordinates and thus to displacement of organisational goals.

There have been otner writers on bureaucracy (e.g. Presthus) who are of the view that the Weberian model is a product of alien culture not quite suitable for transplantation in the developing societies. Observers of bureaucracy in developing countries have noticed behavioural aberration reflecting societal culture of the countries studied. Where the need to fulfil developmental programmes was most urgent, much of the bureaucratic pursuit was directed towards activities other than achievement of goals, as many field studies in India have revealed. A new branch of public administration called development administration has emerged in response to the special administrative needs of the 'developing' countries.

Social scientists like Warren Bennis predict that bureaucracy is likely to go out of use in the wake of new social systems better suited to the 20th century demands of industrialization. According to Bennis, the forecast is based on the evolutionary principle that every age develops an organisational form appropriate to its genius. The vacuum created by the eclipse of bureaucracy, according to Bennis, will be filled up by temporary work-systems which will be more adaptive to rapid social change.[17]

Lloyd Rudolph and Susanne Rudolph have questioned the central theme of the Weberian model of bureaucracy as the most rational construct in terms of production of organisational efficiency As they point out:

"Formal rationality (and technology) can contribute to organisational efficiency, but can also contribute to organisational ineffectiveness by building up the sources of alienation and resistance and fuelling the struggle for power against authority.The persistence or retention of patrimonial elements in bureaucratic administration can mitigate if not eliminate the struggle, just as the presence of bureaucratic features in patrimonial administration can (and did) enhance its efficiency and effectiveness."[18]

In recent times, a very incisive comment on the Weberian model has been made by Claus Offe. The bureaucratic administration, as Offe points out, is "that improbable and conditional form of organisation of social action that precludes the thematization of its own premises." The rule-bound bureaucracy means that the premises of action are not at the disposal of the actors themselves. All that is needed is to blindly and mechanically apply the legal norms to specific situations. This kind of bureaucratic rationality Offe calls "the unadulterated realization of norms" or, in brief, *organisational rationality.* There is a second type of rationality which he calls *systemic rationality.* It refers to the bureaucratic fulfilment of the functional requirements of their societal environment. As Offe observes, "Under conditions of developed, welfare-state capitalism, the rationality of bureaucratic action does not guarantee, but rather perhaps conflicts with, the functional rationality of the political system."

Offe's comment on the Weberian model opens up a new line of analysis that has considerable relevance for the 'third world' countries. Essentially, his typology of rationality - organisational and systemic - raises the question of their congruence in reality. As he points out, under exceptional circumstances when societal conditions permit the highest degree of unrestricted application of rules, the two criteria of rationality may be congruent. But this kind of determinate administrative action tends to freeze administrative autonomy. Under conditions of uncertainty and rapid societal changes, production of results and achievement of objectives become much more important than blind adherence to frozen work norms. To quote Offe's memorable sentence in this connection:

"The premises of administrative action are no longer rules to be imperatively complied with, but are instead treated as *resources* which are to be weighed from the standpoint of their adequacy for specific tasks."[19]

The rule-bound bureaucratic system in a developing country is thus incompatible with the many-faceted and complex tasks of socio-economic development. Organisational rationality and systemic rationality will be at loggerheads in a situation of speedy social reconstruction. Most post-colonial societies are faced with this dilemma and any attempt to innovate new modes of administration is often frustrated by bureaucratic dominance. The kind ofsystemic' rationality Offe has in mind will have its source in the societal environment. Instead of fixed bureaucratic rules predetermining administrative action, the social expectations of programmes and results will be the main motor of government policy and action.

The Gender Issue in Bureaucracy

Bureaucratic theory's standard recipe is the rational organisation administered by impersonal and objective rules and procedures.The Weberian model portrays the bureaucracy as meritocracy in which rewards are determined by technical competence; it rules out any other form of non-rational evaluation such as sexual or racial discrimination. Thus the ethnicity or gender of the employees is of minor concern compared to their formal and technical qualifications. The employees are judged on what they do within the organisation rather than who they are in terms of their gender or ethnicity. As Weber wrote: "The development of bureaucracy greatly favours the levelling of the social classes...."

Mainstream organisation theory has generally accepted this idealized image of the bureaucracy. Very little attention has been paid to the actual work experiences of minority. Only recently, there has been a salutary change in organisational studies and minority groups have attracted the attention of a newer generation of theorists who have focused on the issue of inequalities of power and status that exist in bureaucracies. Far from being a 'rational' organisation, bureaucracies have been found in real life mirroring the prejudices of the larger society. Not until 1869, for instance, the Blacks were allowed to work in the American federal bureaucracy. Outright discrimination against women was ended in the federal bureaucracy not until 1967. So, the "merit myth" of bureaucracy has been questioned by many critics. Kathy Ferguson has pointed out that the so called bureaucratic rationality has in reality worked in such a way that women have been judged unfavourably as potential members of the bureaucracy. It has been argued that a "discourse of bureaucracy" with emphasis on rationality, objectivity and impersonality ran alongside a "discourse of domesticity" that stressed emotional and familial values. Historically, as against domestic principle, bureaucratic principles came to be associated with males and maleness and served to exclude women from the bureaucracies or to confine them to the lower levels.

Researchers like Kanter, Beattie and Abella have successfully discovered the unequal distribution of power in the organisation and the general trend toward restricting women to the lower rungs. Women, they point out, have less chance than men to rise in the organisation. There exists an "opportunity structure" in the organisation which serves to signal women that they are not fully valued organisational members. In India, the constitutional provisions guaranteeing 'equality before the law" and 'equality of employment opportunities' mark a watershed in the history of the civil services. Despite such constitutional guarantee, two problems that persist in India are the lower representation of women at all levels in government and gender inequalities within the service. To illustrate, in 1989 the percentage of women in the Central Government both at gazetted and non-gazetted levels was only 6.6 per cent. In the All India Services as of 1995, there were less than 10 per cent women. In the IFS and IPS in 1992, the corresponding figure was 1.8 per cent only. It seems the picture that emerges in India is that bureaucracy contributes and reflects the biases of a larger societal context and is responsible for creating, maintaining and reproducing such biases.

The several criticisms of the Weberian model show the importance of the original Weberian formulation. Many empirical researches in both developed and developing countries have accepted Weber as the starting point and then gone into the actual manifestations of bureaucracy in real-life situations. These efforts have opened up new ways of viewing Weber's ideas and testing many of the manifest and latent properties of his basic model. At the conceptual level, the attraction of Weber's formulation has never faded away which is a clear proof of its paradigmatic strength.

It is commonly believed that Weber was a champion of bureaucracy and spoke eloquently about the rational character of bureaucratic administration. No doubt, Weber wrote about the technical superiority of bureaucracy in *Economy amd Society.* But, as David Beetham has pointed out in his authoritative study, Weber's political writings had focussed on the negative side of bureaucracy and its essential limitations. Any assessment ofWeber has to take into account the entire corpus of his writings, especially his political writings, where Weber appears as a critic of bureaucracy in real life politics and not so much as a spokesman of an exclusivist'rationality'.

REFERENCES

1. Quoted in Ferrel Heady, op. cit., p. 16.
2. See in this connection, O. P. Dwivedi, William Graf and J. Nef, "Marxist Contributions to the Theory of Administrative State,' *Indian Journal of Political Science,* January-March, 1985.
3. See Nicos P. Mouzelis, *Organisation and Bureaucracy,* Aldine Publishing Company, Chicago, 1975.
4. Martin Albrow, *Bureaucracy,* The Macmillan Press Ltd., London, 1978, pp. 43-5.
5. *"Bureaucracy"* in H. H. Gerth and C. Wright Mills, eds., *From Max . Weber: Essays in Sociology* Oxford University Press, 1946, p. 215.
6. Peter M. Blau *Bureaucracy in Modern Society,* Random House, New 1956, p. 60.
7. Max Weber, *Theory of Social and Economic Organisation,* The Free Press of Glencoe, New York. 1964, p. 337.
8. Gerth and Mills, (eds.), *From Max Heber: Essays in Sociology* op. cit., p. 215.
9. Devid Beetham, *Max Weber and the Theory of Modern Politics,* George Allen & Unwin Ltd., London. 1974. Chapter 3.
10. Alfred Diamant "The Bureaucratic Model: Max Weber Rejected. Rediscovered, Reformed", in Ferrel Heady and Sybil L. Stokes, eds.. *Papers in Comparative Public Administration.* The University of Michigan, 1962.
11. Martin Albrow, *Bureaucracy* op. cit., pp. 47-8.
12. Quoted in Beetham, op. cit., p. 100.
13. Robert K. Merton, *Social Theory and Social Structure,* Free Press of Glentoe, New York, 1949, Chapter 5. Another study on similar lines is by Michel Crozier, The Bureaucratic Phenomenon, University of Chicago Press, 1964.
14. P. Selznick, *TVA and the Grass Roots,* University of California Press, 1949,
15. Robert Merton, *Social Theory and Social Structure,* Free Press, Glencoe, III., 1957, p. 156.
16. A. W Gouldner, *Patterns of Industrial Bureaucracy,* Free Press, New York, 1954.
17. W.C. Bennis and P. E. Slater, *The Temporary Society* Harper and Row, New York, 1968.
18. Lloyd Rudolph and Susanne Hoeber Rudolph, "Authority and Power in Bureaucratic and Patrimonial Administration: A Revisionist Interpretation ofWeber on Bureaucracy", *World—Politics,* January. 1979.
19. Claus Offe, *Disorganised Capitalism: Contemporary Transformations of Work and Politics,* Polity Press, Cambridge, 1985, pp. 300-316.

CHAPTER 6

Behavioural and Systems Approach

Organisation theory has basically been private organisation- based and micro-biased. Its applicability to public organisations has to be carefully considered in view of (a) the public interest philosophy of government that upholds certain values, norms and ethics that are peculiar to public administration; (b) the interconnection among most public organisations as they function on the basis of regular interdependence among different organs (executive-legislature relationships for instance) and (c) the overarching presence of 'democracy' as a guiding norm suggesting participation and openness in government. The 'efficiency' criterion of private organisations may not, therefore, wholly apply to public organisations, as there are other democratic and public interest considerations that weigh heavily in public administration transactions.

TRADITIONAL THEORY

The traditional theorists from Taylor to Weber laid emphasis on the physiological and mechanical aspects of work organisation. They had taken a rather simplistic view of efficiency which they thought could be achieved by following certain specific principles of organisation and management. The environmental and organisational characteristics of the Industrial Revolution in contemporary Europe greatly influenced the thoughts of the traditional theorists.

The mechanistic orientation of the traditionalists has been counterbalanced by the humanistic view of the behavioural scientists. Berelson and Steiner[1] have defined the behavioural sciences thus:

"By the behavioural sciences we mean the disciplines of anthropology, psychology and sociology-minus and plus: Minus such specialised sectors as physiological psychology', archaeology, technical linguistics and most of physical anthropology; Plus social geography, some psychiatry and the behavioural parts of economics, political science and law. In short, we are concerned here with the scientific research that deals directly with human behaviour."

HUMAN RELATIONS APPROACH

Starting with the *human relations,* many and varied contributions from the behavioural scientists have enriched administrative theory and management practice. The human relations approach had its origin in a series of studies conducted between 1927 and 1932 by a group of researchers from Harvard University at the Hawthorne Plant of the Western Electric Company at Chicago. Originally, the research team was headed by Elton Mayo and the studies were published by Roethlisberger and Dickson.[2]

The Hawthorne researchers got the impetus from earlier studies that were based on the scientific management tradition. Initially, a study was undertaken to find out the relationships between intensity of illumination and workers' efficiency as measured by output. The study could not come out with any consistent relationships between the two variables. Strangely enough, with reduction in illumination output registered an increase. This led the researchers to take into account other variables such as length of the working day and rest periods. The research finding was that regardless of any variation in the physical conditions of work, production continued to increase. At this stage, it was hypothesised that changes in output were not due to changes in physical conditions. Rather these were related to changes in social situations at the workplace and changes in the motivation and satisfaction and the style of supervision. The research was pursued in two other phases. In the second phase, the importance of social factors in the work situation was confirmed. In the third phase, small group behaviour was the focus of research. It was found that actual production norms were set by the informal work group and such norms were often at variance with those fixed by the management. The experiment clearly revealed the critical influence of social organisation on an individual worker. The social organisation was the network of relationships among workers based upon attitudes and sentiments. The Hawthrone researchers made a distinction between the formal and the informal structure of the organisation. The former is rule based and structured, while the latter is a product of actual behaviour of organisation members. The most important finding of the Hawthorne Studies was that social and psychological factors at the workplace are the major determinants of workers' satisfaction and organisational output.

Neo-Human Relationists

Scientific management's core assumption has been that the individual worker is simply an operator and not a social being. It is therefore possible to adjust the individual through training and innovative schemes in order that his actions arc fully consistent with the pursuit of organisational goals. The social-psychological need of the individual worker is therefore a non-issue. The other assumption of scientific management has been that money is the chief motivating factor, so far as the worker is concerned. Control over the worker was achieved, in the industrial era, through the application of technological advances supplemented by tighter supervision, more minute tasks and the application of increasingly complex systems of piece rate and incentive payments. This has been the hallmark ofTaylorist method of work specification and supervision.

These assumptions about the low-level members of the organisation led to the gradual introduction of particular kinds of technology to achieve control over individuals who were defined as untrustworthy, lazy and unreliable. To remedy this situation, specific technologies, work designs and organisational arrangements (The so-called principles of classical theory) came to be imposed on the individuals. And this in turn created disaffection and alienation among organisational members. Management looked at it as lack of commitment, idleness and unreliability.

Since the 1960s, it could be seen that much of the writing on organisational behaviour stressed the need for new work designing in order to ensure that the tendency towards low-discretion roles in organisations could be reversed or at least arrested. The literature that dealt with this situation came to be characterised as the 'neo-human relations' movement. The representative writers in this stream of thought are Argyris, McGregor and Herzberg. What they were essentially pointing at was that discretion could be given to lower-level organisation members because of the move towards a 'post-industrial' system of production that had been emerging steadily. In the new production system, greater involvement and commitment would be required of organisation members for the achievement of organisational effectiveness. The organisational arrangements based upon the principles of scientific management would be incapable of achieving the required levels of involvement and commitment. What was needed in the new system was direction - enlargement exercises through job-enrichment, development of autonomous work groups, the use of socio-techmcal concept, etc.[3]

The human relations writers, like the traditional theorists, acknowledged the crucial importance of 'management' in production. They differed from the traditionalists in their basic approach to the organisation which they characterised as a social system consisting of individuals, informal groups and intergroup relationships in addition to the formal structure. To sum up, human relations focussed their attention on the social environment of the job, whereas the traditional theorists concentrated basically on the physical environment.

The behavioural scientists have been contributing to our knowledge of organisational dynamics since the days of the Hawthorne studies. Some of the great names in this school of thought are Carl Rogers, J. L. Moreno, Kurt Lewin and A. H. Maslow. Rogers is well known for his clinical approach to counselling therapy and Moreno for his studies of interpersonal relations. Lewin and his followers pioneered the action research approach to organisational development. Their contributions to group dynamics and field theory have inspired researches in the field of behavioural change through such methods as sensitivity training and other group approaches. Maslows theory of motivation has exerted strong influence on studies of organisational behaviour. He postulated a hierarchy of needs in an ascending order from basic economic and survival needs to social, self-esteem and self-actualisation needs.

Chester Barnard

In this context, the contribution of Chester Barnard, the former President of the New Jersey Bell Telephone Company, deserves special mention. Barnard's approach to organisation can be called behavioural, as he laid emphasis on the psychosocial aspects of management. His book, *The Functions of the Executive* (1938), is a product of ripe experience and abiding interest in economics, psychology and allied fields of knowledge. Like Mary Parker Follett, he viewed the organisation as basically a social system. A formal organisation, according to Barnard, is 'a system of consciously coordinated activities or forces of two or more persons.' He developed an equilibrium theory of organisation by suggesting that the organisation exists by maintaining an equilibrium between the contributions and the satisfactions of its participant members. In elaborating his notion of efficiency, he pointed out that the members participate in organisational activities because they receive actual benefits or they perceive that they are receiving certain rewards. So, both material inducements and psycho-social rewards are important. As Barnard observed, efficiency in organisation is a personal matter related to individual satisfaction; effectiveness, however, is related to the accomplishment of a common organisational purpose. He referred to the existence of informal organisations and noted their significance for the formal structure. His theory of authority in organisation differs radically from the Weberian concept of formal positional authority. In an authority-relation situation, authority in

Barnard's view is a matter of acceptance, of the superior role of the supervisor by the subordinate. It is 'acceptance' by the subordinate and his willingness to comply that lends support to organisational authority.

To quote Barnard's memorable statement:

"A person can and will accept a communication as authoritative only when four conditions simultaneously obtain: (a) he can and does understand the communication; (b) *at the time of his decision he believes* that it is not inconsistent with the purpose of the organisation; (c) *at the time of his decision,* he believes it to be compatible with his personal interest as a whole; and (d) he is able mentally and physically to comply with it."[4]

On the motivation to work, Barnard made the following in-depth and analytical observation:

"...it seems to me to be a matter of common experience that material rewards are ineffective beyond the subsistence level excepting to a very limited proportion of men; that most men neither work hard for more material things, nor can be induced thereby to devote more than a fraction of their possible contribution to organisational effort."[5]

He deemphasised economic motives and stressed such inducements as desirable working conditions, satisfying associations at the workplace, opportunity for participation and distinction and power and a chance to experience pride of workmanship. Individual participants in the organisation look for'the condition of communication that offers opportunities not only for companionship' but also mutual support for personal attitudes. From practical experience Barnard could see how the incentives actually worked in the organisation:

".......... different men are moved by different incentives or combinations of incentives and by different incentives or combinations at different times A second fact is that organisations are probably never able to offer *all* the incentives that move men to cooperative effort and are usually unable to offer adequate incentives."[6]

Barnard looks almost like a full-blown behaviourist. He believed in the importance of persuasion as a means of motivation and underplayed the role of coercion in organisation. He pinned his faith in organisational leadership which, he thought, was the most important factor in organisational management.

Herbert Simon developed Barnard's thoughts further, especially in his collaborative work with March.[7] Simon's contribution to administrative thought will be discussed in much more detail later in connection with decision-making. At this stage, it needs to be emphasized that Simon has been basically concerned with the behaviour of organisations as goal oriented and adaptive entities.

He focuses on the cognitive aspects of organisational operation and emphasises problem solving and rational choice. Instead of the classical, rational economic view of 'maximising' human behaviour, Simon introduced the concept of 'satisfying' behaviour in organisational situations where human beings, according to him, seek really to attain a satisfactory level of performance (as distinguished from maximum or ideal return).

On the theme of organisation-individual relationships, two writers deserve special mention: E. Bakke and Chris Argyris. Bakke belonged to the Yale Labour and Management Centre. He was interested in the realities of organisational life rather than the formal principles of organising. He identified the individual goals as security, progress and justice in respect of acquisition of means, optimum performance, internal harmony, understanding, autonomy, integration and respect. According to Bakke, the individual seeks to use the organisation as a means to further his own goals, whereas the organisation tries to use the individual to attain its own goals.

The 'personalising process' by which the individual makes use of the organisation and the 'socialising process' by which organisation puts the individual to its own use get mixed up in real life. This is what Bakke called the 'fusion process.' To quote his observation:

"The question about loyalty to the organisation is not merely 'what can the organisation do for or to its participants in order to win their loyalty' but also, 'How can *what the participant dees,* i.e., his organisational function, be so arranged that loyalty is generated as a by-product of his organisationally and personally effective participation in organisational activities?"[8]

Chris Argyris, Bakke's former associate and a renowned behavioural scientist, speaks of a basic incompatibility between the needs of a mature personality and the requirements of a formal organisation designed on the classical principles of rigid task specialisation, span of control and unity of command. Strict adherence to classical principles, according to him, is likely to create an organisation that will tend to make the employees dependent and passive.[9]

The notion of participation in organisation has been advanced by a number of theorists. Maslow's ideas on *hierarchy of needs* have influenced administrative thought greatly. Other notable contributions have come from McGregor (his theory X and theory Y will be discussed later), Likert and Herzberg. A more detailed discussion of their writings will be presented in a later section dealing with the problem of motivation in organisation.

The behavioural scientists have given a new orientation to administrative thought by focussing attention on the role *of* the individual, leadership in organisation, group dynamics, motivation and satisfaction. The behavioural studies are a growing body of knowledge and these are increasingly being used in organisational redesigning and problem solving. More importantly, many of the behavioural scientists are now active in the role of change agents. They are not merely satisfied with interpreting the organisation; they are also interested in changing it. As the scientists put it, "Human interventions designed to shape and modify the institutionalised behaviours of men are now familiar features of our social landscape."[10]

Systems Approach

Organisational realities have, from time to time, been investigated from different points of view. The structural aspect, the technological aspect, the human or social-psychological aspect are some of the instances of partial analysis of organisation. Divergent theories have thus emerged out of the microscopic analyses and a need has arisen for looking at the organisation as a whole. In recent years, advances in scientific knowledge in general have made possible the formulation of a general systems theory for the integration of scientific knowledge.

The term, general systems theory, owes its origin to the famous biologist Ludwig von Bertalanffy (1901-1972).[11] Traditional knowledge, according to Bertalanffy, has grown around specific subareas or subject matters. Many a time, similar ideas have been advanced in different subjects without an effort being made to synthesise them. The basic problem in modern science is to promote dynamic interaction among diverse fields. To quote Bertalanffy:

"If we survey the various fields of modern science, we notice a dramatic and amazing evolution. Similar conceptions and principles have arisen in quite different realms, although this parallelism of ideas is the result of independent developments and the workers in the individual fields are hardly aware of the common trend. Thus, the principles of wholeness, of' organisation and of the dynamic conception of reality become apparent in all fields of science".[12]

General systems theory is an attempt to join up the different approaches in science and so as to provide a broad macroscopic view of different types of systems.

The systems approach has been evolving slowly in the social sciences where knowledge-integration has been most keenly felt. For instance, in sociology Talcott Parsons applied the open systems approach to the study of social structures.[13] In the field of individual personality, Kurt Lewin is well known for his application of the tenets of Gestalt psychology *(gestalt* in German means pattern). Purely psychological explanations of personality were found inadequate and emphasis was laid on the socio-cultural forces impacting on personality. The systems approach has thus been spreading fast in both physical and social sciences as a powerful aid to scientific explanations. As Robert Chin observes:

"Psychologists, sociologists, anthropologists, economists and political scientists have been 'discovering' and using the system model. In doing so, they find intimations of an exhilarating 'unity' of science, because the system models used by biological and physical scientists seem to be exactly similar. Thus, the system model is regarded by some system theorists as universally applicable to physical and social events and to human relationships in small or large units."[14]

What is a System?

Webster defines a system as "A set or arrangement of things so related or connected as to form a unity of organic whole". A system is thus a unified whole having a number of interdependent parts or subsystems and it has identifiable boundaries that distinguish it from its surrounding environment in which it is embedded and with which it interacts. Systems are often characterised as 'closed' or 'open'. Biological and social systems are open systems in the sense that they are in constant interaction with their environment. By contrast, physical and mechanical systems are closed in relation to their environment. The concept of 'boundary' is important in understanding the domain of a system. Physical and mechanical systems have easily identifiable boundaries. But the boundaries of social organisations have to be understood from their activities and functions in real life situations. Closed systems have the general tendency toward 'entropy' and disorganisation; open systems, on the other hand, have the tendency to develop through greater internal differentiation and move toward higher levels of organisation. Most social systems fall in this latter category. They grow through internal elaboration of their organisations and tend to develop more and more specialisations leading to increasing organisational complexity.

Relevance of Organisation Theory

The systems approach is particularly relevant to the study of complex public organisations that have elaborate structures and that are embedded in larger social, political and economic environments. According to the open system perspective, an organisation survives and grows by drawing inputs from the environment which are processed internally to produce its output. It is through these input-conversion-output processes that an organisation sustains and develops. The systems thinking help us to have a total view of the organisation including its different parts and their interrelationships. C. West Churchman[15] draws attention to five basic considerations in relation to the systems approach to management:

1. The total *objectives* of the system and the measures of system performance.
2. The system's *environment* acting as constraints.
3. The systems *resources* that are put to use in performance.
4. The systems *components* and their goals and activities (subsystems).
5. The *management* of the system (the regulating and decision-making aspect).

The systems view of organisation was latent in the writings of Mary Parker Follett and Chester Barnard. Herbert Simon's decision-making scheme follows the systems approach which was further elaborated by him and his associates later. Philip Selznick has used the systems framework in his studies of governmental and other complex organisations. To quote Selznick:

"Cooperative systems are constituted of individuals' interaction as a whole in relation to a formal system of coordination. The concrete structure is therefore a resultant of the reciprocal influences of the formal and informal aspects of organisation. Furthermore, this structure is itself a totality, an adaptive 'organism' reacting to influences upon it from an external environment."[16]

The Tavistock Institute of Human Relations in England has produced a number of researches based on systems framework. The organisation has been conceived as a socio-technical system comprising both the social and technical variables.-As Miller and Rice put it:

"Any enterprise may be seen as an open system which has characteristics in common with a biological organism. An open system exists and can only exist, by exchanging materials with its environment. It imports materials, transforms them by means of conversion processes, consumes some of the products of conversion for internal maintenance and exports the rest. Directly or indirectly, it exchanges its outputs for further intakes, including further resources to maintain itself. These import-conversion-export processes are the work the enterprise has to do if it is to live."[17]

The systems approach is now being widely used in organisational analysis. It has proved to be a very useful tool for the conceptualisation of the organisation and its internal and external relationships. Also it has facilitated the 'contingency' or 'situational' view of organisations which mark a radical departure from the traditional approach that emphasised generally the 'one best way' of structuring organisations. Under the influence of systems theory, the current view in organisational analysis is that the structure can vary from situation to situation depending on such factors as their environmental conditions and technology.

Situational Theories

This brings us to the modern approach to organisation theory that underlines the importance of dynamic interaction with environment and other 'situational' factors, influencing organisational design.

In organisation theory, the present trend is to design organisation relative to a situation. The situational point of view does not require that we dismiss earlier ideas about organisations, be it classical design theory or bureaucratic theory. All that is being suggested is that there is no single organisational model which is good in every situation. To be effective, an organisation design has to fit the situation.

Two important lines of thought are significant in this context as they seek to determine the key situational factors. One of these underlines the significance of 'technology' in determining organisation design. The other line of thought suggests the importance of 'environment' in shaping the design.

TECHNOLOGY

'Technology' has been defined differently by different writers. A less controversial definition would be like this: the techniques used by organisations in work-flow activities to transform inputs into outputs.

Technology is a term that is applicable to all types and kinds of organisation. Irrespective of whether an organisation is production-oriented or service-oriented, the role of technology can be seen in the activities that result in the transformation of things coming in (request, raw-material etc.) into things going out.

There have been many studies on the relationship between technology and structure The most influential study on the subject was made by Joan Woodward[18] in England in the 1960s which had a strong impact on organisation theory.This study stimulated a number of follow-up researches in the area of technology-structure relations.

Woodward's was a fairly large scale research involving a detailed analysis of the structure of 100 firms in south-east England. All were manufacturing companies and most were quite small in size. Data were collected on structural indices (e.g., ratio of managers and supervisors to total personnel) as well as on the relative success of the firm in its type of industry (judged on the basis of share of market, profitability, capital expansion, reputation of the firm etc.).

The study first attempted to relate the structural features of the organisations to their size, but found little or no such relationship. Then the research team devised a categorisation scheme based on the type of technology employed by each firm. All the firms were grouped into three primary categories of technology: unit or small batch, mass production or large batch ahd continuous process production.

When this grouping was done, a number of interesting relationships was noticed as follows:

1. Levels of authority increased with technical complexity[19]: Unit production having least, more in mass production and most in process production.
2. Ratio of managers to total personnel increased with technical complexity.
3. Span of control of first line supervisor increased from unit to mass and then decreased from mass to process.

The most intriguing aspects of Woodwards data and the findings that have attracted the attention of organisation Theorists concern the relationship of technology to structure and that in turn to organisational success. There was a distinct tendency for successful firms in each category to cluster about a particular span of control, with the less successful firms seeming to have either a too small or a too larger span for their particular technology.

To quote Woodward, "The fact that organisational characteristics, technology and success were linked together in this way suggested that not only was the system of production an important variable in the determination of organisational structure, but also that one particular form of organisation was most appropriate to each system of production".

An additional important observation was that the administrative or operational procedures that typified each firm varied by the type of technology. At what Woodward calls the 'top and bottom of the technical scale' (i.e. unit and process firms), there was a tendency toward fewer rules, controls and definitions of duties and flexibility in interpersonal relations and delegation of authority, compared to the middle range mass production firms. Firms in a given technological category that deviated from this general pattern tended to be less successful. Strikingly, more successful mass production firms were those which emphasized tight controls, high specification of duties—characteristics that came close to 'bureaucratic' type of organisation.

How Important is Technology?

To what extent technology itself causes oi oaiii-sations to be structured and c j erated in certain ways? Is technology an independent variable? This leads one to think of some kind of technological determinism.

It is not, however, true that technology is not amenable to change dictated by human choice. To say that technology plays an important role in affecting organisation design does not preclude its being considered something that in itself can be changed and altered.

Environment and Organisation

In organisation theory literature, the impact of environment on organisation design has been widely discussed. There have been quite a few influential researches in this area which have sought to highlight the vital influence of environment on organisational structure.

Environment, for this purpose, can be considered as the immediate 'operating environment' of an organisation which would refer to the set of conditions outside the organisation that have a direct impact on the day-to-day functioning of the organisation.

The basic designs of organisations seem to have been critically affected by two inter-related dimensions of the environment:

(a) The environment's relative stability versus its instability; and
(b) The environment's relative simplicity versus its complexity.

Research findings suggest that relatively stable and simple environments seem to permit and indeed encourage the development of highly structured organisations approximating the 'bureaucratic type'. At the other end, environments which have been changing rapidly and which involve considerable uncertainty and unpredictable, tend to lead to more fluidly designed organisations that deemphasize structured relationships.

Also, there is certain evidence to suggest that if an organisational structure is not keeping in step with the salient features of the environment, it is apt to be less effective. It follows therefore that if the environment is highly dynamic and turbulent, the hierarchical and rule-bound bureaucratic organisation would be at a disadvantage. However, within a relatively simple and slowly changing environment, the highly structured, bureaucratic organisation appears to have an edge over the more loosely structured and less rigidly controlled organisation.

The upshot of these findings is that different types of environments require different types of organisational designs for the sake of effectiveness.

Two Studies

The relationship between environment and organisation can be examined in some more details by referring to two very significant studies: one by Burns and Stalker[20] and the other by Lawrence and Lorsch.[21]

Burns and Stalker studied some twenty manufacturing concerns in Scotland and England. They were primarily interested in the types of structure and management practices that developed in relation to the rates of change in the markets for the firms' products and in technological innovation.

From the information they could gather, the

researchers were able to distinguish between two distinct types of systems of management: one called 'mechanistic' and the oc.er 'organic The former seemed particularly characteristic of stable environments and the latter of rapidly changing environments.

The mechanistic system has beer, described as follows:

"In mechanistic systems the problems and tasks facing the concern as a whole are broken down into specialisations. Each individual pursues his task as something distinct from the real tasks of the concern as a whole, as if it were the subject of a sub-contract. 'Somebody at the top' is responsible for seeing to its relevance.The technical methods, duties and powers attached to each functional role are precisely defined. Interaction within management tends to be vertical, i.e., between superior and subordinate. Operations and working behaviour are governed by instructions and decisions issued by superiors. This command hierarchy is maintained by the implicit assumption that all knowledge about the situation of the firm and its tasks is, or should be, available only to the head of the firm. Management, often visualized as the complex hierarchy familiar in organisational charts, operates a simple control system, with information flowing up through a succession of filters and decisions and instructions flowing downwards through a succession of amplifiers."

By contrast, the organic system exhibits the following characteristics:

"Organic systems are adapted to unstable conditions, when problems and requirements for action arise which cannot be broken down and distributed among specialist roles within a clearly defined hierarchy Individuals have to perform their special tasks in light of their knowledge of the tasks of the firm as a whole. Jobs lose much of their formal definition in terms of methods, duties and powers, which have to be redefined continually by interaction with others participating in a task. Interaction runs laterally as much as vertically. Communication between people of different ranks tends to resemble lateral consultation rather thar ve: tical command. Omniscience can no longer be imputed to the head of the concern."

Burns and Stalker did not sav that one system is by itself superior to the other. As they observed,

"We desire to avoid the suggestion that either system is superior under all circumstances to the other. In particular, nothing in our experience justifies the assumption that mechanistic systems should be superseded by organic in conditions of stability."

The other study by Lawrence and Lorsch is much more methodical and its findings have had considerable impact on organisation theory.

Lawrence and Lorsch based their research on detailed case studies of firms in the plastics, packaged food and container industries. The initial study was focussed on six firms in the plastics industry. A number of critical questions was sought to be answered by the researchers. These are:

1. How are the environmental demands facing various organisations different and how do environmental demands relate to the internal functioning of effective organisations?
2. Is it true that organisations in certain or stable environments make more exclusive use of the formal hierarchy to achieve integration and if so, why? Because less integration is required, or because in a certain environment these decisions can be made more effectively at higher organisational levels or by fewer people?
3. Is the same degree of differentiation in orientation and in departmental struc-

ture found in organisations in different external environments?

4. If greater differentiation among functional departments is required in different enterprises, does this influence the problems of integrating the organisation 's parts? Does it influence the organisations means of achieving integration

These four questions summarise the thrust of the research. Three key concepts used in this connection need to be under rood: differentiation, integration and environment.

Differentiation stands for 'the state of segmentation of the organisational system into subsystems, each of which tends to develop particular attributes in relation to the requirements posed by its relevant external environment.' The concept refers in part to structural aspects (division and specialization of labour) and partly to behavioural attributes of employees of subsystems.

Integration is the 'process of achieving unity of effort among the various subsystems in the accomplishment of the organisations' task.' This can be achieved in a variety of ways. The classical theorists relied on creation of rules and procedures governing the behaviour of members. In a relatively unstable environment, integration might be better achieved through plan. In a highly unstable environment, coordination may be achieved by mutual adjustment which would require a great deal of communication through open channels throughout the organisation.

Environment, which is the independent variable in this case, was conceptualised from the perspective of the organisation members as they looked outward.The assumption was that a basic reason for differentiating into subsystem is to deal more effectively with sub-environments.

Lawrence and Lorsch identified three main sub-environments: the *market,* the *technical-economic* and the *scientific.* These correspond to the sales, the production and the research and development functions.

It was hypothesised that the degree of differentiation would vary within each subsystem depending upon the following attributes of the sub-environment: (i) the rate of change of conditions over time; (ii) the certainty of information about conditions at any particular time; and (iii) the time span of feedback on the results of employee decisions.

It follows, therefore, that the greater the differences among the three sub-environments in terms of rate of change, certainty of information and time span of feedback, the greater will be the differences among the three subsystems in terms of organisational structure and behavioural attributes. The greater these differences, that is, the more differentiated are the three subsystems, the more important is the task of integrating these subsystems.

Lawrence and Lorsch propose that the relative effectiveness of an organisation is directly related to the extent to which it achieves required differentiation. Given the attainment of an optimal differentiation in a particular sub-environment, the departments then must be integrated to the degree necessitated by the total environment.

One can calculate three scores for each of the six organisations (mentioned earlier): a score to measure the degree of attainment of required differentiation, a score to measure the degree of attainment of required integration and a score to measure the effectiveness of total organisation. The scores were rank-ordered into high median and low. It was noticed that effectiveness was related to the degree of required differentiation and integration.

Two high performance organisations achieved

both high differentiation and high integration (see Table 1).

Table 1

Differentiation	*Integration*	*Effectiveness*
I	High	High
II	High	High
III	Low	High
IV	High	Low
V	High	Low
VI	Low	Low

The study by Lawrence and Lorsch shows that there is no one best way to organise. Internal st: uctural adjustments would have to be made in tune with the state of the environment. Her ce different organisations can go in for different integrating mechanisms depending on the environment in which they would be working.

Overview

Older and traditional theories of organisation had a limited perspective and in their quest for efficiency they mainly concentrated on the operating level conceiving the organisation basically in mechanistic term. The human relations approach laid emphasis on the psycho-social system without much regard for the structural and environmental aspects of the organisation.

Systems approach, on the other hand, takes an open ended view of the organisation which is considered in the context of an interacting and dynamic environment. The organisation as an open, socio-technical system receives inputs from the environment, uses these for maintenance and production purposes and sends the products out in the environment. The technology and the psycho-social system (because of employment of human beings) are structured properly to conduct the input-conversion-output processes. Being embedded in an 'environment', the organisation has to intelligently relate itself to the relevant aspects of the environment. Internally, various subsystems within the organisation coexist in both differentiated and integrated states. The psycho-social subsystem is represented in the behaviour of human beings at work. The technical subsystem takes care of the mechanistic processing of inputs into outputs. The structural sub-system formalises the relationship between the technical and psycho-social subsystems through definition of jobs and positions, authority allocation and determination of flows of communication and work. Within the structure lies 'management' as a distinct and vital node integrating the different parts together regulating internal relationships and conducting external negotiations.

The systems view of organisation consciously identifies the different sub-systems within the organisation and locates it in the environmental setting. This approach is obviously at a very high level of generalisation. Its purpose is to 'provide us with a macro paradigm for the study of organisations'.

The contingency or the situational view of organisation follows this conceptualisation and seeks to make the systems view implementable in practice. Its focus is on more specific features and patterns of interactions among the organisational sub-systems. Kast and Rosenzweig have explained the relationship between the systems view and the contingency view thus:

"The contingency view of organisations and their management suggests that an organisation is a system composed of sub-systems and delineated by identifiable boundaries from its environmental supra-system. The contingency view seeks to understand the interrelationships within and among sub-systems as well as between the organisation and its environment and to define patterns of relationships or configurations of variables. It emphasises the multivariate nature of organisations and attempts to understand how organisations operate under varying conditions and in specific circumstances. Contingency views are ultimately directed toward suggesting organisational designs and managerial actions most appropriate for specific situations."[22]

This approach departs radically from the traditional theorists' view of 'one best solution'. At the same time, it is much more complex and demands a high degree of managerial talent to identify the different organisational variables and the network of relationships both w'tliin and without.

The Closed and Open Models (CM and OM)

As earlier stated, the two contrasting strands of thought on organisation have also been labelled as 'closed' and 'open' models. At this stage, it will be appropriate to identify their basic differences. The two models can be compared, along following aspects: (i) social role of organisations; (ii) organisational-, view of man; (iii) concept of organisational structure; (iv) concept of organisational order; and (v) perceptions of the environment.

On the first issue of social role, CM seems to be erecting a wall of separation between the organisation and the larger society outside. Rationality has been the organisation's sole prerogative. Hence, society has to be manipulated by organisation. The bureaucracy remains inside the organisation and the client outside. The civil servants are viewed as a class apart from citizens.

By contrast, OM has a different conceptualization of social role of the organisation. Society is looked at as an inter-locking system of organisations and there is no 'non-rational' organisation to be manipulated and controlled by a 'rational' organisation. The bureaucrat and the citizen are one and the same. Thus OM views the organisation as an essential form of society and its purpose and objectives are not different from those of the society in which it is embedded.

In the second issue of concept of man, the views of CM and OM are often presented as theory X and theory Y (a-la McGregor). The CM view is more on the side of stricter supervision and higher level manipulation of man in organisations, as man is thought to be work-avoiding and dependent. By contrast the OM view is more positive about man as seff-actualising and self-controlling. In this view, most men enjoy work and tend to be creative. External manipulation curbs initiative and creativity.

On the third issue, concept of structure, it follows what has been stated above that CM would favour a rigid, hierarchical structure with heavy formalism and ordered communication. The OM view would be just the opposite, as it would support a more participative structure with fairly free flow of communication and considerable flexibility in inter-level relationships.

On the fourth issue of organisational order, maintenance of order and discipline within the organisation is looked at differently by the two models. The CM view would be to characterise order in organisation as an imposed thing coming from the top of the organisation. 'Order' is thus a policed or supervised organisation's atmosphere. According to the OM view, organisational order grows out of spontaneous human behaviour. Men in organisation need it as they need air and water. It need not be superimposed from above. Order is sought to be artificially imposed in a situation of authority crisis in an organisation.

On the fifth issue of environmental perception, CM with its insular and inward looking stance tends to shut the organisation off from the environment in search of stability. In fact, CM thrives on stable environment assumption, whereas the OM view has been that the environment is the soil in which the organisation remains planted. Hence an organisation has to integrate itself with the environment and reorder its internal structure and operations in response to changing environmental situations. OM thus rc resents an appropriate organisational design in situations of environmental instability and uncertainty.

In conclusion, it can be said that both models are ideal constructs. Organisations in reality fall somewhere in between the two extremes. A living organisation is essentially an open organisation; total closure is inimical to organisational survival.

As Nicholas Henry[23] has pointed out, there has been a virtual new school of 'model synthesis' in whose view the closed and open systems need not be looked at as opposites; rather the two are synthesised in practice on the basis of three very reasonable assumptions:

1. Organisations and their environment change.
2. Organisations and the people in them act to survive.
3. Organisations and the people in them learn from mistakes.

To quote Henry: "The essence of the literature of model synthesis is that it starts with the open model (that is, it assumes that organisations are spontaneous collectives of people with their goals and drives, operating in an uncertain environment), but explains organisational behaviour as being motivated by a need to routine and rationalise the organisation's internal workings and its relationships with its environment whenever possible. This is essentially a Darwinian notion (adapt or die). Another way of saying the same thing is that organisations try to become rational. Consider the same concept from another perspective: organisations try to make all variables (such as member behaviour and technological and environmental developments) predictable. From a still different angle, we can perceive that organisations try to achieve closure. Yet another (and perhaps the best) way of expressing the same idea is to say that organisations try to reduce uncertainty."

REFERENCES

1. Bernard Berelson and Gary A. Steiner *Human Behaviour: An Inventory of Scientific Findings.* Harcourt, Brace & World, New York, 1964, pp 10-11.
2. F.J. Roethlisberger and W. J, Dickson, *Manager and the Worker,* Harvard University Press, 1939.
3. Stewart Clegg and David Dunkerbly, *Organization, Class and Control,* Routledge & Kegal Pant, London, 1984, pp.352-355.
4. Chester I. Barnard, *The Functions of the Executive,* Harvard University Press, 1938, p. 165.
5. Ibid., p. 144.
6. Op. cit., pp. 148-9.
7. H. Simon and James March, *Organisations,* Wiley and Sons, 1958.
8. E. Bakke, *The Fusion Process,* Yale University 1953, p, 45,
9. Chris Argyris, *Personality and Organisation,* Harper & Row, New York.
10. Warren G. Bennis, Kenneth D. Benne, Robert Chin and Kenneth E. Cory (eds.), *The Planning of Change,* Holt, Rinechart and Winston, New York, 1976, p. 15.
11. I.V Blanberg, V.N. Sadovsky and E.G. Yudin. *Systems Theory: Philosophical and Methodological Problems,* Progress Publishers, Moscow, 1977, chapter 2.
12. Ludwig von Bertalanffy, *Problems of Life,* John Wiley & Sons., New York, 1952, p. 201.
13. Talcott Parsons, *The Social System, The* Free Press of Glencoe, New York, 1951.
14. "Robert Chin, "The Utility of System Models and Developmental Models for Practitioners", in Warren G. Bennis, et al., (eds.), *The Planning of Change,* Holt, Rinehart and Winston, New York, 1976.

15. C. West Churchman, *The Systems Approach,* Dell, New York, 1968.
16. Philip Selznick, "Foundations of the Theory of the Organisation", *American Sociology Review,* February 1948.
17. EJ. Miller and A.K. Rice, *Systems of Organisation,* Tavistock Publications, London, 1970, p. 3.
18. Joan Woodward, *Industrial Organisation: Theory and Practice,* London 1965.
19. The sc le of technical complexity was devised according to "the extent to which the production process is controllable and its results predictable.
20. T Burns and G.M. Stalker, *The Management of Innovation,* London Tavistock, 1961.
21. P.R. Lawrence and J.W Lorsch, *Organisation and Environment,* Harvard Business School, 1967.
22. Fremont E. Kast and James E. Rosenzweig, *Organisation and Management: A Systems and Contingency Approach,* McGraw-Hill, 1979, p. 115.
23. Nicholas Henry, *Public Administration and Public Affairs,* op.cit, 1986 ed. Chapter 3.

Chapter 7

Goals, Policies and Implementation

Organisations are essentially goal-seeking entities. It is through the achievement of goals that organisations receive continued support from the environment and are legitimised socially. For the managerial cadre, the goals show the way to specific tasks that is to be done at the operative level. For other organisational participants, activities become meaningful in the context of the goals.

Meaning

As Etzioni has defined it,'an organisational goal is a desired state of affairs which the organisation attempts to realise'.The goal concept is, however, not free from controversy.

The meaning of organisational goals is not always quite clear. 'Goals' can be approached from a variety of perspectives. According to the classificatory scheme of Talcott Parsons, at the societal level organisational goals are really an extension of what the society needs for its own survival. At the other extreme is the position that organisational goals are nothing more than the goals of the individual members of the organisation. A critic may, however, quip that if the emphasis is on the variety of individual goals, the whole point of 'organisation' will be missed.

Organisational goals are creation of individuals and groups in the organisation. Yet, the commonly based goals seldom remain constant. New considerations imposed from within or without might deflect the organisation from its original goal. The important point is that the goal of an organisation is an abstraction distilled from the desires of members and pressures from the environment and the internal system.

Herbert Simon, while discussing organisational decision making, develops his own approach to the goal concept which is not rquch different from what has just been stated. According to Simon, 'We must explain organisational behaviour in terms of the goals of the individual members of the organisation, or we must postulate the existence of one or more organisational goals, over and above the goals of the individuals.'[1]

Simon keeps the goal idea (as input to decision) at the level of the individual, but offers the important notion that the goals of an organisation at any point in time are the result of the interaction among the members of the organisation. In Simon's approach, goals become constraints on the decision-making approach. The constraints are based on abstract values around which the organisation operates. Decisions are made within the framework of a set of constraints (goals) and organisations attempt to make decisions that are optimal in terms of the sets of constraints they face.

With slight modification of this stand, it can be observed that organisational actions are constrained not only by goals, but also by pressures from the external environment and by forces generated within the organisation.

When goals are treated as abstract values, it has the merit of showing that organisational actions are guided by more than the whims of individual members. At the same time, organisations need specific guides for actual operational purposes. In this connection, Perrow distinguishes between two kinds of goals. 'Official goals' are the general purposes of the organisation as can be found in statutes, annual reports and other authoritative statements. 'Operative goals' designate the ends sought through the actual operating policies of the organisation; they tell us what the organisation actually is trying to do.[2]

Operative goals reflect the derivation and distillation of a set of goals from both official and unofficial sources. These are developed through interaction patterns within the organisation and through pressures from the external environment. It is the combination of official goals with internal and external factors that defines an existing set of operating goals.

Both for the researcher and the employer, the goal determination is important to make any sense out of existing personnel and resource allocation, organisational structure and processes and output. Also it is important from the point of view of understanding of organisational effectiveness. Official goals are easy to determine from the sources as mentioned earlier. But operative goals have to be distilled from the actual decisions of top decision-makers in the organisation. The kinds of decisions that are taken about allocation of resources such as money, personnel, equipment etc. are a major indicator of the goals of the organisation.

It will be wrong to imagine that organisational goals remain constant through time. These change mainly for three reasons. There is direct pressure from external forces. Secondly, there can be pressures from the very internal system. Thirdly, there are changed environmental and technological demands that prompt the organisation to redefine its goals.

The impact of external relationships on goals has been a fact of organisational life. The classic study in this area is Selznick's *TVA and the Grass Roots* (1966), which documents the impact of bringing new societal elements into the governing structure of the TVA. Currently, in this country students and workers are gradually being brought as members of governing bodies of the universities and industries. This is expected to have some effect on the goal setting of these organisations.

The operative goals of an organisation can undergo drastic changes due to changes in the 'power system' of the organisation. There can be a sudden influx of new kinds of people or leaders in the organisation who might set new standards and change earlier goals.

'Goal displacement' may occur due also to what Etzioni calls 'over measurement' and Bertram Gross labels 'number magic'. When organisations tend to organise their activities around more easily quantifiable spheres, organisational goals become deflected toward the achievement of the easily measured aspect. This may in turn actually defeat the purpose for which the organisation was designed at the outset.

The final source of goal change is a more generalised environmental pressure. New technological developments, for instance, may lead to internal readjustments of strategy and structure of an organisation.

Apart from technology, general values in the environment surrounding an organisation also affect its operation (operative goals). Educational policies in a country may undergo changes, for instance, if general societal values take a turn for, say, the use of only the mother tongue as the medium of instruction. Because of the complex interplay of forces, it is better to talk in terms of a goal structure or a goal set. The goals can be derived from legislations and charters; these can be influenced by managers and other organisational participants. Goals can also be shaped by powerful external influences. As such, the organisation evolves its goals through a continuous process of bargaining and learning.

EFFECTIVENESS

The analysis of goals is rather empty exercise until the second part of the equation is added. Since a goal is something that is sought, the goal-seeking leads to the issue of goal accomplishment, or effectiveness.

Effectiveness is the extent to which an organisation achieves its objectives (goals) within the constraints of limited resources. Efficiency, which is often confused with effectiveness, refers to the process by which the organisation maximises its objectives with minimum use of resources. Organisation can thus be effective without being efficient.

The actual process of evaluating organisational effectiveness is considerably more difficult than one might suspect. Two alternative models have been suggested in this context. One is known as the 'goal model'. This approach emphasises that organisational effectiveness should be evaluated solely in terms of goals or outputs. As a conceptual framework, the goal model is deficient for a number of reasons. For instance, it does not account for the fact that managers must allocate resources to activities which have little to do with goals or outputs. Resources, to cite an instance, must be allocated to recruitment of personnel. Again, for many service organisations (like police), the use of productivity as a major indicator of effectiveness might be misleading. An alternative and a more powerful conceptual framework has been proposed in terms of systems theory. In an open systems perspective, the organisation is viewed as one element of a number of elements which interact interdependently.The organisation takes resources (input) from the larger system (the environment), processes these resources and returns them to the environment in changed form (output). An organisation will cease to exist when it no longer contributes to the larger system of which it is one part; it will no longer contribute when it is ineffective.

The systems concept emphasizes two important elements.The ultimate survival of the organisation depends on its ability to adapt to the demands of its environment and in meeting these demands, the total cycle of input-process-output must be the focus of managerial attention. The criteria of effectiveness must reflect these two considerations and we must define effectiveness accordingly.

Effectiveness can thus be defined in terms of the optimum balance among the various adaptation and maintenance activities. These activities of the organisation, determining performance, can be identified as follows:

1. Acquiring resources,
2. Making efficient use of inputs relative to outputs,
3. Producing outputs—goods/services,
4. Performing technical and administrative tasks rationally,
5. Investing in the organisation,
6. Conforming to codes of behaviour,
7. Satisfying various interests of people/ group.

Effectiveness of an organisation depends upon the extent to which it maintains a balance, that is, achieves an optimum relationship among all its activities.Thus, effectiveness is a composite of a number of activities, each of which is related to the input-process-output cycle and adaptive to the larger environment.

Goal-Setting in Government

In public administration goal-setting posses peculiar problems. The idea of orderly and authoritative goal-setting can be traced to traditional management thought that recommended rigid hierarchy and supremacy of top management in the organisation. With the advent of democracy, as a system of political governance and with the rise of general levels of literacy among workers, a new culture of 'participation' has been slowly gaining ground in business administration. Trade union movements have further pressed for participative decision making.

In public administration, clear-cut goal setting is beset with a number of problems. First, the politicians who are at the helm of affairs as ministers or committee chairmen are birds of passage. They stay in their positions for a limited period. To take a longer term view of things, thus, becomes difficult for them. Long-term goal setting often suffers in government because of the transient nature of the political executive.

Second, politicians are not trained managers. They are essentially mediators in a crossfire of complex and often incompatible demands and pressures. Living in the midst of conflicting pressures and forces, they seek to manage conflict by making compromises and vague statements. These are a far cry from specific, clear-cut goal setting so glibly talked about in management literature.

Third, at the higher levels in government, goals and policies (deduced from the former) are the product of a joint venture between the politician and the administrator. The minister in a department and his secretary work hand in hand together in managing the affairs of the department. The minister is expected to bring in 'values' and the secretary is supposed to internalise it and translate it into definite policies for execution. In real life situations, things are not so neatly subdivided. The two intermingle freely and the goals and policies flow out of this close relationship. So, the process of goal-setting in government is rarely a straight-forward exercise by a single individual. It is much more complex in character and needs the meeting of many minds.

The complicated process of goal setting applies to the government sector as a whole but this does not preclude the possibility of clear-cut goal setting in particular departments such as the agriculture and irrigation. To this extent, goals would be clearly set, these would facilitate formulation of fairly clear policies, which in turn could help in proper designing of the organisation and successful completion of the tasks.

Policy-making in Government

The terms—goals, purposes, policies and objectives—are often used interchangeably. Their differences lie in the degree of specificity. Goals and purposes refer to broad intents for which policies and objectives are formulated. In this sense, goals and policies are value loaded terms referring to a distant state of things that are intended to be achieved. Thus, removal of poverty can be considered a goal which the Government of India wants to pursue. Rural development, urban development and industrial development policies are then geared to attain this broad public goal. Policies, in this context, are major instruments that are carefully formulated to move the society toward the goal. Objectives are more concrete products or end-state to be achieved by pursuing specific policies. It is in this sense the technique is called 'management by objective' seeks to formalise organisational effort to achieve definite results. Objectives are thus much more concrete and often precisely quantifiable.

A subtle distinction needs to be drawn here between policy making and decision making. Geoffrey Vickers makes a distinction between policy making and executive decisions "the first being designed to give direction, coherence and continuity to the courses of action for which the decision making body is responsible, the second designed to give effect to the policies thus laid down." Institutions like municipalities and government departments are engaged in regulating numerous kinds of relationships in society. Roads have to be maintained and developed for the road users. Schools have to be set up and maintained for different groups of students. In most instances, the government institutions are engaged in maintaining the existing relations. Traffic regulations, school enrolment and educational syllabi fall in this category of maintenance of currently held governing relations. However, occasions arise when the governments have to innovate and introduce large-scale changes to cope with rising demands and with new situations. For instance, traffic regulation may accept the present traffic volume with marginal changes and will be satisfied with some additional traffic constables at road crossings, mobile traffic patrol and better utilisation of road capacity through stricter parking regulations. This would involve a number of executive decisions to see that traffic does not go out of control. But, there may be an altogether new situation when mere tinkering with existing regulations may not suffice. The traffic volume and complexity may undergo such dramatic changes over time that these might call for new policy initiative from the government institutions. New roads and by-passes would have to be constructed; much traffic may have to be pushed underground or over ground along a new metro, as it has been done in the Kolkata and New Delhi.

In a situation of rapid change, major policy decisions become necessary as the on-going regulative process can no longer cope with events. The differentiation between executive decisions and policy decisions has been made by Vickers in the following way:

"That element of the regulative function which consists in maintaining the course of affairs in line with the current governing relations I regard as the executive element. That element which consists in modifying the governing relations I regard as the policy-making element."[3]

Need for Policy Analysis

Public policy analysis is concerned with government s behaviour. What the government actually chooses to do or not to do forms the core of policy inquiry. Major policy decisions are taken by the government in such areas as defence, industry, agriculture, education and so on. These decisions involve enormous costs to the nation. Besides financial expenditure, such decisions produce important and wide-ranging consequences. Why particular kind of decisions were taken, how were these arrived at and what would be their likely consequences?—These questions are now being raised by policy analysts. Since policies determine the future shape of the society, scientific knowledge about policy making needs to be built up. Empirical studies in various fields of government operations are expected to yield critical evidences that could be used for creation of a more general body of knowledge called policy science. Yehezkel Dror, who has been passionately pleading for more and more social science applications to public policy problems, presents his point of view thus:

"Policy science can be partly described as the discipline that searches for policy knowledge, that seeks general policy issue knowledge and policy making knowledge and integrates them into a distinct study."[4]

Policy issue knowledge refers to knowledge related to a specific policy. Policy making knowledge has wider concern it deals with the system of policy making activity—how it operates and how it can be improved. As Dror exhorts, "The development of policy science must be speeded up and this advanced policy science put to its fullest use, if critical problems are to be adequately solved."[5]

Further, Dror points out that technology has facilitated effective control of the environment, but the policy makers are unable to design effectively and operate the systems needed for controlling. He pleads for an optimal approach for policy making and evaluation. There should be, in his opinion, the broadest use of information and the best policy should be adopted by a careful examination of goals, values, alternatives, costs and benefits. He insists on the use of extra-rational information to enrich policy analysis. Intuition, value preferences, extraordinary leadership and acute reality perceptions are, according to him, valuable aids to analysis.

For this wide sweep, Dror has often been dubbed an utopian and his views are considered too abstract to be of any use to the practising administrator. Yet, his insistence on rigorous analysis has gained general acceptance. Policy analysis today is emerging as a sub-discipline with its attention focussed on three things:

i) Understanding policies rather than recommendation; the accent is on explanation and not directly on prescription;
ii) Scientific quest for causal relationships in policy issues. Causes and consequences of public policies are now being subjected to rigorous analysis; and
iii) Creation of a body of policy science knowledge; micro or specific policy studies are being used for reaching broader generalisations for universal explanatory purposes.

Political Science and Public Administration

Policy studies have been the confluence zone for the meeting of experts belonging to Political Science and Public Administration. Political scientists have been basically interested in the 'politics' of policy making in specific sectors such as health, education, pollution etc.The questions raised are how the issues surfaced; who are the actors; what kinds of power groups or influences are involved in raising and pursuing the policy objectives. By contrast, the public administration expert is concerned with organisation, decision-process and implementation of policies. While political science has looked into substantive fields (sectors), public administration has chosen to probe into organisational and administrative processes and execution and implementation. More theoretically oriented discussions are thus to be found in Public Administration focussing on organisation theory, political economy and programmes implementation. In a way, public policy field has supported the application of political science knowledge to governmental behaviour. This, of course, does not belittle the importance of public administration as a distinct mode of policy analysis with its emphasis on action-orientation.

Models of Public Policy

There are different ways of looking at public policy.These are of course not mutually exclusive. Each has a distinct focus and each suggests specific things about public policy. Following the classificatory scheme of Dye[6], the models can be presented in the following way:

1. *Institutionalism*

According to this view, public policies have their origin in government institutions that formulate and implement them. A policy becomes public only when it is authoritatively determined by government institutions. Government lends legitimacy to policies. Also, policies assume universalistic character because of their governmental origin. Government policies are thus applicable to everybody in a society.

The institutional approach has been the traditionally accepted the way of looking at policy formulation in government. It assumes that institutional arrangements have their impact on public policy. So, structural changes in government are often attempted to bring about policy changes. In India, institutional changes such as the Small Farmers Development Agency had been introduced to improve the economic condition of small and marginal farmers. Such structural changes may not always produce the desired consequences. Environmental forces may stand in the way of institutional functioning and even direct the operations in such a way that the intended policy impact would become negligible.

2. *Group Theory*

According to the group theorist, public policy at any point of time reflects the equilibrium reached in the group struggle. As different interest groups struggle among themselves to influence public policy, actual policy making in government tends to tilt toward the groups that are gaining influence. By contrast public policy moves away from the demands of the losing groups. To quote Earl Latham, "What may be called public policy is actually the equilibrium reached in the group struggle at any given moment and it represents a balance which the contending fractions or groups constantly strive to tip in their favour.... The legislature referees group struggle, ratifies the victories of the successful coalition and records the terms of the surrenders, compromises and conquests in the form of statutes."[7]

The big farmer lobby in India is often quoted in connection with agricultural price fixation. Similarly, the influence of big industries in changing the industrial regulations is widely acknowledged. These are concrete illustrations of powerful interest groups exerting decisive influences on government policies.

3. *Elite Theory*

Another way of looking at public policy is that it reflects the preferences of a governing elite. A policy is sought to be given a public character, aS if it is the result of accommodation of peoples demands. Actually, the people as a whole do not care much for government policy, nor do they have adequate knowledge about what goes on in government. They are led and manipulated by the elites. Public policies do not, therefore, arise out of the demands of the masses. These flow from the top and do not move up from the bottom.

The elite theory has close resemblance with the group theory, as both refer to policy generation through pressures from specific interests in the society. Group theory, however, is basically pluralistic, whereas elite theory is essentially monistic.

4. *Rational Model*

A policy is rational when it is most efficient. In calculating efficiency, all social, political and economic values achieved or sacrificed by a public policy have to be considered. Maximisation of 'net value achievement' is thus the hall mark of a rational policy.'Net value achievement' means that in framing a policy all relevant values should be explicitly taken into account and sacrifices of some values must be more than compensated by the attainment of some other values.

As Herbert Simon defines it, "rationality is concerned with the selection of preferred behaviour alternatives in terms of some system of values whereby the consequences of behaviour can be evaluated."[8] In formulating a rational policy, the processes will be as follows:

i) All the societal values relevant for the policy in question should be identified and weigh—age should be given to each;
ii) All the alternative courses of action (policy alternatives) should be considered;
iii) All the consequences of each alternative course of action should be identified and evaluated which would mean calculating the ratio between the values achieved and those sacrificed in respect of each policy alternative; and
iv) Selection of one alternative the probable consequences of which would be preferable in terms of the most valued ends.

According to Simon,[9] three kinds of activities are involved in a rational policy-making process: intelligence activity, design activity and choice activity. As he describes the process:

"The first phase of decision-making process—searching the environment for conditions calling for decision—I shall call intelligence activity (borrowing the military meaning of intelligence). The second phase—inventing, developing and analysing possible courses of action—I shall call design activity. The third phase—selecting a particular course of action from those available—I shall call choice activity."

Prerequisites of rational policy-making are many. Firstly, an adequate understanding of societal values is extremely important. Secondly, data and information regarding the alternative courses of action must be readily available. Thirdly, there must be a definite decision-making system in the organisation with adequate capacity to identify relevant data, analyse them properly and predict the consequences of alternative courses of action.

It should be clear by now that there are many barriers to rational policy making. There is no unanimity of views on societal values and giving weigh-age to any one of them is far more difficult.The vast amount of data and information needed to support the policy making process may not be easy to collect and the cost would naturally be too high. The decision-making system itself is many a time very complex that many minds have to meet and there are conflicts of values and personalities impeding the process of reaching decisions. As Meyerson and Banfield concluded in their study of Chicago public housing,"Obviously no decision can be perfectly rational choice since no one can ever know all the alternatives open to him at any moment or all the consequences which would follow from any action. Nevertheless, decisions may be made with more or less knowledge of alternatives, consequences and relevant ends and so we may describe some decisions and some decision-making processes as more nearly rational than others."[10]

In the framing of public policies, 'optimality' on the basis of purely rational calculation is as important as acceptability. That is why even a rationalist like Dror wants policy analysts to broaden their use of extra rational information including intuition and exceptional leadership with acute perceptions of social reality. A recent study of policy making in India reaches a fairly similar conclusion. As the researchers insist, "We believe that neither science, nor an 'optimal' system in policy formulation could replace the decision makers wisdom, experiencejudgment and sensitivity for the environment and compassion for people"[11] and as they observed, "Public policy in a vastly complex techno-social environment like India would have to be concerned with both acceptability and optimality. For without a judicious mix of these two, a policy may fail to have the anticipated impact."[12]

To sum up, rational policy making is more a desired 'thing' than what actually goes on in the government system. In reality, the process of policy making is beset with many problems and pitfalls—institutional, personal, environmental and ethical. To conclude with Martin Rein, "We need a combined standard for judging the desirability of policies able to pass the tests of what is politically feasible, ideologically acceptable and rationally compelling; and such a common standard can never be developed."[13]

5. *Incrementalism*

The incremental model acknowledges the practical difficulties in rational-comprehensive policy making and draws attention to several genuine constraints on administration such as constraints of time, cost, intelligence and politics. The increment disclaimer is best represented in the statement of Charles Lindblom, an eminent economist. Commenting on the rational model, Lindblom writes:

"It assumes intellectual capacities and sources of information that men simply do not possess and it is even more absurd as an approach to policy when the time and money that can be allocated to a policy problem is limited. Of particular importance to public administrators is the fact that public agencies are in effect usually instructed not to practice (this) method. That is to say, their prescribed function and constraints—the politically or legally possible—restrict their attention to relatively few values and relatively few alternative policies."[14]

According to Lindblom, policy makers always start with the accepted programmes and budgets and then try to add new programmes and policies to the existing ones. What actually goes on in government is 'incrementalism' in the sense that past activities are virtually continued with certain modifications. The incremental approach sets up a model of' successive limited comparisons. The assumption here is that in government a historic chain of decisions exists which the administrator can use as a basis for making future choices.

Two concepts used by Lindblom (with Braybrooke) are 'marginal incrementalism' and 'partisan mutual adjustment' to explain the actual policy process in government. The first concept explains the limited and fairly conservative change of policy which is feasible in a specific situation.The second underlines the importance of accommodation of divergent viewpoints and interests in a particular decision situation. The emphasis is more on the practice of 'adjustments' of opinions and interests than merely rational and comprehensive decision-making as a scientific method. Policy making is looked at realistically as marginal and uncoordinated adjustments in situations of conflicting demands and interests and in the face of unforeseen consequences of decisions. Hence it takes the character of 'disjointed incrementalism.'[15]

Lindblom's incrementalist model is diametrically opposite to the rationalist model of Simon and Dror. Criticising the increment stance, Dror points out that in facing new and challenging situations, no historical base exists for a good policy making and the increment is essentially oriented toward stability. To quote Dror, "such models (become) continually less useful for deciding what to do. When the results of past policies have been unsatisfactory, those results count for little in deciding what to do next, since incremental changes in them cannot produce significantly better results."[16]

According to him, developments in management science and empirical research have made it possible to pursue an optimal approach for policy making. Despite such criticisms, the incremental approach has been found in most cases to conform to reality and this seems to fit in properly with the actual administrative situations in government organisations.

An intermediate model has been suggested by the social scientist, Ami tai Etzioni that combines the elements of both rational-comprehensive model and disjointed incrementalism. Two kinds of decision processes identified by him are:

(a) Fundamental policy making that sets basic directions; and
(b) Allied incremental processes that prepare fundamental decisions and develop them further after these have been arrived at. Etzioni's mixed scanning method provides both by first scanning the entire subject area in question very broadly and not in great detail and then concentrating on those aspects revealed that call for more detailed, in-depth scrutiny.[17]

6. *Game Theory*

In situations of conflict as in international relations for instance, game theory has been in use as a method for the study of decision making. The individual decision unit in a game situation may be an individual, a group, or a whole nation, which is not in complete control of other decision units with which it has to interact. Each decision unit has its own goals or objectives. Each must consider how to achieve as much as possible, yet each has to take into account that there are others whose goals differ from its own and whose actions have an effect on all others involved in the situation. The decision units or participants in a game are so situated that there may be many possible outcomes of their actions with different values to them. Decision makers are thus involved in a situation of interdependence. All have to make their independent choices, but the outcome would be conditioned by the choices made by each participant. Game theory is applicable to policy making where there is no independent 'best' choice that one can make—where as the 'best' outcomes depend upon what others do.

As an analytical tool the game theory has been used by social scientists to explain social behaviour in conflict situations. In public policy making, its use is not so common, as the conditions of a 'game' are rarely present in public administration. As Thomas Dye sums up, "Game theory is an abstract and deductive model of policy making. It does not describe how people actually make decisions, but rather how they would go about making decisions in competitive situations if they were completely rational. Thus game theory is a form of rationalism, but it is applied in competitive situations where the outcome depends on what two or more participants do."[18]

7. *Systems Theory*

A very broad 'systems' view of public policy characterises policy decisions as outputs of the political system. According to David Easton,[19] the political system stands for those distinctive structures and processes in a society that is 'predominantly oriented toward the authoritative allocation of values' for the society. The boundary of the system has to be delineated with reference to the activities and processes that are identified as 'political' The system is embedded in an 'environment' with which it is in constant interaction. 'Inputs' are received into the political system from the external environment in the form of demands and supports. The demands seek to activate the process of policy making with a view to get an authoritative decision. These can be directed towards reduction in prices, prohibition, abrogation of a law and similar other public needs. Supports are indicative of acceptance of public policies and results of actions like elections, tax imposition etc.

The authoritative allocations of Easton's formulation are policy decisions. Systems theory thus conceives of public policy as an output of the political system. The systems view has been widely accepted as an useful way of looking at the policy process as it actually works out in government. Policy analysis in terms of both formulation and impact evaluation is greatly facilitated by the systems approach.

Typologies of Public Policy

Policy typologies are useful in understanding why and how certain kinds of policies are made the way they are. Also, such typologies help us understand why some groups do better than others in the realm of policy debates and actual enactment.

The Earliest attempts at making policy typologies generally separated policy into topical categories such as health policy, transportation policy, taxation or fiscal policy and so on. This has no doubt been useful in sorting out different kinds of policy domains but, it has been unhelpful in the matter of drawing general conclusions about the 'politics' of policy making — or, in other words, to understand the kind of 'politics' that underlie these policies.

The modern era of developing policy typologies may be considered to have originated in 1964 when Theodore Lowi laid out his scheme of classic policy types[20]. Lowi divides policies into three basic categories: distributive, redistributive and regulatory. Ripley and Franklin[21] later fine-tuned the typologies by dividing regulatory policy into two categories: protective regulatory and competitive regulatory.

There are different types of 'policies' that are adopted by government from time to time to intervene the socio-economic system. Practically speaking, such policies may be categorized on the basis of method of control. Government control in the form of policy can be used through patronage, regulation and redistribution. Thus public policies fall into three broad categories: (a) patronage policies, (b) regulatory policies and (c) redistributive policies

The first category — *patronage policy* — takes the forms of subsidies, contracts and licenses. Of these, 'subsidy' is a familiar type which can be seen, for instance, in such cases where government wants to promote an activity for public welfare. Take for instance, government wants private transport operators to ply their passenger buses in a route which is initially thought to be a losing concern. Government may issue license at cheaper rate, or may even forego certain taxes, to start with, to encourage the private operators to start the passenger bus.service in a loss-making route initially. Real estate business can be encouraged by initially not levying municipal property tax.

The second category - *regulatory policy* - is generally seen as the most important policy tool used by government to 'regulate' business. For instance, by taxing alcoholic drinks government may try to reduce alcohol consumption. Similarly, by imposing 'effluent tax', government may in effect raise the prices of products of a polluting company. The company may thus lose market in the process because of price increase of their products. Effluent tax may in this way make the company behave and be cautious about pollution.

Following Ripley and Franklin, the two subcategories of regulatory policy may be defined as under.

i) Competitive Regulatory Policy involves policies intended to limit the provision of goods and services to one or a few designated deliverers who are selected from a large number of competing potential deliverers. Ripley and Franklin give the examples of allocation of radio and television frequencies and the awarding of cable television franchises in this connection.

ii) Protective Regulatory Policy is designed to protect the public at large from the negative effects of private activity such as air pollution, unhealthy consumer products etc.

The third category — *redistributive policy* — is intended to manage the economy as a whole. Usually, redistributive policies take the forms of fiscal (tax) and monetary (money supply) policies. Thus a common example is to reduce income tax burden of the poor and the lower middle class and raise the tax burden of the rich and the corporate sector. Monetary policies involve regulating the economy by changing the rate of growth of money supply at any point of time, or manipulating interest rates (like banking loans for housing, car purchase etc.).

A Different Approach

The policy study literature has been divided into two groups, following slightly different approaches. One group has been identified as having the central focus on the *process of public policy making;* another seeks to analyze the *outputs and effects of public policy.* The first group is more descriptive in nature, while the second is more prescriptive. Almost all the models classified by Dye fall in the first category The incremental and rational models are placed, in this new approach, in the second group which takes into account another component which has been called the strategic-planning model (SPM).The SPM suggested by Etzioni originated in the business world in the context of environmental conditions surrounding the business firm of today. SPM blends economic and rational analyses, political values and the psychology of participants in the organisation. In this respect, it is more open minded and free from many constraints. In the first group, in addition to what Dye has presented, a new model called the stream and windows model (SWM) has been given prominence in recent times.The author of SWM is John W Kingdon *(Agendas, Alternatives and Public Policies, 1984)* who has identified three streams in the policy making process: the *problems stream, political stream* and the *policy stream.* As the stream itself suggests, the 'problems' stream involves focussing on the 'problems' attracting policy makers' attention. The political stream explains the process leading to inclusion of the 'problems' in the government agenda, through bargaining among participants in the decision process. The third stream - the policy stream - relates to the decision agenda or alternative specification for policy formulation. Here the major forces are not political but intellectual and personal. The Kingdon approach looks very close to the 'rational' model as suggested by Simon.

Summing Up

The 'goals' or 'end-states' define the objectives of an organisation. The policies are formulated to achieve the goals. The activities that the organisation undertakes and the tasks that are assigned to its different parts flow from the policies that are deliberately adopted.

Public policy analysis has been emerging as an important sub-area of social inquiry since every society is engaged in reshaping and regulating itself with the help of broad-range, imaginative policy interventions. How policies are actually made have therefore attracted attention. The different models discussed in this chapter represent attempts in understanding the reality of policy formulation. These are explanatory devices to find out the causes and consequences of a policy. Hopefully such attempts at model-building will eventually lead to the growth of a policy science, as Dror has envisaged it.

Implementation

The issue of implementation assumes importance in this context. Policy analysis takes a top-down view of government operation. What happens to policies in terms of their actual results on the ground? This raises the issue of implementation; hence, policy analysis and programme implementation are like twins, one is integrally connected with the other. In government administration what worries most is implementation. We owe to Pressman and Wildavsky the interest that later became almost a passion to many, in implementation studies *(Implementation,* University of California Press, 1973).

Due to their writing, students of public administration have been looking at policy making and policy execution as a seamless web in which each strand depends on all the others. In brief, implementation concentrates on the results of administrative action and not merely on its process.

Concern about execution of laws gave birth to the new field of implementation. It is relevant in this context to quote Woodrow Wilson as he said: "It is getting harder to run a Constitution than to frame one". Running is the implementation aspect of government's activity.

Success/Failure

Implementation success or failure is usually linked to the problem of achieving goals that are to be precisely put. For instance, if a scheme of rural housing was intended to build a certain number of houses of particular specification within a time target at specified costs, implementation would mean actual construction of those houses with proper cost, standard and time specifications. There are two ways of judging implementation: *efficiency standard and responsiveness standard.* The former means: What outputs are produced for a given level of inputs? The latter is reflected in the question: Does implementation represent the popular will? In actual administration, there is, always a trade-off between efficiency and responsiveness or accountability.

Performance: Administrative performance, as many implementation studies point out, is dependent on a variety of factors.

First, different kinds of *uncertainties* often accompany programmes. Space, inputs, technology and even staff may not be available at specific time and locations, thereby impeding the take-off of the programme.

Second, *resources* may fall short of requirements and may not be flowing in time. It is customary for government construction programmes to wait for release of funds almost at the fag end of the financial year. Similarly, staff may not be in position because of delays in transfers and appointments.

Third, there are well known organisational problems affecting programme implementation. Within a department, a new programme may not be welcome by all and there may be delay in appointments. A new programme may demand a new organisation which takes time to take shape.

Fourth, a major problem in any organisation is *organisation.* As experience tells us, leadership makes or destroys an organisation and its programmes. Specially, when new programmes are launched in any sector, it is leadership that, to a large extent, determines the outcome. It is relevant in this context to quote Jams Q. Wilson, as he said: "The supply of able, experienced executives is not increasing nearly as fast as the number of problems being addressed by public policy".

Last but not the least, many government programmes cut across departments and therefore success depends on inter-agency coordination. If the partners in an endeavour are not in the same wave length or working at cross purposes, the fate of the programmes can be forecast from this relationship pattern. Now-a-days, under the 'privatisation' philosophy, government programmes are contracted out to third parties like NGOs and private agencies. Success in that event would be dependent on the performance of the 'outside agencies'.

This is a brief checklist of 'problems' of implementation and in reality there can be many more. For instance, inter-personal relations, superior-subordinate relations, inability to monitor results in time are some of the other problems associated with implementation. In this context, the importance of *administrative feedback* needs to be emphasised, as information blockage often poses critical problems for implementation.

Richard Elmore's concepts of 'forward mapping' and 'backward mapping' are of immense significance for implementation research. Conventionally, as Elmore points out, the administrators decide what results they want to achieve and then try to define in details the responsibilities of people at each step in the implementation process. This is what is called 'forward mapping'. In this process, the problem is that the implementers do not control all the facts affecting the process. Elmore's suggestion is that this can be corrected by 'backward mapping', whereby the administrators begin at the end (not the start), working backward and keeping in mind the constraints at each stage. The concept of 'backward mapping' sensitises us to the fact that no part of the policy process acts in isolation. Flence, each phase of the process must be integrated with the others to ensure successful implementation and achievement of goals.

At the end, one cautionary remark may be in order. All failures in programme implementation may not be due to snags in the implementation process. May be, the policy choice was poor and ill calculated; so failure lay in the policy framing process *ab initio.*

Recent Advances in Policy Studies

Today, there are more and more complexities surfacing almost at regular pace in the burgeoning areas of public policy making. Pressures are mounting from different quarters for urgent decisions .in the fields of international trade and military relations, ever-expanding network of information and communication technology, domestic and international environmental management issues (e.g. dams on rivers, forests conservation and expansion and global warming etc.). Governments everywhere are thus constantly being buffeted by pulls and pressures and at the same yme the call is for more well-considered and acceptable decisions — acceptable to variegated groups of stakeholders.

Against this backdrop, serious heart-searching has been going on among public policy analysts whether the contemporary context of policy making calls for a reopening of some of the foundational ideas about 'policy studies and analysis'. Three aspects of policy studies, in this connection, are assuming considerable significance today: (a) renewed emphasis on a special kind of policy termed strategic policy; (b) post-positivist policy analysis; and (c) the phenomenon of 'policy transfer'. Each aspect deserves attention, even if brief.

Strategic Policy

Rooted in the military science, strategy is

what the high command 'commands'. Strategy involves ideas and vision, as well as planned action, expected performance and desired results. In public service management, chief executives - leaders and top managers -- usually engage in strategy formulation in the form of key ideas and thoughts which are conveyed and transmitted to internal staff and managers at different levels as also to outside organisations and institutions for their informed cooperation and collaboration. Strategic policy is thus a mega policy that involves multiple organisations and stakeholders and includes both bold 'visioning' of the future and planned and meticulous issues management to produce desired results. In recent times, many state governments in India, goaded by the central government and the donor agencies (World Bank, DFID etc.) are in the process of formulating strategic policies in the field of 'health reforms', for instance, in order to espouse the cause of fulfilment of the Million Development Goals such as reduction of IMR, MMR etc. Strategic policy making, therefore, needs top level attention and drive that would generate ideas and vision, carry the entire organisation and its ancillaries along, work out performance achievement road maps and build suitable organisational capabilities to comprehend the strategic vision and the actions involved including ways and means to achieve the strategic outcomes. (Paul Joyce, Strategic Management for the Public Svivices, Open University Press, Buckingham, Philadelphia, 1999)

Policy Transfer

Facing new situations and appreciating the urgency of top level decision making, many countries have in recent times taken recourse to what can be called 'policy transfer'.This has led to specialised study of policy transfers inquiring into situations calling for such transfers, modalities of transfers and their consequences for the receiving country. As broadly defined, policy transfer stands for the 'process by which knowledge of ideas, institutions, policies and programmes in time and/or place is fed into the policy making arena in the development of policies and programmes in another time and/ or place'. (Martin Minogue, Charles Polidano, David Hulme (eds.), Beyond the New Public Management, Edward Elgar, 1998).

Policy transfer has historically been practiced on different occasions. The Imperial powers — colonialists like the British or the French — have been known for their policy transfers when it had come to administer their overseas territories. In recent times, many developing nations are emulating the examples of other countries like, for example, the spread of 'Grameen Bank' idea from Bangladesh as a model of micro-credit policy that has fund wide acceptance in rural development field. Many international donor agencies such as the World Bank, the DFID etc. have often been engaged in policy transfers among the grants/ loan recipient countries. After the collapse of the communist regimes in East Europe, the new post-communist regimes have been induced to accept new pro-market policies. Similarly, the world-wide spread of neo-liberal policies have been dictated by many of the donor agencies in the form of shrinkage or 'down-sizing' the state/government, privatisation policies and the involvement of civil society organisations in many of societal problem solving situations.

Students of comparative politics and governance, public administration and others are therefore evincing considerable interest in the phenomenon of 'policy transfer'. Policy transfers can be due to a variety of reasons such as lesson drawing, crisis copying and coerced pushing by donor agencies. There can be many kinds of ready recipients also who are tempted to accept policies for serving their purposes. Politicians, chief administrators, influential consulting firms are among some of the ardent advocates of policy transfers. The 'transfers' can be both 'voluntary' and 'coercive' or a mixture of the two. Voluntary transfers (as in the case of Grameen Bank idea) may take place in the expectation of beneficial results as seen on the ground in the originating country. Coercive transfers are imposed and dictated transfers. The well-known 'structural adjustment policy' of the World Bank in the 1990s falls in the category of dictated and hence, coercive policy transfer. There would of course be willing recipients to dilute the impact of coercion, as it happened in the case of India during the promulgation of 'new economic policy'.

Post-Positivist Policy Study

The policy studies field has traditionally been dominated by the rationalist-technocratic school. Data-based technical decision-making approaches have ruled the roost and thanks to the fast development of data processing and programming-forecasting techniques with the help of computers, rational-technocratic approach has exerted powerful influence on the whole field of decision-making and analyses. This has no doubt brought in a lot of precision and speed in decision-making and enriched policy-making studies from the quantitative perspective. At the same time, the rationality orientation has been overplayed and become almost an obsession, snuffing out alternative ways of exploring policy making efforts.

What used to be called 'muddling through' had not existed for nothing. Public bodies usually consult many stakeholders and take into considerations things 'political'. A major policy in any field, e.g. in pollution abatement or family welfare (also known as population control), has to reckon with many important and powerful societal forces and factors. These are not usually amenable to short-cut, smart and quantifiable solutions, despite best of intentions of computer specialists. Also, a profound truth about public policy that needs to be acknowledged is that policy is about politics which is an arena of contestation, bargaining and negotiation. What are posed as 'facts' are all socially constructed, containing revealed preferences, ideas and emotions. Any worthwhile policy making exercise has to go beyond facts and draw on wisdom and far and hind sight, values and beliefs and 'discourses' of myriad participating actors. (See, for instance, Fischer and Forrester (eds.), Argumentative Turn to Policy Analysis and Planning, 1993)

Post-positivist policy analysis does not altogether shun the well-known 'rationalist' project. The plea is to go beyond rationalist explanation to capture the real-life pattern and flavour of policy grounded in the rough and tumble of practice. The new trend to look for explanations in practice and trace the embedding of policy in values, networks and societal norms and subjective preferences of multiple actors opens up newer possibilities of policy studies and analyses in future.

REFERENCES

1. Herbert A. Simon, "On the Concept of Organisational Goal," *Administration Science Quarterly*, Vol. 9, No. 1 (June 1964)
2. Charles Perrow, "The Analysis of Goals in Complex Organisations," *American Sociological Review*, Vol. 26, No. 6 (December, 1969).
3. Sir Goeffrey Vickers, *The Art of Judgment: A Study of Policy Making*, University Paperbacks, Methuen, London 1968, p. 27.
4. Yehezkel Dror, *Public Policy Making Re-examined*, Chandler, San Francisco, 1968, p. 8
5. Ibid, p.9.

6. Thomas R. Dye, *Understanding Public Policy,* Prentice-Hall, New Jersey, 1975, Ch. 2.
7. Earl Latham, "The Group Basis of Politics", in Heinz Eulau, Samuel J. Eldersveld and Morris Janowitz, (eds.) *Political Behaviour,* Free Press, New York, 1956.
8. Simon, Op. cit, p. 75.
9. Herbert Simon, *The New Science of Management Decision,* Harper, New York, 1960.
10. Martin Meyerson and Edward C. Banfield, *Politics, Planning and the Public Interest: The Case of Public Housing in Chicago,* Free Press; London, 1964, pp.314-5.
11. Ishwar Dayal et al, *Dynamics of Formulating Policy in Government of India,* Concept, Delhi, 1976, p. 74.
12. Op. cit., p. 75
13. Martin Rein, *Social Science and Public Policy,* Penguin, 1976, p. 170
14. Charles E. Lindblom, "The Science of Muddling Through", *Public Administration Review,* 19 (Spring 1959).
15. David Braybrooke and Charles Lindblom, *A Strategy of Decision: Policy Evaluation as a Social Process,* New York, 1963.
16. Op. Cit, pp. 144-5
17. Amitai Etzioni, "Mixed-scanning: a 'third' approach to decision-making", *Public Administration Review,* December 1967.
18. Thomas R. Dye *Understanding Public Policy,* Prentice-Hall, 1975, p. 34.
19. David Easton, *A Framework for Political Analysis,* Prentice-Hall, 1965, pp. 48-50.
20. Theodore J. Lowi, 'American Business, Public Policy, Case Studies and Political Theory', World Politics, 16, July 1964.
21. Randall Ripley and Grace Franklin, Congress, Bureaucracy and Public Policy, Pacific Grove, Calif.: Brooks-Cole, 1991.

CHAPTER 8

Planning, Organisation and Structural Concepts

Planning was the first concept in the classical formulation of the administrative process known as POSDCORB. Even then, administrative planning is very rarely discussed and followed in administration. We are more familiar with economic planning and know very little about the nature and methods of administrative planning. Yet every administrator who has earned some reputation in the profession does follow the same sort of a planned approach to his job. It is understood more as personal skill than transferable knowledge.

For many years government departments have worked with very little formal planning. There are many reasons for this state of affairs. As John Garrett, who was a member of the consultancy group employed by the Fulton Committee in England (1968), pointed out:[1]

There has been a body of opinion in the higher Civil Service, though it is now diminishing, that systematic research and planning has little relevance to its work. Concentration upon the awareness of ministerial responsibility tends to put a low valuation on systematic research-based planning and a high one on rapid reaction to the topic of the day."

Conventionally estimates planning have been done through the budgetary process. This has been accepted as some sort of planning. Also, planning awareness has been low in government often because of lack of clear objectives and standards against which achievement could be measured.

In spite of this deficiency in government operation, the need for planning has been widely acknowledged and various methods and techniques are now being proposed to make planning a reality in government. The socio-economic and political environment of government today is never a static thing and governments everywhere are struggling hard to cope with changes both at home and abroad (e.g. energy crisis). Also, resources are always scarce and they have to be allocated among competing alternatives to maximise production and all round social satisfaction.

All these reasons are compelling enough to accept planning as an essential first step in government's operations.

NATURE OF PLANNING

Planning follows policy making. These two activities are distinct but interrelated. Policies lay down the fundamental principles of governmental action. They provide the framework within which planning has to take place. They set the terms of reference within which plans are formulated.

Planning is a process, while a plan is a product. As a process, planning involves deciding in advance what is to be done and how. Decision making and planning are obviously closely related but there is a difference between a plan and a decision. A plan is oriented towards the future and has an action implication. A decision fundamentally involves selection of an alternative among various choices. Concern for the future and for action need not necessarily be its hallmark. Yet, at all the different stages of planning, decisions are of paramount importance.

The Planning Process

The first step in the planning process is concerned with goal classification and determination of objectives.

No doubt this is not an easy task in government but a hard search is necessary to find out the basic purpose and the major objective. Action has to take place within the framework of purpose and objectives.

The inevitable next step is to forecast the future and try to see through the darkness of the coming years as clearly as possible. The time-horizon of planning may be two years, three years etc. Understanding of the future probabilities starts with an adequate knowledge of existing conditions. Detailed knowledge of the present position is helpful in making future projections.

An alternative course of action in terms of programmes and projects are set forth at the next stage. The planner outlines the alternatives for the benefit of the decision makers who finally make choices out of them.

The next step will involve arrangement of resources to back up the course of action. Finance, manpower and materials have to be quantified and properly assessed.

Another step in the planning process is to be concerned with organisational planning, including planning of methods and procedures. The existing organisation may have to be modified marginally or changed substantially. New procedures may have to be adopted to facilitate action as planned. The plan procedure invariably contains a built-in arrangement for reporting and feedback in order that the results of action can be measured and corrective steps could be taken in case of malfunctioning.

Planning-Programming-Budgeting

As mentioned earlier, various techniques have been evolved to aid governmental planning. To cite one example, the planning-programming-budgeting system (PPBS) has been widely used by the U.S. Government. It has also been put to limited use by the Government of India. This technique grew out of Robert McNamara's quest for economic rationality in defence expenditure, when he was the U.S. Defence Secretary. Very briefly, the steps involved in PPBS are the following:

1. The department's objectives have to be defined clearly and the programmes needed to accomplish the objectives have to be outlined.
2. Out of these, each programme has to be carefully calculated in relation to the objectives.
3. The total costs of the programme have to be worked out as clearly as possible.
4. Within a long-range and perspective view of the future, programme planning has to be undertaken on multi-year basis.
5. The programme objectives have to be rigorously reviewed and their outputs and costs examined carefully. Ultimately, one has to arrive at the most effective means of producing a desired output at the lowest cost.
6. The last step would be to integrate PPB into the budgetary process as it rolls on from year to year.

The introduction of PPBS is just one example. Other techniques like cost-benefit analysis are very much in vogue in current days in government. Planning is thus being slowly accepted as an integral part of normal governmental functioning.

Organisational Structure

Sequentially, the formulation of policy is followed by the creation of the machinery and procedure for implementation of policy. If for instance, a policy is adopted that the rural poverty group has to be specially attended to, in order that their economic condition is brought to a particular level, it will be necessary to create organisations to identify the poverty groups and administer a programme of economic development tailored to their needs. Structural changes in government do not take place very frequently, although minor alterations in procedure are not uncommon. Stability is the hallmark of government. This is especially true of countries having a long tradition of maintaining a particular style of administration. India and many other developing countries have inherited an administrative system that was built during the colonial era to serve the needs of an imperial regime.

The administrative machinery was basically meant for law and order maintenance and surveillance over the people and extraction of revenues. The organisational design and the nature of authority structure were thus influenced by the values and needs of the imperial regime. With the end of imperialism and acceptance of democracy as a form of government, there arose the need for remodelling the system of administration. As the process of change is noticeable in India, governmental functions have been increasing very fast at all levels; the politicians have been articulating various kinds of demands and pressing hard for their satisfaction; the "people" have emerged as a potent force demanding "things" from government and seeking access co the public agencies as participants in the decision-making process. The old colonial form and style of administration will naturally be ill-suited to the needs of the newly emerging society. Change has to be induced and engineered; at the same time the old culture of stability and administrative orthodoxy will be hard to overcome. This is the dilemma before all the developing counties that are striving to achieve speedy socio-economic transformation.

Administrative organisations have their natural growth overtime and in studying them the fact of continuity has to be acknowledged. As the Administrative Reforms Commission of the Government of India had put it:

"The Administration is conditioned by the stage of social, economic and political development of the country and affected by the attitudes and motivations of those who run it. Viewing the problem in this perspective, we have found it necessary to take a realistic view of things and strike a balance between the needs of continuity and those of change."[2]

Organisational changes can be suggested after a careful diagnosis of the "problem" of specific structures. An adequate understanding of the structures and processes of organisation is thus a precondition of change.

Structure

Structure stands for the relatively fixed pattern of relationships among the various parts of the organisation. In an organisation, the total task is subdivided into a number of major components. This is known as internal differentiation. Patterns of relationships are established among the component parts or subsystems on a fairly permanent basis. The formal structure emerges out of internal differentiation and the relatively fixed relationships that are planned among the different parts or components.

The fixed relationships that lead to the formation of the structure result from the decision process are noted below:

1. The total task of the organisation is broken down into smaller components or subsystems.
2. Authority is distributed among different levels and positions.
3. Specific tasks are assigned to different units in space to solve the centralization-decentralisation problem.
4. The differentiated units and tasks are sought to be interconnected to achieve coordination and integration.

Organisational objectives are attained by setting forth the structure of the organisation; thus structure has value only in relation to the fulfilment of objectives. Usually structure is a planned design. In practice, however, the way organisations actually operate does not always follow the lines dictated by the formal structure. Experience shows that informal relationships develop spontaneously within organisations that were not envisaged in the formal organisational chart. In organisation theory, the concept of informal organisation has gained currency to mean those spontaneous activities and interactions amongst positions and groups in the organisation that were not explicitly and formally planned.

Just as structure refers to the established pattern of relationships in an organisation, process refers to the functional aspect of the formal arrangement. The organisation in action is what the process stands for; hence it connotes the dynamic aspect of an organisation.

Departmentation in Government

Before any micro-analysis of structural features, it is necessary to explore the macro-design of government organisations. Here the question that needs to be answered is: Are there any principles governing the formation of government departments and the allocation of functions among them?

Earlier we had discussed how the administrative management theorists (the classical school) sought to evolve a set of"principles" of organisation. Luther Gulick, for instance, identified four principles of organisation: The purpose served, the process employed, the persons or things dealt with and the area or territory covered. Formation of government departments can to some extent be explained on the basis of these principles.The purpose or objective is common to all departments. This is the starting point of organising. Processes stand for the technical or specialised skill aspect of the organisation. The persons or things refer to the beneficiaries or the client served by the organisation. The last principle (area) refers to the geographical or spatial coverage of the organisation. The Department of Agriculture, for example, would have its basic objectives or purposes (to increase agricultural productivity); it would be fulfilling these objectives with the help of certain process or methods (distribution of inputs, for instance); it would serve a group of clients (farmers); and its activities would embrace some geographical areas (agricultural tracts).The difficulty with Gulicks principles is that all seem important.The relative importance of one or two principles cannot be inferred from this formulation while actually dealing with the question of allocation of functions among government departments.

Of all the principles, basic objective or purpose seems most important. It pinpoints the rationale of an organisation; also, it is essentially related to organisational output. The functions of the organisation can be deduced from its objective and its structure will be designed with a view to perform' these functions.

As Peter Self has put it so well, "Any 'principles' of functional allocation must be squared with requirements of political management."[3] At the Federal level in the U.S.A., the bureaux are the basic units which are grouped to constitute a small number of departments. A department in the Federal government is usually very large. Because of the Presidential system in the U.S.A., the Presidents span of control is an important consideration influencing the number of units at the highest level.

Political influences decisively determine the number of ministries and their individual workload in a cabinet system of government as in India. Political coordination makes it imperative that there should not be too many departments. At the same time, different interests and personalities have got to be accommodated in the interest of party politics. Pardy due to the exigencies of departmental management, and partly to distribute patronages, sub functions are allocated to second-rank ministers called ministers of state and deputy ministers. This arrangement keeps the size of the Cabinet small. It is also helpful in subdividing the workload in a ministry so that the senior minister receives assistance from his junior. The junior minister remains an apprentice for some years and gathers experience which helps him climb up the hierarchy

Shifts in public policy have their'impact on the size and arrangement of government departments. Thus, an emphasis on rural development will mean more investment in this sector and more programmes and projects in elaboration of the policy.This is bound to lead de'partmental expansion and complexity.

In the process of social evolution and with the growth of new technologies, functional linkages become important at the highest level. The department formation is thus affected in this process. For instance, 'urban development' assumed importance in the late sixties in India; in consequence, this subject appeared for the first time as part of the Ministry of Works and Housing. Previously, it was the Ministry of Health which used to have some responsibility for this job.

The need for linking up is reflected in joining together Agriculture and Irrigation, or Food and Agriculture. At the state level in India, many state governments have brought a number of subjects related to'rural development, (e.g. cooperation, fisheries, forests and agriculture) within one common fold.This does of course serve the cause of relatedness but at the same time, it has the danger of creating an unwieldy burden for any minister or a permanent secretary.

In a developing country like India, government functions tend to increase in number and complexity'as socio-economic changes are sought to be brought about speedily for larger and larger number of people. New organisations appear to deal with new functions. Illustrative functions are harijan welfare, tribal development, adult literacy and so on.

Also, the political requirements of a developing country including regional and cultural diversities, have their influence on the shape and size of the government organisation at the highest level. Government organisation is also a product of history. Many departments have been existing for ages and have evolved in a particular way.There is also the need for striking a proper balance between stability and change. All these considerations are important in the process of allocation of functions among the different departments.The Administrative Reforms Commission of the Government of India, while discussing this problem, took note of the stage of political development, the relative strength of the party in power, the number of constituent units in the federal systems, regional and cultural variations in the country and similar other considerations. However, the need for rational arrangement was acknowledged by the Commission, as it observed:

"The number of Ministries and departments and the allocation of work to them should be determined on the basis of a scientific analysis of the various functions and tasks to be performed by the Centre—in other words, on considerations of rationality and efficient manageability of the charges, tempered with the need for economy The principle of rationality does not necessarily mean homogeneity of items of work. It implies affinity of subjects and tasks in terms of the operational inputs to attain a particular programme goal or policy objective."[4]

This statement lays emphasis at least on four things, political manageability, economy, affinity of subjects and programme goal or policy objective. The last item is similar to Gulick's principle of basic objective or major purpose.

To sum up, the structure of government organisation and the allocation of functions are the result of a number of needs and influences. It will be wrong to say that the arrangement is wholly political; it will also be wrong to call it wholly rational. The organisation is never static, as new forces and demands call for changes and modifications. What exists at any point of time is the cumulative result of history, politics and rational designing.

Two Aspects of Structure

As one looks at individual organisations like a department or a public undertaking, structure needs to be viewed in its two major aspects.The first aspect refers to such micro considerations as job definition and separating departments, size and shape of the organisation and the number of levels and spans of control. Traditional administrative thought has been deeply concerned with these problems and in spite of many changes in organisational design concepts, the ideas of the traditionalists are not altogether valueless today. The second aspect of structure relates to major operating features such as the degree of specification of activities, the organisation of authority by centralization or dispersion and the nature of controls exercised in furtherance of organisational objectives. The first aspect of structure can be called the anatomical outlines and the second the physiological features. Together they represent the static and the dynamic aspects of organisational structure. The concern about these aspects of structure has been basically expressed for the sake of organisational productivity but in recent times, structural features have been more and more related to the needs of job satisfaction and motivation to work.

Job definition refers to the specification of tasks to be performed by a single person. In less complex organisations, many different tasks are performed by one person. For instance, in a small municipality a head clerk may be found doing a number of tasks such as looking after budget and accounts, stores and equipment and even typing work. In larger organisations, such as municipal corporations, each of these tasks may be entrusted to a separate person." Job specification encourages specialisation and leads to a division of work. How many tasks should a person be asked to perform or what the contents of a job should be, has been an important issue in organisational analysis. Very briefly, it can be said that the current trend seems to be deprecate too narrow specialisation and to make the job interesting and challenging for the performer. New concepts of 'job enlargement' and 'job rotation' have been introduced to alter the content of job in order to make it suit the personality of the worker. Job definition is, however, more a problem at the lower operative level of an organisation. As one moves up the hierarchy, the job, at managerial levels can at best be broadly defined. It is difficult to define, for instance, the precise job contents of a Joint Secretary or a Secretary to a department; but as one moves lower down, the steno-typist, the clerical staff and others at the operative level have fairly defined tasks.

Precise job definition has the merit of communicating to the job holder the organisational expectations. An employee knows clearly what he is expected to do. This may be used by the employee as a reason for not doing any other extra work. The scope of a job is thus important to an employee as well as the organisation. Many times dissatisfactions over the way jobs are structured (job scope), leads to conflicts and tension in the organisation.

Jobs are combined into work groups, as in most large organisations a number of people have to work together to produce results. The members of a work group are engaged in interdependent work and they are a set of people who usually meet each other daily in face-to-face relationship on the jobs. A work group can be formed out of people having the same skills. For instance, typists, computer specialists and statisticians can form a group each. Another way, could be to form a group consisting of different skills that are needed to complete a specific type of work. In a surgical team, for example, there may be an anaesthetist, a surgeon and a couple of nurses. A homogeneous workgroup with a single skill is called a "functional" group; whereas a multi-skill group is known as a "compound" group.

Departments are formed by consolidating work groups. Homogenization of work is the major purpose of departmentalisation. Most big organisations have what may be called *horizontal differentiation* of activities. The Central Secretariat or any State Secretariat in India is a clear example of horizontal differentiation, as the Secretariat consists of a number of departments (e.g. Public Works, Agriculture, Fisheries etc.), each engaged in a specific kind of work. As discussed earlier, departmentalisation can be on the basis of certain principles that were suggested by Luther Gulick. In government,-departmentalisation on the basis of "fuhction" is the usual practice. Each department deals with a specialised field. In this form of organisation, coordination of the different departmental activities becomes a major problem.

HIERARCHY

Horizontal differentiation is the result of division of work at the same level. Division of work also takes place vertically.This vertical differentiation or division of work establishes the hierarchical pattern and creates the different levels in an organisation. The organisational pyramid grows out of vertical differentiation of work. According to Weberian formulation, bureaucracy as a form of organisation exhibits hierarchy as a structural feature. The positions in the organisation are organised in an ascending order, as a number of subordinates are held accountable to one superior at each level and the levels move up in successive layers. The structure of authority and the formal communication pattern follow the organisational hierarchy. As one moves up the ladder, his status, authority, salary and other privileges go on increasing at successive levels.

Hierarchy usually develops out of qualitative changes in work whereby at each higher level the nature of work becomes different and demands a higher order of supervision. By creating the hierarchical pattern, organisations guard against possible work failure at lower levels. When established on the basis of higher competence, hierarchy facilitates quality control in work organisations.

At the same time, the demerits of hierarchy need to be underscored. It has the tendency to make the organisation 'tall' and in consequence the men at the top lose touch with the men at the bottom. Since authority and privileges are unequally distributed in a hierarchical pattern, interpersonal relationship tends to be conditioned by this fact of inequality. Organisational infighting has often been attributed to hierarchy especially where the positions at higher levels are occupied by incompetent officers. The formal role occupation alone does not help in eliciting subordinate compliance. Formal superiority has to be matched by professional competence in organisations. Only then hierarchy can be a meaningful organisational feature.

Authority

Logically, the next concept in this chain of discussion is authority. In traditional management thought, authority has been defined as the superior's right to issue orders directed to the subordinate, who in turn has the duty to obey the orders. In this sense, authority is legitimate power, in which the aspect of legitimacy is important. The exercise of power is legitimate because of the occupation of the formal position by the superior issuing the commands. Hence authority is the attribute of a position and not of a person. It is a facility or a resource that is given to a role incumbent to help him discharge the responsibility entrusted to him. Authority and responsibility are thus closely interlinked.

Traditionally, authority in organisation has been looked at from the superior's point of view. Authority as a resource is organisationally sanctioned. This is authority in possession but authority in use brings the superior in direct relationship with the subordinate. Hence in the dynamic and practical sense authority relationship is what can be found in an ongoing organisation. Research evidence is now available to show why and under what circumstances the subordinates agree to comply with the superiors' orders.[5]

In a relational perspective where the superior and the subordinate are engaged in a behavioural transaction, authority is the legitimate exercise of power from a defined organisational position and at the receiving end the effective use of authority is contingent on the willingness of the subordinate to comply with the superior's directives.

In this connection, Simon makes a distinction between authority and other kinds of influence such as persuasion and suggestion. Obedience, he points out, is an abdication of choice. When authority is accepted, the subordinate "holds in abeyance his own critical faculties for choosing between alternatives". The limits of authority, according to Simon, are set by the "area of acceptance in behaviour" within which the subordinate chooses to accept the supervisor's command.[6]

The pattern of authority in an organisation is known as *authority structure.*

As Katz and Kahn[7] put it: "The supervisors are to instruct, communicate requirements for change, correct any deviations from required performance, in short they are to influence. In turn, they are to accede to the influence of their own supervisors and so on to the top of the hierarchy. The resulting set of role relationships constitutes the authority structure..."

Organisational structure that establishes the different positions and defines their relationships provides the overall framework within which authority structure is laid out. The two are thus closely interrelated.

Other Concepts

The other structural concepts such a *scalar chain, unity of command* and *span of control* have been mentioned in an earlier section. These were developed by traditional management theorists and are still in use in organisational analysis. The *scalar chain* refers to vertical differentiation of work and establishes the hierarchical structure of the organisation. The concept of *unity of command* is complementary to the scalar principle. It postulates a special kind of superior subordinate relationship under which each subordinate will receive orders from only one superior. A related principle is that the *span of control,* which signifies span of supervision. The number of subordinates directly placed under the supervisory control of a superior is his span of control. Traditional management thought suggested a narrow span of control for effective supervision. Current view is that such stipulation cannot be made on ad hoc basis. Actual span of control in an organisation will depend on many factors such as nacure of work, the competence of subordinates and the supervisory staff, the degree of mecharisation of offices and so on.

Graicunas's Theory. In 1933, V.A Graicunas, a French management consultant published a paper under the title *Relationship in Organisation.* He has shown mathematically that a number of direct, cross and group relationships exist between a superior and his subordinates. According to him, the number of cross and group relationships increases in mathematical relation as the number of subordinates assigned to an executive increases. An executive with four subordinates is required to deal with the four "direct" relationships, twelve "cross" relationships and twenty-eight "group" relationships. Graicunas finds that with five subordinates the total relationships go up to 100, with six subordinates to 222 with seven subordinates to 490 and with eight subordinates to 1080. He thinks that an executive can at best manage 222 relationships arising from six subordinates and he prescribes six subordinates as the maximum span of supervision. Other experts are in favour of fixing the span of supervision within a range of four to eight subordinates at the upper level and of twenty to forty subordinates at the foremen s level.

Graicunas has developed relevant mathematical formulas for finding out the number of different types of relationships. The formula for cross relationships is *n(n-l),* where *n* represents the number of subordinates supervised.

For group relationship, the formula is

$$n\left(\frac{2n}{2}-1\right)$$

and for the total number of relationships the formula is

$$n\left(\frac{2n}{2}+n-1\right)$$

How an executive with three subordinates is required to deal with 18 relationships may be shown by the following illustrations:

Three direct relationships These relationships arise from the direct and individual contacts of the superior with his three subordinates - A, B and C.

Six cross relationships These are mutual relationships among the subordinates themselves which are necessary for working under a common superior. In course of work A is required to consult B, or B is required to consult A but the consultation may have different results depending on the response of the other party. Hence, six relationships include: A to B and B to A, A to C and C to A, A to C and C to B.

Nine group relationships These are relationships between the superior and two or more subordinates. As groups may be formed in different ways, relationships too may vary from one group to another. Depending on possible combination of subordinates, nine relationships are as follows: A with B. A with C. B with A. B with C. C with A. C with B. A with B&C. B with C&A and C with A & B.

The theory has been criticised on the following grounds:

First the actual span of supervision is determined by a number of factors which have not been pointed out in the theory. As a result, the maximum span of supervision, as prescribed by Graicunas, is not corroborated by real life practices and there is in reality a wide diversity in the optimum span of supervision.

Second the frequency and severity of relationships have not been dealt with in the theory. They form the core and present the real picture in superior-subordinate relationships.

Third all possible relationships have not been included in the theory. On the list of cross relationships, three other relationships with three subordinates are: A to BC, B to CA and C to AB.

Fourth the theory deals with the downward relationships only but the superior's upward and sideways relationships have been left out.

Fifth like the operating executives, the service department heads exercise line authority over their subordinates and supervise them. That the span of supervision has a much limited application in the sphere of service activity is not clearly indicated in the theory.

Finally with mechanisation of office work and the use of electronic equipment and computer, the old idea of limiting supervision does not hold good in today's technology-advanced world.

Line and Staff

The concept of 'line' and 'staff' in organisation are important and at the same time controversial. The line organisation within an enterprise carries out the enterprise goal. By contrast, the staff organisation contributes indirectly to goal achievement by helping the line to do its work. Simply put, in an irrigation department the engineers who are directly engaged in the construction of irrigation dams belong to "line" The engineers by procuring material and other supplies and keeping accounts fall in the category of "staff". In classical organisation theory, line organisation has the primary source of authority as it performs the major organisational functions. The staff exists in a supportive and advisory role outside the direct chain of command. Executive authority runs vertically down in an uninterrupted flow with more specialised staff to lend support to the line executive but the staff does not exercise any special authority and is not permitted to disturb the hierarchical pattern. It is merely an aid to the executive. As Urwick characterised it, the staff is an extension of the chief executive's *persona,* looking after certain activities on behalf of the chief. The staff is thus attached to an individual and the support is to a person. Line officers, by contrast, perform institutionalised (as distinguished from personalised) functions.

Luther Gulick's POSDCORB represents a pretty long list of staff functions. These can be condensed a bit and even reduced to only planning, executing and evaluating. In any large and complex organisation, continuity demands institutionalization of staff functions. Since top management needs the staff support on a continuing basis, this is what has actually taken place. Most organisations have now institutionalised the staff units. Institutionalisation has also led to specialisation. Staff functions in the fields of personnel, accounting, for instance, are highly specialised jobs now that are looked after by the specialists in most organisations.

Three types of staff can be identified in large organisations personal staff, specialised staff and general staff.

The first category consists of those who attend to details of daily living such as keeping the diary of different engagements, arranging and scheduling meetings, calling people and receiving messages on behalf of the chief and some other work of purely personal nature. It is very common now for ministers to have their personal secretaries who perform some of these jobs. The second category consists of specialists looking after such staff functions as personnel administration, accounts, stores and supplies etc. The third category of general staff assists the chief executive in his policy making role by gathering data and information and analysing them. Many ministries bring in advisers to help them in the specialised branches of work.

The relationship between the line and the staff units is not always a very happy one in many organisations. The line people often criticise the staff unit as a usurper of their legitimate power. Being close to the chief executive, the staff men try to throw their weight about. Secondly, the line people usually complain against the unrealistic plans and ideas of the staff men. The staff is away from reality and the line staff is close to it. Hence the suspicion. At the other end, the staff men argue that the line people have one-track minds and do not bother much about what they suggest. Also, whenever anything goes wrong in the organisation, the line people put the blame on the staff people and very often try to disown responsibility.

Some of these complaints are very common in government and the line-staff conflicts are known to have delayed decisions and caused tension and misunderstanding. Stories are quite common that the engineers have designed a sound and useful project but the finance department has been sitting on it for years!

The line-staff concepts have not become obsolete and are still very much in use. The clear-cut distinction between the two is, however, being increasingly questioned and newer modes of integration are being suggested. It has been argued that the line-staff distinction in its purest form dates back to sin era when technology used to be simple and uniform and the environment of the organisation was relatively stable and much less complex. Newer organisational forms (e.g. matrix organisation) are replacing the old staff-line dichotomy being suggested to suit the complexity of contemporary environment and technology.

Different Kinds of Staff Agencies

Three kinds of staff agencies have been identified whose main mission, despite differentiation, remains the same; to conduct managerial or 'housekeeping' services whereby the substantive function (in charge of line agencies) or the end product is achieved. The three staff agencies are: General Staff, Technical Staff and Auxiliary Staff. Borrowed from military administration, the general staff and technical staff represent two types of command level functions. The general staff assist the commander in carrying out his command function. The technical staff, also called special staff, consist of engineers, supply corps etc. The general staff officer is not a specialist he is primarily an assistant for coordination.

Specialists in public administration suggest that the more purely termed staff activity involves only the advisory function. Auxiliary or special staff functions involve such services as planning, budgeting and personnel activities. There is however no unanimity among experts as to the 'precise scope of the advisory function and that of the auxiliary function, Donald Stone, for instance, has argued that accounting and legal services are more akin to the service (auxiliary) units than they are to the general staff divisions. Another way of specifying the general staff function has been to identify those functions that are "non-delegatable" functions of the chief executive.

Leonard D. White has explained the special

nature of the auxiliary services in the following words:

"The staff function and the function of the auxiliary services are therefore different and ought not to be confused. The auxiliary services are operating agencies, the staff is a thinking, planning and advisory agency. The auxiliary agencies are concerned with the maintenance of an existing organisation and are not concerned with major substantive policies; the staff is concerned with the revision of organisation as new needs may dictate and with the reformulation of major policies".

In conclusion it needs to be noted that sharp distinction and watertight compartmentalisation are not, in actual practice, entertained. Even in the Army, such old ideas are now being replaced by newer formulations like Administration and Operation. As, White has observed: "In actual practice, naturally, the allocation of functions does not always sharply recognize these logical categories; usually staff work is not clearly segregated, the work of the auxiliary services may only partly be placed in special organs and auxiliary agencies may also perform genuine staff functions owing to lack of sharply exclusive differentiation of work".

Centralisation and Decentralisation

An important issue in organisational structuring is how much to centralise and how much to decentralise. Obviously, this problem arises when an organisation becomes very large and the activities grow in complexity. Also, decentralisation has a spatial aspect. When an organisation has its activities spread over a wide geographical space, planning and control of the widely dispersed activities may be done better from points away from the central headquarter. It is an illustration of Gulick's 'area principle *in* operation'. A third argument in favour of decentralisation revolves round the need for organisational autonomy. A decentralised unit can function better when it is organised semi-autonomously without being subjected to a detailed central control. Finally, decentralisation has been supported by the democratic argument that these arrangement facilities lower level 'participation' in decision-making.

Most large organisations try to solve the problem of over-growth and congestion of work at the headquarter level by the twin methods of delegation and decentralisation.

Delegation

Delegation means entrusting part of one's work to others. The municipal commissioner in a city corporation is statutorily authorised to prepare the annual budget. He asks the accounts officer to do this and thus delegates his work to the officer. A scheme of delegation creates a superior-subordinate relationship and has the following features either expressed or implied:

1. A superior, in delegation, assigns duties to the subordinate.What the subordinate has to do is clearly stipulated.
2. Along with such assignment of work, the superior grants authority. This is to facilitate the work assigned to the subordinate, who is thus permitted to spend some money, make some purchases etc.
3. The delegation scheme creates an obligation in the sense that the subordinate becomes duty bound to complete the job assigned to him.
4. An obligation created by a delegation scheme cannot be again delegated. In our earlier example the accounts officer can get the work done with the help of his subordinates but this does not free him from his original obligation.

It is only he who is accountable to the commissioner for the job assigned to him.

Delegation as an organisational principle has been favoured for its skill-producing and confidence-creating attribute. The subordinates who are asked to do the work delegated to them gain experience through this method.The actual way a delegation plan works out in an organisation depends on interpersonal relations. The superior must genuinely delegate and fully trust his subordinate. If the former doubts the latter's capacity and intention, the delegation plan will remain a mere paper plan.

Decentralisation

"The issue of decentralisation", as Fesler has put it, "is more complex in concept and practice than is generally acknowledged."[8]

In organisation theory, decentralisation has been conceived basically as an aspect of intra-organisational differentiations.[9] A complex, large-scale organisation, meeting a dynamic 'task environment", seeks to adapt itself through segmentation and arrangement in self-sufficient clusters, each having its own domain."[10] Decentralised divisions emerge as a consequence, which are sometimes called product divisions or profit centres.

Decentralisation has also been approached from the point of view of organisational decision-making. Organisational complexity entails more numerous and quicker decisions to achieve efficiency. When speed assumes critical importance, decentralised decision-making is usually resorted to. It has been suggested that the degree of decentralisation is greater under the following conditions:

i) Greater number of decisions are made at lower levels of management;
ii) Decisions made at lower levels are important;
iii) Various organisational functions are more influenced by decisions made at lower levels;
iv) There is less monitoring of decisions made by managerial personnel.[11]

Organisational decentralisation, thus conceived, manifests itself in territorial dispersion of units and delegation of authority. Field administration in the form of district and sub-divisional administration, for instance, represents decentralisation through territorial differentiation and dispersion. It is an integral part of state administration. Its peculiarity lies in its physical location away from the state headquarters to provide access to the client. Delegation of authority has naturally to accompany territorial dispersion of the governmental unit.

Theoretical knowledge about decentralisation in politics and organisational designing has been greatly advanced by Kochen and Deutsch in their seminal paper entitled "Toward a Rational Theory of Decentralization: Some Implications of a Mathematical Approach."[12] A functional theory of decentralisation, according to them, has to be related to organisational task performance and ultimate survival. Organisations depend critically on the feedback of information from the environment in order to ascertain the results of their actions and to take corrective measures. The issue of centralisation *versus* decentralisation has to be examined from the point of view of exchange of information and of things and persons with the environment. Kochen and Deutsch thus look at decentralisation as a problem in logistics. Decentralisation is rational or cost-effective if movement of messages, men and materials leads to successful task performance in relation to meet the demands and pressures from the environment.To quote their observation,"For a functional theory of decentralization,... the social tasks to be performed are more important than the historical institutions which currently happen to perform them. Though institutions have a great deal of persistence and tend to protect their own survival, they nonetheless do change. Some of these changes tend toward greater or lesser decentralisation and a functional analysis of the level of decentralisation most appropriate to their chief task is essential in order to evaluate rationally the actual changes which occur in response to technological or political pressures."

This formulation is palpably oriented towards operational effectiveness of organisations. It is a valuable contribution to theoretical knowledge no doubt but the weakness of such an instrumental approach lies in its exclusive emphasis on functionality alone. Decentralisation has more than functional importance. It may reflect commitment to some kind of ethical and political value as well.

To return to organisation theory, decentralisation has generally been conceived as a means to organisational efficiency in limited circumstances of complexity and scale. Its essence has been deconcentration or decongestion of the headquarters unit.

In political science and public administration decentralisation has been discussed basically from the view point of arrangement of government. The different approaches to the concept have been clearly and profoundly presented by Fesler. Following his classification, the approaches can be grouped into four categories: the doctrinal, the political, the administrative and the dual-role.

The *doctrinal approach* seeks to treat decentralisation as an end in itself through a process of 'romantic idealisation'. The Gandhian concept of 'concentric circle' of power distribution and the idealisation of village community in *panchayati raj* have reduced decentralisation almost to a dogma and an article of faith. Instead of treating decentralisation as a means for the achievement of some end-values, such idealisation tends to elevate it to the status of a hardened doctrine.

The *political approach* underscores the essential political character of decentralisation. Initiatives to decentralise and willingness to pass on powers and functions to decentralise units and to allow these units to actually operate within a framework of autonomy are politically determined. Creation of field units of government, away from central headquarters, exemplifies dilution. Decentralisation in the shape of devolution to local self-governing bodies marks an attempt to set up autonomous governments at the level of the locality. Field units of government like district administration are the long arms of the central (state) government and do not pose problems of organisational discontinuity whereas local self-governing bodies that are elected locally to determine local policies and to implement them are, in a fundamental way, detached from the central (state) government. To create and maintain local government is thus a major political commitment. In the absence of such commitment, devolution to sub-national governments, including local self-governing bodies, will remain more in law than in practice. This leads to what Fesler has called 'illusory decentralisation'. Both *panchayati raj* and municipal government in India represent to a considerable extent this sort of facade devolution. Now, of course, with the passage of the 73rd and the 74th Constitutional Amendment Acts (1992), these local government institutions have been accorded a constitutional status with necessary powers and resources.

The *administrative approach* to decentralisation is motivated by efficiency criterion. Enhancement of administrative rationality becomes the desideratum. When field administrative units are set up through a process of dilution, the measure is considered appropriate for field level decision making and prompt problem-solving. In this process, administrative units might come up at many levels between the locality and the central (state) headquarters. With more and more demand for specialised functions, multiplicity of functional departments would appear at the field level.The administrative situation gradually presents a picture of polarisation between general area-based administrative demands and specific function-centred claims of particular functional departments. Currently, district administration in India is faced with this problem of area-function duality. Decentralisation in administrative terms may not therefore always guarantee "clarity of authority and orderliness of operations'. To promote such operational principles conscious attempts are needed to readjust from time to time, the conflicting claims of area and functions in diluted field administration.

Finally, *the dual-role approach*, as Fesler puts it, is a kind of rehearsal of the area-function dichotomy in a new setting. Decentralisation is placed within a larger context of development and change, as distinguished from maintenance of status quo. Conceived in administrative terms, the dual-role approach seeks to highlight the conflict in field administration between tradition and change. Most field administrative systems were evolved in an earlier era mainly to maintain the established order, to collect revenue and to keep things from going wrong. Almost all the developing countries that have inherited the colonial field system are seeking to bring about speedy social and economic change. The functions of field administration have changed radically as a consequence. To quote Fasler,"The intent is to change established ways of doing things so as to carry economic and social development forward rapidly. This contrast with the status quo orientation of a field system geared to maintenance of the established order and may conflict with the personal orientation of field generalists so chosen and trained as to identify themselves with the classes, families and other groups who constitute the'establishment'." Resolution of conflict between two different orientations in field administration calls for adaptation of decentralisation to changing circumstances. The theme is not unfamiliar to Indian administration in general and district administration in particular.

The latest thinking on decentralisation veers around power equalisation and participation. Organisation theory and political science which did not meet very often in the past have now almost come together in explicating the concept of decentralisation concertedly. The concern in organisation theory is increasingly about individual welfare which is considered feasible and desirable through participative management. In political science, decentralisation reappears as a means to the achievement of a more participative 'democracy that goes beyond traditional electoral methods of intermittent representation.

The value being maximised *via* organisation theory is individual employee's 'health'; whereas the value being maximised *via* political science is redistributive politics as a means to community and citizen oriented political "health'.

Contemporary thinking on decentralisation can be looked at from three angles. First, it is thought of as a means to spiritual enrichment and growth of the individual both as worker and citizen. Decentralisation offers opportunity to participate in decision-making. For an individual, it is an aid to the growth and development of personality.

Second, decentralisation has an instrumental value as a means of improving organisational performance. Public administration is related to the operational aspects of government.

The operations are better done through decentralisation which provides access to local information and data and creates conditions for local popular support to administrative action. Administration is opened up in a decentralised system, as it no longer remains a secretive operation of the proud specialists.

Third, the current thinking, very importantly, reflects a paradigmatic shift in public administration as a discipline. The bureaucratic model which has so long dominated the field seems inadequate to explain the contemporary politico-administrative situation. As Thompson pointed out, the Weberian formulation has no concern for the client.[13] As an inward-looking mechanistic construct; it has set up an organisational model without reference to the catchment area of the organisation that determines its locus standi.The decentralisation-participation debate introduces a new perspective in public administration and calls for its reconstruction.[14]

Matrix Organisation

A number of organisations, particularly those dealing with aerospace and weapons production, have in recent times utilized structures that are not easy to analyse along typical anatomical dimensions such as number of hierarchical levels, etc. Their structural arrangements have a variety of names such as "project management", "programme management", "task force", etc. The essence of these structures is that it involves units that cut across segments of both vertical and horizontal dimensions of the organisation. The term "matrix" has commonly been applied to structures that include a number of projects, programmes or task forces.

This form of structure seems to permit greater focus of resources on producing specified target outcomes. There may also be problems of integrating across projects and integrating the projects with other ongoing work of the organisation.

For the individual worker, such structure permits him to keep his attention focussed on tangible output. He can, perhaps, more easily see how his actions at any given moment will be instrumental to some final outcome. He may face at the same time increased ambiguity concerning superior-subordinate relationships. He may find himself with responsibilities both to the project in-charge and to his functional area (e.g., engineering, irrigation). As it used to be in our block administration, the subject specialist such as an animal husbandry man would be administratively responsible to the B.D.O. but technically responsible to his functional chief at the next higher level. Matrix structures are likely to be quite fluid and "temporary" since the structure is created for a time-bound specific purpose, it is expected to be wound after the completion of the project.

To sum up, structure provides the basic framework for the performance of organisational tasks. Thoughts on organisational structure have evolved over the years and the primary motive has been to rationalize the arrangement of work of produce the desired output. Also, structure has been looked at as behaviour-producing; so structural changes have often been introduced to produce a kind of behaviour among the organisational members that is conducive to work performance.

REFERENCES

1. John Garrett, *The Management of Government,* Pelican Books, 1972, p.109.
2. *Report on the Machinery of the Government of India and its Procedures of Work,* Administrative Refomis Commission, Government of India, Delhi, 1968, p.2.
3. Op.Cit. p.58.

4. Op.Cit. p. 17.
5. A.S.Tannenbaum; *Hierarchy hi Organisations,* Jossey-Bass, San Francisco, 1974.
6. Op.Cit. ChapterVII.
7. Daniel Katz and Robert L. Kahn, 77/e *Social Psychology of Organisations,* John Wiley & Sons, 1978, p.323.
8. James W. Fesler, "Approaches to the Understanding of Decentralisation", *Journal of Politics,* XXVII, August, 1965.
9. Paul R. Lawrence and Jgy W. Lorsch, "Differentiation and Integration in Complex Organisations", *Administrative Science Quarterly,* Vol. 12, June, 1967.
10. James D. Thompson, *Organisations in Action.* Mc-Graw-Hill Book Company, New York, 1967, p.76.
11. James L. Gibson, John M. Lyawevich and Janies H. Donnelly, Jr. *Organisations: Structure Processes, Behaviour,* Business Publications, Dalias.Texas, 1973, p.138.
12. Manfred Kochen and Karl W. Deutsch, "Toward a Rational Theory of Decentralization: Some Implications of a Mathematical Approach, *American Political Science Review,* 63, 1969, pp.734-49.
13. James D. Thompson, "Organisations and Output Transaction" in Eilhu Katz and Brenda Danet (eds.), *Bureaucracy and the Public,* Basic Books, Inc., Publishers, New York, 1973.
14. See, in this connection, the *Special Issue of Public Administration Review,* Volume XXXII, October, 1972.

CHAPTER 9

Administrative Processes: Decision Making

The administrative processes represent the dynamic aspect of administration. These can be seen in situations when administration is in action. At any level—the secretariat or the field—administration has to deal with numerous issues and problems.Through a learning process, practices and procedures are evolved to manage the recurrent problems. New problems arise which call for innovations. Within the organisation, many kinds of relationships have to be smoothly conducted to orchestrate the activities of the organisation. Similarly, external relations with clients and other organisations have to be managed. Internal activities need to be planned and controlled. Flow of information within the organisation has to be regulated to facilitate relationships and task accomplishment. So an administrative organisation in action exhibits a number of salient processes.

More important among these are decision-making, communication, control and coordination.

DECISION MAKING

As Fesler and Kettl explain,[1] every approach to administrative decision making involves two issues:

(a) What information can the decision makers use to make their judgments ?

(b) How do political values affect decision?

In a way, these issues remind us about the fact-value distinction as pointed out by Herbert Simon.

APPROACHES TO DECISION-MAKING

Since decision-making is a complex administrative process, many approaches have developed in the course of actual decision-making. Four such approaches can be identified as important and what is being noted is that in all the approaches the two issues of information and values assume considerable significance. Of the four approaches, the rational approach has been taken up later in the course of discussion on Simons behaviour alternative model. This is basically efficiency oriented and seeks to explain production of maximum 'output' by expending a given level of "inputs". Once there are agreements on basic goals, the rational approach works very well. Hence this is applicable mostly to small scale technical problems like, which kind of information technology the police should be using to communicate across the organisation.

The other three approaches are: (a) the bargaining approach, (b) the participative approach and (c) the public choice approach.

One of the main proponents of the bargaining approach, Charles E. Lindblom, has pointed out that decision-making is essentially value-laden and conflict prone. It is always better to conduct limited analysis, as great goals **are generally** beyond reach. Lindblom, thus, prescribes "incrementalism", as it is easier to build support for a series of incremental changes, from the current situation. In decision situation, conflicts are the rule end these cannot be resolved by rational analysis. The bargaining approach suggests that in such a situation "partisan mutual adjustment"—the polling and hauling among decision makers—offers the best hope for the best decisions.

In studying the famous Cuban Missile crisis in 1962 (when American intelligence aircraft discovered Soviet Missile bases in Cuba), Graham Allison[2] argued that the events could be understood from three different perspectives:

Model I : The traditional rational actor approach.

Model II : Organisation—process orientation.

Model III : The bureaucratic—politics perspective.

In terms of Model I, the Cuban Missile crisis could be analysed from a traditional rational - actor approach. According to Model II approach, decisions could be understood in terms of the standard operating (organisational process) procedures of the respective bureaucracies (in USA and USSR). The third approach, Model III, has been called the bureaucratic - politics approach, as decision by this method can be understood as "a resultant of various bargaining games among players in the national government". A decision can thus be understood by understanding "the perceptions, motivations, positions, power and manoeuvres of the players".

In the instant case, the decision to establish a blockade, along with other key decision of the (Cuban Missile) crisis, can be looked at as the result of a bargaining process among the key players. As Allison concludes "What moves the chess pieces is not simply the reasons that support a course of action, or the routines of organisations that enact an alternative but the power and skill of proponents and opponents of the action in question."

Bargaining provides a useful description, how decisions are made in many instances. However, there are important normative problems with bargaining, as not all the interests are invited to the decision situation.Yet, this approach attaches importance to the role of values in decision making and in this it stands in stark contrast with the national model.

The next approach, called *participative decision-making* approach, as the name suggests, is found more directly on the idea of political democracy. It calls at the general level for participation by those who will be affected by the decision. The value of participation in a democracy is universally acknowledged but there are two major ambiguities here that need clarification, *first,* what is meant by participation? Does it mean being consulted for advice by someone who has power to make the decision? Or does it mean showing decision-making power? Again is *consultation* or *sharing* confined to specific aspects of decision-making (say, initiation only) or to all relevant aspects. *Second,* who should be entitled to participate in decision-making? At least four groups may claim entitlement in this context:

(a) The employees of the organisation making decision;
(b) The people the organisation serves or regulates like the client groups;
(c) The tax payers who are affected by decisions;
(d) The whole public or, at least, the voters in a constituency.

Here the problem is that these different kinds of participants may not be in agreement on a specific course of action (decision).

Nevertheless, participative decision-making, as a very powerful method and, is generally being pursued in rural development and urban community development projects.

From the conception of a project to its implementation and monitoring and evaluation, participative decision-making has proved to be extremely useful.

Finally, the *public choice* approach to decision-making has gained considerable prominence in recent times. The main arguments of public choice theory have earlier been discussed in chapter I. Here, suffice it to say that the theory begins with the assumption that human beings are *national* and seek to maximise things that are important to them. It is thus argued that public officials, like all other individuals, are self-interested and they want to avoid risk and promote their own careers. Their motive is to enlarge their programmes and increase their budgets. So, self-interested bureaucrats are likely to produce bigger government that is both inefficient and operating against the public interest. The proponents of the public choice school are in favour of turning over governmental functions to the private sector, wherever possible. They contend that government functions should be contracted out to the private sector and this process of "privatisation', in their view stimulates private-sector competition and dilutes the influence of government bureaucrats. Privatisation is likened to a kind of political guerrilla warfare that directs demand away from government provision of public services, reducing thereby the demand for growth of public budget.

The basic assumption of the bureaucrat as a rational human being, who single mindfully pursues his personal power, security and income and not public interest, is a "terrible caricature of reality. Public service orientation in the bureaucracy is knocked off by a strange kind of one-track assumption. Also, efficiency is not always the only value that public programmes seek to achieve. The public choice theory suggests that both the goals and the motives of the private sector are identical goals like equality and distributive justice, which do not have any parallel "in the market-led private sector". As Fesler and Kettle put it: "The deepest debates are usually one of ends—what should or should not be public functions?—and the public choice movements focus on means begs the most crucial point. There is, quite simply, a *public* interest in public administration".

To sum up, the different approaches to decision-making underline the importance of plurality of ways of decision-making. Clearly, therefore, no single approach can be taken as a solution to the problems of decision-making. "Each approach has its own special virtues and its own idiosyncratic problems."

Mixed Scanning

Etzioni's mixed scanning marks a happy blending of 'incrementalism' and 'rationalism'. As an example of mixed scanning, he refers to the establishment of a worldwide weather observation system utilizing satellite data. In terms of the rational-comprehensive method, complete attempts would be made to survey weather conditions, employing 'cameras capable of detailed observations' and 'scheduling reviews of the sky as often as possible'. In this process, a huge mass of data would be available that would 'overwhelm our action capabilities'. Following the increment path, however attention would be focused on parts of the world whereas, in the recent past, similar patterns had manifested themselves and perhaps on a few nearby regions.

Under Etizioni's mixed scanning system, two cameras would be used, a broad angle one covering all parts of the sky but not in great detail, the other zeroing in on those areas revealed by the first camera to ensure a more in-depth examination. This method might miss an area, where only a detailed camera shot would reveal trouble. At the same time it is less likely, than incrementalism, to miss obvious trouble spots in unfamiliar areas. In mixed scanning the idea is to employ the two levels of scanning flexibly, depending upon the problem. High coverage scanning would be desirable in some cases; the more 'truncated view' would be in others.

The Garbage Can Model

Another model of decision-making known as the "Garbage Can Model" was developed by Michael D. Cohen, James G. March and Johan P. Olsen (ASQ 1972). Decision makers, in their view, function in 'organisational anarchies' characterized by problematic preferences, unclear technology and fluid participation. As a result, the boundaries of the organisation are changing and the audiences and decision makers for any particular kind of choice change capriciously. The reality of choice (as against Simon's national choice) is described as a choice opportunity in the form of "a garbage can into which various kinds of problems and solutions are dumped by participants as they are generated. The mix of garbage in a single can is dependent on the mix of cans available, on the labels attached to them currently being produced and on the speed with which garbage is collected and removed from the science."

This perspective examines, by looking back, how the various unanticipated problem streams flows together to produce what actually happened. Despite its apparent descriptive strength, this model is unhelpful to public administrators who have to deal with decisio situations in real time from within the process rather than after the fact and looking backward.

Nature of Decisions

The concept of decision-making is central to any theory of administration. There is now voluminous literature available on the different aspects of decision-making. The two broad lines of analysis followed in the discussions on decisions are derived from management science and behavioural sciences. The former has formulated a number of techniques such as linear programming, queuing theory etc. which emphasise maximisation principles in arriving at choices among several alternatives. The behavioural sciences, on the other hand, concentrate basically on the individual and the organisation to bring out the social and psychological processes involved in decision-making.

Two points deserve special mention in this context. First, decisions have a sequential character and are rarely one-shot acts. Several decisions are taken over time or at different levels to fulfil the organisations' objectives.Thus, the secretariat department may decide to procure certain quantity of agricultural produce like rice or jute. At the lower level, the district collector may decide how much to procure from which block or subdivision.The second point relates to the quality and relative significance of decisions. At higher levels major decisions are taken in regard to pricing, procurement, cropping pattern etc. These are commonly known as policy decisions, which set the pattern of sub-decision making at lower levels and which usually cover wider geographical areas.

Programmed and Non-programmed Decisions

It is important to distinguish between two polar types of decisions; programmed decisions and non-programmed decisions. The terms are obviously derived from computer language. A programme is a plan for the automatic solution of a problem. When decisions are repetitive and routine, these lend themselves to programming. Each situation need not be treated as a new one and no ad hoc decisions are called for. Detailed procedures are worked out to deal with the recurrent and repetitive situations. Programmed decisions are fairly widely, used in most organisations for routine cases such as tenders and contracts, compensation policy, salary administration and so on. "Decisions are non-programmed to the extent that they are unstructured, new, of high consequence, involve major commitments, or are elusive or complex". Established rules and procedures are inadequate to deal with the new kinds of situations and the organisation has to innovate or improvise. In government, precedents and procedures are generally followed in taking decisions but new situations might arise like demand for unemployment allowance, or the need to undertake new activities (e.g. dairy plant, cold storage etc.), when decisions cannot rely much on past practices and established rules and regulations. Non-programmed decisions thus call for more ingenuity, consultation and a degree of risk taking.

Simon's Behaviour Alternative Model[3]

Herbert Simon is widely known for his model of rational decision making. Imagining the environment of the decision maker as a set of premises upon which decisions are based, Simon makes a distinction between two kinds of decision premises; factual premises and value premises. The factual premises are subject to empirical testing for finding out their validity, whereas the value premises are not subject to such tests. The former are concerned with the choice of means, the latter with the choice of ends of action. To quote Simon:

"Decisions are something more than factual propositions. To be sure, they are descriptive of a future state of affairs and this description can be true or false in a strict empirical sense but they possess, in addition, an imperative quality, they select one future state of affairs in preference to another and direct behaviour toward the chosen alternative. In short, they have an ethical as well as a factual content."

A rational decision, under the circumstances, can be looked at as the right conclusion derived from these two kinds of premises- the value premises and the factual premises.

The behaviour alternative model differs from the traditional ends-means approach where "the initial stipulation of 'ends' forecloses unduly the courses that are considered and to some extent draws the official's attention away from the actual situation in which he is placed." As Simon describes his own model:

"At each moment the behaving object, or the organisation composed of numbers of such individuals, is confronted with a large number of alternative behaviours, some of which are present in consciousness and some of which are not. Decision, or choice", .. is the process by which one of these alternatives for each moment's behaviour is selected to be carried out? The series of such decisions, which determines behaviour over some stretch of time, may be called a strategy. ...The task of decision involves three steps; (1) the listing of all the alternative strategies; (2) the determination of all the consequences that follow upon each of these strategies; (3) the comparative evaluation of these sets of consequences."

In constructing his model, Simon conceives administration largely in terms of planning. The administrator, in taking decisions, must weigh the pros and cons of his action. His administrative man conies close to the concept of the rational economic man that seeks to maximise net satisfaction.

Simon acknowledges the limitations of the actual administrator in the process of his search for appropriate decision premises. First, there are habits and reflexes of the individual which are more or less unconscious. These are important determinants of individual action. Second, the individual's values and loyalties in the organisational context might act as constraints on rational behaviour. Third, data and information are likely to be limited and difficult to get and the decision maker has to work under this basic limitation.

From the decision maker's point of view, the choice of action is actually exercised in a perspective of simplified reality. He defines his own situation and takes decisions within the framework of his situational definition. This subjective frame of reference permits consideration of only a limited number of decision premises. Decision context is thus set by a frame of 'bounded rationality', which means that the decision maker does not have complete knowledge of the situation and he has to make a choice to the best of his knowledge.

Under these circumstances, the decision maker is not searching for the optimal decision but a satisfactory one. The "satisfying" administrative man is thus different from the maximising economic man.

Simon's model of decision making is not free from blemishes. There are difficulties in measuring the costs and consequences of government action in many instances. In the practical world of administration, the elaborate search process may not be feasible, as there is always demand for immediate action than cool contemplation. Yet, with all the imperfections, the Simon model has greatly encouraged the need for the use of various management techniques in public policy making and policy science has received the initial impulse from his formulation.

Organisational Context of Decisions

Decision making in an organisation serves the purpose of fulfilling organisational objectives. Hence the organisation seeks formally to arrange the decisional environment of the individual decision maker. First, the rules and procedures are standardised to help decision making; the process of decision making is thus set in advance for the guidance of administrators. Second, the decisional space is sought to be defined by division of labour and by limiting the span of control. Work subdivision specifies the tasks at particular levels. Decisions will be limited to the tasks assigned at each level. A limited span of control has the effect of delimiting the tasks space of a supervisor. Third, the authority system in an organisation creates a mechanism for structuring the different levels of decision making. Also, it is a way of grading different kinds of decisions in an organisation. As Mouzelis puts it:

"The broad and crucial policy decisions are taken at the top of the hierarchy. They are subsequently transmitted to the lower echelons and become the guiding criteria on the basis of which the inferior decision-maker will take decisions of a more detailed and procedural character. By this process the organisations can be viewed as a means-end chain, on each level of which the supervisor's decisions constitute the major value premises in the decisional enyironment of the inferior (the latter's decision-making) consisting simply in finding the means for achieving the imposed goal)."[4]

The authority system also acts as a quality control device. When decisions taken at lower levels are submitted for the approval of higher authorities, the contents of decisions are subjected to a process of scrutiny. Fourth, the organisational communication system provides a formal framework of information flow in aid of decision-making. Data and information constitute the raw material for decisions. These are supplied by the structured communication system of the organisation. Last but not the least, organisations usually have methods of 'socializing' the participants in the decision making process. Training and the system of 'under study' for officers on probation are quite common in most large-scale organisations. Organisational values, the formal rules and regulations are sought to be injected into the minds of new entrants through these and other allied methods.

Interpersonal relations exert a strong influence on the decision making process in the organisation. Strained relations between two individuals are likely to lead blockages in communication and imperfect flow of data and information. Organisational hierarchy, from this point of view, may in certain situations be an impediment to rational decision making.

REFERENCES

1. James W. Fesler and Donald F. Kettl, *The Politics of the Administrative Process.*
2. GrahamT.Allison, *EssenceofDecision:Explainingthe Cuban Missile Crisis,* Little, Brown, Boston, 1971, p.145.
3. Herbert Simon, *Administrative Behaviour,* The Free Press, New York, 1947.
4. Nicos P. Mouzelis, *Organisation and .Bureaucracy,* Routledge & Kegan Paul, London, 1975.

Chapter 10

Communication, Control, Motivation Leadership

Among the process concepts, communication occupies a central place. Herbert Simon reckons at communication as a process whereby decisional premises are transmitted from one member of an organisation to another. According to Simon, "Without communication there can be no organisation, for there is no possibility then of the group influencing the behaviour of the individual."[1]

The decision-making process is aided by the organisation communication system. Data and information are transmitted to the decision maker through the communication channels. The decision maker can thus be likened to an information processing system.

Nature and Meaning

Communication is a process and information is the 'thing' to be communicated. The word 'communication' is derived from Latin *communis* which means 'common'. In a communication process, the sender of information seeks to establish commonness with the receiver of information. We can now define communication as the use of words, letters, symbols or some other means to have common information about any object of attention. Three aspects deserve emphasis in this connection. Firstly, when interacting with others, words, letters etc. are used. Secondly, two or more persons are involved in communication. Thirdly, the interaction, process is motivated by sharing of information towards a common end.

The contemporary approach to communication has been greatly influenced by cybernetics, a term coined by the famous M.I.T mathematician Norbert Weiner in 1947.[2]

Following almost a Hobbesian line of analysis, Weiner laid emphasis on the natural tendency toward disorder and disintegration in society. Entropy is a measure of the tendency of a system to disintegrate. Since entropy has a natural tendency to increase, it has to be fought back by methodical information processing which is the hallmark of organisation. Information is an antidote to entropy. In a developed system, information is used to collect and transform resources so that the system approaches a state of 'negative entropy.' The natural tendency of the system to disintegrate is thus arrested.

Weiner's theme was that man can control and modify his environment only through information and this information is transmitted *via* messages. He also introduced the idea of monitoring a system *via* a feedback mechanism that signals deviations from the objectives of the system. The flow and feedback of information has a significant effect on human behaviour. The permitted degree of feedback will increase with a manager's uncertainty about handling the problem.

The concern with communication has produced several attempts to develop models of the process. The most widely used model has evolved from the work of Shannon and Weaver and Schramm.[3] The basic ingredients of the model include a source, an encoder, a message channel, a decoder, a receiver, feedback and noise.

The *source* is usually a member with ideas, information and a purpose for communicating.

The function of encoding is to provide a form in which ideas and purposes can be expressed as a message for transmittal.

The message is the actual physical product that is conveyed.

Channels stand for the carriers of messages from the source to the receiver, including written, telephonic and numerous other modes.

The message must be decoded in terms of relevance to the receiver. Each receiver decodes or interprets the message in the light of his own previous experiences and frame of reference.

A *feedback* loop provides a channel for receiver response. This enables the source to determine whether the message has been received and has produced the planned response. Within the communication process, breakdown, interference, or deviation can occur. Shannon and Weaver were the first to identify this concept as noise. They defined noise as those factors that distort the quality of the signal. In the behavioural science context, noise includes those factors in each of the elements of communication that can reduce message fidelity.

Perceptual Process

Communication involves something being sent to a receiver. What the receiver does with or to the communicated message is the most vital part of the whole system. The perceptual process thus becomes a key element in our understanding of organisational communication.

The perceptual process in general is subject to many factors such as emotions, needs, values and interests. This may lead to important difference in the way any two people perceive the same person or message. Sheldon Zalkind and Timothy Costello[4] have summarised much of the literature on perception in fee organisational setting. Most communications take place in interaction with others. How one perceives the 'other' in the interaction process, vitally affects how one will interpret the communication.[5]

Formal and Informal Communication

In any organisation, the formal system of communication is deliberately established. Who should report to whom in what frequency, how should written communications move in the hierarchy, which is the first level where action should be initiated and then passed on to successive higher levels—all these are formally laid down to guide communication along desired lines. But as Simon pointed out, even if there is an elaborate system of formal communications, this system will always be supplemented by a complementary system of informal communications. Information, advice and even orders flow, many a time, along informal channels and not along the deliberately established formal channels of communications. The informal network of communications is based on social relations within the organisation. Two persons at different levels in the organisation may be communicating with each other in a way not formally charted out in the organisation. The social relations like friendship or enmity may create such informal conditions of communication. The phenomenon of informal communication has been acknowledged as the 'grapevine' that creates an actual system of relationships in the organisation which is vastly different from what is formally prescribed. In so far as the 'grapevine' supplements the formal sources of information in the organisation, it has its usefulness in organisational life. Often the tendency, however, is to discourage openness and spread rumour, hence the informal channels may not always play a constructive role. Yet, as Simon observes, "the grapevine is valuable as a barometer of 'public opinion' in the organisation. If the administrator listens to it, it apprises him of the topics that are subjects of interest to organisation members and their attitudes toward these topics."[6]

It needs to be cautioned that too much reliance on the informal channels may lead to the undermining of the system of formal communications in the organisation.

Management Information System: The need for reliable data and information for decision making is now widely acknowledged. Many large organisations, therefore, go for fairly sophisticated information system which is sometimes even computerised. Designing information system has grown into a technical profession. In designing such systems, attempts to develop as much data as possible are quite common. This is likely to lead to collection and storage of heaps of useless data which may not be relevant to management. The information system need not be looked at as a mere technique. Its utility lies in managerial problem solving. So, data and information necessary for decision making have to be organised in support of appropriate decision centres in the organisation.

Control in Organisations

Logically, the discussions on decision-making and communication flow into the larger question of control in organisations. Formal organisations try to maintain a position of equilibrium by using the various control devices properly. The problem of control is thus closely associated with the problem of organisational growth and survival.

In common parlance, control has a negative and restrictive meaning but the organisational control system is a very important means for checking and verifying organisational goal achievement *via* production of intended results. We will first clarify the meaning and nature of control and then indicate some of the control devices that have been evolved in recent times and in the end, the behavioural implications of organisational control will be spelt out in some detail. Essentially, control is a technical problem in organisational goal fulfilment but, its exercise evokes different kinds of responses from the human participants in the organisation.

Nature and Meaning

Control is needed to watch progress of work and to guard against possible result failure. Information about system performance is essential to 'permit timely decisions that emanate as control measures.The most important purpose of control is to make sure that actual operation conforms to established standards. If a typist is expected to produce fifteen typed pages a day, it has to be seen that the typist actually achieves the target. A secondary purpose of control is to provide timely information about actual work performance so that corrective action could be taken in case of any difficulties reported in course of performance.

Three *basic elements of the control process* are the following:

(a) Setting of standards: What results have been planned should be, as far as possible, explicitly stated and made known to all the organisational participants. A village level worker in charge of a number of villages must know in how many fields he has to organise demonstrations in what time period. He should be told clearly how many farmers he should contact and advise in one month (or any other specified period). Performance appraisal becomes easier when expected results are clearly stated.

(b) *Comparison of actual performance against standards:* As the work would be in progress, the results actually achieved should be ascertained for seeing whether actual performance is falling short of planned results or not. This method of control is known as 'monitoring' which stands for mid-course control. When an activity has run its full course and reached the stage of completion, the comparison of final result actually achieved against the planned result is generally known as 'evaluation.' Both monitoring and evaluation do, however, involve comparison of actual performance against preset standards.

(c) *Taking of corrective action:* Information or feedback about actual system performance acts as signals for corrective action. Decisions are called for, on the basis of performance reports, to ensure that appropriate action is taken to remedy the defects and correct mistakes. By taking appropriate action, the management makes sure that actual performance conforms to the planned standards and produces desired results.

In setting standards of performance, the outcome characteristics need to be defined as clearly as possible. Here the key question isrWhat should be accepted as satisfactory performance? The characteristics of results are usually related to the output of an organisation. Services or products are expressed in terms of both quantity and quality and the time dimension is also specified. So, the desired result may be indicated as, for instance, so many metric tonnes output of a particular quality within a specified time period. A second outcome characteristic can be related to the inputs needed for the production of planned output. This is the means aspect of the control process. There would obviously be direct expenses to produce an output. Additional indirect expenses in the form of supervision and other staff assistance should also be considered. Fixed investments in the form of capital expenditure (say, purchase of new typewriter or allied equipment) have to be taken into account.

In *evaluating government programmes,* both output and means or input characteristics have to be carefully defined. Sprue programmes produce precisely quantifiable output. For instance, a dug-well programme creates minor irrigation facilities through the construction of dug-wells. A dug-well is, of course, an output indicator but this is merely an intermediate output. Agricultural productivity and farmers' income have to be ascertained to evaluate the performance of a dug-well programme. Government programmes, many a time, create 'externalities' such as accessibility to a market as a consequence of a roads programme. Evaluation has to take note of these externalities.

In many cases, public programmes take a fairly long time to yield results. The Drought Prone Areas Programme, for example, is a long-term programme which has to be borne in mind while evaluating it. The results flowing from a public programme are easy to find out when the programme is meant for a definite group such as marginal farmers, slum dwellers etc. Programmes meant for specific target groups often suffer from 'leakages'.The benefits may go to non-target groups.This has actually happened in the case of small farmers development programme. A programme like an irrigation dam or a regulated market is likely to have wide spatial impact. The geographical coverage needs to be carefully considered in evaluating such programmes. For example, the impact evaluation of an irrigation project must be done with the help of stratified sampling so that different parts of the command area are included in the sample. Large public programmes are likely to have unintended consequences that may not always be understood at the time of project formulation. Hence continuous monitoring must take note of both planned results and unintended consequences.

An exotic hybrid type of plant introduced for more production may lead to some plant diseases and pests which might not have been foreseen at the time of introduction. Generally speaking, public programmes are launched to produce a series of results. In evaluating them, their comprehensiveness has to be taken into account. A composite index needs to be formulated to ascertain the numerous consequences flowing from multipurpose public programmes.

Besides *productivity,* concerns for *legality* and *morality* assume importance in government programmes. Functional efficiency is reflected in productivity. At the same time, the laws, rules and regulations have to be followed. Productivity in violation of the rules and regulations attracts criticism and censure. Administrators are often heard saying that the rules stand in the way of action.

Administrative morality is a wide-ranging term. Besides observance of rules and regulations, there are certain unwritten expectations about 'integrity' and 'honesty'. More sensitive administrators are careful about their conduct in public affairs and try not to do anything in violation of the sense of morality. Under Indian conditions, it seems there is greater sensitivity to "morality" than 'productivity.'[7]

Control Devices

Organisations that are consciously result-oriented usually adopt a number of measures to see that performance takes place according to planned standards. At whole organisation level, corporate planning has been in use such as the Life Insurance Corporation of India and many other public sector undertakings. A corporate plan (also known as strategic plan) is a long-term plan which spells out the long-term objectives of the organisation. Within this longer-term vision, alternative course of action for achieving objectives are worked out and the choices of action programmes suggested. On this basis, the short-term programmes for actual operations and budgets for the period are formulated. At the top level of an organisation, corporate planning provides a control mechanism by setting standards of short-term activities within a longer time frame. It should, however, be noted that corporate planning in public administration is fraught with many difficulties such as problems of longer term projection of activities. The role of the politician in the planning process is likely to be greatly reduced which by itself is enough reason for disfavouring corporate planning. At the macro or organisation-wide level, *planning-programming-budgeting-system,* or PPBS in short (developed in U.S.A), has been advocated and actually used in many public organisations. Under this system, objectives and programmes are clearly identified at the beginning. Alternative courses of action in achieving a planned output (e.g. reduction in child mortality and traffic accidents) are worked out. Here cost-benefit analysis is applied at the stage of project formulation and choice of projects is made on the basis of this technique In PPBS the results or outputs of the different programmes are identified first; the budgetary process of allocating and controlling funds follows the initial exercise of determination of results.

Even without the application of PPBS, budgetary control is conventionally exercised in most organisations. In allocating funds to different activities (water supply, roads, education, drainage etc.), results are anticipated in rather crude ways. The allocation process has to consider and accommodate competing demands coming fem different departments. It, thus, becomes more than a technical job and assumes a political character.[8] As the activities are carried on, expenditure reporting reflects the progress of funds actually used and the results achieved. Conventional budgeting practices do not always consciously spell out these different processes of identification of planned outputs, balancing of programmes by coordinating the different departmental demands and measurement of results through continuous reporting. PPBS provides a technical support system in aid of financial control specifically and input control generally.

As a management technique, *management by objective* (MbO) is widely used in many private organisations and this has been applied to public sector organisations also. The technique originated with Peter Druckers *The Practice of Management.*[9] Originally, Drucker emphasised the need for spelling out clearly the objectives of every manager in an organisation so that he could then control his performance and direct his efforts toward achieving the objectives. As a control technique, MbO has the advantage of clarifying objectives and tasks at different levels in an organisation and the organisational participants are able to discuss openlv what is to be done by whom and what are the resources or support systems needed to perform the tasks. Also, the various problems and pitfalls in the process of work performance are identified openly d efforts made to overcome these.

The performance of each manager is evaluated against the standards set in course of the initial consultation process when the key tasks of a manager are agreed upon. Control, in this system, is meaningful and purposive, since the objectively and openly defined tasks set the parameters of control. MbO can be successfully applied in a situation where the outputs are fairly precisely quantifiable. Also, the organisational climate must be such that the superior and the subordinate officers interact freely and frankly and there is a fair amount of openness and *camaraderie* in interpersonal relations.

The technique *of performance appraisal,* at the level of the individual employee is conventionally used in government organisations. As a control device, it seeks periodically and collects information on task performance by each employee. It enables the organisation to check whether the performance of each individual participant is going along a planned path and whether the total organisation is thus moving toward the desired direction. Performance appraisal, thus, serves two important purposes. Satisfactory 'work' performance is organisationally necessary. This is the *functional* purpose of appraisal. A s'econd objective is to ensure employee 'health' in terms of personal satisfaction and a sense of well-being. This is the *personal* aspect of appraisal.

As one administrative analyst has observed,"It is really a tool for obtaining certain information and facts about the employee to the higher management with a view to adopt corrective measures, where and when needed; promoting, within the organisation, right personnel practices; and motivating the appraisee to give of his best for achieving organisational success as also his own."[10] The fate of performance appraisal in government organisations in India is fairly well known. Tasks are not always clearly laid down; appraisal, in such circumstances, tends invariably to become highly subjective. In a hierarchy oriented organisation, the superior uses his positional advantage to the fullest extent and seeks to reduce the subordinate to a position of subservience and submission. Personal qualities are often rated higher than work performance.

As in the case of MbO, performance appraisal, to be organisationally useful, has to have a congenial organisational climate. Without a degree of openness and actual (if not formal) de-emphasis of hierarchy, appraisal is apt to be a unilateral process and not an interactional one.

Other Agencies' of Control

Performance of government organisation is controlled in a variety of ways. Within a particular organisation, the devices mentioned above are employed to control performance. Government as a whole is constantly watched by the press and the public. A bad performance immediately attracts public and hits the headline. Complaints can be voiced by the members of the public against specific organisations or activities. Noisy protests and timely complaints serve as useful sources of information for corrective action. A vigilant press and public opinion can be a real controller of government activities, provided the government agencies have the attitude to listen to public complaints and to act on them.

Legislative Control over the executive is one of the basic tenets of democratic government. The legislature frames laws and rules and makes amendments to legislations. The policy control is reflected in legislative changes. Legislative committees like the estimates committee and the public accounts committee are permanent forums through which legislature seeks to control estimated expenditure of executive departments and the actual expenditure incurred by them on completed projects. More specific committees such as the committee on public undertakings are set up to watch over the performance of particular agencies or departments. Legislative control takes the form of debates and discussions that often expose the malfunctioning of executive departments and lead to demands for corrective action.

Government functioning is also subjected to judicial control. Any activity in violation of established laws and regulations can be challenged in a court of law. The executive departments are kept within the bounds of law by the judiciary.

Two other control mechanisms are the *treasury control and the audit control.*[11] The central financial agency of the government as a whole—the Ministry of Finance—plays a major role in government-wide financial control. The budget estimates of different departments are processed, considered and formulated by the Finance Ministry. General financial rules for the guidance of the departments emanate from this ministry. It keeps a constant watch over the departments to make sure that the rules are followed properly and the departments observe economy in expenditure and function within the framework of budget grants. Taxation, borrowings and other revenue raising proposals fall directly within the province of the Finance Ministry's functions.

Audit control is the exclusive jurisdiction of an independent authority—the Auditor General. His major responsibility is to see that the executive departments incur expenditure in accordance with the purposes laid down in the laws, rules and regulations. Also, audit has to make sure that expenditure has been authorised by the competent authorities.

Other forms of input control are personnel control and inventory control. In government the Public Service Commissions and the Ministry in charge of Personnel frame rules and regulations for the common use of different departments, as they seek to recruit and manage their staff. Materials management is a pretty sophisticated job now. This takes care of organisation-wide purchases of inputs such as equipment, raw material etc.

BEHAVIOURAL IMPLICATIONS OF CONTROL

Within an organisation, control involves a process by which a person or group deliberately seeks to influence the behaviour of another person or group. Control is exercised in organisations to 'make the participants conform to organisational requirements. It is, therefore, a means to organisational goal fulfilment. To quote Tannenbaum[12], "It is the function of control to bring about conformance to organisational requirements and achievement of the ultimate purpose of the organisation. The coordination and order created out of the diverse interests and potentially diffuse behaviours of members are largely a function of control."

Since the control process brings two or more persons in a relational situation, the behaviour of the superior who exercises control is as important as the behaviour of the subordinate who accepts it. Control philosophies of the superior become relevant in this context. While commenting on the traditional managerial strategies, Chris Argyris has insightfully observed that such strategies for the direction and control of the human resources of an enterprise are eminently suited to the capacities and characteristics of the child rather than the adult.[13] People at the top, according to McGregor, hold two different views about human nature which affect the control process exercised by top managements.[14] These alternative views have been called 'Theory X' and 'Theory Y'. The assumptions about human nature and human behaviour underlying'Theory X' and 'Theory Y' are as follows:

Theory X

1. The average human being has an inheren dislike for work and will avoid it if he can.
2. Because of this human characteristic of dislike of work, most people must be coerced, controlled, directed and threatened with punishment to get them to put forth adequate effort toward the achievement of organisational objectives.
3. The average human being prefers to be directed, wishes to avoid responsibility, has relatively little ambition and wants security above all.

Theory Y

1. The expenditure of physical and mental effort in work is as natural as play or rest. The average human being does not inherently dislike work.
2. External control and the threat of punishment are not the only means for bringing about effort toward organisational objectives. Man will exercise self-direction and self-control in the service of objectives to which he is committed.
3. Commitment to objectives is a function of the rewards associated with their achievement.
4. The average human being learns, under proper conditions, not only to accept but to seek responsibility. Avoidance of responsibility, lack of ambition and emphasis on security are generally consequences of experience, not inherent human characteristics.

The assumptions ofTheory Y are diametrically opposite to those ofTheory X.These assumptions hold out different conceptions of man as a positive and dynamic being with substantial potentialities for growth and development. The implications for management control are obvious. To quote McGregor, "If employees are lazy, indifferent, unwilling to take responsibility, intransigent; uncreative, uncooperative, Theory

Y implies that the causes lie in managements methods of organisation and control".[15]

Control, according to this line of reasoning, need not be rigid and static. It is the management's responsibility to understand the behaviour of organisational participants and take appropriate steps in specific situations. The manager has to be an able diagnostician and organisational medicine man. A variable and flexible control system follows from this management style.

Maslow's Need Hierarchy Concept

Managerial control is usually conceived in terms of organisational goal fulfilment. The impact of control on organisational participants is important in this context. Exercise of control and its acceptance are also based on certain individual needs which the organisational participants ultimately want to realise through their behaviour in role-performing situations. Abraham Maslow[16] has developed the need-hierarchy concept to explain human behaviour in terms of need fulfilment. This is one of the well-known cognitive approaches to motivation. In an ascending order, the need structure starts from the bottom in the following way:

1. *Physiological needs* including hunger, thirst, sex etc.
2. *Security needs* such as protection against danger, threat etc.
3. *Social needs* such as belonging to groups and associations, friendship etc.
4. *Esteem needs* such as self-respect, ego satisfaction etc.
5. *Self-actualization* needs such as maximum self-development, creativity etc.

These basic needs are interrelated and arranged in a hierarchy. Certain 'higher' needs become important when certain 'lower' needs are satisfied. The needs that, become important as motivator evoke appropriate behaviour in response to them. As the individual grow., psychologically, the relative mix of needs undergoes changes affecting thereby the motivation to work.

From the point of view of control, the significance of the need hierarchy concept lies in its reference to behaviour producing needs in individuals. Why controls are exercised and complied with can be explained with the help of this concept. Controls are institutionally prescribed and individually exercised or received. Explanations in terms of individual behaviour may not therefore present the whole picture.

Control and Motivation

Organisational control has to take care of human motivation to work. What makes a man work or withdraw from work -(that is, motivation) has been the most important question that the behavioural scientists have tried to explore and explain.The cognitive approaches to motivation emphasise the importance of internal needs and processes of individuals. Maslow's need-hierarchy concept, explained earlier, falls in this category. By contrast, the *non-cognitive approach*[17] to motivation treats the internal processes and conditions of individuals as unknown. Motivation, according to this approach, depends on the conditioning effects of reinforcement and is amenable to control because of the consequences that flow from it. Punishment, for instance, will modify or correct deviant behaviour, reward will encourage and sustain a desired behaviour. The non-cognitive approach thus relies on explicit actions of individuals and their consequences as provided by the individual's external environment.

Herzberg's Motivation Hygiene Theory

For managerial control purposes, understanding of internal needs and processes of individuals has been stressed in a number of influential researches. Writings of Frederick Herzberg and Rensis Likert deserve special mention in this connection. The research findings of Herzberg suggest that factors involved in producing job satisfaction and motivation are separate and distinct from the factors that lead to job dissatisfaction. Two different kinds of human needs have been postulated in this context. One set of needs is related to mans animal nature. Man wants to avoid pain from the environment (e.g. threat, insecurity). He has also the learned drives that become conditioned to the basic biological needs. The stimuli, inducing pain-avoidance behaviour, are found in the job environment, or outside the job itself. The second set of needs can be traced to the unique human characteristic— to strive to achieve and to grow psychologically. The achievement and growth needs of the individual inhere in the tasks themselves or the *job content.* As Herzberg explains, "The growth or motivator factors that are intrinsic to the job are: achievement, recognition for achievement, the work itself, responsibility and growth or advancement. The dissatisfaction avoidance or hygiene factors that are extrinsic to the job include: company policy and administration, supervision, interpersonal relationships, working conditions, salary, status and security".[18]

Since management has to ensure best use of human resources to get the organisational objectives fulfilled, Herzberg's motivation-hygiene concept has significant bearing on organisational control system. Appropriate managerial strategy for effective use of human resources has been the subject of research by another eminent behavioural scientist, Rensis Likert. He has evolved four types of management systems called systems 1, 2, 3 and 4. System 1 represents classical organisational design and System 4 its opposite. In terms of motivational process, communication leadership process, decision process, goal-setting process, interaction process and performance goals, the System 4 model encourages greater utilization of the human potential and leads to significant improvement in organisational performance. The assumptions and approaches of McGregors Theory Y are incorporated in Likert s System 4 model.[19] The control process in this model envisages dispersal of decision making throughout the organisation and it emphasises self-control and participative problem-solving.

The researches on organisational behaviour are yielding evidences that seem to suggest that control devices must be adapted to the needs and capacities of individuals. Just as the larger political system postulates participation in the democratic process, the micro-organisation has similarly to create opportunities for participation in decision-making and problem-solving. Political theory and organisation theory thus seem to be converging on the question of participation.

Control Structure

Control philosophies of people holding managerial positions affect the way controls are actually exercised. At the receiving end, the subordinates react to the controls by their varying involvement postures. The pattern of control which characterises an organisation can be called its control structure. On the basis of predominant power base used in an organisation, Etzioni has classified control structures into three basic types[20]: coercive, utilitarian and normative. When controls are exercised basically by using actual physical means, the control structure can be said to be *coercive.* When the method of achieving control is basically the material means, goods and services, the control structure can be called *utilitarian.* Organisations which make use of symbols of affection, prestige and esteem as the predominant means of achieving control can be said to have a normative control structure.

Specific control structures evoke particular kinds of involvement among the organisational members. A coercive control structure generates alienating involvement. The persons being controlled do not feel psychologically involved in organisational affairs. Under a utilitarian control structure, the subordinates exhibit calculative involvement. They work in return for payments being received and there is no intrinsic love for the organisational work. Normative control structure generates a kind of moral involvement. The members perceive the organisational tasks as intrinsically good and valuable and they enjoy doing their work for the organisation in the spirit of a moral duty.

In real life an organisation can have a mix of all the three control structures but most organisations would be having the predominance of one of the three. Organisations like prisons or concentration camps will fall in the first category, while religious and voluntary organisations are likely to fall in the third category. Most government organisations will fall in the second category.

Etzioni's classificatory scheme has implications for top level management in public organisations. Motivation to work in many government organisations is sadly lacking and the inter-personal relations also are none too happy. The involvement of members, in Etzioni's terminology, is highly calculative. It needs an imaginative leadership to transform calculative involvement into a moral one.

Leadership in Organisations

Discussions on control flow naturally into the problem of organisational leadership which provides the basis for influence acts in organisations. Leadership has been variously defined to mean an attribute of personality, a positional characteristic and an attribute of behaviour. Structurally, leadership is related to status grouping in organisations. The formal positions like those of secretary to a department, joint secretary, director etc. fall in the 'leadership' category. Functionally, a leader is partly a manager, as he does not do all the management functions. The distinguishing feature of leadership is its 'ability to persuade others to seek defined objectives enthusiastically'. It is the capacity to influence others to follow which is the hallmark of leadership.[21]

It has been suggested[22] that there are five major bases of power that are used in any influence transaction between a superior and a subordinate. These have been called reward coercive, legitimate, referent and expert powers. The first three types are derived from the formal organisational source. Material reward (e.g. increment) and coercive power, (e.g. suspension) are laid down in organisational rules. Legitimate power is 'authority' to influence others which inheres in the formal position in organisations. The other two powers—referent and expert—cannot be deduced from organisational formalism. Referent power has its basis in personal liking between a superior and a subordinate and expert power depends on the specific expertise or skill of a superior which influences the behaviour of the subordinate. Functionally, leadership exhibits itself in more than routine acts of supervision. As Katz and Kahn put it, "the essence of leadership... has to do with *influential increment* which goes beyond routine and taps bases of power beyond those that are organisationally decreed".[23]

Leaders, according to Philip Selznick[24], are creative men; their profession is politics which involves 'continuous redefinition of public interest and the embodiment of those definitions in key institutions.' Some of the key tasks of leadership identified by Selznick are the:

i) Definition of institutional mission and role,
ii) Institutional embodiment of purpose,
iii) Defence of institutional integrity and
iv) Ordering of internal conflict.

The first task of leadership is to set organisational goals in the light of internal and external demands. Goal setting and policy formulation are the primary tasks of organisational leadership. Secondly, the meaning of policy has to percolate down to the social structure of the organisation. Elaboration and execution of policy would depend on how the whole organisation would be tuned to the thought process of the institutional leadership. Thirdly, the leadership has to maintain the core values of the organisation and its distinctive identity. Lastly, it is the task of leadership to acknowledge the presence of competing interests within the organisation and maintain a balance of power appropriate to the fulfilment of key commitments.

In a related fashion, A.K. Rice conceived leadership in terms of boundary controlling function. "Leadership function is most conspicuous at points of discontinuitics in the organisational structure, where there are breaks between parts of the system."[25]

The key tasks of institutional leadership—the top men in the organisation—are to set the goals and watch over the performance of the whole organisation. At lower levels, leadership tasks would be different in keeping with the demands of the organisational situations at specific locations.

Katz and Kahn[26] identify three levels of leadership acts, differentiated in terms of their effects on organisational structure. At the institutional level, top leadership is concerned with the design of the whole structure and formulation of policy. Lower down, the supervisors at the intermediate level function within the limits of general policy. In specific situations, they piece out the formal structure and make improvisations. The incompleteness of formal structure is thus remedied and the supervisors can perform their tasks by such interpolation of structure. Further down the line, the existing structure is used to keep the organisation in effective operation. The mechanisms and procedures are all laid down: the task of leadership at the operative level is to make the best use of these institutionalised means.

Group activity is the basic characteristic **of** organisations. Leadership is instrumental in **mo**tivating the groups and, in the process, improving organisational performance. **Behavioural** science research has focussed attention on the kind of leadership behaviour that could be related to leadership effectiveness. Four *dimensions of effectiveness*[27] have been specifically identified in this connection. First, leadership has to promote closer and satisfying relationship among organisational members. Second, the individuals and groups must feel that they are important in the organisation. Leadership has to create this feeling among the members of the organisation. Third, leadership has to encourage the members to work toward organisational goal fulfilment. Psychological gearing of organisational members to work and productivity has to come from the leadership. Last, the leadership has to make the resources and other technical means available for successful work performance. Technical aspects of tasks such as planning, organising, scheduling and input supply (e.g. money, material, tools etc.) have to be carefully looked into by the leadership.

To sum up, effective leadership has to care for both 'people' and 'productivity' aspects of the organisation. Providing socio-motional support to the organisational members is as important as ensuring organisational goal achievement.

Leadership has been aptly defined as the increment of influence going beyond the authority of office. In this context, a useful distinction has been made between **transactional** and **transformational** leadership. The former type exchanges rewards for services or performance. As effective guides and efficient managers, transactional leaders encourage improved performance among the subordinates and help them satisfy their needs and desires.

By contrast, transformational leadership 'requires a blend of charisma, individual relationships and intellectual stimulation'.[28] This type of leadership is dramatic in operational nuances and seeks to change the relationship of subordinates and the organisation. As defined by Warren Bennis[29] "Transformational leadership is the ability of the leaders to reach the souls of others in a fashion which raises human consciousness, builds meanings and inspires human intent that is the source of power". Thus, transformational leaders are those who foster *devotion* or commitment among subordinates. Transactional leaders, by contrast, solicit *diligence* or hard work.

To sum up, earlier leadership theories relied heavily on personality traits of leaders. Later researchers have revealed that leaders and followers form a dyad. Leadership requires followers who respond positively to the leader's call for commitment and creativity. Leadership is thus a socially constructed organisational reality (as distinguished from formally constructed hierarchy). Also the nature of the tasks and the situation matter in the effective conjunction of leadership and followership.

Edgar Schein[30] has distinguished between 'management' and 'leadership'. Management may be content with existent values and organisational culture (the way work is done in the organisation). It is the unique function of leadership to get involved in the 'creation and management of culture', creating new symbols and providing a new vision of direction. Interpreting events and action and moving organisations ahead is the essence of creative governance. It is the job of leadership to provide new interpretation and chart out new ways of marching forward, taking the followers along as an inspired and motivated collectively.

COORDINATION

In practical administration, the word 'coordination' is very frequently used to express both a kind of dissatisfaction and a need. With more and more specialisation, organisational differentiation reaches stage when the different segments tend to work in isolation from one another and the achievement of overall objective suffers. Coordination is of an organisation with a view to achieve the goals of the organisation. In classical administrative thought, this has been considered one of the major functions of management.

Herbert Simon has referred to two kinds of coordination.[31] *Procedural and substantive. Procedural coordination is exemplified by the design of the organisation itself that establishes the lines of authority, delimits the spheres of activity, and specifies the relationships among the members of the organisation.* Substantive coordination *is related to 'the content of the organisation's activities'. The organisational form for small farmers' development (SFDA) symbolises procedural coordination. An animal husbandry project (e.g. sheep development) that designs the different activities and the interrelations involved in the project represents substantive coordination.*

In organisation theory, coordination has been sought to be explained in the context of intra-organisational interdependencies. Situations of interdependence have to be objectively identified within the organisation. Appropriate coordinating devices have to be applied to meet the needs of specific situations.

James D. Thompson has conceptualised three types of interdependencies in organisations and suggested three kinds of coordinating devices to match them.

Three types of inter-dependencies identified by Thompson are (i) pooled inter-dependence, (ii) sequential interdependence and (iii) reciprocal inter-dependence. A situation of *pooled inter-dependence* exists when an organisation will be having a number of branches/departments each one of which is fairly autonomous and yet the total organisation depends for its success on the overall performance of the constituent units.

A situation of sequential *inter-dependence* exists where the unifs of an organisation are so organised that the output of one unit is the input for the second one. In such a situation, the second unit cannot function unless the first unit has produced its output and passed it on to the second unit. The third form of inter-dependence called *reciprocal inter-dependence* can be found in a situation where the outputs of each unit become inputs for the others. For example, in an airline, the production of the maintenance unit is an input for the operations unit in the form of serviceable aircraft. At the same time, the output of operations becomes an input for the maintenance unit in the form of an aircraft needing maintenace.

Thompson has suggested three types of coordinating devices: *standardisation, coordination by plan* and *coordination by mutual adjustments.* Standardisation involves framing of explicit rules to guide the action of interdependent units. The relationship of inter-dependence is thus sought to be standardisation through established routine or rules. This type of coordination is suitable for relatively stable and repetitive situations. *Coordination by plan* entails regulation of interdependence through the establishment of schedules prepared in advance. Coordination among the inter-dependent units is thus sought to be achieved through deliberate planning. This type of coordination is appropriate in more dynamic situations where the task environment is a changing one.The last form of coordination, called *coordination by mutual adjustments,* involves transmission of information and communication in the course of action. Inter-dependenceis sought to be regulated not in a structured fashion as in the earlier two instances. This form of coordination proves useful in more variable and unpredictable situations.[32]

Some other devices that are used to achieve coordination are the formal leadership roles in organisation, the committees and the staff units. In the hierarchical pattern, each superior officer at a particular level acts as a coordinator of the activities at his level. The use of committees of various kinds is a universal organisational feature in government organisations. There are permanent standing committees in many organisations (e.g. municipal corporations) which enjoy statutory powers to deal with specific functions such as financial administration, public works, health and education. Special or ad hoc committees are set up in most organisations from time to time to cope with new situations and problems. Committee composition often reflects the need for access to data and information that would be used in decision making; the members of other departments and organisations are taken in or members of the public are co-opted for the purpose.

Specific staff units are often created to facilitate coordination. A data processing unit or a computer centre may be a useful coordinating device in a complex large-scale organisation.

To sum up, organisations in action exhibit a series of important processes such as decision-making, communication, control and coordination. Each of these has its own distinguishing features. There are significant behavioural implications of some of the processes like control and communication affecting motivation and morale in the organisation.

REFERENCES

1. See in this connection, Tom Burns, "Authority and Communications to Subordinates", in Robert Dubin (ed.), *Human Relations in Administration,* Prentice-Hall of India, New Delhi, 1970.
2. Herbert Simon, *Administrative Behaviour,* op. cit., Chapter VIII.

3. Norbert Weiner, *The Human Use of Human Beings*, Houghton Mifflin Co., Boston, 1956. The word 'cybernetics' is derived from the Greek Kybernetes which means helmsman.
4. Claude Shannon and Warren Weaver, *The Mathematical Theory of Communication*, University of Illinois Press, 1948; and Wilbur Schramm, "How Communication Works," in Wilbur Schramm (ed.), *The Process and Effects of Mass* Communication University of Illinois Press, 1953, pp. 3-26.
5. Sheldon Zalkind and Timothy W. Costello, "Perceptions: Some Recent Research and Implications for Administrative"; *Administrative Science* Quarterly, Vol. 7, No. 2 (September 1962), 218-35.
6. The outstanding finding ofTom Burns' study was that "half of the time the boss thought he was giving instructions or decisions to his subordinates, they perceived the same communications as being only information and advice." See Tom Burns, "Authority and Communications to Subordinates" in Robert Dubin (ed.), *Human Relations* in *Administration*, Prentice-Hall of India, New Delhi, 1970.
7. Op cit., p. 162.
8. A survey of administrative behaviour brings this point out very clearly. See Kuldeep Mathur, *Sources ofIndian Bureaucratic Behaviour*, HCM State Institute of Public Administration, Jaipur, 1970.
9. Budgeting as a game and a bargaining process has been very vividly portrayed in Aaron Wildavsky, *The Politics of the Budgetary Process*, Little Brown & Co., Boston, 1974.
10. Peter F. Drucker, *The Practice of Management*, Heinemann, 1955.
11. Bata K. Dey, "Performance Appraisal: Some Techno-cultural Issues", *The Indian Journal of Public Administration*, October-December, 1978.
12. See in this connection, R. B. Jain, *Contemporary issues in Indian Administration.* Vishal Publications, Delhi, 1976, Chapter 9.
13. Arnold S. Tannenbaum, *Control in Organizations*, Tata McGraw Hill Publishing Company, New Delhi, 1968, p.3.
14. Chrig Argyris, *Personality and Organization: the conflict between system and the individual*, Harper, New York, 1951.
15. Douglas McGregor, *The Human Side of Enterprise*, Tata McGraw-Hill Publishing Company, New Delhi, 1960, Chapters 3 and 4.
16. Ibid., p.48.
17. A.H. Maslow, "A Theory of Human Motivation" *Psychological Review*, July 1943.
18. Most representative writing is: B.F. Skinner, *Beyond Freedom and Dignity*, Alfred A. Knopf, New York, 1971.
19. Frederic Herzberg, "One more Time: How Do you Motivate Employees? in Louis E. Davis and James C. Taylor (eds.), *Design of Jobs*, Penguin Books, 1972.
20. Rensis Likert, *The Human Organisation*, McGraw-Hill Book Company, New York, 1967.
21. A. Etzioni, *A Comparative Analysis of Complex Organisations*, Free Press, 1961.
22. Keith Davis, *Human Behaviour at Work*, McGraw Hill Book Company, New York, 1977, p. 107.
23. J.R.P. French, Jr. and B. H. Raven, "The Bases of Social Power", in D. Cartwright and K. Zander (eds.), *Group Dynamics: Research Theory*, Row, Peterson, New York, 1960.
24. Daniel Katz and Robert L. Kahn, *The Social PsychologyofOrganisation5*, John Wiley & Sons, New York, 1978, p. 574.
25. Philip Selznick, op.cit.
26. A.K. Rice
27. Op.cit.
28. Palumbo and Moody, op. cit.
29. Warren Bennis, "Transformative Power and Leadership" in the Thomas J-sergiovanni and John E. Coreally (eds.), *Leadership and organizational* 'Culture: New perspectives on Administrative Theory and Practices University of Illinois Press, 1984.
30. EdgarH.Schein, *Organizationalcultureandleadership: A Dynamic view*, Jossey-Bass, San Francisco, 1985.
31. Op.cit., pp.139-140.
32. James D. Thompson, *Organizations in Action*, McGraw-Hill, New York, 1967, pp.54-56.

CHAPTER 11

Interorganisational Relations

In public administration, interorganisational relationships are evident in multi-level governance. For instance, in a federation, the centre and the constituent states are in constant interaction. Same is the situation in the three-tier *Panchayati Raj* set up.

Organisation theory has been mainly concerned with the internal structure and functioning of organisations. It is now becoming increasingly clear that formal organisations do not exist independently. They interact among themselves and influence each other very decisively. The structure and functioning of a single organisation can be understood better by relating it to the larger family of organisations within which it resides. The traditional concern for interorganisational research has, therefore, been found inadequate and a widening of interest in interorganisational relations is being increasingly advocated. As two researchers observe, "Too much sociological theory and research has been based mainly on the model of a single organisation and attention has been focussed on its internal processes, by and large. Surely this dominant model is not sufficient to analyse newer and more complex organisational forms such as the interlocking networks of organisation in the civil service, the multi-campus State University, regional consortia of educational institutions, multi-outlet distributive organisations in business and multi-plant industrial concerns."[1]

The need for a comprehensive theory of interorganisational relations is widely acknowledged. But it is only in recent times that such efforts have been going on with a degree of seriousness. Studies in social services delivery system have yielded a number of concepts. Levine and White talk of interorganisational cooperative arrangements as a 'system of exchanges.'[2] An organisation-set model of interorganisational relations has been suggested by W. M. Evan.The unit of analysis is taken as an organisation or a class of organisations. The organisation-set stands for its interactions with various other organisations in its environment. Following a systems perspective, an interorganisational system model is constructed with the help of four components: input-organisation set focal organisation, output-organisation-set and feedback effects. The focal organisation is the central point of reference that is in interaction with the environment. The input-organisation set is the supplier of inputs to the focal organisation which produces outputs and services by using those inputs. The focal organisation sends its products out to the output organisation-set. The way the focal organisation relates itself to the output-organisation-set 'has feedback effects on itself as well as on the input-organisation set which again triggers the cycle of interorganisational systemic relations.'[3] By way of illustration, the Calcutta Metropolitan Development Authority (CMDA) may be considered a focal organisation which receives supplies like steel, cement, funds, personnel from many (input) organisations. The inputs are used by the CMDA in producing its outputs such as roads, water works, housing, schools, hospitals etc. These products are received by a number of (output) organisations like the Calcutta Corporation, the municipalities and the State Government departments.The CMDA gets the feedback about its performance from the output organisations which in turn affect the input supply process.[4]

Organisations come together to increase their functional competence and decisional rationality. Two concepts are useful in appreciating the quest for organisational integration: the 'interorganisational field' and 'task environment'. Integration, which is a form of cooperation, is facilitated in a situation where a number of organisations interact among themselves and weave together a network or organisational pattern. The 'social' space in which these interacting organisations exist can be called 'interorganisational field'.

The other concept of 'task environment' stands for "those parts of the environment which are relevant or potentially relevant to goal setting and goal attainment."[5] To gain effective control over their task environment, organisations often enter into integrative co-operations. The aim might be to remove difficulties in procurement of resources or to successfully meet the needs of clients. Thompson refers to three strategies adopted by organisations to better their performance through cooperative means: contracting, coalescing and co-opting.

i) Contracting involves negotiated agreement for the exchange of performance in the future.
ii) Coalescing signifies a combination or joint venture with another organisation in the environment.
iii) Co-opting refers to the process of absorbing new elements into the leadership or policy determining structure of an organisation.

In the field of local administration in India, all the three forms of cooperation can be found. For instance, in the Calcutta Metropolitan Area one local authority has entered into a contract with the Municipal Corporation of Calcutta for supply of water; joint ventures have been resorted to in some instances for common waterworks. Co-opting is rather uncommon, but a very similar device is interlocking membership whereby an improvement trust will be having municipal representation on its executive body.

A very useful conceptualisation of decision-making structures to coordinate service systems has been made by Warren. Four basic models suggested by him are: unitary, federative, coalitional and social choice. In a federative structure each participating organisation agrees to a division of labour but retains its autonomous character. A unitary structure is more integrative and seeks coordination through formal arrangements. The participating units are much more loosely united in a coalitional situation, whereas in a social choice structure the interaction among organisations is still more loosely ordered. Basically, all these typologies of interorganisational relationships point to degrees of convergence and divergence in cooperative ventures to facilitate delivery of social services.

Three Different Perspectives

There are at least three different perspectives from which one can observe the phenomenon of intergovernmvental relations. In the context of public administration, interorganisational relations have *first* to be considered with reference to the different constituent units into which government gets subdivided. Government, in practice, consists of various organs, departments, agencies and branches. The structural differentiation in large-scale administration leads to the formation of so many diverse units that only in a very remote sense 'government' can be thought of as one organisation. Functional specialisation, spatial distance and long existence through time contribute to a process of 'balkanisation', under which each unit of government comes to assume a fairly autonomous existence. In practice, therefore, it looks like so many 'governments', as each department or agency zealously guards its own functional territory and autonomous existence. Interorganisational relations need to be viewed in this perspective of structural differentiation in public administration.

A *second* perspective follows from the theory of separation of powers. The legislature, the executive and the judiciary have, since the ancient formulation of Montesquieu, been considered as separate and distinct organs of government each performing a specific kind of activity. The underlying idea is that there are three distinct kinds of functions which need not be mixed up and should preferably be entrusted to separate public agencies. As governments have evolved over time, their functions have become more and more complex and heterogeneous. The theory of separation of powers conceptualises functional heterogeneity and differentiation. According to Barker, it draws attention to a "distinction of modes of action".[7] The legislative mode, the executive mode and the judicial mode are distinct and different. The legislative mode of action is characterised by deliberation and discussion, the executive mode by quick implementation of the legislative will. The distinctiveness of the judicial mode of action lies in critical sifting of evidence and weighing of arguments. Recognition of these different modes of action does not mean that each mode should be the exclusive domain of a particular organ. In other words, the legislative mode of action may not be the preserve of only the legislature. It may also be partly undertaken by the executive, when, for instance, rules and regulations are framed by the executive in course of elaboration of laws. Similarly, the judicial mode is generally the exclusive field of the judiciary. But the executive may act in accordance with the judicial mode in cases where sifting of evidence and weighing of pros and cons are involved. 'Quasi-judicial' action of the executive is a familiar expression in administration.

The legislature and the executive are known to have conflicting relations in many instances. At the local level, such conflicts have been quite common in our *Panchayati Raj* and municipal government. The reasons for such conflicts are many. Inability to delimit the respective functional jurisdictions of the two organs has been one of the principal causes of tension and conflict between them.

A *third* perspective of intergovernmental relations is provided by the federal principle. Territorially, in a federal country like the U.S.A, and India, there are two basic levels of government. As an organising principle, federalism implies constitutional division of powers between a national government and a number of constituent units of the federation. At each level the federal theory recognises the working independence of a government (national or regional) under the ground rules laid down in the basic constitutional document. The formally codified provisions of the constitution seek to regulate relationships among the different governments in a federation. Still, conflicts are not uncommon between the federal government and the constituent units. The constitution explicitly provides for a built-in mechanism of conflict resolution in anticipation of the need for regulation of centre-state relations. The judiciary is entrusted with this job.[8]

Intergovernmental relations are much less formal at the level of local government. Municipalities and *Panchayati Raj* bodies are created by ordinary state laws, which in a way serve the purpose of local government 'constitution'. In the absence of any guarantee, in the fundamental law of the land—the Indian Constitution—the functions and finances of the local bodies used to be left more to 'politics' than some fundamental constitutional norms. With the enactment of the two Constitutional Amendment Acts—73rd and 74th in 1992, the *Panchayats* and municipalities are now constitutionally guaranteed 'self-government' institutions.

At the level of local government, relationships between two or more local bodies can develop around common issues such as water supply, drainage and planning.

In addition to such horizontal relations, the different units in a multi-level local government system may be vertically linked together. This is the case with our *Panchayati Raj* which creates a hierarchic system with *Zila Parishad* at the top, *Panchayat Samiti* below it and *Gram Panchayat* at the bottom.

The fact of functional differentiation, the theory of separation of powers and the federal principle are important bases for an understanding of the phenomenon of intergovernmental relations as one of the dynamic aspects of public administration.

Interdepartmental Relations[9]

As mentioned earlier, each department of government often comes to assume a fairly autonomous character. The relationships among the different departments can thus be considered as interorganisational relationships. Administrative competition and conflict between departments need closer scrutiny, as these kinds of administrative behaviour greatly influence the administrative processes and outcomes. Competition between departments develops around resources like funds, personnel and enabling powers to achieve their goals. Functional territory in the geographical sense may also be a bone of contention. A municipality and an urban development authority may compete with each other over territorial jurisdiction. Competition may also take place over political support and jurisdiction over a common client group. Competition among the branches of different nationalised banks in a district is very common over both geographical space and clientele. In a competitive situation, the departments usually have their individual areas of operation and separate programmes of activities and their relationships are basically indirect. A competitive situation deteriorates into a conflicting one when interdepartmental relationships become 'more direct and intense.' Conflict between two agencies is more likely in a situation where both are operating the same service. In the Calcutta Metropolitan Area, the Calcutta Metropolitan Development Authority (CMDA) and the Calcutta Municipal Corporation have both been involved in sewage cleaning; and the two agencies have not always had happy relationships.

Lewis Coser[10] has pointed out the importance of conflicts in organisations. On the positive side, interorganisational conflicts bring hostility into the open and serve as shields against absurd perceptions of reality. Organisational ideology, beliefs and goals are moulded by conflicting situations. Conflict, according to Coser, has the merit of creating the identity of the organisation.

This leads us to the next logical discussion on what Peter Self calls agency or departmental philosophy.[11] A government department or agency that has existed for a pretty long time develops its own tradition and culture. The Administrative Reforms Commission characterised this phenomenon as "the desire of the Ministries and the departments to guard their 'preserve' jealously."[12] There are various reasons for the slow but steady development of agency philosophy in government. Long experience of dealing with a specific area of activity, indelible influences of strong personalities connected with the management of the agency activities, deliberate socialisation of the members through training programmes, a fairly well recognisable image of the agency outside are some of the more significant reasons for the growth and steady maintenance of agency philosophy and identity. The image of the Ministry of Home Affairs at the Centre, for instance, immediately comes to mind in this context.

The influence of the *process* and *client* factors, according to Peter Self, is important in moulding the attitudes of agencies. The process factor relates to an agency's methods of work, while the client factor refers to the nature and size of the client group with which the agency has close relationships in terms of its operative responsibilities. Agencies can be classified into bureaucratic and technocratic types on the basis of their methods of work (the process factor). An agency would fall in the bureaucratic category if its work is fairly rigidly fixed by laws, rules and regulations. Uniform application of rules dominates its nature of work and there is very little room for the use of discretion. The method of work is more generalist than particularistic. A technocratic agency, by contrast, is more professionally oriented and much more flexible in rendering services. Technical judgment rather than rigid rule application characterises its basic work norm. These are, of course, pure types. Actual organisations will have a mixture of both types, some tilting more toward the bureaucratic type and some others toward the technocratic type. A licensing department is more likely to fall in the first category, while health and welfare departments will fall in the second.

Relationships with clients (the client factor) are equally important in shaping the attitudes of agencies. Government departments or agencies try to 'protect' the interest of smaller and relatively neglected groups like the tribals and the physically handicapped. Larger clientele group may be much more vociferous in their demands. A government agency dealing with a large group will be at the receiving end. The problem is how to accommodate clientele demands in the policy and operations of the agency. Large and powerful clientele groups like agriculturalists and industrialists try in various ways to influence the working of government agencies in their favour. The usual government practice in India has been to associate influential groups with the consultative committees attached to different departments.

Agency or departmental attitudes are also shaped by significant pressures coming from the political process. Some tasks are more prone to political pressures than others. Also, the level of administration—central or local—determines the extent of percolation of influences. At the level of local government, the tasks are more exposed to political pressures. In terms of method of work, the political method is as good as the managerial method. A single task may have both methods built into it. Building-sanction in a municipality, for example, is partly done technically with the help of technical officers; the sanction itself is however a 'political' decision of a committee on the subject. Generally speaking, with the passage of time, organisations grow in experience and evolve formal rules and procedures for the sake of regularity, continuity and objectivity. Tasks that are initially dealt with politically are likely to be treated more 'managerially' in course of time with the formulation of explicit and well-settled rules and procedures. As an agency grows in managerial strength and stature, its autonomy also increases proportionately.

Semi-independent Agencies

Autonomous agencies are often created on grounds of 'de-politicization' which means taking certain functions out of politics. The assumption is that these functions are basically technical in nature and need more managerial attention than political pressure. The Housing and Urban Development Corporation (HUDCO), the University Grant Commission at the national level exemplify creation of autonomous agencies by the Government of India. There are various other semi-independent agencies (e.g. development authorities, public undertakings etc.) set up by the Central and State Governments. Peter Self[13] suggests three main reasons for setting up semi-independent agencies. First, an *altruistic* reason is advanced that democratic values will be best served by creating an autonomous agency for the performance of some function. By implication, such values will suffer if the government undertakes to perform the function directly. The proposal for the setting up of autonomous corporations for the All India Radio and the Doordarshan (TV) has often been mooted on this ground. Second, a judicial reason is put forward in support of an autonomous agency in situations where certain functions need to be administered impartially and openly with the help of established rules and procedures to the satisfaction of numerous private interests. The Regional Transport Authority in each district is an example of a semi-independent body of this kind. It issues permits authorising the use of motor vehicles for public transit and approves area of operation, routes, stops and fares. Thirdly, there is the persuasive reason for the creation of a semi-independent agency when the government feels that the interests to be served and the potential critics faced could be satisfied by taking such a measure. The creation of the University Grant Commission for the purposes of maintenance of educational standards and financing of higher education illustrates this point.

There are many other important reasons that prompt governments to constitute semi-independent agencies. *Special programmes* needing special administrative effort are often entrusted to an autonomous agency. The Small Farmers Development Agency (SFDA) was a case in point; the purpose was to have a special body to look after the developmental activities meant for the small and marginal farmers. Another reason may be purely *technical and managerial* considerations in undertaking certain activities. A Command Area Development Authority, for example, is usually set up on grounds of technical necessity, an irrigation command area needing a common unified developmental approach. There may be important commercial reasons for setting up some agencies outside the regular government organisation. Financial management has to be different from normal government way of budgeting and expenditure control. Generally, public enterprises are created on this ground. The principle of social control, of course, plays its role in the creation of public enterprises. At the same time, the corporation or company type (e.g. International Airports Authority of India which was carved out of the Civil Aviation Department) of enterprise has to manage its finances in such a way that it earns some profit and does not have to depend much on government. Autonomous agencies are also set up on other *extraneous considerations* such as pressures from the higher level government and from international aid-giving agencies. The origin of most of the specialised rural development agencies such as the SFDA and the DPAP (for the drought prone areas) can be traced to the recommendations of the Central Government. International agencies like the World Bank are known to have put pressures for the creation of special agencies in the interest of 'better' programme management. The Calcutta Metropolitan Water and Sanitation Authority and the Central Valuation Board (for valuation and assessment of property tax purposes) in West

Bengal was, to a large extent, set up under pressure from the international agencies.

It should be clear by now that there are numerous reasons for the creation of semi-independent agencies outside the normal departmental set-up. Formal status as an autonomous agency does not, however, always ensure enjoyment of real autonomy. As the history of public enterprises in India clearly points out, real autonomy needs more than legal backing. Certain conditions must be fulfilled before an agency can aspire after a fairly autonomous existence. First, the functions entrusted to the agency must be actually detachable from the normal departmental functions of government. Second, the agency should have a lucrative source of substantial income of its own. Third, the government (meaning the minister and senior departmental civil servants) must be ready to accept the autonomous character of the agency and would develop a tradition of general non-interference in the affairs of the agency. This, of course, does not rule out major policy control by government. Last but not the least, the agency itself must be able to manage its own affairs with a degree of efficiency so that its public image as a well-run organisation acts as a shield against frequent government interferences. No doubt, the ministers and senior civil servants are often singled out as interfering elements undermining the autonomous status of many semi-independent public agencies.[14] On the part of the agencies themselves, efficient management of their business has, however, rarely been their strong point.

Competition and Conflict

Public agencies are often found to compete among themselves over functions, client, area, resources and political patronage. Efficiency is conventionally considered in government in terms of the volume of expenditure incurred from year to year. Ability to spend money is taken to be the test of agency strength. Hence, competition between agencies is quite common to get as much money as possible for their respective programmes. Big departments (e.g., irrigation and public works departments) get more and more of the budgetary cake than their smaller brethren such as fisheries and small scale industries departments. Interagency competition for client and area is very much evident in the institutional financing of rural development projects for small and marginal farmers. The nationalised banks, the cooperatives and the *Panchayati Raj* bodies (channelizing government funds) are often found to work m the same area for financing minor irrigation and animal husbandry projects. Functional duplication also takes place, when, for instance, pasture development is undertaken in a district by the soil conservation department, the forests department and the animal husbandry department. These agencies may not be competing with each other. Functional duplication[15] in this case is more due to lack of coordination than cut-throat competition. In a really competitive situation, as in the case of bank loms, resource utilisation is likely to be less than optimum and there is a danger of wastage also. It might be necessary in such situations to delimit areas of operation of each agency. Alternatively, financial institutions may be. directed to restrict their operations to limited schemes.

Agencies many a time duplicate their efforts and compete for clientele, when they serve the same public. There are various schemes for the benefit of small and marginal farmers and landless labourers. Since the administering departments for the schemes are different, it is not rare that the same farmers are being served through a variety of schemes, whereas many others have almost received nothing. In this situation also, there is duplication but not so much conscious competition. If there is any competition, it is perhaps manifest in the demonstration of spending capacity. Especially in the last few months of a financial year, the departments become anxious to spend their allotted funds as quickly as possible. There is a certain fear among them that their inability to spend may lead to substantial cuts in their budget next year.

Functional duplication, not so much competition, takes place because of indiscriminate proliferation of programmes and schemes in a particular functional area. This is very much true of the numerous rural development schemes that have been formulated from time to time by the different Central Government departments and agencies in India.[16] Duplication is due primarily to lack of policy coordination at higher levels of government. The other important reason lies in administrative fragmentation, as more and more departments and agencies are created with narrow terms of reference. Animal husbandry department, to cite an instance, is in some cases divorced from live-stock administration. In the name of specialisation, sheep and wool development has claimed autonomy in some states in India. Irrigation had the same fate with different departments and agencies (including public corporations) dividing between themselves the different aspects of the total work. In this situation, the organisations involved compete for more and more funds for their further expansion. In terms of creation of appropriate irrigation facilities and their optimum geographical distribution, this kind of administrative fragmentation is likely to be dysfunctional.

Administrative competition and conflicts can be traced basically to weaknesses at the level of policy formulation. Conflicts have their origin in lack of agreement over desirable course of action. Two agencies may fall out on the issue of what should be done in a situation of common concern. Administrative conflicts form part of the normal administrative process in government. That is why institutional arrangements exist in government to cope with conflicts. Two important institutions in this context are the finance department and the cabinet. Since the public agencies often quarrel over funds to maintain and expand their levels of activities, the finance department can and do play an arbitrative role in conflicting situations. As regards the cabinet, interdepartmental feuds that cannot be resolved at lower levels are invariably pushed up to the cabinet for a final settlement.

Another important device for managing inter-agency conflicts at the sub-state level is the creation of positions of coordination at appropriate points in space. The Divisional Commissioner, the District Collector and the sub-divisional officer have traditionally been performing, coordinating and conflict-resolving roles at their respective levels in field administration.

Interdepartmental committees, ad-hoc mediations, coordination through generalist positions are familiar devices in government for keeping the entire machinery from falling apart. But conflicts need to be firmly tackled at the point where the seeds of discord are sown. The operational level reaps whatever is sown at the policy level.

As Peter Self has rightly observed, a basic cause of inter-agency conflicts "is the frequent inconsistencies or vagueness of public policy goals."[17] Policy inconsistency can be due to a variety of reasons. *Ideologically* induced inconsistency is involved in situations where government takes policy decisions on some broad philosophical grounds. The prohibition policy in India has been pursued from time to time on some ethical-philosophical considerations. The impact of such a policy on the state exchequer has been of no consequence to the policy framers.

Policy inconsistency is, however, basically

traceable to *political expediency.* Government decision to remit all cooperative loans to agriculturalists illustrates this point. Such a decision is obviously intended to win over the peasantry politically; but it is bound to have disastrous consequences for the repayment of other bank loans.

Policy conflicts arising out of inconsistent stances are not always deliberately planned. There are perhaps more unintended policy conflicts than deliberately induced ones. Hence lasting solutions to such conflicts have to be worked out at the level of formulation of policy itself. The emerging discipline of policy science aims precisely at this.

Theoretical Support

Administrative competition and conflicts are a reality in organisational life. Theoretical explanations for these phenomena are not, however, fully developed. The reason perhaps can be traced to the overriding concern of organisation theory for rational coordination. Under the impact of conflict sociology and political science, the phenomena of conflict and competition in administration have been receiving increasing attention today. Lewis Cosers *The Functions of Social Conflict* and Melville Dalton's *Men who Manage* (1959) are outstanding examples of inquiry into this aspect of organisational life.

Competition and conflicts are-the behavioural manifestations of an institutional pattern in a particular country. In a federal system with many levels of government (as in the U.S.A, and India), institutional pluralism is a characteristic feature of the overall arrangement of government. As administrative agencies proliferate in this system, competition and conflicts are more natural in a condition of institutional pluralism. The situation is not much dissimilar in India. An additional factor accentuating administrative proliferation is planning. Successive Five-Year Plans promising more and more investments have led to the creation of numerous departments and special agencies in India.

In a unitary system, as in Great Britain, administrative fragmentation is much less accentuated. Still, with a strong local government system, Great Britain has virtually a two level government. Proliferation of special agencies has not taken place in that country mainly due to the strength and political power of elective local government. The situation is, however, changing now under the impact of New Right philosophy.

Institutional arrangement in a country is reflective of certain dominant cultural values. The American system of government seems to have favoured administrative proliferation and consequent competitions due to a cultural predilection for variety and innovation. Like competition in the economic sphere, administrative competition between agencies has been accepted as the national style of governance. Contrastingly, the tradition in Great Britain has been to minimise competition and conflicts in the administrative sphere. The watchword is coordination which, as Peter Self points out, is rooted in historical acceptance of the unity of the Crown and in the general, administrative attitude toward harmonisation of all public action.[18] Indian administrative tradition flowing out of the bureaucratic state apparatus of the British regime has been to suspect delegation and decentralisation and to support centralised control and integration. Administrative culture has later been reinforced by political culture as the politicians at higher levels have virtually emulated the behaviour of the dominant administrative class in India.

In such a situation, there is a lot of spurious decentralisation and administrative proliferation. Actually, however, control and centralisation continue to remain the basic feature of the Indian administrative system.

Administrative competition can be explained with the help of the political theory of pluralism.

Society, according to the pluralist stand, is a honeycomb of interests and groups that are constantly engaged in competition and conflicts. The administrative system has to accommodate the various demands of the social groups. Creation of a multiplicity of administrative agencies, therefore, reflects a rational response, to societal demands.

Traditional democratic theory, at the other end, contradicts the pluralist explanation. According to democratic theory, the multifarious demands of social groups get sorted out in the political process itself where the different parties and their leaders play arbitrative roles and synthesise diverse demands.The political process produces 'a coherent and consistent programme to be implemented by the administrative system.' Thus the synthesising capacity of the political process acts as a bulwark against administrative fragmentation and competition.

Pluralist political theory supports fragmentation and competition in public administration, while traditional democratic theory favours synthesis and cohesion in public action. These two ideals of administrative arrangement seem bipolar in theory. In practice, however, most administrative situations contain a mixture of both.

REFERENCES

1. NJ. Smelser and J. A. Davis (eds.) *Sociology,* Prentice Hall, 1969, p. 65.
2. Sol Levine and Paul E. White, "Exchange as a Conceptual Framework for the Study of Interorganisational Relationships", *Administrative Science Quarterly,* March 1962.
3. W.M. Evan, "An Organisation-Set Model of Interorganisational Relations", in William M. Evan (ed.), *Interorganisational Relations,* Penguin Books, 1976.
4. A relevant research in this connection is by H.Turk, "Interorganisational Networks in Urban Society", American Sociological Review, vol. 35, February 1970.
5.
6. James D. Thompson, *Organisations in Action,* McGraw Hill, 1967, p. 34.
7. Roland Warren, "Interorganisational Field as a Focus for Investigation" in Merline Brinkerhoff and Philip Kunz (eds.), *Complex Organisations and their Environments,* Iowa, 1962.
8. Ernest Barker, *Principles of Social and Political Theory,* Oxford University Press, London, 1961, p. 258.
9. There are various other provisions in the Constitution of India intended to resolves interstate conflicts. Article 262, for instance, takes care of interstate waters dispute.
10. This aspect has been very lucidly explained by Peter Self in his book *Administrative Theories and Politics,* op.cit (chapter 3).
11. Lewis A. Coser, *The Functions of Social Conflict,* The Free Press, New York, 1956.
12. Op.cit., pp.92-99.
13. Op.cit., p.95.
14. Op. cit, pp.96-7.
15. The Study Team of the Administrative Reforms Commission in its *Report on Public Sector Undertakings* emphasised the need for abnegation of government control to allow the public undertakings a requisite measure of autonomy. It pleaded for a change in the attitude of the minister and senior officials and a degree of parliamentary restraint. See *Report,* New Delhi, 1967, p. 70.
16. To quote Peter Self, "Duplication can be said to arise when two or more agencies provide very similar services for very similar publics, or pursue activities which have substantial overlap in terms of their technical and professional requirements." *See* Peter Self, op. cit., p. 99. Functional duplication may not, however, lead automatically to interagency competition. Duplication is a state of things, while competition is a state of mind.
17. See in this connection, Mohit Bhattacharya, *Bureaucracy and Development Administration,* Uppal Publishing House, New Delhi, 1979, Chapter II.
18. Op.cit., p. 103.
19. Op.cit., p.88.

Chapter 12

Politics and Administration

Two substantive issues that need to be discussed at some length are the relationship between the politician and the administrator and the relationship between bureaucracy and public. Both issues raise questions about the nature of public administration. Politics-administration relationship has been an old theme since the beginning of intellectual inquiry into the structures and processes of administration. The relationship between administration and the public is significant from the point of view of "publicness" of public administration. It is this relationship that defines the nature of public administration.

Politicians and Administrators

Earlier writings on public administration made a clear distinction between 'politics' and 'administration' as two distinct and separate kinds of activities. The distinction was made in terms of ends and means. Politics, being essentially concerned with the processes connected with the shaping and uses of state power has been understood as the fount of value laden policy decisions. Administration is the means for the fulfilment of policy objectives. It is basically an activity concerning the execution of policy decisions in practice. The distinctiveness of the two—politics and administration—was clearly stated by Woodrow Wilson in the following way:

"The field of administration is a field of business. It is removed from the hurry and strife of politics; it in most points stands apart even from the debatable ground of constitutional study. It is a part of political life only as the methods of the counting-house are part of the life of society; only as machinery is part of the manufactured product... Administration lies outside the proper sphere of politics. Administrative questions are not political questions. Although politics sets the tasks for administration, it should not be suffered to manipulate its offices" .[1]

Wilson's line of reasoning has been followed later by many writers. His statement makes a distinction between politics and administration as two separate activities. Institutionally and professionally, the two are considered different. The institutional locus of politics could be found in legislatures, political parties and pressure group; whereas administration is the formalized executive branch of government. In terms of profession, politics is what the politicians do and administration is what the administrators do.The promise of a 'science' of public administration has been premised on the autonomous nature of administration as a tool or means for translating political objectives into practical reality.

Purity of administration as a differentiated function received great intellectual support from Weber's concept of rational bureaucracy.[2] The structural features and the behavioural norms implicit in a bureaucratic form of organisation as conceived by Weber contributed to the growth of public administration as a fairly autonomous institution bound by rigorous rules and uncontaminated by irrational forces. The idealised concept of bureaucracy as it came to be accepted in the West has, according to La Palombara,[3] a number of "behavioural and attitudinal norms that can be added to what has already been said about Weberian bureaucracy." These can be identified as; (i) limited instrumental role in rule-making; (ii) free and open interaction with a plurality of voluntary associations; (iii) maintenance of separate identity and position while dealing with organised voluntary associations; (iv) acceptance of electoral sovereignty and recognition of the legitimate role of elected leaders to specify what is or is not in the public interest; (v) honesty and integrity of public administrators in the performance of their functions and (vi) acceptance of and loyalty to the administrative and political system of which the administrators constitute an integral part. The bureaucratic norms of anonymity, impartiality and neutrality came to be associated with the Weberian model.

The social role of bureaucracy as a neutral instrument in the hands of political masters gained acceptance under certain political and cultural circumstances. Anonymity meant that the civil servant would merely advise the politician from behind and would be protected from being exposed to the din and fury of politics. Impartiality stood for the quality of the civil service to act without bias irrespective of the social pressures and variations in the nature of clients. Neutrality meant a kind of political sterilization, the bureaucracy remaining unaffected by the changes in the flow of politics. The civil servant has been axiomatically considered as politically neutral. There might be changes in political leadership but the civil servant would be unfailingly offering 'technical' advice to the political master keeping himself aloof from the 'politics' of the day. The bureaucracy has thus been portrayed as a universal and permanent institution uncontaminated by the frailties and frivolities of politics.

It is not being debated at this point whether these attributes of bureaucracy square with reality. There are, however, other types of bureaucracy, as Merle Fainsod points out, whose roles may be quite different from what is postulated in Weberian formulation. Relating bureaucracies to the flow of political authority, Fainsod[4] distinguishes five different bureaucratic forms as follows:

1. *Representative bureaucracies*[5]*:* Within political democracies, these "are responsible to and in greater or lesser degree responsive to the political forces which command the support of the electorate and dominate the political organs of government at a given time."
2. *Party State bureaucracies:* These are the by-products of totalitarian regimes and other one-party dominated political systems where the state bureaucracy, has a distinctive structure, "is penetrated, controlled and dominated by the party bureaucracy."
3. *Military-dominated bureaucracies:* These can be found in societies where a strategic power position is occupied by the armed forces "who install their representatives in key civilian posts and endeavour to give direction, to the state bureaucracy."
4. *Ruler-dominated bureaucracies:* These exist in political systems where "bureaucracies are the highly personal instruments of an autocratic ruler or dictator who exercises an approximation of absolute power and who uses his bureaucratic establishment to project his control and impose his purposes on the people whom he rules."
5. *Ruling bureaucracies:* These can be found

in certain phases of colonial rule where "the bureaucracy itself is in effect the ruling element in the political system." Imperial India immediately comes to mind in this context.

This classification of bureaucracies serves an important purpose as it defines the role of bureaucracy in different political systems and relates it to the use of authority. A neutral bureaucracy as a fairly detached instrument of governance is not a universal phenomenon. It can be found only within a particular political framework that accepts the legitimate supremacy of the elected leaders in the administrative and political system. As Almond puts it,"The ideal of a neutral instrumental bureaucracy, responsible to the political arm realised in political systems, comes closest to being where the political culture tends to be secular and rational and where the functions of political choice—that is, the articulation and aggregation of interests and the making of public policy—are performed by specialised agencies."[6]

Bureaucratic role differentiation is thus conceived in terms of the general process of differentiation within a political system. Neutrality and impartiality of bureaucracy can also be traced to the basic class character of the ruling class of which bureaucracy itself is a part. As Donald Kingsley[7] wrote about the British bureaucracy:

'The convention of impartiality can be maintained only when the members of the directing grades of the service are thoroughly committed to the larger purposes the state is attempting to serve; when, in other words, their views are identical with those of the dominant class as a whole... For the past seventy-five years, with very few exceptions, the leaders of all political parties and of the service have been united in regard to fundamentals.Their outlooks and points of view have been uniformly middle class and the identity of their fields of vision made permanent service a possible adventure.

A research study on Malaysian bureaucracy reinforces this argument. The belief in a strong government predominantly interested in peace and order is shared by politicians and administrators alike. As the study points out[8], "... it appears that both civil servants and politicians have accepted the doctrine of political neutrality because, so far at least, it has been possible for political executives to obtain loyal and dedicated civil servants who seem to be prepared to give full support to the party in power. The test will come when another political party takes over the government".

The bureaucracy in England changed with the changing nature of the state. As the old aristocracy gave way to the capitalist state, the character of the civil service changed from an aristocracy-dominated service to a middle-class dominated one. It has been said in this context that bureaucracies are responsible to the extent they are broadly representative of the classes in a state. The socio-economic conditions and the manner of recruitment of the members of the higher civil service (e.g. emphasis on high educational qualification, age, interview technique etc.) favour a particular class that receives a disproportionately high share of the posts in higher public services.[9] Recruitment from a narrow social base, it has been alleged, is likely to lead to the perpetuation of a class in the higher echelons of the bureaucracy, which carries' the danger of entrenchment of a restricted and conservative social outlook in the bureaucracy.

Street-Level Bureaucracy

The focus of bureaucratic theory has conventionally been on the top level in the organisation. It is the employee at the cutting edge level—where the organisation meets the members of the public—that makes or mars the image of the organisation. The frontline employees have been called the street-level bureaucracy. Research on lower level bureaucracy has thrown light on some of the interesting features of employees at the bottom of the organisation like the police constable or the village level worker. It is common knowledge that the primary and basic work of the organisation is done by the lower level bureaucracy. The constable's role in crime prevention is of crucial importance in the police organisation. At the same time, it has been found that the employees at the bottom of the organisational hierarchy are usually a neglected lot. They work hard in poor work environment. Their work is not much appreciated, yet they bear the brunt of organisational work. The police constable, for instance, has to put in hard labour, yet the police station does not provide much of amenities. Nor is his work appreciated by the higher officers. The public image is also of corruption and inaction. The constable's promotion prospect is generally bleak.

In view of the organisational importance of the bottom line workers—the street-level bureaucracy, their characteristics have attracted research attention. Lipsky has noted three important characteristics of this type of bureaucracy:

1. *They are the* front-line staff, *stationed at the bottom of the organisation.*
2. They interact directly with the citizens and often (as in the case of the village level worker) advises the client or *delivers service to the client.*
3. Despite their lower status, they exercise considerable discretion in respect of contacting the citizens and delivering services to them. For instance, it is well known that the police constable may or may not intervene in a local problem-situation.
4. They—the street-level bureaucrats—are not easily amenable to higher level supervision. Although the organisational hierarchy, at least on paper, provides for formal supervision, the location of the front-line worker and his nature of work are such that supervision, in reality, is missing or minimal.
5. Acknowledging the crucial role of the street-level bureaucracy, it has been aptly remarked that this type of bureaucracy would be having a major influence on policy in relation to service as delivered to citizens. "For them policy is not a grand scheme or abstract principle but a constant set of small-scale choice in how to deal with specific individuals in specific settings".
6. Last but not the least, as the lower level bureaucrats exercise discretion, the general trend is towards attending to the calls of the rich and the influential and neglecting the needs of the poor and the down-and-out.

Representative Bureaucracy

The concept of 'representative bureaucracy' has been set against that of neutral bureaucracy. The meaning of representative bureaucracy is not quite clear. It may mean civil service representing proportionately every economic class, caste or religion constituting the population mosaic of a country. Another interpretation has been that it is a bureaucracy consisting of all the social, religious and racial component groups in a society recruited on the basis of ability"[10] For instance, in India reservation of jobs in public service has been provided for the Scheduled Castes and Scheduled Tribes in the ratio of 15% and 7½%

respectively on the basis of the percentage share of each group in the total population of the country as per the 1961 census. Such reservation has been constitutionally guaranteed under Article 16 (4) of the Indian Constitution.

Two important assumptions behind the concept of representative bureaucracy are that (a) all groups have more or less equal political power and rights in accordance with their proportion and (b) the civil servants carry their class attitudes and prejudices into their official positions. As regards the first assumption, political power is nowhere equally shared by all groups in a society, nor is political power structured along the line of microscopic social groups. The second assumption is equally questionable. Attitudes and prejudices of tho civil servant are formed not merely by his location in original social space. These are shaped by such dominant influences as experience on the job, education and socialisation as a member of the bureaucracy. The cause of *harijan* welfare can be best looked after only by a *harijan* civil servant is by no means self-evident. As observed by a critic:

"We are familiar with aristocrats and rich heirs who have passionate sympathy for the working class. On the other hand, the proportion of deviants among the members of the lower classes who work their way up is held by many observers to be high.... It has been suggested that the men who climb out of the lower classes, the upward-mobiles, under present conditions any way, shed their class sympathies either at the beginning of the climb itself or halfway through. The proven existence of deviants from class norms and the probability of their high proportion among recruits from the lower classes, shakes to the foundations the basic argument for representative bureaucracy".[11]

In a plural society with many ethnic, linguistic and religious groups, the concept of a representative bureaucracy would have ominous repercussions. In the composition of the civil service, to emphasise social class identity is to invite parochialism and narrow group interests. The civil service itself will then be a house divided within itself.

Last but not the least, "a system of recruitment that takes into consideration ascribable factors undermines the rationality and logic on which a sound recruitment system is based".'[12]

Representative bureaucracy, in a way, is a contradiction in terms. Bureaucratic identity is based on professional homogeneity.To introduce social heterogeneity is to destroy bureaucracy.

Neutrality versus Commitment

Coming back to the concept of a neutral bureaucracy, three important preconditions of neutrality are (a) cultural or class congruence between the ruling political group and the administrative elite (b) absence of any fundamental disagreement over societal core values and (c) presence of a shared belief system. Kingsley, as quoted earlier, pointed out the first phenomenon in the British political system and the third has been well brought out in a study of Malaysian bureaucracy that shows a common concern among top politicians and senior bureaucrats about the maintenance of law and order. The second precondition is fulfilled by most of the democracies in the West.

By contrast, the developing countries differ sharply from their Western counterparts on all the three counts.The social distance and cultural differences between the ruling political group and the administrative elite are considerable. The two groups do not have a -hared belief system. This is especially true of most of the new nations that have emancipated themselves from western colonialism. There is a hangover of the old imperial culture in the higher echelons of the bureaucracy that is in sharp contrast with the newly emergent political culture demanding speedy socio-economic development and distributive justice. Consensus on social values does not exist in most of the developing nations. In most cases contending groups clash among themselves on the fundamental goals of social reconstruction and on the methods to achieve them.

Neutrality, unde: the circumstances, can be another name for *inertia* and status quo maintenance. Comparing the neutrality of the civil service in Britain and India, a keen observer of the Indian scene has commented thus:

"British genius was given all credit for combining virtues of neutral permanent civil service with the democratic philosophy of competition and alternation of political parties. It was forgotten that neutral, value-free bureaucrat was possible in a society where consensus existed on values but in transitional societies, where situations of dissent and conflict existed, it was too much to expect anyone to be neutral... Can bureaucracy serve all sorts of parties, whose one point spectrum is the CPI (M) and the other Swatantra? Can bureaucracy be neutral while serving secular parties and non-secular parties? Further, what is possible in one society, may not be universally possible. Hence, examples of British practices in this sphere are irrelevant because the social situation in Britain is absolutely different from that in India".[13]

Incidentally, the neutrality concept even in the context of the British civil service has come in for severe attack. Brian Chapman dismisses it as a 'myth' and points out two dangerous aspects of this myth. In reality, the top civil servant is deeply involved in the making of political decisions. Under cover of the myth of neutrality, the civil servants are protected "from the awkward enquiry and demands for justification of motives to which they should be subjected by parliament:, the press and the public."The second danger, according to Chapman, is much more serious. "Neutrality in public office tends in the end to moral corruption. If all governments are to be served with equal impartiality and loyalty there are no grounds at all for criticizing the German official who served Hitler to the best of his ability. In any profession other than government such people would be regarded as dangerous cynics or weaklings".[14]

Neutral bureaucracy, like the concept of bureaucracy itself, seems a highly idealised notion. In actual management of public affairs, the civil servants, especially those at higher, echelons of administration are professionally involved in political decision making. Reality in administration, therefore, refutes neutrality. Moreover, bureaucracy as a group has its own aims and interests. Like any other interest group in society, the bureaucracy is actively involved in the political process in pursuit of class interests.

For developing countries like India where speedy socio-economic development has to be steadily pushed through, the nature and character of bureaucracy assume special significance. The first problem is how to 'declass' a bureaucracy, the. culturally belonged to the colonial era and served the imperial interest. As the Indian experience shows, the colonial administrative structure was allowed to continue even after independence and it was thought that the changed political leadership and institutional framework coupled with proper training and motivation would bring about desired 'cultural' changes in the bureaucracy. .

Another allied issue has been to separate 'development' activities from law and order maintenance and differentiate between 'development bureaucracy' and traditional bureaucracy. For instance, a recent Indian study on the bureaucracy in development of administration suggested that bureaucracies involved in development at the field level, such as agricultural development, tended to be structurally less rigid and behaviourally more flexible than headquarter bureaucracies.[15] The changing role of bureaucracy in the development of administration is characterised in such phrases as 'development bureaucracy' and 'non-Weberian model of bureaucracy'. What is intended is to make the governmental organisations, structurally and behaviourally, geared to the tasks of development.[16]

Bureaucratic performance has been criticised in India since the early days of economic planning. Soon after assuming prime-ministership, Jawaharlal Nehru criticised the civil servants as being 'fossilised in their mental outlook'.[17] Later day critics became more vociferous in singling out the bureaucracy as the main cause of sluggish growth of the economy. It was argued that the conservative and orthodox leadership of the ICS with its upper class prejudices was unequal to the task of socio-economic change along socialist lines. "The creation of an administrative cadre committed to rational objectives and responsive to our social needs is an urgent necessity".[18] Prime Minister Indira Gandhi, at one stage, characterised the administrative machinery as the stumbling block to national progress and wanted "government servants with commitment—to the development of the country and personal involvement in the tasks".[19]

A rather unclear concept *of 'committed bureaucracy'*[20] was born out of this debate over unsatisfactory bureaucratic performance. It came to be looked at as an attempt to create a 'politicised' bureaucracy and commitment was interpreted in terms of acceptance of an ideology and attachment to one political party. Clarifying her stand, Prime Minister Indira Gandhi emphatically denied that she wanted politically committed or servile government employees. What she meant was that the civil servants should be committed to the objectives of the state and should have faith in the programmes they are to execute. Shri Jagjivan Ram, a senior politician and then an important Central Minister, explained the meaning of commitment thus: "...The commitment of a civil servant extends to establish a society in which there will be no exploitation, a society in which every citizen will be provided with equality of opportunity, a society which endeavours to break the past shackles, which discriminated between one citizen and another. It is this broad commitment which is the cornerstone of the edifice and not attachment to any particular party in power. So far as the party in power is concerned, the concept that the civil servant advises the political authority fearlessly and without any consideration whether the advice is accepted or rejected, should prevail."[21]

Since the developing countries are engaged in rapid socio-economic transformation under the leadership of the government of the day, public administration has necessarily a very crucial role to play in this drama of national development. The involvement of civil servants in numerous decisions, be it the location of a steel plant or the setting of a village school building, makes them, partners in development along with the politicians. Questions of value get inextricably mixed up with technical, professional advice. Commitment, in such circumstances, assumes a new meaning and a new significance. The civil servant need not be partisan in his approach but he must have the empathy to understand the mind of a bonafide politician seeking seriously to find a way out of centuries of under development and exploitation. He need not fight shy of being 'politicised' in the sense that politics in the Aristotelian tradition is concerned with social architecture. If the concept of committed bureaucracy stands for the social sensitivity of the civil servant, it is much better to have a committed civil servant than an insensitive, neutral one.

Commitment to social objectives is one thing and to dance to the tune of a political party is another. *"Politicised bureaucracy" seems* apparently an immaculate conception. Bureaucracy has traditionally been conceived in instrumental term (a la Max Weber). It is by definition .a non-political tool to be used by whosoever would be in power in a political system characterised by political competition and party substitutability. A bureaucracy that is "politicised" can be thought of as a different phenomenon deserving to be called differently. The political framework within which such a phenomenon appears is also different. Fainsod's definition of party-state bureaucracy, mentioned earlier, comes closest to this phenomenon. This is a by-product of a totalitarian one-party dominated political system where a monolithic party plays the transcendent role. In such a system, the party penetrates, controls and dominates the bureaucracy so much so that the two are almost indistinguishable. Between technical excellence and political beliefs, the choice is clearly in favour of the latter.[22]

A 'politicised bureaucracy' in a multi-party democracy is an administrative aberration and exemplifies deviant behaviour, if by politicisation is meant[23] involvement of the civil service in party activities (e.g. canvassing for a party in an election) and bending the laws, rules and regulations for the promotion of narrow party interests. Such partisan activities of the civil servant are considered unethical and are not sustainable in law, at least in India, as these are in violation of the civil service conduct rules. The very fact that these activities are usually indulged in secretly for fear of hostile public Reaction and possible court action testifies to their shady character outside the normal run of bureaucratic business. Politicisation, in this sense, should, however, be differentiated from the genuine professional help rendered to the political executive by the top civil servant. Here the real issue is that of political responsiveness of the bureaucracy irrespective of alternation of parties in power. The difference between political responsiveness and politicisation may not always be very clear. The former is an attitude of mind to try to understand the values and social philosophy of the political executive and to offer professional advice fearlessly and frankly in the light of the governing philosophy. The final decision,is that of the political executive. The administrator in this situation, to quote Peter Selfs apt expression, is not so much "a political eunuch as a political chameleon."[24] A politicised civil servant, by contrast, covertly serves the interests of the political party. His style is marked by undue secrecy and breach of established rules and procedures and the objective he serves tends to be narrow private interest, as distinguished from general public interest. To recapitulate, the discussions so far have yielded four organising concepts: neutral bureaucracy, representative bureaucracy, committed bureaucracy and politicised bureaucracy. These are useful guide-posts to an undertaking of the relationships between the administrator and the politician. Their respective roles may, however, be better appreciated referring to what actually takes place in the decision making process.

Areas and Modes of Interaction

The politicians interact with the bureaucracy in different forums in various ways. As legislators, they take part in debates and discussions on the floor of legislature and in many committees of the legislature. As ministers they head the government departments and manage the administrative business. Often the politicians also play the brokerage role by acting as intermediaries between interest groups and the administration. Peter Self identifies four important areas of interaction between the politicians and the administrators. These are:

i) Policy making,
ii) The arbitration of interests,
iii) The treatment of individual and localised claims,
iv) The balance between political accountability and administrative discretion.

As Professor Self observes, "In the first two cases, politicians possess formal responsibility but administrators supply the missing elements of political decisions. In the third case, administrators defend their distinctive methods of uniformity against politicians' frequent interest in influencing particular decisions. The fourth case represents an inevitable point of conflict between the needs and interests of Aie two groups" [25]

Politicians influence *policies* by sensing public demands and making these into election promises. After coming to power, they are expected to formulate government policies to honour their election pledges. Elections are often fought on rhetoric and seemingly ideological grounds rather than on clear-cut policy issues. Still some wide-ranging promises such as removaj of poverty and more welfare measures for the scheduled castes and tribes or land reforms are sought to be translated into public policies. The members of the legislature influence policy-making in a limited way through legislative debates and participation in legislative committees.The civil servant has his own quota of influence at the time of actual framing of the formal policy document. The senior civil servant has the- advantage of long years of experience. Besides, he has the professional skill to put ideas into practice. The policy document is his handiwork. When the minister remains busy in nursing his constituency or managing 'politics' outside, the civil servant initiates policies and gets these approved as an administrative ritual. Other influences come from a variety of sources such as advisory committees, expert group reports and interest group representation.

Arbitration of interests is palpably a political act which falls within the province of the politician. Individual politicians, the political party and the legislature engage in arbitration functions of various kinds. In their constituencies, the politicians often intervene in group disputes. More powerful interest groups like labour, industry, big landlords and even some bureaucratic groups try to tilt public policy in their favour, or at least have their viewpoints ventilated through the mediation of influential politicians. Political parties are expected to aggregate group interests and synthesize them. But parties are rarely homogeneous entities. There may be sympathisers of both labour and capital, the landless and the big landlord in a single party. Political debates within the party bring these interests to the surface and attempts are made, in the interest of party loyalty, to reach compromises and balance the different group demands. The legislature formally does not reveal the presence of group interests and their bargaining process. The different interest groups, whenever their cause has to be defended, get their interests smuggled in through the parties, individual members and senior members of the bureaucracy. The administrators get involved in interest group politics both overtly and covertly. When they receive memoranda and visiting groups representing different interests they deal with group interests in course of their normal official business. There are usually many consultative committees attached to the ministries which act as conduits for the flow of group interests within the administration. Besides, the arbitrative role of the bureaucracy is formally defined by labour legislations and senior civil servants sit in arbitration in labour-management disputes. The government's arbitrative role is quite wide-ranging in developing countries with many ethnic, linguistic and religious groups constituting their social mosaic. When group conflicts erupt, arbitrators are freely chosen from various sources by the government. Leading party members, opposition members, legislators, senior civil servants all are pressed into service on different issues.[26]

Politics of Planning

Planning, as Peter Self points out, has the effect of "foreclosing and reducing the capacity of politicians to effect variable arbitrations and compromises between interests."[27] The process of planning may, of course, take account of the needs of different interest groups and seek to harmonise and balance the various demands. But once a plan document is prepared, the scope for interference by the politician gets considerably reduced. The implementation stage, however, remains exposed to political influences. Planning tells us "what" is to be done and implementation is concerned with "how" the plan objectives have to be realised in practice. As the Indian planning experience shows, the brokerage role of the politician does not end at the planning stage; it extends up to implementation e.g. block development planning may allocate resources among the different sectors such as irrigation, animal husbandry etc. When it comes to actually spending the money on the ground, political interference takes the form of clientele manipulation and site (village) manipulation. The influences (brokerage) come not only from the much-maligned politician but also from the members of the field bureaucracy.

Bureaucratic rule adherence and political intervention in the interest of the client often clash with each other. The relationship between the politician and the administrator tends to move toward a collision course in a situation where the politician is keen to "help" his supporters and constituency members by disregarding bureaucratic rules and regulations.The politician is constantly pestered by supporters for some benefit or the other. It is also in the interest of the politician that the constituency should be nursed properly.As he approaches the administration on behalf of his clients, many a time he finds the bureaucracy "unhelpful" and unwilling to accommodate his requests. Patronage and corruption are closely associated with frequent and numerous concessions that are obtained for their clients by the politician in violation of rules and procedures. The administrator, at the other end, takes shelter under rules and regulations and the general expression of disapproval is that "my hands are tied."

The political weight of the demanding politician does, of course, untie the hands of the bureaucrat occasionally as the latter weighs the pros and cons of his action in terms of his own career prospect in the coming years. There is in this relationship room for genuine differences between the politician and the administrator. The role perception of the politician is different from that of the administrator. The politician is the link-man between the people and the administration and it is his normal job to carry the demands to the appropriate government organisation. The administrator has similarly to function in accordance with the ground rules of his own profession. He has to follow the laws and regulations in treating the "cases" brought before him. In situations of scarcity, the administration has to bear a heavier demand load than what it can actually accommodate. This is true of many developing countries. Both politics and administration are, naturally, to bear the growing burden of public demands. Conscious efforts are needed both by the politician and the administrator to develop 'norms' of mutually acceptable political and administrative conduct. Mutual recrimination is damaging for both, as their images get tarnished equally badly in frequent skirmishes before the public gaze.

The administrator needs autonomy and discretion in much the same way as the politician needs control and intervention.There is thus an mherent clash in public administration between political control and administrative autonomy.The administrator's preference for autonomy might stem from his respect for rules and regulations and uniformity and from his genuine concern for speed and promptitude. The politician from this perspective is a stumbling block in the way of disciplined and expeditious action. On the part of the politician, the administrator might appear as an interloper and a competitor.The politician perceives himself as the ultimate controller of administrative affairs and the real guardian of the public interest. When the administrator wants autonomy and discretion, the politician looks at him as a usurper of political power and an unwanted intruder in the domain of the politician. Cultural disparities (e.g. rural vs. urban) often exacerbate misunderstanding between the two. In developing countries like India, the colonial legacy tends to persist, that public interest is best served by the bureaucrat. Under the thin veneer of seeming acceptability lurks a suspicion of the politician '-hat often turns into explicit hostility.

Political control over the bureaucracy is exercised through the legislature and its committees, apart from the normal ministerial control over the departmental business. Legislative control depends for its effectiveness on a variety of factors such as party composition, legislators' skill, expertise, time and bureaucracy s willingness to part with information. Generally, the departments tend to give out as little as possible, whereas the legislators demand as much as possible.

Effective ministerial control also depends on the intellectual calibre and administrative experience of the minister. Normally most ministers keep busy in politics and can afford little time for administration. The dependence on the civil servant, under the circumstances, is considerable. The acid test of a minister's statesmanship lies in how much he can delegate to the civil servant without losing policy control in key areas of concern.The civil servant, in turn, can serve the minister well if he tries genuinely to enter into the mind of the minister and presents policy alternatives for his final choice. Proposals for administrative action are likely to be accepted if these are submitted in the form of"built-in hedges against risks and uncertainty." In the latter case, the suggestion is to go by stages and experiments which might appeal to the politician better than a rounded and rigid plan of action.

Top Management Level

The top level management is virtually the vanishing point of politics-administration dichotomy. Governmental power is used and directed from the topmost level, where the minister and his secretary and other top advisers have close relationships in the course of identification of problems and framing of public policies. The political executive and the professional civil servant work in close collaboration with each other at the highest level. The ministers occupy position by dint of their political stature, while the senior civil servants hold the positions because of seniority and merit. As Peter Self observes[28], there are significant structural patterns at the top managerial level that "have an obvious effect upon the actual relations between political executives and administrators and upon the ability of the political leadership to get its way".The structural patterns are woven around (a) how members of the two groups come to occupy their respective positions, (b) how sharply the political and administrative roles are differentiated and (c) how far the two groups differ in the degree of cohesiveness in terms of stored beliefs, attitudes and common ties. In addition, the structure of top management is conditioned by the cultural background of the politician and the administrator and their levels of maturity born out of length of experience on the job. The structure is also a product of history that leaves its indelible mark on the participants in the process of management.

Historically, Indian administration, during most part of British rule, was in the hands of the members of the elite cadre of generalist officers, the Indian Civil Service.The politicians were slowly inducted into administration under the Acts of 1919 and 1935. The hegemonic status of the top bureaucracy remained, however, virtually unaltered. It was a "ruler bureaucracy" well-organised and all powerful that framed policies and enforced them with all the support of the Imperial power. After Independence, the roles have been formally reversed.The politician is on top and the administrator is on tap. After Independence, the Indian Administrative Service was modelled on the old ICS pattern. A generalist elite cadre, to maintain historical continuity, has been managing the government at the secretariat and field levels. The administrative culture of British Raj with its built-in hegemonic status of top bureaucracy has thus been hard to erase completely. The relationship between the political executive and the 'senior civil servant, in India has therefore to be understood in the context of the history of the bureaucratic state and the continued existence of an elite corps occupying crucial positions in government.

Under the parliamentary system of government, the superiority of the minister and the subordination of the secretary are axiomatic. It has been a painfully protracted learning experience for the senior civil servant in the course of which, he had to unlearn his past role and accept the politician as his bo'ss. In practice, the civil servant has often regarded the politician as a usurper and an unwanted element. The psychology of avoidance and latent-hatred has also been fostered by institutional arrangements. At the district level, the young IAS officer is the monarch of all that he surveys and he is slowly socialised in a combined role of a politician and an administrator. As he climbs up the service ladder, no sharp differentiation is made between the two roles. Talking about the Malayan bureaucracy, Milne made a similar observation:

"The 'western' view of democracy is that the politicians who constitute the government have been chosen by the people and the civil servants who have not been so chosen were really in a subordinate position. However, in some developing countries which claim to be generally democratic in the western-sense, this relationship may not hold. It may not always be obvious exactly who is a politician and who is a civil servant and in so far as it is discernible, it may not always be the 'politician' who is in control".[30]

The members of the higher civil service, the IAS, cannot be said to be a homogeneous group. They represent the linguistic, religious, caste and regional diversities of India. The members of the service constitute a motley crowd of direct recruits, promotees from state services, special and emergency recruits. There are reserved seats for the scheduled castes and scheduled tribes also. The heterogeneity of the service personnel is not conducive to the development of an *espirit de corps* so badly needed for a top management group like the IAS. The training programme at Mussoorie, initially, used to be for a mixed group of officers from the IAS, Central Services and IPS etc. Professional training for the IAS group exclusively continues for a period of about seven months.This is followed by on-the-job training at state attachments. The duration, design and contents of the training programme cannot be said to be ideal for building up a cadre of top management personnel.[31] Professional pride born out of rigorous management training is not what keeps the group members together. It is basically positional power that keeps the group going. No doubt, there are exceptions to this and surely one can cite a few examples of extraordinary administrative talent that one is bound to witness in a large group. By and large, however, the top management group holds almost an ascribable position as its members tend naturally to climb up by merely being born in a cadre.

With the avowed purpose of maintaining integrity, discipline and political neutrality, the Civil Services Conduct Rules lay down the code of conduct for the civil servant. As the Rules provide:

(a) No member of the service shall be a member of, or be otherwise associated with, any political party or any organisation, which takes part in politics nor shall he take part in, subscribe in aid of, or assist in any other manner, any political movement or activity, (b) It shall be the duty of every member of the service to endeavour to prevent any member of the tamily from taking part in, subscribing in aid of, or assisting in any other manner, any movement or activity which is, or tends directly to be, subversive of the Government as by law established and where a member of the service fails to prevent a member of his family from indulging in any of the aforesaid actions, he shall make a report to that effect to the Government, (c) No member of the service shall canvass or otherwise interfere or use his influence in connection with, or take any part in any election to any legislature or local authority, (d) A member of the service qualified to vote in elections may exercise his right to vote but where he does so, he shall give no indication of the manner in which he proposes to vote or has voted, (e) No member of the service shall, in any radio broadcast or in any document published anonymously or in his own name, or in the name of any other person, or in any communication to the press or in any public utterance make any statement of fact or opinion, (i) which has the effect of an adverse criticism of any current or recent policy or action of the Central Government or a State Government or (ii) which is capable of embarrassing the relations between the Central Government and the Government of any state or (iii) which is capable of embarrassing the relations between the Central Government and Government of any foreign state.

One would expect that the top bureaucracy will be socialised in these norms and will behave in the manner as prescribed in the rules. The reality is, however, very different from what the rules prescribe. As an expert, on Indian administration observes:

"The distressing fact today is that the civil service has lost its elan/and is itself not professional, ready to do anything or everything in the expectation of a reward, or for fear of, say, transfers. The various commissions of inquiry set up by both the Central and State Governments have dutifully confirmed the existence of civil servants who have not bothered about the prevalent laws and professional propriety and freely aligned themselves with the political executive in cynical disregard of public interest."[32]

This may be a very sweeping statement about a group of top managers not all of whom have certainly succumbed to pressures and temptations.

Endemic lawlessness, if it continues unabated, may steadily lead to the disintegration of the administrative class and its ultimate extinction.

At the other end, the ministers are no angels. Political parties in India have not always had steady followers. Nor have they evolved norms of behaviour in their dealings with the bureaucracy and the public. Drawn from diverse cultural, linguistic and regional background, the ministers have had their prejudices and predilections that have occasionally influenced their relationships with the top bureaucracy. The public image of the integrity of ministers has not always been very bright. To quote the Santhanam Committee on Prevention of Corruption:

"There is a widespread impression that failure of integrity is not uncommon among ministers and that some ministers who held office during the last 16 years have enriched themselves illegitimately, obtained good jobs for their sons and relations through nepotism and have reaped other advantages inconsistent with any notion of purity in public life." Fortunately, able and honest ministers have been coexisting with quick-rich and venal types. The quality and character of the minister (being the superior) determines the nature of relationships that develop with the civil servant. Commenting on the relationships between the minister and the secretary, the Administrative Reforms Commission noted that at times differences in approach and manner of work had been the cause of strain between the two. According to the Commission, strains have also arisen sometimes in the personal relationships between the minister and the secretary. To quote the Commission:

"There is a disinclination among quite a number of Ministers to welcome frank and impartial advice from the Secretary or his aid and an inclination to judge him by his willingness to do what they wish him to do. Instances are not wanting of ministers preferring a convenient subordinate to a strong one and thereby making the latter not only ineffective but a sulky and unwilling worker. This has also bred a tendency on the part of an increasing number of civil servants to attempt to anticipate the ministers wishes and proffer their advice accordingly. A further development of this unhealthy trend is the emergence of personal affiliations leading to an element of 'politicisation' among the civil servants."[33]

Armed with powers of transfer and suspension, the minister can browbeat the civil servant and ask him to fall in line. He can also distribute favours differentially. Very few civil servants are able to withstand the pressures or forgo the temptations.

In his analysis of the relationship between the minister and civil servant, Maheshwari points to a pessimistic future. As he concludes,

The relationship between the political and the permanent executive has come to be characterised by a growing feeling of uneasiness, even suspicion and a civil servants uppermost consideration, today, is to play safe and to show only routine initiative and drive in his work. This breeds a tendency for over-consultation and most matters are pushed upward for decision-making.[34]

This is no doubt an alarming trend. For the bureaucracy the contemporary political scenario presents uncertainties, contradictions and genuine problems of adjustment. The future depends on the extent of resilience it can display in the years to come.

In times of despair it is customary to fall back on British examples. As Peter Self explains the British situation, the political-administrative distinction in Britain is well understood and each of the groups is highly cohesive. The general administrators forming the elite group *of* the civil service have maintained a long "tradition of common belief, attitudes and ethics."[35] The general administrator's forte in Britain is his understanding of the wholeness of government and an awareness of ministerial responsibility. Showing a peculiar mixture of compliance and independence, the general administrator as confidential policy adviser to the minister is expected to speak out and then shut up. On the question of relationship between the minister and the permanent secretary, Peter Self observes:

"The senior official has to give not only a personal view (where appropriate) but an accumulated departmental one. Further, his views must be completely innocent of personal alignment with any political party. His task here is not so much to be a political eunuch as a political chameleon He has to enter sympathetically into the political aims of whatever government is in power, as a duty pointing out all the difficulties' in the way of their realisation but resolutely prepared to try and circumvent them if he is so required."

The relationship is thus characterised by flexibility and pragmatism and the minister-administrator partnership is really a coalition of amateurs.

The Fulton Committee on the Civil Service (1968) found the senior administrators in Britain mostly engaged in policy advisory and coordinating roles. Few administrators thought that they were managers.[36] At the highest level, the administrator is expected to understand the wholeness of government and to give advice on policy matters in the larger political context. Organisational management by means of a battery of techniques is a middle management job. It is policy management which is expected of the top echelons of the bureaucracy.

The American federal government is unique in having a changing class of top political executives who join their jobs along with the new President after a presidential election They are personally selected by the President to act as his close advisers, subject to confirmation by the Senate. Most of them belong to the same party as the President. The top executives are drawn from a variety of sources such as business and financial institutions, legal profession, universities and public service.The selection process is obviously guided by considerations of managerial skill and acceptance of the broad political philosophy of the new regime. Ability to get on well with the President and the Congress is of course a prime consideration.

The presidential top advisers are thus temporary incumbents who come and go with the President. In this system, recruitment of the right kind of persons becomes as much problematic as maintaining continuity in top management. The advantages of this system need also to be acknowledged. The President has a fairly free hand to have his own men to manage the executive branch.The top executives share the President's political views. It is thus an openly partisan machinery of administration that is installed after every presidential election. With professional experts at the top, the highest level of management may not however be sensitive to the larger political issue of the day. The top executives may not work always as a cohesive group, as they are drawn from different walks of life and do not represent a general administrative class as in Britain or India. Still, the American system of political executives has worked reasonably well in the political environment of that country.

The top management in France presents a still more interesting picture of bureaucratic ascendancy. The style of government in France is much more bureaucracy-oriented, as the French bureaucracy, well before the Fifth Republic had emerged as the custodian of public interest in the face of frequent political instability. More like the American system, a French minister has a cabinet of his own with the help of which he manages his department. Traditionally, the minister's cabinet used to consist of his politic al supporters. Over the years, however, the cabinet posts have been bureaucratized and these are now occupied by career officials. Thus, in France career executives occupy positions which are clearly political in nature. French public administration is much more permissive in the matter of politicisation of the higher echelons of the civil service. The civil servants are permitted to contest in parliamentary elections and on being elected they can "keep their civil service rights in storage. Political activities of officials as mayors or councillors of local bodies are culturally accepted."[37]

These illustrations from a variety of political systems highlight the importance of 'politics' at the higher levels of government. The structure of top management in various countries has tried differently to arrange politics-administration relationships. There are distinct cultural peculiarities and administrative traditions across the nations that strongly influence the use of politics in the management of governmental affairs at higher levels. The examples certainly point out that in public administration politics is not such an ugly word as it is often made out to be.

REFERENCES

1. Woodrow Wilson, "The Study of Administration, *PoliticalScience*Quarterly,June1887,vol.2,pp.197-222.
2. The Weberian theory of bureaucracy has been fully discussed in the Chapter on Bureaucratic Theory.
3. Joseph La Palombara, "Bureaucracy and Political Development: Notrs, Queries and Dilemmas", in Joseph La Palombara (ed.), Bureaucracy and *Political Development,* Princeton University Press, 1963.
4. Merle Fainsod, "Bureaucracy and Modernization. The Russian and Soviet Case", in Joseph La Palombara (ed.) op. cit.
5. This term carries a different meaning and should not be confused with Kingsley's concept of "representative bureaucracy".
6. GabrielA.Almond,"ResearchNote:AComparative StudyofGroupsandthePoliticalProcess",*American Political Science Review,* March 1958, pp. 279-280.
7. J.Donald Kingsley, Representative Bureaucracy: *An Interpretation of the British Civil Seance,* Antioch Press, Ohio, 1944, p. 278.
8. Mavis Puthucheary, *The Politics of Administration: The Malaysian, Experience,* OUP, Kuala Lumpur, 1978, p. 49.
9. This has proved true of the higher echelons of the Civil Service in India. See in this connection, V. Subramaniam, *Social Background of India's Administrators,* Government of India, Publication Division, 1971; and C. P. Bhambhri, *Administrators in a Changing Society,* National Publishing House, Delhi, 1972.
10. The concept of representative bureaucracy has been related to situation ui a well-written article: Haridwar Rai and Sakendra Prasad "Indian Bureaucracy: A Case for Representativeness", *The Indian Journal of Administration,* January-March, 1973,Vol. XIX, No. 1.
11. V. Subramaniam, 'Representative Bureaucracy: A Reassessment', *American Political Science* Review, Vol. 67, No. 4, December, 1967.
12. Mavis Puthucheary, op. cit., p.64.
13. C.P. Bhambhri, "Some Aspects, of Indian Bureaucracy", paper presented at the International Seminar on Imperialism, independence and Social TransformationintheContemporaryWorld,24-29 March, 1972, New Delhi.
14. Brian Chapman, *The Profession of* Government, George Allen *and* Unwin Ltd., London, 1963, p. 275.
15. VA.PaiPanandikerandS.S.Kshirsagar,*Bureaucracy and Development Administration,* Centre for Policy Research, New Delhi. 1978.
16. Mohit Bhattacharya, *Bureaucracy and Development Administration,* Uppal Publishing House, New Delhi, 1979. p. 13.
17. Nehru's ideas on the bureaucracy and public *administration can be* found in: *Jawaharlal Nehru and*

Public Administration, The Indian Institute of Public Administration, New Delhi.

18. Quoted in Bhambhri, *Administrators in a Changing Society,* National Publishing House. Delhi, 1972, p. 24.
19. See in this connection R. B. Jain, *Contemporary Issues in Indian Administration,* Vishal Publications, Delhi, 1976, pp. 175-6.
20. See, in this connection, T.N. *Chaturvedi, Commitment in the Civil Service.* Government of India, Department of Personnel Training, Monograph, 1975.
21. Jagjivan Ram, "The Role of Indian Administrator Today", *The Indian Journal of Public Administration,* Vol. XXI, No. 2, April-June, 11375.
22. See in this connection, M. K. Whyte, "Bureaucracy and Modernization in China:The Maoist Critique", *American Sociological Review, 38,* 1973, pp. 149-163.
23. See R, B. Jain, "Politicization of Bureaucracy: A Framework for Comparative Measurement", *The Indian Journal of Public Administration,* Vol.XX, No. 4, October-December, 1974.
24. Op. cit., p. 165.
25. Op.cit., p. 153.
26. For example, Mr. Jaisukhlal Hathi, the Governor of Punjab, was invited to arbitrate in the case of the conflict between anti-reservationists and pre-servationists in Gujarat recently.
27. Op. cit., p. 157.
28. The differences in role perceptions are well brought out in Shanti Kothari and Ramashray Roy, *Relations between Politicians and Administrators at the District Level,* Indian Institute of Public Administration, New Delhi, 1969.
29. Op.cit., p. 163.
30. R.S. Milne, Government and Politics in Malaysia, Houghton Mifflin, Boston 1967, p. 157.
31. See, in this connection, C. Bhambhari, Administrators in a Changing Society, National Publishing House, Delhi, 1972, Chapters 5 and 7.
32. Shriram Maheshwari, "The Political Executive and the Permanent Executive: An Analysis of the Emerging Role Patterns". *The Indian Journal of Public Administration,* Vol.XXVI, No.3, July-September, 1980.
33. ARC Report, Op.cit., pp.20-23.
34. Op.cit.
35. Op.cit., p.165.
36. The Civil Service, vol.l, Cmnd. 3633. H.M.S.O., London, 1969.
37. See in this connection, Jean Bilondel, *The Government of France,* Methuen & Co. Ltd., London, 1977, Chapter 8.

Chapter 13

Public Administration and the Public

The instrumentalist view of the machinery and process of government treats public as the recipient of administrative help. A more participative view would place the public at the centre of administration as a decider and the prime mover. In the first view, the public constitutes the client, in the second the agent.

Interaction Typology

Public administration exists for the provision of "public goods" such as law and order maintenance, defence of the political community and so on. Also public administrative activities are concerned with provision of basic services such as health, education, economic security etc. There are many real life situations in which the members of the public interact with public administrative agencies. Analytically, these interactions may be grouped into five main overlapping categories:

1. *Clients:* A most commop form of interaction with public administrative agencies is the "client" form. Here, the essence of the client role is that the citizens seek to obtain a benefit or a service from a public agency. In concrete form, a patient visits a government hospital, for instance, for health check-up.
2. *Regulatee:* As regulatee, the public interacts with many public agencies like the police, income tax authorities, licensing authorities etc. The public has, on many occasions, to submit to various kinds of government regulation in normal course of living.
3. *Litigants:* It is not uncommon to see 'harassed' citizens seeking redressal from the courts. The municipal authority may have withheld building permission; the motor vehicles authority may be delaying issuance of a car license; income tax authorities may have imposed unreasonable tax rates. In all these cases, the affected public moves the courts against "unjust" actions of public agencies.
4. *Cutting-edge level Encounters:* The public interacts more intimately with public agencies at the 'cutting edge' level. Local government, for instance, affects people s lives in various ways. Water supply may have been inadequate and irregular; street lights may not be working, garbage may not have been collected and disposed of. The citizens would, in all these instances, approach the municipal employees who are responsible for these services and facilities. The policeman on beat patrol may be approached by a passer-by for help.

These kinds of interactions are of daily occurrences and the ordinary citizens form opinion about public administration out of these happy/ unhappy interactions.

5. *Participating:* Democracy means people's participation in governance. This theoretical postulate is actually translated into action by structuring participation institutionally and programmatically. A school will be having parents' or guardians' committee; an irrigation project will be associating the farmers with different decision-making processes of the project. The current trend in public administration is toward more and more participative decision-making in public agencies at different levels. It is now widely accepted that public participation democratises administration and brings in new inputs that help sound project designing, implementation and facilitate asset maintenance.

Development Administration

These interaction typologies are helpful in understanding the varieties of ways of people-administration encounters. In the field of development administration, the client typology is further differentiated on the basis of classification of "target" groups. Thus, there are projects that are tailor made for tribals, children and women, scheduled castes and other socially backward classes. Clientele differentiation increases the complexities of interaction between public administration and the public. In the third world situation, it is the poor and the underprivileged who constitute the majority of the population. Nationally conceived development projects have been implemented locally by the technical experts and the field bureaucracy has been treating the target groups as "beneficiaries". Such top-down delivery system has, in most cases, failed to ameliorate the living conditions of the poor. Apart from hijacking of benefits and resources by the village powerful, the centrally planned projects have often disregarded local needs and conditions. The result has been project failure and people's disillusionment about government measures that are ill-suited to local conditions.

People-government interaction, in dealing with mass poverty, has traditionally been looked at from the government end, making the poor more and more dependent on government help. Field researchers are now forcefully arguing that developing people's own capacity to improve their lot is what is needed and not repeated government efforts to design newer and newer projects. As Frances Korten[1] has made the point:

"The very ability of the poor to survive under the most unfavourable circumstances suggests that they are quite skilled in meeting their own basic needs, even if only at standards intolerable to a socially conscious society. Too often government programmes seek to improve their lot not through interventions intended to strengthen their own capacity for "self help" action but through, doing for them, what they previously did for themselves—with the government making the decision and providing the resources. As a consequence the people's former self-sufficiency turns to dependence on government, potentially leaving them even more vulnerable than before to changes in its policies or lapses in its delivery systems".

Participatory and people-centred development activities are now being advocated and actively undertaken both for the real benefit of the people and for building a good image of public administration in the minds of the poor and the under privileged.

Conceptual Issues

The relationship between public administration

and the public, raises a number of important conceptual issues, regarding the role of government machinery and its interactions with the members of the public.

As Katz and Danet explain in the 'introduction' to their edited volume on *Bureaucracy and the Public,* the structure of bureaucratic organisations subsumes a set of guiding norms governing the relationships between the organisation and the clientele. These norms are identified as (a) specificity (b) universalism and (c) affective neutrality. Specificity refers to the strictly limited zone of interaction between administration and the client as formally defined by the organisation. In public transport, the 'passenger' and the 'conductor' have a very specific relationship.The passenger pays the fare and the conductor assures him travel up to a definite distance. *Universalism* stands for equal treatment to a defined group as organisationally prescribed. In our illustration, every bus passenger will have to pay the same fare for the same distance and the conductor is duty bound to behave uniformly in each and every case. *Affective neutrality* means exhibition of unbiased attitude toward the client and by implication, non-display of passions or feelings like anger, affection etc.

Alongside these structural norms of a bureaucratic organisation, a set of factors assumes importance in any interaction between the organisation and the clientele. Interaction means here three things; the manner, the procedures and the resources exchanged. Manner refers to the behavioural transaction in an interactional situation. How does the government officer talk to or receive a member of the public, say in a post office? The procedures refer to the administrative processes involved in an interaction. How many forms does one have to fill up? How long does one have to stand in a queue before a bank counter, for instance? The resources exchanged denote the outcome of interaction. Could a person ultimately withdraw money from his postal savings bank account? Did a person get the building permission from the municipality?

The structural norms and the three dimensions of interaction are useful conceptualisations for empirical examination of bureaucracy-client relationships in specific situations.[2]

Research Findings

'The relational aspect of bureaucracy—its interaction with the public and its subservience to the public interest—is not properly articulated in Weber's theoretical construct. As James D. Thompson has put it,[3] "classic bureaucratic theory is preoccupied with behavioural relations ordered by a single, unified authority structure from which the client is excluded...".The bureaucratic organisation isz a fixed monolith which approximates a steady and depersonalised machine. It is an automation that works uniformly and with unfaltering regularity. The underlying assumption seems to be that the client for whom the machine exists has to be adjustable, as the machine itself is inflexible. The inevitable result that follows is what Merton has called the 'unintended consequences of the bureaucratic structure'. Even if the client could not be served due to procedural rigidity, the organisation would not shed its procrustean character. The Weberian theory is an inward looking structural construct par excellence. Its face is toward the organisation and not the client.

There have been some important studies oh the relationship between the bureaucracy and the client. Of these, special mention can be made of Peter Blau's study[4] of a public welfare agency, William Foote Whyte's study[5] of human relations in the restaurant industry and the research on new Israeli immigrants by Elihu Katz and S.N. Eisenstadt.[6] Concentrating bn the orientation of case workers serving clients in a public welfare agency, Blau points out the rigidities that are produced by administrative procedures, the 'reality shock' which young case workers experience on their joining the organisation, the kind of peer group support that develops in the organisation and how all these influence the relationship between the case workers and the clients. Whyte's memorable study is much more incisive, as it delves deep into delicate human relationship problems in a restaurant considered as a combination of production and service unit. It draws attention to a "high degree of social adaptability" of the worker and the need for client orientation of the whole organisation.The supervision in such a situation has to shed its *laissez faire* attitude and look upon a restaurant or factory as an organisation of human relations, as a system of personal communications, in order to improve client-organisation relationship.

Eisenstadt's earlier writing[7] on the conditions of development of bureaucratic organisations postulated a critical relationship between the bureaucratic organisation and the environment. As he wrote:

'The(se) structural characteristics do not, however, develop in a social vacuum but are closely related to the functions and activities of the bureaucratic organisation in its environment. The extent to which they can develop and persist in any bureaucratic organisation is dependent on the type of dynamic equilibrium that the organisation develops in relation to its environment."

This is a salutary departure from the Weberian introversion and a bureaucratic organisation is sought to be explained more by .referring to the environmental conditions. In this connection, Eisenstadt uses the concept of 'de-bureaucratisation' to connote changes in bureaucratic organisation caused by close interactions between the organisation and the clients.

"In de-bureaucratisation the specific characteristics of the bureaucracy in terms both of its authority and its specific rules and goals are minimised, even up to the point where its very functions and activities are taken over by other groups or organisations."

Katz and Eisenstadt (1960) explored the changes in the bureaucratic organisation in response to the needs of clients. As the new immigrants from the non-Western countries were pouring into Israel, the Israeli organisations had to adapt themselves to cope with the large influx of clients. On a theoretical plane, the notion of "role impingement" as a characterisation of bureaucratisation and de-bureaucratisation marks an important advance on the traditional concept of bureaucracy. This needs some elaboration. It has been suggested that the factors affecting bureaucratisation are many. For instance, when a public bureaucracy has a-monopoly of certain goods and services, the client has little chance of making an effective protest and "under such circumstances,bureaucrats may permit themselves an attitude of detachment and ritualistic formalism vis-a-vis their clients". Using the 'role' concept, Katz and Eisenstadt speculated that the notion of dependence of clients and officials in an interactional situation might be looked at as "a special case of the impingement of other role relationships on a given bureaucratic relationship". De-bureaucratisation can be conceived "in terms of the impingement of non-bureaucratic roles on bureaucratic ones" and over-bureaucratisation would be treated "as either the formalistic segregation of a bureaucratic relationship from all other role relations... or, in its totalitarian form, as the imposition of bureaucratic relationship on relations outside the scope of the bureaucracy".

The upshot of .what Katz and Eisenstadt have said is that the theory of bureaucracy a la Max

Weber does not so much explain the relationship between organisation and environment as it does the formal, structural characteristics of a bureaucratic organisation.The characteristics are not something static: environmental influences do impinge on the organisation. To quote Katz and Eisenstadt, "In effect, over bureaucratisation and de-bureaucratisation represent a disturbance in the relationship between an organisation and its environment that is not envisioned by the classical-model of bureaucracy. This model envisages the roles of both bureaucrat and client as segregated to some extent from their other roles.... However, even in the ideal-type bureaucracy a role is not completely independent of other roles; some outside roles clearly may be, or must be, considered. If an old man, obviously unable to wait his turn in a long queue, is given special attention by a clerk, this is not a case of an irrelevant role relationship being allowed incorrectly to impinge on the bureaucrat-client relationship."

To sum up, the studies just mentioned have focussed attention on organisation-client relationship from different angles. Blau talks of it from the standpoint of 'professionalization' which will further the welfare of clients and at the same time promote a detached attitude toward them. Whytes emphasis is on the reorientation of supervision 'in order to help the restaurant workers to deal with the client successfully. Katz and Eisenstadt have sought to analyse bureaucracy-client relationship within the framework of bureaucratic theory but th\ analysis radically departs from Weberianism by concentrating on the notion of impingement of other role relationships on a given bureaucratic relationship.

The studies by Blau and Whyte shed light on some of the issues involved in the relationship between organisation and the client but as a frame of analysis of the relationship, the theoretical perspective of Katz and Eisenstadt seems much more promising. To recapitulate, the concept of role impingement refers to multiple role relations played by official and client vis-a-vis one another'. How should a bureaucrat deal with a client, would normally be laid down in organisational rules but in an actual encounter, the bureaucrat may tackle the client differently. He may be 'over bureaucratic' or 'under-bureaucratic' depending on his perception of the situations consisting of himself and the client involved in an interaction. In either case, the bureaucrat who deviates from the organisationally prescribed role relations, brings extra-organisational roles to bear on the specific situation, under the impact of the client.

Janowitz and others refer to 'balance' in public administration, which has significance for citizen-administration relations. Public administration will be in a state of imbalance if it becomes too much overbearing or too much subservient. As it has been observed:

"A bureaucracy is in imbalance when it fails to operate on the basis of democratic consent. Bureaucratic imbalance may be either despotic or subservient. Despotic implies that the bureaucracy is too much the master while subservient implies that it is too much the servant. The despotic bureaucracy disregards public preference and demands. It is likely to resort to coercion and manipulation to maintain its power. The subservient bureaucracy finds itself so concerned with the demands of special interest groups that it compromises its essential organisational goals and sacrifices essentially authority."[8]

Bureaucratic dominance has been a constant theme in the literature, on administration in the developing countries due to the legacy of imperial rule in most countries. Alongside bureaucratic ascendancy, the idea of bureaucratic subservience to the powerful economic interests has also been suggested. The contradiction in the two views may be resolved by characterising the higher level bureaucracy as an integral part of the influential social elite in a developing country.

Public administration in the ex-colonial countries like India used to have a 'private' character because of its limited scope, insularity, inequity and methods of operation. Maintenance of law and order and revenue raising were the prime considerations of administration. The administrative operations were undertaken autonomously in the absence of public participation and accountability. The incidence of administration was iniquitous as the benefits accrued mostly to the influential and the powerful. In terms of methods of operation, administration was essentially coercive, formal and apparently procedure-oriented.

Citizen-administration relations were conditioned by the basic nature and operational peculiarities of administration during colonial rule. After winning freedom, the imbalance of a bureaucratic state was sought to be corrected by (a) expanding the scope of government functions, (b) creating institutional infrastructure (e.g. *panchayati raj* in India) to promote popular participation, (c) encouraging political interventions in administration to modify the rigour of formalism (d) instituting organisational and procedural changes in the interest of speed and public understanding of administrative action.

Research findings on citizen-administration relations in India reveal interesting data and information. Based on extensive field survey, the study by Eldersveld, Jagannadham and Barnabas came out with the following finding:

"The attitude of Indian citizens towards their government and its administrative officials particularly is a complex and paradoxical mosaic of support and hostility of consensus and critique. From 75 per cent to 90 per cent view governmental jobs as prestigious, 90 per cent feel that health and community development programmes are worthwhile and less than 50 per cent (20 per cent rural) are critical of the job performance of Central Government officials. On the other hand, the majority feel that 50 per cent or more, of the officials are corrupt, large proportions (60 per cent urban, 32 per cent rural) say their dealings with officials are unsatisfactory and the majority sense that their probabilities of gaining access to officials and being successful in processing their complaints with them are low. Over 50 per cent feel officials in certain agencies are not fair and the citizen can do little by himself and from 60 per cent to 75 per cent feel that political pull is important in getting administrative action."[9]

Studies on police administration,[10] rural developments[11] and urban government[12] reveal citizens' perceptions about public administration in India. Certain common points that come out of these field studies can be summarised as follow:

1. Citizens' ignorance about procedures involved in getting things done.
2. Unhelpful attitude of officials especially lower level functionaries.
3. Inordinate delay and waiting period.
4. Favouritism in administration.
5. Corruption among officials.
6. Need for middlemen (brokers) to get things done.
7. Urban-rural differences in perceptions; urban dwellers being more critical about administration than rural counterparts.
8. Rich-poor discrimination in administration; the rich having easy access to administration and the general tendency of officials to avoid the poor and underplay their needs and interests.

Government Response

At the higher level in government, the problems of citizen-administration relationship have attracted attention from time to time and 'committees and commissions have been set up to deal with them. The Santhanam Committee on Prevention of Corruption[13] felt that discretionary powers exercised by different categories oP government officials opened up "scope for harassment, malpractice and corruption" in the exercise of those powers. The Administrative Reforms Commission[14] took note of the general public complaint about corruption in administration and acknowledged the existence of widespread inefficiency and the unresponsiveness of administration to public needs.

Institutional devices to remedy the. defects .of administration are of particular relevance for the developing countries. Public administration has a built-in tendency in these countries to by-pass the needs of the people at large. The colonial legacy of limited government by an administrative elite stands in the way of universalisation of the benefits of governance. Decision making on major issues of public policy remains a proud preserve of the small politico-administrative elite class. The social structure of the developing societies is characterised by numerous divisions along linguistic, ethnic, religious and economic lines. More powerful groups in the society tend to bend the machinery and processes of government to their side and thus monopolise the fruits of administration.This process of capturing of public administration by the powerful social groups is facilitated by the existence of endemic poverty and illiteracy. Both economic incapacity and lack of education reduce dumb millions into a position of passivity and subservience. Public administration therefore tends to become a very private affair as it usually responds to the demands of a small minority of social elite. The political process many a time fails to achieve integration of interests and tends to create instead rigid social divisions. Once a political party comes to power through the electoral process, public administration becomes a captive agency in the hands of the party. The opposition parties are treated as enemies and not partners in the process of government.

Limits of Publioness

The colonial legacy, social diversity, poverty and illiteracy and the peculiarity of the political process combine together to rob public administration of its publicness in most developing countries. There are three more reasons for this unhealthy transformation of public administration in these countries. First, administrative discretion is fairly widely used by public servants at all levels in the administration. With more and more expansion of government activities, the lower level functionaries engaged in field administration come to enjoy a great deal of discretionary powers. Administrative discretion, when exercised without effective supervision, is apt to breed malpractices and corruption. Second, there has been a consistent increase in the volume of legislations to cope with expanding government activities. With increasing complexity of legislative work, the legislatures have been granting the executive work and more discretionary powers and leaving the details to be worked out by the latter. Delegated legislation has the tendency to magnify executive strength and discretion. Third, the executive in many developing countries has increasingly been assuming the role of dispenser of justice also. Administrative adjudication and the use of administrative tribunals have been on the increase in many countries.

Administrative discretion, delegated legislation and administrative adjudication have the effect of increasing the powers of the executive which is already strong due to the colonial past.

Institutional devices are therefore necessary to check executive inflation and guard against corruption and administrative injustice.

Institutional Devices

In Western democracies, non-legal institutions like political parties, the press and public opinion have been traditionally exercising control over administrative action. Also, the administrative agencies have developed their own internal norms and administrative ethics. Under conditions of economic affluence, these agencies have been able to work fairly efficiently. The Western democracies have still felt the need for institutional control mechanisms to keep the bureaucracy in check and to ensure that public administration really serves the public purpose.

By contrast, the developing countries like India suffer from paucity of resources in a situation where speedy socio-economic development is an imperative necessity. The bureaucratic machinery is a legacy of the colonial past and its essential nature is elitist and isolationist. Tuned to the needs of the imperial regime, the administrative agencies have to slowly adjust themselves to the needs of socio-economic development and the larger public interest. As the monopolist of state power during the colonial days, the basic orientation of the administrative agencies has been towards power and not service to the people. To combat this administrative behaviour, the developing cojintries need strong political will and a steady development of political infrastructure. Effective administration has its own value no doubt but as Lucian Pyel[15] has observed, since the authoritarian organs of government have the tendency "to overshadow the non-bureaucratic components of the political system", these components have to be strengthened first. New social and political institutions have to grow to increase the capacity of the political system to beat the bureaucracy at its own game by subjecting it to effective political control."[16]

With increased tempo of development activities under the aegis of the government, bureaucracy has become all pervasive. There is a search today in most developing countries for effective checks on the administrative agencies that are proliferating in the course of 'development'. One response to this situation has been to identify types of development activities that could be handed over to voluntary organisations. The Planning Commission in India has debated over this issue seriously with of course not much success. De-bureaucratising development activities is also attempted by decentralisation of functions to the local self-governing bodies like municipalities and the *panchayati raj* bodies. The moribund state of most local bodies in India testifies to the lingering strength of the centralising forces of the old bureaucratic regime. Still another attempt, very feeble though, to de-bureaucratise development administration can be traced to sporadic measures for popular participation and political mobilization. Some of the states in India such as Kerala and West Bengal have tried out these measures in recent times fairly successfully in their search for speedier and more effective land reforms.

Decentralisation and popular participation are attempts at decreasing the area of operation of the bureaucratic state apparatus. These are measures for *less bureaucracy*. Alongside these, other institutional devices have been recommended and instituted for *better bureaucracy*. Administrative reform has been a continuous concern of most developing countries in their search for efficient and effective administration. To deal with administrative corruption and to redress citizens' grievances, procedural changes and institutional innovations have been made in many countries.

Three institutional devices deserve special

mention in this connection: the ombudsman system, the procurator system and the system of administrative courts.

The Ombudsman

Created for the redressing of citizens' grievances, the institution of Ombudsman is typically Scandinavian. The office of Ombudsman has been in existence in Sweden since 1809 and in Finland since 1919. Denmark adopted the system in 1955. Norway and New Zealand introduced it in 1962 and the United Kingdom appointed the Parliamentary Commissioner for Administration in 1967. Several countries in the world have since adopted the ombudsman-like institution 'as a bulwark of democratic government against the tyranny of officialdom'.[17]

Ombudsman, a Swedish word, stands for "an officer appointed by the legislature to handle complaints against administrative and judicial action." Although appointed by the legislature, the office of ombudsman is a constitutional post and the incumbent is politically independent of the legislature. Traditionally, the appointment is based on the unanimity principle with all political parties supporting the proposal. As an impartial investigator the ombudsman makes investigations, gets at the facts objectively and reports back to the legislature. The complainant has simply to write to the ombudsman appealing against an administrative decision. The ombudsman can of course investigate on his own initiative. He has the power to inspect the courts and the administrative agencies and he can take up cases on the basis of press reports. His right to investigate does not authorise him to quash or reverse a decision, nor does he have direct control over the courts or the administrative agencies.

The ombudsman system has gained in popularity primarily because of the simple, speedy and low cost method of handling appeals against administrative decisions. Its strength lies in the wide publicity that is given to its working in the press and other forums. The prestige that traditionally goes with the office and the objectivity and competence of the ombudsman have contributed to the legitimization of the institution and its world-wide acceptance.

The Parliamentary Commissioner for Administration in the United Kingdom enjoys a status similar to the Comptroller and Auditor-General. His duty is to investigate cases of alleged mal-administration referred to him by members of Parliament. It is for the Commissioner to define what mal-administration is. The local authorities, hospital boards, nationalised industries, the police, personnel questions in the civil service and the armed forces are excluded from the purview of the Commissioners. Matters on which a right of appeal was open to the complainant and major policy questions that are subject to parliamentary control are also taken out of his jurisdiction. The Commissioner is also debarred from inquiring into the merits of discretionary administrative decisions that are taken legally in accordance with appropriate administrative procedure. He has free access to information except when it is certified by a Minister that the information called for could not be given in the public interest. The investigations conducted by the Commissioner are confidential in nature. Unlike the Swedish system, the institution in U.K. has a much more restricted scope. Its success has, however, prompted the Government to extend the system to other areas of administration such as local authorities, hospital boards etc.

As bureaucratic power tends to increase with more and more expansion of government activities, the search for countervailing mechanisms has been widespread across the nations. It is against this background that the Ombudsman should be regarded as an important new addition to the armoury of democratic government. Like the legislative auditor, he enhances the control and prestige of legislatures in a world in which executive power is growing.

The Procurator[19]

Much like the institution of Ombudsman, the Procurator system in the old U.S.S.R., Czechoslovakia, Hungary, Poland and Romania used to play an important part in redressing citizens' grievances and ensuring observance of legality at all administrative levels.

The procurator system generally consisted of a 'central apparatus' and a number of subordinate offices and the entire system was organised on the principle of subordination of lower to higher procurator. At the apex of the organisation the procurator-general supervised the work of the whole organisation. He was responsible only to the legislature.

The procurator system of the erstwhile East European countries should be distinguished from the Ombudsman system.The latter is really a very small-scale and informal organisation based on the personal investigation of complaints by the Ombudsman himself. By contrast, the procuracy was a large, hierarchic apparatus and its scope was limited almost wholly to the lower levels of government administration. It however took great care to process the complaints submitted to it and was a useful device in the socialist countries including China.

The Administrative Courts

The French system of administrative courts to deal with disputes between the administration and the individual citizens is a unique institution that has spread to many European and African countries (e.g. Greece, Belgium,Turkey etc.). In France, the administrative courts are separate from the hierarchy of ordinary courts. A distinction is made between acts for which a government servant is personally liable and sueable in the ordinary courts (Fautede-Personale) and those which are the result of administrative faults for which service, as an entity, is responsible (Faute-de-service). The latter class of faults is referred to appropriate administrative courts.

The courts of first instance are called Administrative Tribunals and at the head of the system of administrative courts is the Council of State *(conseil d'Etat).* The Council is the government's advisory body on legislation; it is also the supreme administrative court. As the supreme court appeal in all administrative matters, the Council exercises general supervision over administration and possesses ultimate authority over the discipline of civil servants.

The Council consists of over 150 members recruited almost entirely through the School of Administration. It is divided into several sections; the main distinction is between four advisory or so-called administrative sections and a judicial section. The latter has a number of chambers in which five councillors normally decide on cases on the report of more junior members *(mailres des requites and auditors).* Important cases may be decided by ten or fifteen councillors *(conseiliers).* The members of the administrative courts are ordinary civil servants. They enjoy great prestige due to their competence and thorough knowledge of the administrative processes.

Moving the administrative courts is very simple. The plaintiff has to submit two copies of complaints, a copy of the contested decision and an abstract of the legal arguments or factual details in support of the case. The. Council of State makes inquiries and invites the administrator concerned to justify his administrative act. In conducting its proceedings, the council follows the judicial mode and takes any of the two lines of action. It can annul the administrative act or decision on grounds of legality. Alternatively, it can recognise the existence of a subjective right which the administration has damaged and obtain-appropriate redress. Plaintiffs "find in the administrative courts and particularly in the Council of State, some of the characteristics of the Scandinavian institution of the Ombudsman; *the mailre des requites* who is given the task of preparing and reporting on a case will do all the work himself, dig through the administration's files and find what happened, on behalf of the plaintiff who, in some cases, has nothing more to do than file his complaint and pay a very small fee."[20] The gradual spread of this French institution to other countries is proof of its efficacy as the citizens' best friend in a situation of growing executive power and administrative centralisation.

The Indian Response

The need for institutional innovation to deal with corruption and citizens' grievances has been keenly felt in India and suggestions have been made from time to time by committees and commissions to bring about administrative changes and create new controlling agencies. The Law Commission in its fourteenth report drew attention to the wide field of administrative discretion in India where administrative authority may act outside the strict limits of law and propriety without the affected citizen being in a position to get effective redress. The Santhanam Committee on Prevention of Corruption thought that it was necessary to devise adequate methods of control over exercise of discretion by different categories of government servants. As the Committee observed, "In the- more advanced countries various methods of such control have been devised. We recommend that this should be studied and a system of control should be devised keeping in mind the vastness of our country and the basic principles which are enshrined in our constitution and jurisprudence." As a sequel to the Santhanam Committee Report, Vigilance Commissions were set up. at the Centre in 1964 and in the various states later. Vigilance cells have been created in 'several government departments and public sector undertakings.

The Central Vigilance Commission is headed by the Central Vigilance Commissioner appointed by the President of India. He is assisted by other secretarial and technical staff. The Commission receives complaints directly from aggrieved persons. Other sources of information about corruption and malpractices ire the press reports, audit reports, allegations made by members of Parliament etc. On receiving complaints, the Commission may

i) Ask the ministry/department concerned to inquire into it;
ii) Ask the Central Bureau of Investigation to make an inquiry;
iii) Ask the CBI Director to register a case and do the investigation. Prosecution will of course depend on the approval of the appropriate sanctioning authority.

The jurisdiction of the Commission is presently limited to complaints against gazetted officers and officers of equivalent status.

The Central Vigilance Commission is certainly no substitute for an Ombudsman. As it is constituted, the Commission is virtually an extension of the bureaucratic apparatus of the Central Government and its operations are very much hedged in by the overpoweringuninistries and the political forces at the Centre.[21]

The Administrative Reforms Commission set up in 1966 took up on priority basis the matter of redress of citizens' grievances.The Commission felt that the existing institutions to deal Avith this problem were inadequate and found the Ombudsman a "sine qua non of democratic functioning and (as) an essential prerequisite of the progress and prosperity on which the fulfilment of our democracy depends."

The Commission recommended a two-tier machinery of Lokpal and Lokayukta for redressing citizens' grievances. Lokpal would deal with complaints against ministers and secretaries to government in the Central as well as State Governments. The Lokayukta one at the Centre and one in each State, would attend to complaints against the rest of the bureaucracy. The Lokpal would be appointed by the President after consultation with the Chief Justice of India, the Chairman of the Council of States and the Speaker of the House of the People.The legislations for the institution of Lokpal and Lokayukta were introduced in Parliament in 1968 and again in 1971 and 1977. All of them lapsed with the dissolution of respective Parliaments.[22] The ill-fated Lokpal Bill has so far not been able to pass through the parliamentary procedures.

Some of the states in India have set up ombudsman-like agencies but their records do not inspire confidence in the institutions. Maharashtra had the first Lokayukta in 1971. Rajasthan appointed the Lokayukta and the UP-Lokayukta in 1973. In the same year Bihar had the state's first Lokayukta. Not much publicity seems to have been given to the working of these institutions.

The experience of Rajasthan shows that the number of complaints has been increasing over the years (1183 in 1974-75 and 1246 in 1975-76) and the complaints are mostly against gazetted officers and non-gazetted public servants. For instance, in 1975-76 there were complaints against 5 non-officials (ministers, chairmen of municipalities and *panchayati raj* bodies etc.), 401 gazetted officers and 402 non-gazetted public servants. Surprisingly, the Rajasthan Lokayukta[23] could not recommend any tangible disciplinary action or prosecution in a court of law against any public servant involved in these cases.

The case of Bihar[24] is a warning signal for other states who might like to have the institution of Lokayukta. In 1973, the first Lokayukta was named by the Governor, but the Chief Minister wanted to have his own man. This led to a confrontation between the Governor and the Chief Minister. The office of Lokayukta was starved of funds for quite some time as the then Ministry did not like the appointment. In 1974, a new Act was passed providing for appointment of Lokayukta by the Governor after consulting the Chief Justice of the High Court and the leader of the opposition in the State Assembly. When the Lokayukta decided to proceed with an inquiry against two ministers, his appointment was challenged in the Patna High Court; and the State Finance Department was reluctant to give financial sanction to engage legal counsel for the defence of the Lokayukta. The matter even went to the Central level and the Union Home and Law Ministries were approached on how to defend the Lokayukta.

To sum up, the institutional devices available round the world to deal with redress of citizens' grievances are many and varied. So far as India is concerned, several institutional experimentations have been made at different levels—centre, state and local but the problem still remains largely unresolved. Dissatisfaction with governmental operations especially at the cutting-edge point where government meets the people directly (e.g. post office, bank counter, railway booking office etc.) is fairly widespread. Corruption in public administration has again and again come up for discussion at different levels and in different forms."[26] It is against this background of endemic inefficiency in government and general insensitivity to the clientele (the people) that the usefulness of ombudsman or any other grievance-handling machinery should be considered. The ombudsman-type institution presupposes a certain degree of administrative efficiency so that most cases of citizens are generally dealt with fairly and promptly by the regular machineries such as the administrative agencies and the judiciary. The ombudsman is an institution not of first instance but of the last resort. Where normal administration is faulty, slow-moving and corrupt, the ombudsman is likely to be drowned in the piles of cases pushed up to him due to general incompetence and dishonesty down below. As the Administrative

Reforms Commission rightly pointed out, "the setting up of these authorities is not the complete answer to the problem of redress of citizens' grievances. They only provide the ultimate set-up, or such redress as has not been available through the normal departmental governmental machinery and do not absolve the department from fulfilling its obligations to the citizen for administering its affairs without generating, as far as possible, any legitimate sense of grievance." In an environment of administrative inertia and corruption, to get a clear and upright ombudsman may not be easy. Even if one is found out, it is too much to expect honesty and integrity at the top when the entire bottom seems almost rotten. As the recent 'scams' and corruptions show, the top seems equally rotten (possibly more than the bottom). As the Bihar experience reveals, political problems cannot be solved administratively. A democratic system depends for its survival on the honesty and integrity of the politician. In a situation of falling standards of political morality, institutional innovations to deal with citizen's grievances may be of mere cosmetic value and not of real worth. The politicians themselves would pay lip service to the new institutions and even try to sabotage them as they would be having the greatest fear of being exposed by these institutions. Administrative institutions can really work only under conditions of general political acceptance. Where such acceptance is missing, the institutions will either languish or remain mere facade institutions.

Citizens' Charter: This is the latest device to structure citizen - administration relationship. Citizens' charter is aimed at demanding from the government and the service organisations (e.g. hospital, post-office etc.) the fundamentals of accountability, transparency, quality and choice of services supplied to people. The concept of citizens' charter was initiated by 'Common Cause' in 1994. In UK, where the charter has been widely in use, a committee was constituted under John Major, the then Prime Minister; other members were drawn from a cross section of people from industry, academic world, consumer council etc. Once the idea of 'charter' was accepted and given publicity, this committee became responsible for its operationalisation and actual enforcement. The Prime Minister's office was continuously monitoring the progress of citizens' charter in different departments and service organisations. It has now become customary for the Prime Minister to submit a report to Parliament about the progress of the Charter formulated by different ministries. The Prime Minister's report contains comparative estimate of performance over time (previous year and present year) and explains whether efficiency has been up to some standards. If the performance has excelled, it is shown with a 'right' mark and if deteriorated, with a cross (x) mark.

The charter marks are awarded to the personnel in specific ministries and agencies. The nominations are sent by citizens who avail the services. As a mark of honour for the excellent services rendered, the photographs of recipients of charter mark awards are exhibited in the offices. If the standards of performance are not maintained or for any delay or shortfall in performance, the concerned department has to pay compensation ranging from 5 to 75 pounds.

Evaluation: The charter is no doubt an innovative device but its formulation and enforcement are not an easy task. Fairly precise standards of performance have to be set. There has to be some body or authority to monitor performance and watch violations and maintenance. The citizens have to play an active role in giving timely and necessary feedback about services rendered by the government agencies. Within the organisations, the employees must be psychologically and infrastructurally well-prepared to serve the public as per the agreed-upon standards.

Other Countries: Greater concern for accountability to the public has led to innovative schemes in the Philippines and Malaysia. In 1994, the Phillipines Civil Service Commission launched a citizen satisfaction campaign called Citizen, Now, Not later.The Campaign involved the adoption of standard norm, of conduct and courtesy to clients.The Malaysian Administrative Modernization and Management Planning Unit (MAMPU) have designed the Client's Charter, which is a written commitment to the delivery of outputs or services to an agency's clients. Should an agency fail to comply with the stated quality standards, as per its charter, the public can use this as a 'basis for complaints' against non-compliance.

Indian Scenario

In India the Prime Minister inaugurated a conference of the • Chief Secretaries in November 1996 on "an agenda for an effective and responsive administration" in order to restore the faith of the people in the fairness and capacity of the administration at different levels. It was admitted that the public agencies had been inward looking and were alienated from the people. The government of India has since introduced citizens' charters in a number of departments and agencies with public interface (e.g. Income Tax Department, the LIC, the Railways and the CPWD etc). As explained by the Government, the charter places the citizen at the centre of adpiinistration, instead of treating him as a passive recipient of services rendered without regard for quality, cost or timeliness.

Principles Involved

The citizens' charter is based on the following principles:

(a) Wide publicity on the standards of performance of public agencies;
(b) Assured quality of services;
(c) Access to information along with courtesy and helpful attitude;
(d) Choice of and consultation with the citizens;
(e) Simplified procedures for receipt of complaints and their quick redress; and
(f) Provision of performance scrutiny with citizens' involvement.

It is expected that in the coining years the idea of the charter will spread to other organisations at the state and local levels also. It has to be seen that the charter does not remain a mere ritual and serious and sincere efforts are made to involve the citizens in government operations and government agencies and action is taken on the basis of their perceptions about government performance.

In this context, it may be mentioned that the Fifth Pay Commission desired that government transactions should be, whenever possible, made as open as is feasible. A draft Bill on the 'right to information' was appended to the Commission Report. Bureaucratic rules have unduly made government transactions secretive and protective. In near future, the veil of secrecy is likely to be removed with the kind of"right to information" bill being contemplated by the government.

REFERENCES

1. Frances F. Korten, "Community Participation :A Management Perspective on obstacles and option", in David C. Korten and Felipe B. Alfanso (eds.), *Bureaucracy and the Poor,* McGraw Hill, 1981.
2. Elihu Katz and Brenda Danet (eds.), *Bureaucracy and the Public,* Basic Books, Inc., Publishers, New York, 1973, pp.3-25.
3. James D Thompson, "Organisations and Output Transactions", *American Journal of Sociology,* 68, 1962.
4. Peter M. Blau, "Orientation Toward Clients in

a Public Welfare Agency", *Administrative Science Quarterly,* 5, 1960.

5. William Foote Whyte, "When Workers and Customers Meet", *Industry and Society,* New York, McGraw Hill, 1945.
6. Elihu Katz and S.N. Eisenstadt, "Some Sociological Observations on the Response of Israeli Organisations to New Immigrants" in Katz and Danet (eds.), op.cit.
7. Eisenstadt, "Bureaucracy, Bureacratizatjon and Debureaucratization", *Administrative Science Quarterly,* 4, 1959.
8. Morris Janowitz, Deil Wright and William Delany, *Public Administration and the Public Perspective toward Government in a Metropolitan Community* Institute of Public Administration, University of Michigan, 1958, p.6.
9. Sammuel J. Eldersvled, V. Jaganadham. A. P. Barnabes, *The Citizen and the Administrator in a Developing Society,* The Indian Institute of Public Administration, New Delhi, 1968.
10. David H. Bayley, *The Police and Political Development in India,* Princeton University Press, 1969 Chapter 9.
11. Rakesh Hooja, "The Raising and Redressing of Grievances at District Level and Below in Rajasthan", *The Indian Journal of Public Administration,* July-September, 1978.
12. For urban studies, see V. Jagannadham, "Public Administration and the Citizen : How far Public Administration can be Public", *The Indian Journal of Public Administration,* June, 1978.
13. *Report of the Committee on Prevention of Corruption,* Government of India, Ministry of Home Affairs, 1964.
14. *Interim Report: 'Problems of Redress of Citizens' Grievances* Administrative Reforms Commission, Government of India, 1966.
15. *See in this connection Lucian W. Pye,* "Administration, Politics and Development in New States" *in C N. Bhalerao (ed:), Administration, Politics and Development in India.* Lalvani Publishing House, Bombay, 1972.
16. This is an adaptation of what Fred Riggs wrote in
17. "Relearning an Old Lesson: The Political Context of Development Administration", in Bhalerao (ed.), op, cit.
18. The institution of Ombudsman has been studied in great detail and in comparative settings by Professor Donald C. Rowat. See in this connection, (i) Donald C. Rowat (ed.), The *Ombudsman: Citizens' Defender,* Allen Unwin Lond, 1968 and (ii) Donald C. Rowat, *The Ombudsman Flan: Essays on the Worldwide Spread* of an Idea, McClelland and Steward Ltd., Ottawa. 1973. Also see for a comparative review, Frank Stacey, *Ombudsman Compared,* Clarendon Press Oxford, 1978.
19. In Denmark, Norway and New Zealand the Ombudsman does not have the power to supervise the courts and the Ombudsman's investigations are confidential in nature.
20. A Denisov and M. Kirichenko, *Soviet State Law,* Foreign Languages Publishing House, Moscow.
21. Jean Blondel, *The Government of France,* Methuen & Co Ltd., London, 1977, p. 206.
22. See in this connection Kailash Prakash. "The Vigilance Set-up of the Government of India-Some Proposals for Refirm", *The Indian Journal of Public Administration,* October-December, 1972.
23. For comments on the legislation, see S. L. Verma, "Lokpal, Bureaucracy and the Common Man", *The Indian Journal of Public Administration,* October-December, 1978.
24. See in this connection, G. C, Singhvi. "The Lokayukta Institution: Raj as than Experience", *The Indian Journal of Public Administration,* October-December, 1978.
25. For the Bihar story, see R. B. Jain, *Contemporary Issues in Indian Administration,* op. cit., pp. 392-395.
26. See in this connection, John D. Monteiro, *Corruption: Control of Maladministration,* Manaktalas, Bombay, 1966. Also see Haridwar Rai and S. P. Singh, *Current Ideas and Issues in Indian Administration,* Uppal Publishing House, New Delhi, 1979, Chapter XL

Chapter 14

Administrative Reform

Administrative reform is essentially related to the idea of 'change' in administration which is brought about through deliberate efforts. The nature of administrative reform is to be clarified at the outset. Second, reform efforts have to be related to the surrounding conditions that generate or suppress demands for reform. Third, reform strategies differ from situation to situation and aim at solving different lands of administrative problems. The different types of reforms have therefore to be identified and the reform process needs to be explained. Fourth, implementation poses problems perhaps more serious than recommendation. The issues involved in the implementation of reform proposals deserve careful consideration.

Meaning of Reform

Administration being constantly involved in practical action situations cannot afford to remain static. It has necessarily to change for the sake of sheer survival. Four principal goals of reorganisation identified by Mosher are: changing policy and programmes; improving administrative effectiveness; solving personnel problems; and countering pressures and threats from outside organisation. Of these improving organisational effectiveness seems a more generic objective.[1] Paul Appleby in an insightful article on the first Hoover Commission Report in the U.S.A, suggested two basic ,types of changes in administration: constant and episodic.[2] The first type stands for incremental change that takes place in course of spontaneous adjustments to changing situations. New filing system, alterations in procedures of work, reshuffling of postings are examples of this type. Episodic change is called 'reorganisation' by Appleby. It is much more wide-ranging in scope and content involving a major shake-up in government.

Administrative reform has this episodic character. Gerald Caiden defines it as'the artificial inducement of administrative transformation, against resistance'. Three interrelated properties of reform are: moral purpose, artificial transformation and resistance. A reform proposal is aimed at improving the status quo: it marks a departure from existing set-up; and opposition to the proposal is assumed. Caiden makes a distinction between reform and change. The latter is a self-adjusting organisational response to changing conditions, while reform becomes necessary to remedy the malfunctioning of the natural administrative processes.

Administrative development needs to be distinguished from administrative reform. As Fred Riggs has defined it, administrative development is concerned with the growing capacity of administrative systems to make choices and exercise discretion to bring about changes in the environment by deliberate and conscious decisions.

Administrative reform can be considered as a process in the sequential sense.The circumstances in which the demands for reform are articulated, the need for such reform as acknowledged by the reformers, the methods adopted to frame and examine reform proposals and their acceptance and implementation form discrete phases of a continuous process.

Conditions of Reform

Administrative reform is aimed at changing what exists. It is thus related to the existing administrative set-up. Second, many interests and groups get involved in the reform process. Proposals for reform have naturally to weather opposition and conflicting views, as there are 'vested interests' in the maintenance of status quo. What looks good (reform) to some is considered bad by others. Third, administrative reform forms part of a larger political process and should be considered in relation to it. Reform proposals are often conceived in narrow, mechanical terms. This is what Montgomery[6] has characterised as 'adapting static model of administrative perfection to dynamic political reality'. Administration as a machine is sought to be differentiated from its political ecology. Norton Long's warning in this connection is very relevant as he observes that attempts to solve administrative problems in isolation from the structure of power and purpose in the polity are bound to be illusory.[7] Fourthly, a related issue is the status of the bureaucracy in a country where reform proposals are being considered In this connection a distinction has to be made between instrumental bureaucracies and institutional bureaucracies. In the Weberian sense, instrumental bureaucracies are 'instruments' in the hands of the political masters. Once the political leaders frame reform proposals, the governmental agencies are expected to accept and implement them. Institutional bureaucracies, on the other hand, are not dispensable tools or instruments. They might have been created for instrumental purposes, but in course of time they transcend this role and develop expressive or value significance for both their own members and the community at large.[8] The ex-colonial countries like India have inherited institutional bureaucracies with a fairly autonomous character that developed under conditions of administrative hegemony.[9] During the colonial period, the bureaucracy was the master and it ruled virtually unchecked by political overseers. Montgomery has explained the problems of administrative reform under conditions of bureaucratic hegemony thus:[10]

"Bureaucracies are not easily mobilised by external forces. Even when the public does make its demands known, the bureaucracy may lack the empathy necessary to develop a sense of urgency in its response. In most underdeveloped countries, both sides of the demand-response formula are weak; public possesses scanty resources for expressing its interests and the bureaucracy has little sympathy for the conditions under which most citizens live. The forces that compel or induce bureaucracies to follow a desired rationale in these circumstances are much more complicated than the legal relationships, the prestigious hierarchies and the popular demands that have supported reforms in autocracies or Western democracies. Because of the greater difficulty of using reform as a means of changing bureaucratic behaviour in the newly independent countries, a wider range of sanctions and especially those invoking the participation of competing subsystems, is called for".

In the developing countries, administrative reform is badly needed; yet it faces almost insuperable difficulties. The institutional bureaucracies are deeply entrenched in the political systems of these countries. They claim superiority over the political executive and try to 'buy off political leaders and defy public pressures'. They dominate the fora where reform proposals are discussed and the proposals are processed by them. Reforming institutional bureaucracies is therefore more a political issue than a purely managerial one. "The key to the reform of institutional bureaucracies would appear to be

the questioning of the legitimacy of the institution and thereby, its autonomy and self direction, by placing it, along with its values and practices, under the spotlight of public scrutiny".

Acceptance of the real supremacy of the political executive, independent audit of bureaucratic functioning and closer citizens' supervision are necessary to reduce the autonomy .id strength of the institutional bureaucracy. To the extent secrecy in government will be removed and open government promoted, this will lead to the gradual weakening of the institutional bureaucracy and its steady transformation into an instrumentalist role. In other words, administrative reform, to be actually realised, needs political will and political direction. So long as the culture of the colonial bureaucracy lingers on and the top bureaucracy remains entrenched in political positions, genuine reform is unlikely to be proposed and pursued. At any rate, taking the top bureaucracy along is an important precondition of reform.

Types of Reform

Reform proposals vary in their sweep and depth. Their significance also varies depending on what aspects of administration becomes the target of change. Some proposals may attract the attention of the press and the public. There are usually many others that rarely create any commotion. One way of classifying the reform proposals is to refer to the extent of administrative space affected by them. A proposal may have far-reaching consequences for the administration as a whole or for a large segment of it. It may have entire administration-wide significance. By contrast, another proposal may be directed toward one specific aspect or a single department and would thus be of much narrower scope. Creation of vigilance cells ip every ministry or the setting up of the Department of Administrative Reforms at the Centre in 1964 falls in the first group; while creation of the Steel Authority of India (SAIL) or the proposal to split up the Life Insurance Corporation of India for more decentralised decision making, falls in the second.

Another way of classifying the reform proposals is to refer to their substantive contents. If the first classificatory scheme is concerned with 'how much' of administration is being affected, the second is concerned with 'what' is being affected. Substantively, administrative organisations are composed of three inter-related elements: structure, process and behaviour. Administrative reform is often directed toward these three elements either separately or jointly.

Structural reform is very common in public administration. The basic concern here is with division of work, delegation and decentralisation, creation of autonomous agencies and setting up of coordinating mechanisms to harmonise the actions of interdependent units. Most reform proposals concentrate on these themes.

Procedural reform is also frequently suggested and pursued in government organisations. This may involve changes in financial rules, alteration of work procedures (e.g. changes in filing methods, forms etc.) and general attempts to avoid red tape. Much of the work done by the Staff Inspection Unit in the Union Ministry of Finance would fall in this category. Application of a battery of management techniques to different administrative situations also belongs to this class of reform. PPBS, operations research, systems analysis etc. are now widely used in public administration. New technologies like the computer and data-processing machines are being used now-a-days to facilitate better and quicker operations in government. Introduction of these techniques does not of course mean their real acceptance. Techniques and machines in many public organisations remain mere show-pieces or are not genuinely internalised by the employees. Automation has special problems in terms of changing inter-personal relations and role displacement.

Behavioural reform is a relatively new thing so far as government organisations are concerned. Bureaucracy has often been criticised for its impersonal character and dehumanising conseqfcerfves". 'Behavioural changes have therefore been suggested to improve interpersonal and intergroup relationships within the bureaucracy. Also such changes are advocated to make the administration serve the public better. Participative management and sensitivity training have gained wide currency in recent times in public administration. The former is aimed at creating on atmosphere of togetherness by offering opportunities of participation to different grades of employees. Sensitivity training is directly oriented towards attitudinal change and has now become quite fashionable in government training institutions. It remains however a debatable question how far behavioural changes can be really produced by one shot and individual-centred training programmes.

Special importance is attached to organisation development or OD as a technique to bring about planned organisational change. Originally started in business organisations, OD programmes are being tried out in public organisations also. Conceived basically as an ongoing educational process, OD aims at optimum utilisation of human respurces for organisational renewal by laying emphasis on inter-personal processes rather than on structure, procedure, or technology. Major emphasis in OD is on team-building, communication and collaborative problem-solving.

Organisation development programmes have made use of applied behavioural science. Their application to public administration poses some genuine difficulties. As Golembiewski points out, government organisations have special features like openness to many kinds of influences, greater variety of interests, reward structures and values at subgroup levels, absence of a clear-cut management group and weak linkages between executives and operating managers. Also, the 'habit background ot public agencies is unique. Reluctance to delegate, legalism, emphasis on security, stress on caution and procedure and less strongly developed concept of professional management deserve special mention in this context. OD programmes have to face these challenges and constraints in public administration.[12]

The different types of reforms, as described above, are usually considered separately. Structural reform may ignore behavioural implications and procedural changes are often suggested without examining their wider import for the organisation as a whole. The full benefits of reform are thus rarely reaped in the absence of a coherent reform perspective

Reform Process

Administrative reform is never an one-shot job. A progressive government interested in maintaining a certain standard of performance has to continuously adjust its administrative machinery to the various kinds of changes in the society. When performance standards are to be improved, reform becomes much more important. The Government of India set upr as many as eighteen committees and commissions to inquire into one or more segments of public administration. The Administrative Reforms

Commission[13] (1966-70) was set up with most comprehensive terms of reference embracing almost the entirety of public administration in India. The Railway Reforms Committee was set up (May, 1981) to suggest measures for improving the capability of the railways to handle higher volume of traffic in the coming decades. The Committee's work was related to the organisation and working of only one public agency and it could mainly make projective recommendations.

These examples clearly indicate that reform, either comprehensive or sectoral, is a deliberate effort. It is initiated at a particular point of time, discussed at length and carefully formulated for wider dissemination. The reform proposals are then finalised and internalised by relevant organisations for actual implementation. What happens at the time of implementation need to be monitored so that the reform proposals could be suitably adjusted to fit in the real-life situation.

Thus conceived, administrative reform is a process that can be broken down into discrete phases from the perception of problems to the implementation of reform proposals to solve those problems. One way of describing the process is to follow Herbert Simon's model of decision-making. The three stages in Simon's formulation—search, design and choice—apply equally well to the reform process. The search stage refers to the appreciation of the need for administrative change. At the design phase, the different alternatives to cope with change are considered along with their probable benefits and costs. The choice phase is concerned with the selection of one alternative for practical application.

A very similar process-model has been suggested by Caiden.[14] It is much more elaborate and analytical. Caiden's model includes four distinct phases:

(a) Awareness of need for administrative change;
(b) Formulation of goals and objectives, strategy and tactics;
(c) Implementation of reform;
(d) Evaluation of reform in terms of the reformer's objectives.

Effective *awareness of need* for change starts when problems are aired and proposals to solve these suggested. Administrative reform becomes necessary when the administration is:

i) Unable to cope with rising demands coming from clients;
ii) Unable to anticipate future demands those are likely to be put on it;
iii) Lacking in effective methods to cope with its ongoing and protective activities.

Usually, awareness of change is blocked by a number of factors. Tolerance of maladministration may be high in a particular society. The top management may be in favour of status quo. So, reform ideas will not be entertained and are likely to be nipped in the bud. There may be resource constraints and the organisation may not be prepared to invest extra funds for reform. To talk of reform is to deviate from the current state of affairs. Formal organisations tend to socialise individuals into conformist roles. Reform proposals are therefore unconventional. The initiator of reform has to face criticism and even punishment. A reformer is some kind of a rebel who must have the courage and confidence to stand up to the pressures of conformism, social ostracization and organisational intimidation. Administrative knowledge and skill, a sense c politics and a moral commitment to reform are essential prerequisites. Hence, as Caiden observes, 'reform is the work of minority'.

Reform proposals find easy acceptance in situations of uncertainty, disorganisation and dislocation. Ideological commitment to change also facilitates administrative reform.There must be status quo-upsetting socio-economic and political circumstances like regime change, economic crisis, rapid urbanisation, poverty and rising crime rate, which would impel changes in administration to cope with the unusual situations.

The second stage is concerned with proper diagnosis and remedial action. Once a problem has been identified (e.g. low productivity, high turnover of personnel etc.) , one has to go deep into its causes and formulate concrete suggestions for remedial action. Both 'relevant knowledge and creative thought' are necessary to propose workable remedies. Goals and objectives of reform are to be clearly stated and strategy and tactics to push through reform in the face of opposition and suspicion worked out.

Reform proposals can be incremental or comprehensive, imitative or creative. Generally, incremental changes are suggested for practical reasons of acceptability and quick implementation. Similarly, imitation is much easier than innovation. The proposal for reform gives reference to other countries, organisations or situations where a specific method is said to have worked well. This is so very convincing an argument. Innovation would have raised many questions and doubts.

Formulation of reform proposals includes diagnosis of the root causes of maladministration, drafting of feasible proposals, convincing people about their soundness, confronting opposition and keeping some provision of an escape route in case of failure. Complex and sweeping proposals are looked with suspicion and need more time for acceptance and implementation. Usually, reform proposals are judged critically at the initial stages, when these are to be explained clearly to dispel doubts and win s ›port. Acceptance of reforms is more likely

(a) "If they are tailored to local circumstances, implemented through existing institutions and invite local participation; (b) if existing institutions are not condemned out of hand, that is, if attention is given to extolling the virtues of reform rather than the defects of the unreformed; and if they are based on critical rather than uncritical non operationalism."[15]

The reformer has to enlarge his area of support. His strategy could therefore be 'to win over vested interests, opponents and neutrals if possible while strengthening support.' Reforms may preferably be on the basis of a long-term plan and by several stages. There can be a built-in experimentalism within the reform plan so that if things go wrong at any stage, the plan should be flexible enough to permit necessary adjustments in the light of experience. The role of leadership in pushing through reform hardly needs any emphasis.Those who propose reforms must have a large following and should be holding important position in the organisations concerned. Their personalities in terms of leadership qualities and general acceptability help in popularising the reform proposals.

Implementation

While analysing implementation of reforms, Caiden refers to four methods of implementation:[16]

i) Reforms imposed through political revolution;
ii) Reforms introduced to remedy organisational rigidity;
iii) Reforms through the legal system;
iv) Reforms through changes in attitude.

Administration is shaped and influenced by political forces. When one political regime is replaced by another, the change is bound to affect the structure and working of public administration. This happens even in times of peaceful political changes in the course of normal democratic governance. A revolutionary change like colonialism giving place to constitutional democracy or a sudden coup signifies radical transformation of the power elite through shifts in the power base. Sweeping administrative reforms are likely to follow such radical political changes.

In normal times it is the bureaucracy that feels the need for minor administrative changes. Strains and stresses are detected in its operation and excessive rigidity in structure and regulations is sought to be removed. Almost as a kind of defence mechanism, impulses for reform come from within the bureaucracy. The changes take place in several forms such as personnel reshuffling, research, promotion, alteration of structures and regulations, encouragement of innovation and initiative and better public relations.

Administrative reform through changes in the legal system is a very common phenomenon. A new law on land reforms or local government can usher in very significant changes in administration. At the time of framing the law and in course of legislative debates and discussions, the proposed reforms receive wide publicity. The stage of legislation is usually preceded by consultations and deliberations in several fora such as committees or commissions, the press and so on.

Reform through attitudinal changes involves manipulation of the human side of enterprise. Administrative organisations consist essentially of human beings. Formal changes in structures, laws and regulations may not produce the desired results unless these changes are appreciated and accepted by the organisational members. To quote Caiden, "Lasting reforms cannot depend on the superiority of power or the coercion of nonbelievers. Ultimately, those who resist reforms have to be won over in spirit as well as body. Their attitudes must change or be changed."[17]

Attitudinal changes are not easy to bring about. There may be outward signs of change, but really the old ways of doing things may persist. Behavioural sciences have been engaged in researches on various methods of bringing about changes in attitudes to facilitate both organisational growth and individual satisfaction. Administrative reform as behavioural change and adaptation opens up new ways of organisational renewal that are expected to be continuous and informal.

The methods of implementation suggested by Caiden are really 'sources' of reform. Revolutionary change, bureaucratic awareness, legislative intervention and attitudinal transformation provide the impulses for administrative reform. Implementation *per se* is a more mundane job involving organisational arrangement to oversee the actual execution of specific reform proposals. For example, the Department of Administrative Reforms (later called Department of Personnel and Administrative Reforms) became the nodal agency in the Government of India to process and watch over implementation of the reform proposals contained in the several reports of the Administrative Reforms Commission. Usually, the responsibility for 'processing' the recommendations of a committee is entrusted to a smaller committee or to some senior officers. The head of the department/agency has to see that the reform proposals pertaining to his organisation are actually pursued and implemented within a definite time frame. When reforms involve creation of new posts and procurement of new material and equipment, budgetary adjustments have to be made accordingly. Sanctions are also to be obtained from appropriate authorities and tenders and contracts negotiated in time. Implementation would thus mean operationalising of the specific proposals and their enforcement within a definite time frame. Experience shows that reform proposals very often remain in files and shelves for want of attention and supervision. Reforms that adversely affect the interests of the top bureaucracy are likely to be forgotten and those that benefit them are likely to be pursued in right earnest.

Evaluation

Reforms, when accepted and implemented, should be monitored and evaluated. In course of the implementation process many problems and difficulties are likely to arise. The organisation must be prepared to receive these signals of dysfunction and make necessary adjustments to the original proposals. This presupposes a plan of implementation in a phased manner. At each stage the expected result should be predetermined and as the implementation process gets going the actual results should be compared with the expected ones.

Evaluation is concerned with the examination of the final outcome of implementation. The objectives of reforms, as originally conceived, need to be specified and concretised, to the optimum. For example, an original proposal to improve environmental standard has to be made more specific for evaluation purposes. How much reduction in atmospheric pollution is attempted? How many parks and open spaces have to be created or renovated? How many trees have to be planted? What kind of checks should be imposed on automobiles? These and many other questions should be raised and answered at the outset to operationalise the concept of improving environmental standard. Without such specification, the organisational and procedural changes that would be effected to bring about improvement cannot be evaluated scientifically.

Admittedly, there are many methodological problems involved in the evaluation of administrative reforms. Success measured merely in terms of contribution to the ultimate objectives of administrative performance may be illusory.

Even if performance meets the standard, this may not have contributed to 'social efficiency or the public interest'. The end results of reform may not have been due solely to its implementation. Government operations can rarely be attributed to the performance of a single agency. The interactions with the environment (client, politician, business etc.) and the sister agencies are not easy to separate from the single-handed working of a particular agency.

Nevertheless, evaluation of reforms should be an integral part of a reform process. These difficulties are no doubt genuine and to circumvent these, more rigorous methods of evaluation need to be evolved. Unless it can be proved objectively that reforms lead to definite improvement and produce concrete results, further reforms may not be easy to propose and pursue.

Administrative Reforms in Practice

Ideas about administrative reforms (AR)—theoretical conceptual understandings—are derived from the world of administrative practice. AR is intensely practical. In fact the origin of the intellectual field called Public Administration (PA) can be traced to the nineteenth century Wilsonian exhortation for building up a science of administration for reforming administration.

AR efforts are as old as organised government as an institution. The underlying reasons for these may be many such as the birth of a new political regime (e.g. Post-Independence India), emergence of a new vision of collective life (e.g. Development Agenda of Third World countries), major environmental influences buffeting government such as Globalisation and Neo-liberalist trend and externally induced (particularly, donor-driven) change programme, like, the Structural Adjustment Policy of the World Bank.

In the 1960s India had embarked upon a wide-ranging and fairly massive administrative reforms enterprise. The main guiding idea was to 'modernise' public administrative machinery and procedures and to make a close fit between public administration and the developmental needs of the country. China in 1998 initiated a long-drawn-out process of reforms motivated by both internal and external causes. Chinese 'socialism' had to be adjusted to global economic forces and to the need for internal 'market' economy, demand for new employment creation and the restructuring of the large number of public enterprises, particularly the loss-making ones. Similarly, many countries—both 'developed' and 'developing'—have in recent times been engaged in wide-ranging AR efforts.

As regards African countries (particularly Sub-Saharan Africa, it has been observed that one could identify distinct periods of AR exercises starting with (a) post-independence efforts to maintain delivery of public services and sustain public administration; (b) creation of public enterprises in almost all sectors and centrally controlled development projects administration in the 1960s and 70s; (c) reforms under externally induced structural adjustment policy in the 1980s onward — basically 'down-sizing' and wage-bill reduction efforts; and (d) introduction of 'governance' programme in the 1990s with emphasis on rule of law, accountability and transparency, citizens' participation and civil society's involvement in social development.

Broadly, a general sequencing of reforms in public administration can be presented in the following way:

i) Changes in governmental structures, organisations, functions and personnel as first generation reforms;
ii) Reforms in public 'management' as second generation reforms; and
iii) Third generation reforms characterised by broad 'governance' agenda providing for accountability and transparency, citizens' participation and responsive public administration and ethical values in administration.

This is obviously a broad thumb-nail sketch of wide-ranging AR efforts in different continents and countries. Any change programme has always to take into account situational peculiarities of the country concerned—its institutional history, culture and demographic and resources position and external relationships. A rigid blueprint idea ofAR is obviously not a feasible proposition. Also, indiscriminate transplanting of institutions from one country to another without proper regard for the specificities (situational peculiarities) of the recipient country has been found, as per experience, to be non-workable.

World Bank's Reforms Experiences

In this context, it is worthwhile recounting the rich experiences of the World Bank in the broad field of civil service reforms? There have been varied types and complex modes of reform. For instance, governments, have reshaped rigid, hierarchical bureaucracies into flexible, decentralized and citizen-responsive organisations. In quite a few countries, sweeping reforms processes have been on, pushing through radical, systematic transformations based on the 'new public management' model. Reforms have been made in terms of narrower government functions (down-sizing), demands for value for money and a definitive focus on results. More conservative reforms in other countries have attempted incremental improvements, without much of an alteration in the basic administrative structures and functions.

The major highlights of Banks track record in this area are presented here, drawing on the Bank's PREM notes (public sector), no.31,1999. The purpose is not to glorify the Bank's role but to provide a sketch of the complexities and problems of real life reforms efforts in specific (developing country) situations.

In line with first generation 'neo-liberal' civil service reforms ideas, the central concern of Banks reforms policy had been to bring balance to government pay and employment and practices. This is the conventional 'downsizing' exercise that has not been politically acceptable at many places. Hence, a major paradigm shift in reforms enterprise took place soon in terms of formulation of a broader policy embracing 'revamping government functions and organisational structures, improving human resources policies in central, local and sector governments, revising legal and regulatory framework, providing institutional support for decentralisation and managing the process through which these changes are implemented'. Civil service reform, on Bank's own admission, has usually been like 'palliative measures to solve problems that require major surgery'?

Reflecting on whatever has been achieved so far in the area of AR, Bank's creative reminiscences are worth our quotation in this context.

To start with, it has been observed that too often 'technical administrative fixes have been applied to fundamental problems of political economy'. Ignoring critical links with other parts of the larger politico-administrative system, reforms attempts have tended to assume narrow technical exercise. Any worthwhile reforms exercise has to have a comprehensive and realistic framework as well as an outline of indicative instruments of support for it. On the issue of more conventional pay and employment policies reform, the comment has been that such partial policies are 'necessary but insufficient conditions for performance and capacity improvements'. Mere 'downsizing' is not the solution; the goal has to be fixed on long-term right-sizing and performance improvements.

In this connection, some important principles enunciated (implicitly) are:

- Addressing first order questions about the role of the state with important implications for functions, structures and organisations and the processes of government.
- Working out functional links between civil service management and the framework of controls and incentives embodied in the government's financial management systems and forging strong links particularly between personnel and budget functions essential for sound government management.
- Making well-thought-out decisions about decentralisation/dilution keeping in mind implications for personnel, functions and finances and considering, in this context, their linkages with policies related to central civil services departments.
- Ensuring coherence and consistency in reforms programme by taking into account the linkages between central government's civil service reforms and institutional reforms in individual sectors such as health and education with high concentration of government personnel.
- Pursuing a flexible approach to reforms in view of the exceedingly complex nature of governmental reforms as institutional reforms require adaptability and participants' understanding and commitment to reforms goals.
- Avoiding blind adoption of 'new public management' recipes and finding the right reforms strategy to carry out the essential tasks by leveraging scarce resources through, among other things, creative technology application or innovative management initiatives.

Cautionary Remarks

Admittedly, AR initiatives and experiments

are time-consuming, long-gestational and uncertainty-producing, apart from being costly both in monetary and personnel terms. Hence, some cautionary remarks should be in order in this context. First, conventional 'projects' approach to reforms is based on 'engineering model' with emphasis on tight time frame and de-emphasis on the human variables. Second, a highly integrated and long rolling approach to reforms needs to be avoided to obviate overloading of the already burdensome requirements of government reform. Third, reforms initiatives have to make sure that obsolete and discarded systems are not installed in the name of 'reforms' impeding thereby progressive change which is at the heart of any worthwhile AR exercise. Fourth, guidance on the design and implementation of carefully sequenced governmental reforms cannot be provided through a universal (one-size-fits-all) blueprint approach. Countries must be able to choose reforms path and modalities that are appropriate for their specific needs and circumstances. 'Will to change' is very basic to a country's reforms initiative and its determined pursuit and longer term sustenance.

Summing up

To sum up, administrative reform is an important issue in public administration. Its need is widely felt and its modalities are currently receiving considerable attention. Reforms serve a number of purposes and are of various types. There are distinct phases through which reform proposals are to pass. Reforms depend for their success on able leadership, correct diagnosis and grasp of the situation, proper sense of timing, wider support base, careful planning and phasing of proposals, command over resources and above all a sound understanding of 'politics.' The implementation of reforms has to be planned properly and monitoring should be a part of the implementation process. It has to be clearly proved that reforms produce expected results. Hence, evaluation should be an integral part of reform.

REFERENCES

1. Frederick C. Mosher (ed.), *Government Reorganisations: Cases and Controversy,* Bobbs-Merrill, N Y 1967, p. 497.
2. Paul H. Appleby, "The Significance of the Hoover Commission Report" *The Yale Review,* 39 (1); 2-22, September 1949.
3. Gerald E. Caiden, *Administrative Reform,* The Penguin Press, London 1970, p. 65.
4. Fred W. Riggs, "Introduction", *in Frontiers of Development Administration* (edited), Duke University Press, Durham, N. C., 1971.
5. Caiden opts for systems approach, imagining that die process approach is narrow in scope. The process approach need not be narrowly conceived and can be quite comprehensive.
6. J D Montgomery, "Sources of Bureaucratic Reform: Typologv Purpose and Politics,', in Ralph Braibanti (ed), *Political and Administrative development,* Duke University Press, 1969.
7. Norton Long, "Power and Administration", *Public Administration Review,* IX, No. 4, Autumn 1949
8. For a discussion on the distinction between instrumentalorganisationsandsocietalinstitutions, see Philip Selznick, *Leadership in Administration,* Row, Peterson & Co., Evanston, III 1957.
9. Wesley E.Bjur and Gerald E. Caiden, "Administrative Reform and Institutional Bureaucracies", *Dynamics of Development,* edited by Sudesh K. Sharma, Concept Publishing Co., Delhi,Vol. I. 1977.
10. Op. cit., pp. 470-471.
11. Wesley E. Bjur and Gerald E. Caiden, op. cit.
12. See Robert T. Golembiewski and William B. Eddy, *Organisation Development in Public Administration,* Part I, Marcel Dekker, NV 1978.
13. See in this connection, S. R. Maheshwari, *Administrative Reforms, in India.* Macmillan India Limited, Delhi. 1981.
14. Geraid E. Caiden, op. cit., Chapter Five.
15. Caiden, op. cit., pp. 142-143.
16. Op. cit., pp. 145-156.
17. Caiden, op. cit., p. 154.

CHAPTER 15

Comparative Public Administration

As a subfield, comparative public administration (CPA) cannot claim a long history. Since the writings of Aristotle, interest in comparative governmental systems has been a lively field of academic and practical inquiry. Nations have been interested in organising their executive branch of government; and as they tried to innovate administratively, they studied and adopted practices of other countries. In the eighteenth and nineteenth centuries, revolutionaries and reformers in Europe looked across boundaries for institutions to copy or reject. "Undoubtedly the most important comparative research was earned out between 1895 and 1920, not by comparative law professors or participants in international congress, but by a sociologist, Max Weber". We owe to Weber the core concept of the field bureaucracy — as part of a comparative typology of the forms of domination: tradition, charisma and legal-rationality. Since then major comparative studies in the USA had been made by European-trained scholars whose central focus was: the role of bureaucracies in modern government.

Comparative public administration has been widened and deepened by scholarly interest in the administration of third world countries, especially after World War II. But the field had its earlier cultivators in Europe and America such as Finer, Carl Friedrich among others.

BASIC INTEREST AND EVOLUTION

CPA is basically interested in cross-cultural public administration. The founding fathers like Leonard White thought that cultural factors did not make any difference in administrative settings, as in their view, there were universal 'principles' applicable to situations anywhere and everywhere but, writers like Robert Dahl and Dwight Waldo pointed out those cultural factors could make public administration in one nation different from that in another. As Dahl has explained, "The comparative aspects of public administration have largely been ignored and as long as the study of public administration is not comparative, claim for'science of administration' sounds rather hollow.

CPA got real impetus in 1962 when the Comparative Administration Group (GAG) of the American Society for Public Administration (ASPA) received fairly lavish funding from the Ford Foundation at a time when the Cold War was at its height. Ford funding was terminated in 1971, as research was oriented more towards theory-building rather than empirical and practical problem-solving. As Ferrel Heady has put it, CPA addresses five motivating concerns the:

(a) Search for theory;
(b) Urge for practical application;
(c) Incidental contribution of the broader field of comparative politics;

(d) Interest of researchers trained in the tradition of administrative law;
(e) Comparative analysis of ongoing problems of public administration.

CPA is different from public administration in two major respects: First, public administration has generally been culture-bound. The discipline in USA and UK, for instance, is grounded in politico-administrative realities of the two countries. Second, public administration generally differs from CPA in respect of its origins. The discipline, as it has evolved in USA, has been practitioner-oriented and involved in the real world of administration. CPA, by contrast, has attempted to build theory and seek knowledge for the sake of knowledge.

The earlier stage of CPA was enriched by the steady growth of a subfield called development administration. From 1960 to 1970, when development administration dominated CPA, Fred Riggs chaired ASPA's CAG Group. It is small wonder, therefore, that much of the work in CPA has revolved around the ideas of Riggs who had abiding interest in the public administration of the developing countries. As Riggs desired, CPA was to be 'empirical, nomothetic and ecological — that is, to put crudely, factual and scientific, abstracted and generalized, systematic and non-parochial.'[1]

Features of CPA

There are certain distinctive features of CPA. First, it is a relatively young sub-field that emerged only after World War II. Second, there are competing and diverse approaches to the study of CPA which is due to different disciplinary contributions, as also due to the over-enthusiasm of scholars in the field to chart out new directions. Third, by 1962, Riggs could note more and more nomothetic and ecological approaches, indicating thereby application of scientific rigour to analysis. Alongside this movement, there was simultaneously another distinct thrust noticeable among scholars in the wake of post-behavioural revolution in political science. At this phase, emphasis on normative considerations could be seen side by side with empirical analyses. Fourth, the field has been dominated by American scholars mainly due to Ford Foundation's support, as also due to the American scholars' deep interest in the newly independent nations—their culture, politics and administration. Fifth, CPA could be seen having two basic motivational concerns: theory-building and administrative problems of the developing countries.

As one author has summed up the two major reasons for the emergence of CPA (or why compare?): One, the need for comparison as a pre-requisite for the development of a science of public administration (as earlier emphasised by Dahl and others) and Two, the need for comparison in the interest of practical governance and knowledge of facts.

CPA can help students, practical administrators and other experts know and understand more about public administration in other countries. Also, CPA facilitates the possibility of administrative reform in the form of transplantation of certain administrative institutions and practices from other countries.'[2]

Methodologies and Models

CPA has been defined as the theory of public administration applied to diverse cultures and national settings and the body of factual data, by which it can be examined and tested. While this is acknowledged as a laudable objective, there are major methodological and conceptual problems involved in 'theory-building'. For instance, 'democracy' is a concept that is used liberally by most countries, irrespective of the nature of rule actually obtaining in them. 'Administration' itself may not be the same thing everywhere. As R.B. Jain has pointed out,"The study of CPA has given rise to problems of methodological concern and of conceptual focus. Scholars have been greatly preoccupied with the construction of models and typologies of political regimes and institutions and the delineation of geographic cultural areas—an activity prominent also in and shared with comparative politics. The range of concepts associated with the term 'bureaucracy' and its ideal type has been extensively used. The so-called action theory and the concepts and language of (Parsonian) structural-functionalism have often been involved and related and overlapping but different and broader concept of ecology is also frequently set forth as important. Equilibrium theory, particularly the idea of a 'system' with 'inputs' and 'outputs', is prominent. Most of the concepts and phrases of contemporary behavioural science are being used and there is reference, for example, to matters such as communication theory and multi-varian analysis."[3]

Two Models

Although there have been intermittent efforts to construct 'models' of administration, two major 'models' have come up for discussion among students of CPA: The Bureaucratic Model and the Prismatic-sala Model.

The bureaucratic model is derived from Max Weber's conceptualisation of 'bureaucracy' as the most rational organisation. The Weberian model has been discussed in details elsewhere. It has been generally accepted that the legal-rational concept of authority is normally associated with the developed capitalist democracies and they alone are capable of sustaining administrative structures approximating the bureaucratic model. Comparative studies on bureaucracy are numerous. More notable scholars, Eke Morroe Berger, Alfred Diamont, Ferrel Heady and Robert Presthus have come out with revealing conclusions that the bureaucratic structure has functioned differently in different Afro-Asian countries. The studies have brought out close interactions between the administrative sub-system and the broader political system. It is quite common to observe that the boundaries of administrative organisations are difficult to maintain in situations of over-politicisation. The administrators have often crossed over to the political system and the same behaviour of boundary-crossing has been quite common among the politicians also. Personal loyalty, ideological pressures and cultural traits have been found to be influential in real life administrative operations. The size of the public sector measured in terms of certain indices such as economic growth, population, buoyant revenues, social and political changes etc. has been another important dimension of comparative studies on public bureaucracies. Theories of the New Right have advocated down-sizing of government; whereas the developing countries have opted for enlargement of the public sector. Robert Fried has made interesting comparison between 'rich bureaucracies' and 'poor bureaucracies'. Also, his analysis of bureaucratic power in terms of control over state policy and that over society opens up possibilities of new wtys of comparing bureaucracies. Again, the roles of 'military bureaucracies' and 'civil bureaucracies' are interesting typologies for comparative bureaucratic studies.[4]

The phenomenon of environment-administration interaction has been studied in depth by Fred Riggs whose ecological model has been as influential in administrative analysis as Weber's bureaucratic model. Commonly known as the *prismatic-sola model,* this second model has been based on the Parsonian structural functional approach. The Riggsian model, as elaborated in the following chapter, attempts to examine how public administration is performed by different types of social structures. In this highly imaginative model, the administrative sub-system is placed within the framework of a larger system (environment). The grand theory of prismatic society has influenced theorising in development administration—a sub-field which has often been equated with comparative public administration. The idea of 'enclave' development through introduction of micro institutions to push through development within the framework of under development has been one distinct trend in comparative administrative experiments in developing countries.

As a category by itself, 'development administration' has flourished within the larger corpus of CPA literature with contribution from scholars belonging to different disciplines and nations. One recurring stand has been that development administration is not only 'different' from administration in the developed countries; it is also substandard or of lower quality, compared to administration in the 'First World'. As Robert Fried has commented, "The development administration approach to comparative public administration tends to validate a Manichean view of administrative systems—all wonderful in the North, all despicable in the South (or vice versa). It tends to miss the hidden rationalities in Third World administration — the means of being effective and respectful of human dignity in different cultures. It tends to downplay the effectiveness and humanity of pre-bureaucratic, informal social means of controlling behaviour and solving problems (e.g. crime control in Japan). It exaggerates the irrelevance of Third World studies for understanding of the advanced world... and downplays the potentialities for irrational-bureaucratic performance in the advanced world. It produces the same unrealistic view of government bureaucracy performance in the Third World as its objective correlative—the often idealised, just as often demonised, performance of advanced world bureaucracies".[5] What it amounts to is that CPA has not always been a neutral academic field. There have been both overt and covert biases in favour of the administrative models ofWestern developed democracies. This has often led to lop-sided view of administrative reality and a certain neglect of the study of strengths of pre-bureaucratic social control of community life in many of the Third World countries. Only now, for instance, the community management of bio-diversity in some of the so-called underdeveloped societies is being applauded as scientific, rational and resource-conserving.

Problems of Application

Applicability of the models of CPA in specific country situations has its problems. At the time of framing of India's Constitution, for example, the idea of federalism was debated by the founding fathers: and what they actually adopted was different from the traditional model of federalism. India's past history of governance and the special needs of the country weighed heavily in the minds of the framers. The models of CPA thus serve as a framework for analysing different aspects of administrative phenomena in a comparative perspective and they are useful in revealing clearly the social, economic and political bases in which administrative institutions are rooted. As R.B. Jain has observed: "The central problem in the study of CPA is that it is large enough to embrace all the phenomena that should be embraced without being, by virtue of its large dimensions, too unwieldy. The second problem is relating the universal and the unique in one system. The idea of universal runs through administrative study, for example, in the assertions of the 'founding fathers' to the most sophisticated of our contemporaries in the field but to make comparisons implies not only the identification of the universals but also discovering a criterion of differentiation."[6]

Current Status

In USA, the Comparative Administrative

Group disbanded in 1973 immediately after the stoppage of financial support from the Ford Foundation; it merged with the International Committee of the American Society for Public Administration. Reflecting on the gradual decline of CPA, Golembiewski wrote: "Public administration should take note of the fact that comparative administration's failure rests substantially on a self-imposed failure experience It set an unattainable goal, that is, in its early and persisting choice to seek a comprehensive theory or model in terms of which to define itself."[7]

Future Prospect

Lack of financial support, for a time, reduced academic interest in comparative administrative research. The real work of public administration has, however, presented many opportunities, in recent times, for innovative comparative studies. For instance, there is today increasing inter-state interactions due to 'globalisation' and 'liberalisation' policies dictated by international funding agencies and influenced by the forces of international economic transactions. The interactive efforts in the performance of states can thus be a good theme for comparative analysis. The issue of 'human rights' is currently engaging the attention of international institutions and national governments. Comparative studies of 'human rights' enforcement could be another major area of comparative study. There is yet another trend noticeable in governmental circles—the co-production of results in the public sector. Public bureaucracies, private firms, voluntary agencies and community-based organisations are coming together more and more, blurring the distinction between 'public' and 'private' management. Now in different situations, the nations are promoting co-production and creating a climate of networking of 'governance'. All these go to constitute a new thrust toward comparative governmental analysis. This optimistic climate of comparative administrative studies has been aptly described by Robert Fried in the following words: "The international interdependency of bureaucracies... the universalising of demands for human rights; the crucial role of publics in resisting or promoting reform; chancy the nature of status as a member of First, Second or Third Worlds—all of these present students and practitioners of comparative public administration with unexpected challenges to understanding, unexpected opportunities for research and conceptual development, unexpected excitement."[8]

It seems CPA is poised today for resurrection, as the situation worldwide is getting more and more propitious for comparative administrative analysis.

REFERENCES

1. Nicholas Henry, op, cit, p. 31.
2. *Jon S. T Quah.* "Comparative Public Administration: What and Why?" in Ramesh K. Arora *(ed.), Perspectives in Administrative Theory,* Associated Publishing House, New Delhi, 1979.
3. R.B. Jain. "The State of the Study of Comparative Public Administration in India", *The Indian Journal of Public Administration,* January-March. 1991.
4. Robert C. Fried, "Comparative Public Administration: The Search for Theories', in Naomy B. Lynn and Aaron Wildavsky (eds.), *Public Administration: The State of the Discipline,* Affiliated East-West Press Pvt. Ltd., New Delhi, 1990.
5. Robert C. Fried, op. cit. 3. R.B. Jain, op.cit.
6. R.B. Jain, op.cit.
7. Robert T. Golembiewski, *Public Administration as a Developing Discipline. Part I: Perspectives on Past and Present,* Marcel Dekker. New York. 1977, p. 147.
8. Robert C. Fried, op. cit.

Chapter 16

Development Administration

After the Second World War, the new nations emerged out of the dark experience of imperial exploitation and embarked upon a complex process of social reconstruction. Poverty, illiteracy, diseases and malnutrition, low agricultural and industrial productivity together posed a formidable challenge for the governments of the new nations. The idea of 'development administration' as directly government-led effort to intervene in the processes of socio-economic transformation was born at this juncture of Third World history.

Developmental administration need not be equated with administrative development or growth. It is by now widely acknowledged that development administration is public administration with a difference. Its focus is on government-influenced change towards the attainment of progressive social, economic and political objectives. Development, as Montgomery puts it, "is usually conceived as an aspect of change that is desirable, broadly predicted or planned and administered or at least influenced by Governmental action" .[1] To quote Edward Weidner, development administration is "an action-oriented, goal-oriented administrative system."[2] Structurally, development administration is concerned with the organisation of new agencies for development such as a planning commission or a development authority or corporation. It involves refashioning of established agencies like the department of irrigation and agriculture. The internal authority structure and hierarchy within the agencies engaged in development have to be differently conceived. The role of leadership in encouraging and guiding the programmes of development activities needs re-examination in the development context. Efficient management of governmental programmes of development and stimulation of private development activities call for, in brief, a restructuring of public administration. This seems to be the meaning of development administration in its instrumental or practical sense.

The concept of 'administrative development' has for its focus 'administration', which exists as a system like the political system or the economic system. Administrative development refers to the evolving capacity of an administrative system. It takes place everywhere, irrespective of the status of a country (whether it is 'developed' or 'undeveloped'). It is the central task of administration to mobilise resources, use these efficiently and produce desired results through organised efforts under policy direction coming from institutional or political system leaders. Some of the indices of administrative development are (i) increase in size and budgetary allocation; (ii) increasing diversification and specialization; and (iii) more and more professionalisation of administrative personnel. Efficiency and effectiveness of government everywhere is sought to be enhanced by planned administrative development in response to changing societal demands. Development administration, which is focused on 'development' activities also need administrative development to suit the needs of 'development'.

The term 'Development Administration' originated in 1955 with an Indian scholar, Goswami but the conceptualisation and elaboration of the concept were done by the western, especially American scholars. The most important single contribution came from the Comparative Administration Group (CAG) in USA organised in 1960-61 under the aegis of the American Society for Public Administration. Disappointed with the results of the US Government's technical assistance programme for public administration in the developing countries, the members of the CAG—a small group of political scientists and students of public administration—conducted research and seminars on the administrative problems of some of the Third World countries. As the long-time chairman of the CAG, Fred W Riggs came to be regarded as the prime mover of academic interest in the field of development administration.

The Riggsian Model

According to Riggs, development can be seen as 'a process of increasing autonomy (discretion) of social systems made possible by a rising level of diffraction.'This autonomy manifests itself in the form of increased ability of human societies to shape their physical, human and cultural environments. Riggs has pursued what is known as the 'ecological study' of public administration, the basic assumption of which is that public administration operates in different social and environmental settings and adapts itself to environmental conditions in order to achieve a set of social goals.

The origin of the ecological approach to the study of administration .can be traced to the work of John Gaus, L.D. White and M. Dimock. As Gaus described it:

"An ecological approach to public administration builds—quite literally from the ground up; from the element of a place—soils, climate, location, for example—to the people who live there—their number and ages and knowledge and the ways of physical and social technology by which from the place and in relationship with one another, they get their living."[3]

Fred Riggs enriched the concept and gave it a distinct character within the corpus of comparative public administration knowledge. As Riggs has argued, a perfect comparative study of administration should be analytical, nomothetic and ecological, as opposed to normative, ideographic and non-ecological. The basic premise of ecological approach is that the bureaucracy or administration is just one of the many sub-systems in a society and as a subsystem it is in constant interaction with other subsystems, i.e., political, cultural, economic, etc. Hence, for a better understanding of the role and working of bureaucracy, it must be studied in the context of other societal subsystems with which it is interacting continuously. In this process, bureaucracy influences and is in turn being influenced by other subsystems. Hence, it is both an independent and a dependent variable.

The ecological model formulated by Riggs has been the most creative and at the same time a highly controversial model of administration in the developing countries. Along a continuum between agrarian and industrial, Riggs postulates an inductive typology of administrative systems. A social system is a vast network of interrelated parts, each one of which can be understood in relation to other parts and to the whole system. Administrative structure and behaviour being an inseparable and interacting part *of* the whole society could be understood in the context of the social system in which it is embedded. Riggs suggested two ideal types of public administration systems in agrarian and industrial and indicated that similar ideal types could be constructed at various transitional stages between agrarian and industrial.

Riggs had drawn upon the structural-functional approach that gained considerable currency in political science in his times. According to this approach, all societies perform an array of functions such as administrative functions, religious functions, economic functions and so on. Societies usually have a variety of structures that perform the different functions. Thus, the family performs certain social functions, the market performs the economic functions and the legislature and party perform political functions. In traditional societies, one encounters a few structures such as a family or a leader that would be performing a whole host of functions like rule-making, rule-adjudication, economic allocation and even medical and health administration. As society grows and develops, more and more specialised structures appear, each one of which becomes engaged in specific functions. So, differentiation of structures may be looked at as the essence of development. Using an analogy, Riggs pictures the process of differentiation as sunlight passing through a thunderstorm and appearing as a rainbow. Most traditional societies are like sunlight in its natural condition. A few critical structures perform in these societies most societal functions. This mixed state of structures is like pure white light-fused, according to the science of optics. These structures in the traditional societies must be torn apart to make room for more and more specialised functions in the wake of modernisation. To extend the original analogy, the thunderstorm acts as a prism to change the pure white light into a multi-coloured rainbow.

As Riggs puts it, "Traditional agricultural and folk societies (Agraria) approximate the fused model and modern industrial societies (Industria) approach the refracted model. The former is 'functionally diffuse', the latter 'functionally specific'. Intermediate between these polar extremes is the prismatic model, so called because of the prism through which fused light passes to become refracted."[4]

The transitional society is continually in the throes of change. As it moves along, it differentiates in terms of specific structures. This also necessitates integrating mechanisms to hold the parts together. Integration becomes very important as the developing society contains within it both old and new structures coexisting. Thus nuclear medicine and the tribal medicine man will be found to exist together.

Riggs has been primarily interested in social change and in understanding the process of transition which he has termed the prismatic state when structural differentiation goes on alongside efforts toward societal integration. The prismatic society is trapped like light inside a prism. It is not fully fused, nor is it fully diffracted. The new structures are half born and are trying to adjust with the old ones. Modernity and tradition coexist in uneasy companionship. Modern structures and procedures might have been formally introduced, but behind the facade of these new structures, the old and traditional ways of doing things persist in reality. This discrepancy between formal structures and actual modalities has been called *formalism* by Riggs.[5]

On the basis of his empirical research, Riggs has constructed two ideal polar types:

(a) A *refracted society* where every function has a corresponding structure that specialises in its performance;
(b) A *fused society* in which a single structure performs all functions. Riggs con-

ceptualised the 'prismatic society' as a midpoint or intermediate form of transitional society between the two ideal types, combining both fused and refracted features that are characterised by *heterogeneity* (the simultaneous presence, side by side, of quite different kinds of systems, practices and viewpoints), *formalism* (the extent to which discrepancy exists between the prescriptive and the descriptive, between the formal and effective power, between impressions and actual practices) and *overlapping* (the extent to which what is described as administrative behaviour is actually determined by non-administrative criteria). The prismatic society has its appropriate administrative system. Riggs has borrowed the Spanish word 'Sala' for it, which combines both the pure (fused) chamber and (refracted) office traits. In the sala model, both administrative rationality and non-administrative considerations are recognised. To quote Riggs, the prismatic-sala model "enables us to cope with many problems of transitional societies that slip through the net of established social sciences...... whereas it is possible, for example, to speak with some meaningfulness of 'public administration' as a separate institutional sphere and academic discipline in the American setting, it becomes highly misleading to take such an approach in Iran, Indonesia and Malaysia." This insightful observation hints at the surreptitious encroachment of the public sphere by 'private' interests in most developing societies.

Later Modifications

Riggs has since changed his original views about the prismatic society. In his later publication entitled *Prismatic Society Revisited* (1975), he considered his earlier conceptualisation as a mistaken 'one-dimensional approach' and suggested a new definition of prismatic society based on a 'two-dimensional approach'. The original dimension was degree *of differentiation* dnd along this dimension societies were classified into three types: fused, prismatic and diffracted.

In his new formulation, Riggs has introduced the second dimension of degree of integration among structures in a society that is differentiated (a fused society is, by definition, undifferentiated and, hence, integrated). The possibility of mal-integration or lack of coordination among social structures accompanies the process of differentiation. Riggs compares the problem to that of coordination of sounds from the different specialised instruments in a symphony orchestra. It is the conductor's baton that gives proper direction for coordination and achieves integration in the differentiated sounds of the whole range of specialized instruments.

According to Riggs, differentiated social systems can be ranked on a mal-integrated-integrated scale. The two basic societal models of diffracted and prismatic (where differentiation can be found) are further subdivided into finer types on the basis of degree of integration. Accordingly, diffracted societies are reconceptualised as *eo-diffracted, ortho-diffracted* and *neo-diffracted.* Prismatic societies are similarly fine grained into *eo-prismatic, ortho-prismatic anc neo- prismatic.*

This reformulation means that the prismatic model would include any society that i differentiated but mal-integrated. Also, diffracted model refers to any society that differentiated and integrated. Prefixes (eo, ortho, neo) are attached to both the prismatic an diffracted types to suggest stages in the degrc of differentiation.

The two dimensional approach, as Riggs claims, has the advantage of conceding that 'prismatic' conditions need not be confined to less developed countries only but may occur in societies at any level of differentiation including those in developed nations. He refers to symptoms of mal-integration in the United States and other developed nations 'in the form of urban crises, race riots, student uprisings, popular apathy, the hippy phenomenon and the profound turbulence wrought by a continuing war in Vietnam'.

The conditions ofThird World countries provided the initial impetus and data for the construction of the prismatic model. Hence, in spite of the reformulated schema, Riggs has been primarily interested in unravelling the peculiar administrative behaviour in transitional societies which are now reconceptualised as "ortho-prismatic (semi-differentiated and mal-integrated). In the three principal models, the bureaucracies are correspondingly unique. In the 'fused' model, traditional bureaucracies were functionally diffused "each official typically performed a wide range of functions, affecting political and economic as well as administrative functions." At the other end of the spectrum, the differentiated societies (especially well-integrated ones that are reconceptualised as neo-diffracted) have bureaucracies that are much more functionally specific "as the chief—though by no means the only—agent for performing administrative tasks." In the transitional prismatic societies (the orthoprismatic models), the bureaucracies are neither diffuse nor narrowly specific but are intermediate as to the degree of functional specialisation. They do not blend well with the other institutions within the political system and thus tend to fuel the forces of mal-integration. Prismatic societies thus suffer from a serious lack of balance between the rates of the political and bureaucratic growth. Due to bureaucratic hegemony, the bureaucrats often encroach upon the jurisdiction of the politician and try deliberately to affect the political process.

Riggs also refers to the sala model (administration in prismatic societies) as 'basically wasteful and prodigal.' It is associated with institutionalised corruption, nepotism in recruitment and inefficiency in rule application. Self-aggrandisement and self-protection rather than service to the people characterises bureaucratic operation. There is thus always a pronounced gap between formal expectations and actual behaviour.

While acknowledging the pioneering enterprise of Riggs, it needs to be admitted that the prismatic-sala model has lost its specificity, as Riggs himself has later conceded that it is not meant for exclusive application to the developing countries alone. Again, the dysfunctional associated with his model may not always be found everywhere in a tradition-modernity mix. Japan is a glaring example in this context. The Riggsian model suffers from overgeneralization, as the so-called 'developing countries' are not a homogeneous category. Any meaningful conceptualization has got to reckon with the subtle peculiarities of the new nations in terms of their culture, history, administrative tradition, economy and geography.

Bureaucratic Culture

The Riggsian analysis opens up an interesting discussion on bureaucratic culture. In the developing countries, the culture of bureaucracy is a hangover of the colonial regime. Under a system of bureaucratic rule, the general culture of bureaucracy during the colonial period had been authoritarian, centralist and people-avoiding. It was the 'mai-bap' concept that governed the relationship between the ruler and the ruled. With the passing away of colonialism, the popular regimes, that had come to replace imperial rule, were confronted with the problem of transforming the 'ruling bureaucracy' into civil servants accountable to political leadership and the people.

The culture of bureaucracy had been a well-known theme in the Weberian description of the ways of bureaucratic functioning. For instance, Weber referred to the power position of a fully developed bureaucracy and the tendency of bureaucratic administration to keep its knowledge and action secret.

As a general theme, bureaucratic culture may be profitably linked to total societal culture. B. Guy Peters talks of two kinds of modal cultures: rationalist or deductive cultures and pragmatic or empirical cultures.

The bureaucratic concept of universality and impersonality of rules can be associated with rationalist or deductive cultures. Most developed countries exhibit these cultures that tend to emphasise the deduction of specific statements from general statements. The rule-bound administration is generally accepted by the administrator and the client.

By contrast, in a system of pragmatic or empirical culture, generalities are derived from innumerable individual decisions. In some sense, each case is a unique one and the special features of the case call for the modification and even rejection of general rules. This situation comes closest to English common law practices. As Peters observes: "The concept of individuality and individual rights, as one component of the more empirical culture, tends to make the job of the bureaucrat more difficult and forces more attention on specifics rather than on the generalities of the case.[6]

The situation in the developing countries is a mix of these two modal cultures. Apparently, elaborate rules and regulations exist to order administrative, behaviour and operation. In nractice, however, the situation can be described as: 'show me the man, I'll show you the rule'. Thus, formal rules are either decorative pieces or harassing instruments. Whenever it suits the ruling class, the rules are by-passed with impunity.

To sum up, bureaucratic culture in any country is a fairly regular way of administrative functioning conditioned by shared beliefs, norms, values and feelings among t' e members of the administrative class. It grows over time through a steady process of evolution, hence it has a certain permanence about it. At the same time, major societal changes impact on bureaucratic culture and bring about a new or modified culture.[7]

In this context, Crozier's study of French bureaucratic culture is noteworthy. Crozier has focussed less on the effects of national culture on the organisation's relationship with its political environment and more on the influences culture has on the internal workings of the organisation. It has been Czozier's main thesis that each national culture has a unique effect on organisations operating in that culture and that this effect will ultimately constitute the primary pathology of the organisation. *Bon Plaisir,* a symptom long ingrained in the French culture, is a stubborn insistence on personal autonomy that inhibits cooperation in French organisation.[8]

Specificity of Development Administration

Resuming our earlier discussion, development administration as a design or structural problem was not the focus of Riggsian analysis. Nor did Riggs examine the operational problems of development administration in diverse action situations. The structural and operational issues cannot be discussed a *priori;* these have to be explained on the basis of empirical findings on the ground.

The emergence of the new nations out of colonial experience and the urgent need for their speedy socio-economic reconstruction impelled a radical breakthrough in government organisation and operations. It is in this historical context that one has to appreciate the natural beginning of a new administrative paradigm called development administration.[8] The colonial legacy of routine law and order administration along with the associated personnel system and work procedure was found unsuitable for the accomplishment of the tasks of nation-building and programmatic goals fulfilment. The administrative institutions and procedures belonging to the old colonial regime were meant for a different purpose: To preserve and perpetuate a system of colonial domination. These were hot accountable to legislative bodies or to popular representatives at different levels. It was none of the concern of colonial administration to bring about all round agricultural and industrial development. Removal of social and economic inequality and correcting regional economic imbalances were not the objectives of imperial administration. Revenue extraction, export of raw material, minimum essential public services and law and order maintenance constituted the sum of total of imperial rule of the colonies. Security and extraction being the prime concern of the regime, the colonial public administrative system had essentially been centralised, suspicion-ridden and authoritarian.

The distinguishing mark of development administration, by contrast, is its focus on the management of 'development'. As an aspect of public administration, it connotes definite and planned institutional capacity to accomplish the specific goals of development through the formulation of appropriate policies, programmes and projects and their successful implementation. It is not mechanical efficiency of the 'scientific management' brand that is at the core of development administration. Participative, responsive and accountable management constitutes the essence of development administration. The management process has to enlist popular support and involvement; it has to respond to popular needs and demands; and it is ultimately accountable to the people and the popular representatives.

As George Gant has succinctly put it[10], "development administration is characterised by its purposes, its loyalties and its attitudes. The purposes of development administration are to stimulate and facilitate defined programs of social and economic progress. They are purposes of change and innovation and movement as contrasted with purposes of maintaining the status quo". In terms of loyalties, the bureaucracy has to be accountable to the people and not to any vested institutional interests, nor to any king or empire. In terms of attitudes, development administration calls for positive, persuasive and innovative stances from the bureaucracy. The traditional norms or forms of administration must be replaced by flexibility and adaptability to changing needs and situations.The attitude of development administration is outward reaching and not inward looking.

Often, development administration is sharply differentiated from other aspects of public administration such as law and order and judicial administration. Conceptually and practically, such differentiation helps in the focussing of attention on specific public organisations dealing directly with the production of concrete results such as agricultural output, irrigation water, fertilizer production etc. In fact, evaluation of development administration has to be on the basis of sectoral achievements.

Efficiency, in this context, would mean not

merely cost effectiveness; it should also include effectiveness in terms of achievements of results. Considerable investments may go into family planning programme, for instance; but the success of the programme would ultimately depend on the extent of actual reduction in birth rate achieved. This would involve both infrastructural investments (medical facilities, clinics etc.) and large-scale popular support and acceptance. Thus, development administration, in most cases, involves production of planned results in close association with the clientele.

Pai Panandiker and Kshirsagar, in their study of administrative behaviour in development, propose four behavioural parameters,[11] (i) change orientation; (ii) result orientation; (iii) citizen participative orientation; and (iv) commitment to work. They would expect a certain psychological disposition among administrators in development situations based on these parameters. The characteristics of administration that one can infer from this tabulation are change or flexibility, result production, citizen (people's) participation and high morale and motivation in work situation.

Participation has to be more than a mere slogan in development administration. It calls for serious restructuring of administration to facilitate peoples involvement in all aspects of development effort. Inherent in development administration is thus the idea of decentralisation. This means creating institutional opportunities for power distribution. The entrenched 'interests' in the Third World countries can be challenged through a process of decentralisation. Meaningful popular involvement will be possible only when the gross inequality in societal power distribution would be challenged and rectified.

However, the distinction between 'development' and 'non-development' administration need not be carried too far. The routine land revenue or law and order administration creates conditions for development. Unless the routine activities are performed well, development administration is likely to flounder on the rock of routine administration. If the state fails to maintain law and order, no developmental effort will succeed. Similarly, failure of developmental effort may lead to smoulder discontent that might burst into serious law and order problem. Another significant fact of development is the creation of capital assets (e.g. roads, dams, forests, etc.) that must be maintained properly. It is common experience that capital assets like tubewells, roads etc. created out of development fund soon fall into disrepair and the entire investment is wasted. Routine maintenance management is thus as important as development management. This clearly shows the high degree of interdependence between development administration and other routine aspects of administration.

Another important aspect of development administration is its close nexus with politics. An unfortunate trend in academic thinking on development administration has been to shun politics and to apotheosise 'management'. It is glibly overlooked that 'development' means changing the status quo. The development process is bound to affect the societal power structure and generate conflicts and tensions between different power groups. The 'what' and 'how' of development are *ab initio* political questions. Hence, development administrations without 'politics' is like 'Hamlet' without the Prince of Denmark. Essentially what it means is that from policy to implementation development management is inextricably connected with the vital political processes. The 'Third World' has got to break out of the ancient regime of power and privileges in order to reach the goal of a really just society. Development administration is the arena where this political battle is being relentlessly waged.

Evaluation

Criticisms against development administration are many and varied. Some of the important ones can be identified as follows:

1. Conceptually, development administration tends to disrupt public administration as a homogeneous discipline. Practically, the differentiation between development and non-development administration is highly artificial. While admitting some logic in this criticism, it needs to be stressed that the conceptualisation has facilitated analytical distinction between different aspects of public administration. As earlier pointed out, in the practical world of administration, there is a lot of overlapping and interdependence between the cognate arms of administration.
2. Development administration has tended to magnify the role of bureaucracy which has traditionally been a problem in most third world countries. Surely, there is more than a grain of truth in this criticism. The developmentists have exaggerated the role of bureaucracy and, to that extent, underrated other forms of public management. As the Indian experience shows, there have been many innovations in the field of development management. *Panchayati Raj* is an instance in point. Local development with the help of local popular support and involvement has greatly reduced the role of bureaucracy in many areas of rural development. Organisations *like* LAMPS (Large-size multi-purpose societies) for tribal development need to be watched as new institutional devices. In short, there are novel experiments in 'de-bureaucratisation' that have lessons for development management. 'People' as real actors in development drama have now been accepted as axiomatic.
3. It has been alleged that development administration is basically a sugar coated concept trying to cover up the essentially in-egalitarian and unjust nature of the Third World state. This is a serious indictment of development administration and a challenge to the very paradigm of social change through administrative manipulation. The implication here is that radical socio-economic transformation of the Third World is not so much an administrative problem as a political one. So long as the societal power structure would remain static, development administration might at best serve an ideological purpose of concealing the real character of the state. Another challenge to development administration has come from the dependency theorists[12] who go so far as to assert that the phenomenon of underdevelopment has its roots in the developed First World that has caused underdevelopment and has, therefore, a vested interest in it. Exogenous causes that generate underdevelopment are, by implication, beyond the control of the Third World nations. The proponents of social engineering may still stick on to development administration hoping faintly that between a distant 'revolution' and an immediate development enterprise the third world governments have got to choose the latter. After all, government and bureaucracies do not make revolutions!

Earlier Emphasis

As earlier stated, discussion on 'development'

started when the developing 'Third World' was born after the liquidation of colonialism. The national leaders in India, Indonesia and other Afro-Asian countries, immediately after 'independence' expressed their concern about 'development'! Nehru, Nkrumah, Nyarare all desired speedy socio-economic change to get rid of inequality, poverty, ill-health, malnutrition and different forms of social oppression and economic deprivation. At the initial phase, 'development' was conceived in technical terms. Production of food grains, creation of irrigation facilities, construction of roads and buildings and all other production and infrastructural expansion activities called for technical expertise, planning, management and directions from above. In the fifties, when 'development' set out on its journey, the search was on for'goods' and'things'. Roads, buildings, dams, fertilizer, wheat, rice—these were the targets; 'development' meant top-directed 'planned' activities to produce or construct these 'things'.

The first generation development thought was influenced by modernisation theory, the central issue being 'growth'. The Third World was to pursue the path of development which meant, in essence, industrialisation and urbanisation, to emulate the life style of the western developed nations. The euphoria of 'growth' orientation subsided when it was realised in the 70s and the 80s that 'development' did not remove poverty and inequality. The quality of life, so far as the general masses were concerned, showed no signs of substantial improvement. There was a growing realisation that 'development' has been unnecessarily made technical and dehumanised. As leaders like Nyarare reminded us, people cannot be developed, they develop themselves. What was needed was to redirect efforts toward people and their genuine 'empowerment'. The people, especially the poor, all of a sudden emerged as the main actors in development.The call was to put first the diverse priorities of the poor people and it was claimed by experts that to understand and support these were equitable (helping people gain what they want), efficient (mobilising their creative energy) and sustainable (providing incentives for long-term self-reliant investments by the poor). While events, nationally and internationally, were inexorably driving development thought towards 'people' (as distinguished from 'things'), conflicting views persisted, befogging the vision of development.

Perceptual Dilemma

'Development' thinking has never been free from biases—be it 'urban bias' or anything else. Disciplinary approaches of professionals have often been conditioned by their special professional outlook. An economist looking at rural poverty has his distinctive quantitative, projective bias, just as an expert in management science pays special attention to policies, programmes and projects—their formulation, execution, monitoring and evaluation. Sociologists and anthropologists have their own analytical tool-kit like, for instance, the 'moral economy' concept or the idea of primordial loyalties binding different groups in diverse relational ties.

Development 'watchers' have their own perceptions about people in micro-spaces where the poor live. As earlier stated, the first generation developmentalists in the 1950s viewed the micro-space and its people as elements in economic planning and in terms of local resource mobilisation. The same view persisted with some change later, invoking more field-orientation and people's participation in development. As it has been so aptly put: "In the 1950s, blueprints for development were drawn up from an 'aeroplane' perspective. In the 1970s, the field-oriented, participatory approach prompted a 'helicopter' vision, for the experts sitting in the low-flying craft could now claim to have a more accurate perception of their target population. They could even land anywhere amongst the people below to enquire about their views."[13]

What is important to note is that the change from 'aeroplane' to 'helicopter' did not essentially alter the old, top-down vision of reality. The experts, in both cases, thought that 'they knew better than the 'underdeveloped' populations living down below.' In development theorising and practices, perceptions of micro-spaces have often been influenced by 'the field of knowledge and power dominant in political and developmental circles.[14]

It is in this context that the idea of 'reversals', as mooted by Robert Chambers, assumes crucial significance.[15]To quote Chambers:"For the rural poor to lose less and gain more requires *reversals:* spatial reversals in where professionals live and work and in decentralisation of resources and discretion; reversals in professional values and preferences, from a 'first' to last 'list' and reversals in specialisation, enabling the identification and exploitation by and for the poor of gaps—under recognised resources and opportunities often lying between disciplines, professions and departments. Reversals require professionals who are explorers and multi-disciplinarians, those who ask, again and again, who will benefit and who will lose from their choices and actions."

The paradigm of 'reversals', as propounded by Chambers, looks at field realities—ecosystems, farming systems or livelihood stirategies—as non-linear, adaptive and differentiating. Development, in his view, is decentralised and divergent. Bureaucracy and markets centralise, standardise and simplify. By contrast, ecosystems and livelihood strategies become more stable and sustainable by becoming more complex and diverse.[16]

In this connection, it is worth noting that Robert Chambers, has entitled the first chapter of his book *Rural Development: Putting the Last First* as 'Rural Poverty Unperceived'. As he quotes the old English proverb: 'What the eye does not see, the heart does not grieve about; how does the planner, or the rural specialist perceive the rural situation generally and rural poverty in particular? His solutions flow from his perception.The perception riddle that creates distinct biases, has been very succinctly explained by Chambers in the following words:

"Outsiders under perceive rural poverty.They are attracted to and trapped in urban 'cores'which generate and communicate their own sort of knowledge while rural 'peripheries' are isolated and neglected. The direct rural experiences of most urban based outsiders is limited to the brief and hurried visits, from urban centres, of rural development tourism. These exhibit six biases against contact with and learning from the poorer people. These are *spatial*— urban, tarmac and roadside; *project*—towards places where there are projects; *person*—towards those who are better off, men rather than women, users of services and adopters of practices rather than non-users and non-adopters and those who are active, present and living; *seasonal*—avoiding the bad times of the wet season; *diplomatic*—not seeking out the poor for fear of giving offence; and *professional*—confined to the concerns of the outsider's specialisation. As a result, the poorer rural people are little seen and even less is the nature of their poverty understood." Hence, what Chambers has advocated is the need for perceptual reorientation: a paradigm of 'reversals'.

New Orientation

It is a truism to say that development has always been a multi-objective phenomenon. In practice, over the years, the objectives of development have been changing from productivity or growth orientation to poverty-amelioration and social justice to be secured with people's participation.

The oft-cited top-down approach has long been discredited, as the common diagnosis has been that the variegated local situation that has to be treated by development is not amenable to standard bureaucratic and mechanical measures. Alongside this, the development professionals like Chambers have realised from long field involvement that'development' has to be people centred and what is needed therefore is "to reverse the tendency towards concentrating power in impersonal and unaccountable institutions. For development to be locally meaningful, power needs to be returned to the people and communities through the creation of member-accountable institutions and strengthening of local resources control and ownership."

Strangely enough, reorientation in development thinking has, by and large, remained cloistered in academic circles. The world of practice has been living a fairly autonomous life supported by extant political and bureaucratic structures. The paradigm shift from the growth-centric approach to the people-centric one needs corresponding institutional reshaping that is hard to bring about at one stroke. Yet, development theory and practice are moving inexorably toward the people-centric mode.

The institutional rigidities are grounded in the continued acceptance of a concept of development; that is basically top-generated and top-directed. 'Development' is what the 'Centre' visions and plans. Since power and resources have been traditionally centralised and bureaucratic control has dominated public organisations, existence of knowledge, resources and capacity at the local level is ruled out by definitional fiat. All wisdom and science can be found only in the centre and there is nothing at the periphery!

Micro-Level Planning

In this context, micro-level planning, so far announced from the top, has been a centrally guided and straight-jacketed proforma planning. It is a convenience of the centre and not the will and needs of the localities that has been the motive force behind the central advocacy of micro-level planning.

'Development' in this context has meant implementation of a conjured up central vision of what is to be done at the periphery. It has naturally bred uniformity, standardisation, guideline dictated 'planned' activities across the nation. Local diversities in terms of resources, people and culture cannot be accommodated in this steamroller approach to development. As such, one finds JRY, EAS and all other kinds of programmes in every nook and corner of the country.

The standard vision emanating from the centre has sedulously nurtured almost a pathological structure of verticles. The programmes, be it JRY or EAS or any other, have their taproots at the top and these are passed on to the field agencies for implementation *via* the state and its operating departments. There are two kinds of verticality that reinforce centre-domination and therefore local atrophy. One kind of verticality is schemes or programmes-related, while the other is department-related, which also runs from top to bottom. The JRY-kind of scheme weaves its own vertical order. An activity by a department such as Forest Department or Irrigation Department would be usually having its origin in state budgetary allocation. When the Forest Department is engaged in forest-related 'development, it is the departmental vision of development which is necessarily sectoral. There are several such sectoral development activities that cut 'development' into pieces. Linkages among sectors or integrating the different sectoral investments (e.g. soil conservation and forest development) would, in such circumstances go naturally by default. There are many piecemeal developments but no holistic 'development'. What has actually happened in the world of planning is a kind of unholy alliance between schemes and departments. 'Development' has thus been departmentalised. Departmental orthodoxy is hard to break even in normal times; on top of it,'development' has been further fuelling single line piecemeal schematic activities without much care for interweaving and harmonising area-development efforts. Occasionally, lamentations are heard about 'balkanisation' of development and the familiar nostrum invariably suggested has been 'convergence'!

If the verticality of programmes and departmental activities in India has fractured development', the hierarchical structure of the PRIs (Panchayati Raj institutions) has tended to fragment the local will. The three-tier PRI structure is politically hierarchic, 'power' being distributed in a graded fashion between the *Zilla Parishad* and its constituents: *Panchayat Samiti* and *Gram Panchayat.* The programmes (e.g. JRY, EAS etc.) are also situated at different locations. Activities that have to be undertaken at the local *Gram Panchayat* level are often dependent for their start and supervision on either the *Panchayat Samiti* or the *Zilla Parishad.* Fund flow from the higher to lower tiers would many a time be erratic and irregular, creating in the process bottlenecks in on-going operations at the local level. Autonomous local action at the *Gram Panchayat* level in terms of its own need-based planning, funding and implementation is, at present, not formed by the 'system' in vogue.

Thus, the scenario that emerges at this stage is one of multiple interests tending to pre-empt local initiative for local micro-level planning and development. The autonomy of 'locality' is hedged about and there are currents and cross currents that are constantly muddying local development.

Constitutional Amendment

In our context, the 73rd constitutional amendment, against this background, breathes a new spirit of genuine locality-inspired local development. At the same time, it is sure to release institutional shocks that would reverberate across the board in governmental circles and the PRI hierarchy.

The constitutional scheme as envisaged in the 1992 amendment is to institute 'self-government' at the *Panchayat* level that will bring about economic development with social justice through micro-level planning. The locality being the basis of community life will form the foundation on which will rise the superstructure of 'development'. It will be a 'totalising' enterprise, as distinguished from the traditionally pursued *'partial',* schematic and disparate activities. So long, the will of the locality had been superseded by a host of anonymous supra-local authorities.

The locality has been a dumping ground of schemes and projects from above. Henceforward, as the constitutional amendment provides, the genetic code of planning will inhere in the locality—the *Gram Panchayat'and* its constituent gram *Sansads.* Planning for the locality will now be substituted by planning and the locality, firmly establishing, thereby, the proprietorial right of the local people to plan for themselves.

Once the original-status of authentic micro-level planning by the *Panchayats* will gain in legitimacy, it is the higher level planning that has to justify its existence in the context *of Panchayat* planning. The concept of 'decentralised planning'has all along apotheosised the 'centre'. Basically, the image is one of locational change of planning from centre downward.The concept has never accepted the propriety of the locality as the originator of planning. In terms of the new institutional design as crafted by the 73rd constitutional amendment for *Panchayats* and 74th for municipalities, planning is not 'decentralised', it is housed in its proper place—the local community. Locality planning is envisaged as original planning; all other levels of planning will be 'derivative' and not original. In a way, therefore, micro-level planning at the *Panchayat* level bids farewell to 'decentralised planning'. If it actually materialises, a set of conditions is likely to be created to release people's energy that will facilitate taking control of local resources by the people to make their own kind of authentic grassroots planning. 'Development', which belongs really to the people, will at last be rehabilitated.

Along with this re-conceptualisation, 'sustainable development' has been broached as an end-objective. Development is not simply an instant and immediate problem; it has to be a steady and continuing process. Hence, inter-generational equity should be a main objective of development. The natural resources and the bio-diversity—earth's natural capital—should be used in such a way that today's use also takes care of tomorrow's provision. In regard to finite resources like fossil fuel, judicious use has to be made by minimising consumption and if necessary, a new civilisational model has to be designed and pursued to avoid over consumption and prolonged 'rape of the earth'. Here also, people at the grass roots level who are yet to be caught in the western capitalist development model, can, if properly sensitised, be our saviour. Sustainable development needs a people's movement to conserve nature and to counter wasteful consumerist culture.

REFERENCES

1. See John D. Montgomery and William J. Siflin (eds.), *Approaches to Development: Politics, Administration and Change,* McGrawHill, New York, 1966, p. 259.
2. Edward W. Weidner, "Development Administration: A New Focus for Research", in Ferrel Heady and Sybil L. Stokes (ed.), *Papers in Comparative Public Administration,* University of Michigan, Ann Arbor. 1962.
3. John M. Gaus, *Reflections on Public Administration,* University of Alabama Press, 1947, pp.8-9.
4. Fred Riggs, "International Relations as a Prismatic Model," in Klaus Knorr and Sidney Verba, *The International System,* Princeton University Press, 1969.
5. For detailed discussion, see F. W Riggs, *Administration in Developing Countries,* Houghton Mifflin, Boston, 1964 and his *The Ecology of Public Administration,* Asia Publishing House, Bombay, 1962.
6. B. Guy Peters, *The Politics of Bureaucracy: A Comparative Perspective,* Longman, New York, 1978, p. 43.
7. For an extended discussion see S. N. Puranik, "Administrative Culture: Need for Conceptual Clarity and Further Research", *Indian Journal of Public Administration,* April-June, 1978.
8. Michel Crozier, *The Bureaucratic Phenomenon,* University of Chicago Press, 1964.
9. For a critical review of development administration, see O.P. Dwivedi and J. Nef, 'Crises and Continuities in Development', *Administration and Development,* January-March 1982.
10. George F. Gant, *Development Administration: Concepts, Goals, Methods,* The University of Wisconsin Press, 1979, pp. 20-21.
11. V.A. Pai Panandiker and S. S. Kshirsagar, *"Bureaucratic Adaptation to Development Administration"* in S. K. Sharma (ed), *Dynamics of Development,* Vol. 1. Concept Publishing House, Delhi, 1978.
12. For a critical review of "dependency theory", see David Booth, *"Marxism and Development Sociology"* in Martin Shaw (ed.), *Marxist Sociology Revisited,* The MacMillan, 1985.
13. See Robert Chambers, *Rural Development: Putting the Last First,* Longman, 1983.
14. Majid Rahnema, "Power and Regenerative Process in Micro-Spaces," *International Social Science Journal,* special issue on *"The local- global nexus,"* August, 1988.
15. Robert Chambers, *"The state and rural development: Ideologies and an Agenda for the 1990s",* in Christopher Colclough and James Manor (eds.). *State or Markets? Neo-Liberalism and the Development Policy Debate,* Charendon Paperbacks, Clarendon Press, Oxford, 1993.
16. Robert Chambers, *Rural Development: Putting the Last First, op. cit.*

Chapter 17

Public Personnel Administration

We are living in an age of technological revolution. Communication technology has been revolutionised through satellite-based information highways and other computerised information processing systems. Computers are now an integral part of our work processing and word processing technology. Inspite of such awe-inspiring high technology development, human resource remains the most important resource in an organisation. The earlier idea of 'personnel management' in the sense of a manipulative resource management like financial or inventory management has since been replaced by a more dynamic and positive concept of human resources management. The first generation management thought ofTaylorian variety was essentially non-manipulative in the sense that the machine model of organisation tended to play down the role of human resource in an organisation. The other shortcoming in the earlier thought processes could be traced to the exclusive attention that used to be paid to top management ignoring the vital role of human resource at all levels in organisational goal achievement.

There are now authentic organisational studies available that clearly point out that it is quality workforce that has been the main cause of organisational success. An organisations mission is the purpose to which it is dedicated. For instance, to create and disseminate knowledge is the mission of a University. *The goals and objectives* of an organisation clearly spell out what it wants to achieve. For example, a university may have the objective of expanding its library facilities by purchasing more books, creating new reading space, buying more journals and so on. An organisation s strategy is the means by which it seeks to attain its goals and objectives. As it has been well said, if goals and objectives are the organisations destination, then the strategies comprise the route that the organisation follows to reach its destination. Acting in close collaboration with the supervisory personnel, the human resource professionals in an organisation make sure that the quality and quantity of its human resources can live up to the organisation s missions, goals and strategies.

By now it should be clear that personnel or human resource management is a staff function whose basic purpose is to help the organisation achieve its goals. Within the broad framework of strategy, policies and structure of the organisation the personnel function is discharged through a number of processes such as recruitment, selection, placement, training, promotion and career management, compensation and other related activities.

Objectives of Personnel Management

Broadly speaking the objectives of personnel management are:

1. To set up a sound system of employee

recruitment, selection and placement in order that quality manpower could be inducted to properly serve the organisational needs.

2. To ensure fullest utilisation of human potential in order to achieve organisational goals and individual career development. More elaborately put, the objectives of personnel management are:
   i) Effective utilisation of human resourcesforachievingorganisational goals:
   ii) Planned structuring of the organisationtopromoteandpreserve harmonious relationship among the organisational members;
   iii) Creating conditions for human commitment and motivation to work and loyalty to the organisation;
   iv) Providing for right kind of opportunities for individual growth and advancement;
   v) Securing a healthy integration of organisational and individual group goals;
   vi) Planned development of human assets through training, counselling and even selective entry and exit policy, on the basis of scientific monitoring of performance.

The policies and procedures are followed by government for its employees. These are formulated to subserve, the grand purpose of 'public' interest. Public employees have to imbibe certain values like serving the public and making a clear distinction between what is 'public' and what is 'private'. A sense of responsibility to the public is what the government employee has to have. The 'public' responsibility poses a number of dilemmas for personnel managers in government. For instance, public employment has to balance both the 'meric clement' and the 'social equity' element. There are many social groups that need to be accommodated in government jobs. Second, equality of treatment often militates against the merit principle. Third, a public employer has to face the dilemma of working in accordance with his personal conviction or blind acceptance of rules and regulations.

Personnel Functions or Processes

The merit-based public personnel management has four basic steps:

(a) Recruitment, selection and initial placement of employees;
(b) Appraisal, promotion and training;
(c) Compensation or salary payment (including allowances);
(d) Disciplinary control.

Each process is governed by rules and regulations that seek to guarantee openness, fairness and competence. Each has to ensure both democratic opportunity and professional competence.

The Civil Service

The Civil Service through which the will of the state is realised and executed has been an integral part of modern government. We owe to Max Weber the concept of bureaucracy a special type of social organisation characterised by the following salient features:

i) Recruitment on merit basis through open competitive examination;
ii) Functioning on the basis of objective, written-down rules and regulations;
iii) Hierarchical organisation in terms of work distribution and accountability to superior officers;
iv) Impartiality in terms of behaviour;

v) Neutrality in regard to politics;
vi) Regularity and continuity in job performance;
vii) Remaining anonymous in so far as official acts are concerned in course of administration.

The characteristics of bureaucracy have been discussed elsewhere in sufficient details. We are using the two terms-civil service and bureaucracy-interchangeably.The civil service is a system, whereas the civil servant or bureaucrat is a member of the system.

The politicians come and go, but the civil service as a system of administration continues uninterrupted. As Ramsay Muir observes, "It (Civil Service) has become the effective and operative part of our system. The power of the bureaucracy, the permanent civil service, is to be found not only in administration but also in legislation and finance. It not only administers laws, it largely shapes them; it not only spends the proceeds of taxation, it largely decides how much is to be raised and how it is to be realised".

Conceptually, the civil service consists of a body of government officers who are recruited openly on the basis of competitive examinations and who function on the basis of law, rules and regulations and not on the whims and fancies of passing politicians of the day and above all, they follow certain basic administrative norms and ethics geared to public interest and service to the community, as distinguished from private interest of an individual, group or party.

Herman Finer, while referring to the British Civil Service mentioned about three broad types of administrators: the *administrative type* dealing with policy formulation and execution; the *technical type* (e.g., doctors, engineers etc.) that performs tasks of a specialised and technical nature; and the *manipulative type* that is mainly engaged in implementation and execution at lower levels. Analytically, this classificatory scheme sounds all right but actually in reality, all the three types are engaged in'administration' which is the common task of all. Again, the technical category has also to help in policy formulation and execution. Similarly, the administrative class tends tq assume the character of a technical group because of their specialisation in 'administration' including framing of policy and rules and regulations.

The civil service as a career applies to all ranks in the bureaucracy. The idea of a career means an uninterrupted progression from recruitment to retirement, which civil service as a system provides almost in every country. Such a system takes care of entry on merit, training from time to time, periodic promotion on the basis of performance appraisal, disciplinary control, changing compensation plan in terms of changes in career and terminal benefits at the time of retirement. This has been the traditional notion of a career civil service. In recent times, due to emerging demands of professionalization and public criticism of bureaucracy as an 'entrenched interest', contractual engagement and lateral entries are being advocated and practised in some countries to depart from the long term 'career' concept and thus to adapt administration to the changing needs of a dynamic socio-economic situation.

Significance of Personnel Management

Management means getting things done with proper use of materials: human resource, financial resource and material and infrastructural resource. And this involves enlisting human efforts and releasing human energy within an organisation. Clearly, therefore, personnel management forms the core of management functions. Whatever be the position of the senior management people in an organisation be it in financial management sector, or production management wing or any other sector of activities, a manager has essentially to look after two things; work management and personnel management. Management of work is integrally connected with management of personnel. In a large organisation, personnel functions are sought to be concentrated in a personnel department, which, then assumes the character of a staff agency. This does not obviate the necessity of micro or sectional level personnel management at different activity points in an organisation.

In public administration, personnel administration constitutes a vital sector of administration. It is a truism that no administration can rise very much above the quality of its administrators. In other words, the efficiency of the total administrative system depends on the efficient working of its personnel subsystem.

Development and New Personnel System

After the Second World War, many of the Afro-Asian states emerged out of the colonial experience and embarked on radical socio-economic reconstruction in a planned manner.

The central focus of state activity changed from revenue collection and law and order maintenance to speedy development of human and natural resources, removal of poverty and malnutrition and general upgrading of the quality of life of the masses. The role of administration changed from 'executive' mode to 'managerial' mode. To quote Pai Panandiker, 'the executive' type of administration is largely designed to carry out the directions of the government; it seeks to fulfil all the legal requirements of public service. By and large, the functions of this type are to maintain law and order, to regulate social and economic life of the society in accordance with statutory requirements and to carry out governmental directions.

In contrast, the 'management' oriented development administration is programmatically inclined and it focuses its attention not merely on 'carrying out' of the various governmental directions but rather on securing programmatic values or, in other words, on the achievement of goals and successful completion of programmes. At a conference on Personnel Administration organised by the Indian Institute of Public Administration, New Delhi, during March 5-9, 1968, the Chairman of the Administrative Reforms Commission, Mr. K. Hanumanthaiya made the following observation:

"The British left behind an administrative machine which was meant for colonial administration. We have not, however, during the last twenty years since we attained Independence, made any substantial changes in the system so as to reorient it to the goals of development and welfare".[2]

The agenda items of governance have changed after Independence, affecting vitally the philosophy of administration. The self-centred exploitative and authoritarian government has been replaced by a popular, open, developmental and democratic government. Post-colonial administration has to have an ideology of care and concern for the people and a commitment to planned socio-economic development within the framework of a new democratic constitutional order.

Public personnel administration, against this background, has to ensure a people-oriented and action and goal-oriented administrative system. The people in the system have to be properly reoriented, trained and motivated to subserve the overarching needs of development and democracy. As a practising scholar-administrator has put it: "In other words, some new, more promising models or systems of organisation have to be searched out. These systems have to be more oriented to better measurements of their performance; to make more informed and rational choices; to communicate more effectively with their environments; to foresee the consequences of their behaviour on the larger system; to transform themselves in response to change and to being more flexible and open than traditional bureaucracies ever were. In responding to a turbulent environment of rapid technological change and explosive expectations, an adapting bureaucracy has to become more of a learning community than the traditional bureaucracy has been. It has to keep a watchful eye on the moving frontiers of managerial thinking, unleash new motivations for continued learning and personal development. Rather than remaining prisoner of its routines, mechanisms and formally prescribed roles, an adapting bureaucracy is capable of viewing itself in a new way, responsive to the challenge of rapid change and to the growing demands of its environment. In the process, it develops a new orientation different from that of a traditional bureaucracy-more geared to the use of the scientific method in problem-solving and in decision-making, to management by objectives that are compatible with the demands of its larger system, to control by results and to self-regulate more than external control, this is the minimum reform that is necessary in modernising public administration and to make it a carrier of new values."

In 1968 the Fulton Committee Report on the Civil Service in U.K. made very similar observations, as the Report noted: "the structure and practices of the service have not kept up with the changing tasks". On public personnel administration in a dynamic domestic and international situation, the Fulton Report forcefully argued in favour of a professional civil service as distinguished from the traditional, "amateurish" services of the past.[3]

Changing Scenario

Historically, the civil service as a system of public personnel organisation is a late 19th century phenomenon. With the emergence of the 'modern' state and 'rational' administration, the older forms of recruitment on 'patronage system', as in the then U.K. and the politically motivated 'spoils system' earlier prevalent in U.S.A., had to be discarded in favour of a modern system of civil service, impartially selected, administratively competent, politically neutral and imbued with the spirit of service to the community.

Governments everywhere have wily nily been involved in more and more activities in response to changing social, situations. Social change and bureaucratic adjustment have been the central focus of the famous Fulton Report (1966-68) in U.K. As the Fulton Report observed, "The' home civil service today is still fundamentally the product of the 19th century philosophy of the Northcote-Trevelyan Report (1854). The tasks it faces are those of the second half of the twentieth century."

The fast changing world that we live in poses a serious challenge to the civil service in every country In U.K. the memorandum on 'Appointments in Administration (1974)' aptly described the complex nature of work of today's administrators:

"The work of administrators in the government service is demanding, responsible and varied because the activities of departments touch every aspect of the national life and because of the wide range of work that an administrator may be called upon to do within a single department Much of an

administrator's work is done on paper but there is a great deal of personal contact with other government departments, local authorities, both sides of industry and members of the public. A capacity for dealing effectively with other people at all levels is an essential quality as is also the ability to present and defend a case lucidly and persuasively. The other qualities called for are power of critical analysis, sound judgment, a willingness to accept responsibility and a capacity to work hard and quickly.... often they (administrators) work alongside economists, lawyers and scientists and other specialists as members of a team and they may well after their early years themselves specialise in a particular area of a department's interests or, for example, in personnel management or the applications of computer science".

On the role of the civil service in India, the Kothari Committee on 'Recruitment Policy and Selection Methods (1976)' had this to say:

"The great adventure of building up of India, which was Jawaharlal Nehru's inspiring and compelling call to the nation over the years, is the establishment and development of a modern state, wedded to the principles of democracy, socialism and secularism. The national objectives are enshrined in the Directive Principles of State Policy of our Constitution. They involve the stupendous task of social transformation by consent, ensuring economic growth with social justice. They embrace many other aspects of national life such as the development of our composite culture, the spread of education, equality of opportunity for all citizens and measures to strengthen our defences to safeguard our independence. It is in this context of free India's ideals and objectives that the importance of the role of the higher civil services has to be viewed. Their preoccupation is no longer the enforcement of law and order and preserving the status quo. They have a more vital and positive role to play They serve a democratic government formed by elected representatives of the people and assist in formulating and implementing large scale measures of national development. They have to attune themselves to the climate of change and help to translate political programmes into viable statutes and effective administrative acts. Above all, they must accept the totality of the Indian heritage and function without any parochial, linguistic, religious, caste or class prejudice".

In a dynamic domestic and international situation, a civil service that fails to keep in step with the changing times may well prove to be a great hindrance to social development. There is an in-built conservatism in rule-bound and elitist career bureaucracy. A major problem that faces the civil service everywhere is: how can the civil servants be remoulded and continually renewed to cope up with the twin requirements of stability and change.

Types of Bureaucracy

Bureaucracy is usually classified into four types. These are:

(a) *Guardian Bureaucracy:* This type may be defined as that civil service which regards itself as the custodian of public interest and are independent of and unresponsive to the public opinion. It is righteous, incorruptible, efficient, competent and benevolent but authoritarian and unresponsive.

(b) *Caste Bureaucracy:* This type of bureaucracy is caste based and those persons who belong to particular castes can become public officials. Often, a ruling political party favours caste-based appointments and postings.

(c) *Patronage Bureaucracy:* This type of bureaucracy is also known as 'spoils system', as it used to be prevalent in the USA. In this case, public jobs are given as a personal favour or political award to the members of the political party which comes to power. Such a system cannot produce a civil service which is competent and people centric, as the top civil servants tend to exhibit a bias towards party interests.

(d) *Merit Bureaucracy:* This type of bureaucracy has its basis in the merit of public officials. Here, the attempt is to recruit the best men for the public service, merit being judged by objective standards.

Advantages of Bureaucratic System

'Bureaucracy' is often thought of as a term of abuse. As Max Weber conceptualised it, bureaucracy is a special form of social organisation. Because of its special characteristics, its contribution to efficient and rational governmental administration is significant. The following are its advantages:

(a) Its working is based on impartiality.

(b) Since bureaucrats remain in service for a very long time, their knowledge and expertise are of immense help.

(c) Training helps bureaucrats in sharpening their skills.

(d) It is permanent. Governments may come and go but the bureaucracy continues.

(e) Due to increase in the activities of the state, the bureaucracy is the institution which can cope up with the increased volume and complexity of work.

Disadvantages of Bureaucratic System

Bureaucracy has its disadvantages too as all of us are aware of the terms red-tapism, mediocrity, routines etc. The following are the disadvantages:

(a) Lack of humane approach since every decision is taken in accordance with h rd and fast rules and regulations, leading to red-tapes. Rules tend to become more important than fulfilling objectives.

(b) There is virtually no contact with the common masses although the bureaucrats are supposed to serve the masses. Thus the decisions tend to be unimaginative and mechanical.

(c) Since bureaucrats have vast powers, social prestige and economic privileges, they suffer from superiority complex and are prone to corruption as well.

(d) Bureaucracy develops and retains the complicated and laborious methods of work and also each bureaucrat wants to retain maximum powers with himself and seeks to inflate his own departmental budget. The public choice theorists have pointed out the self-aggrandising tendency of the bureaucracy.

(e) Parkinson's Law states that the number and the size of the civil service and the volume of work 'are not related to each other at all'. The personnel go on increasing irrespective of the work load. Bureaucracy has the tendency to multiply its work. It creates new jobs for itself.

The issue, however, is not to banish bureaucracy. How to make bureaucracy more flexible and people-oriented has been the major concern of governments everywhere.

Position Classification

There have been various methods of organising the public personnel system. Position classification is an important aspect of personnel administration. It basically implies classification of employees and identifying their position in an administrative set up. The above concept has been defined in many ways. By classification is meant the grouping of positions on the basis of similarity of duties and qualification requirements. Marshall E. Dimock defines it as the systematic sorting and ranking of position in a hierarchy according to comparative difficulty and responsibility. According to L.D. White, "In its final form, a classification plan consists of a number of classes adequate to enable a place to be found for each existing position arranged in orderly fashion with respect to each other and supplemented by a set of rules and regulations for its administration, interpretation and amendment."

In any personnel system, services have to be classified on the basis of the variety of work and the different grades and kinds of equipment required for different kinds or grades of work. In this respect, classification of governmental position is recognised as indispensable to a career service based on merit. According to Glenn Stahl, "The foundation of a job oriented career system is a position-classification plan. Such a plan is a prerequisite for any system that regards the nature and content of each position as central to good organisation and to motivate based on the work to be performed." Position classification is the organising of all jobs in an enterprise into groups or classes on the basis of their duties, responsibilities and qualification requirements.

The prevailing bases for classification of positions are educational qualifications of the incumbents, competence on the job, level of responsibility attached to the job, rank and personal status of the employee, etc. The precise mix of these depends on a country's administrative value system and culture. There are two well-known systems of classification of positions. These are (i) Rank qualification and (ii) Duties classification.

i) *Rank Qualification:* Here the basis of qualification is the rank and personal status of the incumbent rather than the precise duties inherent in the post. In India we find this system of classification of positions in the all-India 'service' The concept would be clearer when the advantages and disadvantages of this system would be enumerated in the following paragraphs.

Advantages: First it is easier to understand and administer. Second, it promotes mobility by facilitating transfers and it encourages career opportunities. Third, it encourages flexibility in the system. Fourth, it induces loyalty to the totality of the civil services rather than to a specific post. Fifth, it attracts competent and promising personnel and at the same time prefers generalists to specialists.

Disadvantages: First, it violates the principle of equal pay for equal work leading to low morale in the civil services. Second, it overlooks the claims of merit as the basis of holding a particular position, the system being somewhat ascribable. Third, it does not define the contents of any job in detail. Consequently, the performance of its incumbent cannot be rationally measured. Fourth, it is not conducive to the formulation of scientific standards on which selection of personnel, training, transfer, posting, promotion and career development may be organised.

ii) *Duties Classification:* This is also known as position classification. Traditionally, the object of 'duties classification' has been to provide 'equal pay for equal work'. In this system the emphasis is on individual positions in the hierarchy. Each position represents certain well-defined duties and responsibilities, the latter two terms signifying the work assigned to a position and the matters for which an employee is held accountable. A position must remain differentiated from its occupant. The different criteria for evaluation of jobs for purpose of determining their class are: (a) nature of occupational fields; (b) complexity and difficulty in performing duties; (c) scope of responsibility; (d) knowledge and skill needed to do the job.

According to Glenn Stahl, there are four steps in the development of a position classification system: (a) analysing and recording the duties and other distinctive characteristics of the position to be classified (job analysis and description); (b) grouping the positions into classes upon the bases of their similarities; (c) writing such standards or specifications for each class of positions as will indicate its character and define its boundaries and serve as a guide in allocating individual positions to the class and in recruitment and examination; (d) installation by allocating individual positions to the classes thus described.

Let us look into the advantages and disadvantages of 'duties classification'.

Advantages: First, each person under this system gets a clearer understanding of his individual responsibilities as well as of the whole organisation. Second, it induces competitiveness in the totality of the civil service as such. Third, it provides a definite target for recruiting public personnel and paves the way for an objective evaluation of the performance of personnel. Fourth, it provides a basis for equal pay for equal work. Fifth, it provides lateral entry into the civil service from outside the government and postings and appointments are shaped by the requirements of the job to be done. Finally, position classification provides a uniform occupational terminology by grouping similar positions into classes along with uniform, significant and defined terminology for the naming of positions.

Disadvantages: First, its basic assumption that duties and responsibilities of a post are capable of clear identification and must be measured—may be seriously questioned, at least in the developing societies. Duties of many functionaries, particularly those holding line positions, remain, even at the best of times, more undefined than defined. Second, since the pace of change in a developing society is inevitably rapid, the duties of civil servants necessarily undergo corresponding changes quite fast. This implies that the classification plan will have to be kept under continuous revision which would be quite onerous as well as costly. Third, position classification requires for its introduction and installation of technical skills of a wide variety and sophisticated order which is quite expensive and time consuming as well.

It is rather difficult to say whether rank classification or duties classification would be suitable for a country. To uproot any basic administrative arrangement prevailing in a country and to move to a new system would always invoke hostility and create suspicion in the minds of the civil servants, especially those who have been benefiting from the existing system. Administrative reform often fails because of bureaucratic opposition.

Recruitment

Recruitment is a process which is of vital importance to the administrative system as a whole, since it determines the tone and quality of the public services and on it rests the usefulness and relevance of the machinery of government to the society. It constitutes an essential element needed for the stability of the state and in the process it contributes towards preparing for the nation's future. A sound recruitment policy is the key to a strong public service and the cornerstone of the whole public personnel structure.

Generally speaking, recruitment stands for

the search for proper personnel to perform the various activities and obligations in the process of administration. According to one view,

"Recruitment is the process of searching for prospective employees and stimulating them to apply for jobs in organisation". In the words of J.D. Kingsley: "Public recruitment may be defined as that process through which suitable candidates are induced to compete for appointments to the public service. It is thus an integral part of a more inclusive process selection which also includes the process of examination and certification."

The increasingly technical nature of public service and growth of democratic ideas and institutions have made the problem of recruitment much more important today than ever before, As E.N. Gladden has remarked: "Clearly a civil service history can be epitomised as the story of the recruitment of officials since on this first essential step largely rests the nature and degree of usefulness of the administrative machinery," No aspect of personnel administration is more important than recruitment, for unless the basic material is reasonably good, no amount of training, supervision service-rating, classification or research will be able to provide an efficient group of public employees. In short, recruitment is the first step in the employment programme and it is regarded everywhere as the core of the personnel management process.

The credit for developing a scientific system of recruitment for the first time goes to China where recruitment through competitive examinations was first introduced in the second century BC. Prussia was the first country in modern times to introduce a system of recruitment gradually replacing the patronage system from 1857 onwards. In the United States, the 'spoils system' was replaced by the merit principle. In India, the merit system has been in existence since 1853, when it was first introduced in Britain too.

The French system which was introduced after the French Revolution and the British system are two different types, although they have two points in common: (a) the unity of recruitment for all higher administrative cadres made by one single method — competitive examination under the responsibility of one single authority - the 'Civil Service Commission' in Britain and the 'National Bureau of Administration' in France; (b) both the countries have exactly the same notion of public service and public office. If the number of candidates is large, the recruitment is made in two steps: a pre-selection which eliminates all those who are not evidently suitable and a selection proper, through a competitive examination1

Merit System

A merit system in modern government means a personnel system in which comparative merit or achievement governs each individual's selection and progress in the service and in which the conditions and rewards of performance contribute to the competency and continuity of the service. The entrance and usually the promotion features of a merit system are ordinarily founded on a plan of open, competitive examinations (not necessarily written tests) by which candidates are appraised as to their relative fitness for duty in a position, an occupation, or a service (Stahl). The selecting authority, be it a Commission, board or individual, makes no distinction between the candidates on the basis of any party affiliation. Under the merit system, the civil servants remain neutral in politics and promotions take place strictly on the basis of merit. The public servants remain in office till the age of retirement.

Spoils System

As opposed to the Merit System, there has been the age-old spoils system. Under this system, the public offices are distributed to the men of the party victorious at the polls. The public offices are considered 'spoils' to be enjoyed by the political party which has emerged victorious in the elections. When a new party comes into power, it dismisses all the employees appointed by its predecessor and fills the vacancies with its own favourites. This system is also designated as hiring and firing of public officials and employees. It is said in favour of Spoils System that the government cannot put its policies into operation with maximum effectiveness unless its key employees are in active sympathy with its political outlook and programme. The spirit of public service is completely sacrificed and its place is taken by political interests. The employees make an illegitimate use of their offices to promote the interests of their political benefactors to whom they are indebted for their appointment. Politics and administration fall into public contempt in this process.

Process of Recruitment

The process of recruitment and selection includes a number of important steps which may be stated as under:

1. Wide publicity regarding announcement of examination through newspapers and other media;
2. Holding of examination for testing the abilities and preparing an order of merit;
3. Certification—a process by which the selected candidate is sent for an appointment;
4. Selection—an act of choosing from among those qualified and available and the formal act of appointment;
5. Appointment by the competent authority is made which may be permanent, temporary, provisional, on probation, contractual or for an indefinite term, etc.;
6. Placement putting the appointed person in the right place;
7. Orientation and induction into the service and a certain amount of training.

The process of recruitment may be analysed in terms of (i) location of the recruitment authority; (ii) recruitment from within versus recruitment from without; (iii) qualifications required of public officers and employees; (iv) methods of determining qualifications; and (v) administrative machinery for the determination of qualifications.

Location of the Recruiting Authority

The location of the recruitment authority is an essential feature of the personnel system. Generally, there are two methods of locating the recruiting and appointing authority. In one system, the power of recruitment is vested in a special type of government organisation such as the Union Public Service Commission (UPSC) in India, the Civil Service Commission in the U.K. and the Federal Service Commision in the U.S.A, these authorities function as the personnel recruiting agency on behalf of the government.

In the other system, this power is vested in the electorate. This system of recruitment is usually adopted for policy-making posts and in electing personnel of a local administration. But then this latter system has some merit no doubt, but people may nor make wise selection and may be swayed by personal or parochial considerations.

Recruitment from within and Recruitment from without

Different countries follow different systems for recruiting personnel. Direct recruitment, i.e. recruitment from without is done through the prescribed methods from all available sources. Normally, lowest posts in all services are filled by direct recruitment. On the other hand, recruitment from within is done through promotion, i.e. recruitment of persons for new and higher posts from amongst eligible and qualified persons already employed in government services.

Advantagesofdirectrecruitment. Theadvantages of direct recruitment are: (1) it accords with the democratic principle of giving an opportunity to all persons; (2) the source of manpower is much wider; (3) comparatively young and better qualified people can enter the services; (4) it provides inducement to those already employed for improving their qualifications.

The disadvantages of direct recruitment are: (1) Most of those recruited in this manner have no previous administrative experience; (2) incentive to good work among those already employed is reduced; (3) younger men and women come to occupy higher positions than their seniors in age.

There are other methotds of recruitment too. Those are:

1. Individual Recruitment—It is possible and desirable only in cases where the number of posts to be filled is very small and the selection of candidates is generally done through interview.
2. Mass Recruitment—When the number of posts to be filled is large, mass recruiting techniques are to be used for its obvious advantage.
3. Positive Recruitment—It means active search for the best. The positive concept of recruitment implies that the personnel agency must take definite steps to attract the best qualified and most competent candidates.

However, none of the methods of recruitment is entirely satisfactory. In almost all countries a combination of the two systems, i.e. recruitment from within and without is practised to get optimum results.

Qualifications of the Employees

Laying down of proper qualifications is very much necessary in order to recruit suitable candidates to suit the needs of the diverse tasks of administration. Broadly speaking, the qualifications may be of two types: (a) General qualifications entail such factors as citizenship, domicile or residence, sex and age etc. (b) Special qualifications cover such matters as personal qualities, education, practical experience and technical skills. These are being discussed below:

General Qualifications

(a) *Citizenship:* An aspirant for the public service ought to be a citizen of the state. Aliens are excluded from holding any public offices and whenever an alien is employed, it is strictly for a short duration.

(b) *Domicile or Residence:* Domicile qualification was first used in the United States and it continues even today as the federating states are allotted due representation in the National Services.

In India, since the Public Employment (Requirement as to Residence) Act, 1957, domicile restrictions in regard to public appointments were removed.

(c) *Sex:* In the early days, the employment of women in public service was a taboo in most countries. Due to various factors including increasing awareness and spread of education in women, women are gaining entry into the public services. In the Indian Constitution, it has been specifically provided that all citizens in matters relating to appointment to any public office shall have equal opportunity.

(d) *Age:* In countries like the USA, men and women of age group 18 to 50 years are employed in order to get the services of mature men and women. One may enter the American public service at almost any level and at almost any age. On the contrary, in countries like India and Britain, young persons in the age group of 21-28 years are preferred. According to Kingsley, the former emphasises techniques at entry and often favours mediocre maturity.The latter presupposes the existence of a number of career hierarchies and favours the promising youngster and gears the Civil Service to the educational system. However, neither of these systems are adequate to the requirement of the modern public service and any satisfactory scheme of recruitment must combine elements of both.

Special Qualifications

(a) *Educational:* The British system lays down definite educational qualifications for entry into public services. Indian system modelled upon the British also provides for the same. Here, the essential minimum qualification for entry into the administrative services is a University graduate degree.The American system is in sharp contrast to the above system. It does not prescribe any minimum educational qualifications as well as age-limits for entry into public services.

(b) *Experience:* In the USA, an entry to the public services can take place at any age and there the experience of the actual performance of the task is greatly valued and demanded. The Indian system provides for recruitment of young persons fresh from universities and colleges. In case of technical services, experience is treated as desirable qualification.

Personal Qualifications: The public servant should have 'executive ability, tact, resourcefulness, integrity, energy, faithfulness and capacity to get along with others'. According to Pfiffner and Presthus, the personal qualifications of a public servant should be the following:

1. A flexible, but essentially scientific mode of thought, characterised by a recognition of the need for co-ordination;
2. Familiarity with the subject-matter of organisation and management;
3. Facility at problem solving;
4. A highly developed reading and writing ability;
5. Ability to settle vexing situations through inter-personal contact.

Methods of Determining Qualifications

The following methods of determining qualifications have been adopted in most of the countries:

1. *Personal Judgment of the Appointing Authority:* Under this system, the recruiting authority lays down the qualifications of the applicants. The most desirable use of this method can be made if the recruiting authority has to make the appointment from a panel of names prepared by an independent Commission on the basis of competitive examinations.
2. *Certificates of character, ability and educational qualifications:* This method is used to supplement other methods before appointing a person to a public

post.

3. *Record of Previous Experience:* The USA has evolved a scientific system of making records of the work and experience of employees. This combined with the educational record of a candidate may serve as a sound basis of selection.
4. *Examination:* Examinations of some appropriate nature are necessary under a merit system in order to determine the ability of the applicants. Examinations or tests may be either written or oral and of several types.

Written tests: First, there are assembled as well as unassembled tests. The former means that the candidates are required to appear together in order to take the examination. This is the common method prevailing in most of the countries, for the recruitment of a large number of employees. The latter type means that the applicants are examined individually. Such examinations are most often arranged in the case of more responsible positions where it is believed that class-room type of examinations will not help.

Second, the tests may be of two kinds: (i) free answer or essay type; (ii) short answer or objective type. In the former the paper contains about a dozen questions and the candidates may be required to answer nearly half of these in two or three hours but a paper set on the latter pattern may contain fifty to hundred questions requiring very short answers, for example, the multiple choice, the true-false, the matching and a variety of other types. This is followed in the preliminary examination for the all-India services. The essay type is used to get a sample of the applicant's organising ability, his orderly mind, lucidity, imagination and literary achievements.The other type aims at testing the candidates general knowledge. The great virtue of the essay type examination is that it is an effective instrument of measuring the complex mental abilities. Essay tests are designed to measure the ability of the administrator to shape new courses and strategies as policy formulators. He should also be able to motivate others in accepting new challenges and development.The civil servant must formulate and implement developmental works and take up social service meant to transform some aspect of national life. A development administrator must consider it as a part of his duty to educate and consult people and solicit their participation in developmental tasks. Development must be a cooperative endeavour of the people on the one hand and the administrators on the other hand. The questions set are intended to test these abilities and attitudes.

In essay type question, there is a great latitude for the examiner to use his discretion. The personal factor, i.e., the personal like or dislike of the examiner means a great deal in the evaluation of the answers. In the short answer type examination there is very little scope for the use of personal factor. Therefore, it is much more objective and accurate. At the same time, short answer type tests are easier to administer.

Oral Tests: These tests are designed to elicit information about the personal aspects of the candidates' competence. The types of qualifications for which the oral test is appropriate are those that are centred around inter-personal relations involved in the job for which the selection takes place. It is generally believed that the written examination fails to reveal the personality of the candidate. It is quite possible that a person may do exceedingly well in the written examination but he may be lacking in those personal qualities which are particularly required for the specific job.This drawback of the written test is sought to be removed by holding the oral test. It means that the written test is still the basic test, which is supplemented by the oral test. The principal method of oral testing is the use of interview supplemented by an assessment of the past record of the candidates' work. The oral test or interview is particularly suited for the selection of candidates for such jobs as require frequent contacts with superiors or the public. For judging personality and attitudes, oral tests are of special significance.

Determination of Qualifications

The lengthy, complex job of handling the recruitment of the civil services by its very nature demands an independent agency to maintain standards of objectivity and neutrality in personnel selection. Such a personnel of recruiting agency is put in charge not only of the recruitment and examination of public personnel but is also entrusted with personnel management matters, like salary, leave, promotion transfer and classification.

The procedures of recruitment and training have been subjected to debates and discussions in recent years. In Britain, the Fulton Committee was appointed to review the entire range of problems connected with personnel administration with special relevance to recruitment and training. The Committee in its report (1968) initiated the debate on the 'generalist vs. specialist' controversy, making a strong advocacy for relating jobs to organisational objectives and pleaded for increased professionalism in the public services. In India, the Administrative Reforms Commission (ARC) also made a strong plea for the gradual infusion of specialists in the administrative services along with suitable changes in the generalist cadres.

Training

To raise both knowledge and skill levels and increase the versatility and adaptability of public personnel, training is indispensable. It is through training that skilled knowledge is imparted to all categories of civil servants. According to Simon, "Training consists of those conscious efforts that are directed towards the improvement or increase of person's powers, skills or understanding and the development of his beliefs and values". Another personnel expert defines training as 'the process of developing skills, habits, knowledge and aptitudes in employees for the purpose of increasing the effectiveness of employees in their present government positions as well as preparing employees for future government positions'. Thus, training is the continuous and systematic development among all levels of civil servants of that knowledge and those skills and attitudes which contribute to their advancement and efficiency of administration. Moreover, training is essential not only for efficiency, but also for broadening the vision of the employee. It is important for teaching him precision, for making him self-reliant and independent and for creating a capacity to take decisions and make judgements. Training creates the ability to take independent decisions.

Training is a learning experience in that it seeks a relatively permanent change in an individual that goes to improve his or her ability to perform on the job. Edwin B. Flippo defines training as, 'the act of increasing the knowledge and skill of an employee for doing a particular job'. Training helps the recruit to acquire occupational skill and knowledge and contribute his best towards the objectives of the organisation. Training helps mould and shape the entrants to internalise the organisational skills and character and helps them to adapt to new environments. As Felix Nigro puts it, "The function of training is to help employees grow, not only from the standpoint of mechanical efficiency but also in terms of the broad outlook and perspective which public servants need". Training helps build integrity and morale in the public servants by developing the requisite mental attitudes to issues of personal and public conduct. The Committee on the Training of Civil Servants (Great Britain) laid down five major objects of training:

1. Training should endeavour to produce a Civil Servant whose precision and clarity in the transaction of business can be taken for granted.
2. The Civil Servant must be attuned to the tasks which he will be called upon to perform in a changing world.
3. The aim must be to achieve the highest possible standard of efficiency and not to produce a robot like mechanically perfect civil service. He should gain a broader overview of administration.
4. Training must be directed not only at enabling an individual to perform his present work more efficiently but also at making him fit for other duties and at developing his capacity for higher work and greater responsibilities.
5. Substantial regard to staff morale has to be paid—to enliven the nature of routine tasks by making them more interesting.

These aims and objectives hold good for imparting training to civil servants in any country. The training process itself can give the trainee an added sense of dignity. When well conducted, three factors have given particular urgency to training for government servants in developing countries: (i) the need for innovation in administration; (ii) the rapid expansion of governmental functions; (iii) the shortage of trained personnel.

Types of Training

There are a number of types of training. Some may be characterised as pre-entry and post-entry and on the job and off the job training. Some types are suitable for individuals and some for groups. The civil service consists of different types of personnel, so their basic training is of a general character as well as of a special character suiting the requirements of a particular branch. A brief description of important types of training is as follows:

6. *Formal Training:* It consists of an actual study course with lectures seminars, work projects and written reports. It may lead to a professional degree or a certificate. It may be full time or part time, pre-entry or post-entry in nature. It may be given at home or abroad.
7. *Pre-entry Training:* The minimum educational qualification which allows a candidate to opt for the civil services is pre-entry training. However, the term pre-entry training specifically refers to vocational or specialised training. Now-a-days vocational courses are quite common in India.
8. *Post-entry Training:* This type of training is given after one joins the service. It is similar to in-service training which is given after an employee has joined the service. It may be of a formal nature and informal nature or a combination of both with work experience. It may include formal studies and seminars as well as transfers to a variety of posts and special projects designed to afford a variety of experience, new skills and broadened understanding of the government as a whole.
9. *Orientation Training:* It is the planned and guided adjustment of employee to his department or agency and his job. The new employee is introduced to the many factors involved in a new work situation. However, the best training in any service is provided by the actual doing of the jobs in practice.

Methods of Imparting Training: Various methods are used for imparting training. Employees may be allowed to learn about their work by actually working in the office or in the field. This is known as training by experience. Training may be imparted in the form of formal lectures or instructions in administrative academies or training schools. Another method of training is through 'communications', wherein the employees are informed about the nature of work and rules and regulations of the Department in which they have to work. Department concerned may circulate to its employees information about their obligations, the general code of conduct, privileges, etc. Another method of imparting training to the public personnel is by conference or group discussions. In the conference method, the trainees do not receive any formal lectures from the instructor; they themselves discuss the matters, compare notes with one another and put forward their own viewpoint.

Thus, training may be imparted through various methods like discussion, conference, or formal lecturing. Any method may be adopted for giving sound training. Training is initially a function of management and should be a major responsibility of any person charged with the supervision of others. There are today many new ways of inculcating training and the training techniques have changed laying emphasis more and more on audio-visual methods, case studies, sensitivity training and behavioural science techniques. The methods need to be used to fit the objectives of a training programme.

Training in the Third World

Training is the process by which capabilities of the personnel can be improved to meet the changing organisational needs in terms of their knowledge, skills and attitudes that are required in the performance of organisational tasks. This kind of training is primarily directed to routine and operational matters which are necessary for the continuous maintenance and servicing of the administrative machinery. These may include record keeping, office management, accounting, job analysis, job auditing and evaluation etc. The second type is 'development training' directed towards human resource development and geared to manage developmental activities. These are of paramount importance in the case of Third World countries.

The newly independent countries of the Third World have undertaken developmental works on a large scale for national reconstruction; as a result, there has been a tremendous pressure upon the existing administrative structures of these countries. The government has adopted a new role apart from just maintaining law and order and collecting revenues. This calls for redefining the role and function of civil servants who are increasingly required to engage themselves consciously and directly in the task of bringing about socio-economic changes and development. All these require a fundamental change in the outlook, knowledge, skills and attitudes of servants. The role of bureaucracy in development administration has been touched upon in the chapter on Development Administration.

To be an effective administrator in this sense would require a different kind of training. The development administrator must have a proper understanding of the general social structure and knowledge of sociological and economic relationships and principles. He has to be aware of the political social, cultural, economic and environmental constraints and has to formulate and operate development activities often in close association with people and politicians.

The administrator has to understand (i) Sectoral management (e.g. agriculture, irrigation, animal husbandry etc.); (ii) Planning process at the grass roots; (iii) People's 'felt' problems; (iv) National resource management. Specific courses need to be launched for these purposes. Another major dimension relates to politics-sensitivity. Development and politics are twins. The administrator, instead of avoiding the politician, has to understand 'politics' of development. This calls for mounting of imaginative training programs for development administrators.

Career Development

Career development is one of the basic considerations in the personnel policy of a government. The term 'career' has been defined by Glenn Stahl in the following manner:

"It has been widely used to denote the progression of an individual in a field of work throughout the employable years of his life.

A career in business or in profession is a commonly understood concept. Sometimes it means devotion to a speciality, sometimes it means a series of employments which are only loosely related to each other. In either case, it usually implies some degree of success.

Conditions should be created so that it may attract people to enter government service for their whole life. The Commission of Inquiry on Public Service Personnel (USA) clearly described the concept of a government career services, as it stated: "We recommend that the day-to-day administrative work of government be definitely made a career service.

By this we mean that steps shall be taken to make public employment a worthwhile life work, with entrance to the service open and attractive to young men and women of capacity and character and with opportunity of advancement through service and growth to posts of distinction and honour."

Thus, the Commission defined a career as an honourable occupation which one normally takes up in youth with the expectation of advancement and pursues until retirement.

Career development may be initiated in two ways: (i) organisationally; (ii) individually. Thus the study of careers assumes different orientations whether it is viewed from the perspective of the organisation or the individual.

Organisational Career Development: Career development when viewed from organisational standpoint involves 'tracking career paths'. The management seeks information to enable it to direct and monitor the progress of employees and to ensure that capable managerial and technical talent is available according to the organisation's needs. In the changing nature of state and the functions of civil service, organisational career development has become more important today.

Individual Career Development: Here the focus is on the individuals and the central theme is to identify their major career goals and 'to determine what they need to do to achieve these goals. In the latter case, the focus is entirely on the individual and includes his or her career outside the organisation as well as inside. Thus, in organisational career development, individual is groomed to fill the needs of the organisation, but in individual career development each individual's personal work career is analysed irrespective of where this work is performed.

The purpose of career development is to attract and retain men and women of talent and ambition in the government employment. To establish government career service and to attract the best talent in the service certain essentials are to be observed.

These are:

1. There should be 'equality of opportunity' for the citizens to enter the public service.
2. There should be equal pay for equal work.

3. There should be equal opportunity for promotion and advancement. Promotion should be based on merit. There should be suitable outlet for career development opportunities to continuously attract new talents and to create enthusiasm in the existing personnel.
4. There should be security and stability of job.
5. And more importantly, the work culture must ensure job satisfaction.

Significance of Effective Career Development

Career development helps the organisation in more than one way. It adds to the effectiveness of the personnel administration, besides being essential to cope with changing needs. Some of the positive results that accrue from a well organised and properly derived career development plan are:

(a) It ensures needed talents, the right people for the changing staffing requirements of the organisation.
(b) It attracts and retains highly talented personnel.
(c) It ensures equal opportunity for minorities and women.
(d) It removes employee's dissatisfaction by providing opportunities of advancement and better prospects.

Hindrances to Career Development

The growth of career development has been affected by various factors, some of which are as follows:

(a) The first hindrance is the requirement of local residence for a particular job. Only local people are appointed to some jobs. In a federal system as in India residence is considered very essential for the state job. It hinders promotion opportunities, because a talented person may not be a local resident.
(b) Sometimes promotions of employees are made only in the department in which they are serving, e.g., railway employees may be promoted in the Railways only. It restricts the area of promotion of public officials.
(c) There is a widespread feeling that there are no incentives for efficiency in government jobs. This factor has also discouraged many talented persons from seeking public service careers.

Career service is essential for efficiency in administration. This is the only effective way of attracting the best and the talented candidates to public service.

Performance Appraisal

Every organisation has a system of assessment of performance of its employees periodically for determining the output of that employee as well as for deciding on his promotion. Some of the methods of performance appraisal are as under.

The purpose of a performance appraisal system is primarily to assess the capabilities of a person in terms of his contribution towards the achievement of the organisational goals. It, thus, serves a short term purpose of assessing the usefulness of an employee to the organisation and in the long run determines his potential for elevation to higher levels. Conversely, it pinpoints the shortcomings of an employee by pointing these out to him. The superior officers can manage better utilisation of the services of that employee through either correction or position-change.

The performance appraisal system consists of an annual appraisal by the superior of the work of the subordinate. It is usually in the shape of a form which carries entries to determine the adequacy and quality of work done and the general personality and integrity of the officer reported upon. Besides, his fitness for promotion or otherwise is also commented upon. To reduce the ambiguities in relative grading by different officers, certain grades are prescribed. The report is written by the reporting officer in a narrative form, evaluated by the reviewing officer and finally endorsed or countersigned by the senior most officer. This constitutes the Confidential Roll.

If an adverse remark is made regarding an officer which is finally endorsed, that particular officer is shown the report and asked to mend his ways. That officer is also generally given an opportunity to represent to the authorities regarding the contents of the report to be modified or expunged.

This system of performance appraisal has its flaws. Some of the major ones are as follows:

First, in the evaluation form the qualities required of an officer are often not defined nor is there any report on the results of performance of special nature. Besides, the interpretation of the language of the proforma may vary and have subjective elements.

Second, the yardsticks are not commonly accepted and different superior officers attach different values to these terms. Therefore a need is felt for more explicit definition of the yardsticks and even their possible quantification.

Third, both the reviewing officer and the countersigning officer may or may not have any direct or intimate knowledge about the work of the officer reported upon. Again, as the reports are written at the end of a financial year or a calendar year, there are too many to be written and, therefore, the reviewing officers might not do proper justice.

Fourth, the strongest objection against this system is the element of subjectivity which is built into it. Since it is a case of one individual passing a judgement on the other, the element of subjectivity cannot be completely ruled out.

It would be quite relevant to note what the Administrative Reforms Commission (India) had to say about performance appraisal:

1. At the end of each year, the official reported upon should submit a brief resume, not exceeding three hundred words, of the work done by him, bringing out special achievement of his. The resume should be submitted to the reporting officer and should form a part of the confidential report. This should be taken into account by the reporting officer while making his report or comments.
2. Only three gradations are to be made, viz, 'fit for promotion', 'not yet fit for promotion' and 'unfit for promotion' when writing the confidential reports of secretariat officers of the level of under-secretary and above. Further, it has to be indicated whether the officer reported upon has any outstanding qualities which entitle him for promotion out of turn.
3. Good work done during the year should receive prompt appreciation either on a file, or in a tour or inspection note. The official concerned should be allowed to quote these in his resume.
4. The suggestions made above (by the ARC) will ensure that an individual's own estimate of his performance will get a place in his confidential report. It is equally important that his superior officer's assessment made frankly and faithfully is also available in it. This is likely to avoid unnecessary unpleasantness

which might crop up between the officer reported and the reporting officer.

PROMOTION

Promotion is an important constituent of a sound personnel policy besides being a technique of filling vacant posts in public employment. Public personnel system cannot be efficient without providing ample opportunities to the employees to rise high in the administrative set up. To keep the employees efficient, some incentives are required and the greatest incentive to an employee is his promotion from one post to the next higher post.

Prof. Pigor and Myfes has defined promotion in the following manner: "Promotion is the advancement of an employee to better job, better in terms of greater responsibilities, more prestige, or status, greater skill and specially increased rate of pay or salary". In the words of Flippo, "Promotion involves a change from one job to another that is better in terms of status and responsibilities".

The change in duties and responsibilities is the essential characteristic of the promotion process. Promotion means progress from a lower to a higher class leading to change of duties and responsibilities. When an employee is promoted, it leads to increase in his salary also. But a mere increase in salary is not promotion. Increase in the salary is a subsidiary part of promotion; the real promotion is in terms of change in the class status of the employee which involves change of duties and responsibilities.

A well developed promotion policy is very essential for the efficiency of the employees. Promotion is a continuous incentive to efficient working on the part of the employee. The hope of promotion is sufficient to keep the man interested in the job.

Advantages of a promotion policy:

(a) It keeps the personnel efficient.

(b) It ensures rewards for efficient service.

(c) Qualified people are attracted towards the service at the time of recruitment. They know that opportunities exist for progress.

(d) From the point of view of employer a promotion policy is very advantageous. He can fill the higher and responsible posts from the experienced and capable persons who are already in the service. Thus, the employer makes full use of the experience of his employees.

ESSENTIALS OF PROMOTION SYSTEM

W.P. Willoughby has prescribed the following essentials of a sound promotion system:

1. Adoption of standard specifications setting forth the duties and qualifications required for all promotions in the government service.
2. The classification of these promotions into distinct classes, salaries, grades and services.
3. The inclusion within this classification of all the higher administrative promotions except those having a practical character.
4. The adoption, so far as possible, of the principle of recruitment from within for filling up of higher posts.
5. The adoption of the principle of merit in determining the promotion of employees.
6. The provision of adequate means for determining the relative merits of employees eligible for promotion.

Principles of Promotion

Now the question arises as to what should be the criterion for promotion. There are two main principles on which the eligibility criteria for promotion can be fixed. First is the principle of seniority and the second is that of merit.

Principle of Seniority

The seniority principle in government service is widely prevalent as a method of promotion in most countries. Under this principle, promotion is determined on the basis of the length of service of the employee. In general, an employee who has served longer is eligible for promotion. On the basis of this principle an employee is promoted to a higher grade or class. The reasons advanced in favour of the principle of seniority are:

i) It is objective since it is easy to find out seniority of an employee.
ii) Senior man is more experienced.
iii) In this principle, everyone gets an opportunity for promotion.
iv) In case of seniority, there cannot be any interference by the politicians in the promotion of the employees.
v) The principle of seniority gives certainty of promotion to employees, thus better persons are attracted.
vi) Since the promotions are on a just principle, the morale of the employees is expected to be high.

The defects of the principle of seniority are as follows:

i) There is no guarantee that a senior employee will be more competent or meritorious
ii) If seniority alone is the basis of promotion then employees do not make any effort for self-improvement.
iii) Mediocre and un-intelligent persons who cannot compete with the young and meritorious are the greatest supporters of the principle of seniority.

In the words of Pfiffner: "A system of promotion by seniority will frequently result in raising to supervisory and directing positions, persons who have 'crank complexes'... Seniority alone will tend to fill the higher place with incompetent persons. It will discourage the ambitious and remove those incentives which develop personality, courage, self-reliance and progressive outlook. It will foster self-satisfaction, a dead level of mediocre performance and that general let-down which goes with security".

All members of a grade are not fit for promotion and the promotional opportunities are usually few. The organisation has always to balance the need for rewarding merit and that for employee loyalty.

The Principle of Merit

According to this principle, promotions are made on the basis of qualifications and achievements of an employee irrespective of his length of service. This system provides that the most meritorious or the best qualified person should be selected for promotion. According to Flippo, "Merit-rating is a systematic, periodic and so far as humanly possible an impartial rating of an employee's excellence in matters pertaining to his present job and to his potentials for a better job" This principle provides due incentive to the efficient and hard working employees and thus helps in building up the morale and efficiency in public services.

Methods of Testing Merit

A. Promotional Examination

The first objective method of testing a candidate's ability is through promotional examinations. The promotional examination may be an open competition, a limited competition, or even merely a pass. It may be an examination with or without interview.

i) *Open Competition:* Any one, whether in the same development or not, can compete for the post of promotion thereby inviting even outsiders also who are not in the department. This system brings in 'new blood' and 'fresh ideas' into the department.

ii) *Limited Competition:* Under this, only those who are in the department are allowed to appear in the examination. This is also known as the 'closed system' as opposed to the 'open system' under which everyone can compete.

iii) *Pass Examination:* A candidate is just to pass the examination and give proof of his minimum attainments. On the basis of the list of passed candidates, promotions are made as and when vacancies arise.

B. *Efficiency Ratings or Service Records*

On the basis of service records, the performance of the job is evaluated or the relative merit of the employee is evaluated. Knowledge of the work of the branch or department, personality, capacity of taking responsibilities, initiative, official conduct etc. are the qualities judged and gradation made. Methods of efficiency rating in USA are classified under three categories:

i) *Production Records:* This system is applicable to the work of those employees only whose work can be quantitatively compared on the basis of output or production. The production record can be maintained concerning the work of a typist, stenographer, a file clerk, or a machine operator. But this method is inapplicable to the officials who perform administrative or supervisory work.

ii) *The Graphic Rating Scale System:* In it, certain service traits are mentioned on a graph and on their basis the relative efficiency of the employee is usually judged. The service elements judged are accuracy, dependability neatness and orderliness of work, speed with which world is accomplished, industry, diligence, energy and application to duties, knowledge of work, judgement, common sense, success in winning confidence and respect, cooperativeness, initiative, execution, ability to organise ability to delegate authority, self-control, tact, courage, success in improving and developing employees etc. Those traits of the employees are marked and on that basis the qualities of the employees are assessed.

iii) *Personality Inventory System:* This system obtains a record of service by different means; it is illustrated by Probst Rating Scale that was invented and developed by J.Probst in 1927. He mentioned many qualities of an employee in his rating scale and out of these various qualities the rating officer had to select only those titles which were descriptive of the qualities of the employee. Some of the qualities which Probst mentioned are 'lazy, slow, shining, quick and active, too old for work, minor physical defects, indifferent, talks too much, good team worker, pleasant and cheerful, cranky disposition, often grumbling etc.' This is a rather tricky system, as subjective elements are likely to creep in, when characterising an employee.

C. *Personal Judgement of the Head*

Another method of determination of merit for promotion is by leaving it to the judgement of the head of the department who has been in closest contact with the employees and has personal knowledge of the employees and their work in the organisation. Judgement based on personal association is more valuable than any other system of judging the qualities of the employees. However, the importance and utility of the personal judgement of the Head of the Department depends on three factors, i.e., the capacity to make good judgements, the freedom of action enjoyed by him in the department and his good intention.

This system mainly suffers from two limitations. First, this system can work only in small scale organisations; because in a large organisation, it is next to impossible for the departmental heads to keep a close touch with their subordinates, or to form an accurate opinion of their merits and capacities. Second, this system is 'subjective', susceptible to extraneous considerations, leading to unhealthy rivalry and ill-will among the employees.

The above mentioned defects can be removed by constituting Promotion Boards. These Boards may consist of chief officials of the department and on the basis of seniority, service records etc., they may recommend promotions. Again if an aggrieved employee feels that any wrong has been done to him, he may appeal to an agency outside the department. In order to make the reports of the departmental heads more objective and systematic, certain parameters ought to be prescribed.

All these various tests are employed to secure a sound policy of promotion. However the test of the success of a promotion policy is the general contentment, high morale and 'espirit de corps' prevailing among the employees.

In conclusion, it needs to be emphasised that progressive organisations attach considerable importance to human resource development. By contrast, in public organisation human resource is generally neglected. Technological changes like computerisation and use of information technology are demanding new types of professional employees whose management would require special efforts in government in future.

Concluding Observation

Public personnel management has traditionally been 'stability' oriented, rather than 'change' oriented. Weberian 'bureaucracy' has dominated the scene, as a fixed paradigm. Since the 80s of the last century and the advent of 'globalisation' as a phenomenon to be reckoned with by every public authority, personnel management has taken a new turn toward:

(a) Performance monitoring of employees' job;
(b) Quality production of output;
(c) Cost-effectiveness of operations and outputs;
(d) Citizen-satisfaction as an index of good performance;
(e) Inculcation of a spirit of competitiveness in order that public administration functions in a world of choices for the consumer (government being one of many suppliers and not the only supplier).

Following this new philosophy of public management, public personnel management is steadily moving toward a new orientation in terms of contractual (not life-long) job, performance assurance, production-linked remuneration and even separation (called voluntary retirement scheme or VRS, in brief, or the golden handshake).

In future jobs, in government establishments are likely to be less permanent, more challenging, e-governance-based and client-oriented in a more and more competitive world of multiple suppliers of goods and services.

Chapter 18

Financial Administration

Jut as a household cannot be managed without fund, government as the manager of the society can't function without an assured source of fund. The government mobilises resources through taxation, fees and charges and other means. The revenue thus raised is society's or public's money. There is, therefore, a latent understanding that the society is providing fund to government on condition that money so raised from society will be properly spent for public purposes. In the developing countries, government has been responsible for a large number of functions and the private sector is not large enough and unable to undertake most public functions nor can it subserve 'public interest'. Government in developing countries has to raise more and more resources from a variety of sources both for 'maintenance' and 'development' functions. The public sphere has thus expanded over the years to a great extent.

Current Trend

The contemporary trend is toward limiting the public sphere and handing over more and more activities to the private sector. To the extent this will be possible, government activities will shrink and there will be less demand on society to pay for government-run activities. In fact, government expenditure burden will be much less and hence, government will not be raising more and more revenue from the society. This new philosophy of 'state minimalism' can be traced to what is known as the 'Right' reaction or Thatcherism and Reaganomics, as it originated at the time of Mrs. Thatcher regime in U.K. and the Reagan regime in USA. The Third World countries are also now being advised by the World Bank and the international funding agencies to reduce governmental size by unburdening the government and passing on many functions to the private sector. No doubt, the size of government bureaucracy has increased enormously in the Third World countries due to government take-over of many social and developmental functions. There is surely some scope of reduction in the size of government by divesting some of its responsibilities; but the leading role of government in pushing through 'development' and securing a minimum level of quality of life for the general public, specially the poor and the underprivileged, cannot be dispensed with. Hence, the state 'roll back' theory of the 'New Right' philosophy has to be taken with a grain of salt so far as the developing countries are concerned.

The lesson of this argument is that government in the Third World countries has to be an efficient financial manager in two senses: *One,* it has to be prudent in expenditure and must not overtax the society which itself is in the process of growing. *Two,* the government has to frame well planned policies for overall guidance of the economy including the private sector.

Any discussion on 'financial administration' has

to be conducted within this broad understanding of the economy of the developing societies.

Meaning of Financial Administration

Government raises fund from the public to meet 'maintenance' expenditure or the running expenses of public administration. Government has also to raise funds for 'development' expenditure to create new capital assests like big dams, steel plants, new roads, railways, electricity generating plants etc. Financial administration involves planning of public expenditure and revenues, making funds available for the governmental activities and ensuring the lawful and efficient use of these funds. Under democratic government, the legislature is the body to vote the taxes and authorise expenditure. Financial administration has to see that the legislature is not asked to place more tax burden on the people than what is necessary and that the money voted by it for expenditure is used according to its wishes and with due regard to economy and efficiency.

Financial administration thus forms a crucial aspect of public administration. Most administrative acts have their financial implications. They create a charge on the public exchequer or bring revenues to it. Financial operations may be designed to develop and promote particular public policies. Tariffs may be so shaped as to afford protection to the home industries, or taxation may be so designed as to promote economic equality by the transfer of money from the rich to the poor. Finally, financial administration raises important issues of administrative organisation and relationships, e.g., what machinery of financial administration there should be or what the relationship between such machinery and administrative authorities should be or who should have the last word about a proposed item of expenditure, the financial officers or the administrative officers.

Financial administration is a composite term for a number of discrete functions as under:

(a) Preparation of the budget i.e., of the estimates of the revenue and expenditure for the ensuing financial year;
(b) Getting those estimates passed by the legislature or other competent authority;
(c) Execution of the budget i.e. regulation of the expenditure and raising of revenue according to it;
(d) Treasury management i.e. safe custody of the funds raised and due arrangement for the necessary payments to meet the liabilities;
(e) Rendering of the accounts by the executive and audit of these accounts.

The Concept of Budget

Budget making is the first step in government's financial administration. Really speaking, however, the budget does not come from the blue. Its shape, size and details are determined by political perceptions of the ruling class. The government in power has some policies, which are *reflected* in the budget. The term 'Budget' has been derived from a French word, 'Bougette' which means a leather bag or wallet. The term was used in its present sense for the first time in 1873, in a satire directed against Walpole's financial plan for that year. Since then, the term has been used for a financial scheme or statement of annual income and expenditure of the government. Traditional budget acquired the descriptive title of 'line item', as the object was put on the left side and the cost on the right side. As Wildavsky has put it: A budget is 'a series of goals with price tags attached'.

To some, budget is a statement of estimated

revenues and expenditures. To others, budget is synonymous with Revenue and Appropriation Acts. A budget is in reality a statement of the estimated receipts and expenses during a fixed period. It is a comparative table giving the amounts of the receipts to be realised and of the expenses to be incurred, it is an authorisation or a command given by the proper authorities to incur the expenses and to collect the revenues. In a way, the budget is a forecast and an estimate of all the public receipts and expenses and an authorization to incur them and to collect them. The above definitions are defective at least in two ways. First, they do not mention that Budget should contain facts regarding past operations and present conditions as well as proposals for the future. Second, they do not distinguish between the Budget and Revenue and Appropriation Acts. The two things are to be distinguished. The budget represents the act of the Administration while Revenue and Appropriation Acts represent the act of the Legislature.

The budget presents in a consolidated and comprehensive way all the facts regarding the expenditure of the government, past and prospective and the revenue and financial position of the Treasury. The Budget, thus, is something much more than a mere estimate of revenues and expenditures. It is the document through which the executive comes before the fund-raising and fund granting authority and makes full report regarding the manner in which government has managed affairs during the last complete year. The present condition of the public treasury is described and the programme of work for the year to come and the manner in which such work would be financed are explained in the budget.

Thus budget is a plan of government action from the financial point of view. Expressed in financial terms, the budget is a systematic method of gathering information from the past and present, of formulating plans for the future on the basis of this and of reporting subsequently how these plans have been carried out.

Evolution of Budgetary Thought:

Bertram Gross and Allen Schick have classified the different stages of the evolution of budgetary thinking in government (especially American Government). Six periods categorised by them are as follows[1]:

6. Traditional or line item budgeting, with inherent control orientation;
7. Performance budgeting (sometimes called programme budgeting) with its management orientation;
8. Planning-programming-budgeting system (PPBS) with its economic planning thrust;
9. Management by objectives (MbO), with its emphasis on budgetary decentralisation;
10. Zero-based budgeting (ZBB), with its emphasis on ranking programme priorities; and
11. Budgeting as political management, with its centralising and legislative overtones.

As experts like Wildavsky has pointed out, budgeting is draped with the trappings of professionalism, technology and expertise but it is also a system of values and politics.

Economic and Social Implications of Budget

A modern budget plays a very important role in the social and economic life of a community. In early days budget being the statement of estimated receipts and expenditure had only two objectives. First, government had to determine how much money it wanted to take out of the pockets of tax payers in order to maintain its necessary activities with proper standard of efficiency. Second, legislature had to vote funds, so it necessarily wanted to know the plan of expenditure. Thus, in the days of *laissez-faire,* budget was a simple statement of estimated income and expenditure. Modern society, with the rise of the welfare state, had to assure ever-increasing quantity and variety of government activities. The activities of government tend to cover almost all aspects of social life. Government budgeting is one of the major instruments by which the use of public resources is planned and controlled. The budget is thus an instrument for the articulation of government programmes which have ramifications in the entire national economy. It affects development and production, size and distribution of income and the availability of man-power and materials. From the budget citizens can know what benefits they are going to derive from the various plans and programmes of the government and how much tax they will have to pay. Through the budget, various interests, desires and needs of the citizens are consolidated into concrete programmes. The taxation policy of the government as reflected in the Budget aims at narrowing down of class distinctions and social inequalities. The budgetary policy of the government would be directed towards removing poverty, unemployment and mal-distribution of wealth. Thus considered, the budget has tremendous social and economic implications in a genuine welfare state.

BUDGETARY PROCESSES

The important principles and processes involved in the formulation of a budget are as follows:

(I) *Publicity:* The government budget passes through various stages, e.g., recommendation of budget by the executive to the legislature, detailed consideration of the budget by the legislature and administration and execution of the budget by various government departments. Through these various stages, the budget is sought to be made public. Publicity of the budget is essential, so that the people and the press may freely express their views concerning various taxes or schemes of expenditure. Prior to submission to the legislature, budget is a confidential document, as any leakage of budget proposals may benefit sectional interests and hence, harm public interest.

(II) *Clarity and precision:* The budget should be framed in such a way, that it is clearly understood by the general public and items are precisely and unambiguously stated. Any attempt at mystification of the budget should thus be deprecated, as the public will find it hard to understand government's policies and programmes.

(III) *Comprehensiveness:* The entire fiscal programme of the government should be integrated and summarised in the budget. It should give a complete picture of government revenues and expenditures. It should clearly state whether any new debts or borrowings are going to be incurred by the government. Receipts and appropriations should be expressed in details. Through budget, one should be able to know the entire financial position of the government, its assets and liabilities and the future policies of the government in the coming years.

(IV) *Unity:* All government receipts should be consolidated into one general fund for financing all expenditures. Scattering and random expressions would be harmful from the point of view of clarity and precision.

(V) *Periodicity:* The budget is framed within a time horizon. There should be a fixed period for which appropriations should be authorised. If money is not utilised within that period, it should either lapse, or should be re-appropriated. Generally, the budget grants are on annual basis. The budget should be passed by the Legislature, keeping all foreseeable needs in view, in advance of the period during which expenditure is to be incurred. If, for instance, the annual year starts on April 1, it will be convenient if legislature approves the expenditure before April 1. Sometimes due to political exigencies, budget period is shortened and full budget is taken up later.

(VI) *Accuracy:* Accuracy and reliability of budget estimates is essential for any sound financial policy of the government. The information on which budget estimates are based must be sufficiently accurate and detailed in order to facilitate intelligent evaluation by legislators, the public and the media.

(VII) There should be no intentional under-estimation of revenues or concealment of vital facts. In India, the criticism has often been voiced in Parliament that in the framing of budget estimates, there is a tendency to under-estimate revenue receipts and to overestimate revenue expenditure. This distorts the budgetary outlook and the framework.

(VIII) *Integrity:* Government budget, in principle, has to have legislative approval, which is, in theory, people's approval. Fiscal programmes should be carried out faithfully and substantially in accordance with budget provisions. If the budget is not executed as it is enacted, there is likely to be executive-legislative misunderstanding and subsequent questioning from the Comptroller and Auditor-General.

Budget Types

Usually there are three types of budget. These are:

(a) *Legislative:* When budget is prepared by a committee of the legislature on the request of the executive, it is known as legislative type of budget. This type of budget strengthens the importance of legislature. Legislature prepares the budget and approves it. Actually, however, legislature is not competent enough to prepare the budget as the requirements of the various departments are known only to the executive.

(b) *Executive:* In this system budget is prepared by the executive and after it has been approved by the legislature, responsibility for its execution lies with the executive. This is the commonly accepted principle of budget preparation and execution.

(c) *The Board or Commission Type:* In this type, Budget is formulated by a Board or a Commission which may consist wholly of administrative officers or a joint team of administrative and legislative officers. This system is in use in some states of America and in some municipal bodies in USA. The purpose of this arrangement may be either to associate the more important of the independent administrative officers with the Chief Executive in the formulation of budget, or to surround the Chief Executive with a Board so constituted as to restrict his influence in matters of financial planning.

In reality, the Executive type of Budget is the universal practice today. It is felt rightly that the Executive is the best judge of the requirements of the various spending agencies, so it should prepare the estimates of income and expenditure and submit its financial plan to the legislature. The Executive Budget is prepared by experts and in almost all countries, some special agency is provided to help the Chief Executive in the preparation of budget. The Bureau of Budget in the U.S.A., the Treasury in Britain and the Finance Department in India are the expert agencies which prepare the budget on behalf of the executive for placement before the legislature.

Performance Budgeting: Parliamentary vigilance is necessary for proper budget implementation. Parliament should have some machinery to evaluate the expenditure sanctioned to various departments in the Budget. This evaluation should be done to see whether the objectives for which money was sanctioned and spent have been really achieved. Performance Budgeting has been recommended for Railways and other government commercial and Industrial enterprises. Budgetary grants are spent to achieve the purposes and objectives laid down by the Legislature. Review of expenditures has to be made to see whether results have been achieved within the time limit and at minimum cost and maximum economy in expenditures.

Certain conditions are necessary before undertaking the exercise of Performance Budgeting: (i) it would be necessary to have a system of advance programming of government operations on a long-term basis; (ii) the 'end results' of the programme must be measurable; (iii) the outlay shown in the Budget should represent the entire costs; (iv) the programme should be closely monitored by the Budgeting authority; (v) the total outlay should be capable of allocation between fixed and variable costs.

Some kind of Performance Budgeting has been attempted in many results-oriented departments. The Committee on Plan Projects could conduct studies for securing economy and efficiency in the execution of the Plan Projects included in India's five-year plans. The Administrative Reforms Commission in its Report on Finance, Accounts and Audit (1968) recommended the introduction of Performance Budgeting by the departments which are in direct charge of development programmes such as agriculture, irrigation etc.

The Performance Budget should be prepared in the following manner: A programme and activity classification would be made for each department or organisation selected for the purpose of Performance Budgeting. Besides presenting the financial needs of those programmes and activities, expenditures should be classified in terms of 'object', e.g. Establishment. This should be followed by a narrative explanation justifying the financial requirements under each activity. This explanation should include information on targets, achievements, relevant workload factors, comparative performance over the years, etc. All this together will constitute the Performance Budget. It should be accompanied by the demands for grants which will continue to serve as the medium through which appropriation control would be exercised.

Budget is a document but a Budget system is one that makes use of a Budget as the central instrument of financial administration. A budget system has three phases:

1. Formulation of the Budget and determination of the authority for the formulation of Budget.
2. Legislative action upon the Budget.
3. Execution of the Budget: i.e., putting of the provisions of the Revenue and Appropriation Acts into effect.

Before the various phases of Budget system are discussed, it is useful to study the essentials of Budget system. Someone must prepare the Budget and submit it to the legislature. The responsibility lies with the Chief Executive who, with the aid and assistance of an expert agency like the Bureau of Budget or Treasury, prepares the Budget and transmits it to the legislature. The Budget should be accurately and completely prepared and it should state all the facts in detail. The Budget should give a complete picture of government's finances and it should be so laid out and summarised as to make this picture quite clear to the citizens and the tax payers. The procedure adopted by legislature for the discussion of Budget should not be veiled in secrecy. After the Budget has been passed by the legislature, it should be in use throughout the period to which it applies.

The following steps are taken to see the budget through:

(A) *Preparation of Estimates:* First of all, the political executive decides the overall financial policy, on the basis of which estimates are prepared. Budget preparation starts from the lowest level. On the basis of instructions from top nodal agency, various administrative agencies prepare their estimates. These sectional estimates are then examined and scrutinised by departmental heads and then passed on to officers of the Treasury or the Finance Department. After many meetings and discussions, the proposed expenditure plan is consolidated into a single document, which may be again discussed by the Finance Department and the political executive. During the period of preparation of estimates, there is always competition among various Departments, who push their claims for acceptance and the principle of 'survival of the fittest' operates. In the final analysis, the estimates are the handiwork of the Executive Department like the Treasury or Department of Finance.

(B) *Legislative Approval of the Budget:* After the Budget has been prepared, it is submitted to the Legislature with a request for approval. It is discussed in the Legislature in two parts. First, the expenditure side is discussed and then the revenues are discussed. All legislatures make extensive use of Committees for the examination of estimates. In the legislature, two separate Bills are passed; one is the Appropriation Bill which is a legal authorisation to spend money while the second, Revenue Bill, gives authority to impose and collect taxes. After these two bills are passed by the Legislature, the political executive seeks to implement it.

A Budget which has been approved by the Legislature gives authority to the Executive to spend money on particular items as specified by the Legislature. In this way, parliamentary sovereignty is assured.

Agencies of Financial Administration: It is a fundamental principle that a democratically constituted legislature exercises the most important control over the public finances. Legislature, as the fund-raising and fund-granting authority, has the power to levy, abolish, increase or decrease any tax. It has the final authority to sanction money for expenditure. No tax can be levied or collected and no expenditure can be incurred without parliamentary approval.

The Legislature's duties are:

(a) To achieve, between the different services for which the Government accepts responsibility, a reasonably fair distribution of the total sum which the country can afford to devote to Government expenditure;

(b) To ensure that the money so distributed is used for the purposes for which it was intended in accordance with the statutory authority;

(c) To try to secure full value for the money which is distributed. Only a vigilant and knowledgeable legislature can perform the above mentioned tasks. That is why the opposition parties are very particular, about legislative supervision of public finance.

In the same way, in India the Executive demands money from the Legislature by presenting the Budget and Parliament grants it. The Legislature performs its functions cinder Executive leadership. All demands for grants and all proposals for taxation come from the Executive and the Legislature gives its approval to these proposals after thorough scrutiny.

The second agency concerning Financial Administration' and control is the Executive. Control in matters of policy concerning finance vests in the government as a whole. Government decides the expenditure policy. Questions like pay, pension and provident fund to the officials are all determined by the Government. The Executive performs the policy making function concerning finance and then tries to get the approval of the Legislature.

Finance Department: The Finance Department is responsible for the entire Financial Administration of the country. This Department performs a variety of functions. It has control over expenditure of money. It controls and coordinates various spending Departments of the Government. It is responsible for the collection of taxes. It is the duty of this Department to prepare the estimates of income and expenditure of this Department i.e. the annual Budget of the government. Its main business is the proper management of the finances of the country. It exercises vital control and supervision over the expenditure of the Departments. So, first and foremost among the Departments of Administration stands the Department of Finance, or Treasury as it is known in England.

Audit: In all democracies independent audit of public fund as authorised by legislature is vested in a constitutional authority. A very important agency for financial control is this Audit Agency. Honest and sound finance can be ensured by subjecting the public expenditure to the search light of an independent audit. Auditing is the investigation of and report on the fidelity, legality and efficiency of all financial transactions. The audit of public money is conducted by an independent officer on behalf of the Legislature. When the Legislature has sanctioned money for expenditure, it should also see to it that the money is spent economically, legally and honestly. Parliament has to see that money is not misused or mis-appropriated by officials for their own benefit. In India, Parliament gets the audit of public money conducted by the Comptroller and Auditor General, who is a friend, philosopher and guide of Parliament in this respect.

Parliamentary Committees: Finally, two committees of the legislature, commonly known as the Estimates Committee and Public Accounts Committee, exercise financial control on behalf of the Legislature. The Estimates Committee suggests economies in expenditure in various Departments of Government, at the estimates stage, i.e., before actual expenditure and the Public Accounts Committee examines the Appropriation accounts in the light of the audit report of the Comptroller and Auditor General and draws the attention of the Legislature to financial irregularities which might have occurred and makes suggestions for preventing them in future.

The above mentioned agencies are employed for financial control and administration in the government. The purpose of financial control is to secure honesty and economy in expenditure. Government money is provided by tax-payers. These agencies have to see that the tax-payers' money is rightly and properly used. Public money is a trust and financial administration of the country should see to it that a rupee is not spent where a paisa would have been sufficient and that paisa is spent not for the personal gain of any individual but for the good of the society as a whole. Thus, efficient Financial Administration is an imperative necessity for every country.

Accounts and Audit

Proper maintenance of accounts of the public funds and their audit by an agency independent of the Executive control is essential for an efficient administration of public finance. Accounting is constructive and auditing is analytical. Accounting has been defined as the 'art of recording, classifying and summarising transactions, wholly or in part of a financial nature in terms of money and interpreting the results there of'. Auditing is an examination of the books, records and procedures of an organisation to ascertain or to verify the facts with respect to the organisation's financial position and financial operations against certain standards, norms and rules.

Accounts

'Accounting is the science of producing promptly and presenting clearly the facts relating to financial condition and operations that are required as a basis of management. Accounting means maintaining a proper record of the finances of the organisation. So maintenance of accounts is the function of the spending authorities or the executive. Proper accounts also show the legal use of funds and on the basis of accounts report, the spending officers justify expenditure to the superiors. Through a proper system of accounting wrong use of funds can be prevented. Accounting has to ensure that funds have been legally used for the purpose for which Parliament sanctioned it. Accounts should furnish authentic data regarding the financial operations. The spending authorities should produce receipts or vouchers concerning every paise which they spend, against authorisation by appropriate authorities.

Standards of Public Accounting

Some of the essential standards of public accounting are as follows:

(a) *Centralisation of Accounts:* One officer or agency should be held responsible for keeping or supervising the maintenance of all financial records and preparation of all financial reports. Its advantage is that all accounts of the government departments shall be coordinated and unified.

(b) *Character of the Accounting System:* The accounts should be maintained on a double entry basis, with a general ledger maintained on the basis of the following principles:

   i) The classification of the accounts should be in balanced fund assets.

   ii) Those asset accounts of the permanent property which are not available to meet the expenditures or obligations should be set apart from fund assets. The equity represented by them should not be included in the current surplus of any fund.

(c) *Classification of Funds:* Assets, liabilities and proprietorship of every fund or group funds should stand out as a separate balanced group of accounts. A complete balance sheet should be compiled for every fund.

(d) *Budgetary Control Accounts:* A Public Accounting System should include budgetary control accounts, revenues, expenditures, appropriations and encumbrances.

(e) *Revenue Accounting:* In the Accounts reports all items of non-revenue character should be excluded from reports of revenue. Revenues should be classified by fund and by source, in accordance with standard classification.

(f) *Expenditure Accounting:* Expenditure should be classified by funds, by department and by activities (and by object, if desired) in accordance with standard classification.

It is commonly accepted that the above principles should be adopted in preparing the government accounts and the annual accounts reports should be published, showing the correct financial picture of all the departments of the government.

Types of Accounts: There are three types of Public Accounts:

1. *Cash System:* The Cash System of accounts records transactions only when cash has been actually received or disbursed, while the accrual system records transactions at the time the commitment is made. Revenue on an accrual basis means each item of accounts is taken when it becomes due or a bill is issued for it. Thus the cash system never reflects the exact financial situation because it is always behind, while the accrual system is always current. Since some sizeable contracts take months to mature, the difference between the two systems is an important one.
2. *Accrual System of Accounts:* The accrual system makes it possible for management to know exactly where it stands, which is not possible under cash system. Under accrual system, income is taken into account when it is earned and expenditures are taken into account when they are actually incurred. Under accrual system, revenues are taken into account and put under control when they are assessed and expenses are taken into account as they are incurred. The accrual basis affords full current information concerning the realization of the revenue estimates and the expenditure and availability of appropriations.
3. *Cost Accounting System:* It means a system of accounting in which costs are allocated to the various activities in the respective departments. The cost system of accounting reveals the cost of maintaining and operating the several services of the government, the cost of performing the separate functions or activities engaged in, the cost of the different objects or classes of objects of expenditure, etc. If such information concerning costs of various activities is required, a provision is made for a special cost keeping system. The accounts of central and state governments in India are kept under the same heads and sub-heads as those of the budget. The government accounts are maintained on the receipts and disbursements basis and not on 'accrual' basis. The government accounts are based on the single entry basis and not on the orthodox Double Entry System, in vogue, in commercial concerns.

ACCOUNTING IN INDIA

In India, there is the constitutional authority of

the CAG who is responsible for the maintenance of proper accounts of the Government of India. The accounts of the Union and of the States shall be kept in such form as the Comptroller and Auditor-General may, with the approval of the President, prescribe. Under the Comptroller and Auditor General there is an Accountant General in each state, in whose office the accounts of the transactions (Central as well as State), which take place within the territorial limits of the state, are kept.

The Auditor-General compiles the finance and revenue accounts of India in such form as may be prescribed by the President. He may call upon any government officer to furnish any information in such form as may be required for the compilation of these accounts.

The Auditor-General has the power to prescribe the form in which accounts shall be kept in audit offices; provided that no change which would affect the form of the finance and revenue accounts should be made without the previous sanction of the President.

If a doubt or a dispute arises as to the major head under which a particular minor head should be included, it shall be decided by the Auditor-General.

The Auditor-General prepares in each year a review of the balance of the books maintained by the audit departments.

The Auditor-General has the power to determine the form in which officers rendering accounts to the Indian Audit Department shall render such accounts and in which the initial accounts from which the accounts so entered are compiled or on which they are based, shall be maintained.

The Auditor-General has to arrange that officers subordinate to him supply any information required by the President or by a Local Government, which can be derived from their accounts maintained in the offices under his control.

Separation of Accounts and Audit

The present arrangement, under which spending authorities are not responsible for the maintenance of complete and up-to-date accounts related to the transactions for which they are responsible and the duty of compiling and maintaining the complete accounts rests upon an outside authority, namely, the Indian Audit Department, is inconsistent with the various responsibilities of the spending department. They are expected to have effective control over their financial transactions and the discharge of their responsibilities to Parliament to keep within the Budget grants and appropriations. Accounting and Auditing should be maintained as separate functions, because as an essential tool of management, accounting should be under the control of management and at the same time there should be an outside check on management. Auditing and accounting should not be combined in the same agency as a matter of principle. The maintenance of account is the executive function of the spending authorities.

Audit

As earlier stated, audit is one of the most important instruments of parliamentary control over the finances of the country. Independent audit is a very important safeguard of the public money. Auditing is a systematic examination of the books and records of a business or other organisations in order to ascertain or verify and to report upon the facts regarding its financial operations and the results thereof. Audit of government money in a democratic country is done by an independent officer, who performs this duty on behalf of the legislature. It is his duty to see that money has been spent economically and honestly.

Pre-Audit and Post-Audit

Pre-auditing is concerned with the examination of the elements of a transaction before it is completed and recorded in the final accounting records. It is a tool of management and an administrative check upon the accuracy and legality of transactions still in process within a department. Pre-auditing is done to know the availability of funds and legality of expenditure. It can prevent over-expenditure of budget resources, if administered properly.

Post-auditing is concerned with the examination of the records after the transactions have been completed and recorded. Post-audit takes place after the money has been actually spent. Conventionally, audit is understood in this sense.

Functions of an Auditor

An annual audit should be done by one who is independent of executive control and the agency performing the work of conducting independent audit should be responsible to the legislature. This is the principle, as earlier explained.

Generally, the duties of the auditor are mainly three. First, he should examine past transactions. The accounts and reports of all persons or agents having the receipt, custody or disbursement of public money should be examined to ensure proper accountability of fidelity. Secondly, the transactions of public funds, that have been expended, have been received, or that should have been received, should be examined with respect to the question of legality. Thirdly, the auditor should report the result of such examinations to the legislative assembly which is the branch of the government acting as a check upon the executive and administrative branches. The functions of a comptroller, on the other hand, are the settlement of claims, either of or against the state and in this connection the keeping of the central accounts of the state and the prescribing of the subsidiary accounting system in field offices and institutions.

These involve purely administrative duties. The Comptroller and Auditor General will make an administrative pre-examination of all claims for the purpose of determining their expediency, propriety and classification, as measures of administrative control and record.

Comptroller and Auditor-General of India

As earlier stated the Indian Constitution, makers provided for an independent Comptroller and Auditor-General, who conducts the audit of all the public moneys spent out of the Consolidated Fund of India. He is independent of executive control. He has been provided with permanence and security of tenure during good behaviour. All efforts have been made to make his office free from every kind of outside influence and pressure. He cannot be re-employed after his retirement. This independence has been guaranteed so that he can act fearlessly. He can perform his duties of searching criticism and analysis of the expenditure incurred by various executive authorities only if he is independent of executive control free from all pressures. The Constitution lays down his powers and defines his position clearly as under (Article 148):

1. There shall be Comptroller and Auditor General of India who shall be appointed by the President by warrant under his hand and seal and shall only be removed from office in like manner and on the like grounds as a judge of the Supreme Court.
2. Every person appointed to be the Comptroller and Auditor General of India shall, before he enters his office, make and subscribe before the President, or some persons appointed on that behalf by him, an oath or affirmation according

to the form set out for the purpose in the Third Schedule.

3. The salary and other conditions of service of the Comptroller and Auditor General shall be such as may be determined by Parliament by law and, until they are so determined, shall be as specified in the Second Schedule. Provided that neither the salary of a Comptroller and Auditor General nor his rights in respect of leave and absence, pension or age of retirement shall be varied to his disadvantage after his appointment.
4. The Comptroller and Auditor General shall not be eligible for further office either under the Government of India or under the Government of any state, after he has ceased to hold his office.
5. Subject to the provisions of the Constitution and of any law made by Parliament, the conditions of service of persons serving in the Indian Audit and Accounts Department and the administrative powers of the Comptroller and Auditor General shall be such as may be prescribed by rules made by the President after consultation with the Comptroller and Auditor General.
6. The administrative expenses of the office of the Comptroller and Auditor General, including all salaries, allowances and pensions payable to or in respect of persons, serving in that office, shall be charged upon the Consolidated Fund of India.

All these constitutional provisions are intended to make the CAG's position independent and impartial.

Functions

In regard to functions the Constitution states: The Comptroller and Auditor General shall perform such duties and exercise such powers in relation to the accounts of the Union and of the States and of any other authority or body as may be prescribed by or under any law made by Parliament and, until provision in that behalf is so made, shall perform such duties and exercise such powers in relation to the accounts of the Union and of the States as were conferred on or exercisable by the Auditor-General of India immediately before the commencement of this Constitution in relation to the accounts of the Dominion of India and of the Provinces respectively (Article 149).

The accounts of the Union and of the States shall be kept in such form as the President may, after consultation with the GAG, prescribe (Article 150).

The reports of the Comptroller and Auditor General of India relating to the accounts of the Union shall be submitted to the President, who shall cause them to be laid before each House of Parliament (Article 151).

The reports of the GAG relating to the accounts of a State shall be submitted to the Governor of the State, who shall cause them to be laid before the Legislature of the State.

He is 'to audit all expenditure from the revenues of the Union or States, incurred in or outside India and to ascertain whether money shown in the accounts as having been disbursed were legally available for and applicable to the service or the purpose to which they have been applied or charged and whether the expenditure conforms to the authority which governs it. Thus the audit report has to point out any irregularities in expenditure. It has to point out whether budgetary grants have been exceeded or whether there was any proper sanction for expenditure, whether there was any case of misappropriation or waste of public funds. These reports are then presented to the Legislature. He has to bring to the attention of the Legislature any case of waste and extravagance in government expenditures.

The CAG reports on the faithfulness, wisdom and economy of expenditure.

The CAG conducts Audit of Expenditure, Audit against Rules and Orders and Audit of Propriety.

Audit of Expenditure

It consists in examining whether the following essential conditions have been fulfilled:

(a) That the expenditure is covered by sanction, whether special or general, accorded by competent authority;
(b) That it conforms to the relevant provisions of the constitution or laws thereunder and the financial rules and regulations framed by the competent authority;
(c) That it is covered by provision of funds authorised by the competent authority and is within the purpose for which the grant was intended to provide;
(d) That the demand is supported by a voucher in proper form and the person to whom the payment has been made has duly acknowledged the payment and the fact of payment has been so recorded as to make a second claim on the government impossible; and
(e) That the expenditure has been incurred with due regard to the broad and general principles of financial propriety.

Audit against Rules and Orders

Audit work consists in seeing that expenditure conforms to the relevant provisions of the Constitution and of the laws and rules made there under. Audit is also in accordance with the financial rules, regulations and orders issued by a competent authority either in pursuance of any provisions of the constitution or of the laws and rules made thereunder.

Audit against Propriety

It is not only legality but propriety, in the broadest sense of the term, of expenditure also that has to be insured. This delicate task has to be performed by the audit with much discretion and tact.

Zero-Base Budgeting (ZBB)

Another kind of budgeting known as ZBB is sought to be applied to the public sector. It is a private sector system prevalent in US private sector.

In India the then Union Finance Minister, V.P. Singh told a Parliamentary Consultative Committee that the government would be introducing zero-base budgeting at first in a small way in 1986-87 and then in full in budget formulation from 1987-88. However, it is easier said than done. ZBB's applicability to the public sector is fraught with many difficulties.

Problem: The ZBB technique involves a critical review of every scheme before a budgetary provision is made in its favour. In other words, one assumes a zero provision and then starts justifying any that would be suggested. The practice in India or elsewhere under the traditional budgetary process, has been to allot funds on an incremental basis irrespective of whether the scheme in question is doing well or it is even worth continuing. The ZBB technique requires a large mass of quantitative data regarding the impact, targets, objectives, standards of performance and evaluation and a comparison among programmes covering divergent activities. In the Indian context, the ZBB would perhaps enable the government to abandon a large number of schemes along with agencies whether branded as Plan projects or non-Plan expenditure when they are proved to have outlived their utility or to have been non-starters despite investments in infrastructure and personnel. If properly implemented, the technique could help reverse the trend of increased governmental expenditure.

The ZBB approach requires each organisation to evaluate and review all programmes and activities systematically, whether current or new. It involves review of activities on the basis of output or performance as well as cost to (1) emphasise managerial decision-making, (2) number-oriented budgets and to emphasise analysis. ZBB is an approach and not a fixed procedure to be applied uniformly to all organisations. The process must be adapted to suit the specific needs of each organisation. Four basic steps are involved in ZBB approach[2]:

(f) To identify 'decision-units'.
(g) To analyse each decision unit in a 'decision package'.
(h) To evaluate and rank decision packages in order of priority.
(i) To prepare the detailed operating budgets reflecting those decision packages approved in the budget appropriation.

Each budget unit in the organisation will have to develop contingencies for various levels of financial allocation. The most basic level of financial allocation would be the 'survival package'— that is the minimum level of financial allocation for the organisation to survive and to provide for its basic services, so that organisational survival does not suffer.

ZBB is no miracle in financial administration. It would be dangerous to regard ZBB as a sure remedy for financial laxity. The success of ZBB in American industry is largely due to profit motive and organisational resilience. Both of these factors do not usually operate in the governmental setting. Moreover, the bureaucratic temperament is conditioned by the growth impulse which clamours for larger budgets rather than for more challenging assignments. Also, the powerful impact of political pressures on financial decision-making makes the prospects of ZBB very uncertain. In fact the very nature of government decision-making, which is 'muddling through', is ill suited for ZBB.

The advocates of ZBB regard it as a pragmatic approach which offers an extremely flexible management tool. It can lead to substantial savings. Low priority programmes can be eliminated or reduced. Programme effectiveness can be dramatically improved, although it may or may not have a budgetary impact. High impact programmes can obtain increased financial allocation by shifting resources within an agency and tax increases can be checked. With all its much-vaunted benefits, ZBB's application to public finance looks a doubtful starter. More conventional methods of sound budgeting should not be sacrificed for the sake of blind imitations of an ideal system.

REFERENCES

1. Nicholas Henry, *Public Administration and Public Affairs,* Prentice Hall. 1986, chapter seven.
2. See K.L. Handa, *Expenditure Control and Zero Base Budgeting* Indian Institute of Finance, Delhi, 1991.

Chapter 19

The New Public Management

In this concluding section, we propose to examine the basic features of traditional public administration followed by the new conceptualisations of the field generally characterised as Post-Weber and Post-Wilson public administration. In the world of practice, remarkable changes took place in the 80s and the 90s, as governments in the West sought to adapt themselves to new technology, new societal demands and keen competition. This led to a search for a new kind of public administration, known as New Public Management (NPM).

Evolutionary Sketch

Despite the tortuous and unending debate on its disciplinary character, public administration as a special field of study has continued to retain its dynamism since the Wilsonian exhortation for a science of administration in the last century. The sources of dynamism could partly be traced to actual changes, in the real world of governance under the impact of sweeping social change. In part, the roots of dynamism can also be traced to an ongoing search for conceptual and methodological tools on the part of scholars in the discipline. Being both event-pushed and thought-propelled, the discipline has in recent years been causing considerable anxiety among scholars who continue to oscillate between doom and euphoria. To some, public administration is dead, the public sector analysis needs a different discipline. To others, the discipline is now full blown and autonomous. It has been claimed that the absence of a well-knit boundary and considerable porosity of a discipline is symptomatic of its growth and cross-fertilisation. Public administration being deeply engrossed in he intricacies of governance in a fast-changing world has wily-nily to draw on various allied disciplines and so long as this process of dynamic interaction with the diverse knowledge world would be continuing, this should be construed as a positive sign of progressive development of the discipline.

Traditional Public Administration

To refresh our memory, for traditional public administration approach to the public sector, we look for sources in Willoughby, *Principles of Public Administration* (1927), Gulick and Urwick, *Papers on the Science of Administration* (1937), Dwight Waldo, *The Administrative State* (1948), etc.

Theoretical/normative principles were inspired by the writings of Woodrow Wilson, J.S. Mill and Max Weber. The other dominant influences came from the Scientific Management School of the early "twentieth century and later from mainstream organisation theory.

According to the traditional public administration approach[1], the basic principles that would govern the structure of administration, involving the institutional arrangement, motivation of public employees and the status of public interest would be as under:

1. The tasks of public institutions are to be in the hands of the administrators. Politics and administration are two different kinds of activities and their functionaries are different. Administration starts after the initial push coming from politics.
2. Administration is based on written documents, thus making the office (the bureau) the heart of modern government.
3. The tasks are organised on a continuous, rule-governed basis.
4. The rules that regulate work may be technical or legal and for this purpose, trained officials are necessary.
5. The tasks are divided into functionally distinct parts, each furnished with requisite authority and sanctions.
6. Offices and tasks are arranged hierarchically; the rights of control and compliance being specified. All other things being equal, there is preference for centralisation.
7. The resources of the organisation are quite distinct from those of the members as private individuals.
8. The office holder cannot appropriate his/her office for private aims.
9. In performing the assigned tasks, the public employees are to accept their vocational role to fulfil their obligations with a sense of duty.
10. The guiding philosophy in the management of public sector is that *of public interest.* This sets limits to the influence of self-interest in politics and administration.

This is the well-known Weberian/Scientific management model with emphasis on structure, work division, power-differentiation, centralisation and public-private distinction. The whole design is machine-like, rigid and impersonal. As is well known, there are stock objections to this model which need not be repeated here. Broadly speaking, *there have been three kinds of reactions to this traditional model:*

(k) The principles of traditional public administration are primarily normative, sounding like 'proverbs'.

(l) These are lacking in descriptive accuracy. As organisations differ in complexity and character, one-shot enumeration of 'principles' is naive and unrealistic.

(m) The principles fail to identify mechanisms that are conducive to public sector effectiveness and efficiency. They do not have the capacity to explain how the public sector actually works. In fact, the principles are not empirically oriented and are deficient in operational details. The modem state organisation is too complex to be pushed into a list of simple principles.

Post-Weber/Post-Wilson conception of Public Administration

The features other than those identified in the classical public administration model are currently being emphasised on the basis of empirical studies of government administration in the west. The new approaches to public institutions underline the importance of public policy-making, implementation and management within the overarching framework of liberal democracy. It is being suggested that the complexities involved in public policy-making and implementation call for a rethinking about human motivation and efficiency and effectiveness in the public sector.

More pointedly, it is being argued that the classical model of public administration was unconscionably oriented toward rationality, specialization and division of work, rigid hierarchical structure and centralisation. Successful management of the public sector and efficient production of organisational outputs could not be correlated with the principles of classical public administration. As the critics argue, the Weberian claim of bureaucracy representing highest extent of rationality did not fit in with the real-life situation in public administration. In reality, as the critics point out, rational behaviour is not a typical feature of modern organisational life. Organisational rationality as some form of collective expression of reasoned behaviour is rather fuzzy and does not conform to real-life practice in the process of governance. Public policy decisions are often a matter of myriad influences, pulls and pressures and there are multiple actors influencing decisions.

In this context, the behaviour of Simon's 'administrative man' striving to achieve 'bounded rationality' is very relevant. Acknowledging information and data scarcity, time constraint, perceptual limitations, the administrator seeks to eliminate certain alternatives and imagined outcomes in order that a course of action could be adopted purely pragmatically. Most public policy decisions, as Braybrooke and Lindblom observed, involved multiple interest-reconciling and hence essentially synthesising and, accommodating in nature. Rationality-maximisation is not what is intended in the actual process of administering. The 'muddling-through' can be attributed to the nature of public ends or goals in administration, which are not always well-defined and fine-tuned. Even irrationality a component of decision, under such circumstances, may not be ruled out.

The other point relating to specialisation and division of work has been attacked as impractical and injurious to organisational health and productivity.

Post-Weberian view of public organisations has basically been people-oriented as distinguished from structure-oriented as successive research findings have pointed out that people in organisation matter more than formal organisational structure. The classical principles of public administration had held the orthodox view that organisational productivity demanded mechanisation and routinisation of administrative work. The alternative, view, rebutting the classical stand point, has been that instead of sharp delineation of work division and narrow specialisation, the structuring principles must aim at employee job satisfaction. For this purpose organisational work-layout must provide opportunities for employees to work in multiple roles in much more flexible structures. There is considerable research evidence, since the early studies of the human relations school that clearly shows that organisational productivity does not automatically flow from a grand organisational design, defining the functions to be discharged and coordinating the activities of each employee by narrow specialisation and division of work.

The classical public administration model has emphasised hierarchy as a structural design concept. Hierarchy means that power distribution and centralisation have been built into the architecture of traditional public administration.

Contrastingly, it has now been well accepted in organisational analysis that a decentralised strategy is superior to centralised structure. It promotes adaptability, flexibility and mobilisation of local initiative. Decentralisation permits lower level operating units to interpret rules and regulations to suit local needs and to innovate in changed situations. Also, participative decision-making becomes a reality in a bottom-up approach that utilises the full potential of people at basic operating levels and creates conditions for free flow of information within the organisation.

Contemporary view about public organisation is thus not a perfectionist one, as in reality there is no such thing as a rigid and pure model of administration. What happens in actual administrative situations are policy evolution, adjustment and adaptation to shifting circumstances and environmental demands and pressures.

Against this background, the new approach to public administration, superseding the traditional model, can be distinguished with the help of following features:

1. Politics-administration dichotomy is unrealistic, irrelevant and unworkable since the actors on either side frequently change positions and the two activities intermesh in the practical world of governance.
2. In public institutional life, there is no such thing as purely rational decision-making. It is 'bounded (limited) rationality' that characterises actual public decision-making.
3. In a hierarchy-ridden organisation, it is the top that dominates and the bottom has simply to obey and submit. Top-down policy implementation does not, in actuality, work; there cannot be automatic accomplishment of objectives in the public sector or in any sector. Bottom-up communication is helpful in implementation, trusting that basic operating units have the capacity to reinterpret and innovate in dynamic situational changes. Drawing on rich social science research evidences, it is now well accepted that public administration is best looked after by self-steering groups rather than closely supervised groups. Hierarchy is essentially power-oriented rather than work-oriented and is positively threatening in its operations.
4. As practical administration shows, successful public administration is rarely rule-bound. What matters is goal achievement and effectiveness, allowing employees to play multiple roles.
5. Centralisation leads to rigidity. Hierarchy results in implementation deficit. Free flow of communication is impeded by rigid hierarchy and centralisation of power.
6. Public institutions operate efficiently when decentralised, allowing lower level initiative and adjustment.
7. In public administration tendencies towards irrationality are not rare, as many actors and forces impinge upon decisions and compete for accommodation.
8. Public employees do not have any special type of motivation. In real life, they have often been found to act to maximize self-interests like income, prestige and power, rather than public interest.

Thus the old idea of public administration being unique, requiring a sheltered bureaucracy employed for life is now under challenge. The question has been raised why the bureaucratic form of organisation should have the monopoly to provide public goods and services. It has been alleged that bureaucratic failures, that are numerous in reality, affect the society badly both instantly and from long-term perspective as well. There are various options available for the delivery of public goods and services and society may benefit from the many suppliers syndrome. It is not necessary that government should always assume the role of a direct provider of goods and services; instead governments may operate indirectly, allowing non-government agencies to operate directly in a wide range of social activities. This has been forcefully argued by the Public Choice/New Right group.

Rigid, rule-bound and hierarchic public administration does not suit the needs of a dynamic situation demanding speedy action. In this respect, many of the flexible organisational designs and practices pioneered by the private sector may be profitably introduced in public administration system with suitable modifications. The public-private distinction should not be fetishises as a matter of orthodoxy. In the larger interest of societal development, the two sectors should mix freely and collaborate whenever necessary and feasible. Even healthy competition between them should be welcome to improve quality of performance and accelerate the pace of work.

It has been argued that administration must be accessible, transparent and accountable. The citizen has every right to question how public fund is being spent and whether he is getting his money's worth. The civil servant has to be result-oriented, responsible and responsive. The bureaucracy has enjoyed security and anonymity at the cost of transparency. There must be more openness in administration and accountability for whatever is done or not done.

Changes in Advanced Countries

In the 1980s and early 1990s, for a variety of reasons remarkable changes took place in public sector management practices in most advanced countries:

(a) Structurally, the change was from rigid, hierarchical and bureaucratic form of public administration to a flexible, market-based form of public management.

(b) The change was not merely in form/style. There was remarkable change in the role of government in society and (ii) similarly, there was a change in government-citizenship relationship. These objective conditions engendered opportunities for the emergence of almost a new paradigm in public sector analysis.

The 1990s saw the emergence of a new model of public sector management. This has been variously called: 'Managerialism' 'New Public Management, market-based public administration', 'Entrepreneurial Government' etc. The thrust has been toward a determined effort to implement the 3Es: Efficiency, Economy and Effectiveness.

The new public management has following salient features:

1. Focus on management, not policy—on performance appraisal and efficiency.
2. Desegregation of public bureaucracies into agencies which deal with each other on a user-pay basis.
3. Use of quasi-markets and contracting out to foster competition.
4. Cost-cutting.
5. A style of management which emphasises output targets, limited term contracts, monetary incentives and freedom to manage.

For a more positive perspective, within this stream of thought, there has been the path-setting publication by Osborne & Gaebler (*Reinventing Government,* 1992). They suggest a ten-point programme for what they call entrepreneurial governments (EGs):

1. EGs promote competition between diverse providers of goods and services.
2. They empower citizens by pushing control out of bureaucracy.
3. They measure performance of their agencies focusing particularly on outcomes, not inputs.
4. They are driven by their missions and not by their rules/regulations.
5. They redefine their clients as customers and offer them choices.
6. They prevent problems rather than cure them after they blow out.

7. They put their energy into earning money, not simply spending it.
8. They decentralise authority, embracing participatory management.
9. They prefer market mechanisms to bureaucratic mechanisms.
10. They focus not simply on providing public service but on catalysing all sectors - public, private, voluntary — into action to solve community problems.

These are fairly clear-cut and straight forward identification marks of a type of government which the new inventors call entrepreneurial. Although, the characteristic features are being bandied about as 'empirically derived', these are more accurately, preferred qualities than actual attributes.

These features of Entrepreneurial Government yield a multi-faceted government system with the following characteristics:

1. **Catalytic Government**
   Acting as catalyst 'leveraging' private-sector actions to solve societal problems.
2. **Community-owned government**
   Pushing control of many services out of the bureaucracy and into the community, (empowering families and communities)
3. **Competitive government**
   Encouraging competition to increase the level of performance and minimise cost (e.g. competition among public schools to improve quality of education)
4. **Mission-driven government**
   Defining fundamental missions, developing budget systems and framing flexible rules to free employees to pursue goals, without being enslaved by rules.
5. **Results-oriented government**
   Instead of focusing on 'inputs', paying attention to 'outcomes' or results.
6. **Customer-driven government**
   Spending is tied to results and for this purpose resources are given directly to the consumers to let them choose appropriate providers at minimum cost.
7. **Decentralised government**
   By decentralising or getting authority down to the lowest level, organisational functioning is improved, as information, communication and decision-making would then be located at the actual site of problems.
8. **Market-Oriented government**
   By restructuring the market (as in housing or environmental management) and by leveraging many private decisions, government can accomplish more than what it can do by financing administrative programmes. In a market-oriented approach, for instance, fees are attached to pollution, forcing producers to pay full costs of their undesirable activities.

As David Osborne has summed up the position: "We don't need more government; we need better government. To be more precise, we need better governance. Governance is the act of collectively solving our problems. Government is the instrument we use. The instrument is outdated and it is time to remake it."

While the general tone of the prescription is in order, the preference for market as implied in it may not wholly suit the situation in many 'Third World' countries.

Reinventing Government immediately caught the attention of anti-bureaucracy campaigners and the publication was accorded a warm welcome, heralding, as it were, the birth of a new form of public management.

Government Response:

With considerable caution, the practical world of governance in the West responded to this new paradigm change in the following manner:

— Improving public management through performance measurement and evaluation.

— Reducing budgets,

— Cutting the size of government,

—Privatisation of public enterprise,

— Contracting out in selective areas.

The overall emphasis has been on changing bureaucracies into result-oriented organisations, in which managers would be accountable for achieving targets and results. Reduction in the size of government, reducing the functional load of bureaucracies, speed, results production and accountability soon became the buzz words. Historically, bureaucracy had always been under attack as power grabbers, secretive, rule-bound and inward looking rather than client-oriented. But, the contemporary scenario seems unique in that it marks a savage onslaught on bureaucracy as the mainspring of mal-governance, as if other causes are of no consequence. The complexities of a post-modern society, the crumbling ideologies of politics and the overall social development puzzle of the dying century are all side pushed and 'bureaucracy' is singled out as the villain of the piece.

As Caiden has summed up the situation: All blamed the dead hand of bureaucracy, especially the poor performance of public bureaucracies and the daily annoyances of irksome restrictions, cumbrous red-tape, unpleasant officials, poor service and corrupt practices.

The CAPAM Conference[2]

There was a ripple effect of this new paradigmatic shift in public administration thought. In this context the inaugural conference of the Commonwealth Association for Public Administration and Management held in Charlotte town, Canada, in August, 1994 assumes considerable significance. For the first time in the history of the Commonwealth such a high-level conference addressed itself exclusively to the issues of public management in today's context dubbed as 'government in transition'. There was a general consensus that strong environmental forces have been buffeting the public sector and governments all over the world are being forced to cope with them. Some of the impinging forces are knowledge-based production, the communication revolution and a massive explosion in world trade. In a multi-polar world, trade negotiations need to be worked out both bilaterally and multilaterally. The information technology revolution has led to shrinkage of distances among partners and facilitated almost instant electronic networking. Globalisation has become a reality, setting the stage for professional networking and collaboration in the development and sustenance of a new public administration.

Components of NPM

The 'new paradigm' called the New Public Management, that has steadily emerged, emphasises the role of public managers in providing high-quality services that citizens value and advocates increasing managerial autonomy, particularly by reducing central agency controls. It demands quick corrective measures and rewards both organisational and individual performance. It recognises the importance of providing the human and technological resources that managers need to meet their performance targets and is receptive to competition and is open-ended about which public purposes should be performed by public servants as opposed to private sector.

The new paradigm[4] has several interrelated components that cut across traditional ways of organising government.

The *first component* relates to the delivery of high-quality services that citizen's value. The consumers are reconceptualised as active customers and not just passive recipients. Hence, serious attempts are being made to find out what the customers expect. Public sector organisations, as in UK, Singapore and some other nations are setting performance targets, measuring performance and publicising results for the wider public. The most dramatic such initiative is UK's Citizens' Charter, a global statement of the government's service quality commitments. This was launched by Prime Minister John Major in 1991. Singapore has set up a Service Improvement Unit (SIU) in the Prime Minister's office to keep a watch on departmental efforts.

The second component of the new paradigm emphasises that, to achieve high-quality standard of services, the managers need increased autonomy. In UK, Australia, New Zealand and Singapore a distinct trend is noticeable toward shifting operating responsibilities from the central departments to specific agencies. Infrastructural development in Singapore, for example, has been transferred to agencies with clear performance targets and increased autonomy. Also, greater flexibility in working conditions such as contractual appointments, work place bargaining etc. is being permitted to make use of more expertise and employee creativity.

Organisational structures are being simplified and hierarchies flattened to create conditions for more positive and productive managerial leadership. In the field of financial management, freedom to manage within consolidated running costs of programmes is being encouraged in countries like UK and Australia. The general trend is to increase the autonomy of local managers by devolving more power to them.

The third component of the new paradigm relates to fairly rigorous performance measurement of individuals and organisations. Rewards including pay structures are based on fulfilment of performance targets. Both UK and New Zealand are moving from a tenure system to fixed-term contracts. In financial management, public agencies are changing, from cash to accrual accounting, thus making them more cost-conscious and resource-saving. In Canada, Australia and UK, periodic review of government programmes has become almost customary.

The fourth component concerns managerial support services to facilitate achievement of pre-set performance targets. Successful managerial performance needs to be backed up by proper human and technological resources. In the area of human resource management, recruitment policy has to be directed toward drawing the best available talent from the market, assuring them attractive salary and other allied benefits while constantly exposing them to skill-improvement training programmes. Australia is using competency-based training that starts by defining competencies relevant to a given organisational level. UK and Mauritius are tailoring training to the job-needs of rank.

Equity initiatives are being taken up in some countries. For instance, Australia has drawn up a strategic plan targeted at women, the disabled, the aboriginal and those with non-English backgrounds. This is expected to expand the pool of talent available to the government.

It is being increasingly recognised that leading edge information technology is an essential facilitator of service improvement initiatives. By 1990, Singapore civil service described itself as being fully computerised. Both for internal communication and service provision, information technology is spreading fast in many commonwealth countries.

Alongside the need for autonomy for agency/departmental management, it is also being asserted that managerial performance at any level has to be responsive to the overall, central policy directives. The organisation of the Cabinet has thus been streamlined in many countries. Australia has established systems of Cabinet Committees, reduced the number of departments and grouped programmes more rationally Some of the Commonwealth countries have recognised institutions for giving support to Cabinet functioning. Jamaica has created a Permanent Secretaries Board and facilitated Cabinet review of key areas of administration.

The fifth component of the new paradigm is an advocacy of "receptiveness to competition and an open-minded attitude about which purposes should be performed by the public sector as opposed to the private sector". In many commonwealth countries, there is currently more and more private sector involvement in activities that were formally reserved for the public sector. In the field of infrastructure development such as roads, electricity etc., private sector is being invited to undertake constructional and extension activities. Non-government organisations are taking up projects in many countries (e.g. India) in the social sector (especially health, education, nutrition and child health and women's development). In Bangladesh, the, role of the Grameen Bank in providing micro-credit to the rural poor, particularly women, has attracted international attention.

'Privatisation' has been adopted as an official policy in some of the nations. In Singapore telecom, airlines and shipyards have been privatised. UK has gone ahead with an aggressive policy of privatisation (47 privatisations since 1979). There are also examples of public-private joint ventures in some countries (e.g. Singapore, India), removing in the process the traditional rigidity about the 'Public' sphere.

Policies supportive of private sector activities have been adopted in most commonwealth countries. Important among these are dismantling price controls, deregulation and narrowing down of the public sector (also called downsizing).

An Overview

The new public management with its explicit 'market'-orientation and over reliance on the private sector has varied responses from the Commonwealth countries. It looks as though neo-classical economics has captured the public sector all over the world.

The negative feelings toward government and the public sector so dominant in the eighties have, however, now been changing; and there is growing concern today about government's crucial role in macro-management and in creating sound policy environment for the society and the economy to function smoothly. Government has to lead the whole socio-economic system and find alternative ways of providing services and facilities. It is good to know how private management works; but at the same time the unique policy role of the higher civil service should not be diluted in our craze for phoney managerialism. Government' especially at the higher echelons, has its peculiar ways of accommodating interests, feeling the pulse of the nation, intervening in conflicting situations and calculating pay-offs in difficult bargaining situations.

Above all, there is a thing called 'public interest' which lies at the heart of government operations and it is irreplaceable by any market philosophy.

The other point of view that has come up sharply in the CAPAM conference is the need for strengthening the civil society in many of the developing countries. Operating almost as a third sector there are institutions run and sustained by citizens, sometimes with assistance and advice from NGOs. Countries in the developing world have to build infrastructural facilities, improve peoples access to resources and conserve natural resources by promoting sustainable use. 'Empowering' the citizens assumes crucial significance in this context. Outside the sphere of big government and macro-management, there are the grass roots people's efforts to organise themselves against deprivation and exploitation from above. The new paradigm of public management is centred on the core and almost oblivious of the periphery. There is, therefore, a lurking suspicion that the new paradigm might as well lead to hijacking of the state by the 'private' and the 'powerful'. The public sphere may ultimately remain only with the grass roots where people strive hard in their own way to build a democratic space away from the big state's massive management enterprise. There is thus a fear in certain circles about the balkanisation of the state by different interests—a theme so dear to the heart of the pluralists.

The CAPAM conference came out with a new paradigm of public management no doubt. But, there were other voices also, suggesting alternative ways of organising government. Narrowing down the scope of government, it was pointed out, may not be the universal recipe, in view of the diverse development trajectories of nations.

The new public management philosophy was basically triggered by a combination of economic issues and geopolitical changes (e.g. collapse of the Second World) resulting in reduced financial resources for governments. Managerial rethink, therefore, became an imperative necessity to optimise scarce resource use and find alternative ways of delivering public services by developing a new synergy between the public and private sectors. As Mohan Kaul has summed up: "The broad objectives of these reforms have been to shift emphasis from developing plans to develop key strategic areas, to shift emphasis from inward-looking systems to develope partnerships, to shift emphasis from inputs and processes to outputs and outcomes; and to shift emphasis towards managing, diversity within a unified public service. Finally, managerial pragmatism and political conviction are highlighted as essential to motivate management innovation in government"[3].

NPM and Traditional Public Administration

At this stage, the relationship of NPM with traditional public administration needs to be clearly highlighted.[4]

First, under the NPM, public sector decision-making structures are so designed as to let managers manage; political leadership would be concerned only with macro policies and goals. All other matters are taken out of day-to-day democratic insight and delegated to professional bureaucrats who would be deciding on the basis of economic rationality. In this garb the NPM essentially involves reasserting the Wilsonian separation of administration from politics with a vengeance.

Second, the NPM has emerged as a method of management technology for reaching a set of goals for state action. Thus conceived, it 'reduces the public sector's traditional reliance on process accountability and enhances the role of results accountability'. Ensuring fair and honest administration of public affairs, eliminating patronage and other misuses of the state apparatus have been the hallmarks of bureaucracy's 'process accountability'. But in contemporary situation marked by communication revolution, information processing and flexible, cost-sensitive managerial needs, traditional bureaucratic administration seems a misfit.

The NPM 'stipulates that public servants should

have to accept more personal accountability for the actions of their agencies in return for this enhanced autonomy and flexibility'. This is clearly a significant departure from the concept of 'anonymous' bureaucracy in traditional public administration.

Third, the NPM has to be viewed not so much as an altogether new 'paradigm' as a refreshing reconstruction of the evolving discipline of public administration. It needs to be recalled that there has been a long tradition of 'implementation' research pioneered by academic stalwarts like Pressman and Wildavsky. The main issue raised by them has been: How public organisations transform policies into results? Implementation studies 'moved the issue from a focus on organisations, especially on their structures and processes, to public programmes and the results they produced'. It was "performance" that took the centre stage in public administration.

Again, as these studies progressed, there had been the realisation that diverse disciplinary inputs were necessary to go deep into the problems and issues surrounding implementation performance and production of results.

As it has been rightly suggested, the NPM did not emerge all of a sudden as a new paradigm. These two trends: a focus on performance more than organisational structure and process and efforts to explore the problem from many different disciplinary bases—gave birth to the NPM which, therefore, had its roots in the earlier implementation research in traditional public administration.

The advocates of the NPM sought a far more positive view of government and its programmes and in focussing on what managerial autonomy could do instead of how organisations behaved they rejected traditional public administration.

A more dispassionate review of the field would, however, have revealed that the NPM came 'to resemble less an accumulation of knowledge and more a family feud'. No doubt, the NPM has symbolised something very new sweeping the study of governance and public policy. Yet, both implementation research and traditional public administration had much to contribute to the new movement. As Donald Kettl has summed up the situation: 'Implementation established the importance of the programme as a fundamental unit of analyses'. Public administration argued the need for a solid budgetary process, the right human resources system and functional organisation. In their headlong rush to build something new, some public management scholars have glossed over the critical building blocks that public administrators lovingly laboured so long to build and that, even in a short time, implementation students had created. Nevertheless, NPM has exposed the over-protected 'bureaucracy' to models of management, which, if carefully adopted, can bring about improvement in traditional public administration.

REFERENCES

1. Jan-Erik Lane: *The Public Sector: Concepts, Models and Approaches,* —SAGE, 1993.
2. *Government in Transition,* The Inaugural Conference of the Commonwealth Association for Public Administration and Management, Charlotte town, Prince Edward Island, Canada, 28-31 August, 1994, University of Toronto Press, 1995.
3. Mohan Kaul, "The New Public Administration: management innovations in government', *Public Administration and Development,* vol. 17, 13-26, 3997.
4. Ewan Feriie, Andrew Pettigrew, Lynn Ashburner, Louise Fitzerald, *The New Public Management in Action,* OUP, 1996.

Chapter 20

Good "Governance"

The Context

In the vocabulary of public administration 'good governance' is a recent entrant within a context. There are three ways of understanding this new developments.

One: It is an attempt to widen the scope of public administration by going beyond formal government.

Two: It is an externally dictated term invented to prescribe aid-conditionality.

Three: It is a genuinely democracy-intensifying concept - to make public administration more open, transparent and accountable.

Good governance need not be narrowly conceived in the manner the World Bank and other funding agencies have sought to present them. A more creative approach would be to treat the issues as new opportunities to have a fresh look at state-society relationships in today's complex world of governance. To quote Kooiman[1] in this context:

"In many countries, the main tendency in recent years has been to shift the balance between government and society away from the public sector and more towards the private sector. Partly, this added up to privatisation and sometimes to deregulation. But there are also efforts to shift the balance towards a sharing of tasks and responsibilities; towards doing things together instead of doing them alone (either by the 'State' or by the 'market'). New patterns of interaction between governments and society can be observed in areas such as social welfare, environmental protection, education and physical planning. These new patterns are apparently aimed at discovering other ways of coping with new problems or of creating new possibilities for governing".

It is this search for 'new possibilities' that brings out the true meaning of good governance.

Meanings: *The fist connotation* in terms of widening the scope of public administration has been very well explained by Rosenau. Writing in the context of contemporary global politics he explicates the term 'governance' in the following way:[2]

"Governance is a more encompassing phenomenon than government. It embraces governmental institutions but it also subsumes informal, non-governmental mechanisms whereby those persons and organisations within its purview move ahead, satisfy their needs and fulfil their wants... Governance is thus a system of rule that is as dependent on inter-subjective meanings as on formally sanctioned constitution and charter... it is possible to conceive of governance without government—of regulatory mechanisms in a sphere of activity which function effectively even though they are not endowed with formal authority."

A straightforward definition of governance is: "The capacity to get things done without the legal competence to command that they be done." The concept of 'governance', thus, frees administrative studies from conventional formalism. At the same time, it opens up possibilities of drawing on society's alternative collective problem-solving fora and devices. Governance, so conceived, is more a network of multiple agencies and organisations than a fixed 'government' agency or department.

Governance, in this context, stands for establishment, operation and networking of social institutions. Concretely, it manifests itself in formal rules and regulations, decision-making procedures and programmatic activities that serve to define social practices. In real life, there are many forms of community organisations or voluntary, collective self-help approaches through which a group of people organise themselves to achieve common purposes, such as irrigation, water distribution, resolution of local disputes and community defence. Governance, in this context, is a way of crafting social institutions as a matter of public concern. To get things done through formally constituted governments is not, therefore, the only way available for collective problem-solving.

The *second meaning* of governance is closely linked to international aid-conditionality.

Referring to the background conditions of the 'good governance' concept, Leftwich points out that contemporary western aid and overseas development policy have three defining features. First, the aim of aid has been to promote open, market-friendly and competitive economies. This policy was embodied in the new conditionality of structural adjustment lending, developed in the 1980s. Later, in the 1990s, two further features have been added to structural adjustment. These are support for democratisation and improvement of human rights records and insistence on what has come to be called 'good governance'.

Development assistance to the Third World countries in the post Cold War era has, thus, been, subject to the new *politics of 'good governance'*. In 1989, the concept of 'governance' was for the first time highlighted in a World Bank document on Sub-Saharan Africa. By good governance was meant, at that time, sound development management. Four key dimensions identified in this context were: (a) public sector management; (b) accountability; (c) legal framework for development; and (d) information and transparency. The Bank document on Sub-Saharan Africa had this to say: "Improving governance would begin with an assessment of the institutional environment (with emphasis on the key governance elements of accountability, rule of law, openness and transparency) which determines the patrimonial profile of the country: high when all other factors are absent and low when they are present."

As the Bank's document, entitled *Governance and Development (1992),* puts it, "governance is defined as the manner in which power is exercised in the management of a country's economic and social resources for development." From its lending experience in many developing countries, the Bank came to realise that "good governance is central to create and sustain an environment which fosters strong and equitable development and it is an essential complement to sound economic policies". Three distinct aspects are identified in the conceptualisation of 'governance': (a) the form of political regime (parliamentary or presidential, military or civilian and authoritarian or democratic); (b) the process by which authority is exercised in the management of a country's economic and social resources; and (c) the capacity of governments to design, formulate and implement policies and in general, to discharge government functions. The first aspect, it is admitted, falls outside the Bank's mandate. The focus of 'governance' is, therefore, basically on the second and third aspects.

Recounting its wide experience, the Bank

document narrates vividly the problems of 'governance'. For instance, despite technical soundness, programmes and projects have often failed to produce desired results. Laws are not enforced properly and there are often delays in implementation. Privatised production and market-led growth do not succeed unless investors face clear rules and institutions. In the absence of proper accounting systems, budgetary policies cannot be implemented or monitored. Many a time, procurement systems encourage corruption and distort public investment priorities. Again, failure to involve beneficiaries and others affected in the design and implementation of projects has often led to substantial erosion of their sustainability.

Against this background of malgovernance, the Bank has attempted to focus on some of the key dimensions of 'governance', such as public sector management, accountability, the legal framework for development and information and transparency, as already stated.

Economic, human and institutional development is considered important in bringing about sound development management. The conditionality's of 'good governance' are thus carefully spelt out and as the Bank document sums up:

"Governance is a continuum and not necessarily unidirectional: it does not automatically improve over time. It is a plant that needs constant tending. Citizens need to demand good governance. Their ability to do so is enhanced by literacy, education and employment opportunities. Governments need to prove responsive to those demands. Neither of these can be taken for granted. Change occurs sometimes in response to external or internal threats. It also occurs through pressures form different interest groups, some of which may be in the form of populist demands. Although lenders and aid agencies and other outsiders can contribute resources and ideas to improve governance, for change to be effective it must be rooted firmly in the societies concerned and cannot be imposed from outside".

More pronounced political meaning of 'governance' appeared in the policy directives of the OECD countries, laying down conditionality for receiving economic assistance. The OECD documents sought to link development assistance, with (a) participatory development, (b) human rights and (c) democratisation. The key components of 'governance' were identified as:

- Legitimacy of government;
- Accountability of political and official elements of government;
- Respect for human rights and the Rule of Law (including individual and group rights and security, a legal framework for economic and social activity and participation).

What emerges out of the combined efforts of the aid-giving countries and the international funding agencies is that entitlement to aid would depend on the degree to which a client country would be having a liberal -democratic state in a pluralist society.

The third meaning of 'governance' is implied in the explanatory ideal, as governance highlights the importance of rule of law, human rights, participatory development and democratisation. As against the managerial slant of governance, the ethical-normative dimension links 'governance' to some of the older issues in political theory. State, as the ancient Greeks said, stands for good life. It is not enough that administration is run on sound managerial lines. The equity and legitimacy aspects are as important, or perhaps more important, than good management. The governing process should provide opportunities for the people to actively participate in decision-making and the fruits of government must be universally shared and not captured by an influential minority. People's perception about how the governing process is going on serves as the barometer of legitimacy of governance. Empowerment is thus a precondition of good governance.

Summing up: So far as the first and third aspects of "governance are concerned, it has been commented that the concept of 'good governance' is a salutary departure from the overly formalistic character of conventional public administration. In today's complex world of governing, government alone is not capable of coping with myriad problems. A degree of networking with other societal organisations will enhance the capacity of governance in the society as a whole. Also, this will facilitate development of 'social capital' in terms of social groups' agreed involvement and co-sharing of problem-solving.

Civil Society

The 'good governance' paradigm and the current concern about administrative decentralisation have brought to surface the role of civil society in local collective social problem-solving. The concept is not easy to define. As commonly understood, civil society represents 'the realm of organised social life that is voluntary, self-generating, largely self-supporting and bound by a legal order or set of shared values.' (Diamond, 1999).

We owe to Alexis de Tocqueville the foundational work linking civil society to democracy in his writings in the mid-1800s. American democracy, Tocqueville thought, was sustained by the richness and diversity of a wide range of voluntary associations. Among the neo-Tocquevillians, the name of Robert Putnam, the Harvard Professor, readily comes to mind. His work in recent times, on the political development of Italian regions has helped revive the concept of civil society. In evaluating the work of regional governments in Italy, Putnam observed that 'social capital' understood as features of social organisations such as trust, norms and network rather than socio-economic development was the central explanatory variable. In Putnam's analysis, the propensity of individuals to join private, voluntary associations contributes to the effectiveness of democracy.[5]

In this connection, Larry Diamond's recent work on *Developing Democracy* deserves special mention. To quote Diamond, "Democracy - in particular, a healthy liberal democracy - requires a public that is organised for democracy, socialized to its norms and values and committed not just to its myriad narrow interests but to larger, common, civic, ends. Such a civil public is only possible with a vibrant civil society".[6]

Public administration, particularly development administration, has in recent times relied considerably on civil society conceptualisations in its quest for people-centric and participative decentralized governance.

To the extent governance would be bringing in transparency, openness, rule of law and human rights observance, this will facilitate strengthening of democracy.

The second aspect— to tie up 'good governance' with aid-giving— has been critically reviewed by many commentators. One set of arguments has been that the World Bank is seeking to 'politicise' the otherwise technical issue of financial aid to the third world countries. How does one measure 'good governance' remains an open question. There are others who point out that 'good governance' is a simplistic notion, as there are diverse ways of governing in multi-cultural contexts. Good governance, as the critics point out, seems in a rehash of the one-best way principle of classical administrative theory resurrected naively the contemporary world situation that demands more open-endedness in governance than rigidity of any kind.

Nevertheless, public administration has been widened and deepened through the introduction of the concept of 'governance'.

REFERENCES

1. Jan Kooiman (ed.), *Modern Governance: New Government-Society Interactions,* New Delhi, Sage Publication,1993.
2. James N. Rosenau, "Governance, order and change in World Politics", in Rosenau and Ernst-Otto Czempiel (eds.), *Governance without Government: Order and Change in World Politics,* Cambridge University Press, 1992.
3. A. Leftwich, "Governance, The State and the PoliticsofDevelopment", *DevelopmentandChange,* Vol. 25 (1994), 363-386.
4. The World Bank, *Governance and Development,* Washington D.C., 1992.
5. Robert Putnam, *Marketing Democracy Work: Civic Tradition in Modern Italy,* Princeton University Press, 1993.
6. Larry Diamond, *Developing Democracy: Toward Consolidation,* The John Hopkins University Press, 1999.

Chapter 21

Governmental Accountability

Two contrasting concerns of public administration, in recent times, have been (a) managerial orientation as noted earlier in New Public Management; and (b) accountability and citizen's participation. The first concern involves more management, while the latter focuses on taming bureaucratic power and bringing the citizen back in administration.

Governments everywhere - in both developed and developing nations - are powerful institutions run by the bureaucrats. Expanding government functions have brought in their trail bureaucratic expansion and the bureaucracies have a daily impact on the quality of life of the citizens. There is an increasing concern today about how the bureaucracies are using 'power'. At the heart of these concerns is 'accountability': for what and to whom are bureaucracies answerable? How are the bureaucracies held accountable?

The substance of accountability places at least four requirements on the public administrators:

1. Make laws work as intended with a minimum of waste and delay;
2. Exercise lawful and sensible administrative discretion;
3. Recommend new policies and propose changes in existing policies and programs as needed;
4. Enhance citizen confidence in the administrative institutions of government.

For a wider perspective, one has to place the accountability question along the democracy question with its in-built 'public interest' value. To quote Bernard Rosen:

"Economic and social forces impact on administrators in a variety of ways, causing them to consider in a political context information that reflects the diverse conditions, attitudes and values of a pluralistic society. It is in this political process, as individuals and groups exercise the right of access to the decision makers with resulting adjustments and compromises, that the accountability of public administrators in a representative democracy is put to the most sophisticated tests; because it is then that the definition of the 'public interest' is honed" (Rosen, 1998).

Accountable to Whom ?

The question, accountable to whom, has several answers in view of the varied meanings and purposes of accountability. Five straightforward answers are:

i) Accountable to the internal hierarchy
ii) To the legislature
iii) To the judiciary
iv) To the citizens; and
v) To the media.

Excepting the first one, all other accountability relationships are external to the organisation in question. This shows that public administration's 'publicness' is primarily due to its external linkages. Beyond internal supervisory accountability, public organisations are answerable to the two principal organs of government: the legislature and the judiciary. The citizens, who are at the receiving end, are the best judge of the quality and quantity of services administered for their benefit. But they have hardly any means to hold the administration accountable. Third world public administration is post-colonial administration with distinct hangover of the structure and culture of a dominant bureaucracy. Again, unequal distribution of economic and political power is a hindrance to impartial rule and there is strong evidence to suggest that the bureaucracy tends to serve the rich. Last, but not the least, the media in democracy is to keep a regular vigil on whether public administration is really serving public or private interest.

Bureaucratic accountability is thus at the core of public administration in a democracy. Under a constitutional system of government, it is axiomatic that the bureaucrats should be subordinate to the mandates and constraints of the constitution as interpreted by the judiciary and to their hierarchical superiors within the organisation. Democratic government also postulates the subordination of the bureaucrats to the people and their elected representatives.

As Fesler and Kettl point out, *bureaucratic responsibility has to be seen* from two stand *points.* One is *accountability* as briefly mentioned earlier; the other is ethical behaviour. Bureaucratic ethics needs to be discussed separately because of its many-sidedness. "The two elements overlap and are generally compatible, but not always. Morality may call for disobedience to superiors or reporting of superiors' unethical behaviour to their superiors, to legislators, or to the public". (Fesler and Kettl, 1991).

In discussing accountability, the major concern is how to ensure that who wield power exercise it responsibly, so that they can be held accountable for their action. According to classical democratic theory, the line of accountability is fairly straightforward. The people elect their representatives on the basis of their stand on issues. Administrative agencies carry out the policies made by the people's representatives. The administrators are accountable to their political chiefs who in turn are answerable to the legislature. In modern day administration, this policy-making and policy-implementation dichotomy does not quite hold good. The administrators do participate in policy making and their discretion in today's big government is enormous. As the state has grown big and there have been frequent abuses of power by the bureaucrats, incessant demands have been made by the public and the media that there must be clearer and more transparent public administration and the moral fibre of public officials must improve. In other words, the public demand in most democracies has been that *there must be responsible use of power and authority and clearer means of administrative accountability.*

TWO CONNOTATIONS:

The notion of political accountability carries *two basic connotations: answerability,* the *obligation of public officials to inform about and explain what they are doing;* and *enforcement,* the capacity of accounting agencies to impose sanctions on power-holders who have violated their public duties. According to Romzek and Dubnick (1987)., the answerability concept is too narrow to capture the full reality of accountability relationships. In their view, public administration accountability involves means by which public agencies and their workers manage the diverse expectations generated within and outside the organisation, which is a very wide-ranging conceptualisation.

Accountability can be viewed from the perspective of domesticating power. There are three different ways of preventing and redressing the abuse of potential power:

i) Subjecting power to the threat of sanctions;
ii) Obliging it to be exercised in transparent ways;
iii) Forcing it to justify its acts.

Accountability involves the right to receive information which is the *informational dimension of accountability.* There is then the corresponding obligation to release all necessary details.

It also implies the right to receive an explanation and the corresponding duty to justify one's conduct. This is the *argumentative dimension* of accountability. As it has been aptly put: "Power should be bound not only by legal constraints but also by the logic of public reasoning. *Accountability is antithetical to monologic power. It establishes a dialogic relationship between accountable and accounting actors.* It makes both parties speak and *engages them both in public* debate. It is therefore opposed not only to mute power but also to unilateral speechless controls of power". (Shedler et al, 1999).

Simply stated, accountability is answerability for one's action or behaviour. Public services accountability involves the methods by which a public agency or a public official fulfils its duty and obligations. It includes the process by which that agency or the public official is required to account for such actions.

Types of Accountability

Admittedly, accountability is a very complex concept which need not be mixed up with the commonplace idea of tackling corruption. It is really the 'driving force' that generates pressures for the key administrative actors to be responsible for and to ensure good public service performance. Accountability has both a substantive part and a procedural or means part. On the substantive side, the focus may be on mundane things such as 'regularity' in following the prescribed rules and regulations of the organisation and observing the formally prescribed authority pattern. Then, there is the notion of *performance accountability* that focuses *on effectiveness and achievement* of goals. Also, there is the attendant concept of financial accountability involving evaluation of goals achievement and checking on the actual delivery of a pre-planned service. Based on these considerations, three major kinds of accountability have been suggested: fiscal accountability, process accountability and programme accountability. *Fiscal accountability* is the most traditional form of accountability involving scrutiny of records of financial transactions to ensure that the expenditure was legally made. The legislature maintains, in this way, its power over the purse. By reviewing financial records, the investigators often uncover and prosecute kickbacks in contracts and abuse of welfare programmes.

How the public agencies perform their tasks is at the core *of process accountability.* Procedural irregularities (such as improper tenders and contracts) in roads and buildings construction and other government activities are detected and remedies suggested in this form of accountability.

Programme accountability focuses on results or effectiveness. Government funds and procedures are merely means to ends. It is not enough to show that funds have been fully spent on, say, anti-poverty programmes. The real issue is: was the beneficiary correctly identified? Has the programs been able to improve the living standard/economic status of the beneficiary? Programme accountability looks beyond mere efficiency and searches for effectiveness.

Dwivedi and Jabbra have defined public service accountability in terms of "methods by which a public agency or a public official fulfils its duties and obligations and the process by which that agency or the public official is required to account for such actions". Seen in the context of public policy and administration, accountability in their view, should include at least five elements (Jabbra and Dwivedi, 1998):

- Organisational or administrative;
- Legal;
- Professional;
- Political;
- Moral.

Organisational accountability is the traditional hierarchical accountability within the organisation, as laid down in the classical Weberian bureaucratic form of administration.

Legal accountability relates actions in the public domain to the established legislative and judicial process. This is achieved either by a court action or by a judicial review of an administrative action: the public organisation or its officials are held accountable for not following legislative intent or legal delegations.

Professional accountability involves balancing the code of profession (of doctors, engineers etc.) with the larger purpose of protecting the public interest. Today, governments rely more and more on the expert advice of the professionals, who, in course of discharge of their duties, define public interest in their own way. It is not unlikely for the public interest and the professional codes to collide in reality. However, it is public interest which, in the ultimate analysis, should determine the responsibility and accountability of the professional.

Political accountability is concerned with the legitimacy of a public programme and even the survival of the involved organisation. In a democracy, the administrators are 'duty bound to recognize the power of political authority to regulate, set priorities, redistribute resources and to ensure compliance with orders'.

Last but not the least, moral accountability is at the core of public administration. It is more than obedience to laws and bureaucratic norms. A moral public official is one who 'strives for a moral Government'. As instances of administrative and political corruption become more and more widespread, the demand for moral accountability in the management of public affairs gets articulated more and more in different forums such as the media, the legislature and the judiciary.

Three different purposes of accountability assume importance in this context. *One:* the most commonplace objective has been to control abuse of bureaucratic power and discretion. *Two:* there must be an assurance that performance will be in accordance with standard and quality. *Three:* accountability is not just one-shot pursuit; it involves learning in pursuit of continuous improvement in governance and public management. On top of it, there is the human dimension of accountability subsuming values and ethics and creating trust in government. As it has been aptly put: "If there is no transparency and no living democracy with a free press, the control of abuse and the advanced performance evaluations will lead nowhere. Accountability in public administration cannot be reduced to a technical question of designing control procedures and institutions. It is a question of democracy". (Wolf, 2000).

In western democratic models of governance, public employees face multiple sources of legitimate authority and competing expectations for performance. "Authority relationships and legitimate performance expectations can derive from supervisors, elected chief executives and legislators, the courts, external auditing agencies, professional associations, co-workers, clients and the general public". (Romzek and Dubnik, 1987).These multiple sources of authority, obviously, create complex relationships and present challenges for serving public officials. Four types of accountability that can be identified as hierarchical, legal, professional and political have their corresponding behavioural expectations as depicted below: (Romzek, 2000):

Types of accountability
Behavioural Expectations

Hierarchical	Obedience to organisational directions
Legal	Compliance with external mandates (laws, rules etc.)
Professional	Deference to individual judgement and expertise
Political	Responsive to key external stake holders

Accountability, in this context, has been conceptualised as "the dialectics of accountability for performance". As one moves away from traditional Weberian model of bureaucracy to a more flexible, non-hierarchical, results-oriented and citizen-friendly public administration, demanded by the new civic culture of the new century, there is growing need now to attend to issues of 'accountability alignment'. The important managerial implication of accountability alignment is to make sure that performance evaluation criteria matches the managerial emphases and behavioural expectations (as noted above) which the management hopes to elicit from the employees.

Tools of Accountability

There are different tools or means available to make public servants accountable and particular tools are designed to suit particular purposes. Because of the essential multi-dimensionality of the concept, several tools are employed simultaneously in practice. As the following table shows, the different tools sub-serve different purposes (Hayliar, 1991):

The Tools for Accountability

Ends (to facilitate/ enhance)	Means (Tools)
Legitimacy of decision-makers	Constitutions, electoral systems for government and decision-making bodies; bureaucratic systems of representation; Royal prerogative; legislation; letters of appointment; standing orders and formal delegation of authority.
Moral Conduct	Societal values, concepts of social justice and public interest; professional values; Training/induction programmes
Responsiveness	Public participation and consultation; debates; advisory bodies; public meeting, freedom of speech
Openness	Parliamentary question times; public information services; freedom of information laws: public hearings: green and white papers; annual reports
Optimal resource utilisation	Budgets; financial procedures; rules of virement; parliamentary public account committees; auditing; public enquiries and participation; formal planning systems
Improving efficiency	Information systems; value
and effectiveness	for money audits; setting objectives and standards; programme guidelines; approval feedback from public.

Accountability and Paradigms of Public Administration

The accountability question needs to be cast in the background of paradigms of governance. Classical public administration based on the functioning of bureaucracy within the framework of democracy has so far been the staple of accountability theory. In the practical world of public administration today, two closely competing but complimentary, paradigms seem to hold away: *one* has gained wide currency as 'New Public Management' (NPM); and another is known as 'good governance'. 'Reinventing Government', although an innovative title falls in line with the main current of thought advocating quality (as against size) of governance and entrepreneurial spirit.

Historically, the liberal-democratic set-up evolved several basic mechanisms of accountability such as ministerial control, parliamentary debate, legislative committees, media scrutiny and the ombudsman system. In recent times, there have been some major changes a sort of paradigmatic transition in the mode of public governance under the rubric of 'new public management', 'reinventing' or 'reengineering' government. In essence, what is being advocated is a market-centred, neo-liberal approach to governance under which its objectives are shifted to economic growth and productivity and its normative standards are redirected toward efficiency, competition, profit and value for money. The standards that are being set for public governance are those of business management. This marks a radical departure from the traditional norms and objectives of governance: enhancing human progress, maintaining law and order, removing poverty and unemployment, providing public welfare, ensuring impartiality and equal treatment, safeguarding citizens' rights and guaranteeing justice and fairness.

As it has been aptly put, in contemporary public management 'the new diction is the language of the market, of competition, of enterprises, customers and, in a nutshell, of entrepreneurial management' (Haque 1998; Konig 1997). There has thus emerged a unique set of challenges to the realisation of accountability in the current phase of public administrative changes everywhere. Haque has explained in details the current dilemma of accountability in today's public governance ambience (Haque, 2000). As he argues, the contemporary change in governance toward efficiency, outcome, competition, value for money, catalytic role, autonomy, partnership and customer orientation pose formidable political, managerial and methodological challenges to accountability in terms of three specific dimensions:

i) The standards of accountabiiity (accountability for what);
ii) The agents of accountability (accountability to\whom);
iii) The means of accountability (how accountability is ensured)

So far as the *standards of accountability* are concerned, these have under the current mode of governance, become instrumental in nature placing emphasis more on procedural, economic criteria such as efficiency and productivity than on substantive public concerns like equality and representation. To quote Haque, "It is essential to understand that the accountability of public governance for market-based economic performance does not necessarily imply its accountability for citizens' rights, its accountability for competitive and productivity does not guarantee its accountability for representation and equality and its accountability for higher profit does not connote its accountability for welfare and justice. In short, therefore, the growing primacy of business-like criteria adopted in contemporary public governance has the tendency to displace its accountability in terms of established democratic standards.

As regards, agents of accountability, through the evolutionary process governments in democratic societies have increasingly become accountable to diverse groups and classes of citizens entitled to social services such as education, housing, health and social security. The people-centred tradition of accountability had "evolved with the emergence of broader civil society, an organised working class and an increase in the entitlements of rights of common citizens". Under the new paradigm of public management (NPM), citizens have been redefined as customers or clients- which are a commercial view of citizenship, reducing the social rights associated with collective citizenship, to narrow commercial prerogatives of individual customers governed by exchange relationship.

The third dimension- the means of accountability has been under challenge in today's context of neo-liberal mode of governance which has brought in its trial new sets of institutions, structures and norms. Following Haq's analysis, the first change to note is the growing power of ministers or political executives to exert influence on the public service leading to the politicization of civil servants by ministers in violation of the principle of political neutrality. Recent policy to do way with permanent tenure of senior public servants and introduce contract-based appointments makes the public servants more vulnerable to political executives exercising control over the job contracts and careers. Ministerial control as a means of accountability marks the public servants extremely loyal to ministers ignoring their accountability to the general public.

Second, the existing means of accountability may be affected by the structural and procedural autonomy granted under the current governance system. Most developed countries such as UK, Canada, New Zealand, France and others have desegregated and corporatized various ministries and departments into autonomous entities. Autonomy of public agencies for the avowed purposes of economy and productivity has reduced the opportunities of political representatives to scrutinize their activities and diminished the scope of legislative debates over programmes undertaken by the agencies almost like private corporations with maximum operational autonomy. Unprecedented managerial autonomy poses a serious challenge to the traditional means of accountability and even opens up opportunities for abuse and corruption by the chief executives of the autonomous agencies, who may use the public offices for private gains and overlook laws and rules that generally govern public administration.

Third, under the 'new management' regime, many developed and developing countries have shifted from process-oriented to result-oriented performance of public agencies with increasing focus on outcome than inputs. On the face of it, the result-oriented administration may look quite attractive; but such mode of governance is likely to render the existing means of accountability ineffective. As Haq has observed, it is difficult to put such outcome-based administrative system under legislative scrutiny due to the qualitative and controversial nature of public sector outcomes such as environmental security, poverty alleviation and community development. The result-oriented public administration tends to focus more on 'what' is being achieved. In consequence, there is likely to be the "diminishing relevance of such means of public accountability as internal control and supervision over various inputs and processes in the public sector.

Last but not the least, under the current mode of governance public-private partnerships and exchanges pose a threat to certain means of accountability, since these modalities are less answerable to normal legislative scrutiny and ministerial supervision. It is often difficult to find out if joint ventures or business deals have been made to the detriment of public interest or no. Stories are often heard of contracts of different kinds involving extra-legal tactics and opportunities for substantial 'kickbacks'. To sum up, as Haq rightly points out, "the current proliferation of public-private partnership and exchange represents a challenge to various legislative and executive means of accountability.

Accountability under 'good GOVERNANCE

The World Bank's lending conditions under the rubric of 'good governance' has been reviewed by many authors from the standpoint of conceptual elaboration of 'governance' and its implications for Third World development. (Bhattacharya 1998) Good governance is itself an accountability-oriented concept applicable to a specific target group - the Third World countries. To follow the line of thinking of its sponsor (the World Bank), good governance is synonymous with sound development management; it is an essential complement to sound economic policies. Governments are the main producers of public goods and they frame rules for the market to work efficiently. The institutional frameworks conductive to growth and poverty alleviation do not evolve on their own; rather the emergence of such frameworks needs incentive and adequate institutional capacity to create and sustain them. It is in this context that the World Bank pinpoints accountability as an essential prerequisite of 'good governance' (World Bank 1992).

Bank's accountability concern, in the context of Structural Adjustment Policy, has pervaded both public and private sectors. The phenomenon of 'capture' of public services and resources by relatively narrow special interests has been a common-feature in most countries. Governments often keep their transactions secret and the public in general is not prone to demand information about performance. Accountability assumes importance in respect of ensuring efficiency in investment as well as in production and distribution of public goods and services. Government has also to ensure accountability in the private sector through appropriate company and securities legislation, competitive policy and regulatory oversight, especially when 'down-sizing of government takes place through disinvestments, privatisation and contracting.'

Public accountability, the Bank document points out, involves three interrelated groups:

(a) The general public and particularly recipients of public services, who are interested in service providers being accountable to them;
(b) Political leaders and supervisors of service providers who would like the service providers to be accountable to them;
(c) The service providers themselves, whose objectives and interests often differ from those, of (a) and (b)

To follow the Bank's argument, historically accountability has revealed three features:

One, the salience of *micro-level accountability,* as due to expansion of state activity it has become difficult to apply broad accountability to numerous functions of government;

Two, the *focus in accountability* tends to be on *inputs,* especially public expenditure, rather than *outputs or effects;*

Three, accountability has mostly been by

internal administrative control exercised by political leaders, government agencies and bureaucrats acting as proxies for the public.

Two broad types of accountability identified by the Bank are: *micro-accountability,* and *macro-accountability.* Micro-accountability remains critical, especially in ensuring government responsiveness to the views and needs of the public for which services are intended. The concepts of 'exit' and 'voice' which originated in Albert O. Hirschman's classic work, *Exit, Voice, and Loyalty: Responses to Decline in Firms, Organisations, and States (1970)* have been used to underscore the importance of *micro-accountability.* For instance, competition or scope for the public to 'exit' when dissatisfied with a service, may have a salutary effect on the agency concerned by reducing its revenues and then by making the careers or pay of the staff less secure. Similarly, 'Voice' in the sense of participation of the public may influence the quality or volume of a service through some form of articulation of preferences of demand. Accountability is increased, if such 'Voice' makes the public agency more responsive to public demands.

It has been the Bank's policy to find out ways of increasing 'exit' and 'Voice' at the design stage of service delivery projects. Accountability at the micro level can, however, be sustained only when the government and society at large are committed for doing so.

Decentralisation in the form of strengthening local government has been widely viewed as essential to ensuring greater responsiveness and accountability for many kinds of infrastructure and service that have hitherto been in the control of the central government.

The other kind of accountability - *macro-accountability* - has two major dimensions: *financial accountability* and *accountability for overall economic performance.* Financial accountability involves, as the Bank document identifies:

i) A properly functioning government accounting system for effective expenditure control and cash management;
ii) An external audit system which reinforces expenditure control by exposure and sanctions against misspending and corruption;
iii) Mechanisms to review and act on the results of audits and to ensure that follow up action is taken to remedy problems identified.

As it has been rightly emphasised, without a well-functioning system of financial accountability, government efficiency is poor and the probability of corruption increases greatly.

Accountability for economic performance involves review of resource use in public investment programs and general strengthening of the capacity of governments to monitor and evaluate their own economic performance including proper resource use.

A complex concept: Accountability, though simple sounding, is an extremely complex concept. Traditional public administration considered it basically as an internal organisational issue seeking to bring about a congruence between top-down policy and bottom-line implementation. There have been many constitutional and institutional changes to enhance public accountability of government agencies. In the developed countries initially and later in the developing nations as well, the philosophy of 'new public management' sought to make public administration more productive and efficient through a variety of devices. Accountability, under 'new public management' has undergone a radical change, although, as discussed earlier, the focus has continued to remain on the 'management'. For the developing 'Third World' in the grip of serious debt crisis, the World Bank came out with the new 'good governance' prescription with its accompanying micro-accountability and macro-accountability formula. Institutional capacity-building became the central point and the Bank's primary objective has been to promote sound development management by removing, as far as possible, the possibilities of 'capture' of benefits by the socially powerful. But, the real issue seems to have been by-passed by the Bank. The Third World's socio-economic power structure has been such that the machinery of government has virtually been 'privatised' by the elite and the affluent. So long as the ground reality continues to be the same, 'accountability' to the general public will remain a mere rhetoric and not a reality.

REFERENCES

1. C.P. Bhambhri, 'Social Context of Accountability', in T.N. Chaturvedi (ed.), *Administrative Accountability,* IJPA, New Delhi, 1984.
2. Joseph G. Jabbra, 0 P Dwivedi (eds.), *Public Service Accountability,* Kumarian Press, Inc., 1998.
3. Adam Wolf "Symposium on accountability in public administration reconciling democracy, efficicncy and ethics: Introduction," *International Review of Administrative Services,* vol. 66, 2000.
4. Barbara S Romzek and Melvin J. Dubmck, Accountability m the public sector: Lessons from the challenger Tragedy", *Public Administration Review,* 1987, 47.
5. M. Shamsul Haque, 'Significance of accountability under the new approach to public governance', *International Review of Administrative Services,* vol. 66, 2000.
6. Mohit Bhattacharya, 'Conceptualizing good governance" *Indian Journal of Public Administration,* Special Issue, July-September 1998.
7. Richard Mulgan, The Process of Public Accountability", *Australian Journal of Public Administration,* 56(1): 25-36, March 1997.
8. Michael G.O. 'Loughhn, 'What is Bureaucratic Accountability and How can we measure it? *Administration and Society,* vol. 22, No. 3, November 1990.
9. World Bank, *Sub-Saharan African: From Crisis to sustainable growth: A Long-term Perspective Study,* Washington, 1989.
10. *World Bank, Governance and Development,* Washington, 1992.
11. Ray Kiely, 'New Liberalism revised? A critical account of World Bank concepts of good governance and market friendly intervention", *Capital and Class,* Spring, 1998.
12. James W. Fesler and Donald F Kettl, *The politics of the Administrative Process,* Chatham House Publishers, New Jersey, 1991, Chapter 13.
13. P Guy Peters and Donald J. Savoie (eds.) *Governance in a changing Environment,* Mcguill- Queen's University Press, Montreal/ Kingston, 1995.
14. Barnard Rosen, *Holding Government Bureaucracies Accountable,* Praeger, 1998.
15. Andreas Shedlar et al., *Conceptualizing Accountability,* 1999.
16. M. Hayilar, "Accountability: Ends, means and Resources", *Asian Review of Public Administration,* vol. 3(2), 1991.
17. Albert O. Hirschman, *Exit, Voice* and *Loyalty. Responses to Decline in Firms, Organisations, and States,* Yale University Press, 1970.

Chapter 22

Social Accountability

The two words—'social' and 'accountability' - have their distinct meanings. In a broad sense, 'social' refers to non-governmental, civil society organisations where people work on the basis of voluntarism and not compulsion or coercion. Accountability stands for submitting the 'accounts' of something/some activity entrusted to somebody To put it simply, 'accountability' is the obligation of power-holders to take responsibility for their actions. In a straightforward sense, 'accountability' is answerability in respect of the performance of the tasks entrusted to somebody. In public administration context, it refers to the obligation on the part of public officials to report on the usage of public resources and answerability for failing to meet stated performance objectives. In conventional administrative practice, accountability is an in-house arrangement through which the designated supervisors hold the subordinates accountable for their assigned activities. The social dimension of accountability is a relatively recent phenomenon, making 'administration' accountable to outsiders — the society.

Social Accountability: No doubt governments can do a great deal on their own to improve accountability through actions such as strengthening top-down oversight, professionalizing staff through civil service reform, empowering internal comptrollers, establishing performance contracts and creating new independent public oversight agencies. However, it is now being strongly argued that pro-accountability reform is much more effective when societal actors play a central role as well. This is what is being called 'social accountability'. To follow the-World Bank definition: Social Accountability is "an approach towards building accountability that relies on 'civic engagement', i.e. in which it is ordinary citizens and/or civil society organisations who participate directly or indirectly in exacting accountability".

There is a growing literature now, in this context, on 'civic engagement' emphasizing society's role in improving government accountability — a process increasingly being termed as "social accountability"[1]. According to Ackerman (whose concept paper is often cited as a general reference on the subject), "We should welcome this paradigm shift as an opportunity to rethink accepted categories and as a chance to give a dynamic boost to development thinking".

The effectiveness of conventional supply-side (government) mechanisms of accountability and elections (the principal traditional demand-side mechanism of accountability) has proved limited. Citizens need not be satisfied only with participation in five-yearly election processes.

To quote, in this context, the landmark document — World Development Report, 2004[2]:

"Citizens are combining electoral accountability and participation with what would traditionally have been considered the official accountability activities of the state. These initiatives address accountability at various levels. Some are aimed at strengthening voice in service delivery by enabling answerability and some at pushing further for enforceability. These initiatives and the state's response, employ a number of old and new tools, including tools based on information technology."

Government operations constantly impinge on the lives of citizens; hence, it is imperative that the citizens keep a close watch on normal government activities like licensing, imposition of varied regulations, distribution of many scheme-related benefits etc. at different levels. It needs to be closely watched whether the government agencies are actually operating keeping in mind the basic public interest concerns. By involving citizens in monitoring government performance, demanding and enhancing transparency and exposing government failures and misdeeds, social accountability mechanisms are potentially powerful tools against public sector corruption. In addition to improved government, social accountability 'empowers' citizens. 'Empowerment', in this context stands for 'a person's capacity to make effective choices; that is, as the capacity to transform choices into desired actions and outcomes'.[3]

The concept of social accountability underlines both the *right* and the corresponding *responsibility* of citizens to expect and ensure that government acts in the best interests of the citizens. As contrasted with within-organisation accountability, social accountability is 'external' and yet governmental, organisation is considered as an integral part of the civil society within which it is embedded.

'Social Accountability' Defined

Social accountability may be looked as "an approach towards building accountability that relies on civic engagement'. Ordinary citizens and/or civil society organisations participate directly or indirectly in exacting this kind of accountability. Social accountability initiatives include 'traditional' forms, such as public demonstrations, advocacy campaigns, investigative journalism and the recent ones such as citizen report cards, participatory public policy making, public expenditure tracking and "efforts to improve the effectiveness of "internal" accountability mechanisms of the government, for example by involving citizens in public commissions and hearings and oversight committees."[4] It has also been suggested that social accountability initiatives are most effective when these are 'institutionalized' and when the states' 'internal' (horizontal) accountability mechanisms are "more transparent and open to civic involvement." Transparency is thus inextricably linked to accountability. It has been found that the poor people are the greatest beneficiaries of effective social accountability initiatives. Social accountability activists also maintain that by involving citizens in initiatives geared towards demanding accountability of elected leaders, social accountability has the additional importance in respect of democratic strengthening.

Clearly, social accountability is about affirming and operating direct accountability relationships between the citizens and the state. Thus conceived, it refers to the broad range of actions and mechanisms, beyond voting, that citizens can use to hold the state's agencies to account. Participation of citizens in the formation of government is not the only method of democratic governance. It is perhaps much more important to ensure government's accountability to the lay citizens in course of actual functioning or governing.

Social accountability has both *intrinsic* and *instrumental* values. Its **intrinsic** importance is reflected in (a) the strengthening of democratic relationships and (b) people's empowerment. Its **instrumental** value is reflected in (a) development effectiveness in terms of improved service delivery and(b) better governance (which is, obviously, a holistic concept). More importantly, social accountability introduces a salutary **'ethics of governance'** by deepening democracy and ridding society of the vices of corrupt practices.

Two Kinds of Accountability

Government accountability falls broadly into two classes: 'supply-side' accountability and 'demand-side' accountability. Discussions on accountability have traditionally been oriented toward supply-side or government-side accountability as against demand-side or people (citizens)-side accountability. Improving supply-side accountability involves using methods such as political checks and balances, administrative rules and procedures, auditing requirements and formal law-enforcing and adjudicating agencies like the police and the judiciary. All these devices represent 'top-down' accountability. Additionally, independent pro-accountability agencies like vigilance commission, ombudsmen etc. have been constituted in many countries to improve government accountability. Again, in some instances public institutions have been privatised or services have been contracted out to the private sector to bring market accountability in the public sector.

Despite introduction of many newer devices and institutional mechanisms to improve government (supply-side) accountability, more recently attention has been paid to the institution of 'demand (people)-side' accountability mechanisms. This has been necessitated by two reasons: one, perceived inadequacy and limited success of the 'supply-side' mechanisms of accountability and two, to forge direct links between government agencies and the citizens and to 'empower' citizens. The basic objective of introducing 'demand-side' accountability mechanisms is to strengthen the voice and capacity of citizens, particularly the poor-and the socially marginalized communities, to enable them to directly demand greater accountability and responsiveness from public officials and service providers. This trend toward instituting demand-side accountability mechanisms reflects a growing attention to issues of good governance, people's empowerment and rights-based approaches to development.

Building Blocks

Five key steps are identified for enabling a social accountability process mechanism.

- **Mobilizing around an entry point:**This involves the identification of an entry point and developing of a strategy to address the problem. Potential strategies for addressing issues could include, for example, budget analysis/advocacy activities, tracking of inputs and/or expenditures, participatory evaluation of service delivery etc.
- **Building an information base:** A key process involves accessing or generating relevant information, both supply-side and demand-side, for building a credible evidence base. Relevant data/information must be interpreted and analyzed in order to be rendered operationally useful. This would be useful in produce meaningful findings that can be used in the dialogue with stakeholders.
- **Going Public:** A critical aspect for enabling social accountability is dissemination of information to the public and public debate around them. Effective communication strategies and mechanisms are,

therefore, essential aspects of social accountability.

- **Building Coalitions:** Informing citizens of their rights and responsibilities, engaging their interest and mobilizing them to build coalitions and partnerships with different stakeholders are core aspects of social accountability. The need for collective action and the capacity of CSOs to facilitate and support such mobilization, especially that of the poor and marginalized are crucial to the success of social accountability initiatives.
- **Advocating and negotiating change:** The most crucial and challenging element of a social accountability strategy is to be able to elicit a response from public officials and effect real change. The most effective strategies usually involve direct interaction and negotiation with the concerned government counterparts and in some cases, the institutionalization of mechanisms for ongoing consultation and dialogue.

Social accountability approaches primarily include accessing information, making the voice of citizens heard and engaging in a process of negotiation for change.

Information:

A critical aspect of social accountability is accessing or generating relevant *information* and making it public. Both 'supply-side' and 'demand-side' information need to be garnered in support of credible evidence. The supply-side information from government and service providers and demand-side information from users of government services, communities and citizens have thus to be collected and analyzed. This process calls for transparency of government operations including capacity to produce and provide data and accounts for accessing supply-side information such as policy statements, budget commitments and accounts, records of inputs, outputs and expenditures and audit findings. Initially, therefore, social accountability interventions would involve lobbying for enhanced information rights and public transparency. At the other end, a wide variety of participatory methods and tools—such as community scorecards, citizen report cards and participatory monitoring and evaluation techniques—have been developed to generate data on demand-side information. Efforts would have to be made alongside this to raise awareness and promote local-level mobilization and organisation.

Voice:

Giving *voice* to the needs, opinions and concerns of citizens is another key element of social accountability.There are many forceful strategies evolved by practitioners to strengthen citizen voice. These include creating spaces for public debate and platforms for citizen-state dialogue, building citizen confidence and rights awareness, facilitating the development of coalitions and alliances that can speak with a strong, united voice and making strategic use of modern and traditional forms of media. It has to be seen in this process that the voices of poorer and more marginal groups get due priority.

Negotiation:

To elicit favourable response from public officials and achieve real change is of crucial importance for which the *negotiation* processes have to be properly thought of. Among the several forms of such negotiations are community-level meetings with government officials or indirect, mediated forms of consultation and negotiation. Citizens groups have been found to employ a range of both informal and formal means of persuasion, pressure, reward and sanction with a view to creating public pressure. Experience shows that often in many situations, the citizen's groups have opted for legal and/or institutional reforms to facilitate meaningful negotiation.

These core elements of social accountability have been used in real-life situations in various combinations in different places. Various alternative forms are being worked out and tried in field situations by creative civil society groups.

New Generation of Social Accountability

Traditionally, citizen or civil society-led efforts to hold government accountable have included actions such as public demonstrations, protests, advocacy campaigns, investigative journalism and public interest lawsuits. In recent years, the expanded use of participatory data collection and analysis tools combined with enhanced space and opportunity for citizen/civil society engagement with the state have led to a new generation of social accountability practices. They emphasize a solid evidence base and direct dialogue and negotiation with government counterparts. These include, for example, participatory public policy-making, participatory budgeting, public expenditure tracking and citizen monitoring and evaluation of public services, called 'social auditing' — being discussed later in this paper in some details.

The concept of social accountability underlines both the *right* and the corresponding *responsibility* of citizens to expect and ensure that government acts in the best interests of the people. The obligation of government officials to be accountable to citizens derives from notions of citizens' rights, often enshrined in constitutions and the broader set of human rights. Social accountability initiatives help citizens understand their civic rights and play a proactive and responsible role in exercising those rights. In other words, opportunities to hold government accountable through the exercise of social accountability facilitate people's understanding of the governance processes and their eventual 'empowerment'. Social accountability, as it is exercised by the 'society', has the benefit of familiarizing the citizens with the processes of governmental operations. It 'empowers' citizens and has considerable educative value in terms of creating 'good citizens' depend exclusively on state horizontal mechanisms as there could be instances of manipulation. It is equally not desirable to depend on civic organisations, as their efforts could be thwarted by the state. Therefore, the synergy between these two sectors is vital for producing best results in the public accountability regime.

Social accountability initiatives have proliferated all over the world in recent times. In India, *Mazdoor Kisan Shakti Sangathan* (MKSS) or Workers and Peasants' Power Association, Rajasthan: Public Affairs Centre (PAC), Bangalore, are some of the important civic groups that have rendered valuable services in holding state and local government officials accountable. India's Right to Information law has facilitated greatly civil society's efforts to hold the administrators accountable. There were many administrative abuses in the past (and these are still persisting) such as non-payment of wages or under-payment, personal aggrandizement of council officials and so forth committed by local bodies and grassroots government officials against the rural poor. The non-political movement known as *Mazdoor Kisan Shakti Sangathan* (MKSS) was launched to face these abuses and rectify them with aggressive local people's activist postures. Earlier there have been diverse strategies such as sit-ins, rallies, lobbying with the government, like music, puppets and street theatre etc. After prolonged struggle, the MKSS became victorious when the government of Rajasthan incorporated the government notification that the people would have access to the records on *Panchayat* expenditure and can have photocopy records. The government finally enacted the Right to Information Act in 2000.

In Rajasthan, the MKSS used public hearings through which the discrepancies between what was written on paper and what was given to the rural labourers could easily be identified. Through this, the labourers got fair wages, fictitious names on the pay roll could be identified and other kinds of anomalies could be detected. The MKSS message has now inspired many Indian states where the NGOs have been pressing for 'social audit' and access for information under the right to information law. The Government of India eventually passed the Right to Information Act in 2005.

In India, it is common knowledge that most citizens, particularly the poor, face serious problems relating to the delivery of essential public services such as water, electricity and health etc. In view of recurring mismanagement and corruption, smaller movements have been organised in the past against unresponsive and corrupt public officials. In this context, the role of the PAC, Bangalore, deserves special mention. PAC, a Bangalore-based NGO, came forward with the imaginative idea to improve civic services delivery system of essential public services. They introduced what is known as 'report cards' that seek citizens' opinions about their real-life experiences in getting day-to-day essential local public services. These reports are widely publicized in local media and through other methods to pressurize the local authorities to improve services delivery. PAC now conducts surveys using report cards for all essential services on all-India basis.

Relation with Traditional Mechanisms

Conventional accountability mechanisms are not to be replaced by social accountability mechanisms. Rather the latter need to be viewed as complementary to conventional internal (government) mechanisms of public accountability. Usually, governments have internal control mechanisms to ensure accountability of public servants. These may be identified as follows:

i) Constitutional mechanisms such as CAG audit, separation of powers, Public Accounts Committee and so on;
ii) Political mechanisms such as debates and legislative investigative commissions, media reporting and political party agitations etc.;
iii) Fiscal mechanisms including formal systems of auditing and financial accounting;
iv) Administrative mechanisms including hierarchical control and reporting, norms of public sector probity, public service codes of conduct, rules and procedures regarding transparency and public oversight
v) Legal mechanisms like corruption control agencies (vigilance commission), ombudsmen and the judiciary.

Ideally, the two sets of accountability mechanisms — internal (within formal governmental set-up) and external (citizens/ civil society) mechanisms of accountability — should be mutually reinforcing. Social accountability includes efforts to enhance citizen knowledge and use of conventional mechanisms of accountability (for example, through public education about legal rights and available services) and efforts to improve the effectiveness of internal accountability mechanisms through greater transparency and civic engagement (for example, citizen and community participation in public commissions, hearings, advisory boards and oversight committees). Strengthening legislative oversight and links between parliamentarians, citizens and civil society organisations are also important ways to enhance social accountability.

At the ground level, the socio-economic and political contexts of most developing countries pose in reality, serious constraints in realizing the objectives of social accountability. There are many evidences to suggest that even the best objectives of social accountability are being thwarted by unfavourable social and political contexts. In the developing world extreme inequality, poverty and undemocratic political situations pose considerable threats to the autonomous actions of social-actors-led civic organisations.The undemocratic elements within the state structure always create hurdles and they are usually reluctant to give any space to civic organisations. There are instances of corruption and capture by those who are either at the helm of the power structure or allied with the power structure through the client list networks. Access to information is another crucial element for social accountability initiatives. Unless relevant information and documents are made available to civic groups, they cannot generate pressures.

The strength of local civic organisations is crucial for effective social accountability initiatives. The civic groups should have the ability to sway initiatives, attract local supporters and members and mobilize them. In many countries, their strength is impaired by internal strife, undemocratic elements within the groups, client list nexus with state decision makers and so forth. In order to extract better results, civic organisations and the state have often to work in tandem. Since the efforts of local civic agencies can be thwarted by unhelpful state agencies, the synergy between these two sectors is vital for producing best results in this area. In fact, the civil society's attempts to improve the performance of public (government) projects need to be appreciated by the political leaders at the highest level. Once cooperation is assured from the highest level, normally, lower level officials come forward to extend help and assistance in the functioning of local civic groups.

Cross-Cultural Evidences

Over the last two decades or so, social accountability initiatives have proliferated all over the world. A number of major social accountability initiatives undertaken in different parts of the developing world are listed below.

Participatory Planning and Policy Formulation: Participatory planning and policy formulation has become an increasingly common trend. Decentralized planning has been institutionalized in West Bengal and Kerala. Participatory budget formulation, though less common, has been used at the local level in Brazil in over 100 municipalities.

Participatory Budget Analysis: This may involve analyzing the impact and implications of budget allocations, demystifying the technical content of the budget, raising awareness about budget-related issues and undertaking public education campaigns to improve budget literacy. CSOs also play a key role in building public awareness about policies in key areas such as poverty reduction, gender equity, environmental protection, employment and social services.

Participatory Expenditure Tracking: This involves citizen groups tracking how the government actually spends funds, with the aim of identifying leakages and/or bottlenecks in the flow of financial resources or inputs. Examples include participatory tracking of primary education expenditures in Uganda, Jan Sunwais or participatory audits in Rajasthan and Delhi, People's Estimate in Andhra Pradesh (for monitoring and execution of rural public works), etc.

Citizens' Surveys/Citizen Report Cards: These are survey methods where feedback from individual citizens is aggregated to provide report cards and survey reports on a range of issues. These could pertain to service delivery assessments, opinion polls, awareness exercises etc. While surveys have been used extensively the world over, their use to generate Citizen Report Cards have been made in India and Philippines.

Citizen's Charters: A charter is an explicit statement of what a public agency is ready to offer as its services, the rights and entitlements of the people with reference to these services and the remedies available to them should problems and disputes arise in these transactions. Citizen's Charters have been used in various departments at the Centre and States within varying degree of success.

Community Score Cards: These are used to assess service delivery in a participatory manner at the community level. Typically, the process involves ratings of service delivery by users and self-assessments by providers who then participate in an interface meeting to identify and sort issues and differences.

In addition, other important methods are campaigns for electoral reforms, public interest litigations and social audit.

What is Social Audit (SD)?

As earlier mentioned, in recent times 'social audit' has emerged lately as a powerful tool to bring about governmental accountability to the lay people. Social auditing is a process that enables an organisation to assess and demonstrate its social, economic and environmental benefits and limitations. It is a way of measuring the extent to which an organisation lives up to the shared values and objectives it has committed itself to.

It provides an assessment of the impact of an organisation's non-financial objectives through systematically and regularly monitoring its performance and the views of its stakeholders.

Social auditing requires the involvement of stakeholders including employees, clients, volunteers, financing agencies, contractors, suppliers and local residents interested in the local organisation and the local development schemes under review. Stakeholders are defined as those persons or organisations who have an interest in, or who have invested resources in, the organisation.

Social audits are generated by the organisation themselves and those directly involved. A person or panel of people external to the organisation undertakes verification of the social audit's accuracy and objectivity.

What does SD Involve?

The social auditing process requires an intermittent but clear time commitment from a key person within the organisation. This social auditor forges links with others in the organisation and designs, co-ordinates, analyses and documents the information collected during the process.

Social auditing information is collected through research methods that include social bookkeeping, surveys and case studies. The objectives of the organisation are the starting point from which indicatory of impact are determined, stakeholders identified and research tools designed in detail. For this purpose, local NGOs may be of considerable help to mobilize local people and motivate them to undertake the SD exercise. The local people need to be told about the nature and importance of SD and they have to be trained in the methods and techniques of SD. In other words, the local people being the chief stakeholder have to take the lead with, of course, help and assistance of some NGOs who know the area's governance system and its development activities.

The collection of information is an on-going process, often done in 12-month cycles and resulting in the organisation establishing social bookkeeping and the preparation of an annual social audit document/report.

Experience has shown that it is important to provide training to the social auditor as well as mentoring during the first few years. If well facilitated, social auditors from different organisations can become self-supporting for subsequent years. Also, local people with support from active local NGOs, can pursue social audit as a regular institutionalized (as against one-shot) mechanism to closely monitor and evaluate local development programmes and projects of government.

HOW COULD IT BE OF USE TO LOCAL COMMUNITY?

A social audit can complement an organisation's annual financial audit by providing clear and succinct information on performance against social objectives. The results can be fed into the organisation's strategic review and planning processes to improve overall performance and social impact. It has been shown to increase accountability of the organisation to its stakeholders and to enhance democratic practice.

The *advantages of social audit* can now be synoptically put as

- Community training on participatory local planning,
- Encouragement and stimulation of local participative democracy,
- Facilitating community participation,
- Social inclusion of disadvantaged groups,
- Experimentation in collective decision making and sharing of responsibilities,
- Developing human resources and local 'social capital'

To elucidate further the concept of 'social audit', it is the process of vigilance and monitoring kept by the society to ensure that the public money is being spent in the most prudent way adhering to all the stipulated guidelines. The major principle that guides social audit is that it should be done by the society itself, of course, with assistance from the trained people. The process of the audit itself should act as a process of capacity-building of the citizens. Independent people — bona fide NGOs and experienced trainers who do not have any interest in the implementation of any local development scheme should help the Society in conducting social audit. There should be well-worked-out mechanisms to address the grievances or findings that come out as a result of the social audit. The findings of the social audit should be taken seriously by the administration at the highest level and corrective actions have to be initiated immediately on receipt of the report of the Social Audit. To reiterate the main objectives of social audit are to:

1. Assess the physical and financial gaps between needs and resources available for local development;
2. Create awareness among beneficiaries and providers of local social and productive services;
3. Increase efficacy and effectiveness of local development programmes;
4. Examine the various policy decisions,

keeping in view stakeholder interests and priorities, particularly of rural poor

5. Estimate the opportunity cost for stakeholders for not getting timely access to public services.

Effectiveness

It is not always easy to conduct social audit without community preparedness on one side and institutional help and cooperation on the other. Therefore, to be effective, the social auditor must have the right to:

1. Seek clarifications from the implementing agency about any decision-making, activity, scheme, income and expenditure incurred by the agency;
2. Consider and scrutinize existing schemes and local activities of the agency
3. Access registers and documents relating to all development activities undertaken by the implementing agency or by any other government department.

This requires transparency in the decision-making and activities of the implementing agencies. In a way, social audit includes measures for enhancing transparency by enforcing the right to information in the planning and implementation of local development activities.

Appropriate institutional level

It might be advisable to statutorily endow the *Gram Sabha (gram sansad,* in the case of West Bengal) *with* power

- to inspect all public documents related to budget allocations, list of beneficiaries, assistance under each scheme, muster rolls, bills, vouchers, accounts, etc., for scrutiny;
- examine annual statements of accounts and audit reports;
- discuss the report on the local administration of the preceding year;
- review local development for the year or any new activity programme;
- establish accountability of functionaries found guilty of violating established norms/rules;
- suggest measures for promoting transparency in identifying, planning, implementing, monitoring and evaluating relevant local development programmes
- ensure opportunity for the rural poor to voice their concerns while participating in social audit meetings.

Statutory 'social audit committees' may be constituted (although this might be violable of the principle of voluntarism) at the level of each tier of the PRI. These committees need not be permanent and can be set up depending on the nature of programmes/ schemes to be audited. The members can be drawn locally from among the different programme stakeholders. The services of retired functionaries of different organisations, teachers or persons of impeccable integrity and known expertise residing in the vicinity of the organisations may be taken on board as facilitators and members of such committees. Efficient and locally acceptable NGOs may come forward to 'train','advise' and assist social audit groups and committees to make social audit a success.

Concluding Observations

Accountability is acknowledged as the heart of democratic governance. Over the years, various strategies have been used to improve government accountability. It is now being increasingly felt that to remove the distance between the government and the governed and to accommodate rising people's demand for direct participation in 'governance'. It is not enough to rely merely on traditional intra-organisational accountability mechanisms. Wherever feasible, the governance process needs to be opened up and made accessible to the 'public'. Social accountability may thus be looked at as a timely institutionalization of a long felt demand for openness, transparency and accessibility.

REFERENCES

1. See, in this context, the excellent foundational work of Ackerman on 'Social Accountability'. John M. Ackerman, Social Accountability for the Public Sector: A Conceptual Discussion, January 18, 2005.
2. World Development Report, 2004, Making Services Work for Poor People, A Co-publication of World Bank and Oxford University Press. See particularly Chapter 5 on 'Citizens and Politicians'.
3. Malena, Forster and Singh, Social accountability: An Approach Paper, World Bank, 2004.

Chapter 23

Administrative Ethics

Since-the days of ancient Greek civilisation, virtuous life, citizens' direct participation in public life and obligations of public servants had been major components of political philosophy. Contemporary discussions on administrative ethics can be traced to such discussions in the past. But, more importantly, the growth of democracy and democratic consciousness has, in recent times, led to searching questions about bureaucracy's expanding role and autonomy which it is feared, may overshadow the core values of a democratic polity.

Against this backdrop, two major frameworks of ethical standards in public administration can be identified as (a) bureaucratic ethos and (b) democratic ethos.

The **bureaucratic ethos** that has been the dominant mode of public administration can be traced to the Weberian model of rational bureaucracy, Wilsonian dichotomy of politics and administration and the Taylorian scientific management theory. "The content value of bureaucratic ethos are chiefly contained in five pervasive concepts: efficiency, efficacy, expertise, loyalty and accountability. In one form or another, these concepts and their inclusion as positive behavioural norms for public administrators have remained viable in both theory and practice."[1]

The **democratic ethos,** by contrast, is less precise and more eclectic and open-ended. It has been an evolving framework subsuming such content values as regime values (what could be enshrined in the constitution), citizenship, public interest and social equity. As has been rightly observed, such a set of values "clearly places the framework in the realms of political theory."[2]

Weber's formulation: In his seminal discourse of 'Politics as a vocation', Max Weber introduced a crucial distinction between (i) an ethics of ultimate ends (ii) an ethic of responsibility. This has relevance for public management. In the first ethic, the responsibility for **consequences** is lacking. To quote Weber, "There is an abysmal contrast between conduct that follows the maxim of an ethic of ultimate ends—that is, in religious terms, the Christian does rightly and leaves the result with the lord —and conduct that follows the maxim of an ethic of responsibility, in which case one has to give an account of the foreseeable result of one's action."

Weber did not consider these two ethical orientations as polar opposites. As he said, "an ethic of ultimate ends and an ethic of responsibility are not absolute contrasts but rather supplements, which only in unison constitute a genuine man . . . . . .".

The principle of 'ethical neutrality' supposed to originate in Weber does not hold well in this context. Neutrality seeks to avoid the consequences of action. It may be recalled that the New Public Administration movement (Minnowbrooke I) in the late sixties of the last century rejected value neutrality in public administration. There was, on the contrary, a strong advocacy of value, relevance, change and equity. Since the days of the NPA movement, serious searches have been on to evolve workable ethical principles in public administration. It was felt that administration helps to shape decisions and (as Simon observed) establish priorities among competing values.

Search for Values: Paul Appleby's[3] advocacy of the virtues of honesty and loyalty in public administration has influenced generations of scholars. Going beyond these, Stephen Bailey[4] argued that "Three essential moral qualities in the public sector are optimism, courage and fairness tempered by charity."

Frederickson and Hart[5] talk of a public service model that they refer to as the 'patriotism of benevolence', which is a blend of patriotism and benevolence (or love of others).

Discussions on public service values and duties reflect a mixture of institutional arrangements (such as accountability), instrumental values (like efficacy) fundamental or ontological values (like honesty, fairness etc.).

One forceful view has been that the basic cores of tenets that together define the moral foundation of public administration are honour, benevolence and justice.[6]

Honour stands for the adherence to the highest standards of responsibility, integrity and principle.

Benevolence (as Frederickson explained) is the disposition to do good to others and to promote the welfare of others.

Justice stands for fairness and regard for the rights of others, including respect for the dignity and worth of each individual. Justice finds full philosophical explanation in John Rawls's famous work, *A Theory of Justice* (1971).

These three imperatives taken together constitute the moral foundation of public administration.

Internal Checks Vs. External Accountability

The discussion on administrative ethics must take note of the classic debate between Finer and Friedrich—which is really a debate between internal constraints and external controls. Writing against the background of rising bureaucratic power and responsibility, Finer argued that the only sure protection against this phenomenon is the establishment of a set of external checks in the form of laws and administrative powers to discipline erring civil servants. Carl Friedrich, on the other hand, argued in a pragmatic fashion that external checks, cannot eliminate all abuse and wrongs. The remedy lies in recruiting the right kind of people and socializes them carefully into a set of public service values.[7]

Lying hidden in these debates are suspicions about deviant bureaucratic behaviour. In real life, bureaucratic corruption and highhandedness are not uncommon and administrators are known to have been 'secret' in public dealings and using considerable discretion unregulated by laws and rules.

Three Perspectives: Against this background of real life administration, three broad perspectives can be drawn to establish ethical standards for public service:

(a) Regime values;
(b) Situational ethics;
(c) Personal ethics.

As earlier mentioned, the regime values rely on the Constitution as the repository of the core values of a nation and, administration has to function within the four corners of these values as enshrined in the Constitution.

The situational values point out the impossibility of regulating all bureaucratic behaviour by laws and rules and the Constitution. There are innumerable situations where the administrator has wily nily to exercise his or her judgement in the context of the cases being dealt with. Flexibility is necessary rather than rigid adherence to rules.

The personal values are closely linked to situational values but these form a different kind. After all, in an administrative situation, it is the individual who has, each time to take an 'appropriate' decision. Underlying this behaviour is a concept of personal ethics. In public administration literature, there are many instances of leading authors (e.g. Paul Appleby or O. Glenn Stahl) urging public officials to build their own ethical framework consciously and carefully. Stahl's wise counsel is worth our quotation in this context:

"Our immediate obligation as a society is to imbue more young people with a selfless vision, with the excitement and satisfaction that derives from most governmental activity. Recruits in all fields—engineers, technicians, social scientists, even clerical workers—must be infused with a sense of mission, an ethical passion for the public interest."[8]

Societal Culture and Ethics

Administrators function within the large framework of societal culture. We owe to Fred Riggs the ecological approach to public administration that situates administrators within the broader social-environmental framework. How administrations function and the way administrators behave cannot be explained only by reference to intra-bureaucratic operational modes. Administrative ethics, is a determinant of the wider socio-economic culture that exerts deep influence on administration.

The other influence on administrative ethics can be traced to what Guy Peters calls 'bureaucratic culture'. There are distinct differences between different kinds of public organisations. For instance, a police organisation has its distinctive ways of doing things. By contrast, a social development agency engaged in child welfare or anti-poverty management will be more client-serving and de-bureaucratized in its operations. For a fuller understanding of administrative ethics, therefore, the culture of organisation has to be reckoned with as an important variable.

REFERENCES

1. Darrell L. Pugh,'The origins of Ethical Frameworks in Public Administration', in James S. Bowman (ed), Ethical Frontiers in Public Management, Jossey-Bass Publishers, San Francisco, Oxford, 1991.
2. Pugh, op. cit.
3. Paul Appleby, *Morality and Administration in a Democratic Government,* Louisiana State University Press, 1959.
4. Stephen Bailey, "Ethics and the Public Service", *Public Administration Review,* December 1965.
5. Frederickson and Hart, "The Public Service and the Patriotism of Benevolence", *Public Administrative Review,* Sept.-Oct. 1985.
6. Kathryn G. Denhardt, "Unearthing the Moral Foundation of Public Administration. However, Benevolence and Justice", in Bowman (ed.), op. cit.
7. Herman Finer, "Administrative Responsibility in Democratic Government", PAR, I (Summer 1941). Carl Friedrich, "Public Policy and the Nature of Administrative Responsibility", in Friedrich *et al* (eds.), *Public Policy,* Harvard, Cambridge, 1940.
8. O. Glenn Stahl, "A Public Service for the Twenty - First Century", in Ali Farazmand (ed.), *Handbook of Bureaucracy,* Marcel Dekker', New York, 1994.

CHAPTER 24

Globalisation and Public Administration

The phenomenon of 'globalisation' is a much-talked-about theme today. Enthusiasts look at it as creating for humanity almost a borderless human existence with the traditional sovereign slates melting away in a fast-growing web of interconnectedness. Pessimists perceive the evolving situation as creating a grossly unequal international states system with massive gainers on one side — particularly the western developed nations—in a historically structured uneven economic playing field and miserable losers on the other especially the 'developing countries' (the Third World, so to say) that had embarked upon a long-drawn-out and complex process of nation building and speedy socio-economic reconstruction after coming out of a long era of exploitative colonial rule. Drawing on the bitter experiences of many Third World countries, apprehensions have been expressed in some quarters that 'globalisation' would in reality mean pernicious control over economy, polity and culture by powerful multinationals aided and abetted by the irresponsible domestic elites—the compradors, so to say. So, surrounding 'globalisation', the central point that is being raised is: is it going to be an unalloyed promise of prosperity for everybody, or, is it going to bring in its trail a pathological process of 're-colonisation' whereby the Third World would again be reverted back to the old historical process of subjugation to the First World's politico-economic hegemony.

MANAGING GLOBALISATION

Against this mixed backdrop of expectations and uspicions, globalisation needs to be understood, not so much in terms of dreamy-eyed philosophy as a concrete managerial-administrative issue with the state being enmeshed willy-nilly in a network of complex relationships. In this connection, the detailed observations of Guido Bertulucci, Director of the Division for Public Economics and Public Administration, DESA (United Nations) are worth our quotation:

"Managing the public sector in today's environment of constant change, particularly in view of globalisation, has become an increasingly demanding challenge for national decision makers, policy advisors, service delivery managers and civil servants at large.

The functions and role of the State have been transformed substantially. The general configuration of its responsibilities has changed and this has introduced important modifications both in the policy arena and in the State's requirements for high-level skills, qualitatively and quantitatively. Overall, the course of change points to a shift of focus away from hands-on management and the direct production of services and goods towards strategic planning with a view to the establishment and maintenance, refinement and reform of an enabling framework for private enterprise and individual initiative. A parallel shift has moved the State's centre of gravity and with it the locus of power. Decentralization, debureaucratization and deregulation are adding to the importance not only of local government, but also of non-state actors on whom significant functions are devolved or outsourced. At the same time, a range of tasks and policy decisions, traditionally handled by national bureaucracies in their respective capitals, is being increasingly transposed to an inter-governmental or supranational level as a result of increased flows between countries of goods, capital, labour and information. Increasingly, the State is called upon to act as 'linking pin' of processes of planning, consultation, negotiation and decision-making involving diverse actors. State and non-state, at different levels of governance. The State is the hub of activities connecting multiple partners and stakeholders from very varied fields, regions, cultures, occupations, professions and interests. It has also become apparent that the benefits of globalisation have been so far uneven. Experience suggests that one of the main causes of the crises plaguing developing countries and the inability of some of them to integrate in the world economy is state capacity deficit. Globalisation is certainly presenting many opportunities, including foreign direct investment, trade, access to information technology; however, only countries that have in place an effective public administration solid political and economic institutions, adequate social policies and a committed leadership can ensure that all sectors of society benefit from greater integration into the world economy."

In order to make full use of the opportunities provided by globalisation, as Bertulucci observes, developing countries need, among other things, to reinvest in their public sector and enhance their capacity for policy analysis, formulation and implementation. Hence, what countries need most in order to enable people to enjoy the benefits of globalisation is to focus on strengthening their institutions, develop human resources capacity and achieve technological adequacy. This alone can enable them to capture the economic gains which participation in globalisation may bring and at the same time help them to mitigate globalisation's social costs.

Perspective of Public Administration

Depending on the specific perspective taken, the theme of globalisation along with its varied ramifications has been the subject of conflicting interpretations. Economists and international trade experts have been adopting their own disciplinary angles. Political scientists and sociologists have taken their respective viewpoints. Public Administration has basically been an inward looking discipline concerned with the management of a country's domestic public affairs. Very recently, it has woken up to the need for focusing on the pulls and pressures of the on-going processes of globalisation and their impact on domestic administrative management. Since then, the search has been on to 'reinvent' or reposition' the discipline in the context of a newly emergent world order.

Traditionally, public administration has been concerned with the policies and actions of a country's formal governmental machineries including their organisational structures, decisional processes and behavioural dimensions. Globalisation, as it is being currently perceived, has considerable implications for the management of a country's public affairs contextually as well as substantively. To revert to Bertulucci's significant comments, globalisation that involves greater integration of a country into the world economy, demands well-designed state capacity building. The state has to emerge in a new 'linking-pin' role with enhanced capacity to engage in strategic planning, negotiations and consultations with varied actors. To reap the full benefit of economic gains and to reduce the likely social costs of globalisation, there is the urgent need to strengthen appropriate institutions (e.g. the bureaucracy and especially the policy level leadership, decentralised, local governance system etc.), develop human resources and update technological capacity.

The purpose of the present discussion is to clearly bring out these implications by planning public administration within the framework of contemporary globalisation process and discourse. There is almost universal recognition today of the urgent need for realignment of a country's public administrative system, but the direction and contents of reform are far from clear. Note, in this context, the comments of the UNDP:

"The pressures of globalisation have focused more attention onto the public sector. While globalisation could serve to integrate people, it has demonstrated a capacity to marginalise many. To combat this requires governance approaches that embrace transparency, accountability and stakeholder participation in policy debates, as well as a government that uses its resources efficiently to allow its citizens to compete in a global market and to reduce the gap between the poorest and richest inhabitants of the world. Globalisation not only increases the need for strong international and regional venues for dialogue, global policy-making and enforcement of international agreements and regulations, but also enhances the pressures for strong national governments, competent to integrate and negotiate in a global environment and capable to stand up to global forces that neglect the particular claims and challenges of developing countries, in particular the 'Least Developed ones.'

Special emphasis, thus, needs to be laid on the perceived impact as well as actual consequences of globalisation on the public administration system of the Third World countries. More precisely, the discussion focuses on five major interconnected aspects of the core theme:

- Meaning of 'globalisation' and the present status of 'globalisation' discourse
- Implications of 'globalisation' for traditional public administration as an operative system in a country situation
- Need for repositioning of the discipline of Public Administration in the face of 'globalisation' discourse
- Exploring special kind of relationship, if any, between 'globalisation' and development administration in view of the fact that the developing countries have been pursuing their 'development' programmes for the last five decades or so
- Implications of globalisation for administrative 'ethics' in general and for 'development ethics' in particular

THE GLOBALISATION DISCOURSE

Globalisation has been defined in various ways and its newness has also not gone unchallenged. Economic and market integration of the countries of the world through increased flow of goods, services, investment and capital fund flows and labour mobility has been the common marker of 'globalisation'. It might sound over-economist, yet at the heart of contemporary globalisation discourse is the central fact of increase in international transactions, particularly international trade, in markets for goods, services and some factors of production. Along with this noticeable trend, there is remarkable growth and expanded scope of many institutions that transcend national boundaries including multinational firms, international institutions and nongovernmental organisations (NGOs) operating globally. There has also been the expansion and international exchange in many other fields such as foreign direct investments, role of multinational corporations and integration of world capital markets. At the national or domestic level, the extraterritorial reach of government policies has been quite common in many areas of concern such as trade, international investments negotiation and even social development policies in vital sectors like health, education and poverty reduction.

In the process, governments are facing constraints on their functioning because of their subjection to certain rules and regulations framed and 'imposed' by a number of international institutions (WTO, for instance) of which they are members. We can now refer to David Held et al for both an 'informal' and a 'formal' definition of globalisation as under:

- An informal one 'as the widening, deepening and speeding up of worldwide interconnectedness in all aspects of contemporary social life, from the cultural to the criminal, the financial to the spiritual'.
- A formal one as a 'process (or set of processes) which embodies a transformation in the spatial organisation of social relations and transactions—assessed in terms of their extensity, intensity, velocity and impact—generation of transcontinental or interregional flows and networks of activity, interaction and the exercise of power'.

Discussing at the Open Democracy Forum on January 24, 2002. Held commented that worldwide interconnectedness was not a new thing; it existed for some hundreds of years. But if one traces its increase, 'there is now an on-going transformation, from economics, politics and migration to culture and law, which is creating a new kind of world order'. Quoting Kant that in the fabric of everyday life 'we are all unavoidably side by side'. Held argued that truly today we are side by side 'not just at moments of catastrophe, but in trading and trading arrangements, in the nature of financial markets, in the nature of environmental change from ozone depletion to global warming, in areas that are fundamental to human health such as welfare, sexuality and AIDS, right the way through to new questions posed about genetic manipulation'.

Held's two other comments are of considerable significance in this context: *one,* 'globalisation is not an end state, or a single thing, any more than is democracy or industrialisation. These are processes, involving changing relations of human affairs...; and *two,* it should not mean that local does not matter anymore. Rather 'local' does matter in a different way. 'It is being re-contextualized in a more complex world of economics, politics, culture and migration'.

VALUE QUESTIONS

Globalisation has its winners and losers. Its processes are prone to affecting both the human societies and the bio-physical environment within which the humans live and survive. Hence there are deep ethical issues involved in the globalisation process. Two comments are worth our quotation in this context.With respect to the changing configuration of the public and private spheres, Farazmand (1999) maintains that, with the increasing dominance of the corporate sector, government's role, "in the allocation of resources the equitable distribution of wealth, the stabilization of economy and economic growth has been overruled by the globalising corporate elites". As a result, the public sphere and citizen participation has shrunk. Therefore, "public administrators should resist shrinking this realm of public service by engaging citizens in the administration of public affairs and by playing a proactive role in managing societal resources away from the dominant control of globalising corporate elites". In Farazmand's view, nothing less than the future legitimacy of public administrators is at stake.

Second challenge — the shift from civil administration to non-civil administration — is even larger. According to Farazmand, the traditional administrative state balanced corporate elite interest with broad public interests. But now "the balanced administrative state has been replaced by the corporate-coercive state".Thus, public administration is being transformed from administering public affairs to administering the public itself, "for social control and facilitation of capital accumulation". Public administrators with a social conscience, he argues, should resist this change.

Third is the challenge of privatisation, which Farazmand claims "promotes greater opportunities for corruption". "Public administrators," he contends, "must resist the market-based concepts of treating citizens as consumers and degrading them to market commodities".

Fourth is globalisation's tendency to promote elitism and elites who operate as subsidiaries or agents of transnational corporations. Many of these 'corporate mercenaries' in less-developed nations "run repressive regimes which violate the human rights of their own people" (p. 518). The paradox is that, "globalisation has produced a massive concentration of corporate power and has centralised its organisational structure while at the same time governmental decentralisation has been promoted across the world".

Finally, Farazmand asserts that, "globalisation challenges the human conscience of the public administration community". Public administrators, who are "professional citizens of the global community," are responsible for addressing many moral issues, "including the conditions and deprivations of the poor, wage slavery and sweatshops in global factories, environmental destruction, global warming inequity and injustice". Public administrators can raise global consciousness about global issues, "question the sincerity of the elites, oppose exploitation and resist being used for undemocratic, unjust and inequitable purposes around the globe". Farazmand suggests that the Internet and other communication systems can be helpful in this regard. The upshot of Farazmand's position is that public administrators in both more- and less- developed nations are guardians of global community interests who "have a global responsibility to act ethically and morally in a coordinated manner".

John McMurtry's (1998) *Unequal Freedoms: The Global Market as an Ethical System* demonstrates the need for establishing and elaborating a moral framework for globalisation and a system of justification. McMurtry focuses on the underlying values that drive globalisation including what he refers to as the value program in which assertions such as "We must compete in the new global marketplace" are seen as given, natural, unalterable. As McMurtry states, in value programme, all people enact its prescriptions and functions as presupposed norms of what they should do. All assume its value designations and value exclusions as given. They seek only to climb its ladder of available positions to achieve their deserved reward as their due. Lives are valued, or not valued, in terms of the system's differentials and measurements. All fulfil its specified roles without question and accept its costs, however widespread, as unavoidable manifestations of reality.

According to McMurtry, the value program underlying the global market system consists of "efficiency of factor allocation, comparative advantage, increased export earnings, rise in market share, increased GDP performance and annual incomes and, above all, vastly increased returns on investment in an area of chronic under investment". The master assumption is that the global market system is superior to any other. The underlying premise is that the private sector is efficient and the government is inefficient. Thus, "whatever the market does is good and whatever government does is bad, unless it can be shown to serve the market".

The value programme of globalisation is a closed system of choice, which the acquisition of money drives society and the impact on the civil commons is either ignored or discounted. But as McMurtry asks, if the common interest is not protected and advanced by the stale, then the state loses the justification for its existence.

Operating Issues

As Daniel Bell has put it, globalisation has created conditions under which governments look too small in the face of big issues (e.g. global warming) and at the same time governments sometimes look too big to deal with small problems, as for instance when it comes to local environment and ecology, it is the local people who are more suited to deal with those problems than big government.

In practice today the traditional operating style of government as sovereign authority functioning on the basis of formal authority in an exclusivist and insular fashion has come under questioning. Most problems today tend to elude the monopolistic grasp of government and need interlinking with many other agencies, be it the private sector or the civil society, i.e. domestic governance. When it comes to conducting external relations — economic, diplomatic, environmental or financial — government has to operate in association with many important agencies and institutions at the international plane (e.g. WTO). Hence, it has been observed by public administration analysts that contemporary public administration has to have 'networking' capacity — the ability to function in association with many agencies and organisations both at home and abroad.

Capacity-building

Against this background of complexity and networking, capacity-building in government has been considered to be of paramount necessity. How to interact with international organisations and agencies, how to involve citizens and the private sector in the domestic sphere — these are important issues that need to be brought in as new public management issues for which a new breed of public administrators need to be specially groomed up. Globalisation has consequences for the management of public affairs in both 'developed' and 'developing countries' and these are not the same for both. Because of resources constraint and 'dependence' on the 'developed' countries, as also weak administrative managerial capacity, the developing countries are likely to suffer more and lose rather than gain as the processes of globalisation would be unfolding themselves in the years come. Some balancing act would therefore have to be institutionalized to lend support to 'developing' countries and help them compete in an unequal playing field.

CHAPTER 25

Postmodernism and Public Administration

Public administration, since its formative years, has always been receptive to new ideas and explanations in order to delve deep into the structures and processes of institutional governing systems. In the process, it has drawn eclectically on many disciplines and modes of thinking. Postmodernism emerged as a massive thought-shaking, overarching vision that influenced almost all branches of human knowledge. Public administration reacted to the new 'paradigm' rather late and, that too, rather half-heartedly. There is not much literature dealing comprehensively on postmodernist public administration as such. At the same time, this line of thinking has drawn the attention of many public administration scholars, particularly in the USA. Most postmodern scholarship within public administration can be traced to Denmark, The Netherlands and USA. Interestingly, the organisation theorists have been more receptive to the broad formulations of postmodernism whereas, the public administration scholars have been much less receptive to the new trend.

MODERNITY

Postmodernism is not easy to define. One has to understand the meaning of 'modernity' before trying to grasp the meaning of 'postmodernism'. Modernity with its roots in European Enlightenment had produced a post-medieval civilisation culture based on science, secular humanism (not God but Man is the author of his destiny) and progressivism (the world is changing toward better future led by science and reason). Modernism pervaded every aspect of human endeavour — be it scientific pursuit, cultural studies, or social analysis. For more than a century and a half, the social analysts have been preoccupied with modernity and the characteristic features of modern society. There were famous original master analysts such as Marx, Durkheim and Max Weber. As it came to be defined, modernity stood for rationalization, specialisation and bureaucratisation, centralisation and industrialisation. Science and rationalisation were privileged over any other human knowledge forms, closing as it were the myriad options of knowledge creations in history. The organisational hallmarks of modernity were posed as the industrial corporation and the bureaucratic welfare state. Economic and social developments were construed to have been the products of 'rational' use of resources and application of advanced 'scientific' knowledge.

POSTMODERNISM

Postmodernism is much like a pointer without precise content — at best an exciting new way of looking at the 'objective' world. There is clear indication in postmodernist thinking that the previous cultures and the philosophical advances are at an end and something else is emerging to take its place. Postmodernist ethos resists unified, all-encompassing and universally valid explanations — the grand narratives. Thus incredulity to meta-narratives (like, for instance, class conflict as the motor of progress, or bureaucracy as the most rational organisation etc.) is at the core of postmodernist thinking. Postmodernism respects difference and celebrates the local and the particular at the expense of the illusory universal. Modernity is associated with the uses of science and technology that are credited with bringing in an era of unprecedented industrial productivity, faster transport and communication, spread of representative democracy and complex web of bureaucratic governments. Postmodernists are not much enamoured about all these; rather they point out the darker sides such as instead of liberation of mankind, the growth processes, in their view, have brought in oppression, repression and depletion (like vanishing rain forests and fast depletion of biodiversity). As Scott (1998) commented, a strong state with a well-organised bureaucracy imposes upon society the rigid scientific categories and bureaucracy-designed simplifications that characterise the modernisation discourse.

Cognitive Relativism

Science, the postmodernists argue, seeks out 'truth' on the basis of 'facts'. But, in their view, science is just one of the many ways to find out meaning in this world — one among many other equally deserving 'discourses'. Facts are not neutral; they are social constructions made and maintained by discourse. The postmodernists talk of many discourses that go to constitute multiple realities. Hence postmodernism favours celebration of multiplicity of cultures, discourses and knowledge. Methodologically, thus, post-modernists promote 'cognitive relativism' that de-privileges science.

Much of the theoretical inspirations of postmodernism are drawn from the terse and sometime, abstruse writings of great contemporary European philosophers like Foucault, Derrida and Laclau. Foucault's concepts of 'power' and 'government' have been influential in breaking away from the modernist notion of power as an institutional fix; instead it is something that permeates all spheres of life. Following Foucault, the postmodernists would look at power as 'strategic possibilities of variance' putting actors in relationships, developing through 'discourse' in terms of speech. The concept of 'government', an innovative thought which Foucault formulated after considerable historical studies, has now been partly pre-empted by the modern-day 'governance' theorists, very inadequately though. Turning to Derrida, his ideas on language are extremely helpful in understanding 'signifiers in ambiguous structures, always in play, vibrating and under change'. It is therefore futile to search for 'general truth'. One can at best aim at interpretation concerning 'how knowledge is constituted, oriented towards ambiguity and the unsettled'.

The other famous philosopher is Laclau who, following this line of reasoning, treats language as a structure, a form and not a substance: 'The meaning of a word is not to be found in the physical referent but its meaning in our heads'. Relational and meaningful 'totalities' should therefore be analysed as 'discourses'; the totality is a combination of linguistic and extra-linguistic components.

The postmodernists have been staunch critics of the modern, rationalistic model of the actor and the public organisation. For instance, the much-vaunted bureaucratic efficiency has been sought to be 'deconstructed'. The argument has been that it is a social construct, as efficiency is culture specific — modernist, Weberian and linked to enhancement of production. Efficiency is privileged in a society that lays emphasis on 'control'—a phenomenon liked by the modernists but not by the postmodernists. This kind of 'deconstruction' helps to understand what lies under seemingly well-established categories like bureaucratic efficiency.

Methodologically, postmodernists have been characterised as 'social constructivists'. As against 'fundamentalism', social constructivism's stance on 'objective knowledge' has been that, unlike the Durkheimian and modernist line of argument (facts are measurable and quantifiable and as something being there unrelated to the observer), the world around us is understandable as an ongoing discussion of our subjective perceptions of social conditions. The other important methodological point to note is that the postmodernists give preference to hermeneutic analysis, contextual and inductive reasoning as against modernist positivism, empiricism and deductive logic. Modernists' attempts at generalisation, synthesis and prediction are replaced by exceptions, difference and indeterminacy. As Farmer has explained this point, many postmodernists focus on the conditions of the marginalised, the oppressed and the peripheral; by contrast the modernists to a large degree seek the governors, the powerful and the liberated.

In this context, Fox and Miller deserve special mention for their fairly comprehensive presentation of the postmodernist version of public administration. Briefly, in their *Postmodern Public Administration* the focus has significantly shifted from the logic of the bureaucratic system to broader democratic consequences of the system for the citizenry. Following Habermassian discourse theory, a model of authentic discourse has been presented in the interest of active citizenry functioning as worthy participant-agents in public affairs. At the core of Fox and Miller analysis is a deep dissatisfaction with the 'loop model' of democracy: It is essentially an input-output-feedback understanding of democratic decision-making with dividing lines between politics and administration and the idea of the neutral public employee having the voter as a client to serve.

The plea is for authentic and sincere discourse — for the development of inter-associational form of democracy through 'extra bureaucratic policy networks and other formations'. To quote Fox and Miller, "When community is reduced to a series of otherwise atomized individuals brought together usually by the coincidence of their consumptive activity, the community does not develop political skills...meeting-goers are not participants". Participation in authentic discourse requires 'warrants for discourse'. Trust and intentionality — basic orientation towards problem-solving — are the prerequisites of involvement for which, on the part of administration, there has to be attentiveness and ability to listen that makes for 'creative engagement'.

Postmodernist Public Administration

As discussed above, the postmodernist trend is rather recent in public administration study and research. It will require a full-length book to present a comprehensive account of Public Administration's recent turn to Postmodernism. There is, however, no unifying, integrated postmodern approach to Public Administration. The use of the term 'postmodern' in conjunction with public administration can be traced to Hummel (1989) and Dennard (1989). Hummel looked at postmodern organisation, whereas Dennard wrote about radical humanism in a satirical narrative form. Marshall and White (1990), in their attempt to 'deconstruct' the Blacksburg Manifesto (constitutionalist interpretation to counter the market trend), introduced postmodernism as a method of public administration analysis. Farmer (1997, 1999) has drawn attention to the limitations of the 'grand narratives' in public administration such as Taylorist efficiency, specialisation and aspirations to science of public administration. His focus is on the voices marginalised in public administration —women, minorities etc. and he looks ahead toward radical listening to the 'other' that might bring about the liberation of the marginalized voices.

Concluding Observations

This is a thumbnail sketch of the rich contributions that have been forthcoming in recent times from a group of innovative front line researchers in public administration. From the standpoint of enrichment of the discipline of public administration, postmodernism opens up newer possibilities of disciplinary growth. There is considerable scope for carefully following the extremely challenging and innovative methodological and substantive thoughts of postmodernism — especially those relating to the understanding of 'truth', working out alternatives to the conventional bureaucratic paradigm, building up of authentic, participative, citizen-centric democracy and focusing on the marginalised and the exceptional in the context of contemporary societal fragmentation. The postmodernist outlook has the potentiality of giving birth to an altogether new public administration that would break away from the age old, conventional Weberianism and bring back the 'public' in public administration. Its other contribution lies in the demystification of bureaucratic rationalism and in forcefully exposing the latent designs of the corporate interests surreptitiously trying to co-opt public interests.

From the perspective of the Third World, postmodernism has been characterised as basically 'Western' and 'ethnocentric', since the evolutionary trajectory from 'modernity' to 'post modernity' refers to the specific historical developmental path of the Western developed nations. The other major criticism has been that postmodernism's rejection of 'grand narratives'is directed toward the rejection and undermining of Marxist socio-historical theory keeping in view the historical evolutionary specificities of the post-communist western world. At the same time, postmodernist's emphasis on micro-movements and the problems of the marginalized, the women and others has lent considerable intellectual support to the study of such social movements. Another aspect of postmodernist discourse on authentic, communitarian and participative democracy has direct relevance to the world-wide movement today towards decentralisation and civil society and people's empowerment.

REFERENCES

1. D.J.Farmer (1997) 'Derrida, deconstruction and public administration', American Behavioural Scientist, 41(1), September.
2. ....(1999) 'Public Administration Discourse: A Matter of Style', Administration and Society, 31 (3).
3. C.J. Fox and H.T. Miller (1995) Postmodern Public Administration, Towards Discourse, Sage Publications, London.
4. O.C. McSwite (1997) Legitimacy in Public Administration: A Discourse Analysis, Sage Publications, London.
5. C. S. King and C. Strivers (1998) Government Is Us: Public Administration in an Anti-government Era, Sage Publications, London.
6. James C. Scott (1998) Seeing like a State. How Certain Schemes to Improve the Human Condition Failed,Yale University Press, New Haven.
7. Frank De Zwart (2002) 'Administrative Practice and Rational Inquiry in Postmodern Public Administration Theory', Administration and Society, 34 (5).

Chapter 26

Civil Society and Governance

In recent years, there has been a widespread acknowledgement of civil society's role in improving governance. United Nations Millennium Project Report *(Investing in Development)*, for example, claims that 'strong civil society engagement and participation are crucial to effective governance'.

Background

In the long tradition of Western social and political thinking, since the enlightened philosophers, especially Montesquieu, Hegel and Tocqueville, the concept of civil society has been quite an influential theme for centuries. In the post-World War II situation, reflecting on the great bloodbath of the century, many social thinkers used this concept (civil society) in their inquiry into the causes why some democracies survived the Great Depression while others collapsed and gave rise to Fascism. Almond and Verba's classic *The Civic Culture* can be cited as one of the major examples in the 1960s. During the last two decades the resurgence of the concept of civil society can be attributed, to a great extent, to the inspiration aroused by the civil societies' resistance to the post-totalitarian regimes in Eastern Europe and the former Soviet Union. The democratic transition in these areas as well as in many Third World coun ries during these two decades — what Huntington has characterised as the 'third wave' — inspired scholars and researchers to probe further into the makings and functioning of civil society.

Two Modes of Social Development

In this context, mention may be made of two contrasting modes of social development: *one,* state or government-led development and *two,* society or community-led development. Historically, the state in Western societies got involved in 'welfare' activities during the exploitative phase of early Industrial Revolution in the late eighteenth century. The 'welfare state' concept struck roots to ameliorate the adverse social situations created by Industrial Revolution. Similar kind of lead role was taken by the state/government in the Third World countries as they emerged out of the exploitative clutches of colonial rule in the post-World War II situation.

The other contrasting mode of social development has been the community or society-led welfare and development activities. Both in the West and in Third World societies, there has historically been a fairly well-accepted society or community-centric self- development tradition. The Church in the West has long been associated with social development activities along with numerous voluntary associations such as the Rotaries and other organisations. In India, Gandhi's 'Sevagram' model and Tagore's 'Shriniketan' model of rural development have been typical of community-based people's autonomous social development enterprises. Similarly, when Julius Nyerere— the famous African (Tanzanian) leader — said that 'people cannot be developed, they can only develop themselves', he was placing emphasis on the importance of community's internal strength as the firm basis of authentic development. This train of thought was later conceptualised and put into actual operative practices in local development by eminent field researchers and social analysts like Robert Chambers and David Korten — Chambers in his idea of 'putting the last first' and Korten in his concept of 'people-centric development'.

Contemporary Background

For a variety of reasons, state's traditional role as the primary developer, organiser and supplier of most social services has been undergoing a sea change in recent times. In many countries, state-driven welfare systems and government-sponsored associations going down to grass-roots level were used to build trust and legitimacy around policies and programmes that were essentially developed at central level. The styles of governance are undergoing major changes in recent decades under the impact of rising public demands for social services that the state alone is unable to meet successfully. Also, there are strong socio-economic forces challenging the hegemonic position of the state as the sole decider and supplier of social services. The recent 'globalisation' trend has further fuelled the urge to look for alternative ways of making provision for social services beyond the known exclusive role of the traditional supplier — the state. Liberalisation policies under the impact of what is called 'neo-liberalism' have widened the roles, responsibilities and burdens of social actors outside the state. They have led to a refocusing of the relationship between state and non-state actors in shaping and implementing public policy. Also, in the post-Cold War period, the collapse of the Soviet system led to a resurgence of the idea of 'civil society' as a necessary social space for building and sustaining democracy through the capacity building of liberty-loving citizens as the bulwark of a strong democratic state.

The prominence of 'civil society' can also be traced to successive waves of democratisation, beginning in Latin America and Eastern Europe and spreading across the developing world. Civil society has been characterised as acting as an increasingly crucial agent for limiting authoritarian government and working toward popular empowerment. The other salutary aspects relate to reinforce democratic accountability and improve the quality and inclusiveness of governance. Civil society's role in the provision of public goods and social services in supplementation of state/government provision and its particular role during civic emergencies like floods and earthquakes have received universal acknowledgement and acclaim.

Against this background, civil society has been considered to be an essential prerequisite of 'good governance'. Its contribution has been particularly recognised in nurturing an ethical and open democracy by working steadfastly toward ensuring transparency, effectiveness, openness, responsiveness and accountability; the rule of law; and the acceptance of diversity and pluralism. Civil society has also a glorious track record of espousing the special interests of the excluded sections of society — the marginalised, the poor and the women.

Definitional Problem

There are numerous definitions of 'civil society' and the different interpretations are often due to alternative social and political philosophies that are not always easy to reconcile. If we focus mainly on political and sociological conceptions, politically conceived, civil society is rooted in the Anglo-American tradition of liberal-democratic theory which identifies civic institutions and political activity as an essential component of the emergence of a particular type of political society based on the principles of citizenship, rights, democratic representation and the rule of law. The sociological conception of civil society is that of an intermediate associational realm situated between the state on the one side and the basic building blocks of society on the other (individuals, families and firms), inhabited by social organisations with some degree of autonomy and voluntary participation on the part of their members.

These two notions are often used simultaneously in confusing ways. The political definition is often criticised on the ground that (a) it tends to assume that all societies - no matter how diverse in cultural, social and political terms — are destined to follow the path of liberal democratisation and (b) even granting a close nexus, historically speaking, between civil society and the evolutionary process of liberal democratisation in the West, the latter idea itself has a variety of versions and inherent problems in practice.

There are also problems with the sociological definition. For example, should the Mafia and other such secret and criminal societies be included within 'civil society' umbrella? Two conceptions of civil society dominate modern social and political thought and both are rooted in liberal democratic theory. It was Adam Smith who first articulated the classical bourgeois understanding of it as a market-organised sphere of necessity which is driven by the self-interested motion of individual proprietors but Smith drew heavily on Locke's earlier position that civil society is constituted by property, labour, exchange and consumption.The rapid development of markets soon encouraged bourgeois political economists to theorise civil society as an autonomous self-governing sphere which can transform individual strivings for particular advantage into the public good. Hegel built his theory of the state and civil society on this understanding and Marx's development of Hegel continues to inform the thinking of much of the left.

The second and related strand of liberal thinking is Tocqueville's notion that civil society is an intermediate sphere of voluntary association sustained by an informal culture of self-organisation and cooperation. His finding that Americans are uniquely disposed to associate in defence of local interests has rested at the heart of the effort to reconcile liberty with equality for some time. This view informed a good deal of the civil society literature of Eastern Europe and, supplemented by Madison, has become integrated with pluralism and communitarianism in the United States. Dwelling on his 19th century American experience, Tocqueville placed maximum value on 'experiences of association helping to cultivate the capacities of citizens'. As he observed, 'In democratic countries, knowledge of how to combine is the mother of all other forms of knowledge; on its progress depends that of all the others' (Tocqueville, 1835).

Again, autonomy and voluntary participation — the hall marks of civil society — may not be present in many state-dependent organisations In many third world countries, groups and organisations that form part of civil society operate secretly either because they are declared illegal, or because they suffer from systematic state repression. Should these be included as civil society organisations?

The idea of 'civil society' is intrinsically linked to liberal democratic discourse espousing plurality of social views. As such, the notion of civil society is associated with certain characteristics such as voluntary participation and separation and autonomy from the state. Social organisations in the real world only embody these characteristics to varying degrees: the boundaries between state and civil society are often blurred, the two organisational spheres may overlap and individuals may play roles in both sectors.

In this context, Larry Diamond's very comprehensive definition of civil society is worth our quotation:"Civil society is . . . the realm of organised social life that is voluntary, self-generating, (largely) self-supporting and autonomous from the state, bound by a legal order or set of shared rules. It is distinct from 'society' in general in that it involves citizens acting collectively in a public sphere to express their interests, passions and ideas, exchange information, achieve mutual goals, make demands on the state and hold the state officials accountable. Civil society is an intermediary entity standing between the private sphere and the state.

Civil society is concerned with public rather than private ends. . . civil society relates to the state in some way but does not aim to win formal power." (Diamond 1994)

Civil Societies in Developing Societies

Civil societies in developing countries fall into many categories. Distinctions need to be made between 'modern' interest groups such as trade unions, professional and business associations and 'traditional' organisations based on kinship, ethnicity, culture or religion; between those organisations with specifically political aspirations and roles and those which are either outside politics or only intermittently involved; between associations which accept the political status quo and those which seek to transform it by changing the political regime or redefining the political community; between highly organised and well resourced interest groups such as trade unions and business/professional organisations and other forms of organisation such as NGOs or community associations which have different operating procedures and organisational objectives; between organisations which are intended to protect and extend the narrow interests of their members and those with a wider social or political agenda; and between organisations with extensive membership and those with quite limited membership (but sometimes with broad support from non-members).

Roles and Activities

In terms of their roles and activities, civil society organisations vary widely such as (a) those engaged in mobilisation of social actors (women, labour, dalits etc.); (b) others representing the interests of specific groups in government-society interactions; (c) some others monitoring and evaluating government activities on behalf of society; (d) many others who are engaged in developmental activities — commonly known as 'development NGOs'. Civil society organisations contribute in diverse ways to socio-political development such as seeking to transform an authoritarian rule into a democratic one, to further deepen an existing democratic regime. Improving equity or stimulating particular kinds of developmental action which enhance the well-being of the poor and the socially marginalised would be the objective of many development NGOs. Civil society groups may have wide or narrow interests depending on the respective charters and composition of these groups.

Civil society organisations play an active and constructive part in political life. They help foster fairer, more honest, transparent, democratic and accountable governance which is more tolerant of diversity and pluralism. They can be a role model to others by practicing this sort of governance themselves within their own organisations. They can create opportunities for the people to gain participatory experience that inculcates the skills needed to make such governance a reality.

Civil Society and Governance

The contribution made by civil society to good governance is essentially concerned with the means by which organised interests seek to influence and engage with state institutions. In doing so, they usually help to strengthen state legitimacy and relations of trust between public officials and ordinary citizens.

There are many ways of looking at the relationships between civil society and state or governance. One influential view of the positive democratising and developmental role of civil society is linked to Robert Putnam's well-known research on 'social capital' (1993). In his path breaking research on comparative study of Italy's regional governments, Putnam comes to the interesting conclusion that 'economics does not predict civics, but civics does predict economics, better than economics itself'. He actualises on 'civicness', or a sense of civic community — the creation and sustenance of it, in his view, is provided by 'a dense network of secondary associations' which are the main source of 'social capital'. To quote Putnam, "Participation in civic organisations inculcates skills of cooperation as well as a sense of shared responsibility for collective endeavours. Moreover, when individuals belong to 'cross-cutting' groups with diverse goals and members, their attitudes will tend to moderate as a result of group interaction and cross pressures." In his view, citizen participation in different social groups such as parent-teacher associations, chorus groups and other civic groups generates 'mutual reciprocity, the resolution of dilemmas of collective action and the broadening of social identities', all of which together contribute directly and indirectly to social cohesion and democratisation. Putnam can surely be called a Tocquevillian, as he harks back to Tocqueville who in his classic *Democracy in America,* as earlier pointed out, attached considerable democratic value to associative communal life inhering in civil society.

Apart from its 'democratising' worth and democracy-strengthening value, four major areas can be identified where civil society can positively contribute to 'good governance'. These are: (a) public policy and decision-making; (b) transparency and information; (c) social change through social activism; (d) supplementing government effort; (e) working for social justice.

1. Civil society organisations can play a role in mobilising particular constituencies to participate more fully in politics and public affairs. Poor and socially disadvantaged groups — marginal farmers, sharecroppers, landless labour, artisans, informal sector workers, urban slum dwellers, disabled people and socially oppressed women — are usually much less able to exercise influence over public policy and resource allocations. Higher rates of political participation often result from institutional innovations — such as democratic decentralisation — designed to promote local involvement in decision-making. But such innovations will only be effective if grassroots organisations and social movements can organise the poor and articulate their demands at local and higher levels.
2. Civil organisations contribute to better governance by improving transparency and increasing the availability of information about the making and implementation of government policy. Activities from within civil society to promote these goals include the discovery, publication and dissemination of information about issues on legislation, legal provisions, public expenditure allocations, the implementation of policy and programmes

and special enquiries. Such information may be directly published and circulated by groups within civil society for wider public knowledge.

3. The civil society groups often successfully mobilise citizens to put pressure on governments to achieve various social goals such as changing forest development policy, transferring erring officials, providing housing and medical aid to the poor and slum dwellers and so on. These are examples of a more activist role of civil society, in which civic actors back up information and dissemination activities with mobilisation and public advocacy work.
4. Civil society organisations can contribute (and they actually do so) by working directly with government in shaping, financing and delivering public services in a variety of ways. These can take the form of public-private partnerships in which civil society organisations work closely with state institutions in designing and providing health and educational services, by mobilising funds from among client groups and other sources, by providing services directly and by monitoring quality and coverage. In some cases this can create the basis for synergy, in which state institutions acquire greater legitimacy and improve their performance by developing responsive working relationships with civil society that draw on reservoirs of social capital built up in local communities.

The fourth area where civil society can make a contribution to good governance is in the field of social justice, rights and the rule of law. There are two main dimensions to this:

- The *advocacy role* of specialist human rights organisations in pressing for the implementation of existing laws, plus fresh legislative initiatives and institutional reforms to improve the functioning and accountability of state policing and security organs;
- The *protective role* of civil society in sheltering individuals threatened by repressive states, defending their rights through the official legal process, for example by providing paralegal services to groups of citizens who do not have ready access to the courts (such as Association for Protection of Democratic Rights).

Civil Society in the Context of Globalisation[1]

The grassroots action we have been witnessing on the streets of Porto Alegre, in cyberspace, outside the headquarters of the World Bank and IMF and on the roads and railways to Davos is emerging in direct response to a perception that, increasingly, important decisions affecting people's lives and well-being are being made in non-transparent ways in supranational institutions that are not accountable to citizens and not accessible to citizen engagement. Decisions about trade rules, intellectual property rights, macro-economic restructuring policies, privatisation of vital public services and debt relief are made behind closed doors in ways that are largely perceived to be undemocratic.

1 This section draws extensively, with suitable modifications, on the outstanding speech delivered by Dr. Kumi Naidoo, CEO and Secretary General, CIVICUS, at the World Bank Headquarter as Presidential Fellow of the World Bank on 10th February, 2003. The author is grateful to Dr. Naidoo for his kind permission to use his speech in this discussion.

It is against this backdrop that the notion of 'civil society' has re-entered mainstream discourse. Civil society is, of course, not a new concept, but it is one that has been re-discovered over the past decade with this rise in citizen activism. What the World Social Forum and recent global civil society gatherings have come to represent for many people around the world are spaces where the voices of average citizens 'count' in discussions around social, political and economic justice.They are venues where people and groups who feel increasingly alienated from the prevailing global system can join together to explore alternative visions for a more ethical form of globalisation that works for the benefit of average people, rather than simply for the benefit of powerful interests.

Since the Rio Earth Summit, the civil society has come into its own as an important political, social and economic actor. The last decade has witnessed a dramatic growth in the number of citizen groups, as well as in their capacity, scope, reach, public profile and influence. This 'global associational revolution,' as it has been called, is being driven by the same forces that are producing globalisation — democratisation. the spread of new technologies and global integration of various forms.

Historically much of the work of civil society organisations or CSOs, has occurred at a micro level, where they are involved in providing important services to vulnerable communities in areas as diverse as health care, education and professional training, legal advice, humanitarian relief, women's empowerment, technical assistance in agriculture and environmental protection and so on. Civil society groups have often stepped into the uneasy vacuum of post-conflict situations and have compensated for the state (not without debate) in the growing number of instances where vital public services have been rolled back due to macro-economic reforms. Many CSOs have become actively engaged in advocacy work, campaigning and policy-making. Public campaigns on issues such as landmines, debt relief and the international criminal court have had a definable impact.

As civil society has matured, its credibility with outside audiences has grown. Many governments seek to harness the expertise and local knowledge of civil society groups in policy-making. High-profile civil society groups, particularly those working around environmental issues, have developed a certain 'brand recognition'; their endorsements or criticisms of business practices, for example, carry weight with the public and have become an important force with which the private sector must reckon.

Challenges Facing Civil Society

Accordingly, civil society is attracting a new level of scrutiny in its role as a major public actor. It is being forced to grapple with both external and internal challenges, from those who are seeking to make civil society stronger and more credible, as well as from those who question its right to play certain roles. I would like to touch briefly upon five of these challenges.

The first is a challenge of power and power imbalances within civil society. The sector is vibrant and extremely diverse. It encompasses both major transnational NGOs with multi-million dollar operating budgets and tiny citizen-based organisations with highly constrained resources, access to information and capacity. It embraces highly structured groups such as trade unions alongside loose issue-based social movements. While this diversity adds to the sector's richness, it also throws up fundamental questions about whose voices are heard and in which venues, how resources are accessed and distributed and who is speaking for whom.

The second challenge internal to civil society

is about bridging narrow interests and broader goals. Many civil society actors are committed to advance a specific issue, whether this involves protecting rainforests, promoting fair labour practices or advancing women's rights. While recent civil society activity has been noteworthy for the alliances that have been formed among groups with different areas of interest, there remains a type of 'silo mentality' which prevents CSOs from working across areas of speciality, toward common goals.

For example, dialogue between human rights organisations and development organisations has historically been weak and many potentially productive synergies have evaded us. With many human rights organisations now embracing social and economic rights and with many development organisations adopting a rights-based approach to their work, it is an opportune time to bridge this divide. The dichotomy between the world of volunteering (defined as the provision of direct services to communities in need) and the world of social activism (defined as those that are more concerned with structural and policy changes) remains a challenge. We also need to create an environment where, for example, NGOs rise to defend workers' rights of association in cases where trade union rights are threatened and where trade unions vocally defend the rights of NGOs.

A third internal challenge for civil society is to articulate a coherent vision for a more just and equitable global system. One of the frequent criticisms of the so-called 'anti-globalisation' movement, is that it is *against* everything imaginable, but not *for* anything discernible. Although many within the movement are working proactively for social and economic justice, civil society is challenged to move beyond debate and *ad hoc* mobilisations and to formulate a strategy for achieving its vision. The core issue, however, may not be an absence of alternative visions but rather the fact that the world's powerful governments appear unwilling to engage with these alternatives.

The fourth challenge is one that emanates from outside civil society. The allegation is made that citizen activism threatens to undermine democratic systems by 'short-circuiting' established procedures for decision-making. This kind of argument is short-sighted and oblivious of the fact that an active, engaged citizenry is essential for a healthy democratic society. There is a wrong notion that needs to be vehemently resisted that elections equal democracy, that a victory at the ballot box is a blank check to rule without any interface and dialogue with citizens in between election periods. To reduce democracy to the singular act of voting once every four or five years is clearly an error. Civic activism complements democratic practices and makes them more effective by drawing citizens more fully into public life and providing a constant check on official accountability. Engagement with citizen voices leads to more effective policies that better address the concerns of primary and secondary stakeholders, that integrate innovative ideas and knowledge from the local level and that result in greater impact and ownership within communities.

The fifth challenge is perhaps the most complex of all and is heard both inside and outside civil society: the challenge of legitimacy and the related issues of transparency, representation and accountability.

Challenges to civil society's legitimacy come from many quarters. They are often voiced by national political leaders and occasionally by prominent voices at global institutions. It is frequently said that civil society groups don't represent the views of anyone but themselves and that if they are accountable at all. It is usually 'upward' to their funders, rather than 'downward' to those they purportedly serve.

Legitimacy cannot be taken for granted and must continuously be earned and civil society groups are taking up this challenge head-on. Self-regulation mechanisms such as codes of ethics and standards of excellence have been adopted at the national level by civil society in several countries; a culture of transparency in governance structures is also gaining strength across the sector. Civil society groups work to derive mandates and legitimacy for their activities through extensive consultative processes.

There is also a powerful accountability factor at play with the functioning of CSOs which can be called the principle of perform or perish.' Not a single cent secured to undertake CSO activities is secured on the basis of obligation. Whether funding is derived from a government department, individual, foundation, business organisation or multi-lateral institution, resources will not continue to be available if civic organisations are not performing on the basis of their vision, mission and objectives.

The issue of civil society legitimacy is a valid one and need not be lightly brushed aside — particularly when it is voiced with an eye to building up the long-term credibility and effectiveness of civil society as an actor. All too frequently, however, the critique is lodged by those who would dismiss the right of civil society groups to give voice to citizen concerns and to engage in decision-making processes.

Civil Society and the 'Democracy Deficit'

It is rapidly becoming a truism that the old notion of government as the sole repository of knowledge and wisdom is breaking down in an era of globalisation and with the emergence of a devastating 'democracy deficit' in several local and national contexts and certainly at the global level. Surveys reveal declining levels of citizen trust in political institutions. In many democratic systems 'form' has largely overtaken the 'substance' of democracy: elections nlay be held but fewer and fewer people are choosing to vote and the meaningful interface between citizens and the elected is minimal between election periods. Affiliation with traditional political parties is on the decline as the parties themselves are characterised by a lack of internal democracy or fail to address issues that citizens believe are important. The influence of moneyed interests in many political systems is also turning citizens away from traditional engagement in favour of participation.

Although faith in traditional political institutions is waning, this should not be taken as a sign of citizen apathy. On the contrary, people are finding new and more direct ways to get involved in public life and decision-making — marking a shift from representative democracy to what is often called participatory democracy. Citizens are arguing for a new notion of governance that requires political leadership to engage with citizenry in ways that allow for ongoing input into decision-making and policy formation. Finally, civil society groups are slowly carving out a more active role in actual decision-making processes, as witnessed in their direct participation over the last decade in UN conferences with some national governments including civil society participants in their delegations. Certain innovative international commissions involve civil society groups as equal stakeholders in policy-making, rather than in an after-the-fact consultative role.

To understand the silence of most citizens, one should look more deeply at the discourse around social exclusion. In the coming decades humanity should judge itself not on the basis of the progress made by the most privileged sections but on the basis of the progress made by those that have been historically marginalised.

This includes not only uncontested minority communities, such as people living with HIV/AIDS, people with disabilities, racial, ethnic, religious and cultural minorities, indigenous people, people with alternative sexual orientations, people who are not literate and so on. It also should include constituencies not often thought of as minorities *per se.* Young people are becoming increasingly alienated from public life. We must also consider older people and take note of the levels of alienation they feel and the fact that we deprive ourselves of their learned wisdom. We must acknowledge the scandalous fact that, after decades of activism for full gender equality, women still occupy on average less than 10% of leadership positions in government and business.What does it say about the quality of our democracy when women are so heavily under-represented even in long-standing democratic countries, let alone in those that are fledgling democracies? When we add up this all, it becomes increasingly difficult to deny that democratic voice does not prevail in public life and that we are facing a serious 'democracy deficit' on multiple levels. It is not being suggested that civil society is intrinsically good and that governments are intrinsically bad. However, it should be recognised that effective democracy needs a vibrant civil society as well as an effective and accountable government. Both face struggles of accountability but they bring a vital diversity to governance and provide complementary and mutual accountability systems. We can anticipate that this arena will always be contested — but this should strengthen democratic practice, rather than weaken it.

Concluding Observations

Civil society has entered the vocabulary of both development politics and development administration. In politics, the nexus between civil society and democracy has been discussed from a variety of points of view (Schmitter, 1997). The general argument has been that civil society functioning has a salutary capacity-building effect on democracy. Also, active civil society and strong democracy has been found to be closely related. The other aspect of civil society's nexus with development administration is relatively under-researched. Only now, mainly inspired by Robert Putnam's research on Italy, administrative researchers are delving deep into the ways civil society organisations. They have been contributing to 'development management', basically at the locality or grass roots level. Government-civil society synergy has thus come to occupy centre stage in contemporary development administration studies, particularly in relation to researches focused on poverty amelioration and accessing public services and government project benefits to the poor, the socially marginalised and the women and children.

REFERENCES

Alexis de Tocqueville, Democracy in America (Vols. I and II) 1835.

Gabriel Almond and Sidney Verba, The Civic Culture: Political Attitudes and Democracy in Five Nations, Princeton University Press, 1963.

Larry Diamond, 'Rethinking Civil Society: Toward Democratic Consolidation', Journal of Democracy, Vol. 5, No. 3 (July 1994).

Larry Diamond et al. (eds.), Consolidating the Third Wave Democracies, Johns Hopkins University Press, 1997.

Philippe Schmitter, 'Civil Society, East and West' in Larry Diamond et al. (eds.) op. cit.

Robert Putnam et al., Making Democracy Work. Princeton University Press, 1993.

Michael Foley and Bob Edwards, 'The Paradox of Civil Society', Journal of Democracy, Vol. 7, No. 3, 1996.

Chapter 27

Right to Information

James Madison writing in 1822 gave eloquent expression to the urgent need for 'popular information' in a democracy. As he said, "A popular government without popular information, or the means of acquiring it, is but a Prologue to a Farce or a Tragedy, or, perhaps both. Knowledge will forever govern ignorance. And a people who mean to be their own Governors, must arm themselves with the power which knowledge gives." Implicit in Madison's remark is the essence of democracy which is rule by the people. It is well known that reality is, however, very different and actually 'ruling' is left to the bureaucracy functioning in tandem with the political group in power. The tradition in the Third World countries has been worse. During colonial rule, the administrative culture had been basically inward-looking, people-avoiding and secrecy-practicing. Even after formal 'Independence', the phenomenon of bureaucratic domination persisted for a variety of reasons — poverty and lack of 'real' citizenship being a major causative factor. Thus, democracy has, in most countries, remained a 'procedural' facade. As it has been rightly said:

"The right to information is a product of both *institutions* and *culture.* Institutions are shaped by laws and the structure of government. Culture is rooted in the history and practice of government as well as in the broader traditional understandings of the accountability of leaders and of what constitutes representation. Culture is often more powerful than formal arrangements, particularly in societies that are undergoing a process of democratic transition and/or whose political systems still reflect traditional social methods of interaction." (UNDP Practical Guide Book on RTI, 2006)

Background: Democracy and RTI

The 'third wave of democracy', to quote Huntington, coupled with the spread of 'governance' philosophy in the last decade of the twentieth century, ushered in a new era of democracy-strengthening along with emphasis on its essential attributes such as 'openness', 'transparency' and 'accountability'. There has been a worldwide trend in recent times toward more openness in the system of governance. Various factors have contributed to the new upsurge for governmental openness. More important among these are changing socio-economic milieu, increased awareness of the public about their rights, the need to have a fully accountable and responsive administration and growing public opinion that views continued practice of bureaucratic secrecy as a potent factor in enhancing the chances of abuse of authority by government functionaries. In most of the countries where large-scale administrative reforms have been attempted recently, emphasis has been laid on liberalising the extent to which details of policy, performance and other information about government activities are made available to the general public.

There is universal recognition now that the people's right to information is the foundation of a healthy and functioning democracy. The cardinal element in the formation of democratic societies — the element most feared and suppressed by totalitarian rulers — has been an informed and active citizenry. Experience tells us that the more the citizens know, the better prepared and more motivated they are to effectively participate in the decisions that affect their lives and property and their physical and economic well-being. The people's right to official information is an indispensable element of a functioning democracy. The ideal of a 'government by the people' presupposes that the people have access to information on matters of public concern in order to effectively exercise its governing power. The free flow of information about the affairs of government paves the way for debate in public policy and fosters accountability in government.

The people's right to official information is also essential in economic life. A free flow of official information results in better government policies. It provides the institutional foundation for a more responsive government planning by enhancing the capacity of the public to provide timely feedback to government. The availability of official information widens the base for the generation of more knowledge about key development issues, not only by researchers and academic institutions, but also by the public at large. It promotes constructive and informed debate between and among government and stakeholders and builds consensus around policy objectives and design. All these promote more informed government interventions supported by a solid and broad-based constituency.

Need for the Right to Information

On the question of why the right to information', apart from what has been stated above, certain strong grounds have been advanced for its promotion. First and foremost, availability of this right makes for the empowerment of the people who would otherwise be ignorant about the processes of governance. Second, the right to information creates conditions for 'open governance' which is the foundation of democracy. By contrast, secrecy in governmental functioning tends to promote corruption and misuse or abuse of public authority. Third, the right to information is an investment in people's trust in government which is the real basis of democratic governance. Fourthly, what J.S. Mill regarded as the educating influence of local government is the product of openness affording access to government departments and documents and thus enabling citizens to acquire knowledge about the goings on in government. Fifth, the right to information, by removing unnecessary secrecy surrounding the decision-making process in government makes the citizens 'co-sharers' in public policy making and administration. This helps improve the quality of overall governance in public interest. Sixth, grassroots democracy — the government at the cutting edge level — becomes much more authentic and people-centric when people participate directly and observes at firsthand how the government functions in reality. Participative governance is a sure safeguard against 'secret' government. Last but not the least, people's right to information brings about a major change in the 'quality' of government by making it really 'public'. People's easy access to information about governmental operations as a matter of 'right' makes these operations open and transparent. It ensures accountability and responsiveness to people's needs and demands.

UN and Donor Agencies

Currently, international pressure, particularly from

the UN and donor agencies, has been mounting on country governments for making governance more open, transparent and accountable.The UN General Assembly's Resolution 59 (1) adopted at the 65th Plenary Meeting on December 14, 1946 reads as under:

"**Freedom of Information is a fundamental** human right and the touchstone for all freedoms to which the United Nations is consecrated."

In this connection, the provision of another historic declaration — the Universal Declaration of Human Rights — adopted by the UN General Assembly on December 10, 1948 is worth our quotation:

"Everyone has the right to freedom of opinion and expression; this right includes freedom to hold opinions without interference and to seek, receive and impart information and ideas through any media and regardless of frontiers (Article 19)."

World Bank Policy

We can quote in this context an excerpt from a paper prepared by the World Bank Information Centre:

"People have a right to information from public institutions and a right to participate in the development policies and projects that affect their lives. Transparency in World Bank operations will help to reduce corruption, not in the least by helping foster a 'demand side' of governance. Key concerns and recommendations related to transparency and corruption:

- The World Bank's **Disclosure Policy** provides an important framework for the timely release of information about the institution's policies and operations. We are pleased that the Bank is reviewing this important policy in 2007 and urge Bank management to require in-depth public consultations on the policy document in the coming months.
- The Bank should subscribe to the **Global Transparency Initiative's 'Transparency Charter for International Financial Institutions'** to show its clear commitment to better governance and accountability.
- **Contract and revenue transparency** is critical to create an environment conducive for civil society and media to monitor revenue-generating projects throughout implementation. This is particularly important in high risk sectors like extractive industries. The GAC framework should explicitly mention the importance of promoting **contract transparency** as a critical step forward to reducing corruption in high-risk sectors and projects. Moreover, the World Bank should adopt the principles put forward by the Publish What You Pay Coalition which is copied below for reference.
- **Greater openness and information disclosure throughout the project cycle is critical** — from project preparation through Board approval to project completion and evaluation. In particular, the release of project supervision and evaluation documents facilitates meaningful civil society monitoring of Bank operations. The Bank should release more information during project implementation to the public and this should be a major area of focus in the forthcoming review of

UNDP Policy[1]

For UNDP, the right to information is a key underpinning for work in democratic governance and is vital for promoting 'open governance' and the accountability of public decision makers as well as for strengthening transparency, participation and the rule of law. The right to information is not only fundamental for an open and democratic society but is a key weapon in the fight against poverty and in accelerating human development. In 2006, over 68 countries had comprehensive laws to facilitate access to state records and many more are in the process of enacting such a legislation. This illustrates the growing recognition on the part of governments of the importance of access to information for enhancing democratic engagement, building confidence in government institutions and strengthening their credibility and effectiveness. However, in many States, including democracies, people are routinely denied access to official information, indeed information that should be in the public domain. Only 32 of the countries in which UNDP is present have laws requiring the disclosure of government records. The UNDP Oslo Governance Centre convened a seminar on the right to information to explore how UNDP can strengthen its support to promoting and protecting the right to information in countries where UNDP is working. The seminar built on several guidance materials and resources that have been developed under UNDP's Access to Information service line, particularly the Practical Guidance Notes on Right to Information Programming and Measuring the Impact of Right to Information Programmes.

Key points that emerged from the seminar are:

1. The right to information is a cross-cutting area that contributes to the overall strengthening of democratic governance, primarily by increasing participation (including CSOs and media), accountability, transparency, access and distribution of power and delivery of public services.
2. The right to information is of vital importance to poor and marginalised people.
3. UNDP can support right to information in a number of ways without necessarily having a dedicated right to information programme but it is critical that right to information is systematically integrated into all programming (not just governance), country office (CO) policy advice and other CO activities such as multi-stakeholder dialogue meetings.
4. There is a real need for COs to develop right to information strategies to support their poverty reduction/governance programming. The Common Country Assessment (CCA) or equivalent should include an analysis of the Access to Information (A2I) context which would inform such strategies
5. Responding to right to information challenges concerns both the 'supply' and 'demand' sides of information. Capacity and capabilities are central factors for both. On the supply side, UNDP can be most directly engaged working upstream. The right to information is a cultural and service delivery issue (like the delivery of other state public goods and services).

CHRI Workshop

Just before the framing of the Right to Information Act by the Government of India, a workshop was organised on the theme by the Commonwealth Human Rights Initiative (CHRI) at New Delhi on September 7, 2001. CHRI's position in this regard was explained 'as a right that was central to the realisation of all other human rights, as a tool for fighting corruption, for ensuring transparency and accountability and most of all for enabling informed participation by the people'.The ideas that came out of the workshop were as follows:

Donor's to look at relevance of Right to Information: - There was a feeling among the participants that the Right to Information was a new area for NGO's and Donor's and these groups need to look at relevance of the Right to Information for their work.

Public Education: - There is a need to build greater awareness on the issue of right to information and take the issue to a wider audience and only then will the government be forced to act. The media should be used in order to develop awareness; in addition Right to Information is also the responsibility of the media. Local media should be used as a channel of delivery, in addition. Donors should come together to inform media to generate demand for information and to supply information.

Supply and Demand of Information: - There was a view that it is necessary to access people's need, one could conduct a user survey to find out what people want, develop a data base of this and ensure these needs are met. All states in the country are taking initiatives in the Information Technology sector, there are many e-governance projects being undertaken. Providing access to information through these means is nothing but giving effect to the right to information. This really is the supply side of the information flow.

Repositioning right to information: - Right to information has been looked at from a legal point of view and we now need to move away from the legal definition and look at the delivery of information. If one were to convince government officials using the language of rights would not be the right approach.

Involvement of the Corporate Sector: - Some of the participants felt that the corporate sector should be brought within the purview of the law on the right to information. Internationally legislations on right to information have referred to only access to government held information, only the South African law on the point tries to bring in the private sector within the purview of the law.

Providing access to relevant information: - There is a need to provide relevant information that people can use, merely providing access to government information that no one can understand will not be useful for anyone. Organisations must get involved in processing information that people can use and this information should be accessible to people in a timely manner. Budget analysis for instance is a very useful exercise, organisations involved in this should do greater advocacy around this issue.

On the issue of Right to Information vis-a-vis the donor community, the following suggestions came up in course of deliberations at the workshop:

1. The Right to Information should be incorporated into their areas of funding.
2. Right to Information will not be effective until and unless people have knowledge of the law and are empowered to use the same, the law will be ineffective, therefore there is a need to spread awareness by including components on right to information into existing programmes.
3. Assessment of information needs of people by various organisations with respect to the work they are associated with is necessary.
4. The donor community should encourage its partners to use the law on right to information to access information and disseminate this to the groups and people they work with.
5. NGO's must act as intermediaries to make information available to people from the government and in this regard should get involved in processing information relevant to people.

6. One of the donors working on issues related to children is keen on incorporating right to information in their work on participatory development involving children.

The Role of NGOs

In creating public awareness and holding the government socially accountable, the NGOs have a major role to play Most innovative approaches to ensure people's access to information have come from the NGOs in developing countries. For instance, in rural Rajasthan it is almost a household word now that the revolutionary zeal shown by the Mazdoor Kisan Shakti Sangthan — a local NGO — brought about remarkable changes in field-level government operations through 'awakening' of the rural masses. It is through the untiring efforts of the MKSS that the 'right to information' grew into a local movement and ultimately Rajasthan Government on public demand came forward with a new legislation on the right to information. MKSS has been highlighting corruption in government expenditure in field projects. It exposes bribery and malfeasance and alleged 'payments' made to labourers and suppliers of construction material. Information is further cross-checked through a system of public hearing - locally called*Jan Sunwais* — which are held face to face and allow workers to testify personally. In this process, the MKSS helps overcome illiteracy and other forms of social backwardness. Through the medium of *Jan Sunwais,* MKSS makes relevant public information accessible to the poor villagers.

Subsequently, the Open Democracy Forum (ODF) in South Africa, learning from the MKSS experiences, concentrated more on creating awareness among the rural masses on similar lines. The ODF was established basically to monitor and support South Africa's access to information law.

Implementation Processes of RTI

Ab initio, there may be genuine difficulties in a country to push through a radical legislative measure like the Right to Information Act. Even if the initial huddles are crossed and a law is enacted, there might be many more impediments to the law's actual implementation.The law itself may be couched in language with numerous provisos to make sure that very little is actually disclosed to the public. Again, there may be too many officers designated for the purpose and the formalities/rules and regulations may be too lengthy and cumbrous to be easily understood and followed by the lay public. More importantly, the bureaucratic mindset has to change from age-old secrecy-proneness to openness. To have a right to information is one thing and to have 'access' to it is another thing. 'Access' means gate-keepers who may be set in such a way that the enjoyment of the 'right' would be extremely problematic in reality. Particularly, to the poor and the socially marginalised sections of society who normally avoid the governmental system or at best approach the system through middlemen, any administrative innovation remains unknown and hence, unusable.

In this context, the implementation processes of the right to information, as depicted clearly in the UNDP Guidelines, are presented in the table:

Implementation of right to information legislation by government involves many activities covering the whole range of issues from 'baseline information' to 'outcome indicators' as shown in the Table on next page.

(a) There has to be clear evidence of institutional reform to facilitate access to information. Proper regulations need to

Baseline assessment			
Example of Baseline information	*Information sources*	*Outputs*	*Example Outcome indicators*
Training programmes for public officials; Managerial arrangements for dealing with access to information including senior level responsibility; Budgetary provision for implementing ac cess to information system; Specialist body charged with overseeing access to information.	Relevant international reports such as Transparency International Corruption Perceptions Index, reports by international financial institutions, polling data; Decisions by the administrative body overseeing access to information; Relevant media coverage.	System in place for monitoring access to information requests; System in place for dealing with appeals impartially and quickly; Requests for information being disposed of in a timely manner; Designated officials in charge of information requests trained and discharging obligations efficiently; Creation of effective administrative appeals body to supplement the courts; Managerial arrangements for dealing with access to information including senior level responsibility; Existence/creation of a specialist body charged with overseeing access to information.	Percentage of requests dealt with in a timely manner in accordance with the law/ regulations/policy; Decisions of appeals bodies where requests are refused; Number of officials trained; Monitoring by public officials of information requests; Disaggregated percentage of requests refused by public agency (an average for the public sector as a whole might conceal high rates of refusal by those agencies of most concern to the poor/ women, i.e. police, Ministry of Health, Ministry of Education).

(b) be framed to support the rights such as charging reasonable fees for petitioning, simplifying application and appeal procedures.

(c) A regular budgetary provision has to be made for implementation — particularly keeping in view the need for information system upgrades and training of both government employees and political leaders.

(d) An agency within the bureaucracy needs to be designated to take the lead on administering the access regime, managing implementation and monitoring access. A specialist office has to be created (i.e. an Information Commissioner) or designated to oversee and/or promote access to information with proper staff and budget.

(e) A specialist, independent office, autonomous and independent of government interference, has to be created or designated to deal with appeals.

(f) A regular system of monitoring implementation of the law needs to be urgently instituted. Records should be kept by relevant department or public body on the number of requests made and granted/refused.What is the average response to an information request? Are responses provided in a timely manner or is delay being used as a means of undermining the law in practice? How effective is the appeal system? If information requests are refused, are there reasons given for the refusal and if so, are these documented and recorded? How many appeals against refusals are made and how many upheld?

(g) At the highest level in government, there has to be clear evidence of awareness of problems of implementation, which are likely to be many and complicated at the outset. Press coverage of the problems should be invited and public debate encouraged.

There are many other intricate operational problems involved in any new system aimed at giving a fair trial to an altogether unfamiliar regime of 'right to information'. Both political will and bureaucratic zeal would be necessary to usher in and sustain this new regime.

Comparative Experiences

As earlier stated, under popular pressure and contemporary democratisation movement throughout the world, openness and transparency in governmental operations have become quite trendy in recent times. Right to Information laws are being enacted in many countries in keeping with the currently prevailing mood.

Sweden was the first to enact a law — Freedom of the Press Act — as early as in 1766. The Act now forms part of the Swedish Constitution under which every citizen has full access to official documents held by public authorities. A detailed list of 'exemptions' to access has been provided in the Secrecy Act of 1980. Information can be withheld on such grounds as national security and foreign relations, public economic interest, privacy, prevention or prosecution of crime etc. 'Open Sweden Campaign' is the latest move in that country to 'encourage openness coordinated by representatives from the national government; county councils, municipalities and trade unions with a view to increasing public sector transparency, raising the level of public knowledge and awareness of information disclosure policies, encouraging debate and active citizen involvement."[2] Over forty nations today are credited with having their freedom of information laws (FOI) and some more are in the process of framing their legislations on the subject.

United Kingdom has been slow in opening up the governmental proceedings. The latest legislation — Freedom of Information Act, 2000 — provides for general access to information held by public authorities. The UK law, however, contains many exemptions relating to a host of issues such as investigations and proceedings, ministerial communications, policy formulation, evidence of health hazards and so on. Political activists and NGOs have been critical of the UK law for being rather conservative on the issue of genuine 'openness' of governance. The Information Commissioner looks after the Freedom of Information regime. His decision may, however, be overruled by the Minister of the Department.

In the United States, there is a federal law — the Freedom of Information Act, 1966 (amended several times) and separate state laws in each state. Under the provisions of the federal law, any person can ask for government records held by executive and military establishments, government corporations and other organisations performing government functions. There are nine exempted categories: (i) national security; (ii) internal agency rules; (iii) information protected by law; (iv) business information; (v) inter-and intra-agency news; (vi) personal privacy; (vii) law enforcement records; (viii) financial institutions data; (ix) oil wells data.[3] After the 9/11 incident, many Western nations including USA have tightened a bit on the question of openness of government under the threat of international terrorism.

In France, freedom of information and accountability of public servants are an integral part of constitutional right, according to the historic Declaration of the rights of Man and of the Citizen. The French law — Act No. 78-753 of 17 July, 1978 — sets as a general rule that citizens can demand a copy of any administrative document in paper, digitized or other form and establishes the Commission d'Acces aux Documents Administratifs — an independent administrative authority to oversee the process.There exist a number of exemptions as under:

- Documents established in the process of justice.
- Documents of cases before the national Ombudsman.
- Documents carrying an appreciation or judgment over a named or easily identifiable person, or containing private information of that person (such as medical records), when the person requesting the document is not the person described in the document or, in some cases, from his or her family; such documents may often still be obtained after the names of the persons involved are erased.
- Documents for which that are already available to the public.
- Documents with secrets regarding national defence or national foreign policy (though they may often be communicated after erasure of certain passages).
- Internal deliberations of the national executive.
- Documents from fiscal, customs, criminal enquiries.

Certain exempted documents may still be available according to other statutes. For instance, some tax-related information about any taxpayer is available to any other taxpayer from the same tax district.

The freedom of information law in Japan[4] came into effect in 2001, allowing access to administrative documents held by administrative agencies in electronic or printed form. Following the practice in other countries, six broad categories under the exemption clause are:

- Information on public security or public order
- National security or international relations related information
- Information on internal deliberations (in case such information is likely to harm free exchange of opinion or neutrality of decision-making)
- Information that puts audits, inspections and contracts in danger
- Information about an individual, unless the information is necessary to protect a life and a public official on duty
- Information about a corporation that risks harming its interests or information given voluntarily in confidence

In Canada, the Access to Information Act, 1982 gives all Canadian citizens the right to have access to federal government records that are not of a personal nature. Steps have been taken to ensure that information about government activities are broadly available to the people, with exceptions being limited and narrowly defined. There are provisions for resolving any disputes over the application of such exceptions independently of the government. To investigate complaints from the members of the public, an Information Commissioner has been appointed who functions autonomously.

In Germany, the federal government passed a freedom of information law in 2005. Six of the sixteen Bundeslander (provincial governments) have their own separate laws on the subject.

Among Scandinavian countries, Finland enacted the Freedom of Information (FOI) legislation in 1951, followed by Denmark and Norway in 1970. Austria and The Netherlands passed this legislation during the 70s, while Australia, Canada and New Zealand enacted it in 1982-83. Various states or provinces of the United States, Canada and Australia have also enacted their own FOI legislations.

Certain common features of the FOIs in different countries are:

- Defining the scope of access to governmental information
- Putting limits to access on such grounds as national security, external relations, personal privacy and other sensitive documents related to law and order
- Setting up administrative machineries and procedures for receipt of applications from the members of the public, timely disposal of such applications and appellate forum for hearing appeals from lower level decisions

Information Law in India

Many civil society groups and the Apex (Supreme) Court in India have been arguing in favour of people's right to information—with a view to empowering people and enriching Indian democracy. As earlier stated, the MKSS in Rajasthan played a pioneering role in mobilising the rural masses to compel government to disclose information about expenditure in rural public works projects. Rajasthan soon came out with a state RTI which was emulated by many other states. Other major NGOs that demanded from time to time electoral reforms and freedom of information are Lok Satta, People's Union for Civil Liberties, Association for Democratic Reforms and others.

The Supreme Court of India, in the landmark case of State of Uttar Pradesh vs. Raj Narain (1975) observed that the right to information is implied in the right to freedom of speech and expression under Article 19(1) and right to life guaranteed under Article 21 of the Constitution. Among many of its memorable judgments, the Court's famous verdict in the case of S.P. Gupta vs. Union of India (1981) is worth our quotation: "There can be little doubt that exposure to public gaze and scrutiny is one of the surest means of achieving a clean and healthy administration. Today it is a common ground that democracy has a more positive content and its orchestration has to be continuous and pervasive. This means *inter alia* that people should exercise sound judgment on the conduct of the government and the merits of public policies, so that democracy does not remain merely a sporadic exercise in voting but becomes a continuous process of government — an attitude and habit of mind. But this important role people can fulfil in a democracy only if it is an open government where there is full access to information in regard to the functioning of the government." This is a full-throated endorsement by the Apex court of the imperative need for open and transparent democracy in India.

Going out of its way, the Fifth Central Pay Commission (1994-96) dwelt at length on the need for 'openness' in government defined as 'easy and speedy access to right information'. As the Commission observed, "Experience of other countries shows that we will have to initiate the process by passing a Right to Information Act, somewhat on the lines of Canada and the United Kingdom."

In 1997, the Government of India had set up a Working Group on Right to Information and Promotion of Open and Transparent

Government. The terms of reference of the Group included the examination of feasibility and the need to introduce a full-fledged Right to Information Act with a view to meet the needs of an open and responsive government. For framing the legislation, the following broad principles were accepted by the Working Group:

- Disclosure of information should be the rule and secrecy the exception
- Exceptions should be clearly defined; and
- There should be an independent mechanism for adjudication of disputes between citizens and public authorities

The Working Group prepared a draft bill but there was hardly any taker, as national politics drifted into other directions.

Transparency in governmental operations was very much on the agenda of the Conference of Chief Ministers held on 24 May, 1997. A statement was issued at the end of the conference along with an Action Plan for Effective and Responsive Government at the Central and State levels. The Chief Ministers recognised that secrecy and lack of openness in government business is largely responsible for corruption in official dealings. The government set for itself a time limit of three months to ensure easy access of the people to all information, except to the extent required to be excluded on specific grounds like national security.

With rapid changes in the national political scene, the issue of openness and transparency became a backburner. In 1998, the National Agenda for governance of the multi-party coalition named the National Democratic Alliance (NDA) declared:"Our first commitment to the people is to give a stable, honest, transparent and efficient government capable of accomplishing all-round development. For this the government shall introduce time-bound programme of needed administrative reforms".

Accordingly, the NDA Government introduced the Freedom of Information (FOI) Bill, 2000 in Parliament, which, however, could not be pushed through because of lack of determined political will. Subsequently, the Freedom of Information Act (2002) was passed providing for accountable government and ensuring for every citizen the freedom to secure information from the Central and State public authorities. Strangely enough, the Act could not be enforced due to lack of notification and non-framing of Rules by the bureaucracy. This amply demonstrates the hostile politico-administrative environment of the projected people's right to information.

The next political regime that emerged was the United Progressive Alliance under Congress leadership with the Left Parties lending support to it. A National Common Minimum Programme was drafted in May 2004 to give policy direction to the new regime. The Programme included, among other things, a commitment to 'provide a government that is corruption-free, transparent and accountable at all times and an administration that is responsible and responsive at all times.' Another important item in the Minimum Programme was 'to set up an Administrative Reforms Commission to prepare a detailed blueprint for revamping the public administration system. The Programme laid emphasis on the need for promotion of E-governance on a massive scale and desired that 'the Right to Information Act will be made more progressive, participatory and meaningful'.

The Right to Information Act, 2005

Ultimately, the new law — the Right to Information Act — was enacted in keeping with the commitment of the UPA regime. The Freedom of Information Act, 2002 was repealed and the new Act came into force on 12 October, 2005. The preamble to the Act affirms that 'democracy requires an informed citizenry and transparency of information which are vital to its functioning and also to contain corruption and to hold Governments and their instrumentalities accountable to the governed.' The objective, as stated in the Act, is 'to provide for setting out the practical regime of right to information for citizens to secure access to information under the control of public authorities, in order to promote transparency and accountability in the working of every public authority. . . '.

With the coming into force of the new Act of 2005, the earlier Act of 2002 has been repealed. But, curiously enough, the old colonial law — the Official Secrets Act, 1923 (OSA) — has not been repealed. An overriding clause in the new Act — Clause 22 — has of course been included which provides: "The provisions of this Act shall have effect notwithstanding anything inconsistent therewith contained in the Official Secrets Act, 1923 and any other law for the time being in force or in any instrument having effect by virtue of any law other than this Act." No doubt, this provision is reassuring enough; yet the continuity of the 1923 Act remains suspect. In this connection, the observations of the Second Administrative Commission are significant: "The OSA would not come in the way of disclosure of information if it is otherwise permissible under the RTI Act. But OSA along with other rules and instructions may impinge on the regime of freedom information as they historically nurtured a culture of secrecy and non-disclosure, which is against the spirit of the Right to Information Act." The ARC has therefore categorically recommended as follows:

"The Commission firmly believes that the Official Secrets Act, 1923 in the current form is antiquated and unsuitable to emerging needs."

Logically, thus, the Commission concluded that the OSA 'should be repealed and substituted by a chapter in the National Security Act, containing provisions relating to official secrets.'[5]

The RTI Act (Clause 3) provides that 'subject to the provisions of this Act, all citizens shall have the right to information'. The Act has defined the two terms — information and authority — very widely.

- 'Information' means any material in any form including records, documents, memos, e-mails, opinions, advices, press releases, orders, circulars, contracts, reports, papers, logbooks, samples, models, data material kept in any electronic form and information relating to any private body which can be accessed by a public authority under any other law for the time being in force.
- 'Public Authority' has been defined as any authority or body or institution of self-government established or constituted (a) by or under the Constitution; (b) by any other law made by Parliament; (c) by any other law made by State legislature; (d) by notification issued or made by the appropriate government and includes any (i) body owned, controlled or substantially financed, (ii) non-government organisation substantially financed, directly or indirectly, by funds provided by the appropriate government.

Exemptions clause: Reasons for 'exemptions' include national security, sovereignty and integrity of India, strategic and scientific or economic interests of the state, foreign relations, incitement to offence, contempt of court, breach of parliamentary privileges, commercial interests, trade secrets, intellectual property rights, cabinet papers and purely personal information.The law provides that information that cannot be denied to any legislative body would not be denied to any person.

Records maintenance: The Act makes it

obligatory on the part of every public authority to maintain its records properly to facilitate the right to information and publish relevant information and data regarding its organisation, duties, functions and roles played by all its officers and employees including the organisation's decision-making process.

Information Commissions

Under the RTI Act, the Central Government has constituted a *Central Information Commission* consisting of the Chief Information Commissioner and Information Commissioners not exceeding ten in number. These Information Commissioners would be persons of eminence in public life having wide knowledge and experience in law, science and technology, management, social service, journalism, mass media or administration and governance. The commissioners are appointed for a term of five years on the recommendation of a committee consisting of the Prime Minister, Leader of the Opposition in the Lok Sabha and a Union Cabinet Minister nominated by the Prime Minister.

The *State Information Commission* is constituted by the State Government, consisting of the State Chief Information Commissioner and other State Information Commissioners not exceeding ten in number. The State Chief Commissioner and other Commissioners are appointed for a term of five years by the Governor on the recommendation of a committee consisting of the Chief Minister, the Leader of the Opposition in the Legislative Assembly and a Cabinet Minister nominated by the Chief Minister.

Public Information Officers

Under the provisions of the Act, every public authority is required to designate its specific Public Information Officer (PIO) in all administrative units for providing information to the applicants and giving reasonable assistance to them.

Procedure

A person desiring information has to make a request in writing or through electronic means along with a certain prescribed fee. On receipt of such request, the Information Officer concerned shall as expeditiously as possible and in any case within thirty days of the receipt of request, either provide the information on payment of prescribed fee or reject, giving the reasons for rejection as per the legal provisions. In case of rejection, the person concerned should be told within what period he/she can prefer an appeal along with the particulars of the appellate authority.

Concluding Observations

The RTI Act, prima facie, surely marks a major step forward toward openness and transparency in governance. But there are many challenges that this Act has to face in course of its implementation.

The bureaucratic culture of 'secrecy' is not easy to change. Structurally, procedurally and behaviourally, bureaucracy in India has to culturally prepare itself to accept 'openness' as a criterion of good governance.

The politician in India, often in league with the bureaucracy, has to accept that democracy means people's rule, not politician's rule. It is no use blaming the bureaucracy all the time; our politicians today have often been found lacking in 'big visions'.

- People in India, in many places, suffer from a variety of 'bondages'. The social bondages — be it of caste, religion or anything — stand in the way of enjoyment of the rights which are enshrined in the constitution or provided in any statute. Thus, 'social freedom' through education and popular movements is the key to real assertion of popular right.

- Often in the past it has so happened that a liberating and progressing legislation (e.g. abolishing child marriage or Sati, for instance) would be taking the lead in terms of advance 'conscience' of the society. Such legislation will be actually internalized by the society only when appropriate 'people preparedness' will be taking place through liberating social movements. The example of MKSS in Rajasthan is a case in point in this context. The success of RTI Act will ultimately depend on people's understanding of its real worth in day-to-day living.
- Currently, the trend has been toward 'privatisation' and 'outsourcing' of many erstwhile government activities, shrinking, in the process, the 'spheres' of public administration. Under the circumstances, the ambit of the RTI law might have to be widened to bring within its purview many organisations working for the public authorities in different garbs.

It has been argued that the 'open government' idea has often been broached in terms of the prevailing consensus that looks at secrecy and democracy as two sides of the same coin. Governments would like to keep certain things 'confidential'; but citizens demand information about how they are governed. Ultimately, a sensible and genuine democracy has to strike a balance somewhere and find out a golden mean.[6]

REFERENCES

1. UNDP and the Right to Information, Seminar report, Oslo, Norway, 22-23 May, 2006.
2. Asok Kumar Mukhopadhyay (ed.), Right to Information, Administrative Training Institute, Government of West Bengal, Kolkata, 2007.
3. Mukhopadhyay, op. cit.
4. Mukhopadhyay, op. cit.
5. First Report, Right to Information: Master Key to Good Governance, Second Administrative Reforms Commission, Government of India, New Delhi, June 2006.
6. See in this connection, Richard Chapman and Michael Hunt (eds.), Open Government in a Theoretical and Practical Context, Ashgate Publishing Ltd., 2006.

Chapter 28

Participation and Governance

People's participation is axiomatic in democratic governance. In the context of 'development' efforts of the Third World countries, participation has assumed added significance, as the rich experience gained through decades of development convincingly proved that 'participation' is the key to meaningful and authentic people-centric development. Current upsurge in 'participatory governance' is, however, a more generic concern related to 'good governance' paradigm.

Participative Governance

The Sixth Global Forum on Reinventing Government held in Seoul (South Korea) came out with a forceful argument in favour of 'participative governance'. To quote the deliberations of the Forum: "The institutionalisation of participation by all people is a cornerstone of good governance. Participatory governance provides citizens with access not only to information but also to decision-making power. Participatory governance entails the close involvement of people in the economic, political, cultural and social processes that affect them and facilitates access of individuals and groups to a wide range of opportunities that in turn promote responsiveness of governance actors toward people-centred development. Accordingly, participatory governance means a convergence of social and political participation and the scaling up of participatory methods, state-civil-society partnerships, decentralisation and devolution, participatory assessment and other factors."

Participation, in a generic sense, has been conceptualised in terms of right of citizenship; it is a 'right' on its own strength. With such extended meaning of participation beyond traditional voting and political rights, there is a serious search going on in all democratic countries for more participatory approaches to processes of democratic governance.

Background of 'Development'

It is by now an old story to reiterate that 'development' as a concept made its appearance in the post-World War II global situation when the newly independent ex-colonies had embarked on a long-drawn-out process of socio-economic reconstruction. Development effort was basically donor-funded and spearheaded by the 'bureaucracy', in the absence of alternative action agencies such as the private sector or active citizenry. Decades of bureaucracy-led top-down development efforts soon came under close scrutiny as there was scanty evidence on the ground of any appreciable trickle-down effect. Rather there were evidence-based reports of cornering of benefits by the elite and the powerful and rural poverty showed no appreciable signs of abatement. The 'failures' sensitised the planners and administrators, at national and international levels, to the need for closer understanding of complex field problems from the eyes and ears of the local people. Through the 1960s and 1970s, policy changes took place in quick succession from community development to integrated rural development to basic needs programmes.

Responding to the 'failures', particularly, in the area of poverty amelioration, eminent field researchers and social activists came out with alternative visions of development assigning centrality to the people as architects of their own destiny and active participants in the drama of development. For instance, Paulo Friere, one of the famous Liberation Philosophers, wrote:

"Policies carried out by a rigid bureaucracy in the name of the masses to whom they are transmitted as order are one thing; policies carried out with the masses are quite another thing with their critically conscious participation in the reconstruction of society, in which the necessary directions never become slogans."

David Korten, another renowned social scientist with a long record of sustained field research, made a distinction between two contrasting visions of development which he called 'growth-centred development' and 'people-centred development'. As Korten has contended, 'the prevailing growth-centred vision of development has not only failed a substantial majority of the world's people, but is also systematically deepening human misery and destroying our planet's life support systems'.

Robert Chambers, whose name is associated with a particular technique of participatory development, widely known as PRA (Participatory Rural Appraisal), has been a staunch advocate of 'doing' participation in the actual field situation for effective and efficient people-led development. As the title of his book suggests — *Rural Development: Putting the Last First* — Chambers wants the 'people' to be the real actors, not just passive beneficiaries, of 'development'. PRA (sometimes called PLA) has been a very popular technique used by grassroots development agencies involving the people in problems identification and local planning and problems solving. Besides PRA, a complementary technique often used by social planners is FGD or focus group discussions where specially planned group meetings are organised to elicit the special problems of a 'group', say tradesmen, fishermen, senior citizens or any other relevant group.

In this context, the observation of the South Asian Commission on Poverty Alleviation (1992) is worth our quotation:

"Participation... is seen not in narrow terms pointing towardsformalactivitieseffectedthroughrepresentatives. Instead, it is defined as a socially vibrant grassroots process whereby people identify with the process as their own, with occasional help from facilitators. The process is inherently educative, leading progressively to a higher level of consciousness which evolves through newer experiences of facing reality. They are then able to participate as active subjects in the development process rather than as passive objects."

The quotation above brings out the essence of participation' as a conscience-raising exercise that has a transformative role in bringing about a kind of 'rebirth' of the people as shapers of their own destiny. Participation, thus, need not be narrowly conceived in instrumental term — as a tool to use people to achieve some project targets. It has a wider emancipator connotation.

Critique of Participation and Participation Ladder

There is a critical difference between going through the empty ritual of participation and having the real power needed to affect the outcome of the process. It has been rightly pointed out that participation without redistribution of power is an empty and frustrating process for the powerless. It allows the power holders to claim that all sides were considered, but makes it possible for only some of those sides to benefit. It maintains the status quo or at best 'uses' participation for the benefit of the power holders.

A typology of eight levels of participation may help in the analysis of the issues surrounding the practice of 'participation' in real-life situation. For illustrative purposes the eight types are arranged in a ladder pattern with each rung corresponding to the extent of citizens' power in determining the end product. (See Figure below)

The bottom rungs of the ladder are: (1) Manipulation and (2) Therapy.These two rungs describe levels of 'nonparticipation' that have been contrived by some to substitute for genuine participation.Their real objective is not to enable people to participate in planning or conducting programmes, but to enable power holders to 'educate' or 'cure' the participants. Rungs 3 and 4 progress to levels of 'tokenism' that allow the have-nots to hear and to have a voice: (3) Informing and (4) Consultation. When they are proffered by power holders as the total extent of participation, citizens may indeed hear and be heard but under these conditions they lack the power to ensure that their views will be heeded by the powerful. When participation is restricted to these levels, there is no follow-through, no 'muscle,' hence no assurance of changing the status quo. Rung (5) Placation is simply a higher level tokenism because the ground rules allow have-nots to advice but retain for the power holders the continued right to decide.

Further up the ladder are levels of citizen power with increasing degrees of decision-making clout. Citizens can enter into a (6) Partnership that enables them to negotiate and engage in trade-offs with traditional power holders. At the topmost rungs, (7) Delegated Power and (8) Citizen Control, 'have-not' citizens obtain the majority of decision-making seats, or full managerial power. Obviously, the eight-rung ladder is a simplification, but it helps to illustrate the point that so many have missed — that there are significant gradations of citizen participation. Knowing these gradations makes it possible to cut through the hyperbole to understand the increasingly strident demands for participation from the 'have-nots' as well as the gamut of confusing responses from the power holders. (This is taken from a well-known paper by Sherry R. Arnstein, "A Ladder of Citizen Participation", JAIP, Vol. 35, No. 4, July 1969)

In practical situations, Arnstein's typology can be an excellent evaluator tool to probe into the motives behind the use of participatory methods.

Development as Enlargement of People's Choice

Development, as it should be clear by now, has traditionally been conceived in economic terms like how has gross national product increased, or what has been the status of per capita income etc. It is now being defined in human terms with participation of people as a crucial factor. To quote the Human Development Report, 1990:

"We are rediscovering the essential truth that people must be at the centre of all development. The purpose of development is to offer people more options. One of their options is access to income — not as an end in itself but as a means for acquiring human well-being. However, there are other options too such as long life (India's ancient exhortation is *jeevema sharadah shatam*, may you live a hundred years), knowledge, political freedom, personal security, community participation and guaranteed human rights. People cannot be reduced to a single dimension merely as economic creatures. What makes the study of the development process fascinating is the entire spectrum through which human capabilities are expanded and utilised to the fullest."

The emphasis of development study has thus shifted to the role of human agency and enhancement of human capability. Development is being understood as empowerment, as the enhancement of human capability to intervene in policy and decision-making in the public sphere. Participation in developmental decision-making is being viewed both as a matter of right as well as a step towards democratisation. With the passage of the Constitution 73rd and the 74th Amendments in 1992, we, in our country have also taken some major steps towards ensuring people's participation in development. It is against this background that proper clarification, understanding internalisation of the concepts of participation and development has become so much crucial.

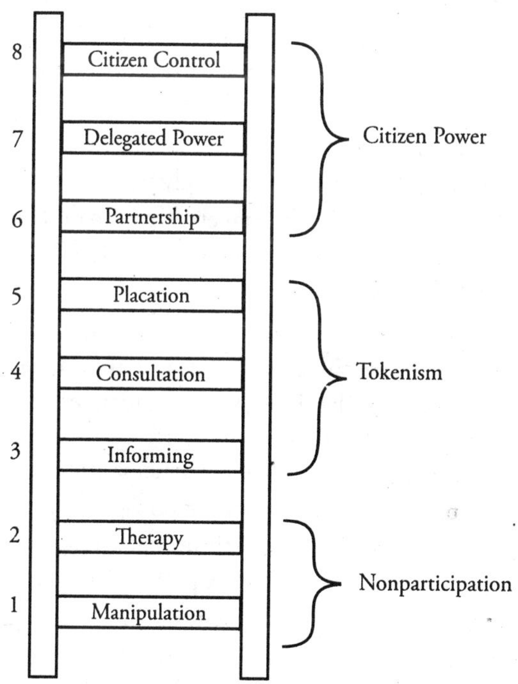

Eight rungs on the ladder of citizen participati

Meaning of Participation

Conventional Meaning

Participation is usually interpreted as people

(i) contributing cash or free labour for developmental schemes such as road construction or school building construction, or (ii) identifying would be beneficiaries of developmental projects, or (iii) offering some suggestions in respect of some programmes. Cash or in-kind services are recommended as ways to create a sense of ownership on the part of the poor. It is also an obvious way to cover part of the project cost. This usually takes place at the implementation stage. People do not, by and large, participate either in the planning stage or in the stage of project formulation. Their participation at the implementation stage is also rare. They are not called upon to monitor, review or evaluate the scheme. If this is the situation, how do we define participation?

Operational Meaning

Participation can be interpreted in various ways. The practice has been evolving — from treating participation as 'user' group consultation to a much wider citizen-oriented rights-based participation. Today the emphasis is on 'rights-based' participation. This means all policy and decision-making in the public sphere and all expenditure incurred must have an in-built and direct system of public participation. It may also be considered as an essential part of the *process of democratisation.* This means all administrative decisions and actions must be subjected to public control and scrutiny. Participation has thus to be viewed as *empowerment.* In other words it means enabling the people to influence public policy and to take decisions in matters concerning their lives. For some, participation is the *essential feature of freedom and human development.* It is also one of the conditions. This denotes participation is both the *means and the end of development* because it enhances the capabilities of human beings and helps them take control of their own lives.

As a guide to action, *we may define participation as a process through which the stakeholders in a project or activity influence and share control over decisions, which affect their lives.* If development means capacity building of the poor so that they can voice their choices and exercise their options, which are essential conditions of democracy and freedom, then participation becomes an inherent component of development. But participation is also necessary for very practical reasons. It is often noticed that much of the effort going into 'development' is not always producing the desired results. So far as distribution of resources and benefits are concerned, the record is often discouraging. Development programmes have not been able to change the living conditions of the poor in most cases. They have often favoured the rich. Why this is so? There has been a general belief that the poor illiterate villagers are incapable of thinking and organising themselves for their development. They have neither the required knowledge nor the capacity. So it has to be sponsored and directed from outside by experts and implemented through the government agencies. Under this system there is little scope for involvement of the rural people in the planning process. It has generally been assumed that decisions in this respect are the sole preserve of the government officials, the experts and the elected representatives. Now it is being realised that non-involvement of the poor and the socially marginalised in the planning and implementation of the development projects meant for them is the prime cause of neglect of their interests and perpetuation of their poverty.

Stakeholders

The notion of 'stakeholders' is important in this context. *Stakeholders are those who are affected by the outcome — negatively or positively — of a project/scheme or those who can affect the outcome of a proposed scheme.* By popular participation we usually mean participation of the poor and the disadvantaged, either defined in terms of wealth, education and social status, or ethnicity and gender, or even in terms of physical incapacity They are in most cases the intended beneficiaries. They are invariably the 'voiceless' in the development process and in general are the major stakeholders. But all of them may not be the direct stakeholders. Take the case of any water supply project in a dry district. If you have observed the life of the poor in the villages, you must have noticed that management of water in the family is generally a woman's job. Women collect water against all kinds of odds which is then used for drinking, cooking, washing, cleaning, feeding the domestic animals and so on but everyone in the family uses water. So in this particular project of water supply, women among the poor households are the primary stakeholders and others are secondary stakeholders. There are other kinds of stakeholders as well. They include individuals and parties or even institutions that are likely to be affected directly and indirectly. Stakeholders also include the community based organisations (CBO), the non-government organisations (NGO) and even the local government and representative organisations in a significant way because they are also participants in the development initiatives.

Forms of Participation

There are various modes of participation. At one extreme we have an absolutely non-participatory mode. Here the whole institutional arrangement is such that there is little scope for participation of the people. Here the state is the only actor and the whole process of development is driven by the state's bureaucratic machinery. Power and decision-making is centralised and there is little transparency and hardly any accountability to the people.

Next is the ***manipulative*** mode. Here participation is encouraged only in a very limited manner, mostly to reduce cost by mobilising some resources from the people.

The third mode is called ***incremental.*** Here the situation is ambivalent. In some cases people are consulted in planning and implementation but not in the formulation of policy. Here the bureaucratic control is still there but at the same time the value of participation is to some extent recognised. But this recognition does not lead to any institutional change.

There is another kind of participation where people are the central actors and they are not just the passive beneficiaries of projects that are conceived elsewhere and thrust on them from above. This kind of participation needs to be distinguished from incremental participation. We can call it ***developmental participation.*** In the former the people are the targets of development. In the latter however they are the real actors.The former treats the beneficiaries as passive. The latter on the other hand treats them as agents. The former dis-empowers. The latter empowers. In the latter mode the goal is not just the successful implementation of schemes but also the enhancement of the capability of the people in a progressive manner. *Involving the user group or setting of beneficiary committees, although useful, still falls far short, of the developmental participative mode. In the ideal participative mode of development there is no power differential between the donor and the receiver, between the administrator, the representatives of the people and the people themselves who can freely come forward to air their choices and preferences. It provides the means for joint learning and action.* Participation to be meaningful must lead to joint production of knowledge and strategy of action. Participation to be really effective must create a situation in which cooperative decision-making is possible.

Advantages of Participation

The major objective of participation is to involve the people in planning, project formulation, implementation, monitoring and review of local level developmental initiatives. Once the process starts, it leads to involvement of local people, which in turn facilitates the process of social acceptance. When development projects are thrust from outside these in most cases remain non-integrated with the local social system. People do not develop a sense of ownership about them. It is because of this that we find that when a tube well goes out of order people do not come forward to mobilise their resources to repair it but wait for the concerned department to do the job. On the other hand, *when people are involved, they take direct initiative for the operation, maintenance and repair of a facility, which benefits them. Thus participation leads to the building of beneficiary capability.* Again, *participation means sharing of information not just about needs and deficiencies but also about possible means of solution.* This brings an additional resource of local knowledge and expertise, which leads to better planning. The advantages of the participative mode get clearer at the implementation stage. At the outset, *it facilitates mobilisation of local resources in a significant manner because of the sense of collective ownership that is generated.* These resources may be of various kinds — material, human or financial. These may also come as local level experiences and expertise, which are particularly relevant in disaster management programmes. Involving the people at the implementation stage also ensures direct and regular monitoring of the project, which ensures timely completion. Thus *the possibility of time and cost overrun is minimised.* After the project is completed people tend to take initiatives to develop ways and means for operation and maintenance of the new facility. When the people participate in the implementation stage usually the possibility of leakage is minimised in comparison to departmental or agency managed projects. As such *it ensures maintenance of quality. The process also tends to eliminate what is known as 'contractor raj' with all its problems. Last but not the least it ensures transparency and accountability,* because the project work is always under the critical gaze of the local stakeholders. *Participation makes a right balance between technical and local expertise.* It is only the local people who can finally say whether the technologies and methods being followed are sufficiently effective and efficient. They can also provide proper feedback for mid-stream corrections, if necessary.

Participation also creates a condition of looking forward and backward. It is a process by which the participants relate an ideal future vision with the realities of today and list the key events and factors where interventions are necessary as per their priorities.

Preconditions of Participation

It is obvious that participation, in the real sense of the term, depends on a number of preconditions such as literacy, presence of 'social capital'(feeling of trust and togetherness in the community), a degree of equality of wealth and political power and above all, a sense of collective life informed by a democratic ethos. Apart from these, some other steps also need to be taken:

- First and foremost among them is a proper environment. Institutionally, the 73rd and 74th Constitution Amendments have created this environment to a great extent. The Constitution has also provided for the involvement of the Gram Sabha or people's assemblies in the planning of development projects.
- Apart from the legal provision, processal and procedural reforms are necessary to free 'development' from 'departmentalism' as the government departments invariably seek to put the departmental priorities above people's perceptions. Hierarchically arranged departmentalism makes local level integration of functions all the more difficult.

At the end of the day, however, participation would not be meaningful unless resources are transferred to the appropriate level. By resources here we mean financial and administrative resources.

Barriers to Participation

Despite the advocacy of 'participation' as a desirable thing for development, in real life there are many obstacles to participation. Some of the major obstacles are identified as under:

Caste Barriers

In many states of India, caste plays a major role in social relations. The spectacle of domination of upper caste over the lower caste people is too well known to be repeated. Even though many of the oppressed castes are beginning to assert themselves, people belonging to the lowest castes, particularly the scheduled castes and the tribal people, are still at the receiving end.

Class Barriers

People are unequal not only socially but also economically.The division between the rich and the poor is a crucial element of the ills associated with social inequality. In economic matters mutual interests of the rich and the poor may be contradictory to each other. It may therefore become difficult for the poor to participate in collective activity together with the rich. Because of their economic strength the rich have greater opportunity for influencing public decisions. The poor are deprived of this opportunity, since generally they do not have effective institutions of their own from where they can make their voices heard and in other public institutions or forums they do not find access in equal footing with the affluent people.

Gender Inequality

Our Society is unequal not only in terms of caste and class but also in terms of gender. In a male dominated society, women suffer from many kinds of discrimination. Women's participation in public activity, in particular, is often socially discouraged and opposed. In traditional thinking women's domain is confined to the inner world (that is, the family), public activities being the exclusive concern of the male. The reservation provisions introduced by the 73rd and 74th Constitution Amendments have brought many women in the leadership position of Panchayati Raj and municipal institutions. Still, numerous instances can be shown where elected women representatives of local bodies have been subjected to harassment. At the same time, it can be hoped that given adequate opportunity and encouragement, women will be able to assert themselves and make useful contribution to the development of the community. In recent years, women have come forward to form and run efficient self-help groups from where they have launched public actions for the benefit of the members of the groups.

Lack of Motivation

The people of our country have long been subjected to centralised governance under which decisions that affect their lives are taken at levels which are inaccessible to them. They feel powerless while dealing with an institution of the state. They seem to believe that their participation, even where solicited, is not going to create any impact upon the holders of the state power. Hence, the general tendency has been to shy away from participating in government programmes.

Lack of Capacity

Lack of capacity in managing institutions is an obstacle to the growth of civil society organisations of the marginalised people. Once they would be organised, there would be opportunities for their members to participate in public action for their own benefit. But, such institutions have to be created and then managed properly for the benefit of their members. All this requires new kind of skills not generally available with people who have no experience of engagement in public activity.

Political Constraints

Political parties in a democracy mobilise people around major issues and during elections. Political parties by their nature are centralised organisations and leader-oriented. Their mission is to change the society from above. Micro space at the local level does not generally exist in their scheme of things. The scope of participation of the masses in political matters is typically restricted to voting for a party or joining a political programme of the party. The policies and activities of political parties may work against participation in, at least, three ways: one, polarisation on the basis of loyalty to political parties tends to create obstacles to the formation of strong civil society. Besides this, parties — particularly those with strong ideological bias — tend to use the masses for their own broader party interest rather than the small but burning local problems of the poor and the marginalised. Above all, political parties being highly centralised and leader-oriented often pay lip service to the cause of decentralisation. The dilemma here is: decentralisation is a pre-condition of participation whereas political parties may not in reality favour participatory governance.

Participatory Development

Development in the participatory mode generates a durable form of social learning and commitment.

- In this mode, the stakeholders internalise both the purpose as well as the means of a jointly developed strategy of development planning and implementation. This leaves a long lasting and stable impact on the people and the social system.
- The social learning, which is generated through the process of participation usually, leads to a collective endeavour towards problem solving.
- Consequently, this leads to social invention in which the participants, with the help of external actors, creatively assess and employ their own knowledge and practice for dealing with their problems as identified by them.
- The stakeholders invent the new practices and institutionalised arrangements they are willing to adopt. In the process, they individually and collectively develop insight and understanding of the new behaviour required to attain the objectives that are set collectively.
- With all the stakeholders working, learning and innovating together, it helps reduce the risk of failures. The commitment on the part of the people also increases substantially.
- When the process that produces a project or a development plan is participatory from the start, it creates a network of support and commitment as well as a sense of ownership. This is a net gain which remains unattainable in any non-participatory mode.

Participation in Use

Field researchers and non-government and voluntary agencies engaged in development projects have come out with evidences of success stories showing that common people have ideas and skills as well as a rich storehouse of local knowledge. These are essential ingredients of local level planning. Even ordinary villagers have rich resources, both material and human, to contribute to the development process. They can significantly contribute to the implementation of the projects. There are also evidences of a few successfully implemented departmental schemes where the field level administrators showed initiative to directly involve the people. The joint forest management project at Arabari in West Bengal is one such evidence. The Human Development Report published by UNDP commented as early as in 1992 that, "Peoples' participation is becoming the central issue of our times".

After the Constitutional 73rd and 74th Amendments, the Governments at all levels are showing interest in participative development. The Universal Primary Education Programme of the Government of India is an instance to the point. Emphasis is placed on locally rooted, participatory micro development organisations with scope for involving voluntary and non-governmental organisations. In our country the micro-watershed projects have put a lot of emphasis on local level participation. Participation in these cases is seen as a socially vibrant grassroots process whereby people identify the development activities as their own. This mode of participatory development produces the twin benefits of project success and democracy-strengthening.

Repositioning Participation

It is now being strongly suggested that 'participation' as a concept needs to be repositioned. Conventionally, participation has been more instrumentally conceived and planned. The basic objective has been to make 'use' of participation in projects planning and implementation. An alternative concept of participation as 'social citizenship' has recently been broached by active social researchers. To quote Andrea Cornwall and John Gaventa (of IDS Sussex group) in this context:

"...more functional concepts of participation, through which beneficiaries participate as users or consumers of pre-determined public services, are of limited utility. Not only do they fail to include people in broader aspects of the policy process, but they also ignore their contribution to self-provisioning outside formal government arenas. Most importantly, they fail to recognise or realise the potential of more active citizens engagement in making and shaping social policy and with it opportunities for enhanced service responsiveness, transparency and accountability."

It is toward this mode of active citizen engagement that one looks forward to in future which has been broadly defined as 'social citizenship'.

Overview

The current wave of 'participatory approaches' has touched on the core of the 'governance' process. Earlier approaches had been directed more toward influencing planning in general and planning for poverty eradication in particular. To the extent, participation mobilises the 'voice' of the people it has positive impact on action planning and on the functioning of democracy as people-driven governance. At the same time, one has to be cautious about the 'real' intentions of power holders who often invoke 'participation' as a method of cooptation of the 'opposition' and a way of defusing popular resistance.

By way of a counter-discourse, one of the first books to challenge the almost universally fashionable rhetoric of participation is *Participation: The New Tyranny* (Zed Books, 2001). It looks at participatory development's promises of empowerment and appropriate development compared with what actually happens on the ground.

Citing instances of failed participatory practices and presenting refreshing conceptual analyses, this book has sought to unmask some of the lofty moral promises of participatory development. The book is edited by Bill Cooke and Uma Kothari, Institute for Development Policy and Management, University of Manchester.

Researchers on 'participation' need thus to approach the subject with an open mind and critically examine the field situations where 'participation' is being invoked as a tool to facilitate 'development'.

CHAPTER 29

E-Government

The discussion on E-governance needs to be contextually placed. Faced with new challenges in the wake of rapid social and technological changes and mounting public demands for more efficient and transparent public administration, governments worldwide are now striving hard to transform and reinvent the government systems. The compelling objective is to deliver efficient and cost-effective services, information and knowledge through innovative information and communication technologies. To quote Guido Bertucci, Director of United Nations Department of Economic and Social Affairs:"Public sector reforms throughout the world embodying ICTs are part of an on-going effort to build trust in defining the terms of a social contract between the diverse groups that make up a society. New forms of dialogue and collaboration among public, private and civil society organisations enhance transparency and accountability that can create conditions of fair and open competition while expanding access so that everyone can participate and benefit from today's knowledge-based economy. E-inclusion, one of the many pre-occupations of modern government, can broaden access to social and economic opportunities, thereby creating new markets in developing countries." (Newsletter of DPADM/UNDESA, Issue 1, No. 113, 2007)

E-GOVERNMENT VS. E-GOVERNANCE

In this context, two terms that are now being frequently used are E-government and E-governance. Their meanings need to be distinguished at the outset to dispel doubts about terminologies in use. 'Government' as the action arm of state has been a familiar concept; by contrast, the term 'governance' is a relatively new entrant in public administration vocabulary. It stands for, to quote the World Bank's formulation, 'the traditions and institutions by which authority in a country is exercised, this includes the process by which governments are selected, monitored and replaced, the capacity of the government to effectively formulate and implement sound policies and the respect of citizens and the state for the institutions that govern economic and social interactions among them'. Implicit in this formulation is an attempt to extend the traditional understanding of 'rule and regulation' beyond formal machineries of 'government' and include other social actors like the private sector and the civil society organisations as co-actors in steering the processes of social life.

Following the World Bank/UNDP definition (which has gained more or less universal acceptance), *E-government* can be defined as the application of Information and Communication Technology (ICT) — particularly Internet-based information technology — by government agencies to improve the efficiency, effectiveness, transparency and accountability of government. In this definition 'technology' is the means and efficiency, transparency etc. are the consequences that are expected to flow from the use of ICT. Contrastingly, *E-governance* is about the use of ICT to support the guiding and steering of an organisation — be it a private agency or a civil society organisation (other than government) to achieve its goals. In the political context, E-governance is about the use of ICT to steer society and promote public interest. For example, 'e-procurement' that is concerned with the use of ICT to support the purchasing departments of public or government agencies falls in the category of E-government. By contrast, an ICT application designed to help lobbyists (e.g. farmers, industrialists etc.) to participate efficiently in the political processes, like influencing a public subsidy policy or new electricity tariff would fall in the category of 'E-governance'.

Following the common practice, however, we will be using the term 'E-government' to connote the application of ICT to public administrative purposes in the public interest. Basically, E-governance is distinguished from E-government with a view to highlighting the democratic qualities of the new ICTs. These ICTs support not only the activities of governments, but also foster new forms of political mobilisation and multi-stakeholder participative governance.

Defining E-Government

'E-Government' (as defined by the World Bank Group) refers to the use by government agencies of information technologies (such as Wide Area-Net-works, the Internet and mobile computing) that have the ability to transform relations with citizens, businesses and other arms of government. These technologies can serve a variety of different ends: better delivery of government services to citizens, improved interactions with business and industry, citizen empowerment through access to information, or more efficient government management. The resulting benefits can be less corruption, increased transparency, greater convenience, revenue growth and/or cost reductions.

Traditionally the interaction between a citizen or business and a government agency took place in a government office. With emerging information and communication technologies it is possible to locate service centres closer to the clients. Such centres may consist of an unattended kiosk in the government agency, a service kiosk located close to the client, or the use of a personal computer in the home or office.

E-government aims to make the interaction between government and citizens, government and business enterprises and inter-agency relationships more friendly, convenient, transparent and inexpensive.

Background

The United Nations Committee of Experts on Public Administration, at its first session held from 22 to 26 July, 2002 discussed at length the issue of capacity of the public sector to support the creation and application of knowledge, innovation and technology for development. Two guiding thoughts of the Committee have been: (a) public sector organisations must become 'learning organisations' that are recognised as strong and strategic organisations; and (b) capacity-building in support of state governance would require the harnessing of the power of information and communication technologies in support of innovation.

The Committee urged upon the member countries to shift public administration towards a culture of performance of the whole organisation, mission and results, lifelong learning, innovation, life employability with safeguards, horizontal teams and networks and an outward orientation towards all segments of society. In this connection, the committee recommended capacity-building by capturing knowledge and supporting innovation through the building of a learning infrastructure, connectivity and network. Public sector organisations would thus encourage transparency and accountability, improve service delivery and provide services in a citizen-centred way. This process would forge a link between governance and transformative innovation in public administration supported by knowledge, innovation and technology — more specifically ICT.

The United Nations Millennium Declaration (2000) provides another important background for this analysis. Calling upon member countries to promote 'good governance', the Declaration laid emphasis on the need for strengthening capacity to implement the principles and practices of democracy and the rule of law and to work collectively for more inclusive political processes, allowing genuine participation by all citizens and ensuring the right of the public to have access to information. All this places ICT application in public administrative operations in the position of a servant of people-centred, democratic and participative governance as a means for human development.

The Moral Framework

The United Nations World Public Sector Report (WPSR) — E-government at the Cross roads — describes the moral purpose of E-government as a public administration which is in the process of transforming its internal and external relationships with the use of modern ICT, which is about communication among people being the quintessence of human society. In the context of public administration, e-government is bound to have an impact on the creation of public value — a notion rooted in people's preferences. E-government, to quote the WPSR, is justified if it enhances the capacity of public administration to increase the supply of public value — the outcome of a high quality of life. E-government development 'must be put within the context of a vision of the kind of society with which the people want to identify and make part of their life experience'.

Constraints and Facilitators

Public administration being a mix of political will and guidance on the one hand and bureaucratic professionalism on the other, the application of ITC has to reckon with the complexities that are inherent in the structure and processes of public management. Government administration has unique characteristics like the pivotal role of merit-based and trained bureaucracy and politically influenced decisions that are not always driven by efficiency or productivity considerations. Also, public sector organisations are subject to certain constraints of financial, legal/regulatory, contractual, personnel and institutional nature. Under the circumstances, it is much more challenging in the public sector to make ICT infrastructure investment decisions. Often, the lure of ICT becomes a kind of fad and organisations try to 'mimic' others who have already introduced ICT In this connection, interesting indicators may be quoted which have been classified as (a) barriers, (b) inhibitors, (c) drivers (d) enablers.[1]

Barriers: Certain impediments or road blocks can be identified that stand in the way of introduction of ICT in a public organisation. These are

- Inadequacy or lack of fund provision
- Poor infrastructure

- Insufficient or non-existent skilled personnel
- Bureaucratic tendencies (rule-following as against work achievement)
- Dominance of unhelpful, narrow, self-interested politics

Inhibitors: These are factors that *ab initio* make it difficult to induct ICT in the organisation. These are

- Absence of ICT departments and mobility of ICT champions
- Lack of an appropriate legal and regulatory framework
- Poor data systems maintenance
- Lack of staff motivation
- Lack of a coordinated approach to organisational development

Drivers: These are support systems for ICT introduction consisting of

- Government and political support
- ICT champions within the organisation
- E-government strategy formulated by the top management
- Internal pressure and rising user expectations
- External pressure, technological change and modernisation drive

Enablers: These are facilitators creating the right ambience for ICT introduction and use, as listed below:

- Availability of trained staff within the organisation
- Easy engagement of outside consultants
- Positive attitudes toward ICT as a real aid to organisational development
- Internal source of fund
- 'Good practice' development including local improvisations and design divisibility

Broad Objectives

E-government through planned Introduction of ICT creates a web of connectivity or 'networking' that has the following relational dimensions:

(a) Intra-organisational connectivity or within organisation networking, (b) connectivity between government and citizen, (c) government to business connectivity, (d) government to employee connectivity (e) government to government connectivity.

To elaborate the points earlier made, the benefits of ICT application can be synoptically identified as:

- Organisational efficiency enhancement
- Improved services delivery — better service, more convenient, more reliable and lower cost
- Greater participation of citizens in government affairs
- Lower transaction costs
- Helpful in building trust between government and citizen
- Providing greater people's access to government information
- Making government more accountable by making the operations more transparent
- Enhanced control of fraud and reduction of corruption
- Providing wider development opportunities, especially benefiting rural and traditionally underserved communities and marginalised sections of society (e.g. Women, Scheduled Castes, Scheduled Tribes)
- Challenging existing ways of doing work
- Creating a general climate of organisation-wide reform
- Harnessing organisational energy/resources through networking or organisational synergy

Administrative Reform

As already pointed out, E-government should not be looked at as a standalone kind of effort to bring about some patchy changes in the organisational work processes. To optimise the efforts and costs involved in the introduction of ICTs, E-government initiatives in any country should advisably be cast within the broader framework of the country's administrative revamping efforts. In this context, the appointment of the Second Administrative Commission in India (2005) readily comes to mind. The Government of India, in appointing the Commission, asked for the 'preparation of a detailed blueprint for revamping the public administration system'. The Commission is, 'required to suggest measures to achieve a proactive, responsive, accountable, sustainable and efficient administration for the country at all levels of the government'. What is noteworthy in our context is that the Commission has to inter alia consider (a) citizen-centric administration and (b) promoting E-governance. Thus, E-governance has not been thought of in insular term as a kind of one-time change through the introduction of ICTs. Introduction of ICTs has very rightly been made an integral part of wider and systemic governmental reform.

E-government as a New Paradigm

The question that can be raised at this point is: how the introduction of ICTs in public administration is going to bring about a transformation of the nature of traditional public administration? Four stages in the evolution of public administration can be identified in this connection:

The Bureaucracy Model with which we are familiar has been undergoing change with emphasis basically on internal structural, operational reform and individual officers' work style transformation through the introduction of the ICTs.

- The Information Management Model that is steadily emerging seeks to forge a link between citizens and government in terms of electronic public service.
- The Citizen Participation Model which is an emerging way of doing things creates conditions for strong citizen's participation in government decision-making process through two-way interactions with an emphasis on information technology as a device to promote transparency and invigorate democracy.
- Finally, the E-governance Model with multiple transactions through widest networking between diverse social entities and all political and administrative activities. This model represents a virtual merger of E-governance and E-government by synergising the efforts of all social actors including 'government'.[2]

REFERENCES

1. Dr. Dan Ramenyi (ed.), ICEG 2006, the Second International Conference on E-government, University of Pittsberg, USA, 12-13 October, 2006.
2. Seang-Tae Kim, Toward a New Paradigm of e-Government: from Bureaucracy Model to Governance Model, unpublished paper presented at the 26th International Congress of Administrative Sciences (Seoul) 2004.

CHAPTER 30

Techniques of Administrative Improvement

Public administration as a discipline had its origin in the search for a 'science' of administration that, as Woodrow Wilson envisaged, would 'straighten the paths of administration'. Internal administrative structures and processes have, since the times of Wilson, have passed through momentous changes under pressures from within and without.

BACKGROUND

Looking back, classical administrative thought, particularly Taylorism, paid almost exclusive attention to productivity-related work processes improvement.The first generation administrative thinking had been interested in micro-level work improvement practices such as proper 'structuring' of organisation, manipulating the span of control, working out proper line-staff relationship and so on. Caring for the 'human' element and motivating the staff later attracted managerial attention; yet, the issue of proper organisational structuring and work process streamlining continued to be the major concern of productivity-oriented managers. Next generation administrative thinking concentrated more and more on 'decision-making' processes with supportive data base and information management. Technological breakthrough, particularly computer-aided data processing and information management, steadily moved managerial thinking from micro to macro organisational concerns such as organisation-wide policy and decision-making, performance monitoring, business-process re-engineering and results or output-outcome-based monitoring and evaluation.

In earlier chapters, discussions have been made on 'Administrative Reforms' and 'E-government. Introduction of Information and Communication Technology (ICT) has opened up vast opportunities of much more sophisticated internal work process re-engineering and organisation-environment interface management.

WORK AND METHOD STUDY

Despite all these changes in work process reordering and much improved information and data management, Taylor's basic ideas about 'work', 'method' and 'time' management continue to have their validity and application. To quote Taylor, 'It is not 'Rule of Thumb'when you consider that piece work based on arbitrary quotas was normal practice. The use of work study/measurement to determine a fair quota was a step forward for both management and the workers. 'Taylor's contribution lay in the scientific study of 'work' and its 'standardisation'.

WHAT IS WORK STUDY?

Work study is a generic term for those techniques, particularly method study and work measurement, which are used in the examination of human work in all its contexts. This exercise helps systematic investigation of all the factors that affect the efficiency and economy of the work situation being reviewed, the objective being to bring about improvement. Briefly stated, 'work study' is the systematic study of an operation or process to ensure the best possible use of the human and material resources available. The application of work study to a department is made to improve the existing method of operation and thus to enhance organisational productivity. In course of application of work study techniques, widespread consultations with employees would be helpful to understand the existing work processes as well as to tap the reactions of all concerned to suggested changes in the work process.

Benefits of Work Study

Application of work study brings in concrete benefits to the organisation and the employees in general. Some of the expected benefits are:

1. Increased productivity
2. Reduced costs - labour, material, overheads
3. Improvement of working conditions
4. Improved quality of work and production
5. Better control of costs
6. Procedural streamlining
7. Better incentive schemes for employees on objective basis
8. Precise information and data availability for work scheduling and accurate costing

Components of Work Study

Work study consists of two main components:

(a) Method Study
(b) Time Study - Work Measurement

The first component deals with the investigation into work methods, while the second is concerned with calculation of time in work accomplishment.

Method Study

Method study, as the name suggests, is concerned with the study of 'method' of work. The systematic recording and critical examination of ways of doing things in order to make improvements is known as Method Study. The objectives of 'method study' are broadly as follows:

i) Analyse methods of work
ii) Gain insight into how work is performed
iii) Document methods of work
iv) Bring about improvement in methods of work
v) Facilitate data-based planning
vi) Provide information for Time Studies
vii) Explore opportunities for mechanisation
viii) Help work out methods of wage calculation and incentive Schemes

Benefits

A Scientific Method Study is helpful in (a) the better understanding of work performed, (b) improved work performance (c) ensuring more safety in terms of less risks from hazards for health and assets.

Procedure

In a Method Study exercise, the following steps are taken:

1. A specific job is selected for study (e.g. Midday meal in schools)
2. Current performance of the job is observed and facts are recorded

3. Major features of the job are taken into consideration such as activities performed, functionaries involved, tools and equipment used and kinds of materials processed or moved
4. After detailed examination of the job, its components are questioned in regard to their feasibility and necessity
5. Alternative methods are then explored
6. After weighing the pros and cons of each method, the most suitable one is selected
7. This becomes the basis of new work instructions
8. Training of operators will start as per the new work instructions
9. Performance measurement will then be on the new operative system
10. Steps would be taken to ensure that old methods of work are discarded and control methods are devised to monitor work performance as per the new regime

Time Study

Measuring 'work' is as old as Taylorist practice. Work Measurement is the application of techniques designed to establish the 'time' (Taylor's stop watch) for a trained and qualified worker to carry out a task at a defined rate of working. Time Study is a form of Work Measurement.

The objectives of 'time study' are to:

- Establish 'Standard Times'
- Rate the performance of operators
- Collect authentic information to calculate overall production capabilities for capacity planning.
- Firmly work out total work content of finished products

Benefits

The benefits of time study are the following:

- Knowledge about Standard Times (may be, negotiation would be necessary on this issue with workers' unions)
- Ability to estimate total work content
- Factual evaluation of work performance of operators
- Incentive schemes can be planned properly to motivate workers to perform well

Inputs and Outputs

The inputs required for a Time Study are:

- Documented results of a method study for the job to be measured
- Observations of the job to be studied
- Time readings for the job to be measured from the Stop Watch (Taylorist method)

The outputs would be as follows:

- Standard times for the job that has been measured
- Completed Time Study Sheet with ratings and times
- Knowledge about the work content for specific products and processes.

Defining Gantt Chart

A Gantt chart is a horizontal bar chart. It was developed as a production control tool in 1917 by Henry L. Gantt, an American engineer and social scientist. Frequently used in project management, a Gantt chart provides a graphical illustration of a schedule that helps to plan, coordinate and track specific tasks in a project.

A Gantt chart is constructed with a horizontal axis representing the total time span

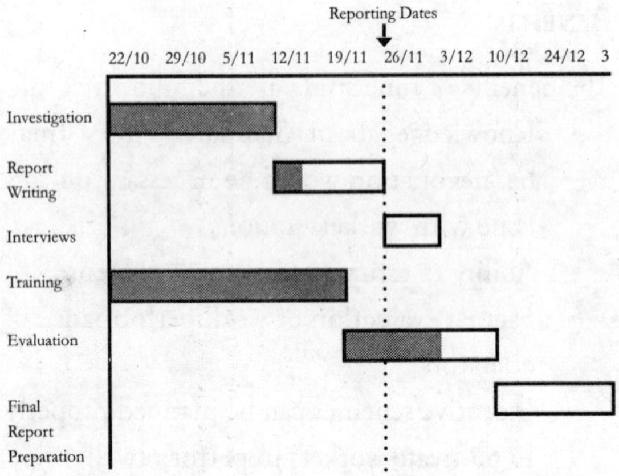

Gantt Chart

of the project, broken down into increments (for example, days, weeks, or months) and a vertical axis representing the tasks that make up the project. Horizontal bars of varying lengths represent the sequences, timing and time span for each task.

Gantt charts give a clear illustration of project status, but one problem with them is that they don't indicate task dependencies - you cannot tell how one task falling behind schedule affects other tasks. The PERT chart, another popular project management charting method, is designed to do this.

CPM & PERT

The Critical Path Method (CPM), the Programme Evaluation and Review Technique (PERT) and other forms of network analysis are the recent innovations and extensions of the Gantt chart.

Critical Path Method (CPM). CPM was developed by the engineers of the Du Pont Company in the 1950's for its application in all scheduling work, construction projects, research and development programmes and in many other situations that require estimates of time and performance. CPM calls for dividing a programme or a project into its elementary parts in their chronological order of sequence. By breaking a project into its interconnecting parts, the CPM technique is helpful in finding out the more strategic elements of a plan for the purpose of better designing, planning, coordinating and controlling the entire project.

Main features. A network of events and activities is presented pictorially in CPM with the help of several circles and arrows. Each circle represents an event and each arrow represents an activity. An event involves a specific point of time at which a part of the programme is completed. An event signifies the beginning of one activity and the end of another activity. Events are assigned serial numbers for expressing their sequence and their separate identification. An activity, on the other hand, implies time-consuming efforts or actions required for achieving an event. The flow of sequential activities is indicated by the arrow-head and such flow calls for estimating time in number of days or weeks in respect of each activity between any two events. That is, there must be an elapsed time for each activity between events.

After a network of events and activities has been prepared and times for all activities have been shown, the critical path is computed with reference to those strategic events and activities which take the longest time to complete the whole project and which thereby leave the least slack time. Slack time is the difference between the target time and the project-completion time. In other words, the critical path involves the minimum expected time in which the project as a whole can be completed. Although attention is focused on one critical path in network system, there exist several critical paths in order of importance. Figure illustrates a simple network with its critical path.

Advantages. The network analysis through CPM leads to a number of benefits:

11. It focuses attention on the timely

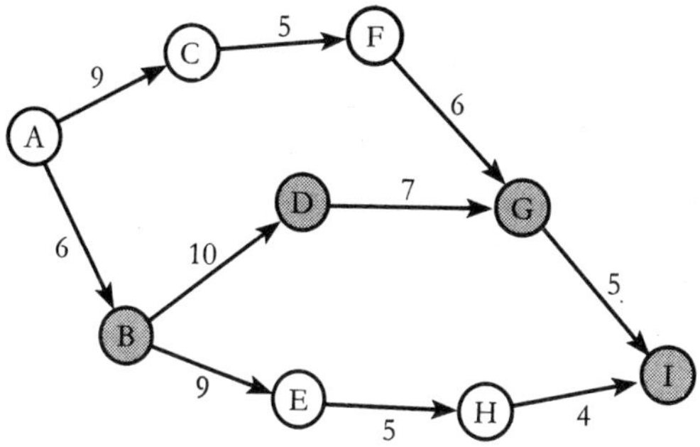

A simplified network with its critical path in black shade.

completion of the whole project or even on shortening its time span by several means.

12. It permits to place special emphasis on each activity for securing its improvement by way of putting greater resources, changing the technology or adopting other like methods. Briefly, it results in the optimum utilisation of resources and facilities.
13. It enables managers to make advance planning for all activities, to identify strategic events, to detect potential bottlenecks to the flow of work and to avoid an unnecessary pressure on other paths.
14. Because of concentrated thinking and attention on each activity of the project rather than on the whole of it, it improves the quality of planning, organising and controlling in a number of ways.

*Limitations. **CPM has some limitations:***

1. In repetitive or routine operations and for recurring projects, it has limited use and applications. It is well adapted for non-recurring projects.
2. As the time estimate for each activity is based on a single time without any consideration of future contingencies and impending difficulties, time allotted for different activities may prove to be unrealistic.

The Programme Evaluation and Review Technique (PERT). PERT is a sophisticated version of the network technique comprising a larger number of events and activities. It was first developed for use in the U.S. defence projects in connection with the execution of Pollaris missile programme in 1958. PERT has refined the CPM technique in two respects. *Firstly,* it has adopted statistical methods for estimating the time required for each activity. Instead of using one single time as in CPM, PERT calls for computing the expected time for each activity on the basis of weighted arithmetic mean of three different estimated times, viz., the optimistic time, the most likely time and the pessimistic time.The expected mean time is further tempered with the principles of standard deviations of the probability theory. *Secondly,* the PERT system can even be applied to new projects for which no past experience is available. PERT can encompass too many events and activities of a very complex project with the help of electronic computers and can provide managers with alternative decisions in respect of the time required, resources to be put in and the adjustment of quality specifications for each activity.

PERT applies basically the same principles of network analysis as are used in CPM. The PERT chart also requires the graphic presentation of events with the help of circles and the activities with the help of arrows. The critical path is also computed on the same considerations as are involved in CPM.The diagram given in Figure illustrates the nature of PERT chart. PERT was originally-introduced for putting emphasis on time and performance of the work and it did not concern itself with the cost of the work. In subsequent years, PERT/TIME has been refined further by the introduction of PERT/COST. But the translation of time factor in PERT into the cost element has made the PERT system complicated and imperfect in character, thereby restricting its wide use in complex projects.

Advantages. There are five special advantages of PERT:

1. It compels managers to make advance planning for fitting the relevant parts into an integrated whole.
2. As it encompasses a number of events and activities at different levels of the organisation, it calls for systematic planning all down the line.
3. It is instrumental for concentrating attention on critical or strategic elements that may need any correction or modification.
4. It requires a system of forward-looking control with a view to completing sequential events and activities in proper time.
5. It fosters all-round co-ordination by way of looking into the time, quantity and direction dimensions of co-ordination.

Limitations. ***PERT is subject to some limitations:***

1. The expected time for each activity of any nebulous programme cannot be determined on a basis of certainty.
2. PERT has special application in creative planning and it is not worthwhile for adoption in routine planning for recurring events that take place in mass or process production.
3. PERT gives emphasis on time only and ignores costs. As a result, it is suitable for programmes where time is of essential consideration or where time and costs have a close relationship. In other cases, it has limited applications.

Chapter 31

Network Theory: Impact on Public Administration

Public administration has been traditionally concerned with the internal structures and processes of governmental organisation. The familiar concepts associated with our discipline are 'authority', 'hierarchy', 'division of work' or 'departmentalization', 'organisational control' and 'communication' and so on. By contrast, the real world of governing, particularly in recent years, has witnessed a very different administrative scenario where formal government has been found actually functioning in an interactive mode in close contacts with a variety of organisations — public, semi-public, non-governmental organisations and even the private sector. It is in this context that the idea of 'network' caught the attention of public administration scholars. We are especially indebted to Laurence O'Toole who in his seminal paper published in Public Administration Review (Jan../Feb. 1997) had drawn our attention to the phenomenon of 'networks' that, in his view, needs to be studied carefully to gain realistic understanding of public governance as also to advance 'theory building' in public administration. To quote O'Toole, 'Public administration increasingly takes place in settings of networked actors who necessarily rely on each other and cannot compel compliance on the part of the rest.Yet the standard writings to which most administrators turn for advice to improve performance devote relatively little attention to acting effectively in such situations'. It is this phenomenon of practice-theory disjunction that O'Toole thought needs to be seriously attended to.

O'Toole's Description

To borrow O'Toole's expressions:

"Networks are structures of interdependence involving multiple organisations or parts thereof, where one unit is not merely the formal subordinate of the others in some larger hierarchical arrangement. Networks exhibit some structural stability but extend beyond formally established linkages and policy-legitimated ties. The notion of network excludes mere formal hierarchies and perfect markets, but it includes a very wide range of structures in between. The institutional glue congealing networked ties may include authority bonds, exchange relations and coalitions based on common interest, all within a single multiunit structure. In networks, administrators cannot be expected to exercise decisive leverage by virtue of their formal position. Influence in larger networks is more difficult to document, predict and model than it is in relatively simple two- or three-party relationships."

Empirically, inter-unit patterns — networks — are increasingly evident in public management operations. As O'Toole points out, such inter-unit structures often 'involve webs of public, not-for-profit and business organisations in crosscutting configurations. Even at the international level, agreements on issues such as environmental quality have been translated into policy in many nations and domestic programme managers find themselves linked in multilevel and cross-national webs 'from the negotiating table to the shop floor.' While the reality at one end is 'networked', the actual public organisational response at the other end continues to be traditional. Most administrators, in real life, cautioned O'Toole 'are now either operating with inappropriate organisational models or adapting conventional structures to meet the more challenging demands'.

Administrative Reality

At the functional level, 'government' in reality has to operate, almost always, in a large 'relational' context. There are the different branches of government, within-department sections and rules-governed relationships within which the actual operations are conducted. Departments often have to depend on other cognate agencies for major decisions such as recruitment of personnel, budgetary allocation and sanctions beyond certain limits etc. Files move from one section to another, one level to another, one organisation to another within the governmental set-up. Many a time, references are made to Public Service Commissions or Personnel Department to sort out a department's personnel problem. Similarly, financial issues are often referred to the Finance Department for clearance. Beyond such within-government relationships, historically, in the pursuit of successful management, governments have usually developed extensive collaborative relationships with 'outside' agencies such as charitable organisations, private agencies and associations. That is why Frederickson[1], the eminent public administration specialist, has introduced, in this context, the 'theory of administration conjunction' which, in his considered view, 'shows the possibilities for building theories indigenous to public administration that tackle the important questions of governance'.

The Concept

The term 'network', as used by different disciplines, has not been free from ambiguities. Castells who is commonly associated with the idea of 'grand theory' of 'Network Society', has used the term 'network society' as a synonym for a new 'collective capitalism'. As Castells argues, 'as an historical trend, dominant functions and processes in the Information Age are increasingly organised around networks'. In his formulation, 'A network is a set of interconnected nodes. A node is the point at which a curve intersects itself. What a node is, concretely speaking, depends on the kind of concrete networks of which we speak'. As Castells asserts, the contemporary networking forms of management and production do not imply the demise of capitalism. Rather, in its various institutional forms, the network society is, for the time being, a capitalist society.[2]

The concept of 'Network' has been put forward, as earlier pointed out by O'Toole, to represent qualitatively different means by which diverse organisations and actors bring about change in their terms of work. In the process, they change the environments through which public goods and services are defined and produced.

The 'network' form has thus been characterized as the signature form of organisation in today's information age. The expression has been used as a kind of timely metaphor for increasingly contrived as well as naturally evolved communication among social actors engaged in complex social interactions. More particularly, governance network can be defined as:

- A horizontal interaction and articulation of interdependent but operationally autonomous actors/agencies engaged in the performance of a commonly agreed upon task
- The 'family' of actors/agencies interacting through, negotiations among themselves
- The inter-organisational transactions taking place within a regulative, normative, cognitive and imaginary framework
- The interactions among participating agencies being to a certain extent self-regulating in character
- The inter-organisational transactions contributing to the production of public purpose in a particular area or sphere of activities

Contemporary Governance

The last few decades have witnessed the proliferation of the phenomenon of 'network governance'. The stark reality of 'governance' today is evident on the ground in the shape of formation and functioning of *actual networks* of public agencies, private organisations and diverse groups and citizens associations.This governance scenario impels the need for rearticulating our conventional understanding of government and authority.

Contemporary governmental operations are driven by a variety of factors such as broader changes in the economy and society (citizens, for instance, demanding quicker and more adequate remedies) and major advances in technology. These circumstances call for 'networked' forms of organisation – 'a networked trend greater in breadth and different in kind than anything seen previously'. Traditionally, the familiar governmental system has been 'hierarchical', 'rule-bound' and 'process' (as against 'result')-oriented. This model of organising and running government has been fast giving place to a more web-like, inter-organisational and inter-sectoral relations-seeking pattern, as governments everywhere are today getting involved in complex problems situations that demand creative responses to such problems. As it has been succinctly put[3]:

"This push and pull is gradually producing a new model of government in which executives' core responsibilities no longer centre on managing people and programs but on organising resources, often belonging to others, to produce public value. Government agencies, bureaus, divisions and offices are becoming less important as direct service providers, but more important as generators of public value within the web of multi-organisational, multi-governmental and multi-sector relationships that increasingly characterize modern government."

Need for Change

Governments in contemporary complex societies are confronted with tasks that are not always amenable to the traditional command and control reactions. In view of the ambiguity and complexity of the tasks, governments have to abandon the. 'silo' mentality and enter into partnerships with other parties like private sector agencies and non-government organisations. There is emerging today a distinct trend towards striking relationships with 'outside' organisations, as much of the work involves complex links among multiple organisations – public and private that need to be coordinated. How to reconcile traditional top-down hierarchy built along vertical lines of authority with the emerging 'networks' built along horizontal lines of action is the central issue to be tackled in contemporary public administration.

From the functional perspective, network governance is a contrivance to create a synergy between diverse competencies and sources of knowledge to come to grips with complex interlinked problems such as planning highways, building irrigation dams, mitigating floods, coping with global warming or large interconnected environmental management problems and so on. As it has been characterized[4], "a typical network... combines the voluntary energy, legitimacy of the civil society sector with the financial muscle, interest of business, enforcement, rule-making power, coordination and capacity-building skills of states and international organisations".

'Governance' and 'Network'

The present trend towards 'networked' government is closely related to the contemporary paradigm shift in public administration from 'government' to 'governance'. In this context, we may profitably refer to the four basic elements which, according to Peters and Pierre[5], characterise discussions on 'governance'. These are: (a) the dominance of networks, (b) the state's declining capacity for direct control, (c) the blending of public and private resources and (d) the use of multiple instruments.

In terms of (a), what is implied is that contemporary governance is characterised by a collection of actors (as against one actor) having influence over the production of public goods and services.

In terms of (b), the power of the state today is connected not so much with direct performance but with its ability to negotiate and bargain with multiple actors in policy networks and the members of such networks are treated as equal partners in the policy process.

In terms of (c), in the process of production of goods and services, public and private actors often coalesce in mutual exchanges – each using the other in the procurement of resources which they are often unable to obtain unilaterally.

Lastly, as regards (d), governance today involves increasing employment of non-traditional methods such as using tax incentives (instead of command and control regulations) for making and implementing public policies.

Background of Networking

It has been pointed out[6] that 'governance by network represents the confluence of four influential trends that are altering the shape of public sectors worldwide'. These trends, as clearly identified by Goldsmith and Eggers, are:

- *Third-Party Government:* increasing use of private firms and non-profit organisations to deliver services and fulfil policy goals
- *Joined-up Government:* multiple government agencies, often at multiple levels of government, joining together to provide integrated service
- *Digital Revolution:* contemporary technological advances (ICT/Fax etc.) enabling multiple organisations to collaborate in real time for the production of goods and services
- *Consumer Demand:* mounting citizen demand for control over their lives and for more and better 'public goods' to match the (technology driven) customized service provision on the model of the private sector

Reality of Governance

The reality today is that the world of governance is not the sole preserve of either the private or the public sector. While facing a complex socio-economic situation and responding to increasing citizens demands for more choices and better services and goods, the traditional public-private distinction is fast becoming obsolete and governments of all ideological hues are collaborating everywhere with private organisations and non-profit agencies to fulfil societal demands and expectations.

The issue in today's governance scenario is:

'how to manage a government composed more and more of networks instead of people and programs'.

This issue is of considerable practical significance. The governments organisational, management, financial and personnel systems have historically been designed to operate within the framework of 'hierarchical', not 'networked', model of government. It has thus been rightly observed that the increasing trend today towards the practice of 'government by network' is at odds with the traditional Weberian theory of bureaucratic hierarchy that has so far dominated public management theory.

In a way, 'governing by network' can be regarded as the twenty-first century model of public system management. New models of governance are being forced on the public officials by the shifting and ever-widening situational complexities. The old Taylorist model of one-size-fits all solutions is ill-suited to meet the challenges of contemporary socio-economic complexity that calls for more and more 'customized approaches' to suit situational specificities. Again, to quote Goldsmith and Eggers[7]:

"The traditional, hierarchical model of government simply does not meet the demands of this complex, rapidly changing age. Rigid bureaucratic systems that operate with command-and-control procedures, narrow work restrictions and inward-looking cultures and operational models are particularly ill-suited to addressing problems that often transcend organisational boundaries."

At the same time, it should not be thought that all that is in 'traditional' administration needs to be thrown overboard. In this context, O'Toole's sensible comment (at the annual meeting of the APSA, Toronto, September 4, 2009) is worth quoting:

"It has sometimes been claimed that network researchers assume that this structural form (of networking) is supplanting hierarchical organisation but this is untrue. The *observable* dynamic is rather more interesting: Public administration now confronts the challenge of coordinating action both within and across organisational boundaries, with the use of formal authority and also via other means."

Realistically, horizontal relations between network actors are at the core of the governance network concept. The networks phenomenon directs our attention to the fact that 'public purpose' is many a time produced through negotiation among relatively autonomous actors. It needs to be emphasized that the distinguishing feature of 'governance network', as against other forms of networks, is that it marks a deliberate attempt to contribute to the production of public purpose through horizontal negotiations.

Hierarchy versus Network (NW)

When is the 'network' model appropriate? Alternatively, when is the traditional 'hierarchical' model suitable? The advantages of 'network governance', as pointed out by Goldsmith and Eggers[8], are:

(a) Network (NW) frees government to concentrate on its 'core functions' by handing over and dispersing many activities to other providers — both public and private.

(b) The other benefit of NW lies in the opportunity it creates to requisition best possible talents and expertise available outside the governmental system.

(c) By involving a variety of providers, NW encourages 'experimentation so critical to the innovative process' – which is often faced with difficulty in the hierarchical model of bureaucracy.

(d) As is well known, bureaucratic organisations being rule-bound and hierarchic, tend to be rigid and inflexible. By contrast, NW governance can avoid these structural constraints and be 'more nimble and flexible'.

(e) NW can help (by associating with the private sector) 'expand reach without incurring huge capital costs' and at the same time it enables governments 'to engage the non-profit sector's innovative spirit and creativity in efforts to solve major social problems'.

(f) Another signal advantage that augurs well for the deepening of democracy is the ability of NW governance to enlist the support of the civil society organisations in the process of solving many complex social problems such as drug addiction, infant mortality, immunization etc. This method facilitates bringing the citizens into the mainstream of 'governance' and social problem solving, making them more self-governing than passive recipients of government benefits.

In this context, we are presenting below, in a tabular form, the 'factors determining Government's choice of a Governance Model' (Goldsmith and Eggers, 2004).

Three Levels of Networks

In public sector management, collaborative ties have become influential in policy framing and program development at three levels. With the crafting of substantive tools and strategies involving domain-linkage in this situation, some form of 'network governance' will emerge as a new mode of public management superseding both bureaucratic government and markets.

The first domain having direct importance for public policy is 'inter-organisational network'.

Table: Networks Model vs. Hierarchical Model

Factors Favouring Network Model	Factors Favouring Hierarchical Model
Need for flexibility	Need for stability
Need for differentiated response to clients or customers	Need for uniform, rule-driven response
Need for diverse skills	Need for a single professional skill
Many potential private players available	Government predominant provider
Desired outcome or outputs clear	Outcome ambiguous
Private sector fills skill gap	Government has necessary experience
Leveraging private assets critical	Outside capacity not important
Partners have greater reach or credibility	Government experienced with citizens in this area
Multiple services touch same customer	Service is relatively stand-alone
Third parties can deliver service or achieve goal it lower cost than government	In-house delivery more economical
Rapidly changing technology	Service not affected by changing technology
Multiple levels of government provide service	Single level of government provides service
Multiple agencies use or need similar functions	Single agency uses or needs similar functions

Here, groups of public and private organisations are tied up in non-hierarchical relationships through partnerships and contracts based on joint tasks domain and mutually agreed-upon resource sharing plan.

The second domain is characterized as 'inter-actor networks' of leaders and advocates. In this networking, what matters most are the personal ties developed among bureaucrats, politicians and administrators-politicians interactions. Linkages with significant 'stakeholders' are also of considerable importance in this kind of networking.

The third domain has been called the 'inter-agency network' which has also been described as 'delivery network' or 'service network', as this kind of networking refers to the ways in which various interacting agents join up and collaborate in the provision of a common service or project management.

Of the three types, the inter-agency network is considered most useful and more frequently pursued type in the production of an array of public goods and services.

It is being contended that network management strategies will have to become part of the standard operating procedures of public management. At the same time, one has to admit that the content, conditions and implications of the network approach as a prescriptive theory of public management need to be further developed, tested and evaluated.

Practical Problems

In this connection, attention needs to be drawn to a number of practical issues of considerable significance:

- The network management strategies in terms of concrete techniques and supporting instruments need to be further elaborated by working out a proper road map for practicing administrators as-participants in active networks.
- More attention needs to be paid to the institutional conditions for the introduction of network management strategies. Potential institutional barriers need to be identified and removed to successfully move towards such network strategies. There is need particularly to identify the positive and negative incentives for inter-organisational cooperation and collaboration.
- The practical implications of network strategies and their impacts on administrative arrangements need to be carefully considered. Applying network theory in practice would involve a redefinition of the traditional roles of politicians, administrators, interest groups and citizens at large. For instance, what would be the role of democratic 'politics' and 'accountability' in a system of network management? How can citizen participation be fitted into the network arrangement?
- Even if network strategies are adopted, these need to be rule-governed and properly directed to achieve planned results. How will such rules be framed and what kind of directing authority would be in charge of steering the network?
- Even if resource-sharing and mutual collaborative efforts are found to be useful in a network arrangement, how will the sharing principles be worked out and how can such sharing and collaboration be sustained over longer periods?
- Network governance has to be carefully designed with all actors in the network understanding clearly their respective roles in order that each actor can play its role as per design.

GENERATIONS OF NETWORK THEORISTS

Two generations of governance network theorists may, in this context, be briefly mentioned. It goes to the credit of the *first generation theorists* to coin the term 'governance' as a label for a specifically new theoretical and empirical research agenda denoting plurality of actors in the processes of societal problem solving.The central idea in this new perspective has been the uncovering of the role of networks of multiple actors and agencies in the governing of an increasingly complex and fragmented society.

The *second generation* of network research is currently engaged in more detailed operations of the concept of networks governance and in fleshing out different types of such networks. The other important objective of the second generation networks theory is to work out and elaborate the implications of networks governance for the democratic functioning of the polity.

In a recent paper by Berry et al (Public Administration Review (64[5], 2004) entitled 'Three Traditions of Network Research', three parallel streams of literature about network theory and research have been highlighted: (i) social network analysis, (ii) policy change/political science networks (iii) public management networks. As they have remarked; there has been an abundance of network research since the publication of O'Toole's seminal article in PAR in 1997. Against this background, they have called for 'a variety of methods for studying public management networks and cultivating discussion among those who employ different methods or whose work is guided by different theoretical orientations, including the value added by social network analysis'.

CONCLUDING OBSERVATIONS

At the end of the day, the sustainability and general acceptance of networks governance would depend squarely on its capacity to enrich, not undermine, the performance standard of democratic governance. Crucial elements in this context are the linkages between network governance and the forms of representative democracy as a functioning governance system. Thus, networks governance theory has to deliberate on how to accommodate such crucial democratic parameters as 'access and accountability', 'representation', 'legitimating' and 'transparency and openness'. In the ultimate analysis, the current trend and spread of network governance have to stand the acid test of ensuring, above all, a more efficient 'democratic' functioning. It has been rightly argued that drawing on the different theories of democracy, one has to develop a set of criteria for judging the extent to which the governance networks, themselves are 'democratic' and not merely techno-managerial recipes. It should be clear by now that the new regime of network governance marks a paradigm shift in public administration. At the same time, it needs to be acknowledged that both designing network and its proper management call for a new breed of innovative public managers. Governments have to develop certain core capabilities for this purpose. For instance, conceptualizing 'network' and its application in specific situations require high quality policy leadership in government. Operation of network involves a lot of in-house activities such as proper structuring, formulating functional ground rules, actual ICT-based networking, inter-agency communication formatting, indicators-based monitoring and evaluation and so on.

The new network governance system is bound to have repercussion on the extant public personnel management system — covering the entire gamut from recruitment to training, career development, performance evaluation and pay and emoluments. By way of conclusion, we can quote no less an authority than Donald Kettl who had clearly pointed out the contributions of network theory in his scholarly and profound article (presented at the Fifth National Public Management Research conference, Texas A&M University, December 4, 1999):

"The growing interconnections among public, private and non-profit organisations profoundly disrupt traditional notions of public administration. Different strategies and tactics demand new approaches to ensure effectiveness and responsiveness...The field's response has been to develop a new theory of network-based relationships. Both formal and informal ties link organisations seeking a common purpose. This work has made several important contributions. First, it has helped public administration escape the pathologies of theory deeply rooted in hierarchical authority. Second, it has helped reconcile theory to new-and obvious-patterns of administrative practice. Third, it has led to intriguing new approaches to coordination that do not rely solely on authority. Fourth, it has helped to provide the foundation for linking the study of governance with an understanding of the workings of government."

REFERENCES

1. H. George Frederickson and Kevin B. Smith, The Public Administration Theory Primer, Westview Press, 2003.
2. Manuel Castells, The Rise of the Network Society, Vol. 1, Blackwell Publishing, Cambridge, MA, 1996.
3. Stephen Goldsmith and William D. Eggers, Governing by Network: the New Shape of the Public Sector, Brookings Institution Press, Washington, D.C., 2004.
4. W.H. Reinicke and F. Deng, Critical Choices: The United Nations, Networks and the Future of Global Governance, International Development Research Council, Ottawa, 2000.
5. Guy B. Peters and John Pierre, 'Governance without Government? Rethinking Public Administration', Journal of Public Administration Research and Theory, 8, 1998.
6. Goldsmith and Eggers, op. cit.
7. Op. cit. p.7.
8. Op. cit. Ch. 2.

Chapter 32

Feminism and Public Administration

Essentially a political movement, 'feminism' is a multi-faceted phenomenon. In a generic sense, it stands for a distinctive theoretical orientation toward political, social and economic equality of the sexes and organised activity to promote women's rights and interests. Public administration as the action arm of government cannot escape the influence of feminist movements and orientations; yet, as we will have occasions to mention in course of the present discussion, the discipline of public administration has been a laggard in regard to its response to the feminist calls for 'gender justice' and general 'gender orientation' toward public organisations and public policy issues and their implementation. Possibly, the answer to this relative passivity of the discipline can be found in part at least in Carole Pateman's characterization of feminist theory. As she forcefully argued:

'Feminist theorists place themselves in an exposed position. Their arguments are as potentially subversive of conventionally radical theory, including Marxism as of other theories and those radicals who might be expected to be the allies of feminist scholars are as often as not hostile, or at best indifferent. To ask embarrassing questions about the relation between women and men and to argue that sexual domination is central to, although unacknowledged in, modem social and political theory, is to touch on some emotions, interests and privileges very different from those disturbed by arguments about class.'[1]

Historically, 'feminism' emerged as a political movement on the belief in equality of women and men committed to 'the elimination of gender-based injustice'. Many of these injustices have been institutionalized in laws and public policies that patently discriminated against women. Specific rights (e.g. right to vote), immunities, privileges and opportunities were granted to men and systematically denied to women. Public law and public policy have, therefore, been targeted as the site for contestation in the western countries during the course of the past two centuries.

'Waves' of Feminism

To meaningfully associate itself with 'feminism', administrative thought needs to appreciate the successive shifts in feminist thinking. Basically grown and developed in the 'Western' socio-cultural milieu, feminist movement has passed through successive and sometimes overlapping, stages of evolution (that is why the term 'wave' is not universally accepted).

It was only by the late nineteenth century and early twentieth century that organised feminist movements became really visible. This can be considered as the period when the *first wave of feminism* hit the world. Strange though, women were considered as private properties to be purchased in marriage and they had no right to vote in a democratic setup or any right to property. That was the time for the rise of the 'first wave', seeking equal rights for women, exemplified by the Suffragettes who sought the vote for women and were against abortion.

The *second wave of feminism* is associated with the period of 1960s and thereafter till 1980s. It came as an explosion in America and then spread across the world. The movement was especially vocal in matters like civil rights, sexual liberation, childcare,, health, welfare, education, work and reproductive rights including the right to abortion. Cultural and social equality for women was a major issue in the second wave of feminism. The second wave of feminism especially campaigned against the social and cultural stereotyping of women as "only capable of becoming a housewife" and nothing more. It advocated for equal rights for women as of men to pursue a work life and career.

The *third wave of feminism* is in fact a continuation of the second wave of feminism beginning from the early 1990s. It focuses on the perceived failures of the second wave of feminism. The third wave also focuses on issues like race, gender and feminism. Further the movement broadens into global dimensions with different shades of feminism becoming visible based on issues specific to a particular society or a culture.

It will be wrong to suggest that the feminist movement has come to a stop. It is very much alive and vibrant today raising many significant questions regarding promotion of more egalitarian workplace, recognition of 'emotion' in human relational context and similar other issues of importance not only for women but also for a safer and better holistic human condition.

Impact on Public Administration

Feminist administrative theory, in its explicit form, needs to be traced to Camilla Stivers' seminal work — *Gender Images in Public Administration (993).* In this pioneering work, Stivers raises the fundamental question of 'legitimacy of public administration'. She traces the sources of this legitimacy to the formative days of Public Administration in the writings of Woodrow Wilson (1887) and to his idea of politics/administration dichotomy. Wilson's version of administration is legitimate because it is neutral. With the rise of the administrative state and public hostility towards the bureaucracy, many public administration theorists have come forward to build a strong defence of public administration. The legitimacy of this administrative state essentially derives from the three main qualities of individual civil servants: expertise, leadership and virtue. Armed with a gender lens and backed by many feminist theories, Stivers sets to deconstruct the gender bias that characterizes the definition of these qualities.

Stivers' Main Thesis

Stivers' central thesis is that dilemmas of gender are embedded in the images of expertise, leadership and virtue that are used to legitimate the administrative state. According to her, these images "have masculine features" and they "help keep in place or bestow political and economic privilege on the bearers of culturally masculine qualities at the expense of those who display culturally feminine ones." This masculinity "contributes to and is sustained by power relations, in society at large that distribute resources on the basis of gender and affect people's life chances and their sense of themselves and their place in the world".

The feminist movement generated new theories of power, of virtue, of the nature of organisation and of leadership and professionalism. Stivers' main interest in 'Gender Images' has been basically to establish a truth.

She warns that her book contributes very little if "justifying public administration involves simply mobilizing support for administrative business as usual." Focusing on traditional gender images of expertise, leadership and virtue, Stivers deconstructs the three main characteristics which are used to defend the legitimacy and power of the administrative state. Her approach may be considered historical. She uses the experience of women in the past and current societal expectations to conclude that the future has much in store for public administration's ability to truly and fully, include women at all levels of the hierarchy and decision making. She argues that "the justifications of public administration [exist!] in a space that (1) depends for its coherence on the subordination of women through their assignment to a set of duties that, no matter how necessary, are generally regarded as less worthy or significant and (2) limits both women's opportunities to participate in public life and the time and energy they have to devote to it." In Stivers' view, these are paradoxical dimensions. This paradox largely contributes to the legitimacy crisis of the administrative state. Expertise is deconstructed on the basis of "its aura of objectivity", its assertion of autonomy, its hierarchy and its norm of brotherhood. Stivers' main argument is that "the image of expertise is fundamentally inconsistent with widely accepted notions of womanhood and requires a social order that subordinates women". For 'expertise' to be an engine of excluding certain segments in society is not a surprising reality. One would only have to look at the historic under-representation of certain societal groups in the public sector professional categories to realize how 'expertise' could be made an exclusive quality.

The point to note here is that 'expertise' has the potential to exclude not only women but also many other segments of the population. Public administrators are expected to hold the ship together as a coherent and not fragmented, enterprise.

In this context, Stivers discusses four images of leaders: *the visionary, the decision maker, the symbol* and *the definer of reality*. All four images are masculine. Images of virtue are also "fundamentally gendered and linked to a sex-based division of social life into public and domestic spheres that disadvantages women and hinders public administration from promoting a politically compelling version of virtue". Stivers argues that these images have for long been a masculine domain. According to her, this creates a conflict between being feminine and being a leader.

To be a feminist in public administration, according to Camilla Stivers[2], binds one to three things:

- To the idea that gender is a crucially useful category of analysis, a framework or lens that enables one to see important things that otherwise remain invisible or obscured;
- To a critical perspective on women's current status and prospects and
- As Gerda Lerner once put it, to "a system of ideas and practices which assumes that men and women must share equally in the work, in the privileges, in the defining and dreaming of the world".

It is important to note that within the broader field of 'governance' that has emerged almost like a new 'paradigm' today, the 'gender' concern has not received the centrality it eminently deserves. This point has been clearly put forward by Martha Nussbaum in her well-argued 'introduction' to the volume entitled 'Essays on Gender and Governance'[3]. As she argues:

"The relationship between gender and governance has too often been neglected in both theoretical and empirical work. Until very recently, most influential political thought has been built around a conceptual distinction between the "public" realm of politics, military affairs and administration and the "private" realm of family and domestic life. Women's role, in a wide range of traditions and in theoretical work influenced by them, has typically been associated with the "private" realm and men's role with the public" realm. The public/private distinction has been thoroughly criticized as being in many ways misleading and untenable. Nonetheless, it continues to influence both theoretical and empirical work, with the result that women's efforts to gain a voice in governance have often been ignored." When it comes to conventional studies of public administration or public organisations, the feminist approaches to administration/organisation have been generally concerned with two basic issues: (a) identifying and reducing gender-based inequalities and (b) promoting more egalitarian workplace. As regards the second issue centred on workplace, the feminist concerns are focused on the disadvantages faced by women in their workplaces and on the diverse social, organisational and individual factors that produce and reinforce women's subordination to men in the workplace.

Compared to other social science disciplines, public administration theory has rather been a late comer in the otherwise burgeoning field of feminist thought. There is truth in Camilla Stivers's forthright statement[4]: 'At present there is virtually no published theoretical work from a feminist perspective in the field of public administration'. Of course, many PA scholars have, in recent years, started reflecting on this status of our field. Women's scholarship and experiences, within the discipline of public administration, have still largely remained on the periphery with discussions limited to a rather narrow range of topics. Usually, most common themes have been (a) numerical representation in public organisations, (b) comparable worth, (c) affirmative action, (d) equal opportunity (e) subordination to men (masculinity). As we will be discussing later, the contemporary trend has fortunately been toward undertaking more wide-ranging research themes like questioning the taken-for-granted Weberian 'hierarchy' and 'rationality', organisational 'leadership issues', impact of 'emotional' psychology on organisational performance and similar other topics with deeper organisational and functional concerns[5].

Stivers's 'Bureau Men, Settlement Women'[6]

In this context, special mention needs to be made of Camilla Stivers's recent (2002) ground-breaking work (based on the life and work of an eminent social worker and administrator – Jane Addams. During the first two decades of the twentieth century in cities across America, both men and women struggled for urban reform but in distinctively different ways. Adhering to gender roles of the time, men working for independent research bureau sought to apply scientific and business practices to corrupt city governments, while women in the settlement house movement laboured to improve the lives of the urban poor by testing new services and then getting governments to adopt them.

Although the two intertwined at first, the contributions of these "settlement women" to the development of the administrative state have been largely lost as the new field of public administration evolved from the research bureaus and diverged from social work. Camilla Stivers now shows how public administration came to be dominated not just by science and business but also by masculinity, calling into question much that is taken for granted about the profession and creating an alternative vision of public service.

Stivers's innovative and analytical narrative offers a rare look at the early intellectual history of public administration and is the only book to examine the subject from a gender perspective. It recovers the forgotten contributions of women—their intense engagement in public life, concern about the proper aims of government and commitment to citizenship and community. In the process, it reveals that they were ultimately more successful than their male counterparts in enlarging the work and moral scope of government.

Literature on Feminism

The theoretical literature of feminism is complex and multifaceted. It is difficult to cull out from the ongoing multipronged discussions any common defining concern within it. The contemporary articulations are also fraught with internal debate over explications of gender itself.

In broad terms, two types of 'feminism' have occupied the centre stage of feminist thought. These are commonly known as (a) liberal feminism[7] and (b) radical feminism. *Liberal feminism* is the dominant ideology of modern society and is grounded in classic liberal thinking that individuals should be free to develop their own talents and pursue their own interests and should be treated according to their individual merits rather than on others basis's such as in the feminist's case, sexual characteristics but because liberalism evolved in a context in which the private sphere of the family was excluded from political demands for equality, in which traditional social arguments remained strong and in which the Church upheld women's subordinate role in the family, liberal feminism developed a distinction between the 'public' and the 'private', relegating women's 'problems' to the 'private' sphere.

Radical feminists find the reforms called for by liberal feminism to be inadequate and superficial. The main goal for radical feminists is not to introduce equal rights; they do not want women to become like men, but to free women from patriarchal control — the main challenge to patriarchy being in the form of separatism. While liberal feminists wish to create equality in society and are quite happy to live with men so long as they are not treated as lesser citizens, some radical feminists wish to see a policy, which would see women, cut themselves off from men entirely both socially and sexually.

The *third group of feminists* ('postmodernist') envisions an encounter, a strategic engagement between feminism and post structuralism that transforms both sides in significant ways. The attempt here is to meld the analytical and critical power of both strands, to "combine a postmodern incredulity toward meta-narratives with the social-critical power of feminism".

Postmodern feminist argument has been that sex and gender are socially constructed and it is rather difficult to generalize women's experiences across cultures and histories. Post-structural feminism uses various intellectual currents for feminist concerns. Many post-structural feminists maintain that difference is one of the most powerful tools that women possess. Feminist projects of "rewriting," "re-inscribing," or "redeploying" key concepts of political and historical vocabulary have emerged as one primary outcome of the encounter between feminism and post-structuralism. There are feminists who aim to rewrite the terms, experience and discourse and, by implication, the notions of agency, subjectivity and identity. Specifically, their purpose is to untangle the relationships between discourses and experiences by exploring the ways in which subjects mediated or transformed discourses in specific historical settings.

Among the many uses of 'deconstruction' in feminism, the most successful is in line with the use of deconstruction to criticize masculinity.The main goal of the feminist stance is to change the social world. Hence, the most interesting query regarding the use of deconstruction for feminist theory is whether and to what extent it has been possible to convincingly unravel that there is nothing natural, objective or scientific about any given practice or description of masculinity and that all things attached with it are nothing but social constructs.The'de-constructivist'arguments are too elaborate and terse to be fully discussed in our context (of administrative theory).

Equity Feminism

A familiar orthodoxy manifest in the writings of many public administration scholars is what can be called "equity feminism".This is the body of theory that documents and demands rectification of the problems of social and economic discrimination arising from gender. The general pattern that we can see in the writing that has been produced by feminist scholars in public administration has started from the broad framework of justice. The so-called Equity Feminism, at its essence, has been concerned with fair treatment or justice in the way women are treated in employment. Moreover, it is concerned with the way present management processes and policies are being used to the disadvantage of women, specifically. This traditional stream of literature addresses some of the basic structural issues in the bureaucratic set-up. Scholars following this stream question the number of women in government agencies, their rank or success as compared to men or other minorities and conduct and encourage similar types of research. In essence, this traditional literature does not aim at changing the way in which government is administered so much as it aims to open up opportunities for women within current structure, methodology and practice. In the large crop of Equity Feminist literature, discussions usually revolve round issues like the number of women participating in various levels of government, alleged biases against them and the conditions preventing them from increased participation etc.

All of these works are directed at improving, in one way or another, the level of participation of women in the institutions of public administration and 'redressing' organisational wrongs within the 'male dominated' bureaucratic set-up. They do not offer any alternative management, leadership, or organisational structure or process practices based on a feminine perspective, let alone guidance for taking pragmatic action based on such a perspective.

'Other Voice' Feminism

A second category of feminist thought, one with a more psychological and philosophical cast, is often referred to as "other voice" or "difference" feminism. Its concern is to identify the ontological and epistemological characteristics that attach to gender distinctions. This literature represents the point of view that women constitute an alternative form or capacity of mind to that represented by men. The argument is that this other mental and emotional frame or paradigm, which can be loosely identified by a set of oppositions to the dominant male frame, could be of substantial benefit in the operation of the social world were it to be acknowledged and given venues for expression. This view ascribes a unique perspective or viewpoint to women as gendered beings who are then seen to contribute a unique perspective to methods of managing or administering in government institutions. A number of important research pursuits can be found in this area, among them are those that explore: how governance is changed by the very nature of women participating at senior levels, the effects of gender on moral development, the gendered nature of the Weberian bureaucracy, variations in male and female behavioural styles of management and leadership and those tha directly or indirectly build on Stivers' work.

Related literature describes types of behaviours or management styles that are often ascribed to women or a feminine perspective, e.g., methods of authentic participation or bureaucratic listening. The work of Kathy E. Ferguson deserves special mention in this context. Ferguson's[8] groundbreaking book examines bureaucracy and describes an alternative constructed out of the "concrete and shared experiences of women". In her view, liberal reforms – placing more women in management positions, for instance — are not enough What is needed is the emergence of an alternative voice grounded in the experience and perceptions of women that will challenge the patterns of control found in every aspect of modern life. Her concern basically is for an alternative public discourse, as she argues that the public discourse today is not the language of women even when women speak it. Ferguson's presentation is an admirable blend of the feminist literature and the literature on organisation theory and practice. In the face of increasing incursions of bureaucracy into daily life, her call is for a feminist discourse that would inject into public debate a reformulation of the basic political questions of power, reason and organisation which would, in the process, bring about a legitimacy of the contemporary concern for both autonomy and community. Ferguson thus goes beyond the narrow confines of public administration and contributes to the larger project of human liberation.

The broad scope of her interest has been:

- To clarify and render intelligible the structures and processes of power in bureaucratic society and the effects these structures and processes have upon individuals caught within them
- To offer a basis for opposition to bureaucratic discourse and bureaucratic structures
- To suggest an alternative, non-bureaucratic approach to the problem of organisation, one that criticizes and rejects the forms of organisation and the terms of self-understanding embedded in bureaucratic discourse and calls instead upon the theoretical and practical terms of a specifically feminist discourse.

There are other eminent scholars contributing to this 'feminist' discourse in public administration. For instance, Georgia Duerst-Lahti and Rita Mae Kelly explore leadership and governance by offering:

1. The concept of 'gender power' is crucial to our understanding of leadership and governance;
2. To build upon prior empirical research in sex and sex roles in order to move beyond into a richer conceptual and explanatory realm;
3. To illustrate concrete ways to deploy the concept of gender power in a spectrum of leadership and governance arenas. Asserting that "gender power exists as a central construct of the political world of governance," the discussions aim at examining 'gender power' through explorations of leadership roles[9].

Leadership Discourse

Leadership discourse has been a familiar theme in feminist literature relating to public administration theory and practice. One major contribution in this respect has come from

Carol Edlund. She has identified the significant concepts of women' leadership style and how they are a "necessary element in the developing multi-versalist paradigm". To quote Edlund in this context:

The [feminine leadership style] concept refers not to leadership by women but rather to a leadership style that contrasts with the dominant masculine leadership style. The qualities of either style can be possessed by both men and women; in addition, in individual instances the styles are likely to be mixed. The basic assumption here is: men and women, in order to be successful in bureaucratic organisations, have had to adopt the masculine style almost exclusively, one that is dysfunctional in the interconnected world of today. A feminine leadership style incorporating traits usually attributed to women offers more potential for management and problem-solving in the present environment than does the masculine style alone.

Further on she suggests that: The traditional, bureaucratic model of leadership by itself is not adequate because it fails to meet the needs of an enlightened workforce and to take into account the totality of the human psyche. A masculine leadership style with its emphasis on rational (head) thinking gives little value to the relevance of feminine (heart) thinking. A new reality is emerging in the public workplace in which there seems to be an awakening to the human needs of workers. Employees yearn for a more caring, liveable work environment. They believe that love, family and labour can be integrated. Edlund's work provides a very rich source of data for filling in characteristics of the feminine-based practical administrative alternative. She envisions a worker "who relies on an ethic of self-development"[10].

The volume edited by Bailey and Mayer (1992) carries a fascinating paper by Camilla Stivers entitled '"A Wild Patience": A Feminist View of Ameliorative Public Administration'. In fact, this anthology is a gold mine of really challenging and innovative papers on the 'feminization' of Public Administration.

Core Thinking on 'Equity'

It is, of course, 'equity feminism' that has most often been taken to be the core of all feminism. It fits the familiar category of a political protest that is demanding justice through a material pay-off. 'Other voice feminism' is sometimes seen in this light as well, though more as a move to increase the influence of women than to gain them specific economic or social benefits. The social principles that women are taken to represent—caring, inclusion, mutual communication and so on—are presented as preferable to the principles of social organisation that attach to the stereotype of men.

Post-modernist Thinking

The third category of feminist thought might be called 'post modernist or de-constructivist feminism'. This category embraces the most heterodox, subtle and philosophically sophisticated ideas about human identity and social reality. This genre of thought is too variegated co suggest briefly with any accuracy. In general, though, its project is to demonstrate that the opposition that creates gender—male and female—is not grounded in any real or essential difference. The point is that the sexual distinction is an artefact of human consciousness.This idea has a number of profound implications.The most general is that men and women, as actual people, are simply in a sense wearing a "uniform" or playing a certain role at the level of social behaviour, one that reflects and expresses the requirements of the structure of mind that the human species is carrying at present. It is important to distinguish how this perspective is different from other voice feminism. The other voice position is that men and women, either because of biology, social position and socialization, or location in the archetypal structure of life, exhibit a different mind and behaviour. The deconstructionist argument, by contrast, is that the structural position of the woman is where a certain function, essential to the operation of consciousness, is performed. This means that even were human beings to develop bodies that were completely indistinguishable from one another as genders, if consciousness remains the same, "something" would still have to be in the position of the woman to provide a venue through which the necessary function could be performed.

This statement highlights the profundity of this brand of feminist theorizing. If gender is implicated in the generic structure of contemporary consciousness, it behoves us to develop a more general understanding of it in these terms and explore its implications. Misunderstanding the function of gender could produce the most serious kinds of distortion and problems, perhaps even fatal ones, for social processes and institutions. Furthermore, if the sexual distinction, characterized at the most fundamental level, sustains our current pattern of consciousness, shifts or changes in the social structures and processes that consciousness creates are intimately tied to it. In structural terms, our very mind and the world it makes are products of a dialectic that oscillates from the position of the woman.

This characterization of the outlines of a deconstructive feminism, even as approximate as it is, reveals the exotic quality of this brand of thought. The full implications of the line of analysis it indicates are even more obscure. One thing is clear, however: To understand this form of feminism in conventional liberal terms, as just another protest movement that is seeking to get something for itself, is a critical mistake.

Masculine Imagery

Feminist scholars of public administration have uncovered and critiqued the dominance of culturally masculine imagery in public administration theory and practice. In particular, expertise, virtue, leadership and bureaucracy —the much lauded characteristics of public administration — are based on male perspectives on the world. In Ferguson's critique of bureaucracy, for example, public administration discourse emphasizes the control and subordination of employees by upper management, mirroring the control and subordination of women by men throughout history. This emphasis on control and subordination leads lower-level bureaucrats to resort to "feminization" as a means of coping with their secondary status, a strategy that includes deferring to superiors and conveying favourable images to them. From Stivers's perspective, images of expertise, virtue and leadership are not only culturally masculine but also deliberately unteminine in their cultural construction. Expertise based on science pits objectivity against emotion, culturally masculine autonomy against culturally feminine responsiveness, scientific authority against lay perspectives and professional expectations against societal expectations (which, for women, revolve around family). Leadership is culturally masculine not only in objective terms (more leaders are men) but also in subjective terms (leaders should look male and pale). Public virtue is portrayed in decidedly culturally masculine overtones, in terms of paternalistic guardians, autonomous fame seekers, commanding heroes (not heroines) and citizens who have historically been identified as white and male. Duerst-Lahti and Johnson suggest that public organisations may actually be more culturally masculine than other organisational types given the influence of the "manly" Weberian bureaucracy and its undervaluation of the culturally feminine.

Though the critique of public administration practice and theory is both well founded and well-articulated, recent public administration scholarship has become more mindful of gender.

PA Theory and Feminism: A Summing Up

As hinted earlier, unlike other social sciences, public administration theory has been a late comer in the otherwise burgeoning field of feminist thought. One has to refer again, in this context, to Camilla Stivers, whose contribution in this field is of seminal importance. To recapitulate, Stivers suggested 'four current areas in public administration theory where feminist thought might be productively used':

- The question of administrative knowledge;
- The model of the ideal public servant;
- The nature of administrative discretion; and
- The dimensions of the administrative state'.

In her estimation, each of these issues might serve as the focus of in-depth feminist treatment. In her earlier 1990 paper in *Women and Politics,* Stivers followed through this line of argument and made detailed observations on each issue separately.

Almost in a similar vein Hutchinson and Mann wrote in a recent paper[11]: "there is as yet no defining body of feminist theory in our field'. They traced the lack of feminist theory to the historic exclusion of women from positions of power and to the liberal, narrow model of administration in public administration that reduces the potential for ongoing feminist praxis. As they have argued, the liberal historic concern with equity has no doubt led to many advances for women in public administration but it has restricted the creative development of a feminist public administration theory.Their suggestion in response is that public administration scholars should 'develop a body of feminist theories as well as a distinctly feminist praxis to add to the growing body of theoretical work in other disciplines'.

Refreshingly enough, another paper by Patricia Shields[12] invokes 'Classical American Pragmatism' as an untapped source (though already linked to feminist discourse) 'that (in her view) can add and enrich PA feminist theory and praxis'. This line of thinking – to link PA theory to 'pragmatism' – has found eloquent expression in Camilla Stivers's later work (earlier mentioned) *Bureau Men, Settlement Women: Constructing Public Administration in the Progressive Era.*

Significantly, Karen Hult, in her well-researched paper on 'Feminist Organisation Theories and Government Organisations', has drawn attention to two complementary but analytically distinct concerns in recent feminist work on organisations: (a) the first one draws attention to the 'disadvantages' that women as a group confront in organisations and (b) the other concern relates to the exploration of the 'diverse individual, organisational and societal factors that produce and reinforce women's subordination to men in the work place'. Such research, in her view, spotlight the range of ways organisations are 'gendered'[13]. The issue of 'glass ceiling', for instance, has been raised by many researchers.This relates to unwritten but actually followed policy in organisations whereby a 'ceiling' is imposed limiting upward mobility of women employees. The term 'glass' stands for transparency as the limitation in regard to 'advancement' is not immediately apparent and remains normally an unwritten and unofficial policy.

Research Findings

The notion of gender as an explanatory and intermediary variable within the framework of public management has drawn considerable attention in recent times. With more and more women joining the public organisational work force, hard evidences of job performance and styles of functioning and behavioural dispositional changes need to be collected to form definitive ideas about 'gendered' public organisations.

Nevertheless, there has been a significant research focus on contrasting the managerial behaviours and leadership traits of men and women. Research in this area has been conducted in many academic disciplines and tested in a variety of organisational contexts—like legislatures, state and other public sector agencies including law-enforcing agencies, local governments and so on. Despite arguments concerning the gendered nature of public organisations, consensus on the differences between the genders playing their respective organisational roles remains somewhat elusive.

There is now fairly substantial research literature available (mostly in the Western developed countries) pointing toward fundamental gender differences in organisational values, management styles, policy preferences and leadership strategies. The implied suggestion, therefore, is that women offer notable emotional labour to an organisation, have different motivations for work in the public sector and they are more democratic and are "less hierarchical and more participatory, interactional, flexible, consociation and multifaceted". There is research evidence to prove that women are more likely to report using an interactive style of management resulting in more effective training/coaching, development and interpersonal communication. Stivers[14] (2002) has been prophetic in suggesting that the "images of professional expertise, management, leadership and public virtue that mark justifications of administrative power contain dilemmas of gender." Research evidence points toward women's leadership styles differing from men's; and at the same time both genders learning from each other. Studies on leadership style seem to suggest that significant differences exist in regard to the tendency to lead democratically or autocratically, with female administrators. Also, significant differences have been observed between the genders with respect to emotional intelligence. The other oft-applied conceptual model is that of 'representative bureaucracy' which is explained below.

Representative Bureaucracy

Women's presence in public organisations on some 'quota' basis is often advocated on the notion of a 'representative bureaucracy' which was first articulated by Donald Kingsley in 1944. Kingsley coined the term "representative bureaucracy" in response to what he observed in the British civil service during World War II. He argued that the British civil service was effective in implementing the policies of the political party in power because they both shared a middle-class economic orientation. This common economic background, Kinsley argued, led to shared values and norms and such similarities made it more likely that those working in bureaucracy would naturally agree with and implement, the ideas of those working in elected offices[15]".

Formal recruitment of women employees on the basis of 'representative bureaucracy' has however to be linked to performance or results produced in civil service through this system. In other words, it has to be empirically proved if just passive or formal representation of a subset of the population — women — leads to policy outcomes more in line with their specific needs and preferences. Despite substantial research examining if and how gender differences are seen and manifested, research linking the management strategies of male and female administrators to organisational outcomes is more limited and inconclusive. Available research literature on 'gender' in public administration does seem to suggest that gender matters with respect to leaders' behaviour and organisational outcomes, albeit in varying ways. However, more research (particularly in the context of the developing countries) linking gender and outcomes is needed to connect and further delineate the broad findings about gender to the conceptual and empirical research in public management.

Concluding Observations

The critique of public administration practice and theory from the 'gender' perspective is both well founded and well- articulated and it is indeed heartening to note that recent public administration scholarship has become more mindful of the role of 'gender'. Modern public organisations are becoming more complex knowledge-users and employers of multi-skilled personnel due to the formal accommodation of women and minorities. This is bound to be reflected in their personnel composition in terms of greater degree of diversity in skills and knowledge, cultural values, abilities and attitudes and leadership styles. Literature analyzing the contributions of women to effective functioning of the organisation recognizes gender-based behavioural differences among men and women. Women are often considered to be "nurturing, interactive, intuitive, sharing and more personalized in their dealings with their fellow employees and organisational public (customers)."[16] There is urgent need, therefore, for a careful analysis of these qualities in the interest of their effective utilization in the contemporary public sector organisations. By promoting integration, diversity and cultural and behavioural pluralities public organisations can enhance the quality of human resources and, through this, in all probability, public organisational productivity.

NOTES

1. C. PATEMAN, 'The Theoretical Subversiveness of Feminism', in C. PATEMAN and E. GROSZ (eds.) Feminist Challenges: Social and Political Theory, Northeastern University Press, Boston, 1986.
2. Camilla Stivers, 'Dreaming the World: Feminisms in Public Administration', Administrative Theory and Praxis, Vol. 27, No. 2, June 2005.
3. Martha Nussbaum, 'Gender and Governance: An Introduction', in Martha Nussbaum, Amrita Basu, Yasmin Tambiah, Niraja Gopal Jayal, Essays on Gender and Governance, Human Development Resource Centre, UNDP, New Delhi 2003.
4. Camilla Stivers, 'Toward a Feminist Perspective in Public Administration Theory', Women and Politics, Vol. 10 (4), 1990. Her classic work is a landmark in public administration literature: Gender Images in Public Administration: Legitimacy and the Administrative State, Sage (2nd Edition), 1992.
5. See in this context the other seminal contribution to PA theory from the feminist perspective by M. E. Guy, 'Three Steps Forward, Two Steps Backward: The Status of Women's Integration into Public Management', Public Administration Review, 53 (4), 1993.
6. Camilla M. Stivers, Bureau Men, Settlement Women: Constructing Public Administration in the Progressive Era (Studies in Government and Public Policy), University Press of Kansas, 2002.
7. There are other types of feminist thought such as socialist /Marxist feminist thought, Lesbian feminist thought and so on. The socialist/Marxist variant is often invoked in social development analysis. But it has its own internal epistemic problems. In terms of traditional Marxist account of power, domination is understood on the model of class exploitation – domination is linked to the capitalist appropriation of the surplus value. Socialist feminists have argued

that Marx's analysis of class domination must be supplemented with a radical feminist critique of patriarchy in order to yield a satisfactory account of women's oppression. The resulting theory is referred to as dual systems theory. As Iris Young puts it, "dual systems theory says that women's oppression arises from two distinct and relatively autonomous systems. The system of male domination, most often called 'patriarchy', produces the specific gender oppression of women; the system of the mode of production and class relations produces the class oppression and work alienation of most women"(Iris Young, Throwing Like a Girl and Other Essays in Feminist Philosophy and Social Theory, Indiana University Press, 1990).

8. Kathy E. Ferguson, The Feminist Case Against Bureaucracy, Temple University, 1984.
9. Georgia Duerst-Lahti and R. M. Kelly (eds.), Gender Power, Leadership and Governance, University of Michigan, 1995.
10. Carol J. Edlund, 'Humanizing the Workplace: Incorporating Feminine Leadership', in Mary T. Bailey and Richard T. Mayer (eds.), Public Management in an Interconnected World: Essays in the Minnowbrook Tradition, Greenwood Press, Westport, 1992.
11. Janet R. Hutchinson and Hollie S. Mann, 'Feminist Praxis: Administering for a Multicultural, Multigendered Public, Administrative Theory and Praxis, 26 (1), 2004.
12. Patricia Shields, 'Classical Pragmatism: Roots and Promise for a PA Feminist Theory', Administrative Theory and Praxis, Vol. 27, No. 2, 2005.
13. See Public Productivity and Management Review, Vol. 19, No. 2, December 1995.
14. Stivers, 'Introduction', Public Administration Review, First Published on Line, December 2002.
15. J. D. Kingsley, Representative Bureaucracy: An interpretation of the British Civil Service, Yellow Springs, OH: The Antioch Press, 1944.
16. See, in this context, Bonnie G. Mani, "Gender and the Federal Senior Executive Service: Where is the Glass Ceiling?", Public Personnel Management, 26, 1997.

CHAPTER 33

Disaster Management

Every year disasters like earthquakes, tsunami and floods suddenly strike many parts of the globe and often take the lives of people and livestock and cause damage to property and crops in the affected areas. Disaster mitigation in all its aspects has, therefore, assumed a major public policy and management concern today all over the globe. Large scale disasters tend to wash away the hard earned gains of 'development' of the developing countries that are struggling hard to bring about speedy socio-economic 'development' of the masses steeped in poverty, ill health and malnutrition.

DEVELOPING COUNTRIES

What is particularly worrying is that during the last quarter century (1980-2004), over 95% of natural disaster deaths occurred in developing countries and their direct economic losses averaged US$54 billion per annum[1]. Speedy economic development is of paramount importance for the developing countries. Yet, a single natural disaster like tsunami can stunt their economic growth for many years due to lost production, damaged infrastructure and the diversion of scarce development resources for recovery efforts.

To start with, we may refer to the almost regular annual visitations of different kinds of 'disaster' in India. On account of the unique, geo-climatic conditions, India has been traditionally vulnerable to natural disasters. Floods, droughts, cyclones, earthquakes and landslides have been recurrent phenomena in the Indian subcontinent. In India, about 60% of the landmass is prone to earthquakes of various intensities; over 40 million hectares is prone to floods; about 8% of the total area is prone to cyclones and 68% of the area is susceptible to drought. In the decade 1990-2000, an average of about 4344 people lost their lives and about 30 million people were affected by disasters every year. The loss in terms of private, community and public assets has been astronomical. These introductory observations speak volumes about the need for disaster management as an integral part of a country's overall national plan exercise.[2]

DEFINING DISASTER MANAGEMENT (DM)

For public administration in any country – especially in the developing countries – managing or coping with disaster — poses the biggest challenge for public policy planning and overall public management. Hence, today 'disaster management' is steadily emerging as a sort of distinct discipline demanding multiple skills of management – political, administrative, economic, financial, social and behavioural.

DM: A Special Type of Public Administration
As a special kind of public administration, DM's unique characteristics can be identified as under

1. As earlier mentioned, it is a multi-

skilled job requiring inputs from various disciplines and departments.

2. Procedurally, it has to be innovative requiring conventional rules-modification, as unprecedented job requirements often call for imaginative and creative improvisations.
3. Structurally, DM has to mobilize all possible resources which impel evolving a new multi-functional organisation drawing on a diverse array of departmental people and resources.
4. Because of the blurring of line of government and non-government organisations, the traditional public-private dichotomy vanishes in DM.
5. 'Coordination' which is supposed to be the heart of public administration has to be carefully modulated taking everybody on board.
6. 'Hierarchy' and 'authority' — the staples of humdrum public administration — have to be replaced by persuasion and camaraderie.
7. DM's other peculiarity is its multi-level character, as it has to rely on all the levels — central, state and local. Even international agencies like the Red Cross and others get involved in large scale disaster management.
8. Above all, in the process of actually running a DM, 'public interest' takes a new meaning; a new kind of humanitarianism informs the entire management process

Disaster management, simply stated, is the art and science of managing disasters. It consists in addressing an event — usually a natural hazard like an earthquake, cyclonic storm, landslides etc. – that has the potential to seriously disrupt the social fabric of the community. Disaster management involves a whole-of-government approach to using community resources to fight the effects of an event and assumes the community will be self-sufficient for periods of time until the situation can be stabilized. It may not be possible to completely counteract the damage. Yet, it is possible to substantially minimize the risks through early warning, provide developmental plans for recuperation from the disaster, generate communication and medical resources and aid in rehabilitation and post-disaster reconstruction.

Today, DM is considered much more broadly. It is more than just response and relief, i.e. it assumes a more proactive approach. It is a systematic process and is based on the key management principles of *planning, organising* and *leading* which includes *coordinating* and *controlling.* DM aims to reduce the negative impact or consequences of adverse events. Disasters cannot always be prevented but the adverse effects can be minimized. DM is a system with many components.

Types of Disasters

Disasters are often classified according to their: (i) causes – natural vs. human and (ii) speed of onset – sudden vs. slow. While the first type, such as a massive flood disaster or an earthquake, is well-known, the second, like for instance, 'drought' has deeper implications for development planning. Drought is called 'creping disaster' as, due to lack of rains or erratic and woefully inadequate rains, the distress unfolds gradually and slowly

1. Natural Disasters: These types of disaster naturally occur in proximity to and pose a threat to, people, structures or economic assets. They are caused by biological, geological, seismic, hydrological, or meteorological conditions or processes in the natural environment (e.g., cyclones,

earthquakes, tsunami, floods, landslides and volcanic eruptions).

2. Human-Made Disasters: These are disasters or emergency situations of which the principal, direct causes are identifiable human actions, deliberate or otherwise. Apart from "technological disasters" this mainly involves situations in which civilian populations suffer casualties, losses of property, basic services and means of livelihood as a result of war, civil strife or other conflicts, or policy implementation. In many cases, people are forced to leave their homes, giving rise to congregations of refugees or externally and/or internally displaced persons as a result of civil strife, an airplane crash, a major fire, oil spill, epidemic, terrorism, etc.

Impacts: Disasters usually have serious impacts on community life. Some of these can be identified as under:

- Infrastructure damage
- Telecommunication loss
- Flooding
- Landslides
- Power disruption
- Health and water problems
- Agricultural damage in all its aspects like crop, cattle loss etc.
- Loss/damage to housing
- Damage to inland and coastal environments
- Disruption of standard of living, lifestyle, etc.

Need for Sustainable Development

As distinguished from proactive and long term sustainable development, earlier approaches to disaster management had usually been reactive and basically 'relief' oriented. Contrastingly, one of the strongest links with development today is the planned promotion of sustainable livelihoods and their protection and speedy recovery during disasters and emergencies. Where this goal is achieved, the affected people have a greater capacity to deal with disasters and their recovery is more rapid and long lasting. In a development oriented disaster management approach, developmental considerations are strongly represented in the 'mitigation' and 'preparedness' phases of the disaster management cycle. The components of DM are now discussed below in seriatim.

A. Mitigation

Mitigation activities actually eliminate or reduce the probability of disaster occurrence, or reduce the effects of unavoidable disasters. Mitigation measures include building codes; vulnerability analyses updates; zoning and land use management; building use regulations and safety codes; preventive health care and public education. Mitigation will depend on the incorporation of appropriate measures in national and regional development planning. Its effectiveness will also depend on the availability of information on hazards, emergency risks and the countermeasures to be taken. The mitigation phase and indeed the whole disaster management cycle, includes the shaping of public policies and plans that either modify the causes of disasters or mitigate their effects on people, property and infrastructure.

B. Preparedness

The goal of emergency preparedness programs is to achieve a satisfactory level of readiness to respond to any emergency situation through programs that strengthen the technical and managerial capacity of governments, organisations and communities. These measures can be described as logistical readiness to deal with disasters and can be enhanced by having response mechanisms and procedures, rehearsals, developing long-term and short-term strategies, public education and building early warning systems. Preparedness can also take the form of ensuring that strategic reserves of food, equipment, water, medicines and other essentials are maintained in cases of national or local catastrophes.

During the preparedness phase, governments, organisations and individuals develop plans to save lives, minimize disaster damage and enhance disaster response operations. Preparedness measures include plans; emergency exercises/training; warning systems; emergency communications systems; evacuations plans and training; resource inventories; emergency personnel/contact lists; mutual aid agreements and public information/education. As with mitigations efforts, preparedness actions depend on the incorporation of appropriate measures in national and regional development plans. In addition, their effectiveness depends on the availability of information on hazards, emergency risks and the countermeasures to be taken and on the degree to which government agencies, non-governmental organisations and the general public are able to make use of this information.

C. Response

1. *Humanitarian Action*

During a disaster, humanitarian agencies such as Red Cross, Ramakrishna Mission, CARE etc. are often called upon to deal with immediate response and recovery. To be able to respond effectively, these agencies must have experienced leaders, trained personnel, adequate transport and logistic support, appropriate communications and guidelines for working in emergencies. If the necessary preparations have not been made, the humanitarian agencies will not be able to meet the immediate needs of the disaster affected people. They, however, have necessarily to function in a concerted manner, usually under the coordinating umbrella of some government agency like the District or Subdivision Administration.

2. *Proper Response*

The aim of emergency response is to provide immediate assistance to maintain life, improve health and support the morale of the affected population. Such assistance may range from providing specific but limited aid, such as assisting refugees with transport, temporary shelter and food, to establishing semi-permanent settlement in camps and other locations. It also may involve initial repairs to damaged infrastructure. The focus in the response phase is on meeting the basic needs of the people until more permanent and sustainable solutions can be found. Humanitarian organisations are often strongly present in this phase of the disaster management cycle.

D. Recovery

As the emergency is brought under control, the affected population is capable of undertaking a growing number of activities aimed at restoring their lives and the infrastructure that supports them. The aim of the recovery phase is to restore the affected area to its previous state. It differs from the response phase in its focus; recovery efforts are concerned with issues and decisions that must be made after immediate needs are addressed. Recovery efforts are primarily concerned with actions that involve rebuilding destroyed property, re-employment and the repair of other essential infrastructure. There is no distinct point at which immediate relief changes into recovery and then into long-term sustainable development. There will be many opportunities during the recovery period to enhance prevention and increase preparedness, thus reducing vulnerability. Ideally, there should be a smooth transition from recovery to on-going development. Recovery activities continue until all systems return to normal or better. Recovery measures, both short and long term, include returning vital life-support systems to minimum operating standards; temporary housing; public information; health and safety education; reconstruction; counselling programs and economic impact studies. Information resources and services include data collection related to rebuilding and documentation of lessons learned.

The main aim of disaster management is to reduce, or avoid the potential losses from hazards, assure prompt and appropriate assistance to victims of disaster and achieve rapid and effective recovery. The disaster management cycle illustrates the ongoing process by which governments, businesses and civil society plan for and reduce the impact of disasters, react during and immediately following a disaster and take steps to recover after a disaster has occurred. Appropriate actions at all points in the cycle lead to greater preparedness, better warnings, reduced vulnerability or the prevention of disasters during the next iteration of the cycle. The complete disaster management cycle includes the shaping of public policies and plans that either modify the causes of disasters or mitigate their effects on people, property and infrastructure. The mitigation and preparedness phases occur as disaster management improvements are made in anticipation of a disaster event. Developmental considerations play a key role in contributing to the mitigation and preparation of a community to effectively confront a disaster. As a disaster occurs, disaster management actors, in particular humanitarian organisations become involved in the immediate response and long-term recovery phases. The four disaster management phases – mitigation preparedness, response and recovery as earlier explained — do not always, or even generally, occur in isolation or in this precise order. Often phases of the cycle overlap and the length of each phase greatly depends on the severity of the disaster.

Early Warning System

In recent years the continuity feature of emergency management has resulted in a new concept – Emergency Management Information System (EMIS). EMIS is aimed at supporting the emergency management process by providing an infrastructure that integrates emergency plans at all levels of government and non-government involvement and by utilizing the management of all related resources (including human and other resources) for all four phases of emergencies. In this connection, the importance of 'early warning system' needs special mention. With improved technologies developed over the years, early warning systems have been extremely helpful in many situations. Desktop systems and computer communications emerged as a technology for linking emergency professionals on a global basis in the eighties. With the 1990s, computer equipment became more powerful and is now an essential component of disaster operations worldwide. Today Earth observation satellites provide basic support in pre-disaster preparedness programs: in-disaster response, monitoring activities and post-disaster reconstruction.

In the United States of America, the national nodal agency in charge of disaster management is the Federal Emergency Management Agency or FEMA as it is called. Two main components of the strategy formulated by FEMA are (a) to increase public awareness of natural hazard risk and (b) to significantly reduce the risk of loss of life, injury, economic cost and destruction of natural and cultural resources due to natural disasters.

Five key elements of the overall strategy are:

- Hazard identification and risk assessment,
- Applied research and technology transfer,
- Public awareness, training and education,
- Incentives and resources
- Leadership and coordination.

Disaster Risk Reduction

There are three requirements for disaster risk reduction strategies:

- They need to be mainstreamed into development planning;
- They must be multi-sector
- They must invest in ecosystem management.

INTEGRATED ECOSYSTEM APPROACH

In this context, special mention needs to be made of the 'ecosystem approach' to disaster planning and management. From the sustainability point of view, ecosystems matter to disaster risk reduction and they can be managed to reduce disaster risk more effectively. Ecosystems provide valuable protective services, including barriers such as mangrove forests and coastal wetlands. Better management of ecosystems can assist disaster-ridden societies in alleviating poverty and achieving economic growth.Taking ecosystem management into account in disaster preparedness and post-disaster situations can decrease the vulnerability of people's lives and livelihoods.

It is now generally agreed that a more effective integrated 'ecosystem approach' is needed to reduce the impacts of the disasters. Hence, currently what is being proposed is an approach that integrates ecosystem management, development planning and risk reduction strategies to reduce disaster impacts and improve both livelihoods and biodiversity outcomes. Ecosystem management can contribute to more effective reduction of disaster risk in two major ways.

- Well-managed ecosystems can mitigate the impact of most natural hazards, such as landslides, hurricanes and cyclones. In addition, productive ecosystems can support sustainable income-generating activities and are important assets for people and communities in the aftermath of a disaster.
- For ecosystems to make these contributions, it is essential that they be factored into relief and rebuilding efforts in the post-disaster response phase. Not taking care of critical ecosystems after a major disaster can cause significant economic and environmental losses and impose hardships on already vulnerable communities.

The environmental sector needs to act in conjunction with the humanitarian and emergency sectors to make real changes in how they prepare for and manage future natural disasters. Natural disasters are increasing in number and intensity and taking a terrible toll in human lives and social and economic infrastructure. Most disasters are exacerbated by poor development planning and human-caused vulnerability. They also severely compromise poverty alleviation goals.

More effective and comprehensive disaster risk reduction strategies are needed that decrease people's vulnerability to the impacts of natural disasters. A comprehensive approach to disaster risk reduction should include several components:

- Integrating risk reduction into ecosystem management and development planning;
- Post-disaster strategies that focus on communitv livelihood recovery while

minimizing damage to the ecosystems that are essential for livelihood security;

- An emphasis on ecosystems as natural barriers;
- Community preparedness.

Integrating disaster risk reduction can occur only if people and organisations in various sectors make a collaborative effort. What is needed is an integrated effort by emergency, humanitarian and environmental agencies.

Environmental issues might not be the main focus during a disaster; yet, it is now being increasingly realized that environmental concerns — along with poor governance of natural resources — are part of the underlying causes of many, if not most, humanitarian crises. The aim should thus be to integrate basic environmental issues into the operations of emergency response agencies and to provide basic environmental training to relief and reconstruction sta. This will facilitate the accelerated implementation of key environmental provisions in post-disaster situations. For example, rapid environmental assessments could have helped to reduce the environmental impacts — such as oozing, water contamination and human-animal contacts.

Livelihood Planning

Reconstructing livelihoods, while traditionally the domain of development planning, also depends on environmental factors, including post-disaster waste management and mitigation using natural and articifial barriers.These activities need to be coordinated with land-use decisions. Reducing the impact of future disasters involves mapping hazards (using ecosystems to buffer these risks), enforcing zoning regulations and building capacity. Ecosystem management, development planning and disaster risk management need to be integrated and institutionalized at regional, national and local levels in order to have a real on-the-ground impact in reducing the risk of natural disasters.

At least ve important reasons may be advanced in defence of the need for integration of ecosystems and long-term livelihoods concerns with disaster risk reduction:

1. It can decrease vulnerability to natural disasters. There is mounting evidence that climate change is increasing the frequency of extreme hydro-meteorological events such as heat and cold waves, tropical hurricanes, windstorms, oozing and mudslides. Serious human consequences are escalating due to the greater number of people in high-risk areas such as flood plains, coastal areas, small islands and steep slopes.
2. Natural disasters have a high cost. They have a negative impact on economic growth and disproportionately affect the poor. They have a disproportionately high impact on less developed countries and poor populations, impeding progress toward achieving Millennium Development Goals, or for that matter, the country's national development goals.
3. It costs less to prevent disasters than it does to the damage they cause. Preventing loss is significantly less expensive than reconstituting livelihoods and prevention measures need to be mainstreamed into disaster risk reduction. Such measures include investing in ecosystems such as sand dunes, mangrove belts, coral reefs, wetlands conservation and use of forested slopes as barriers. Community preparedness and reducing population vulnerability through development planning are also important in this context.
4. At-risk populations depend on ecosystem services for their livelihoods. The poor are more vulnerable to natural disasters;

they depend on environmental resources for protection and livelihoods. Therefore, investing in natural barriers and mainstreaming disaster risk and ecosystem management in development planning is likely to make a major contribution to the goal of achieving sustainable livelihoods for the poor.

5. Disasters can affect biodiversity through the spread of invasive species, mass species mortality and loss of habitat. Poorly planned post-disaster response and reconstruction work often do more damage to biodiversity than the disaster itself. This in turn threatens the ecosystem services — including food, medicinal plants and animals, clean water, air and buffers from extreme natural events — that are critical to people's livelihoods.

Development and Disaster

The upshot of what has been stated above is that disaster mitigation should not be looked at as an ad hoc stand-alone affair; it needs to be integrated with national development planning within the framework of a longer term overall development vision. As India's 10th Plan document clearly laid down[3]:

"Five Year Plan documents have, historically, not included consideration of issues relating to the management and mitigation of natural disasters. The traditional perception has been limited to the idea of "calamity relief", which is seen essentially as a non-plan item of expenditure. However, the impact of major disasters cannot be mitigated by the provision of immediate relief alone, which is the primary focus of calamity relief efforts. Disasters can have devastating effects on the economy; they cause huge human and economic losses and can significantly set back development efforts of a region or a State. Two recent disasters, the Orissa Cyclone and the Gujarat Earthquake, are cases in point. With the kind of economic losses and developmental setbacks that the country has been suffering year after year, the development process needs to be sensitive towards disaster prevention and mitigation aspects. There is thus need to look at disasters from a development perspective as well."

International Response

There has in recent times been a universal recognition of the need for international efforts to study, disseminate useful information and to develop internationally accepted standards of disaster reduction and mitigation efforts. It is acknowledged that disaster loss is on the rise with grave consequences for the survival, dignity and livelihood of individuals, particularly the poor and hard-won development gains of the 'developing countries'. Against this background, disaster risk is increasingly being recognized as a matter of global concern. Its impact and actions in one region, can have an impact on risks in another and vice versa. The entire globe today is confronted with increasing vulnerabilities related to changing demographics, technological and socio-economic conditions and unplanned urbanization, unplanned development within high-risk zones, underdevelopment, environmental degradation, climate variability, climate change, geological hazards, competition for scarce resources and the impact of epidemics such as HIV/AIDS. All these point to a future where disasters could increasingly threaten the world's economy, its population and particularly the sustainable development of developing countries. All over the globe, on average, more than 200 million people have been affected every year by disasters in the past two decades.

Disaster risk arises when hazards interact with physical, social, economic and environmental vulnerabilities. Events of hydro-meteorological origin constitute the large majority of disasters. Despite the growing understanding and acceptance of the importance of disaster risk reduction and increased disaster response capacities, disasters and in particular the management and reduction of risk continue to pose a global challenge. In this context, the recently concluded international conference, widely known as the Hyogo Conference, deserves special mention.

The Hyogo Conference[4]

The World Conference on Disaster Reduction was held from 18 to 22 January 2005 in Kobe, Hyogo, Japan and adopted what is widely known as the Hyogo Framework for Action (HFA) 2005-2015. The Conference provided a unique opportunity to promote a strategic and systematic approach to reducing vulnerabilities[5] and risks to hazards. It underscored the need for and identified ways of building the resilience of nations and communities to disasters.

The HFA identified specific gaps and challenges in the following five main areas:

(a) Governance: organisational, legal and policy frameworks;
(b) Risk identification, assessment, monitoring and early warning;
(c) Knowledge management and education;
(d) Reducing underlying risk factors;
(e) Preparedness for effective response and recovery.

These are the key areas for developing a relevant framework for action for the decade 2005–2015. The World Conference resolved to pursue the following expected outcome for the next 10 years:

'The substantial reduction of disaster losses, in lives and in the social, economic and environmental assets of communities and countries.'

It was further resolved to adopt the following strategic goals to attain the expected outcomes:

(a) The more effective integration of disaster risk considerations into sustainable development policies, planning and programming at all levels, with a special emphasis on disaster prevention, mitigation, preparedness and vulnerability reduction;
(b) The development and strengthening of institutions, mechanisms and capacities at all levels, in particular at the community level, that can systematically contribute to building resilience[7] to hazards:
(c) The systematic incorporation of risk reduction approaches into the design and implementation of emergency preparedness, response and recovery programmes in the reconstruction of affected communities.

It was enjoined that in their approach to disaster risk reduction, states, regional, international organisations and other actors concerned should take into consideration the key activities listed under each of the following five priorities and should implement them, as appropriate, to their own circumstances and capacities:

1. Ensure that disaster risk reduction is a national and a local priority with a strong institutional basis for implementation.
2. Identify, assess and monitor disaster risks and enhance early warning.
3. Use knowledge, innovation and education to build a culture of safety and resilience at all levels.
4. Reduce the underlying risk factors.
5. Strengthen disaster preparedness for effective response at all levels.

As earlier stated, the starting point for reducing

disaster risk and for promoting a culture of disaster resilience lies in the knowledge of the hazards and the physical, social, economic and environmental vulnerabilities to disasters that most societies face and of the ways in which hazards and vulnerabilities are changing in the short and long term, followed by action taken on the basis of that knowledge. Key Activities identified in this connection are:

A. National institutional and legislative frameworks

(a) Support the creation and strengthening of national integrated disaster risk reduction mechanisms, such as multi-sector national platforms, with designated responsibilities at the national through to the local levels to facilitate coordination across sectors. National platforms should also facilitate coordination across sectors, including broad based dialogue at national and regional levels for promoting awareness among the relevant sectors.

(b) Integrate risk reduction, as appropriate, into development policies and planning at all levels of government, including in poverty reduction strategies and sectors and multi sector policies and plans.

(c) Adopt, or modify where necessary, legislation to support disaster risk reduction, including regulations and mechanisms that encourage compliance and that promote incentives for undertaking risk reduction and mitigation activities.

(d) Recognize the importance and specificity of local risk patterns and trends, decentralize responsibilities and resources for disaster risk reduction to relevant sub-national or local authorities.

C. Resources

(e) Assess existing human resource capacities for disaster risk reduction at all levels and develop capacity-building plans and programmes for meeting ongoing and future requirements.

(f) Allocate resources for the development and the implementation of disaster risk management policies, programmes, laws and regulations on disaster risk reduction in all relevant sectors and authorities at all levels of administrative and budgets on the basis of clearly prioritized actions.

(g) Governments should demonstrate the strong political determination required to promote and integrate disaster risk reduction into development programming.

C. Community participation

(h) Promote community participation in disaster risk reduction through the adoption of specific policies, promotion of networking, strategic management of volunteer resources, attribution of roles, responsibilities, delegation and provision of the necessary authority and resources.

Today, the HFA Declaration – an extremely useful, detailed and informative document – remains as some kind of a Bible for all nations, regional, local communities and agencies dealing with the different and complex issues involved in 'disaster management planning'. Also, to note carefully, the most important international organisation today is the United Nations Inter-Agency Secretariat of the International Strategy for Disaster Reduction (UN/ISDR) which is located in Geneva.

Disaster Insurance

Problems: In this context, the issue of 'disaster insurance' assumes considerable significance. It needs to be remembered, however, that disaster insurance is distinct from other forms of insurance for the following reasons:

1. Disaster risks are difficult to estimate;
2. Disasters can affect large portions of the population or risk pool at the same time;
3. Informal safety nets (family and friends) tend to break down during disasters;
4. Disasters cause multiple losses simultaneously to life, health and property (covariant risk).

As has been rightly pointed out, 'disaster insurance' should not be thought of as a stand-alone measure; rather it should be looked at as an integral part of an integrated 'disaster management' plan. "Insurance instruments are only one of many options in managing risks of natural hazards. The first and arguably the highest priority in risk management, is to invest in preventing or mitigating human and economic losses. Disaster prevention can take many forms: reducing exposure to risks, (e.g., land-use planning); reducing vulnerability (e.g., retrofitting, in earthquake prone zones, high-risk buildings); or creating institutions for better response (e.g., emergency planning).The residual risk can then be managed with insurance and other risk-financing strategies for the purpose of providing timely relief and assuring an effective recovery. Disaster risk management thus consists of risk reduction and risk coping."[5]

Nature of Insurance: Technically, disaster insurance is a monetary agreement between an insurance company and an affected individual, entitling the individual to compensation for losses incurred during disasters. A few common examples include natural disaster insurance, earthquake insurance and tsunami insurance and so on and so forth. When affected by large-scale disasters, such as floods, people can benefit greatly from having natural disaster insurance. These policies cover flood insurance, emergency insurance, tsunami insurance and insurance on the risks associated with storms. This type of insurances is also known as "catastrophe risk insurance."

In this connection, special reference needs to be made of the role and efforts of the US Federal Government's Disaster Agency — the FEMA. The Standard Flood Insurance Policy (SFIP) for home owners in earthquake and flood-prone areas, issued by the Federal Emergency Management Agency (FEMA), specifies the terms and conditions of the agreement of insurance between FEMA as the Insurer and the Named Insurers. The 'named insurers' in participating communities include owners, renters, builders of buildings that are in the course of construction, condominium associations, owners of residential condominium units and mortgagees/trustees (applicable for building coverage only)[6]. Kunreuther, in his paper just cited has evaluated alternative measures for mitigating losses to residential structures from natural disasters. He has discussed four extreme cost-bearing approaches (in the US context) to cover losses from natural disasters: (i) total federal responsibility, (ii) self-insurance by the homeowner, (iii) required insurance protection, (iv) land use restrictions and building codes. Also, he has suggested a plan for mitigating future losses based on comprehensive disaster insurance coupled with land use measures and building codes regulations. In this connection, two critical questions are whether disaster insurance should be voluntary or compulsory and to what extent higher level governments need to subsidise insurance plans. In the context of the developing countries, in view of widespread poverty and inequality, the governments and public authorities at all levels have necessarily to play a more proactive and direct role to formulate, implement and finance disaster mitigation plans with, of course, active local community support .

Overall, natural disaster insurance may

cover human beings, cattle, residential property, movable property, industrial risks and other risks of a similar nature. Situations in which it may be beneficial to have disaster health insurance may arise during riot, strike and malicious damage. In applicable cases, it covers earthquakes and allied perils.

Disaster Health Insurance is applicable in the cases of community perils such as plague, cholera and contagious perils such as Swine or Bird flu. The monetary compensation levels in the case of both disaster health insurance and natural disaster insurance like earthquake insurance and tsunami insurance are usually high. It is advisable for people living in catastrophe-prone areas to take out a natural disaster insurance policy in order to be compensated in times of emergency.

Because of many technical aspects associated with disaster loss assessment, initially at least, the private sector companies might be reluctant to venture out in the area of 'disaster insurance'. It is expected that because of non-experience, at the beginning, poorer people may not want to trust the Insurance companies and pay the premium (which may be high and beyond their means) for disaster Insurance. Therefore, an imaginative public awareness programme needs to be mounted initially to convince the people, particularly the poor, about the costs and benefits of disaster insurance. Also, government subsidy will be needed to keep the premium low and within the reach of poorer people. Even 'community disaster insurance' for a large community group may be planned initially to make the people insurance-oriented through propagation of a kind of new culture dissemination programme.

Insurance markets in the majority of developing countries are undeveloped and coverage for natural disasters is extremely limited. Where hazard coverage exists, it is usually limited to major industrial and commercial properties and some wealthier households. The demand for risk transfer instruments in emerging markets is often constrained by market gaps, lack of regulatory frameworks, lacking data on disaster risk, a lack of a culture of risk financing and the reluctance of large reinsurance market players to invest in the development of small risk markets. With little to no access to formal insurance mechanisms for disasters, the poor are forced to self- insure, depleting their savings when disaster strikes. Other consumption-smoothing strategies include taking emergency loans from microcredit institutions or money lenders and relying on family or community support. Community support measures may break down in times of disaster, as entire communities are affected at once. Without adequate coping strategies, poor households are locked into the poverty cycle, taking out high-interest loans or defaulting on existing loans, selling assets and livestock, or engaging in low-risk, low-yield farming to lessen their exposure to extreme events. Reliance on government or donor assistance is often inadequate, as this support can be ad hoc, poorly targeted and slow in disbursing. Moreover, disaster assistance can discourage governments and individuals from taking advantage of the high returns of preventive action.

Role of Microinsurance[7]

The use of micro insurance to indemnify against losses caused by severe or catastrophic natural disaster is only just emerging. The aim of disaster micro insurance is to provide low-income households and businesses with easily accessible and affordable life and health insurance as well as insurance to cover the loss of small-scale assets, livestock and crops in the event of a flood, typhoon, or other natural disaster. A limited number of schemes offering micro insurance cover against disaster risk already exist, which, if properly planned and administered, can help to break the poverty cycle by providing low-income households, farmers and businesses with rapid access to post-disaster liquidity, thus protecting their livelihoods and providing for reconstruction. As insured households and farms are more creditworthy, insurance can also promote investments in productive assets and higher-risk/higher-yield crops. In addition, insurance has the potential to encourage investment in disaster prevention if insurers offer lower premiums to reward risk-reducing behaviour.

At the same time, it has to be kept in mind that without sufficient back-up capital through reserves or reinsurance and/or sufficient geographic diversification, the payment of insurance claims is jeopardized affecting thereby the viability and credibility of the micro insurance program. Disaster insurance schemes should therefore be based on sound estimates of low-probability, high-consequence risks so that premiums can be properly priced and the requisite capital reserves or reinsurance can be assured.

The science underlying the models and risk estimates must be independent, verifiable and viewed as reliable by insurers, investors and donors. Where there is a high degree of ambiguity with the risk estimates of extreme disaster events, international donors, on the advice of national governments, may come forward to provide incentives for private sector involvement in such schemes.

To be acceptable and popular to poorer people, micro insurance has to be affordable to low-income clients. Disaster insurance premiums include the costs of handling many small contracts, distributing the product often to remote areas, as well as assuring sufficient capital to cover dependent claims. These elements combine to make insurance more costly than the purchaser's expected losses from the insured events. A major dilemma in such situations is to calculate and peg premiums in such a way that even the very poor in high-risk areas can avail of the benefits of the scheme.

There are several ways to reduce disaster insurance premiums. The most obvious is 'subsidies' from public authorities and international donors for those at lower risk in the insurance pool. There are many such examples in developed and transition countries. The Hungarian government is providing subsidies to poor households as part of a recently legislated flood insurance pool. In the UK extensive cross subsidies in the private flood insurance system make it affordable to low-income households. In developing countries, transaction costs can be minimized by offering policies to groups or communities and through established microfinance institutions. The high costs of capital reserves and reinsurance can be lowered through government or donor provision of reinsurance. An example is the Turkish Catastrophe Insurance Pool, where the World Bank reinsures a layer of risk for the pool.

Disaster insurance, particularly aimed at the poor and the socially marginalized, is obviously a high-risk business. Hence, one cannot expect the private sector – the market – to come forward in aid of the poor. A concerted effort is badly needed among scientists, micro insurance and risk-transfer experts, the research community and representatives from civil society, governments and bilateral and multilateral donor institutions to work out a viable pro-poor disaster insurance system[8].

To conclude, because of huge human tragedy and colossal 'development loss', disaster management today deserves serious attention from planners, researchers, administrators, all levels of public administrative institutions, civil society and even the private sector. As earlier stated, the role of the

FEMA in USA, particularly in pioneering the flood insurance policy, is worth our emulation. In India, the NIDM under the Union Home Ministry may initiate similar insurance measures on pilot basis for adoption by State Governments with appropriate subsidy from the Union Government within the framework of a national disaster management plan.

NOTES

1. Joanne Linnerooth-Bayer and Reinhard Mechler, Insurance against Losses from Natural Disasters in Developing Countries, Background Paper for United Nations World Economic and Social Surveys, July 25, 2008.
2. See Disaster Management in India, Ministry of Home Affairs, Government of India, 2004.
3. Tenth Five-year Plan (2002-2007), Planning Commission, New Delhi, 2002, Ch. 7.
4. See in this connection Hyogo Framework for Action 2005-2015: Building the Resilience of Nations and Communities to Disasters, International Strategy for Disaster Reduction (ISDR), United Nations, Geneva, 2005.
5. Bayer and Mechler, op. cit.
6. See in this context Howard Kunreuther, 'Disaster Insurance', The Journal of Risk and Insurance, Vol. 41, No. 2, June 1974.
7. See Reinhard Mechler and Joanne Linnerooth-Bayer with David Peppiatt, Disaster Insurance for the Poor? A Review of Microinsurance for Natural Disaster Risks in Developing Countries, A ProVention/IIASA Study, July 2006.
8. See, in this connection, an excellent review on the theme of our discussion: Jerry R. Skees, Barry J. Barnett and Anne G. Murphy, Creating Insurance Markets for Natural Disaster Risk in Lower Income Countries: The Potential role for Securitization, Paper Prepared for the 101st EAAE Seminar on 'Management of Climate Risks in Agriculture', Berlin, Germany, July 5-6, 2007.

CHAPTER 34

Administrative Corruption: Concept, Causes and Cure

In a treatise on public administration dating back to the fourth century B.C. in India, Kautiliya wrote in his monumental classic Arthasastra[1]:

"Just as it is impossible not to taste the honey (or the poison) that finds itself at the tip of the tongue, so it is impossible for a government servant not to eat up, at least, a bit of the king's revenue. Just as fish moving under water cannot possibly be found out either as drinking or not drinking water, so government servants employed in the government work cannot be found out (while) taking money (for themselves)." In another passage, Kautiliya states that there are "forty ways of embezzlement" and then goes on to enumerate these ways.

This shows that there is historical evidence of corruption being an ancient phenomenon. Its damaging effects have only now been recognized as a matter of grave public administrative concern generally and a special problem for 'development' in the context of the developing nations.

WHY CONTEMPORARY INTEREST?

Note in this context the observation of the Report on Human Development in South Asia (1999):

"Corruption is one of the most damaging consequences of poor governance. It undermines investment and economic growth, decreases the resources available for human development goals, deepens the extent of poverty, subverts the judicial system and undermines the legitimacy of the state. In fact, when corruption becomes entrenched, it can devastate the entire economic, political and social fabric of a country . . .corruption breeds corruption – and a failure to combat it effectively can lead to an era of entrenched corruption".

As Treisman's authentic study suggests, in the developing countries[2], corruption, concentrated 'in countries that are poorest and have the lowest levels of human capital' and assumes a major development issue. Kofi Annan, former Secretary General of the United Nations, while alerting the nations against the scourge of 'corruption', wrote in the Preface to the historic UN Convention Against Corruption[3]:

"This evil phenomenon is found in all countries—big and small, rich and poor—but it is in the developing world that its effects are most destructive. Corruption hurts the poor disproportionately by diverting fund intended for development, undermining a Government's ability to provide basic services, feeding inequality and injustice and discouraging foreign aid and investment. Corruption is a key element in economic underperformance and a major obstacle to poverty alleviation and development."

Indian Case[4]: Though India is credited with having made considerable progress in terms of economic reform over the past few years, corruption is perceived to be widespread and entrenched at all levels of the political and administrative system. India ranks 87 from 178 countries surveyed in Transparency International's *2010 Corruption Perception Index (CPI),* with a score of 3.4. Since the first iterations of the index, India has scored between 2.7 and 3.5, indicating that – despite some progress – corruption continues to be perceived as rampant and endemic by the various CPI sources.

Identifying 'weak governance' as the main reason, the Second Administrative Reforms Commission[5] emphasized three factors in particular which, in its view, have aggravated 'corruption' in India.

- First, there is a colonial legacy of unchallenged authority and propensity to exercise power arbitrarily.
- Second, for historical reasons, there is enormous asymmetry of power in Indian society. Nearly 90% of our people are in the unorganised sector. Quite a number of them lead a precarious existence, depending on subsistence wages with no job security. Nearly 70% of the organised workers with job security and regular monthly wage are employed by the state directly or through public sector undertakings. Their employment in government comes with all the trappings of power. Such asymmetry of power, without effective checks and institutional safeguards, reduces societal pressure to conform to ethical behaviour and makes it easy to indulge in corruption.
- Third, in the early decades after Independence India chose a set of policies whose unintended consequence was to put the citizen at the mercy of the State. Over-regulation, severe restrictions on economic activity, excessive state control, near–monopoly of the government in many sectors and an economy of scarcity – all created conditions conducive to unbridled corruption.

However, the main issue today is an abysmal and pathological 'governance deficit' in India. The remedy lies in strengthening 'governance' at all levels – national, state and local[6].

It is widely known that corruption manifests itself in a number of ways. It ranges from petty to grand in nature, from political to bureaucratic in focus and from incidental to systemic in scope. Essentially originating out of exploitation of public office for private gain, corruption radiates from governments through agencies and impacts upon the individuals and/or organisations required to liaise with those agencies in order to obtain basic services. In view of the range and impact of corrupt behaviour, any anti-corruption strategy must be cognizant of the basic causes of corruption, the political and socio-economic environment in which corruption thrives and its broader links with organised crime and even international illicit goods and capital flows. In the Indian situation today, this big picture needs to be kept in mind to plan out any worthwhile and effective strategy to combat widespread corruption.

Definitional Issues

Modern social science defines corruption in terms of three basic models:

1. First, corruption is related to the performance of the duties of a public office. According to J. S. Nye[7], corruption is "[b]ehaviour which deviates from the normal duties of a public role because of private-regarding (family, close private clique), pecuniary or status gains; or violates rules against the exercise of certain types of private-regarding influence. This includes such behaviour as bribery (use of reward to pervert the judgment of a person in a position of trust); nepotism (bestowal of patronage by reason of ascribable relationship rather than merit);

misappropriation (illegal appropriation of public resources for private regarding uses)".

2. Second, corruption is related to the concept of exchange derived from the theory of the market. One view has been that the bureaucrat views his public office as an enterprise from which to extract extra-legal income. The civil servant's compensation package is not related to ethical evaluation of his usefulness for the common good but upon the market situation. The civil servants, under conditions of high levels of government regulations, may devote most of their time and effort to assisting entrepreneurs in evading state laws and statutes. They, in exchange, earn extra-legal income.
3. Third, the definition of corruption is couched in terms of the public interest, as argued by Carl Friedrich[8]: "[t]he pattern of corruption may therefore be said to exist whenever a power holder who is charged with doing certain things, that is a responsible functionary or office holder is by monetary or other rewards, such as the expectation of a job in the future, induced to take actions which favour whoever provides the reward and thereby damage the group or organisation to which the functionary belongs, more specifically the government". According to Friedrich, the opportunistic activities of corrupt bureaucrats can severely damage the public interest and should be considered important variables in the study and evaluation of corruption.

The same connotation can be found in the broad definition of corruption by Gould and Amaro-Reyes[9] as a phenomenon 'taking place in a public organisation when an official or civil servant in defiance of prescribed norms, breaks the rules to advance his personal interest at the expense of the public interest he has been entrusted to guard and protect.'

Public choice theory and corruption

Economists have turned to public choice theory, which sees corruption as post-constitutional opportunism designed to generate benefits for individuals or groups at the expense of the rest of society. According to public choice theory, the scope and extent of corruption in a country is basically determined by that country's institutional arrangements and not necessarily by the character of its civil servants and politicians. Once the constitution has been designed and adopted and a government established, there is an incentive for individuals and groups to subvert the rules in an effort to generate benefits for themselves. Rules subversion, if successful, can allow individuals to secure benefits above and beyond what would have accrued to them otherwise. This kind of behaviour can occur in both democratic and nondemocratic societies.

Bureaucrats, whose job it is to design and execute public policies, may attempt to use the process to maximize their private objectives at the expense of serving the general public efficiently and equitably. The desire by civil servants to maximize their private objectives and the effort by organised interest groups to subvert the rules and to extract benefits for themselves create opportunities for corruption.

Public choice theorists argue that bureaucratic corruption is directly related to the scope and extent of government intervention in private exchange (i.e., in markets). Effective control of corruption, then, must be based on a modification of existing rules in order to change incentive structures and constrain the ability of the state to intervene in private exchange and create artificial scarcities.

MANY FORMS[10]

Briefly, these forms (of corruption) are: acceptance of money and other rewards for awarding contracts, violation of procedures to advance personal interests, kickbacks from developmental programmes or multi-national corporations, pay-offs for legislative support, diversion of public resources for private use. overlooking illegal activities, intervening in the justice process, nepotism, common theft, overpricing, establishing non-existing projects and tax collection and tax assessment frauds[11].

Four Divergent Views

We may refer, in this context, to four divergent views on the definition of corruption traceable to moralists, functionalists, social censurists and social constructionist realists.

(a) The moralists view "corruption as an immoral and unethical phenomenon that contains a set of moral aberrations from moral standards of society, causing loss of respect for and confidence in duly constituted authority"[12] . One of the well-known proponents of this view, Nye, portrays corruption as "a behaviour that deviates from the formal duties of a public role (elective or appointive) because of private-regarding (personal, close family, private clique) wealth or status gains, or violates rules against the exercise of certain types of private-regarding influence"[13]. This way of defining corruption tends to individualize a societal phenomenon and attempts to dichotomize as to what is good and what is bad.

(b) The functionalists usually look at corruption in terms of the actual function that it plays in socio-economic development. Claims are made by functionalists that corruption flourishes as a substitute for the market system; offers an acceptable alternative to violence; increases public participation in public policy. Some functionalists believe that political and bureaucratic leaders may see a national interest in actively pursuing or tolerating a certain degree of administrative corruption.

(c) The proponents of 'social censure' believe that in understanding corruption one should take into consideration the capacity of the state to produce a particular form of social relations and shift the theoretical emphasis to the interplay of law, ideologies and political economy.

(d) 'Social construction reality' views corruption as problematic and the actors involved can be studied by relating them to contextual information on their social positions, interests and stakes in the system as well as on the political, economic and social conditions within which they function.

Diverse Approaches

In view of the multitude of approaches and views on corruption it is not easy to agree on any unanimous definition of the term. Two definitions of corruption can prove handy. The shorter definition of corruption includes "abuse of authority, bribery, favouritism, extortion, fraud, patronage, theft, deceit, malfeasance and illegality"[14]. The broader definition of corruption refers to "use of one's official position for personal and group gain and that includes unethical actions like bribery, nepotism, patronage, conflict of interest, divided loyalty, influence-peddling, moonlighting, misuse or stealing of government property, selling of favours, receiving kickbacks, embezzlement, fraud, extortion, misappropriation, under-or over-invoicing, court tempering, phony travel and administrative documents and use of regulation as bureaucratic capital[15].

Political and Administrative Corruption[16]

Political corruption[17] is "the behaviour of (elected) public officials which diverges from the formal components – the duties and powers, rights and obligations – of a public role to seek private gain"[18]. By contrast, administrative corruption is defined as "the institutionalized personal abuse of public resources by civil servants."[19] In both cases public officials (elected and appointive) can convert public office into private gain in many ways.

The effects of corruption on the agencies of public administration can be particularly damaging. When corruption is believed to be the way the public sector, or any of its agencies, routinely operates the damage goes beyond the loss of misdirected resources, public administration risks losing both its capacity to be effective and the trust of citizens in the fair and impartial application of public resources and authority. In the public domain it becomes difficult to guarantee compliance with public standards or respect for the rule of law. A particularly damaging institutional consequence for the public administration is that competent and honest employees can be lost or deterred from working for government at all further reducing its capacity for integrity and effectiveness.

A more elaborate approach based on aspects of the corrupt transaction is offered by Syed Alatas[20]. He distinguishes six forms of corruption:

i) "Transactive" corruption involves the mutual arrangement between a donor and a recipient;
ii) "Extortive" corruption implies some form of compulsion usually harming a party; "defensive" corruption refers to the act the victim of extortion is compelled to engage in;
iii) "Investive" corruption involves an act with no immediate payoff but an expectation of a favour sometimes in the future;
iv) "Nepotistic" corruption relates to family members being appointed to positions in the government;
v) "Autogenic" corruption entails one person acting alone with no official-citizen exchange:
vi) "Supportive" corruption refers to acts designed to protect and strengthen existing corruption.

Often a distinction is made between 'grand' corruption and 'petty' corruption. The first type is more likely to occur among high level government officials/politicians who have limited interaction with the public and are involved in large public investment projects. "Petty corruption" tends to take place among low-level, bureaucratic workers who regularly interact with the public say, the police constable or a municipal octroi collection clerk.

Interestingly, Mark Robinson[21] has identified three forms of corruption:

(a) "Incidental" corruption, which is confined to malfeasance on the part of the individual and is thus rare;
(b) "Institutional" corruption referring to certain institutions that may be riddled with corruption due largely to the absence of controls;
(c) "Systemic" corruption which reflects situations where corruption is deeply entrenched and pervasive throughout society.

A similar sort of distinction contrasts "centralized" and "decentralized" corruption depending on the level of control exercised by the political elite over local officials. As Pranab Bardhan[22] writes, "it might be that local governments may be captured much more easily or proximity may make collusion between elite or special-interest groups much easier".

A final approach distinguishes types of corruption based on the motives, purpose or outcome of the corrupt act. The range, of course, can be rather extensive. Does the corrupt act – for example, allowing a murderer to go free – result in the diversion of millions of dollars from a program designed to help the poor or simply in speeding up the award of a license that would have been granted in time anyway? One easy distinction based on motive separates corruption that promotes purely personal interests from corruption that benefits a clique, a political party or an institution which may be more systematic.

In a discussion of the link between organised crime and corruption, for instance, Margaret Beare[23] offers a non-exhaustive taxonomy of corruption based largely on motive or outcome. She identifies four types:
"bribes/kickbacks", which are paid or demanded in return for being allowed to do legitimate business; "election/campaign corruption", designed to ensure continuing influence;"protection corruption", payments in exchange for being allowed to engage in illegitimate business; "systemic top-down corruption", where the nation's wealth is systematically siphoned-off by the ruling elites.

Systemic corruption that is all pervasive and most worrisome and difficult to eradicate has been described vividly in the following words[24]:
Systemic corruption is (a) endemic and (b) institutionalized. In systemic corruption, corrupt activities are the norm rather than the exception. Officials routinely engage in corrupt practices and citizens are well aware that bribes are crucial for receiving extra favours (e.g., an advantageous court ruling) or simply what they are legally entitled to (e.g. the timely issuance of trade licenses or birth and death certificates). Myriads of networks are built within the state apparatus and between public officials and private citizens; their main purpose is the facilitation of corrupt exchanges. Patron-client networks connect lower to higher officials. Lower officials usually buy their positions and share illicit gains with their superiors. An informal hierarchy of clientelism[25] overlaps with the official state hierarchy. Networks are also built between businesspeople and officials to further each other's interests. Often public officials' involvement in private business and entrepreneurs' political aspirations are so extensive that the boundary between public and private spheres is permeable and ambiguous.

Fine-tuning the various approaches, another effort has been to classify corruption into five groups:

- Public-interest-centred,
- Market-centred,
- Public-office-centred,
- Public-opinion-centred,
- Legalistic.

i) Proponents of the public-interest-centred approach believe that corruption is in some way injurious to or destructive of public interest.

ii) Market-centred enthusiasts suggest that norms governing public office have shifted from a mandatory pricing model to a free-market model, thereby considerably changing the nature of corruption.

iii) Public-office-centred protagonists stress the fact that misuse by incumbents of public office for private gain is corruption.

iv) Those who believe in public-opinion-centred definitions of corruption emphasize the perspectives of public opinion about the conduct of politicians, government and probity of public servants.

v) Others have suggested looking at corruption purely in terms of legal criteria in view of the problems inherent in determining rules and norms that govern public interest, behaviour and authority.

Again, corruption has been differentiated into three types – collusive, coercive and non-conjunctive.

(a) In collusive corruption, the corruptees themselves are willing and active participants in the process and use of corruption as an instrument for inducing wrong action or inaction on the part of authorities, deriving benefit greater than the costs of corruption on their part.
(b) In coercive corruption, those in the position of power and authority force corruption upon the corruptee.
(c) In non-conjunctive corruption, benefits are obtained at someone else's cost and victims are unaware of their victimization.

State Capture

In corruption literature, 'state capture'is a broader concept in that it encompasses the formation of laws, rules and decrees by a wider range of state institutions, including the executive, ministries and state agencies, legislature and the judiciary. Who can capture the state? Often, the "captors" are individuals, groups, or firms from the private sector seeking rents or other advantages from the state.Yet any actors with access to public officials and the capacity to provide private benefits to these officials in order to obtain advantages in the governing process can be seen as potential captors. Indeed, public officials themselves can capture the state if they abuse their authority to shape institutions and laws primarily to further their own private financial interests at the expense of the broader public interest. In a seminal paper on the politics of reform in the post-communist transition countries, Joel Hellman[26] explained the phenomenon of 'state capture' in the transition countries. His insightful analysis helped understand the processes of how in some countries the powerful oligarchs manipulate politicians, shape institutions and control the media to advance and protect their own empires at the expense of 'social or general public interest'.

Corruption: Causal Variables

Usually, the causes of corruption are complex and are rooted in a country's policies, bureaucratic traditions, political development and social history. Discussions about the causes of corruption have tended to explain how and why corruption occurs rather than identify deterministic causes. Studies generally produce a mixture of situations, attitudes and processes that might be better understood as enabling factors, indicators or conditions that allow or facilitate corruption. Few of these factors can, in isolation, be said to cause a corrupt act to occur. Neither are they strictly causal in the sense that corruption will occur if they are present in a given location. Instead they are observed — or perceived – phenomena which may make it more possible for corruption to occur. They are similar to risk factors for diseases or accidents that combine —or align – in a given time and place to create an environment that is conducive to an individual perpetrating a corrupt act.

Explanations vary with the analytical framework applied so that the act of bribing a public official will look to an economist like rent seeking, to a prosecutor like a crime and to a public administrator like a failure of accountability. Each perspective employs a different diagnostic toolkit and is likely to recommend a different kind of response. One study[27] identified six kinds of causes in the theoretical anti-corruption literature together with the causal chains that they indicate:

i) Public choice theory – official makes a rational choice to act corruptly

ii) Bad apple theories – official with "bad" character necessarily acts corruptly
iii) Organisational culture theories – group culture and aspects of the workplace encourage the official to act corruptly
iv) Clashing moral values – the official's societal or personal values and norms permit corruption
v) The ethos of public administration theories — pressure on the official to perform, overrides integrity, considerations and allow corruption
vi) Correlation theories — no casual theory only correlations.

The most cited causes of corruption include: (1) the absence of rules, regulations, policies and legislation; (2) weak systems of enforcement; (3) weak systems of oversight (i.e., the absence of a watchdog institution); (4) lack of accountability; (5) lack of transparency; (6) lack of checks and balances in the system (e.g., institutional weaknesses in the legislative and judicial systems); (7) lack of integrity; (8) monopoly of power; (9) high degree of discretion; (10) low salaries; (11) high rewards compared to risks; (12) low detection rate.

Klitgaard Formula

One common approach, focused on accountability, has been to adapt and extend a hugely influential, although not wholly undisputed, formula by Robert Klitgaard[28]. His formula is represented in the form of an equation as set out below.

$$C = R + D - A$$

In the above equation, C stands for corruption, R for economic rent, D for discretionary powers and A for accountability. The equation states that the more opportunities for economic rent (R) exist in a country, the larger will be the corruption. Similarly, the greater the discretionary powers (D) granted to administrators, the greater will be the corruption. However, the more administrators are held accountable (A) for their actions, the less will be the corruption and hence a minus sign in front of A. Mathematically speaking, we can say C varies directly with R and D and inversely with A.

In sum, this formula suggests that the absence of accountability, transparency and integrity in addition to monopoly and discretion, result in corruption.

The UNDP[29] modified Klitgaard's formula by adding other dimensions: integrity and transparency. This creates the formula $C=(M+D)-(A+I+T)$, where C is corruption, M is monopoly, D is discretion, A is accountability, I is integrity and T is transparency. This suggests that the absence of AIT (primarily as a consequence of weak governance) in addition to monopoly and discretion, results in corruption. This formula strengthens the theory that corruption is primarily a failure in governance.

Multi-causal Phenomenon

Obviously, a complex phenomenon like corruption would be in reality, multi-causal. Leslie Palmier used a three-factor method to study corruption in some parts of Asia:

An individual is likely to commit a corrupt act if he or she (1) is paid a low salary; (2) is provided with the opportunities for corruption; (3) perceives corruption to be low risk, high reward activity. In other words, corruption thrives when the individuals concerned receive meagre salaries, have ample opportunities to be corrupt and are unlikely to be caught and not severely punished even if they are caught. At the end of his comparative study of the control of bureaucratic corruption in Hong Kong, India and Indonesia, Palmier concluded:

"bureaucratic corruption seems to depend not on any one of the [three] factors identified but rather on the *balance* between them. At one extreme, *with few opportunities, good salaries and effective policing, corruption will be minimal; at the* other, *with many opportunities, poor salaries and weak policing, it will be considerable* (Palmier[30], 1985).

The causal variables of 'corruption' are too many in fact. A rather simplified categorization is in terms of four main factor-groups namely: political and judicial factors: historical factors; social and cultural factors and economic factors.

1. Political Factors

The political factors capture the democratic environment of a given country, the effectiveness of its judicial system and the origin of its legal system. It is widely believed that corruption is related to the deficiencies of the political system and that democracy, by promoting political competition and hence increasing transparency and accountability, can provide a check, albeit an imperfect one, on corruption. Other characteristics of the political environment, including electoral rules and the degree of decentralisation may also be important in explaining corruption. The judicial system is also expected to play a role in controlling corruption. The role of the legal system and the rule of law have featured prominently in many recent studies on the quality of governance and its consequences for development.

2. Historical Factors

To a large extent, it is difficult to separate the historical factors from the political and judicial factors. The effectiveness of the judicial system is dependent on the colonial heritage of the country in question. It has been argued that those countries that were former colonies of Britain and who adopted the common law system appear to have more effective judicial systems than those who adopted civil law systems associated with former colonies of continental European countries.

3. Social and Cultural Factors

This group of factors captures the social and cultural characteristics of a country that may impact upon the pervasiveness of corruption in a given country. For example, religion shapes social attitudes towards social hierarchy and family values and thus may determine the acceptability, or otherwise, of corrupt practices. Religious and ethno-linguistic fractionalization may also have an impact on corruption and other characteristics associated with the quality of government.

4. Economic Factors

Proponents of economic determinants of corruption have focused typically on three factors: the degree of openness, a country's endowments of natural resources and the size of the public sector. Less open countries restrict trade and impose controls on capital flows. This creates rents and hence enhances the incentives to engage in corrupt activities. It has been argued that increased competition reduces corruption and that more open economies are less corrupt.

Natural resource endowments have also featured in cross-country studies of corruption, the justification here being that the concentration of exports on natural resources is a proxy for rent-seeking opportunities. Several studies on the causes of corruption have emphasized the size of the public sector. Tanzi[31] notes in his exceedingly detailed and well-analyzed paper that the significant role of the public sector in the economy affords public officials some degree of discretion in the allocation of goods and services provided and hence increases the likelihood of corruption. This mechanism is reinforced if the wages public officials receive are relatively low.

Remedies and Strategies

At the outset, it needs emphasizing that first and foremost, there has to be a genuine political consensus and commitment to deal with corruption firmly. To quote in this context the cautionary comments of Daniel Kaufmann, an acknowledged authority on the subject[32]: "One of the challenges. . . . . . is to be able to distinguish

between a seriously committed programme to control corruption and politically convenient rhetoric, on the other . . . . . . In the bandwagon

of making pronouncements, passing decrees and creating special governmental anti-corruption units, there are many whose commitment to really address the problem is seriously in doubt."

Three Strategies

Generally, three concurrent strategies are suggested to curb and control corruption. First, the formal machinery of monitoring officials and politicians needs to be drastically improved. There is a need for political will to implement this. Second, this social will can be generated by informed popular pressure. We cannot expect the bureaucrats and politicians who benefit from the political system to reform themselves. Third, the public must be educated to exert moral and political pressure to outlaw corruption. The mobilization of such public pressure depends on a clearer understanding of the modern concepts of public office and public service and a more widespread public awareness of the social costs including 'development' retardation, grave political and institutional risks and distortions which corruption, particularly 'systemic corruption', entails.

In this context, we can quote C.V. Narasimhan[33], a former Director of the Central Bureau of Investigation (CBI) in India, who has also similarly recommended three types of anti-corruption measures: preventive, punitive and promotional. Preventive measures refer to those electoral and administrative reforms concerned with making all government transactions "more transparent and accountable to the people." Punitive measures include the "laws, rules and the mechanism for effective investigation, court trial, departmental disciplinary action and other means to deter the corrupt functionaries." Finally, promotional measures focus on the "encouragement of value-based politics, inculcation of moral and ethical principles among the younger generation in schools and colleges and the build-up of a kind of social ostracising of corrupt people by the society" (Narasimhan, 1997).

The anti-corruption strategies can be divided into four broad categories:

- Economic/Market Reforms,
- Administrative/Bureaucratic Reforms,
- Accountability/Transparency Enhancing Reforms,
- Political Accountability Enhancing Reforms.

To combat incidences of corruption, the mainstream approaches argue that corruption is largely caused by the greed of public officials who have the discretion to offer citizens benefits or cause damage to their activities but who are inadequately monitored or face inadequate punishments for violating laws. If bureaucrats or politicians have the power to offer selective benefits or cause selective damage and if their risk of detection or risk of punishment is low, they are likely to engage in corruption to enrich themselves. The similarities between them on the core drivers allow us to collectively describe it as the *greed plus discretion theory* of corruption.

The standard policy response to corruption

is entirely based on attacking the drivers of corruption identified in greed plus discretion theories. The well-known collection of measures to attack corruption derived from this analysis include:

i) Reducing the discretion of public officials through liberalization and privatisation,
ii) Improving salaries of public officials, thereby addressing their low living standards in many cases but also increasing the opportunity cost of corruption since they stand to lose their positions if detected,
iii) Improving the rule of law to punish and prosecute corrupt bureaucrats and politicians,
iv) Encouraging greater transparency of government decision-making through deepening democratisation, decentralisation and the creation and encouragement of civil society watchdogs.

If corruption in developing countries was indeed entirely or even largely driven by the factors identified in the greed plus discretion theory of corruption, the adoption of these anti-corruption measures in a wide range of developing countries would by now have produced significant reductions in corruption in the countries adopting them. Unfortunately, we know from detailed econometric and country case studies that many of the core policy tools identified in the greed plus discretion theories have limited if any effect on corruption.

UN Document (2003)[34]

The UN Guide landmark document quoted above has laid down the broad outlines of 'anti-corruption strategies and institution-building'.

To quote the document:

"In constructing overall strategies, institutional reforms can be grouped into "pillars of integrity" that are mutually supportive and include elements from government and elements of civil society. Key public-sector groups that must usually be included in such strategies are the executive and legislative branches of Government at the national, regional and local levels; the judicial branch and its supporting institutions; key "watchdog" agencies, such as auditors or inspectors; law enforcement agencies and other elements of criminal justice systems.

From the private sector, there should also be inclusion of the media, relevant academic individuals, institutions and other organisations, such as trade unions, professional associations and general or specific interest groups, who play a vital role in promoting integrity and ensuring transparency and accountability. The final pillar is the general population itself; public awareness of reforms and expectations of the standards set by those reforms ultimately hold the reformers and the institutions accountable for the success or failure of programmes."

The following Table illustrates some of the key "pillars" that may need to be incorporated into institution-building projects.

(Basic Principles) Quality of Life; Rule of Law; Sustainable Development

'PILLARS' supporting National Integrity System

1. Political Will
2. Administrative Reforms
3. "Watchdog" Agencies
4. Parliament
5. Public Awareness
6. Judiciary
7. Media
8. Private Sector

Main Motive Force: Public Service to Serve the Public.

As the document enunciates the principles

in this regard, "As with the pillars of a physical building, the pillars of integrity are interdependent. A weakening of one pillar will result in an increased load being shifted on to the others. The success or failure of the overall structure will thus depend on the ability of each element to support the loads expected of it. If several pillars weaken collectively, or if any one pillar weakens to an extent that cannot be compensated for by the others, the entire structure will fail."

In articulating the concept of a 'national integrity system' (NIS), the founding director of Transparency International, Jeremy Pope, sought to demonstrate that the task of building a robust framework of integrity into social institutions involved many more elements and a greater diversity of strategies. In this connection, it needs special mentioning that the concept of 'National Integrity System', as a comprehensive method of fighting corruption, has been explained and elaborated by Langseth et al. in a seminal paper published under the auspices of the Economic Development Institute of the World Bank[35]:

Corruption and Governance

Corruption is a problem which all governments, at any level of development, have to deal with. The literature abounds with efforts to understand and measure its magnitude and impacts. "Good government" plays an important role in the development process and "requires the highest standards of integrity, openness and transparency". The main requisites for good governance include:

1. Political legitimacy for the state through democratic elections and transfer of power and an effective political opposition and representative government,
2. Accountability and transparency in the sharing of information,
3. Separation of powers,
4. Effective internal and external audit,
5. Effective means of combating corruption and nepotism,
6. Competence of public servants,
7. Impartial and accessible justice systems,
8. The absence of arbitrary government power.

Action towards curtailing corruption is perceived as a commitment towards creating good government. As such, discussion of corruption is almost always conducted within the framework of good governance. Corruption and governance lie on a continuum but occupying opposite poles. Whereas governance, with its end goal of creating a good government, aims to serve the interest of the people, corruption, through the use of public office and resources, serves the narrow interest of family and allies. Good government is bound by rules aimed to create a transparent and accountable government; corruption plays discreetly and sometimes directly on these rules to make decisions which will benefit those who have access to power and the highest bidder. Thus, more insidiously, corruption has a far reaching negative effect on the national psyche which eventually goes back to undermine the whole system of good governance itself. Systemic corruption breeds a culture of corruption and skews the people's perception of what is right and wrong. For a number of countries where it has been effectively institutionalised, where wealth and power have become the measure of success, corruption has become socially acceptable, sometimes even aspired to. Energies of a large number of people are channelled towards occupying positions in the government to partake of the fruits of a corrupt system.

Strategies to limit corruption have to be realistic and achievable and tailored to the needs of particular countries. In other words, policies intended to address corruption have to be consistently implemented over the long term. Corruption being essentially a governance issue, increased governmental accountability and transparency, enhanced public participation in decision making, strengthened public sector and civil society institutions and greater adherence to the rule of law will not only improve governance but will help counter corruption. Free and open competition is ultimately the greatest weapon against corrupt practices – whether political, economic or bureaucratic.

At the national level, specialised agencies and anti-corruption bodies can be extremely effective, provided they have sufficient independence, authority and resources to function efficiently. Beyond government actions, a broad coalition against corruption, encompassing governments and the public, is necessary. The NGOs and the civil society, the press and the business sector all have a crucial role to play. Public opinion has to be supportive to anti-corruption efforts and public opinion is the major force in creating an environment in which corruption is not accepted or condoned. Public education as to the detrimental effects of corruption is important in creating public awareness and an active public response in support of anti-corruption measures.

One way of looking at 'corruption' is to describe it as the conscious attempt or deliberate diversion of resources from the satisfaction of the general interest to that of selfish (personal or particular) interest. The disdain for corruption is clearly felt mainly on ground of morality as it inflicts some sorts of adverse effects on any society where it exists and persists.

Corruption has been defined by scholars of governance and public administration in various ways. Khan[36] defines corruption as an act which deviates from the formal rules of conduct governing the actions of someone in a position of public authority because of private – regarding – motive such as wealth, power or status. "Corruption is the perversion of integrity or state of affairs through bribery, favour or moral depravity" ... It takes place when at least two parties have interacted to change the structure or processes of society or the behaviour of functionaries in order to produce dishonest, unfaithful or defiled situations". In other words – corruption is a systematic vice in an individual, society or a nation which reflects favouritism, nepotism, tribalism, sectionalism, undue enrichment, amassing of wealth, abuse of office, power, position and derivation of undue gains and benefits.

Corruption also includes bribery, smuggling, fraud, illegal payments, money laundering, drug trafficking, falsification of documents and records, window dressing, false declaration, evasion, underpayment, deceit, forgery, concealment, aiding and abetting of any kind to the detriment of another person, community, society or nation. Again, corruption transcends bribery but includes "treasury looting and also the deliberate bending of rules of the system to favour friends or hurt foes. It is clearly the evidence of absence of accountability, law and order."

Corruption in the government involves three broad layers:

- First is corruption within the broader political system which includes the demands of electoral politics, the extensive use of patronage in political appointments and the extensive use of "pork barrel" funds.
- Second is corruption within the public sector, which is usually focused on three major problems: spotty performance of mechanisms for identifying and sanctioning employees engaged in corrupt and illicit behaviour, considerations of pay and employment and government procurement.

- Third is corruption within specific agencies, which involves grand corruption (involving widespread syndicates and millions of dollars); petty corruption (which involves smaller amounts of money, such as 'grease money' to facilitate the delivery of goods and services).

Certain types of corruption may not necessarily involve money. It may involve gift-giving or influence-peddling. It can also come in the form of future benefits. With this type of corruption, the boundary between a corrupt and a non-corrupt behaviour becomes quite thin.

World Bank's latest Policy Document

In this connection, special mention needs to be made of the World Bank's latest policy pronouncement[37] to firmly link the Bank's governance agenda with anti-corruption strategy. To quote the policy document:

"The strengthening of country institutions remains central to the governance agenda but several systems are required and there are no simple, unequivocal shortcuts to putting them in place. Three sets of institutions are central to the governance and anti-corruption agenda: those relating to cross-cutting core government systems (*e.g.*, for managing policy development, finance, people, information, assets); those relating to specific sectors (*e.g.*, forestry, education, transport, natural resources) and those relating to the ways in which the executive is held accountable to citizens (*e.g.*, parliaments and parliamentarians, ombudsmen, anti-corruption authorities, the judiciary, third-party mechanisms at various levels, civil society)."

Corruption and Development[38]

From the perspective of the developing countries, much research has been done on the detrimental effect of corruption on 'development'. Studies show that a corrupt country is likely to achieve aggregate investment levels of almost 5 per cent less than a relatively incorrupt country and to lose about half a percentage point of gross domestic product per year. It is also shown to slow down FDI. Investing in a relatively corrupt country, as compared with an incorrupt one, is estimated to be equivalent to 20 percent private tax on investment.

High levels of corruption reduce economic growth. It can distort the allocation of resources and the performance of government in many ways. It has a pervasive and troubling impact on the poor, since it distorts public choices in favour of the wealthy and powerful and reduces the state's capacity to provide social safety nets (UNDP, 2000). It exacerbates poverty, most especially in developing and transitional economies. Among the identified effects of a corrupt regime are:

- Lower level of social services
- Infrastructure projects biased against the poor, since public officials will design public projects that will maximize bribery receipts and minimize the chance of detection
- Higher tax burdens and fewer services
- Lower opportunities for farmers to sell their produce and for SMEs to flourish, as their ability to escape poverty using their livelihood will be severely restricted by corruption of the state regulatory apparatus.

Strategies[39]

The anti-corruption strategies can be classified in different ways by the:

- Type of *policy instruments* suggested, for example whether it is monitoring and controlled focused or focused on the motivation of the corrupt agents;
- *Motivation of the campaign,* for example whether its major aim is to improve

- the efficiency of government, or rectify injustices, or to get rid of political opponents;
- *Position of the agents targeted,* for example whether they are clustered in a few sectors or are in high or lower level positions and so on;
- Likely *effect of the policy;*
- Type of *organisation initiating* the anti-corruption strategy.

Research on corruption often underscores the importance of formal institutions in consolidation of democracy and good governance. It is argued that well-functioning legal, administrative and institutional institutions are necessary requirements for development. However, research on corruption in poor countries should also look beyond the formal structures of the central state to the informal networks of patronage and social domination (clientelism) that often determine how political power actually is wielded, including the local community or district level. The concrete inter-linkages between state institutions and society ought to be probed, to explore the multiple ways in which they influence and shape each other. Weight should also be given to the legacy of historical antecedents (e.g. colonialism).

Institutions may have traditional and patrimonial functions in addition to their formal roles. Usually, however, citizens relate to and are dependent on the formal institutions (constitutions, electoral arrangements, party systems, legal orders and administrative procedures) to gain their full and basic political and civil rights. When it comes to democratic consolidation, the concerns are for the spread of democratic norms, of political crafting and the design of political institutions. Research on corruption has thus to focus on both informal and formal institutions.

The implementation of anti-corruption strategies will need a focus on formal public agencies. For instance, reforming tax administration has emerged as a priority in many anti-corruption plans. While there is some clarity regarding what type of improved agency is desired, there is considerably less understanding on how to make this happen. Accordingly, what is the link between the level and arbitrariness of taxes and regulations, the resulting corruption and bribery and the evolution of the shadow economy? Another specific area of research is to study the role of institutional checks and balances (the power sharing formulas as well as the actual power balance) between the executive branch, the legislative branch and the judiciary. There are various forms of power sharing mechanisms and the way power is institutionalized goes to some extent to determine the forms as well as levels of corruption.

Anti-Corruption Agencies

At the outset, a cautionary comment may be added. It may not be difficult to create agency/agencies for combating corruption. But there are many practical questions involved here about the organisation and jurisdiction or scope of its activities, personnel or staffing and resources. Also, the relationships between the 'new' agencies and already existing controlling machineries may be a tricky issue. As a well-documented and researched monograph has succinctly put it[40]:

"Anti-corruption strategies are deemed to have a number of intrinsic weaknesses including over-reliance on the judiciary, police and financial sector without appreciating that, in many countries, such institutions are weak and corrupt themselves. Anti-corruption efforts often attempt to create an ethical standard by which individuals are supposed to abide, ignoring the fact that if such officials were moral beings, the corruption would not occur in the first instance."

Against this apposite observation, as is well known, there have in recent times been numerous strategies and institutional responses to reduce and weed out the 'scourge' of corruption. Usually, a prompt and hurried response has been to establish an anti-corruption agency but as Patrick Meagher[41] has posed the right questions in this regard: "This ostensibly straightforward nostrum actually poses a lot of difficulties. How much authority and which specific powers, to give it? How big should the agency — and its jurisdiction — be? What should we expect of such an agency and how will we know whether it has been successful?"

While there is today a legitimate concern about how to effectively combat corruption, a well-argued paper[42] has sounded a timely caution that ' anti-corruption commissions fail to reduce public sector venality in all but a few special circumstances.' As the paper has pointed out, "those governments that have established successful anti-corruption commissions have done so in response to demands for reform from a broad base of domestic constituents. Demands for reform generally occur after a precipitating crisis has caused deep economic hardship and a national consensus exists that reforms must be implemented. Anti-corruption commissions are effective when they respond to that national consensus and a broad domestic coalition supports reform."

Types of Agencies

Two broad types of anti-corruption agencies all over the globe are (i) single-agency models and (ii) multi-agency models. Regarding the first, the most cited cases are the agencies in Hong Kong and Singapore. The alternative strategy, used in most countries, is to add one or more special anti-corruption bodies to the traditional mix of judicial and administrative institutions. This kind of more traditional multi-agency models can be found in most countries such as India and USA. In fact, most countries — particularly the larger ones like India and the USA — address corruption using multiple agencies, rather than concentrating powers and leadership responsibility in a single agency.

To illustrate, the experiences of Hong Kong's Independent Commission Against Corruption (ICAC) and Singapore's Corrupt Practices Investigation Bureau (CPIB) are worth our citation. It will be wrong to think that under the single-agency strategy *all* anti-corruption functions are concentrated in a single bureau which would be impossible under almost any constitutional arrangement. The single-agency approach places a number of key capabilities, responsibilities and resources under one roof-thereby creating a powerful centralized agency able to lead a sweeping effort against corruption. The centralized agency has still to interact with other entities having jurisdiction in this field — notably the courts and in most cases, prosecutors, as well as line ministries in areas likely to be affected by corruption, e.g. revenue and public works.

Contrastingly, the multiple-agency approach is less ambitious. It consists in creating one or more additional units or agencies with specific anti-corruption responsibilities that either did not previously exist or were scattered among departments. This strategy avoids setting up a strong "lead" agency in the anti-corruption field. This modality poses a lower risk than the single-agency approach of upsetting the balance and separation of governmental powers.

Singapore Case: Corrupt Practices Investigation Bureau (CPIB)

Singapore's CPIB was founded in 1952, replacing the Anti-Corruption Branch (ACB) of the Police Department's Criminal Investigation Department. A scandal in 1951 revealed widespread corruption in the police. The main objective of the reform appears to have been to make the anti-corruption effort more effective by removing the ACB's functions from the police force. The corruption problem remained unresolved, however and the government of Lee Kwan Yew in 1960 decided to strengthen CPIB and enact a new Prevention of Corruption Act strengthening penalties and calling for the forfeiture of corrupt gains. The Act also increased CPIB's powers to include arrest and examination of any suspect's bank accounts. Since that time, Singapore has amended the Act and enhanced the powers and resources of CPIB. Among the changes was an expansion of criminal liability for corruption to include those who may not accept a bribe but intend to commit the offense and those who accept a bribe but do not provide the expected favour in return. CPIB has been able successfully to establish its credibility as a serious anti-corruption force.

Hong Kong Case: Independent Commission against Corruption (ICAC)

Hong Kong's chief concern was entrenched and systematized police corruption, which facilitated drug trafficking gambling and prostitution in return for huge rents and also included bribery and extortion related to routine police functions such as traffic control. The system appears to have allowed for collection and passing of percentages of graft up the hierarchy to the Chief Superintendent. By the late 1960s, when Hong Kong was looking for a way to grapple with its corruption problems, it turned to Singapore as a successful model.

The immediate crisis giving rise to ICAC's founding was a corruption scandal involving Peter Godber, then Chief Superintendent, who escaped and later was extradited for trial from the UK. A Commission of Inquiry was convened and the Governor subsequently called for the establishment of ICAC, which was set up in 1974 under the ICAC Ordinance. The agency was separated from the police, headed initially by a distinguished former government official and senior company executive named Jack Cater. This decision especially signalled the government's desire to rescue Hong Kong's reputation and establish its credibility on the anti-corruption front[43].

Hong Kong: Broadly, Hong Kong's ICAC is charged with: "fighting corruption through effective law enforcement, education and prevention to help keep Hong Kong fair, just, stable and prosperous." The three main functions are handled by three separate departments: Operations, Community Relations and Prevention.

Operations: The offenses that ICAC investigates include those under the ICAC Ordinance, the Prevention of Bribery Ordinance and the Elections (Corrupt and Illegal Conduct) Ordinance, as well as blackmail committed by a civil servant through misuse of public office and corruption in the private sector — including bribery and white-collar crime. The ICAC Ordinance requires the Commissioner to investigate "any" suspected corruption.

Prevention: The Prevention Department has the responsibility and authority of examining practices and procedures of government entities with a view to identifying and reducing opportunities for corruption — and advising private organisations on measures to prevent corruption. It provides a report to the client organisation (but does not submit bills to the legislature or policy papers to the executive).

Community Relations: The Community Relations Department carries out public awareness and education programs, handles complaints and inquiries about corruption and maintains liaison with anti-corruption agencies in the mainland.

Hong Kong's ICAC (as well as Singapore's CPIB) has authority both to respond to complaints and to undertake investigations on its own initiative. ICAC does not have power to prosecute but transmits its investigative findings to the Attorney General.

Singapore: The functions of Singapore's CPIB include: to receive and investigate complaints alleging corrupt practice; investigate misconduct by public officers with an "undertone" of corruption and prevent corruption by examining the practices and procedures in the public service for purposes of minimizing opportunities.

The Investigation Branch deals with the first two functions. CPIB's stated objective has always been "swift and sure" action against corruption covering both the public sector and the private sector (especially payment of commissions and kickbacks). It is authorized to investigate *any other offense* that is disclosed in a corruption investigation. CPIB cannot itself prosecute but some cases get filtered out during investigation and after referral.

A Data Management and Support Branch handles the preventive function, along with the related tasks of collecting information and screening candidates for official positions.

An Administration Branch provides general support to the agency's overall functions.

CPIB, in carrying out its investigative functions, has both the regular powers of the police as well as special powers. This includes powers of arrest as well as search and seizure — based on information or reasonable suspicion and without necessarily obtaining a judicial warrant in advance.

CPIB may also examine bank accounts, enter and search the books of banks, require explanations of disproportionate wealth and of transfers of assets abroad by the suspect and her/his immediate family members. It has jurisdiction over corruption offenses and offenses discovered during corruption inquiries, by both the public and private sector. The statutory provisions give CPIB a wide scope of authority — but this stops short of prosecution, which can only be done by the Public Prosecutor.

CPIB's hand is strengthened by its authority to impose heavy sanctions. These include stiff penalties for offenses, legal duties to furnish information and stringent prohibitions on obstruction or failure to comply. Administrative restraints on civil servants are quite rigorous, including a prohibition on unsecured debts, borrowing from anyone with whom they have official dealings and engaging in any additional employment without approval. (Ah Leak 1999, www.gov.sg/pmo/cpib/lawenforcement.htm) The threat of losing government employment on these grounds surely encourages compliance and cooperation.

Tan Ah Leak, a former CPIB Director, has attributed the success of CPIB to five factors[44]:

1. Singapore's cultural climate which opposes corruption;
2. A well-paid civil service which discourages civil servants from being corrupt;
3. Effective administrative measures such as disciplinary proceedings by the Public Service Commission, careful scrutiny of government expenditures by the Auditor-General's Department and the Public Accounts Committee of Parliament and the Ministry of Finance's control of public spending;
4. A highly literate and sophisticated society which readily reports corrupt behaviour with no fear of reprisal; and
5. The CPIB's ability to investigate prominent

persons, which in turn has enhanced its credibility among Singaporeans,

In his statement to Parliament in January 1987, the former Prime Minister LEE Kuan Yew identified the following five factors for the success of Singapore's anti-corruption strategy:

i) The law against corruption contained in the Prevention of Corruption Act;
ii) A 'vigilant' public that was ready to report all suspected corruption;
iii) A CPIB which was 'scrupulous, thorough and fearless' in its investigations;
iv) The fact that the CPIB had the 'full backing' of the Prime Minister;
v) A public opinion that 'censures and condemns' corruption that brands a guilty party with a stigma of corruption that 'cannot be washed away by serving a prison sentence'.

'One-size fits all approach' to anti-corruption strategies is no longer acceptable or practical; given that the focus of anti-corruption reform will be unique to every country[45]. In order to be holistic in approach, anti-corruption strategies need to incorporate policies in relation to a number of sectors vulnerable to corruption and amenable to change. Underpinning dedicated efforts in relation to those sectors are a number of guiding principles which influence the nature and direction of the anti-corruption strategy.

Huberts[46] (1998) has distinguished six strategies:

1. Economic — emphasizes the need for the economic stimuli for corruption to be reduced and suggests that such might be achieved by, inter alia, paying higher civil service salaries;
2. Educational — aims at altering the attitudes and values of the populace and civil servants alike via training and education campaigns and engagement of the media;
3. Cultural — ensuring that the behaviour and attitudes of those in power are subject to stringent codes of conduct and their behaviour filters down to civil servants;
4. Organisational or bureaucratic — strengthening internal control systems such as auditing to detect corrupt activity and staff rotation to reduce the propensity for individuals to establish themselves in entrenched corruption;
5. Political — increasing in transparency in terms, e.g., the monitoring of party finances and more broadly, a clearer and more definite separation of powers in terms of the judiciary and the state;
6. Judicial measures — advocates harsher penalties for corrupt practices but also the creation of independent anti-corruption agencies.

Four broad themes may be said to form the basis of most anti-corruption strategies:

- The first seeks to utilize regulation as a counter to corruption.
- The second seeks to provide financial aid with conditions of non-corrupt behaviour attached.
- The third seeks to employ the media as a means of investigating corruption and publicizing its effects.
- The fourth seeks to engage the NGO and allied sectors in pricking the consciences of governments and international organisations which can in turn bring pressure to bear upon corrupt countries.

In this connection, reference may be made to a well-documented field study which examined three patterns of corruption control operating within Hong Kong SAR, India, Mongolia, Philippines and Singapore:

(a) The first pattern involved the introduction of anti-corruption legislation with no independent anti-corruption agency. Mongolia has the *Law on Anti-Corruption* and three provisions restricting bribery in the *Criminal Code.* However, the task of curbing corruption is divided among police, the General Prosecutor's Office and the courts.

(b) The second pattern involved the introduction of anti-corruption legislation with several agencies. In India the *Prevention of Corruption Act* is implemented by the Central Bureau of Investigation, the Central Vigilance Commission, the state anti-corruption bureau, the State Vigilance Commissions and the State Lok Ayuktas.

(c) The third pattern involved the creation of anti-corruption legislation with one independent agency. In Singapore the *Prevention of Corruption Act* is implemented by the Corrupt Practices Investigation Bureau (CPIB). The third pattern was deemed the most effective given that Singapore and Hong Kong SAR had been determined by Transparency International to be more successful than the other countries in minimizing corruption.

Code of Conduct

It is common practice to have a code of conduct for civil servants specifying 'do's' and 'don'ts' as a matter of routine control mechanism of bureaucratic behaviour but this is often reduced to a regular administrative ritual with little force in terms of really 'controlling' behaviour. The UN document[47] (2003) has offered some concrete tips to vigorously activate the 'code of conduct'. The recommendations are as follows:

"Distributing a Code of Conduct across the public service is in most cases not enough to change the performance and/or the behaviour of civil servants. Experience has taught us that the issuing of a Code of Conduct is 10% of the entire job needed to improve the performance of public servants. In order to succeed you need to have an integrated approach including actions and new institutions in the following areas:

1. *Ethics training* to make all civil servants aware of the new performance standards and also about the consequences when not complying.
2. *Public awareness campaign* to make the public aware of their rights and where to complain if they are not served according to the standards prescribed in the code of conduct.
3. Implement a credible and responsive Public *Complaints System* known to and trusted by the public at large.
4. Independent and credible *Disciplinary Mechanism* with the necessary mandate to enforce the Code of Conduct."

The last point is of particular importance to make the code of conduct really useful. But, as Professor Bardhan[48] has rightly observed: ". . . getting rid of many of the dysfunctional regulations remains a major first step in anti-corruption policy, whatever the nature of the state. In addition, it is imperative to institutionalize the various kinds of accountability mechanisms at different levels of the government".

Concluding Observations

Continuing with the same refrain and endorsing Professor Bardhan's apt remark, without being pessimistic, it needs reinforcing the argument that there is no single magic formula available to weed out, or even to reduce overnight, a complex problem like corruption. As experiences across the globe point out, a sustained and integrated effort is necessary to move steadily toward the ultimate objective, taking many interdependent socio-political, economic and administrative-judicial factors into account. At the same time, 'it is important to recognize the fundamental role that political will and support for reforms at the highest levels of government can play in bringing about practical results and in raising the credibility of and public support for, anti-corruption progress'[49].

Two contrasting demands need to be noted, in this connection, while studying 'corruption and its remedies'. On one side, the practical need to diagnose and combat corruption in the interest of 'good governance' and 'democracy' weighs heavily in the minds of scholars and administrators studying corruption. On the other side, the interest of theory-building takes a back seat because of the more practical concerns of governance. This dilemma has been aptly addressed by Diana Scmidt with her veiled suggestions for 'theory' building in this fertile field of scholarly research[50]. In this context, the observations of Diana Scmidt are worth our quotation:

"Anti-corruption research needs to move beyond output-centred towards more process-oriented analysis. It also remains to be linked analytically to the past and ongoing transformations in their multiple dimensions and with due attention to national and local contexts and differences regarding economic reforms, democratisation or authorisation and civil society formation as well as historical and cultural factors. Anti-corruption research is less ordered along scholarly disciplines and more influenced by and oriented towards practice. It is lacking a coherent theoretical basis or debate.

The field of anti-corruption studies is still in the midst of defining itself. Some scholars have made proposals for conceptualizing anti-corruption, suggesting further development of existing approaches to corruption, such as principal-agent frameworks or institutional approaches based on democracy and political culture theories or government legitimacy.

Research on corruption has triggered numerous strategies for reform and recent insights about the results of reforms have caused new demands for research. Some more steps remain necessary for breaking new ground in connecting political science anticorruption research to policy. While a wide range of academic, policy, think tank and NGO communities are active in the area, many of them are still looking for each other. From a research perspective, strategies for analyzing anti-corruption in its many dimensions remain ill-conceptualized. In general, different approaches need to be elaborated for studying the various actors and structures, the processes of designing and implementing anti-corruption initiatives and the mismatches between expectations and results, including unintended side and counter-effects and the encounter of cultural-specific biases."

NOTES

1. R. P.K ANGLE, Kautiliya Arthasastra, tr. 3 Vols., Laurier Books, Motilal, New Delhi 1997.
2. Daniel Treisman, 'The Causes of Corruption: A Cross-sectional Study ', Journal of Public Economics, 76, 2000.
3. United Nations Convention Against Corruption, United Nations, New York, 2004.
4. See in this connection an India-focused well-argued paper: O. P. Dwivedi, 'Bureaucratic Corruption in Developing Countries', Asian Survey, Vol. 7, No. 4, April 1967.
5. See Ethics in Governance, Second Administrative Reforms Commission, Government of India, 2007.
6. See in this connection an excellent paper on India: Sunil Sondhi, Combating Corruption in India: The Role of Civil Society, (Delhi University): paper prepared for the XVIII World Congress of International Political Association, August 1-5, 2000, Quebec City, Canada.
7. J. S. Nye, "Corruption and Political Development: A

Cost-Benefit Analysis." American Political Science Review 61(2), 1967.
8. Carl J. Friedrich, 'Corruption Concepts in Historical Perspective', in Arnold J. Heidenheimer and Michael Johnston (eds.), Political Corruption: Concepts and Contexts, Transaction Publishers, New Brunswick, New Jersey, 2009.
9. D. Gould and J. Amaro-Reyes, "The effects of corruption on administrative performance: Illustrations from developing countries". World Bank, Staff Working Paper No. 580. Washington D.C., 1983.
10. For details about different types of corruption, see UN Guide for Anti-corruption Policies, Chapter II, United Nations, New York, November 2003.
11. United Nations, Corruption in Government. Report of an Interregional Seminar held in The Haque, The Netherlands on December 11-15, United Nations, New York 2000..
12. D.J. Gould, "Administrative Corruption: Incidence, Causes and Remedial Strategies in A. Farazmand ed. Handbook of Comparative and Development Public Administration, Marcel Dekker, Inc., New York, 1991.
13. Nye, op. cit.
14. G. E. Caiden, "What Really is Public Maladministration?" Indian Journal of Public Administration, Vol.37, No. 1:1-16, 1991.
15. Quoted in M. M. Khan, op. cit.
16. See in this connection a brilliant paper based on rich theoretical and practical issues: Mohammad Mohabbat Khan, 'Political and Administrative Corruption', prepared for Transparency international, Bangladesh, 1997.
17. The concept of 'political corruption' has been very ably elaborated in: Mark Philip, 'Defining Political Corruption', Political Studies, XLV, 1997.
18. J. M. Kramer, J.M. (1997). "Political Corruption in Post- Communist Russia: The Case for Democratization", paper presented at the 17th World Congress of International Political Science Association (IPSA) held in Seoul, Korea on August 17-21.
19. D.J. Gould, Administrative Corruption: Incidence, Causes and Remedial Strategies", in A. Farazmand (ed.), Handbook of Comparative and Development Public Administration. New York: Marcel Dekker, Inc., New York, 1991. Also see Gould and Amaro-Reyes, The Effects of Corruption on Administrative Performance: Illustrations from Developing Countries. World Bank Staff Paper No. 580. Washington, D.C.: The World Bank, 1985.
20. Quoted in Paul Heywood, 'Political Corruption: Problems and Perspectives', Political Studies, XLV, 1997,417-435.
21. See Mark Robinson (ed.), Corruption and Development, Frank Cass Publishers, New York, 1998.
22. Pranab Bardhan, 'The Economist's Approach to the Problem of Corruption', World Development, Vol. 34, No. 2, 2006.
23. M. E. Beare, 'Corruption and Organised. Crime: Lessons from History', Crime, Law and Social Change, 28, 1997.
24. Christoph FL Stefes, Governance, the State and Systemic Corruption: Armenia and Georgia in Comparison, Caucasian Review of International Affairs, Vol. 2(2), Spring 2008.
25. First elaborated by anthropologists and sociologists, clientelism describes the hierarchical patron-client social relations/bonds that have long marked the countryside in peasant societies
26. These bonds are founded on mutual material advantage: the patron furnishes excludable resources (money, jobs) to dependents and accomplices in return for their support and cooperation (votes, attendance at rallies.
27. Joel S. Hellman, 'Winners Take All: The Politics of Partial Reform in Postcommunist Transitions', World Politics, 50 (2), 1998
28. G. de Graaf, "Causes of Corruption: Towards a Contextual Theory of Corruption" Public Administration Quarterly Spring 2007: 39-86
29. Robert Klitgaard, Controlling Corruption, Berkeley: University of California Press, 1988.
30. Anti-corruption, UNDP February 2004.
31. Leslie Palmier, 'The Control of Bureaucratic Corruption: Case Studies in Asia', Allied Publishers, New Delhi, 1985.
32. Vito Tanzi, 'Corruption around the World: Causes, Consequences, Scope and Cures', IMF Working Paper, May 1998.
33. Daniel Kaufmann, 'Revisiting Anti-corruption Strategies: Tilt Towards Incentive-driven Approaches?', in Robert Williams and Alan Doig (eds.), Controlling Corruption, Edgar Elgar Pub. Cheltenham, 2000.

34. C. V. Narasimhan, 'Prevention of corruption: To –wards Effective Enforcement', in S. Guhan and Samuel Paul (eds.), Corruption in India : Agenda for Action, Vision Books, New Delhi, 1997.
35. UN Guide for Anti-Corruption Policies, United Nations, New York, November, 2003.
36. Petter Langseth, Rick Stapenhurst, Jeremy Pope, The Role of a National integrity System in Fighting Corruption, Economic Development institute, The World Bank, 1997.
37. Mushtaq H. Khan, "A Typology of Corrupt Transactions in Developing Countries" IDS Bulletin, Vol. 27, Issue No. 2, April 1996.
38. Strengthening Governance: Tackling Corruption, the World Bank Group's Updated Strategy and Implementation Plan, The World Bank, March 6, 2012.
39. A seminal paper on this theme is: Pranab Bardhan, 'Corruption and Development: A Review of Issues', Journal of Economic Literature, Vol. 35, No. 3, September 1997.
40. An extremely informative document, in this context, is: Research on Corruption: A Policy Oriented Survey by J. C. Andvig et al., commissioned by NORAD, Oslo, December 2000.
41. Rob McCusker, 'Review of Anti-corruption Strategies', Technical and Background Paper, No.
42. Australian Institute of Criminology, Canberra, 2006.
43. Patrick Meagher, Anti-corruption Agencies: A Review of Experience, Submitted to the World Bank: PREM-ECA, IRIS Center, University of Maryland, August 2, 2002. This is an excellent study of the comparative institutional experiences all over the globe.
44. John R. Heilbrunn,'Anti-Corruption Commissions: Panacea or Real Medicine to Fight Corruption', World Bank Institute, The World Bank, 2004.
45. See Robert Klitgaard, Controlling Corruption, University of California Press, Berkeley, 1988.
46. See an excellent paper on Singapore: Jon S. T. Quah, 'Combating Corruption Singapore-Style: Lessons for other Asian Countries', School of Law, University of Maryland, No.2, 2007 (189)
47. See in this context A. Doig, Dealing with corruption: the next steps, Crime, law & social change 29(2—3), 1998.
48. L. W J. C. Huberts, What can be done against public corruption and fraud: expert views on strategies to protect public integrity. Crime, law & social change 29:1998.
49. UN Guide for Anti-corruption Policies, United Nations, New York, November 2003.
50. Pranab Bardhan,'Corruption and Development: A Review of Issues, Journal of Economic Literature, Vol. XXXV, September 1997.
51. Rob McCusker, op. cit.
52. See in this context Diana Scmidt, 'Anti-Corruption: What Do we Know? Research on Preventing Corruption in the Post-Communist World', Political Studies Review, Vol. 5, 2007.

Chapter 35

Public Administration in Transition

In this last section, an attempt is made to identify and present some of the major currents of thought that have emerged in recent decades to highlight and clarify the administrative and governance' riddles in today's turbulent times.

To start with, Phillip Cooper et al in their seminal volume 1 entitled *Public Administration for the Twenty-First Century* reminded us that "history is valuable but only their prologue. The hard part is keeping those lessons of the past in mind while focusing on the future". Since its inception, public administration has been concerned with making government work better. This eternal quest for better governance has always taken place within changing contexts. Contemporary search for better governance has to reckon with the changes in the nature of today's world in which we live and work.

The themes that seem extremely important in today's context include the globalisation of public administration, the increasing complexity of intergovernmental and inter-sector relations particularly in the domain of trade, industry and economy. Harnessing and making the best use of global technological revolution, acknowledging the importance of social diversity and social inclusion (particularly in view of multi-cultural and feminist movements). Dealing with major environmental issues at local/regional, national and international levels and, above all, fulfilling the internationally sponsored Millennium Development Goals aimed at overall improvement of human resources globally.

The UN Perspective

From the perspective of the United Nations, Guido Bertucci and Adriana Alberti[2] have drawn attention to what they call'a cumulative paradigm movement away from public administration and towards governance via public management'. They strongly pose the emerging challenges of public administration today, especially from the standpoint of the developing countries. As they argue,

"Perhaps the greatest challenge facing the UN Programme in Public Administration these days is that of contributing to the constantly evolving knowledge of public administration issues by highlighting the emerging challenges that are of crucial importance for developing countries. Three of them seem of critical relevance in the years to come, particularly in view of the challenges posed by the Millennium Declaration and by recent events of great impact such as the September 2001 terrorist attack and the December 2004 tsunami in the Indian Ocean. The first one is how to revitalize public administration and reassert its pivotal role in development while capitalizing on the important lessons of the NPM and governance movements; the second is to reconcile the current shift in public administration focus from social service delivery to the provision of security with the need to foster economic and social development; the third is the need to strengthen transparency and accountability systems for the increased development and emergency aid necessitated by natural disasters and by increased efforts to achieve the MDGs."

They refer, in particular, to three contemporary needs to establish the 'central anchoring role of public administration'. *First,* they lay special emphasis on the need for recognition of the central position of public administration 'as a vital determinant in the practice of public management and good governance'. *Second,* they affirm the need for a redefinition of the 'core functions' of public administration with special emphasis on 'those functions that would be jeopardized if left to the private sector or civil society'. In their view such functions include 'justice and security, regulatory control and the delivery of services critical to the process of human development such as education, health and environmental protection'. *Third,* they lay down the conditions for the revitalization of public administration — to give it a new life forsaking the 'archaic role of exclusive regulatory control and (its) paternalistic and monopolistic approach to service delivery'. To quote, in this connection, their valuable and timely recommendations: "Public Administration must recognize the value and virtue of partnerships among the various sectors, cooperating with actors in the private and civil society sectors at local, national, regional and global levels to galvanize experience, knowledge, skills and to utilize resources for effective response to public needs. Partnerships constitute a major component of the process of giving new life to public administration. The revitalization of public administration entails bringing together the best attributes of the three concepts (public administration, public management and good governance) to construct a sharp instrument for effective, responsive, transparent and accountable functioning of the state".

As spokespersons of the United Nations, Bertucci and Alberti obviously take everybody on board in their prescriptions for a 'revitalized' public administration irrespective of any consideration for the vexed compatibility issue in this regard. For instance, to what extent the principles of traditional (Weberian) public administration can coexist with the NPM principles? What would be the 'revitalized' role of public administration in the event of adoption of a 'governance' perspective? These and many other kindred issues are associated with the notion of a rather simple-sounding 'revitalized' public administration.

Rethinking Public Administration

In this context, the UN document (1998) entitled *'Rethinking Public Administration: An Overview*[3] admirably sums up the contemporary administrative situation in the world.The major highlights of the report are as follows:

1. **Role of the State**: While the role of the State in national development continues to be important, consensus is shifting about the precise functions to be assigned to the State vis-a-vis other institutions and non-governmental organisations and the appropriate modalities for discharging different national functions.
2. **Democratisation trends:** Democratic institutions are becoming more widespread and democratisation movements are manifesting themselves in many countries. The number of politically aware individuals demanding empowerment is also on the increase in most countries.
3. **The changing nature of public policy management:** Public management is being affected by two seemingly contradictory forces. On the one hand, many national issues have been redefined by globalisation trends: environmental concerns; human rights; economic, trade and aid imperatives and the need for in-

ternational standards. The increased speed of and access to, communications have also catapulted national problems into international arenas. On the other hand, there are demands for independence, greater autonomy and decentralisation within multi-nation and nation-State systems. Unitary systems of planning and administration are no longer acceptable in many countries of the world.

4. **The many voices of the policy process:** Emerging concerns have dramatically shifted social agendas. For example, environmental concerns, labour costs and international labour mobility have become major preoccupations. Similarly, human rights and the role of women and other disadvantaged groups have become major issues. Natural and human-made disasters create new problems and demand urgent government attention and resources.

5. **The imperative use of information technology.** The development of microcomputer and data communications technologies, computerization and information systems development have become essential in improving the effectiveness and efficiency of public administration and an organic part of the economic and social development process. Effective use of modern information technology leads to opportunities for speeding up development as well as to the challenge to manage these changes. At the same time, management of information systems provides both a more objective basis for decision-making and a demand for targeted training and resource utilization.

As the UN document suggests, 'To effectively meet these challenges and their consequences, public administration needs to modify both its traditional style and substance. In many cases, far reaching institutional changes are required and involve strengthening inter-institutional cooperation to promote harmony among changing administrative, political, market and non-governmental institutions. Administrative processes also need to be reviewed and/or reengineered'.

Similarly, the United Nations document (2004) on *'Revitalizing Public Administration'* deserves special mention as it marks another bold attempt to gather together the diverse experiences internationally as also to chart out broad guidelines for 'reforms' in public administration worldwide. The document contains both a brief overview of what has gone on so far as 'public administrative reform' in different countries and a concise guideline for the future directionality of 'reform'. As described in this UN document:[4]

"...since the latter part of the 1970s, the meaning of public administration has gradually become diluted, giving way to the concept of public management. Since that time, initiatives for public sector reform geared towards introducing and popularizing management approaches and methods of private sector enterprises have been undertaken in many countries, paving the way for a modified concept of public administration known as 'public management', which puts emphasis on issues of effectiveness, efficiency, economy, deregulation, client orientation and rolling back the frontiers of the State".

The Experts Committee openly expressed their anxiety regarding steady erosion in the core concerns of the state and its impact on society. To quote the Committee report: "After more than 20 years of public sector reform, the results of public management have been mixed. It is increasingly suspected that the emphasis put on market forces and deregulation, as well as on efficiency and savings in the public sector, may have had a negative impact on the traditional mandate of the State, leading to irregularities, including inadequate protection of the vulnerable in the provision of public services such as health and education, causing lapses in the management of issues related to State security. In being overly eager to adopt the management behaviour of private enterprise, the public sector may have lost touch with its responsibility to the general public interest in a number of respects. In this context, the concept of governance has gained increasing respect because of its focus on participation, people's interest, equity, transparency and accountability in the management of public affairs. However, public administration still needs new life in order to refocus its efforts in the management of public affairs on the critical missions of the State as well as on guaranteeing the general public interest".

This presentation (by an Experts Committee) does not negate either public management or governance concepts but rethinks public administration, public management and governance with a view to constructing a renewed conceptual basis for the 'revitalization' of public administration.

Some of the concepts that emerged as benchmarks in this quest for the revitalisation process are given below:

- Redefining and reaffirming the fundamental missions of the State, including its role in ensuring peace, security and stability and the rule of law and order, as well as creating a sustainable environment conducive to individual and private sector initiative and economic growth and human development;
- Developing and sustaining partnerships and collaboration among the institutions of the public sector, civil society and the private sector;
- Promoting cooperation among institutions of the State and public administration in different countries in order to facilitate the exchange of successful experiences in renewing public administration
- Selectively integrating principles and practices of public management and governance in public administration so as to build and promote public administration systems that are efficient, economic and effective as well as participative, responsive, equitable and accountable to the public;
- Instilling, within the sphere of public administration, structures and a culture of research, including the application of new information and communication technologies which can play a critical role in giving new life to public administration;
- Encouraging the attraction, recruitment and retention of the best human resources in the public sector.

In summing up, the Expert Committee observed:

'A search for public administration revitalization should integrate the three concepts of 'public administration', 'public management' and 'good governance'. It needs to be recognized that at the core of public administration are the mottos of serving the general public interest and the higher missions of the State. A revitalized public administration will give vibrancy to the interaction among the various actors in the public, private and civil society sectors to encourage effective participation and collaboration in the process of human development, encouraging transparency and accountability. Without effective public administration, the threads that bring together the efforts of all these actors will weaken, common efforts will become disorganised and there will be undue emphasis on individual survival to the detriment of the general interest. This is likely to breed corruption, widespread unethical behaviour, lack of integrity in the management of public affairs, inadequate regulatory action, which may lead to increased criminal activity, insecurity, as well as unplanned development, which will leave the vulnerable, including children and the disabled, without proper support, thus increasing poverty. Public administration as an instrument of State action and the guarantor of the general interest should be revitalized to champion the ongoing efforts to achieve the Millennium Development Goals'.

These are important issues on which the

Experts had laid considerable emphasis in their bid to rehabilitate public administration.

Scholarly Responses

Eminent researchers studying the public system have been reflecting from time to time on the kinds of changes that have been taking place in the practice and study of public administration. Slowly and gradually but constantly and extensively, a change is being nurtured in the public systems and in the attitudes of public managers, politicians and citizens to the usually conservative role of public institutions. These changes carry many challenges, as well as risks, that the citizens, governments and administrators of the future will have to confront and address. They all represent new alternatives for the evolution of public administration as an art, perhaps also as a science and as a profession[5] (Lynn, 1996).

Commenting on the changes that have taken place in public administration study over the years, one serious scholar has observed[6]: "Today, public administration is already very different from what it used to be forty, thirty and even twenty or ten years ago. In the coming years it is going to be even more different."

B. Guy Peters[7], the well-known public administration expert has observed in this context: 'The comfortable world of the then conventional public administration has been altered dramatically in recent years. The transformation in public administration has come about in part through practice itself, with political leaders, their loyal advisors and their sometimes less loyal civil servants, developing new mechanisms for achieving public sector goals. Most of these mechanisms for enhanced performance have been founded on the basic premise that public and private administrations are fundamentally the same.'

The other important aspect of change not mentioned by Peter is the increasing role of the 'public' and the 'civil society' being admitted and asserted in contemporary public administration discourse. We would be focusing on some of these current themes and would refer in this connection to some of the more significant UN documents and reports dealing with the recent developments in public administration.

Traditional Public Administration

According to Peters, five fundamental assumptions defined functioning of public administration in the traditional model. These five assumptions were:

1. *An assumption of self-sufficiency.* This characteristic of the traditional system assumed that if government is to do anything it will organise and equip itself in order to make and implement the program. Stated differently, government is a self-sufficient actor that can act autonomously from the economy and society.
2. *An assumption of direct control.* As well as being self-sufficient in relation to society, government is also internally structured by authority and hierarchy, so that the individuals at the top of organisational pyramids were assumed to be capable of exercising control within their own organisations.
3. *An assumption of accountability upward.* In this conception of government, accountability was to flow upward, with career officials answering to their political "masters" and those masters as ministers answering to legislatures. This mode of accountability was to be the principal form of connection of administration with the political system and with the surrounding social system.
4. *An assumption of uniformity.* Government was supposed to treat all citizens equally and to provide the same benefits and deprivations to all similarly situated

people. This was seem as a fundamental conception of fairness but by producing formal equality the doctrine may have produced inequities.

5. *An assumption of a civil service system.* This principle of the traditional system as "standardized establishment procedures" — meaning that personnel in the public sector were to be governed through a formalized civil service for recruitment, pay grading and other aspects of internal management.

The five assumptions above described how conventionally governments performed their constitutionally assigned tasks. In terms of this conventional conception of public administration, public sector organisations are autonomous from society but at the same time its linkages with society came through the open, democratic political system. In this conception of governing, the internal management of public organisations was to be carried out through 'rule-based' rather than 'market-based' criteria and there was to be a great deal of internal consistency in the recruitment and reward of public employees.

The various principles of public administration discussed above defined a stable and comfortable way of governing for much of the public sector. That system of governance was far from exciting but it did provide for an honest, politically neutral and generally effective public service. It also exhibited a number of important political values, such as the equal treatment of all citizens. Those virtues were not enough, however, to satisfy many critics of the bureaucracy in and out of government.

The traditional conception of administration relied on a limited and representative conception of democracy. It had a clear sense of public administration within a 'political context', served by an institutionalized, depoliticized, professionalized and neutral career personnel system. There was open admission that all administrative activity was (should be) animated by political actors and by political values and the main 'driver' of government would be 'politics'. In this 'traditional' concept of governing, there was thus a 'paradoxical mixture of political dominance and de-politicization'.

'Six Old Chestnuts'

Interestingly, Peters refers to 'six old chestnuts' that, in his opinion have guided traditional public administration. In his earlier publication — *The Future of Governing: Four Emerging Models8* (1996) — Peters focused attention on what he termed 'extraordinary changes' in public sector reform during the 1980s and 1990s. As he argued, 'change in the public sector is the rule rather than the exception' and 'each solution tends to create its own new set of problems, which in turn will create a new set of reforms'. Thus, it is a fact that in most countries the 'cycle of reforms' in the public sector goes on uninterrupted, although the causalities for such 'reforms' are unlikely to be uniform in each country situation. Peters draws attention to the changes in the economy and in the popular mind that had come about in Western Europe and North America at the end of what he calls the 'period of consensus politics' of the 1950s and 1960s. In his view, 'with that change has come a change in the definition of what constitutes good government and acceptable public administration'. In other words, the traditional model of public administration — its role and structures in particular — had come under serious public scrutiny.

In this context, Peters refers to what he calls the 'six old chestnuts' that have guided our thinking about the public service and its role in governance. These six basic ideas are no longer as sacrosanct as they used to be in the past. To follow his line of argument, briefly stated, these six ideas are as under:

i) Apolitical Civil Service,
ii) Hierarchical and Rule-bound Management,
iii) Organisational Permanence and Stability,
iv) Institutionalized Civil Service,
v) Internal Regulation,
vi) Equality of Outcomes.

There is considerable overlap here with the presentation of the 'five assumptions' above about traditional public administration. We would briefly touch upon each of the 'six old chestnuts' as explained by Peters.

Apolitical Civil Service (APS): The assumptions of 'politics-administration dichotomy' and 'neutral competence, are at the heart of APS. The basic idea is that the career civil servant must function neutrally irrespective of whatever political masters would temporarily come to power.

Hierarchical and Rule-bound Management (HRM): This stands for the classic Weberian model of bureaucratic organisation with assumptions of HRM within the public service including the authority of civil servants to implement and enforce regulations outside it.

Organisational Permanence and Stability (OPS): The assumption here is that as an organisation, public bureaucracy is permanent and stable and the public servant is conceptualized as enjoying a secure life-time employment.

Institutionalised Civil Service (ICS): An allied concept that traditional public administration is an institutional civil service — a distinctive and professional civil service that is governed as a corporate body.

Internal Regulation (IR): Another assumption that has been associated with the Western (particularly Anglo-American) democracies is that 'the civil service should be acquiescent and respond almost without question to policy directives issued by nominal political masters'.

Equality of Outcomes (EO): The traditional model of governance holds that there should be as much equality of outcomes as possible. Within the civil service, the governing principle is 'equal pay and conditions of employment for similarly qualified employees'; in respect of clients, the principle is 'clients with same objective characteristics should receive the same benefits'.

With changing circumstances, these six old chestnuts that have for decades guided thinking about public service and its role in governance, 'are no longer as canonical as they once were'. They seem to have fallen out of grace and the search is on to replace the old model by some other 'models' that would hopefully bail the governments out of the contemporary governance crisis.

Four Emerging Models

Traditional public administration based on the above assumptions worked fairly successfully for decades but due to a number of unprecedented socio-economic changes, a large-scale rethinking of governance was necessitated during the 1980s and the 1990s. Significant shifts in the economy and slow but steady demographic changes compelled most governments in the developed West to respond in terms of 'governance rethinking'. Among major reasons for this change was the fact that 'the economies and societies that governments are meant to control and regulate have become less governable'.

Faced with this large socio-economic transformation, few governments in the West remained untouched by some reform or the other. It has been alleged that in their frantic search for instant remedies, most reforms had been 'off the shelf' type of reforms. As Peters explains, his purpose in suggesting the 'four models' of reforms is to explicate more integrated visions of possible futures for the state and its bureaucracy. To quote in this connection Peters cautionary comment: "If the implications of these alternative visions are more fully explored, understood and contrasted with the traditional conceptualizations of governance, then there is some possibility of producing more effective planned change in government. There is certainly no guarantee of success even with more coherent programmes and the possibility that even the best-planned administrative changes will be diverted and subverted is inevitably present".

The four 'models' of reforms identified by Peters as alternatives to the traditional public administration are now being presented in some details below. These models are:

i) Market Model,
ii) Participatory State Model,
iii) Flexible Government Model and
iv) Deregulated Government Model.

Let us now look into the architecture of each 'model' as identified by Peters:

1. **The Market Model:** As Peters observes, "If there is a single alternative to the traditional model of public administration . . . it must be the market model". A widely circulated prescription has been that the private sector methods of managing activities are inherently superior to the traditional public sector management methods. A number of 'problems' of traditional public sector management are mentioned in this connection. One such problem is lack of sufficient incentives for government employees to perform the jobs as efficiently as they might. Another view (problem) has been that a common tendency among bureaucrats has been that they try to maximize the size of their agency budgets in order to enhance their own personal power and income. A third 'problem' mentioned in this context is that the bureaucrats are sometimes overzealous about the exercise of public policy — especially those policies that are alleged to damage industry — and impose 'internalities' on the society as a whole. In the process of regulation, the original legislative intentions of regulation are often subordinated to undesirable bureaucratic hassles to the detriment of the basic interests of the regulated industry. The 'market model' is flaunted as a better alternative, under these circumstances, to 'cure this set of complaints concerning traditional public administration'.

2. **Participatory State Model:** Almost antithetical to the 'market model', the 'participatory model', as the name suggests, searches for 'more political, democratic and collective mechanisms for sending signals to government'. This model lays emphasis on employees' and citizens' consultations in public policy making and implementation. The advocates of participation are highly critical about organisational hierarchy and top-down management style which, in their opinion, restrict employees — particularly lower level employees — to get involved in their jobs. To quote Peters in this context, "The fundamental assumptions informing this (participatory) approach are that a great deal of energy and talent lies fallow and underutilized in the lower echelons and that workers and clients closest to the actual production of goods and services in the public sector have the greatest insight and information about the programs....if those ideas and talents were harnessed adequately, then government would perform better".

3. **Flexible Government Model**: This is the least clearly articulated of the four models; yet, this model 'captures several important realities of public complaints about government and contemporary proposals for reform'. The basic idea behind 'flexible government' is that it is not

rigidity or conservatism but *flexibility* in terms of organisation, personnel and operations that is of crucial importance in the face of turbulence and change. Flexibility in this context 'refers to the capacity of government and its agencies to make appropriate policy responses to environmental changes rather than merely responding to habitual ways to inherently novel challenges'. It has almost become like some sort of a canonical truth that public organisations and employment should be stable and permanent. As against this, it might sound heretical to suggest that instead let there be experiments, at least in limited ways, in terms of innovative proposals to decrease the permanence of budgets, organisations and employment in the public sector. Due to age-old habits and diehard conservatism — a sort of culture of being locked-in to the ideas of the past — most public organisations lead a cosy and comfortable existence and are reluctant to think of and invest in change. By contrast, contemporary environmental situation of governance marked by 'globalisation', 'global warming', cultural pluralism, civil society and general popular activism calls for 'flexibility' in public organisations, personnel policy and programmes innovations. Stability, it has been critiqued, is no doubt an important source of organisational memory but it is also a potential barrier to future learning. What is needed at this juncture is a 'learning organisation' capable of investing in change.

4. **Deregulated Government Model:** This model is focused on 'deregulation'; it seeks to unleash the potential power and creativity lying within the public sector by 'deregulating government'. Deregulation, in this context, refers not to economic policy but to the internal management of government itself. Some examples are, for instance, removing internal constraints over personnel management, materials purchasing, procuring and similar other functions in the public sector which are presently so strictly rule-bound that in many instances rule-observing gets precedence over efficient performance. A major assumption of 'deregulation' is that if some constraints on action are selectively eliminated, government agencies could then function much more efficiently. The suggestion here is that in today's circumstances when government has to compete with private organisations and expeditiously deliver goods and services to the public. It would be able to function much more efficiently and could even take up newer and more creative activities, if some of the shackles impeding its operations would be removed.

These four 'models' represent four alternative plans for moving government away from the traditional model of public administration. These reforms need not be seen as discreet systems to be implemented as exclusive models of public sector reform. In practice, the models would be adopted, depending on the country situation, in mixed forms. What is intended more often by country governments is to propose reform models to create governmental systems that would function better or bring about improved governmental performance. The general search in reform efforts has been toward producing efficient and effective policy outcomes along with their successful implementations. In this connection, Peters makes a few interesting comments such as 'the four models raise new issues about accountability and the public interest' being dominant concerns for the designers of democratic political systems. Again, the advocates of reform have more 'collective faith' in manipulating formal structures and procedures than in transforming the culture of an organisation. Excessive zeal for 'entrepreneurial ideal' or 'unrestrained management' may in reality, spell danger for governments in the absence of a positive value framework supporting democratic ethos and the public interest. As Peters admits, "The contingencies for selecting one or another of the models of reform have been explored from a normative perspective — what governments should do?" Obviously, normative questions are not always amenable to empirical verification. It will depend on specific country situations — their politics, institutional history, wider societal culture — to choose between alternative reform models.

The cautionary comments in this context are that the models are good in terms of diagnosis but lack clear strategies for intervention. In conclusion we can quote the balanced view of Peters in this regard that each model does have its merits, but each will also impose some costs on society. As he observes, "Any choice of paradigms for government and administration is unlikely to be Pareto optimal but the benefits and sacrifices should be clear in making judgments about governance."

Donald Kettl on Changing Public Administration

Confronted with new challenges, public administration as a discipline today is hard pressed to live up to dual expectations: the discipline's growth and development on one side and responding to the needs and requirements of the practitioners on the other. The practitioners faced with new challenges and buffeted by unprecedented changes look toward helpful responses from the discipline. As Donald Kettl, a well-known expert in the field, describes the situation thus

"Public administration, as a subfield within political science, thus finds itself in an interesting position. It is struggling to define its role within the discipline even as governments around the world are looking more to public administration to resolve public performance and citizen confidence problems. Indeed, one of the most striking features of modern governance is the universal attention that puzzles like devolution, privatisation, deregulation and public interest receive. In many ways, therefore, the dawn of the 21st century ought to be prime time for public administration….. "

Kettl has not only posed the question but also tried to give an answer to it. As he remarks: "It is tempting to seek to rebuild public administration on the greatness of its past. Indeed, one of the field's great is the eternal nature of its fundamental questions. The Key, however, lies in understanding that the problems with which today's government administrators are wrestling are categorically different from many of the problems earlier theories charted. The interconnections among the public, private and non-profit sector are unprecedented. So too is the increasing globalisation of public policy. Faced with these tough challenges, administrators are blazing their trail through a thick forest with few guides. Their paths—the issues with which they are grappling and the solutions they are finding—offer valuable clues for the future of public administration research. Making public administration and the study of governance forward looking requires grounding it in the field's ageless questions; using the new problems, administrators face to define new theoretical puzzles and learning from the successes and failures of administrators to chart the field's empirical research. That requires using practice to inform theory—asking the questions that most need to be answered and identifying the answers that are most persuasive".

Broadly, Donald Kettl's views on the state of the discipline today are as under:

The dilemma faced by the discipline of public administration, since its birth in the late nineteenth century, has been to develop disciplinary knowledge scientifically or to assist and advise practitioners to solve their intricate, real life administrative problems. As it has attempted to build disciplinary knowledge, it has risked distancing itself too much from practice. Anxious public officials have sought quick solutions wherever they can find them and those solutions have been easiest to grab in the private sector. At the same time, public administration experts—preoccupied with regaining their place in the discipline by producing more-scientific work orentrappedinoldhierarchical—andauthority—based models that fit new government problems poorly—have failed to engage the cutting-edge issues. Disappointed at the discipline's perceived inability to come out with instant answers, government reformers have looked instead to journalists, consultants, private management gurus, other nations and even to each other.

The key to redefining public administration's future lies in shaping the future by building on its past and in recognizing that the critical linkage is a keen diagnostic sense of the new twists that fresh problems present. Understanding administrative coordination today must include the wholesale interconnectedness of the public and private sectors and of federal, state and local governments. Understanding administrative effectiveness today must incorporate new approaches to making large and complex bureaucratic organisations more responsive to citizens and their needs. Understanding administrative accountability today must build on charting the new relationships among elected officials and the administrators who implement the programs they create.

Public administration scholars have usually been drawn to administrative studies by the excitement of real people tackling real problems most but it has weakened our ability to understand the questions that need answering. That, in turn, has weakened public administration's theoretical development. Theory without the ability to predict and understand something real and important is not worth doing; theory well-grounded in questions central to government officials and scholars alike is inescapably lively and exciting. The keystone to public administration's rich future lies in solid social science, grounded in enduring puzzles that help provide answers to the future's problems. In other words, Kettl's recommendation is that public administration has to have a good grounding on the realities of administrative practice but that should be done on the basis of social scientific theory building.

Frederickson's Observations

In this context, special mention needs to be made of the famous Gaus Distinguished Lecture delivered in 1999 by the legendary figure in our discipline, H. George Frederickson under the title: 'The Repositioning of American Public Administration'. The emergent public administration, in his view, has a new language and its own unique voice. Although his observations relate basically to 'American' public administration, yet these have major implications for the generic study of public administration. As he commented: . . .'the contemporary practices of public administration have jumped ahead of theory. The theoretical perspective I will propose, therefore, is based on contemporary practices that appear to be specifically designed to solve, ameliorate, or at least to address issues associated with the disarticulation of the state, high jurisdictional and disciplinary fragmentation and diminished bureaucratic capacity'.

Three important features of contemporary public administration to which Frederickson had drawn our attention are

(a) Declining relationship between jurisdiction and public management,
(b) Disarticulation of the state
(c) Need for a broadly based redefinition of what it means to be 'public'.

To elucidate these three features, the *jurisdictional issue* can be understood by referring to the practical problems faced by contemporary states, regions, cities and other local units to deal with a wide range of spill-over problems spanning the economy ('the new global economy', for instance, has been characterized and the 'end of geography') and the environment, floating population and satellite-based information flow.

The second allied feature — *disarticulation of the state* — can best be described in terms of steady erosion of the state's capacity to deal with complex social and economic issues that (e.g. acid rain, immigration flow etc.) often cut across state borders and hence elude the sovereign power of the state.

The third feature relating to the *'publicness'* of public administration can be traced to the proliferation of agencies and institutions that today are engaged in doing the public's business. Traditionally, the term 'public' has usually been associated with formal 'government'.

As Frederickson depicts the picture of contemporary public management scenario:

"Public management is now understood to include government but also all of those organisations and institutions that contract with government to do governmental work, those institutions and organisations that are essentially public-serving — the so called non-governmental organisations and the wide range of organisations and institutions as privately held utilities". This has led to the blurring of the line between 'public' and 'private', rendering the public-private distinction somewhat fuzzy. The theories and practices identified by Frederickson, in this connection, are (1) new institutionalism, (2) network theory and (3) governance theory.

There has been a noticeable contemporary trend toward a steady shift from 'government' to 'governance' which is indicative of efforts to widen the number of members engaged in the management of public's business.

Institutionalism: In this context, Frederickson's ideas about 'institutionalism' deserve special attention. Through his terse and dense expressions, Frederickson has incisively brought home the point that 'the most influential ideas of contemporary public administration are now a part of a broadly defined "institutionalism". To borrow his extended arguments in this connection, 'institutionalism sees organisations as bounded social constructs of rules, roles, norms and the expectations that constrain individual and group choice and behaviour'. It covers the core ideas of contemporary public administration: results, performance, outcomes and purposefulness. It combines the structural or organisational elements of institutions and their managerial and leadership characteristics. Finally, in Frederickson's view9, institutionalism is not confined to formal governmental organisations only. It 'includes the empirical and theoretical considerations concerning the full range of so-called "third sector" organisations and fully recognizes the fuzzy distinctions between public and private institutions'.

Network: Referring to the phenomenon of 'network governance', Frederickson describes the characteristics of 'network' in public management thus:

'Public sector networks are understood to be structures of interdependence. They exhibit both formal and informal linkages that include exchange or reciprocal relations, common interests and bonds of shared beliefs and professional perspectives'.

In this context he approvingly quotes O'Toole10 who had earlier drawn attention to the emerging significance of 'networks' in contemporary public administration: "In more concrete terms, networks include interagency cooperative ventures, intergovernmental program management structures, complex contracting arrays and public-private partnerships. They also include service-delivery systems reliant on clusters of providers that may include public agencies, business firms, not-for-profits, or even volunteer-staffed units all linked by interdependence and some shared program of interests."

As Frederickson has remarked, "It is evident that network theory accounts for an increasing percentage of the activities of public programs, operating through 'networked constellations'."

Governance: As regards, 'governance theory', Frederickson looks at it in terms of the 'expansion of public administration's scholarly arena'. Reflecting on the contemporary administrative situation, he points out11 that 'the definition of public must now include a broad variety of institutions and organisations traditionally considered outside the realm of government, as well as the relationships these organisations have with each other and with policy making authorities. This new definition dramatically increases the number and complexity of the explanatory targets public administration theory must account for'.

Concluding Observations

Admittedly, this is a highly selective presentation of key ideas about changes in public administration in recent decades. Deficiencies and defects of public administration in real life will continue to provoke new ideas and practical innovations. But one should proceed with caution in adopting intellectual fashions and best practices. As Allen Schick[12] cautioned in his well-argued paper, reforms should be grounded in contexts and cultures and market type (privatisation oriented) reforms should be preceded by robust public sector management innovations.

James Q. Wilson[13] made the significant remark that 'public management . . . is a world of settled institutions designed to allow imperfect people to use flawed procedures to cope with insoluble problems." This is a profound statement worth remembering in today's circumstances of fluidity and uncertainty when Pundits of administration go on spinning ideas of 'reforms' that need to be accepted with a degree of caution and circumspection. Living in today's 'globalised' world in these 'fluid times' with, on one side, emerging rich possibilities created by science and technology and on another, increasing feelings of uncertainty about international trade and economic relations and particularly 'security', any universal blueprint of governance and public management at this juncture is bound to raise suspicion rather than hope.

Above all, public administration is basically to serve 'public interest' which gives it the legitimacy it enjoys as a separate 'field'. Any dilution of its basic nature is bound to affect the discipline's core characteristics.

NOTES

1. Phillip J. Cooper, Linda P. Brady, Olivia Hidalgo-Hardeman, Albert Hyde, Katherine C. Naff, J. Steven Ott, Harvey White, Public Administration for the Twenty-First Century, Harcourt Brace & Company, Orlando, Florida, 1998.
2. Guido Bertucci and Adriana Alberti, 'The United Nations Programme in Public Administration: Reinventing Itself to Help Reinvent Public Administration', International Review of Administrative Sciences, Vol. 71 (2), 2005.
3. Rethinking Public Administration: An Overview, Division for Public Economics and Public Administration, United Nations, 1998.
4. United Nations, Revitalizing Public Administration as a Strategic Action for Sustainable Human Development: An Overview, Committee of Experts on Public Administration, Third Session, 29 March-2 April, 2004, New York.
5. L. E. Lynn, Public Management as Art, Science and Profession, Chatham House Publishers, NJ., 1996.
6. B. Guy Peters, 'The Changing Nature of Public Administration: From Easy Answers to Hard Questions', Asian Journal of Public Administration, Vol. 24, No. 2, December 2002.

7. B. Guy Peters, The Future of Governing: Four Emerging Models, University Press of Kansas, 1996.
8. H. George Frederickson and Kevin B. Smith, The Public Administration Theory Primer, Westview Press, Boulder, Colorado, 2003.
9. L. J. O'Toole, Jr., 'Treating Networks Seriously: Practical and Research-Based Agendas in Public Administration, Public Administration Review 57 (1), 1997.
10. Frederickson and Smith, op. cit.
11. Allen Schick, 'Why Most Developing Countries Should Not Try New Zealand's Reforms?', The World Bank Research Observer, 13 (1). February 1998.
12. As quoted in Laurence E. Lynn, Jr., 'Public Management', November 15, 2001. prepared for the Handbook of Public Administration, Sage Publications.

Index